ISBN 978-1-333-97243-1
PIBN 10656611

1 MONTH OF
FREE
READING

at

www.ForgottenBooks.com

By purchasing this book you are eligible for one month membership to ForgottenBooks.com, giving you unlimited access to our entire collection of over 1,000,000 titles via our web site and mobile apps.

To claim your free month visit:

www.forgottenbooks.com/free656611

English
Français
Deutsche
Italiano
Español
Português

www.forgottenbooks.com

Mythology Photography **Fiction**
Fishing Christianity **Art** Cooking
Essays Buddhism Freemasonry
Medicine **Biology** Music **Ancient
Egypt** Evolution Carpentry Physics
Dance Geology **Mathematics** Fitness
Shakespeare **Folklore** Yoga Marketing
Confidence Immortality Biographies
Poetry **Psychology** Witchcraft
Electronics Chemistry History **Law**
Accounting **Philosophy** Anthropology
Alchemy Drama Quantum Mechanics
Atheism Sexual Health **Ancient History**
Entrepreneurship Languages Sport
Paleontology Needlework Islam
Metaphysics Investment Archaeology
Parenting Statistics Criminology
Motivational

DISSERTATION

ON THE

PROPHECIES

RELATIVE TO

ANTICHRIST AND THE LAST TIMES;

EXHIBITING THE

RISE, CHARACTER, AND OVERTHROW

OF THAT

TERRIBLE POWER:

AND A

TREATISE

ON THE

SEVEN APOCALYPTIC VIALS.

BY ETHAN SMITH, A. M.

PASTOR OF THE CHURCH IN HOPKINTON, N. H.

SECOND EDITION.

In the last days perilous times shall come....PAUL.
Ye have heard that Antichrist shall come....JOHN.
The Beast that ascendeth out of the bottomless pit....ANGEL.
The Lion hath roared; who shall not fear....AMOS.
The destroyer of the gentiles is on his way...JEREMIAH.
Blow ye the trumpet in Zion; sound an alarm in my holy mountain....JOEL.

———

BOSTON:
PRINTED AND SOLD BY SAMUEL T. ARMSTRONG,
No. 50, CORNHILL.
1814.

CONTENTS.

RECOMMENDATIONS.

The testimonies kindly given, by those Divines, to whose inspection and advice the manuscript of the first edition of this work was submitted, will not be here inserted; (as they were inserted in the first edition;) except the two following, as a specimen of them.

Rev. Dr. Hemmenway's. "Having heard a considerable part of the Dissertation above mentioned read, I can heartily concur with the others, who have recommended the publication of it, as ingenious, seasonable, and highly worthy of the public attention.
MOSES HEMMENWAY."

Wells, Nov. 28, 1809.

—————

Rev. Dr. Thayer's. "Having attended to a Dissertation in manuscript, of Rev. E. SMITH, on the Prophecies, relative to Antichrist and the last days; including a Treatise on the seven Vials; I am fully of opinion, that new light is thrown upon the subject; that the predictions, and the events stated as their fulfilment, better accord with each other, than in any publication that I have seen upon the interesting subject. The work appears to be handsomely and judiciously executed; and calculated to afford important and necessary instruction and warning to the present generation. For these reasons it is wished that it may be made public. ELIHU THAYER."

Kingston, July 2, 1810.

PREFACE

SINCE the publishing of the first edition of this work, the signs of the times continue to be very interesting. And the evidence, that a new era of affairs has indeed commenced, is *decisive.* Nothing has occurred to evince that any material point in this publication, is incorrect. As far as the author has understood, the sentiments of it have met with general approbation. He is hence encouraged, as the first edition has for some time been disposed of, and a second has been requested,— to submit this to the public.

The work has been diligently revised, and enlarged. A new chapter has been inserted, on the Revelation of St. John: And one on the millennial Kingdom of Christ: A new section also, on Ezekiel's chambers of Imagery: And a section on the illegitimate dynasty in modern France. Some other sections are revised, and enlarged. To some of the vials, especially the fifth, considerable additional attention has been paid. In the chapter on the Revelation, two *charts* are given, to facilitate the explanation of this mystical book. An introductory chapter was prepared, to ascertain the origin and use of the figurative language found in the Bible, and to explain many of the symbols usual in prophetic imagery. But this has since been given to the public in a small separate publication, as *A Key to the figurative language found in the sacred Scriptures.* Hence it is here omitted.

The late signal *reverses* in the affairs of the French Empire, it is believed, furnish no serious objection against the views given of that Empire, as the last head of the secular Roman Beast. They indeed furnish the fulfilment of a feature, found in the prophecies, relative to this last part of the Roman Power, which, till lately, has been wanting;—that "the feet and toes" of the great image should be "part of iron, and part of clay;" that "the kingdom should be partly strong, and partly *broken.*" That the earth should help the women, (the Church) and occasionally open her mouth, and swallow up the floods, cast from the mouth of the dragon, with a view to sweep her from the world. That "the wrath of man shall praise God," when he comes down in the last days, to save all the meek of the earth; "and the remainder of that wrath," or, what would exceed the divine purposes, "he will restrain." That after the infidel Power, Dan. xi, 36—45, shall have done according to his will, and have magnified himself above every god, or legitimate ruler, and spoken marvellous things against the God of gods, and Jesus Christ; after the same nation shall have received a god, or ruler, whom their fathers knew not;—an emperor of foreign descent;— and shall have been led by him to overrun the most strong holds of neighboring nations; and this foreign god shall have divided out the Roman earth for gain, to his vassal kings *of an hour,* — at the time of the end, (when these things are thus far accomplished,) a kingdom of the south shall *push, (butt)* at him; and a kingdom of the north shall come against him like a *whirlwind,* which prostrates all in its way. A whirlwind, or tornado, for so many centuries predicted, composed of a vast coalition of powers, might be expected to sweep its way, and prostrate opposition.

An incipient fulfilment of these prophetic strokes, has of late *caused a smile upon the face of the world;* and revived hopes, which had become almost extinct. To how great a degree these reverses may proceed, God only knows. Should the *brokenness* of this last part of the Roman Power be now made in a considerable degree as conspicuous, as has been his antecedent *strength;* (as the text seems to warrant us to expect; "the kingdom shall be partly strong and partly broken,") that wicked Power would indeed, for the present, be *prostrated!* But should this be the case, should all the horns of the Antichristian Beast be torn off, and the wretch lie bleeding and fainting; yet it appears evident that all his work is not yet done. This great Roman Beast does not go into his final perdition, till the battle of that great day of God, which is subsequent to the restoration of the Jews to Palestine.

The enormous Power, or Influence, symbolized by the *Beast from the bottomless pit,* probably depends on no one man;— though it has been accommodated hitherto with a leader truly prepared for the work of judgment. In the first reign of the imperial head of the Roman Beast, emperors were set up, and deposed, and numbers slain, in thick succession. And it repeatedly seemed as though destruction had fallen upon the Empire Still that imperial head continued. That genius of the people continued, which would be governed by nothing short of a military despotism. And this, we may expect, will be the case, henceforth, on the Roman earth, till the Millennium. Should revolution succeed revolution, it would not alter the case.

The principles of atheism, licentiousness, and disorganization, taught and supported in a profound system, and which constitute the very essence of the Beast from the bottomless pit, are so extensively and deeply disseminated, that the infernal current of them will not be effectually controled nor regulated, even though prime leaders be destroyed, and the earth open her mouth and swallow up their floods of efficient rage! The fountain of the extensive mischief remaining, it will, in some shape, fill all up again. The *nature* of the Beast from the bottomless pit is not *changed.* It rests on the *broad basis* of a general systematic corruption, which will never be purged, but with the exterminating fire of the great and notable day of the Lord; which is subsequent to the restoration of the Jews.

Most joyfully would I participate in the fond hopes of those, who with some confidence expect, that the arm of the oppressor is either *already finally broken*, or will *very soon be no more;* that the horrors of Atheism are nearly expired;—that the modern system of licentiousness will now immediately be banished from the world;—and that the Church of the Redeemed will speedily and joyfully *rise*, with but little more depression or interruption, into her millennial Glory. God in mercy grant, that this may be the case! Gladly would I resume this my former fond sentiment upon the subject, and acknowledge that my subsequent fearful apprehensions have risen too high, relative to the prophetic warnings of this period.

I have no doubt but God's people have every thing to excite their hopes, and their exertions. Their expectations cannot be too sanguine, relative to the *final termination* of their struggles. But I still apprehend that the rising sun of the Millennium is at some distance; and that the inspired *warnings* to the people of God, relative to the events between the present time, and *that day*, are solemn and interesting. Hopes, that are too much elated, may be of real disservice to the people of God, by leading them to imagine the work is done; and their warfare is accomplished; and by throwing them off their guard against the enemy. And such hopes may be of service to the enemy, by enabling them the more fatally to plan and prosecute their deeds of intrigue and mischief. It is *while men sleep*, that the enemy sows tares. The deep system of iniquity, (copied from the code of the Jesuits, with vast improvements,) which has produced the unprecedented scenes of modern date, and has brought the civilized world within a hair's breadth of ruin, will not be annihilated, on receiving the first, or second *check*. Men may fondly hope for the affirmative, and lay their fears to sleep. But they will find new attacks. That diabolical system, after some of its "floods are swallowed up," its "kingdom partly broken," and its "wrath restrained,"—will rally and form again in deep recesses. Its masks and disguises may be shifted. But probably the nations have more yet to hear from it. The three unclean spirits like frogs are, after the sixth vial, to terrify the world; and are to gather the antichristian nations to the valley of slaughter; where, *in the most hostile array against Christ*, they will be utterly destroyed. Then "the whole earth shall be devoured with the fire of God's jealousy;" and "he will sweep the sinners thereof out of it." This burning up of all the wicked and the proud, and leaving them neither *root* nor *branch*, is an event *still future*. Between the present time, and its fulfilment, possibly as great intervals of light *may* be experienced, as might be expected to form a *transition* from the events of one great vial of wrath, to another. But whatever joyful hopes and anticipations may, in such intervals be excited;—it will appear, that the summer itself is *future* of the unerring tokens of its approach. April days may be dark and lowery. And even the bloom of May may for once be overcast with a storm of hail.

It has usually been the case, relative to the trials of the Church, that nothing is more *illusory*, than present *appearances*, in relation to the final termination of an impending calamity. As "the kingdom of heaven cometh not with observation;"— but the *coming of Christ* is like the *coming of a thief*;—so when light has seemed to be dawning, it has often proved, in event, that scenes of great darkness were still in reserve. On the other hand, when all things have seemed full of despair;—light has suddenly broken upon the astonished sight of the sufferers. Human wisdom must be baffled. "Salvation is of the Lord." The knife must be at the throat of the Church, in Isaac, before the angelic voice stays the slaying hand, and proclaims relief. After the bitterness of death is thus in a sense *past*, in the critical moment *relief comes*. The proverb is hence annexed, "In the mount (of distress) God will appear."

Let an ancient mirror reflect light upon the present state of things. After darkness, which might be felt, had filled and astonished the kingdom of Egypt, while light rested upon all the dwelling of Jacob, and Pharaoh in consternation, commanded Israel to *go*, with their little ones, and serve the Lord; it seemed as though relief was at the door. But after this, the tyrant's heart was hardened; and he would not let Israel go. Another tremendous portion of wrath was to be discharged on the enemies of the Church, in the death of their firstborn. After this, salvation seemed to be complete. Laden with the riches of the Egyptians, they were thrust out at once from the house of bondage, and under the immediate leadings and smiles of the Almighty, they commenced their march toward Canaan. Certainly now (would Israel naturally say) "*The darkness is past, and the light shineth.*" *Farewell, thou vanquished tyrant; and all the slavery of Egypt, farewell! We are upon the wing for our long promised land of rest! Your chains and your menaces we now defy! God has broken your power, and taken us out of your hands!*

Divine promises, and circumstances seemed to warrant such triumphant language. But what was the result? Israel's slavery in Egypt was indeed *at an end*. But events the most terrifying of all, were still before them. The tribes of the Lord were after this, and before their final release from the land of Egypt, to be driven to their *wits end;* and to give up *all for lost!* The sea in front; an enraged enemy in arms pressing upon their rere; and unpassable ways in each hand, united to threaten their inevitable destruction. *All*, within human sight, was desperation!

The call of heaven by Moses was;—"Fear not; stand still, and see the salvation of the Lord!" Nor was the call in vain! De-

liverance came from the Almighty arm. The sea was divided.
The cloud of God removed, and came between Israel, and the
persecuting foe. To the former it was a protecting light; to
the latter, darkness and terror. The Egyptians were plunged
in the deep. The Church was safe. And she sang the song
of Moses,

And is not the song of Moses and of the Lamb to be sung at
a period *still future?* The destruction of the persecuting enemies of the Church, and her deliverance which will occasion
the song of Moses and of the Lamb, at the close of the vials,
must surely be *future events.* The deliverance of Israel at the
Red Sea was among the "shadows of good things to come." It
was a type of events just at the dawn of the Millennium.
Some of the preparatory *lucid intervals* have indeed already
dawned upon the people of God. The Most High has undertaken their deliverance and enlargement. His holy arm is
made bare in the sight of all nations. But in the joys of the belief of an approaching Millennium, it does not behoove the
tribes of the Lord to lose sight of their danger; nor to overlook
the *Antitype of the scene at the Red Sea.* Though "God will
finish the work of judgment, and cut it short in righteousness,
because a short work will the Lord make in the earth;" yet he
will take time enough to accomplish this work in the best manner;—and to have some of the most signal displays made o
human depravity; of divine justice; and of the grace and faithfulness of God.

Under the fifth vial, in this edition, it is ascertained, that a
new and signal period of judgments, in the last days, was clearly to *precede,* and to be *distinct from* the battle of that great
day of God Almighty, *the seventh vial:* And that we are notified, that men would naturally mistake the *former* for the *latter:*
But that the latter, when the former becomes tremendous, *"is
not yet,"* but is *future.* This thing appears in most of the
prophecies, which most clearly describe the events of the last
days. The "sun is to be turned into darkness, and the moon
into blood, *before* the great and notable day of the Lord shall
come;" Joel ii, 31. An unprecedented cutting off of the nations, desolating their towers, making their streets waste, destroying their cities, and greatly sweeping off their inhabitants,
must precede, and be distinct from God's rising up to the prey,
gathering the nations, assembling the kingdoms, and pouring
upon them his indignation, even all his fierce anger, when the
whole earth shall be devoured with the fire of God's jealousy;—that he may turn to the people a pure language, that
they may all call upon the name of the Lord, and serve him with
one consent. Zeph. iii, 6—9. Unusual divine "judgments are
to be *abroad in the earth; and God's hand is to be lifted high,"*
—*before* he gives the warning, "Come, my people, enter into
thy chambers, shut thy doors about thee, hide thyself for a little
moment until the indignation be overpast. For behold the

Lord cometh out of his place to punish the inhabitants of the world for their iniquity; the earth also shall disclose her blood, and shall no more cover her slain;" Isa. xxvi, 9, 11, 20, 21. At a new and amazing period of judgments, in the last days, between the second and third woes, seven thunders of unprecedented wars utter their voices. These are mistaken for the finishing scenes of judgments. But the angel decides that the "finishing scene "*is not yet*;—but in the days of the seventh angel, when he shall begin to sound, the mystery of God shall be finished, as he hath declared to his servants the prophets;" Rev. x, 3—8. The *hour of God's judgment* was to be announced to the world, as come, (at the same time with the flight of the missionary Angel through the midst of heaven,) as an event clearly preceding, and distinct from the appearing of the destroying Angel upon the white cloud, to reap the harvest and to gather the vintage of the earth, then ripe; Rev. xiv, 7, 14—20. Wars and rumors of wars new and terrrifying to the world— were to prove but the *beginning of the sorrows* of the last days. But it is at the same time expressly ascertained, that "*the end is not yet*" Many interesting things are yet to be accomplished, before the sign of the Son of man coming in the clouds of heaven, shall be presented; Matt. xxiv, 6, 8, 29, 30. The *pushing* of the king of the south, and the coming of the king of the north like a whirlwind against the infidel Power, clearly precede, and are distinct from the event of this Power's coming to his end between the two seas in Palestine; Dan. xi, 40, 44, 45. A temporary prostration by such a military whirlwind—for twenty four hundred years *predicted*—precedes, and does not *prevent* the going forth of the same Power, with great fury, utterly to make away many after the restoration of the Jews to the Holy land. Here is the expedition of Gog and his bands in Ezek. xxxviii. These synchronical prophecies all unite in the sentiment, that the seventh vial, (the battle of the great day) is *after* and distinct from a new scene of terrors, which were to indicate its approach. The fifth vial fills the kingdom of the Papal Beast with gross darkness. But terrible as the events of this vial are, they are by no means to be confounded with the events of the seventh vial. The sixth and seventh vials are future and distinct from it. The Turkish government must be destroyed, and the Jews restored, and the great subsequent coalition formed against them, of what is called, "the kings of the earth and of the whole world," to prepare the way for the seventh vial. What intervals of light, or of respite to a sinking world, may take place between some of the last vials;—what short intervals of general peace may induce mankind to hope that the most fatal scenes of judgment are past, *God only knows.* But it is believed that a new era of judgments has commenced, which will terminate only with the des-

truction of *all that is Antichristian;* and with the full preparing
of the way for the millennial glory of the Church.

In one of the prophets we learn that *three signal overturnings,*
were to precede and introduce the Kingdom of Christ. Ezekiel
(chapter xxi) predicts a *sharp sword,* sharpened for a sore
slaughter, and furbished that it may glitter;—given into the
hands of the slayer;—a sword of the great men to be slain. The
prophet is directed to cry, and exhibit tokens of distress. "Smite
thine hands together, and let the sword be doubled the *third
time;* the sword of the slain.—Ah, it is made bright, it is wrapped up for the slaughter."—"Thus saith the Lord God, Remove the diadem, and take off the crown! this shall not be the
same; exalt him that is low, and abase him that is high. I will
overturn, overturn, overturn *it;* (the *crown;* or will show myself terrible to the wicked kings of the earth) and it shall be no
more, until he come, whose right it is; and I will give it him."
The ultimate accomplishment of this is clearly the introduction of the Millennium. *One* great overturning we have seen;—
that of the Papal Beast. *Two* overturnings are still future;—
that of the Turks; and of a subsequent coalition against the
Jews. Christ will then come, and take the Kingdom; and fill
the earth with his salvation.

That the friends of Zion may devoutly search the scriptures, and learn their true sentiment, and their warnings relative to these last days, is the desire of

                                        THE AUTHOR.

Hopkinton, N. H. Sept. 1, 1813.

PREFACE

THE events of the period, in which we live, are of great magnitude. To open in a connected and judicious manner the sacred Prophecies relative to the last days, with their fulfilments, must be a desirable object.

I am not insensible of the arduousness of this undertaking; and that some worthy men discountenance attempts to explain prophecies, till a long time after their fulfilment. Doubtless the prophecies generally will be more clearly understood, when they shall be viewed at a considerable distance past. But this should not preclude our *present* attempts to form correct opinions relative to those which are not fulfilled; much less, relative to the accomplishment of those, which are recently fulfilled; and of those, which are now in a train of fulfilment. The Jews were by our Lord reproved for not understanding the signs of the times; i. e. for not understanding the fulfilment of prophecies, then taking place before their eyes.

The prophecies were given, not only to evince the divine origin of Revelation, by being viewed *after* their evident fulfilment; but also to *direct* and *animate* the people of God in the prospect of, and *during* their fulfilment. But this implies our duty to study them, while the events, which they predict, are taking place, and while they are *future*. Accordingly, when the Revelation was made to St. John, it was prefaced with this admonition; *Blessed is he that readeth, and they that hear the words of this prophecy, and keep those things which are written therein; for the time is at hand.* Repeatedly is it given in charge, in the midst of some of the darkest prophecies; *Let him, that readeth, understand.* We read; *None of the wicked shall understand; but the wise shall understand.* They shall know the judgments of the Lord. Daniel previously understood by books the return of the Jews from Babylon. This knowledge excited his prayer for the accomplishment of the event. Simeon, Anna and others, who waited for the consolation of Israel, understood by prophecies the coming of the Messiah; and they discerned the accomplishment before their eyes, in the Babe of Bethlehem. We are told; *The secret of the Lord is with them that fear him:* And, *The Lord God will do nothing, but he will reveal it to his servants the prophets.* Not by new revelations; but by leading to a correct investigation of those already given. All the directions given to the people of God, relative to the perilous times just preceding the Millennium, clearly imply, that the Church will, at that day, understand the most interesting prophecies then about to receive their fulfilment. Otherwise, how could the embassadors of Christ, as commanded, Joel ii, 1, "Blow the trumpet in Zion, and sound an alarm in God's holy mountain," when the day of the Lord is nigh at hand? Hence there is much encouragement to *pray* and *study*, that we may form correct views, in the light of prophecy, *of the great events of our days.*

The Church of Christ has been premonished respecting most of the signal events, in which she was to be much interested, in every age. In this the care and kindness of her divine Lord have ever appeared. And he has graciously so ordered, that his people should be led to form essentially correct views of the fulfilment of those premonitions. Shall the great events of this period of the world then, be an exception to this general rule? Shall the events of our days, more interesting than events of former ages, and which for more than twenty years have been alarming the world, and demonstrating the commencement of a new and important era, be supposed to be veiled in impenetrable mystery? It cannot be probable! Some of the most interesting prophecies of Revelation have recently received their accomplishment; which is leading on a train of events most important, and clearly predicted. And it must be important to Zion to be able rightly to view, in the light of Divine prophecies, the present, and the subsequent designs of Providence.

Attempts to write upon the prophecies have been, in the estimation of some, brought into disrepute, by the *failing* of even able and good men, in their conjectures upon the subject; and especially by the injudiciousness and enthusiasm of others. But shall occasion be hence taken to neglect this important and useful part of the word of God?

The author of the following work is not insensible of the perils of the times, and the delicacy of his subject, at such a day as this. Permit him once for all to *protest*, that he is not knowingly governed, in any thing he has written, by the party interests of the day, viewing them merely as *political events*. He confidently appeals to all, who for twenty years have known the tenor of his public ministry, and of his life, that he is no *party man*. What he has written, is written under a solemn conviction of the infinite weight of evangelical truth; and of his accountability to God, as a minister of the Gospel. Events of a political nature are noted, to show their fulfilment of the word of God; to ascertain moral duties, moral turpitude, and the dangers of the times from the just displeasure of the Most High. In this point of light, it is the duty of every minister of Christ to have his eyes open to political events. I am indebted to Mr. Faber for my conviction, that the prophecies concerning Antichrist, instead of being exclusively applicable to the Romish hierarchy, designate an Atheistical Power of *later date;* and am indebted to him for finding in Dan. xi, 36,— a prediction of this

Atheistical Power; and finding a fulfilment of it in the *French nation.* But this author wrote before the government of France had assumed its Imperial form. There are striking traits of character in the above noted prophecy, and in various others, overlooked, or misapprehended by this author. On reading his application of the prediction in Dan xi, 36,— to the French nation, I felt a difficulty from the seeming *abruptness* of such an application. But on consulting the preceding parts of the chapter, in connexion with chapter xth, and learning, as I apprehended, the object of the revealing Angel, I found my doubts removed, and my confidence in the correctness of the application of the passage to the French nation, established. With this clew I have endeavored to examine various other prophecies, which respect the same period, and some preceding, and subsequent periods; with what success, the reader will judge. I acknowledge *many* expositions, given in this work are *new;* at least they are so to me; which has excited my fear and solemn attention in the investigation of the true sense of those passages. I have endeavored to consult and compare authors on this subject; and have long been in a habit of perusing them with some pleasure. But it will be seen that I have not been governed wholly by old opinions; but have endeavored to compare Scripture with Scripture, and to adopt its most obvious and natural meaning. I have no other apology to make for presenting this Dissertation to the public, than the fact, that gentlemen, whose judgment I venerate, have advised to it; and my own conviction of the truth of the scheme, and the weight of the subject here presented.

THE AUTHOR.

Hopkinton, July, 1810.

DISSERTATION.

CHAP. I.

We are taught in the prophetic parts of the sacred Scriptures, to expect the rise of a terrible, atheistical Power, and a vast influence of Infidelity, in the last days, or just before the Millennium.

THERE are many predictions of this event, both in the Old and New Testaments; some of which will be noted in the following sections. This terrible power is to exist *after* the predominant reign of Popery, and not long before the battle of that great day of God Almighty, which is to prepare the way for Christ's millennial Kingdom. This Power is not a *fifth* Monarchy on earth; but is comprised in the *fourth;* or is the last head of the old Roman Beast. It is, in the language of prophecy, the old bloody, persecuting Roman Empire revived, after it had long lain dead: Ascending out of the bottomless pit, in the last days; to accomplish God's works of judgment; and then to go into perdition. This I shall endeavor to substantiate. The rise of this Power is predicted as a new and terrible event.

SECTION I.

Preliminary remarks upon the Xth and XIth chapters of Daniel.

The first passage, which will be adduced to prove the proposition stated in Chap. I, is Dan. xi, from the 36th verse, to the end. To prepare the way for the consideration of this passage, let the following things

4

be premised. The prophet Daniel had twice predicted the existence of the Roman empire; in the legs of
iron;* and in the fourth beast strong and terrible, having great iron teeth.† Popery had been before predicted, under the emblem of the little horn of the Roman beast, speaking great things against the Most
High.‡ Mohammedism had been predicted, under
the emblem of the little horn of the he-goat;§ as Mr.
Faber has ingeniously shown.‖

In Dan. ix, we have an account of the prophet's
fasting and supplication, relative to the return of the
Jews from Babylon; upon which he has his vision of
their return; of the seventy weeks; of the coming and
death of the Messiah; and of the destruction of Jerusalem.

Then, in the beginning of chap. x, we are informed,
In the third year of Cyrus, king of Persia, a thing was
revealed unto Daniel, *and the thing was true; but the
time appointed was long.* And the whole of the succeeding chapter is taken up in preparing to present this
far distant thing to view. In verse 14th, the Angel
says, *Now I am come to make thee understand what shall
befal thy people*, in latter days; *for yet the vision is
for many days.* No such formal preparation was made,
nor notice given, *of the great distance of the event*,
when the prophet was about to, predict the Roman empire; or the introduction of Popery; or of Mohammedism; although the two latter were then ten or twelve
hundred years future. Here was a new subject, a most
interest thing to be revealed, the time of which was
to be *long posterior* to those which had just before been
predicted. The revealing angel seems to have but
one thing in view: *A thing was revealed to Daniel.* It
was to be *a thing* closely connected with what should
befal the Jews *in the latter days.* This could not refer
to the destruction of Jerusalem by the Romans. For
this had been before predicted;¶ and it was not by far

---

*Dan. ii, 34, 40.   † Dan. vii, 7.   ‡ Dan. vii, 8, 24.
§ Dan. viii, 9.   ‖ Vol. i, p. 158.   ¶ Dan. ix, 26, 27.

so distant, as was the thing now to be revealed. The letter being what is to befal the Jews in the *latter days*, evinces, that it was to be something beside Popery. The Papal imposture never so materially affected the Jews, as a nation, as appears to be here indicated. The thing to be revealed then, must be an event to take place near the time of the final restoration of the people anciently in covenant with God; and just before the Millennium; and an event, which will deeply affect that people at that period. It was also a thing *before predicted* by the other prophets. Dan. x, 21, *But I will show thee that, which is noted in the Scripture of truth.* Popery was not *much* before noted in the Scripture of truth; till this prophet himself had just before predicted it.* But concerning the restoration of the ancient people of God, in the last days, it had been *abundantly* before noted by the prophets, that a terrible Power will, soon after their return to the land of their fathers, attack and greatly afflict them.† Some expositors have applied this prediction of Daniel (which is to be particularly noticed in the next section) to the Papal hierarchy. But in view of the preceding remarks, it appears unnatural thus to do. And the picture there drawn does not apply to Popery, without unnatural distortions of its features. The power there predicted is to remain in the tide of his glory, till the battle of the great day of God Almighty;‡ a thing which cannot now be believed of the Papal hierarchy. This power then, can be no other than the atheistical Antichrist of the last times. The way being thus prepared, the Angel says, chapter xi, verse 2, *And now I will show thee the truth*, i. e. I will draw towards the *great object in view.* But before he comes *directly* to it, he begins, as is usual in such cases, with a line of preceding kings and events. When the Romish hierarchy was to be predicted, chap. vii, the prophet introduces that wicked power, by giving the preceding succession of the eastern monarchies. When Mohammedism was to be predicted, chap. vii,

---

* Dan, vii, 8, 24. † See Chap. III, Sec. 2 and 4 of this book.
‡ See the close of Dan, xi.

the prophet ushers in that vile imposture, by briefly alluding to the succession of the preceding powers, in the line of which it came. So in the case before us, the Angel describes a line of kings from the then present period, in order to introduce, not the atheistical Power in view immediately, but *Antiochus Epiphanes,* a noted king of Syria, *as a type of the atheistical Power, who was to rise in the last days.* This terrible Power the prophet predicts, first by his *type* Antiochus. St. Jerom informs us of its being a generally received maxim, "that it is the manner of the holy Scriptures to deliver beforehand the truths of futurity in *types.*" (Bp. Hurd, p. 57.) We find much of this. When the Millennium was to be predicted, in Psalm lxxii, it was introduced by its type, the reign of Solomon. And the Holy Spirit there, without any formal notice, slides from the type to the antitype. This is a common thing in prophetic writings. In like manner, this terrible Power of the last days is predicted, first by a description of his *type.* It is an old opinion of expositors, that Antiochus was a notable type of Antichrist, even while they supposed the Romish hierarchy to have *been* Antichrist. But much more strikingly do the type and the antitype agree, if the latter be the terrible infidel Power of the last days, as I trust will appear. The type Antiochus was to afflict the Jews grievously, after their restoration from Babylon. And the infidel Power, then about to be predicted, is to afflict them much more grievously, soon after their final restoration, just before the introduction of the Millennium. The revealing Angel proceeds. Three kings he notes, who were to arise in Persia, after Darius, then on the throne. Then a fourth, richer than all the three, who should meddle with the realm of Greece to his ruin. Alexander is then noted. Then his four generals, among whom his empire was divided. Then the wars of the two most distinguished of them, called the king of the north, and the king of the south, or Syria and Egypt; in which wars the Jews were deeply interested;—till the Angel, verse 21, introduces *Antiochus,* the type of the terrible Power then so far future. On this type he dwells for fifteen verses. And from the prophetic description, we learn, in the character of Antiochus, something of the character of Antichrist. In this description we observe, that Antiochus, the type of Antichrist, was a vile person; not the heir of the crown of Syria; but obtaining it by flatteries. He overflowed his enemies *with the arms of a flood.* He deposed the prince of the covenant, or Onias, the Jewish high priest. He *wrought deceitfully,* even after the obligations of solemn treaties. He did *what neither his fathers had done, nor his father's fathers.* He reduced strong holds, *by forecasting devices against them. He scattered the prey among his favorites. He stirred up his courage and power against the king of the south,* who checked his progress by a furious, though unsuccessful effort of defence. Ptolemy was overcome through the treachery of some of his own subjects. Antiochus returned from Egypt with great riches. He was elated with pride; and his heart was against the holy covenant, or the church of God.* He makes another attack upon the king of the south; but not with his former success. He is annoyed with the navy of a rival power, (the ships of Shittim, or Rome,) and is obliged to return. His indignation again rages against the holy covenant, or the church of God at Jerusalem. *He has intelligence with them that forsake the holy covenant;* or he intrigues with apostate Jews. *Arms stand on his part;* or armed soldiers are sent into Judea, to enforce his abominable orders. *The sanctuary of strength* or the temple at Jerusalem *is polluted. The daily sacrifice is taken away. The abomination, that maketh desolate, is set up.* Apostate Jews are *corrupted by flatteries. But such as know their God, are strong and do exploits. They who understand, instruct many; yet they fall by the sword, by flame, and by captivity, and by spoil, days,* (as in the original.†)

---

* He slew forty thousand of the Jews; he sold as many more for slaves; and polluted the temple at Jerusalem.

"† The desolation of the temple, and the taking away of the daily sacrifice by the commissioner of Antiochus continued three years and a half, according to Josephus." Newton on the Prophecies. Vol. i, p. 310.

*Yet when they fall, they are aided with a little help. But
many cleave unto them with flatteries. And some of the
people of understanding fall, to try them, to purge, and
to make them white, even to the time of the end.* *

'* A celebrated modern author supposes, that the Angel here
leaves the events of the days of Antiochus; and from verse 31st
to 35th gives a prophetic sketch of events down to the sixteenth century of the Christian era: That verse 31st predicts
the destruction of Jerusalem by the Romans, forty years after
the ascension of Christ: That verses 32d and 33d predict the
persecution of the primitive Christians under Pagan Rome: that
verse 34th predicts the conversion of Pagan Rome to Christianity, in the revolution under Constantine, and the subsequent
corruptions of Christianity in that empire, which gave rise to
the Man of sin: And that verse 35th predicts the Papal persecutions of the witnesses down to the sixteenth century. This
scheme I cannot conceive to be correct, for the following
reasons:
1. Simply to predict the line of events, from the time then
present, till the rise of the Power, which he had in view to predict, appears not to have been any part of the object of the revealing Angel. If it had been, it would not have been said,
chap. x, 1, A thing *was revealed unto Daniel; and* the thing
was true; but the time appointed was long. (See also verse
14th.) But it must have been said, that *many things* were revealed to Daniel; some of which were far distant, and some of
which were near. To reveal that *one thing* appears to have
been the *sole* object of the Angel, in chapters x, and xi. And
the *manner* of his doing this appears to have been, not the predicting of a course of events, which should reach to the time of
the rise of the Power; but the predicting of the Power by his
type, Antiochus Epiphanes; and then passing immediately to
the antitype. If the object of the Angel were to predict simply the course of great events, which should reach down to the
rise of Antichrist, why did he dwell for at least ten verses,
(from v. 21st to 31st, according to the scheme of this author,) on
the wars of Antiochus Epiphanes; and then touch so lightly on
the subsequent events, which were of far greater magnitude,
and which were to occupy seventeen or eighteen centuries?
Why should he, after dwelling for ten verses on the affairs of
Antiochus, appropriate but *one* verse to the *great event* of the
coming of Christ in the destruction of Jerusalem, and of the
Jewish nation by the Romans; two verses to the ten persecutions of the primitive Christian church, under Pagan Rome;
one verse to the conversion of Pagan Rome under Constantine,
and the subsequent corruptions, which issued in the Papal apostasy; and but *one* verse to all the Papal persecutions of the wit-

' Thus the Angel proceeds in his description of Antiochus, the type of the terrible Power to be predicted,

nesses down to the sixteenth century? Who can account for
such an amazing want of proportion in the communications of
the Angel, if simply a prediction of *facts* were his object?

2. When a person or event is predicted by his type, it is not
usual for the prophet, after predicting the type, to give a sketch
of events, which should take place between the type and the antitype. This is usually no part of his object. But the writer,
in such cases, slides from the type to the antitype, without regard to the length of time, or distance of place. This we find
in Psalm 72d, in the predictions of the kingdom of Christ, with
its typical reign of Solomon. This we find in the various predictions of the *coming of Christ;* and of the battle of the great
day. We should hence be led to expect, that after the revealing Angel had presented to Daniel the *type* of the POWER in
view, he would pass immediately to the antitype. And this I
apprehend is the fact.

3. The language from verse 31st to 35th appears in perfect
unison with the preceding prediction of Antiochus. But it
does not seem at all to apply to a variety of new subjects, and
distant events, without a most unnatural and forced construction. Let us examine. For the ten preceding verses, it is a
given point, that Antiochus is the subject. In the last of the
ten, or verse 30th, we read, "For the ships of Chittim shall
come against *him,* (Antiochus on his expedition in Egypt,)
therefore *he* shall be grieved, and return, and have indignation
against the holy covenant: so shall *he* do; *he* shall even return
and have intelligence with them, that forsake the holy covenant. Verse 31. And arms shall stand on *his* part." On *whose*
part? What does grammatical construction, what does the
common sense of the reader reply? Does the word *his* here
relate to the person, who is the subject of the preceding verse,
and of the *ten* preceding verses? Or does it relate to a new
subject; a subsequent empire; and to events some centuries
after the events of the preceding verse? If liberty may be taken to say the latter, may not any expositor take liberty to fix
any sense to a text, which he may please? There is sometimes
a shifting *in relatives,* to a different person from the antecedent, when *type and antitype* are the subject. The antecedent
may be the type, and the relative may respect the antitype.
But in no other cases can this be admissible. But, says the ob-
jector, does not the substance of this 31st verse decide that it
relates to the siege of Jerusalem by the Romans? *And they*
(the arms that shall stand on his part.) *shall pollute the sanctuary of strength, and shall take away the daily sacrifice, and they
shall place the abomination that maketh desolate.* Does not our
Lord, Mark xiii, 14, apply this very text to the seige of Jeru-

and in a detail of events under his tyranny, till verse
36.   Here he drops the type, and takes the antitype, as

salem?   Answer. By no means.   Daniel had spoken of the
abomination of desolation, in three passages; chap. ix, 27, relative to the destruction of Jerusalem by the Romans; chap. xi,
31, (the passage under consideration) relative to the persecutions of the Jews by Antiochus; and chap. xii, 11, relative to
the rise of Popery, or Mohammedism, or both, at the beginning
of the 1260 years.   And now, to which of these did our Lord,
Mark xiii, 14, refer, as he applied it to the destruction
of , Jerusalem?   Surely to the passage in chap. ix, 27,
which relates to the destruction of Jerusalem by the Romans;
and not to either of the two *other* passages, which relate to different periods and events.   A desolating abomination is a common prophetic figure, to denote an invasion of the rights of
conscience.   It is found in different passages; and in relation
to different invasions.   We may as well say, Christ referred to
the passage in Dan. xii, 11, which relates to the beginning of
the 1260 years; as that he referred to that in chap. xi, 31; and
thus confound the whole order of those prophecies. , The very
thing predicted, in the passage under consideration, forbids
that it should be applied to the destruction of Jerusalem by the
Romans.   For *polluting* the sanctuary of strength, and *burning*
it, are two very different things.   The latter was performed by
the Romans: But the former by Antiochus; and the whole
verse was fulfilled by him, when he with armed forces plundered, and defiled the temple; called it the temple of Jupiter O-
lympius; placed in it the image of this heathen god; forbade
the Jewish sacrifices; and compelled the Jews to eat swine's
flesh, and to conform to the idolatrous rites and manners of the
heathen.

Verses 32, 33. *And such as do wickedly against the covenant,
shall be corrupt by flatteries; but the people, that do know their
God, shall be strong, and do exploits.   And they that understand
among the people, shall instruct many, yet they shall fall by the
sword, and by the flame, and by captivity, many* days.   Who
shall corrupt by flatteries the apostates from the covenant?   It
is said *he* shall do it.   Antiochus has been the subject of the
whole paragraph, without the least interruption, or notice of
the introduction of a new subject.   The unity of the whole
passage seems to decide, that the people spoken of were the
Jews under the persecution of Antiochus, and not the promiscuous Christians of other nations many centuries afterwards.
Verse 34: *Now when they shall fall, they shall be holpen with a
little help; but many shall cleave to them with flatteries.*   To apply this to the revolution in Rome, and those lucrative establishments in the Church, by which Constantine designed to set
the Church superior to the violence of her enemies; but which

is common in prophetic writings; and he immediately describes *the thing, which was to be revealed.*

SECTION II.

This Infidel Power predicted in Dan. xi, 'from the 36th verse to the end.

THE way being thus prepared, the Angel comes to the Power, who was to be revealed, whose time was *long;* or who was to exist just at the close of the wicked ages of the world.

And the king shall do according to his will, and he shall exalt himself and magnify himself above every god; and shall speak marvellous things against the God of gods; and shall prosper, till the indignation shall be accomplished; for that, which is determined, shall be done.

Upon this verse let the following things be noted:

proved, as some say, the occasion of the rise of the Papal hierarchy, appears to violate the unity of the whole prophecy. Verse 35; *And some of them of understanding shall fall, to try them, and to purge, and to make them white, even to the time of the end, because it is yet for a time appointed.* And does this relate to a new subject *still?* to the persecuted witnesses under the Papal hierarchy, down to the sixteenth century? Will not such a mode of exposition open the door to the wildest conjectures of men, in the interpretation of prophecy? There appears to be a perfect unity in the whole fifteen verses, (from the 21st to the 35th inclusive,) which is incapable of being broken, or of permitting the different parts to be applied to a variety of different powers, and in far distant ages. And it is a fact, that events took place under Antiochus Epiphanes, which appear to answer to every part of the predictions. (See 1 Macc. i, 21—23, and from the 41st to the end; and chap. ii; 2 Macc. the 2d, 5th, 6th, 7th, and 8th chapters; and Heb. xi, 35 —38.) Its being said, that *some of them of understanding should fall to try them—to the time of the end, because it is yet for an appointed time,* does not necessarily carry our thoughts to the battle of the great day, nor to the end of the world, nor to the sixteenth century; but to the end of the tyranny and persecutions of *Antiochus,* the subject then under consideration. As Antiochus was presented here as the type of Antichrist; so the *end* of his persecution was typical of *the time of the end of the* antitypical Antichrist.

5

1. That here is a change of. characters, or a new subject introduced, is acknowledged by expositors; and is evident from all that follows.   What precedes was but a few centuries after Daniel's time.   But what follows, or what the Angel had in *view* to reveal, was to take place at a time then *far distant*, just at *the time of the end*.   This we learn from verse 40th; *And at the time 'of the* end *shall the king of the south push at him; and the king of the north shall come against him.* What precedes the 36th verse, is spoken *of* the king of the south, and king of the north; in order to exhibit Antiochus, as has been shown.   But now, at the time of the end, many centuries *after* the time of Antiochus, we find those two powers uniting against a *third* Power; who is the new Power introduced verse 36th.   *And the king*, says the Angel; q. d. The king, that I have in view; who has been described in his *type;* and is now to be described in his *own* character.

2. By a king, in the language of prophecy, is generally to be understood a dynasty, or government; a kingdom, or civil power; whether monarchical, or republican; and not an individual person.   In this sense we are to understand the king in this text. Instances of this kind in prophecy are numerous.   Antichrist is by no means an individual person; but a vast *Power.*

3. In this passage we are presented with a great *atheistical* Power, who in his commencement is to be *anarchical;* raised up to be an instrument of the Divine indignation; and who is to exist till that work of judgment shall be accomplished.   His licentiousness is first noted; *he shall do according to his will;* breaking every restraint.   His anarchy follows; *and he shall exalt himself and magnify himself above every god;* i. e. above every *king* or legitimate ruler.   That this is the sense of the passage, is evident. The following clause decides it; where the Most High is called, *The God of gods;* i. e. the King of kings, and Lord of lords. Kings and earthly rulers are, in Sacred Writ, called *gods. I said, Ye are gods.*   *Thou shalt not revile the* gods; i. e. thou shalt not speak evil of the *rulers* of thy people. *God standeth in the congregation of the mighty; he judg-*

eth among the gods. In such passages, kings, and
other lawful rulers are called *gods;* which passages
may suggest the true sense of this Power's exalting
himself above every god. War with kings was to be
among his first characteristics. His Atheism follows;
and shall speak marvellous things against the God *of
gods.* He shall blaspheme and deny the God of heav-
en; the King of kings. And a train of astonishing successes shall follow, or attend his arms; till the work of
judgment, for which he is raised up, shall be accomplished. For the Divine counsel has originated the
event for judgment; and nothing can frustrate its accomplishment.

Verse 37; *Neither shall he regard the god of his
fathers, nor the desire of woman; for he shall magnify
himself above all.* Kings, and the God of heaven, were
before denounced. Now his fathers' god, their pretended *head of the church,* so long venerated, even as a
god, in all Popish countries, is by this Power rejected.
Antiochus deposed Onias the Jewish high priest. And
the Antitype of Antiochus deposed, and reduced to
beggary the pope of Rome. And the Seed of the
woman, to be the mother of whom was the fervent desire of the Jewish women, before his incarnation, and
whose vicar the god of the fathers of this infidel Power
pretended to be, is impiously disregarded, and his religion abjured. Eve upon bearing her first son, exclaimed, *I have gotten* the man, the Lord, as in the original.
Her desire to be the mother of the promised Seed,
suggested to her fond imagination, that this babe was
the person. This same general desire continued in
after ages. And it was perhaps chiefly on this account,
that barrenness in Israel, where the Seed of the woman
was to be born, was deemed so great a reproach. *The
desire of women,* therefore, seems a suitable enigmatical
appellation of the Messiah then to come, and then thus
desired by women.

How exactly does the character here given to the
infidel Power, accord with the New Testament characteristics of Antichrist! *He is Antichrist, who denieth
the Father and the Son. Denying the Lord who*

bought them. Denying the only Lord God, and our Lord Jesus Christ. Despising dominions; speaking evil of dignities. Such predictions in the New Testament probably allude to this very passage in Dan. xi, 37. They identify the subject of their description, with that of the prophet; or show that the Power predicted in both is the *same*. For the first thought of the application of *the desire of women* to Christ, I am indebted to Mr. Faber. At first, the application appeared to me doubtful. But on deliberation, I apprehend it to be correct; so perfectly does it agree with the characteristics of Antichrist in the New Testament, as is noted above, and as may further appear.

The supposition that the clause, *Neither shall he regard the desire of women,* is the same with the characteristic of the Papal hierarchy, *Forbidding to marry,* cannot be admitted. For the Power under description is a Power different from Popery, as has been suggested, and as will more fully appear in the course of this Dissertation. And the two passages literally express different things. The *desire of women* must mean what women desire. It must mean the object of the desire, which women did then entertain, when the passage was written. But *forbidding to marry* is quite another thing.*

Verse 38; *But in his estate shall he honor the god of forces.* When this Power shall view himself established, although he deny God, and Christ, and all legitimate authorities, yet shall he acknowledge *Mozim,* (in the Heb.) translated by Mede and others, *gods-protectors; i. e. tutelar gods.* He shall adopt his fancied deities, like the country-gods of the ancient heathen.

---

* Should any doubt relative to this exposition of the passage, let them examine the following; Neither shall he regard, but shall destroy the monarch of his own nation: And his queen, and hundreds of thousands of innocent females, shall he destroy, as though the desire of women for their lives, for the lives of their children, and for that protection, which is their due from man, were wholly disregarded. The queen, and 250,000 females were murdered in France, during the reign of terror there; furnishing an unprecedented trait of character, and of diabolical cruelty, in the history of man.

Some things highest in popular estimation, shall be reputed as gods.' Or some deceased champions of their Infidel order shall, in the impious fancy of their followers, be deified; and perhaps their bones deposited in some temple.

Or, after this Power shall gain national importance, he shall honor *military munitions;* or pay his first attention to the arts of war; a sense which the term *Mozim* may bear.

The last part of verse 38th; *And a god whom his fathers knew not shall he honor with gold and silver and precious stones and pleasant things.* Although his fathers' god, and all gods have been rejected; yet a god, or *ruler*, of foreign descent, shall by and by come to be acknowledged by this power, and honored with the greatest magnificence.

Verse 39th; *Thus shall he do in the most strong holds with a strange god, whom he shall acknowledge and increase with glory; and he shall cause them to rule over many, and shall divide the land for gain.* This infidel Power shall overrun strong holds, and powerful nations, with this foreigner at their head, who shall be received as their supreme ruler, and honored with the highest dignity; and he shall lead them to subdue states and nations; and shall distribute their governments among his favorites, for his own aggrandizement.*

Verse 40th; *And at the time of the end shall the king of the south push at him; and the king of the north shall come against him, like a whirlwind, with chariots and horsemen, and with many ships; and he shall enter into the countries, and shall overflow and pass over.* After this Power shall have been for a time in existence, trouble shall arrest him from powers here called, *the king of the south, and king of the north.*

---

* The Hebrew word *Mehir*, rendered by our translators *gain*, signifies a *price, worth, value.* See Micah iii, 11, and 2 Sam. xxiv. But the *radical* idea is *to exchange.* He shall divide out the nominal crowns of his conquered nations, for an *exchange* of homage and aid, which in his turn he is to receive.

These names, in the preceding parts of the chapter, are
applied to Egypt and Syria. These countries are now
under the dominion of the Turks. These appellations, in the above passages, *may* be designed to denote
the Turkish empire. This empire, it is thought, is
soon to be subverted; that the way for the return of
the Jews may be prepared. (See section on the sixth
vial.)

The sixth trumpet established the Ottoman empire,
by loosing the four Turkish sultanies, which were
bound upon the river Euphrates.* And it is expected
the sixth vial will effect the ruin of the Turks; and this
at a period not far distant.† The attack in this passage in Daniel, of the king of the south, and the king
of the north, upon the infidel Power, may probably be
an event introductory to the judgment of the sixth
vial. The Ottoman empire may in some way be engaged in a war with the infidel Power, to its own
ruin. Whether this will be the case, or whether some
other powers, on the south, and on the north of the infidel Power, will prevail to check the common enemy,
time will decide. In favor of this being the case, it
may be remarked, that the leading *subject*, in this chapter, preceding the 36th verse, changes, in this verse,
from the *type* to the *antitype.* In like manner *the*
kingdom of the south, and kingdom of the north, spoken
of after this change in verse 36th from the type, to the
great Power of the last days, may relate to *different*
powers from the kingdom of the south and kingdom
of the north, in the preceding parts of the chapter.
Some nation in the *south* of the infidel Power may
push (butt) at him, and prevail so far as to impede
his ambitious projects: And some mighty power in
the north may lead a numerous host against him.
The coming of this king of the north against him like
a *whirlwind, with chariots and horsemen,* (armies of infantry, artillery, and cavalry) *and many ships,* seems
clearly to intimate, that a vast coalition is formed in the
north against him, in connexion with some naval pow-

*Rev. ix, 13.   †Rev. xvi, 12.

er. And the phraseology seems to intimate also great *success* against the infidel Power. For a mighty whirlwind usually prostrates every thing in its way. This great *reverse of things* perhaps, fulfils the predictions in parallel prophecies;—that the last part of this Roman Power—being part of iron, and part of clay,—should be partly strong, and partly broken;—that its parts should not cleave one to another;—that the earth should open her mouth, and swallow up the floods;—or the remainder of that wrath God would restrain.

A *new turn* seems in this passage to be given to the operations of the infidel Power: Or he is, afterward, found making *new invasions.* He *enters into the countries; overflows, and passes over.* Some distant expedition is set on foot. Something new and wonderful must be done, perhaps to retrieve the tarnished fame of his arms; and to accomplish some deep plot formed against the enemy. He is by and by found in the *Holy land.* The way must be prepared for another vial of divine wrath to be discharged.

Verses 41st—43d; *He shall enter into the glorious land, and many countries shall be overthrown; but these shall escape out of his hands, even Edom and Moab, and the chief of the children of Ammon. He shall stretch forth his hands also upon the countries, and the land of Egypt shall not escape. But he shall have power over the treasures of gold and silver, and over all the precious things of Egypt; and the Libyans and Ethiopians shall be at his steps.* Great success, attending the arms of the infidel Empire, in this his first expedition into the east, is here indicated. Having entered into the *countries*, probably of Turkey in Europe, and having overflowed, and passed over the ancient Hellespont into Asia Minor, he enters into Palestine, from the north, laying all the Turkish provinces at his feet. The south eastern Arabs, in Arabia Felix, escape, as being far out of the line of his tour. But the express exception of these, implies, that the other countries generally, in those parts, will fall be-

fore him. He beats his way round into Egypt, where
he makes a thorough conquest, and finds access to
whatever treasures the subdued people may have in
their possession; or may have been conveyed thither
by Turks, fleeing in consternation. Ethiopia, (probably not the African, but the Arabian,) and Libya, or
the States of Barbary (now subject to the Turks) are
to become subservient to his views. Thus he finishes
a most extensive expedition; in which probably, the
judgment of the sixth vial is fulfilled, in the subversion
of the Euphratean empire, that the way of the return
of the Jews and Israelites to the land of their fathers,
may be prepared.

Verses 44th and 45th; *But tidings out of the east
and out of the north shall trouble him; therefore he
shall go forth with great fury to destroy, and utterly
to make away many. And he shall plant the taber-
nacles of his palaces between the seas, in the glorious
holy mountain; yet he shall come to his end, and none
shall help him.* These tidings out of the east, and
out of the north, probably will relate to the return of
the ancient people of God. Their return may be expected soon to succeed the overthrow of the Turks.
And the infidel Power evidently feels his interest extremely affected by this event. To have such an influence set up within his lately acquired territories, in favor
of the Christian Religion, and of those powers, who support it, will fill him with rage. These tidings *may* be
said to be out of the *east*, and out of the *north*, as they
will relate to the collection of the Jews and Israel from
eastern and *northern* regions, to the Holy land. Repeatedly the restoration of the Jews is predicted as being from the land of the north, See Jer. xvi, 14, 15,
and xxiii, 7, 8. The infidel Power will therefore be
excited to collect "the kings of the earth, and of the
world," for a *new* expedition into Palestine;* and to

* That this passage in Daniel xi, from the 40th verse to the
end, predicts two expeditions of the infidel Power into Palestine, and at some distance of time from each other, I trust will
appear very evident from collateral prophecies, which will come
into view in the course of this Dissertation. This concise proph-

unite in a vast confederacy for the utter extirpation of the new church of God in Jerusalem.† The seventh vial finds him there, in Armageddon, at the head of his vast coalition of the kings of the earth, and of the false prophet; and it plunges him in ruin.‡ Here, under the most signal judgment of the great Head of the church, he *comes to his end, and none shall help him.*

Other passages in the Old Testament predict this infidel Power, and his overthrow in Palestine. But as the way may be better prepared to form a right understanding of them, the consideration of them will be deferred till the third chapter of this dissertation.

ecy in Daniel makes no mention of this Power's crossing the Mediterranean, to return home from his first expedition; or of any events, after he subdues Egypt, and has the Ethiopians and Libyans at his steps; till the tidings out of the east and out of the north trouble him, and call him again to Palestine. But we cannot infer from this, that he returns to Palestine from Egypt; or that the event takes place immediately, or before he returns home from his first expedition. The contrary of this will doubtless appear to be the fact. This first expedition prepares the way for the restoration of Israel, by the subversion of the Ottoman empire; as I trust will appear. And the return of God's ancient people, their conversion to Christianity, and the preparing of the way for the last coalition against them, must occupy *some time;* as long a time, I apprehend, as the space between the sixth and seventh vials. For I believe it will appear, that the first expedition of this infidel Power will fulfil the sixth vial; and that the second will open the way for the fulfilment of the seventh. To suppose that this prophecy in Daniel predicts but one expedition of the infidel Power into Palestine, is to involve the subject in great obscurity. The first expedition being said to be *at the time of the end,* (verse 40,) amounts to no great objection against there being two expeditions. The slaying of the witnesses is said to be, *when they shall have finished their testimony.* Yet some authors suppose that the event may consistently with this be more than three centuries before they shall have actually finished their testimony. This I believe to be *incorrect.* Yet I think it very consistent with the language of prophecy, where the year is not specified, to say, a thing is *at the time of the end,* when it is yet as far distant, as is the time of the sixth vial from that of the seventh.

† See chapter 3d of this Dissertation.
‡ Rev. xvi, from the 13th verse to the end; and xix, 19, 20, 21.

6

SECTION III.

Antichrist another Power, beside the Papal hierarchy.

It has been the general opinion of ·Protestant divines, that the predictions concerning Antichrist were fulfilled in the Papal hierarchy. Some of late doubt the correctness of this sentiment. It probably *may* be doubted I shall in this section note some prophecies, and make some remarks, not so much with a view to find the certainty of the rise of a great Power subsequent to the reign of Popery, as to show that this terrible subsequent Power is emphatically the *Antichrist* of the New Testament. In the prophecies now to be noted, and in the remarks to be made, both the above objects will be ascertained.

. No doubt the Romish hierarchy was indeed *antichristian;* and was so to a fatal degree. It was the blasphemous horn of the Roman Beast, into whose power the saints were to be delivered, for 1260 years; Dan. vii, 8, 25. It was the apostasy predicted by Paul, 1 Tim. iv, 1, 2, that "in the last days some should depart from the faith, giving heed to seducing spirits, and doctrines of devils." It was the second Beast, in Rev. xiii, 11, which rose out of the earth, had two horns like a lamb, but spake like a dragon. It was the woman, Rev. xvii, called "Mystery, Babylon the great, the mother of harlots, and abominations of the earth." It was the subject of various prophecies; a terrible power; an awful judgment to the world; and as abominable, as any have ever conceived.

But it appears evident, that the Papal hierarchy was not the last great and terrible Power, foretold to be raised up in judgment to the wicked nations, in the last days. Another Power was to be raised up, for the execution of divine judgments, to be a rod of iron, a battle axe of destruction, to execute divine wrath on that Mother of harlots, to hate the whore, to make her desolate and naked, to eat her flesh, and burn her with fire, and to dash in pieces the nations of God's enemies. This work of judgment was not to be done by a *Papal hierarchy!* but by a *tremendous Power*, raised up for the purpose, *subsequent* to the reign of the Papal hierarchy.

In the predictions to be noted in this dissertation, it is evident, that it is the secular Roman Beast, under his last head; and not the *Papal* Beast, the little horn, the false prophet, that is, the great leader in battle array against Christ, at the time of the end, or of the seventh vial. This appears in Dan. vii, 11, "I beheld then, because of the voice of the great words, which the *horn* spake, I beheld even till the *BEAST* was slain, and *his* body destroyed, and given to the burning flame." It is important to note here, that the great Power upon the stage, predominant when Christ appears at the battle of the great day, is the *Roman Beast*, which in verse 2, rose out of the sea, or the tumultuous state of the nations, before the Christian era. This *Beast* is here spoken of as distinct from the Papal power, which in the same passage is mentioned as the *horn* of this same Beast. The Beast is the great Power *then to be slain*, and his body destroyed and given to the burning flame. This event, of his body's being destroyed and given to the burning flame, none can pretend has yet taken place. It must be future. The *Roman Beast* then, great and terrible, must be found in existence, distinct from Popery, either now, or at a time still future. This secular Roman Beast is the great Power in hostile array against Christ; and is the Leader of the contending nations, in that last battle of the great day of God.

The above passage in Daniel accords *with*, and is explained *by*, Rev. xix, 19, 20; where we have a more full account of the same period and event. After a description is there given of Christ in battle array, occasioned by a war against him by the terrible Power of the last days, we read, "And I saw the *Beast*, and the kings of the earth gathered together to make war against him, who sat on the horse, and against his army. And the Beast was taken, and with him the false prophet, that wrought miracles before him, with which he deceived them, that had received the mark of the beast, and them that worshipped his image:—These both

were cast alive into a lake of fire burning with brimstone. And the remnant were slain with the sword of
him, who sat upon the horse." It is thus evident, that
the great Power of the last days, leading the battle
against Christ, is the *old Roman Beast*, distinct from
the Papal hierarchy, and *managing* this hierarchy, as a
puppet in his hands; which hierarchy in the above passage, is noted, as the *false prophet;* and in the corresponding passage, in Daniel, as the *horn* of that Beast.
In various other passages these two Powers are found,
at the same period, in the same connexion; the *Beast*
and the *false prophet.* The *Beast* is first, or is the great
mischievous *Power,* then in existence. And the *horn,*
the *false prophet,* is a mere subordinate tool of mischief in his possession.

In Rev. xvii, this Power is found ascending, in the
last days, from the bottomless pit, to go into perdition.
(A passage which will be explained in another section.)
The going of this Beast into perdition, is there twice
spoken of, as nearly connected with his rise from
the infernal world, and from his state of long inactivity;
indicating, that the time of this his revival is in the *last
days,* or but a short time before he goes into perdition.
This idea we repeatedly find. The apostles inform,
of the same Power, "that his judgement lingereth not,
and his damnation slumbereth not;" that he bringeth
upon himself *swift destruction;* as did the rebelling
angels, and various most notorious transgressors of
old; Jude 5—8 verse. And 2 Pet. ii, 1—10. But so
short a reign cannot be attributed to the Papal hierarchy; which continued for a great course of centuries.
The great Power of the last days then, must be subsequent to, and distinct from Popery.

In the above noted chapter, Rev. xvii, this great
Power is represented as distinct from Popery. The
one is the scarlet colored Beast, full of the names of
blasphemy. The other is a woman, with all the characteristics of the hierarchy, borne by this Beast, and by
his horns executed, verse 16. This Beast must be the
tremendous Power of the last days, noted in the aforecited passages, Dan. vii, 11; and Rev. xix, 19, 20.

In Rev. xvi, 13, we find this Beast, distinct from Popery, and placed before it, as a greater enemy. The passage informs of the three unclean spirits like *frogs*, from the mouth of the dragon, (the devil) of the *Beast*, (the newly raised terrible Power, placed next to the dragon) and of the false prophet; (the skeleton of Popery and false religion) spirits of *devils*, going out into the kingdoms of the earth, and of the whole world, to gather them to the battle of that great day of God Almighty. Here is a Beast, at that time, *beside*, and superior *to* Popery. These three Powers, the devil, the *Beast*, and the false prophet, are found again in the same connexion, in Rev. xx, 10, being cast together into the lake of fire. ' From the view of these passages, it clearly appears, that a great and terrible Power was to rise posterior to Popery. The same appears, as will be noted, in Rev. xiv, 8—11, where, after Papal Babylon is *fallen*, a most terrible *Beast* is presented.

The present state of the Romish hierarchy forbids, that it can be that terrible Power of the last days. That hierarchy has already fallen under the iron grasp of a far superior Power who is inflicting on its nations the denounced judgments of heaven. To whatever degree of mischief, to the people of God, the dependant skeleton of the hierarchy may be yet made an occasion, before the battle of the great day; (and the indications concerning this are thought to be not uninteresting,) yet this false prophet will be only an engine of policy, and perhaps of desperate malice, in the hands of a far superior Power, who most heartily despises all true religion.

The great Power of the last day is, (Dan. vi, 40—43,) *at* or *near* the time of the end, engaged in a war with the king of the south, and the king of the north, and probably a coalition united with them. This was never fulfilled in the Papal hierarchy. If it were, it must have been in the attacks of the Saracens, who fulfilled the first wo trumpet, Rev. ix, 1—12; or in the invasions of the Turks under the second wo trumpet, Rev. ix, 12—21. No other events can have the least even apparent claim, as having been a fulfilment of that prophecy. But the former of these events was more than 1200 years ago; and the latter more than 350. But the time of the end, when this war, with the king of the south and king of the north, is to be undertaken, must be still *future.* Consequently, that war must be with a Power subsequent to the hierarchy, viz. the terrible Power of the last days. The king of the south was Egypt: The king of the north, Syria. Those nations are now under the government of the Turks. The Turkish government is soon to be subverted, under the sixth vial of wrath; Rev. xvi, 12. The fulfilment of the prediction, relative to this war, with the king of the south, and the king of the north may soon commence. And some power *may* be found in union with the *latter* or the Turks, which may give an emphasis to his being called, at this late period, *the king of the north.* However this may be, the argument in this paragraph shews, that a great and terrible Power was to be raised up subsequent to the reign of Popery.

Popery was a very different thing from a rod of iron to dash wicked nations to pieces. It was an abominable corrupting system; a harlot, to pollute, and to prepare the nations for judgment. But it was very far from being that great new threshing instrument, having iron teeth, to beat the nations to powder, which was to be furnished in the last days, Isa. xli, 15. It required an instrument very different from the *Papal hierarchy,* (represented as a *delicate female,)* to beat small the mountains of wicked potentates and kingdoms of the earth, and to make the hills as chaff. And a very different instrument was, for this purpose to be furnished, and is indeed furnished, before the face of the world.

When the reformation under Luther, the art of printing, and the revival of learning in Europe, after the dark ages, had unveiled the abominations of Popery; there were many millions whose pride of heart would not permit them to embrace the doctrines of the reformation, and who would easily be induced to deny the Christian Religion, and its blessed Author.

This was a process very natural in old corrupt Popish countries, after the mummery of their false religion was exposed, and became ridiculous. Especially was this the case in a nation constitutionally licentious, volatile, haughty, and impatient of every restraint. Such a people would need only an association of infidel philosophers, under the instigation of the infernal dragon, to institute a scheme, which would give birth to the terrible Power of the last days. And such will appear to have been his origin.

A question now arises:—Is this the Power, that was to be known by the name of *Antichrist;* The Papal hierarchy *was* indeed predicted to exist; a most abominable apostasy. But a posterior, and most terrible Power, raised up for the work of divine judgment, was also much more abundantly predicted to exist. And the apostle John speaks of *Antichrist,* who, they had heard, was to come. Now which of the two above noted Powers was to be that Antichrist of John?

Reply. A decision of this is not very material. The leading sentiment of my dissertation is not materially effected, be the question decided as it may. For it is *that great Power of the last days,* of which I treat; whether that prediction of John, relative to Antichrist, apply exclusively to this Power, or not. If it do *not* apply exclusively to it; still there are many predictions that *do;* and *these* contain the subject of my dissertation.

I have taken the liberty to apply to this Power, the name of *Antichrist;* being of opinion, that this Power is essentially *included* in the Antichrist of John, if not most immediately the very Power designed.

Several of my reasons for this opinion I will now state.

1. It is the express characteristic of John's Antichrist, that he is an *Atheist;* denying the Father and the Son; denying that Jesus is the Christ; denying that Christ is come in the flesh. And we find it to be the leading characteristics of the terrible Power of the last days, (as has appeared in Dan. xi, 36—, and as *will* appear in the next section, on the writings of the apos-

tles,) that he denies *God* and *Christ;*—"privately bringing in damnable heresies;—denying the Lord, who
bought them;—and bringing upon themselves 'swift
destruction:"—"Denying the only Lord God; and our
Lord Jesus Christ." Abundantly this Power is represented, as Antichrist is represented to be, *a gross
infidel.*

But the papal hierarchy did not deny the Father, nor
the Son. It did not deny the only Lord God; nor the
Lord Jesus Christ. It did not deny that Jesus Christ
had come in the flesh. It professed the highest veneration for God, and Christ, and the Christian Religion.
And though this profession was not *gracious*, but was
abominable hypocrisy; yet this profession (uniformly
constituting an essential part of their system from the
beginning) is not to be blended with the personal wickedness of its subjects. It is in itself *proper* to profess
a veneration for God and Christ, and the Christian
Religion. And this profession lying at the foundation
of a system, constitutes a feature in the basis of that
system, very different from the *atheism* of Antichrist.
Antichrist, at his developement, takes to himself the
character of a *gross atheist*. Whatever "form of Godliness" (while he denies the power of it) he may afterward find it most convenient to his diabolical views, to
adopt, yet he is a *noted atheist.*

2. Another argument in favor of the idea, that the
terrible Power of the last days is the Antichrist in
John's epistle, is as follows: This Power is abundantly
represented as engaged in an *actual war with Christ.*
This war is represented as carried on with such *spirit*
and *power*, as to bring down the Captain of our salvation from heaven, with all his retinue and apparatus for
the most terrible warfare. Christ is represented as en-
gaging in this war, with unprecedented attention; and
pursuing it to a final and most decisive victory over the
Beast, and the false prophet, the kings of the earth, and
all their armies.

In Dan. xii, 1, after the great infidel Power of the
last days, described in the preceding chapter, has
reached Palestine, to make war with God's ancient

covenant people there, "Michael (Christ) the great
Prince, stands up for the children of his people; and
there shall be a time of trouble, such as never was since
there was a nation, even to that same time." Here is a
war greater than any ever before known, between this
very Power, and Christ. In Rev. xiii, 7, we learn,
that the great object of this *healed head* of the Roman
Beast, (the great Power of the last days,) is *war* with
the people of God." "And it was given unto him to
make *war* with the saints." In Rev. xvii, 14, we find
the same. Of the ten horns of this very Beast from the
bottomless pit, it is said; "These shall make *war with
the Lamb.*" Of the same Beast it is said, relative to
the witnesses, Rev. xi, 7, "And when they shall have
finished their testimony, the beast that ascendeth out of
the bottomless pit, shall make *war against* them."
Rev. xii, 13, "And when the dragon saw, that he was
cast out unto the earth, he *persecuted the woman,* that
brought forth the man child." His floods of rage,
falsehood and violence, now poured forth, to cause the
church to be carried away; and the voice of wo, at the
same time from heaven, against the inhabiters of the
earth and of the sea, because the devil had come, with
great wrath, knowing he had but a short time, (or the
Millennium was about to dawn) *all indicate unprecedented war at that time against Christ.* In Rev. xiv,
12— to the end, the same thing is indicated. After the
missionary Angel had begun his flight through the
midst of heaven, to preach the Gospel to all nations;
after it was ascertained that Papal Babylon had fallen;
and a third warning voice was heard, warning mankind, as they would escape inevitable damnation, to abstain from all affinity with the *Beast,* (the horrid blasphemous Power of the day,) solemn indications follow.
This warning will not be taken in good part, by the
powers implicated. And it follows; "Here is the patience of the saints: Here are they, that keep the commandments of God, and the faith of Jesus. And I
heard a voice from heaven, saying unto me, Write,
Blessed are the dead, who die in the Lord, from hence-

7

forth; yea, saith the Spirit, that they may rest from their labors; and their works do follow them." A signal *war against the church* is here implied. And what follows confirms the indication. For the Captain of her salvation immediately appears in arms. The next verse presents him upon the white cloud, with his sharp sickle. The harvest of the earth is reaped. The clusters of the vine of the earth, *fully ripe*, are gathered for the pressing. The wine-press is trodden; and a river of blood is emitted. All this implies, that the great Power of that day is in *arms against heaven;* having instituted a most furious *war with Christ*.

The same is found in Rev. xiii, 13—. To prepare the way for the seventh vial, the agents of the dragon, the Beast, and the false prophet, (unclean spirits, like frogs, called spirits of devils,) go out unto the people of the whole world, to gather them to the "BATTLE of that great day of God Almighty." War virtually against Christ, is the object. And the Beast (the great Power of the last days) next after the infernal dragon, is the great instigator of it, by his threefold, diabolical influence. Christ upon this proclaims, that his coming should be sudden and dreadful. His enemies are convened in battle array at Armageddon. There he comes upon them, and decides the contest.

A sublime description of this warfare, and of its final decision, we find in Rev. xix, 11— to the end. Christ, as a great triumphant general, upon a white horse, an ancient emblem of victory, *rides forth.* His eyes are as a flame of fire. Many crowns are upon his head, His vesture is already dipped in the blood of his enemies. All the armies of heaven follow him, upon white horses. The *war against him* has become most serious. Out of his mouth goeth a sharp two edged sword, by which to smite the nations. He is now going to rule them with his rod of iron, and to tread the wine-press of the fierceness of the wrath of Almighty God. On his vesture and on his thigh his titles appear, in capitals, KING OF KINGS, AND LORD OF LORDS. The occasion of this tremendous order of battle, following verses unfold. "And I saw the *Beast*, and the kings of the earth, and their armies, gathered together, *to make war* against him, who sat upon the horse, and against his army. Here is the great Power of the last days, at the head of the coalition *against* heaven. This is the Power, concerning whom we have so many express predictions of his being in *ar-ray against Christ.* Is he not then, the *Antichrist?* What is *meant* by *Antichrist?* The word signifies *against Christ.* Does the word of God inform of any *other Power,* as having been more expressly *against Christ,* than this Power of the last days? Can one third so much of *war language* be found in the word of God, relative to the Papal hierarchy, or any other power, as is found relative to the great Power of the last days? Let the analogy of Scripture then, decide who is the *Antichrist* of the New Testament.

3. Another argument, that the Antichrist in John is this great infidel Power, is this:—John says, "*Ye have heard that Antichrist shall come.*" He here refers his readers to an event well ascertained in prophecy. This was before his Revelation was written, or the books of the New Testament collected, or filled up. His reference then, must have been chiefly, if not wholly, to the *Old Testament.* This was *their Bible.* And it was *there* they had heard that *Antichrist was to come.* But in the Old Testament they had read but very little, and that in one or two obscure hints, relative to the *Papal hierarchy:*—While they had read *much, very much,* relative to the terrible Power of the last days. See section ii, and v, chap. iii, of this dissertation. This terrible Power, predicted Dan. xi, 36— to the end, we find, was a Power much predicted before by the prophets. Chap. x, 21, "But I will shew thee that, which is *noted in the scriptures of truth.*" This Power had been the great subject of Eezekiel xxxviii, and xxxix chapters; Gog, the land of Magog;—and of other prophecies of the Old Testament. So that, when his destruction is predicted, Rev. x, 7, by the seventh trumpet, or third wo, it is there said to be, only "as God hath declared to his servants the prophets." And in Rev. xvi, 14, when the abominable, slippery and

crooked agents of this Beast collects the kingdoms of the world, it is said to be "to the battle of THAT GREAT DAY of God Almighty." *What* great day? THAT great day so well known in the Old Testament; as in the above quotation, Rev. x, 7, "as he hath declared to his servants the prophets." John's Antichrist then, being the Power, that his readers had heard *was to come*, (1 John ii, 18,) must, I think, be the great Power, that leads the coalition in the battle of *that* great day of God Almighty.

I might multiply arguments: But it seems needless. It will appear in the next section that John's Antichrist, when he appears, is soon to be destroyed. But the Papal hierarchy was to exist 1260 years. Which argument seems sufficient to show, that Antichrist was to be a Power subsequent to the reign of the Papal hierarchy.

SECTION IV.

Antichrist predicted by the Apostles.

IN 1 John ii, 18, we read, *Little children, it is the last time: and as ye have heard that Antichrist shall come, even now are there many antichrists; whereby we know that it is the last time.* This Epistle is said to have been written with a principal view to the Christian Jews. A principal object of the writer probably was, to exhibit the beauties of the Christian character, in contrast with the bitterness of the unbelieving Jews, and of the carnal heart; and to evince the great doctrine, that Jesus Christ is the true Messiah; in opposition to the infidelity of the Jews.*

*It has been supposed by some, that St. John, in this Epistle, had his eye upon the heresies of the Gnostics and Ebionites. The Gnostics, a heretical, gentile sect, from Simon Magus, boasting of their knowledge sufficient to teach men the things of God, denied the humanity of Jesus Christ; and held that he suffered only in appearance. The Ebionites, a heretical sect of Jewish Christians, denied the Divinity, and the miraculous conception of Jesus Christ; yet pretended to hold that he was sent of God. Possibly the sacred writer had his eye upon these heretics. They virtually denied the Father and the Son, and thus were antichrists. But the infidelity and bitterness of his

This Epistle is supposed to have been written just before the destruction of Jerusalem; which was one coming of Christ, or a lively type of the destruction of Antichrist, at the battle of the great day. Some, it is true, have conjectured, that it was written upwards of twenty years after the destruction of Jerusalem. But there is no evidence of this; as good expositors acknowledge. I think those have the most evidence on their side, who think it to have been written before the destruction of Jerusalem. Doctor Guyes was of this opinion; and thinks, that the individual antichrist spoken of, chap. ii, 18, and iv, 1, were the Judaizing teachers, predicted by Christ, Matt. xxiv, 24, to come before the destruction of the temple. · These were forerunners, or typical, of the false teachers of the last days. This circumstance, that the Epistle was written just before the fatal catastrophe of the Jews, by Titus the Roman, accounts for the writers sayings, "It is the last time." In the original, it is—*the last hour.* It was then, as it were, the last hour, previous to the coming of Christ, in the fatal catastrophe of the Jewish nation. There were at that time many violent opposers of the doctrine of the Divinity of Christ, especially among the Jews, and the Judaizing teachers;* from which event the Apostle infers, that it was the last hour with that unbelieving nation. And so it proved in fact. For *wrath soon came upon them to the uttermost.*† Eleven hundred thousand Jews perished by the sword, at the siege and taking of Jerusalem by the Romans. And more than fourteen hundred thousand were destroyed in that war. Their temple was burnt; their city destroyed; and the small remnant of the Jews were sold for slaves to different nations. *Ye have heard that Antichrist shall come.* He alludes to predictions of an event, which was then *far future.* — When he adds, *even now are there many antichrists,* he could not mean,

---

nation, the Jews, and the hordes of Judaizing teachers, whom Paul calls *dogs, evil workers, and the concision,* Phil. iii, 2, probably were one great occasion of his writing this Epistle.

*Titus i, 10, 11.

†See Josephus on the destruction of Jerusalem.

that these many antichrists constituted *that* Antichrist, who they had heard was to come. He distinguishes between that Power *then far future,* and the petty, individual antichrists of his day, putting one in the singular, and the other in the plural. We may view the passage, as amounting to what is expressed in the following paraphrase: Ye are assured in various predictions, that a terrible Power, which may properly be styled Antichrist, on account of his enmity against the Christian cause, shall arise in the last days; and shall bring upon himself swift destruction: So that the appearance of that wicked Power shall be a certain token of its then being the *last time* with the enemies of the Church. And even now are there many among our countrymen, of the same bitter, infidel spirit; by which we know it to be the last time with the Jewish polity. Josephus informs, that in the last tremendous scenes of the destruction of the Jews, it was common for them "to make a jest of Divine things, and to deride, as so many senseless tales, and juggling impostures, the sacred oracles of their prophets." They were given up to the most gross and barefaced infidelity; and thus they were the antichrists of that day. Or they may be viewed as a *type* of the great Antichrist of the last time. *Who is a liar, but he that denieth that Jesus is the Christ? He is Antichrist that denieth the Father and the Son.** *And every spirit, that confesseth not that Jesus Christ is come in the flesh, is not of God: and this is that spirit of Antichrist, whereof ye have heard that it should come, and even now already is it in the world.*† Here it is the decided *character* and *spirit* of Antichrist, that he is a gross Infidel: Not merely loving to have pre-eminence; or corrupting the ordinances of Christ; as did the Romish hierarchy; but expressly *denying Christ;* having the very spirit, which the infidel Jews possessed. The Apostle in the above passages teaches, that the Antichristian spirit, then existing, indicated that it was the *last hour* with its subjects. But it was the last hour only with the Jews. It

*1 John ii, 22.   †1 John iv, 3.

was *their* gross infidelity then, which he calls the spirit of Antichrist. His inference, that the spirit of Antichrist, then existing, indicated that it was the last hour with its subjects, was deduced from this fact, which he understood to be a truth, viz. that the rise of Antichrist was to be but a short time, *like an hour*, before his utter destruction. The reasoning of the Apostle rests on this ground. For surely if Antichrist might exist many centuries, as did Popery, before he *goeth into perdition*, the Apostle could not have inferred from the existence of the spirit of Antichrist in his day, that it was the *last hour* with its subjects. We arrive then at this conclusion from the remarks of St. John, that Antichrist is another Power beside the Papal hierarchy; and that his rise was to be but a short time before the battle of the great day. And these ideas we find clearly exhibited in various prophecies.

The other apostles, Paul, Peter and Jude, predict this Power, and his abominable agency and influence. I shall first note the writings of Jude. He inscribes his Epistle to the people of no particular place; but to the true people of God; "to them, that are sanctified by God the Father, and preserved in Christ Jesus, and called." From various considerations, which I shall proceed to note, it is evident, that his Epistle is *prophetic;* or that the events of it, when he wrote, were *far future;* and were to take place but just before the Millennium. I shall first make this appear; otherwise, my remarks upon the Epistle will be of no avail to my object.

1. In verse 4, the writer hints what he was going to do; by informing, that the characters, he was about to describe, "were of old ordained to this condemnation." In the original it is, "of old forewritten to this judgment." Alluding to the ancient predictions, in the prophets, relative to the great Power of the last days. It is as though Jude had said; I am now going to describe the characters and agents of that tremendous enemy of the church in the last days, just before the millennial Kingdom of Christ, *so much predicted* and *described* in the *prophets;*—the people there "forewritten

to this judgment;"—or, predescribed to this character
and destruction. If the descriptions in this Epistle
had some primary reference to the Judaizing teachers
of that day; it is evident, from the above clause, of
their having been "of old forewritten to this judgment," that they had their ultimate reference to the
characters, that introduce the battle of that great day
of God Almighty. For these are the characters *forewritten*, in the ancient prophets, as has been noted,
and as will more fully appear.

2. In verse 14, of this Epistle we have another clew
for our guidance, in our inquiry for the period and
characters described. "And Enoch also, the seventh
from Adam, prophesied of *these* (these characters, that
I describe) saying, Behold the Lord cometh with ten
thousands of his saints, to execute judgment upon all,
and to convince all, that are ungodly among them, of
all their ungodly deeds; and of all their hard speeches,
which ungodly sinners have spoken against him!"
Here we learn, that the characters described are those,
who shall be in existence on earth, when the Lord shall
come; with all his retinue of war, to sweep the wicked
from the earth:—That it is their malice against him,
(in his people) their hard speeches and ungodly deeds,
which will be the immediate occasion of that tremendous judgment:—And that their wickedness and their
ruin are to be so terrible, that Enoch was inspired to
predict the events, more than seven hundred years before the flood!

How striking, that this solitary and precious fragment of most ancient prophecy should be preserved
now for fifty centuries, to designate, with other scriptures, the period, character and overthrow of the terrible Power of the last days! And how exactly its language, of the *Lord's coming with thousands of his saints*,
comports with the descriptions of the same battle, in Rev.
xix, 11,— to the end; "*all the armies of heaven* following him on white horses:" Joel iii, 11, where Antichrist
is gathered to the valley of decision; and the prophet
adds, "Thither cause thy *mighty ones* to come down,
O Lord:" As Zech. xiv, 5, upon the same period and

event; "and the Lord my God shall come, and *all the saints with thee.*

3. In verses 17, 18, the point under consideration is *decided.* "But, beloved, remember the words, which were spoken before of the apostles of our Lord Jesus Christ; how they told you, there should be mockers in the *last time,* who should walk after their own ungodly lusts." Here the characters, whom he was describing, are the *mockers of the LAST TIME!* And they are the very characters described by the *other apostles;* that, "in the *last days* perilous times shall come;" "there shall come, in the *last days,* scoffers.".

Thus we may consult Jude's Epistle with an *assurance* that those whom he describes, are the abominable characters of the *last days.*

In his introduction of the subject is a solemn caution to duty. "Beloved, when I gave all diligence to write unto you of the common salvation, it was needful for me to write unto you, and exhort you, that ye should earnestly contend for the faith, which was once delivered unto the saints." He then begins his subject. "For there are certain men crept in unawares, who were before of old ordained to this condemnation; ungodly men, turning the grace of our God into lasciviousness, and denying the only Lord God, and our Lord Jesus Christ." Here is the same character, given of the terrible Power, Dan. xi, 36—, rejecting *God* and the *Savior.* 1 John ii, 22, "He is Antichrist, that denieth the Father and the Son." These characters have "crept in unawares:"—come, as from some dark recess: Under fatal disguises:—Are *among* a people, and have effected their mischievous plans, before they are known.

The writer now, to fortify the minds of his readers, before he leads them over the ground, or unfolds the terrific picture, introduces the idea, which generally attends the description of this terrible Power, that his reign shall be short; he shall soon be destroyed. This he does, in verses 5, 6, 7, by noting the signal ruin of the ancient most inveterate enemies of God, as an emblem of what is just ready to be executed on these

8

wretched characters of the last days, when they should appear. "I will therefore put you in remembrance, though ye once knew this, how that the Lord, having saved the people out of the land of Egypt, afterward destroyed them, that believed not. And the angels, who kept not their first estate, but left their own habitation, he hath reserved in everlasting chains under darkness, unto the judgment of the great day. Even as Sodom and Gomorrah, and the cities about them, in like manner giving themselves over to fornication, and going after strange flesh, and set forth for an example, suffering the vengeance of eternal fire." He goes on, "Likewise also these filthy dreamers defile the flesh, despise dominion, and speak evil of dignities." They are here noted by the Holy Ghost as *dreamers*. Their plans are *wild dreams*. They are as much at variance with the established and most useful institutions among men, and the approved paths of experience, as dreams are at variance with common sense. And they are notorious for despising virtuous dominion, and vilifying all dignified characters, who stand in their way. "Yet Michael the Archangel, when contending with the devil, he disputed about the body of Moses, *durst not (could not endure to)* bring against him a railing accusation; but said, The Lord rebuke thee.

But these, (i. e. the characters of the last days) speak evil of those things, which they know not; but what they know naturally as brute beasts, in those things they correct themselves." Characters and institutions, whose excellency is beyond their perverted conceptions, *they slander*. And their natural powers are utterly vitiated.

"Wo unto them! for they have gone in the way of Cain, and ran greedily after the error of Balaam for reward, and perished in the gainsaying of Core." *Cain* hated and slew his brother, because his own works were evil, and his brothers were righteous, 1 John iii, 12. *Balaam* was hired to curse, and labored to corrupt and to destroy the people of God. *Korah*, and his impious company rose against the order of Religion and government established in Israel; and all perished under the immediate avenging hand of God. See

Numb. xvi, 1—38. These characters of the last days are, in all these particulars, *followers of those men.*

"These are spots in your feasts of charity, when they feast with you, feeding themselves without fear; cloulds without water, carried about of winds; trees, whose fruit withereth, without fruit, twice dead, pluck- ed up by the roots; raging waves of the sea, foaming out their own shame; wandering stars, to whom is re- served the blackness of darkness forever." Amazing descriptions of the diabolical *deceivers* of the last days! The last above mentioned is *striking;* "wandering stars!" or comets with fiery tails, sweeping awry over every land; crossing the orbits of all other planets; and deemed harbingers of war and judgments. The afore- noted passage, relative to the prophecy of Enoch, fol- lows. This has already been noted. The description then continues.

"These are murmurers, complainers, walking after their own lusts; and their mouth speaking great swell- ing words; having men's persons in admiration because of advantage." Murmuring and complaining, under some sly pretence, against whatever impedes their pur- poses: Their words being abundant and very stout: While they flatter the tools, and cringe to the more im- portant agents of their cause.

"But, beloved, remember the words of the apostles of our Lord Jesus Christ; how that they told you, there should be mockers in the last time, who should walk after their own ungodly lusts."

The next characteristic is remarkable. "These be they, who *separate themselves; sensual,* having not the *spirit.*" Their plans are formed *separately* from the mass of mankind. All is done in the *dark.* The great spring of their vast machine is designed to be kept out of sight. Their object is designed to be kept *conceal- ed,* till it is *effected.* The world is to be bound by in. *visible hands!*

And their *leaders* are not only *graceless,* but grossly "*sensual.*" Sensuality and selfishness are their highest motives. "*Having not the Spirit.*" The mass of mankind *have* usually been subjects of the striving,

checks and restraining influences of the Spirit of God.
Even the violent people of the old world were thus.
God said of them, "My Spirit shall not always strive
with man;" which implied that he was then still striving. But with the diabolical seducers of the last days,
the Spirit of God has *ceased to strive!* It is emphatically announced of them, even in comparison with the
rest of the impenitent part of mankind, that they *have
not the Spirit.* A spirit very opposite to the Spirit
of God, has leavened their whole souls. The whole
scheme is, in other scriptures, represented as being
under the agency of the *wicked one*, instead of the Spirit
of God. "For they are spirits of devils," it is said of
these three unclean spirits like frogs. In one passage
they are represented, to be "an habitation of devils; a
hold of every foul spirit, and a cage of every unclean
and hateful bird." This Beast "ascendeth out of the
bottomless pit." "And the *dragon* gave him his power,
and seat, and great authority." "Wo to the inhabiters of the earth and of the sea; for the *devil* is come
down unto you, having great wroth, because he knoweth he hath but a short time." No wonder then, that
it is said of them in Jude, *"having not the Spirit."*
They have a *reprobate* spirit, the spirit of the *wicked
one.* Hence David, predicting the Kingdom of the
righteous Ruler, (Christ,) and the scene of its introduction, concerning these very characters in Jude,
writes thus; "But the sons of Belial shall be all of them
as thorns thrust away, because they cannot be taken
with hands; but the man, who would touch them, must
be fenced with iron, and the staff of a spear; and they
shall be utterly burnt with fire in the same place."
2 Sam. xxiii, 6. 7.

Jude informs, (as we have seen,) verses 17, 18, that
the other apostle also predicted these mockers of the
last time. We may then turn to their writings with
an assurance, that we shall find their predictions of these
wretched characters. *And we do find them.*

Paul described this terrible Power of the last days,
and the agents of his mischief, not only in the Man of
sin in an Epistle to the Thessalonians; (see sect. viii,

chap. 1 of this dissertation;) but also in 1 Tim. iii, 1—8. In this *first* Epistle, he had predicted the apostasy and superstition of the church of Rome, chap. iv, 1—3. "Now the Spirit speaketh expressly, that in the *latter times,* (mark here! it is not in the *last days;* but *latter times)* some shall depart from the faith, giving heed to seducing spirits, and doctrines of devils; speaking lies in hypocrisy; having their conscience seared with a hot iron; forbidding to marry; and commanding to abstain from meats, which God had created to be received with thanksgiving of them, that believe and know the truth." Here was predicted, not a system of *infidelity,* but of *superstitious religious rites;* "doctrines of demons," the papistical worshipping of saints and images, as some expositors explain it. But in his second Epistle, iii, 1—8, Paul makes an advance; and predicts the rise of *another later* Power; and *one* of a *different* character. "This know, also, that in the *last days* perilous times shall come." q. d. This know, over and above what I before predicted concerning the Papal apostasy. That was to be in the *latter* days; this in the *last* days. "For men shall be lovers of their ownselves, covetous, boasters, proud, blasphemers, disobedient to parents, unthankful, unholy, without natural affection, trucebreakers, false accusers, incontinent, fierce, despisers of those that are good, traitors, heady, high-minded, lovers of pleasure more than lovers of God, having a form of Godliness, but denying the power thereof; from such turn away. For of this sort, are they, who creep into houses, and lead captive silly women laden with sins, led away with divers lusts; ever learning, and never able to come to the knowledge of the truth. Now as Jannes and Jambres (the pagan magicians of Egypt) withstood Moses, so do these also resist the truth; men of corrupt minds, reprobate concerning the faith." Here we have a striking description of the malignant passions of men let loose from the restraints of Religion, and of a good education; as is abundantly predicted to be the case, in the last days, in the reign of infidelity and of terror; when the rage of the times will be; "Let us break their bands asunder; and cast away their cords

from us." Even these characters, after they have fixed
their characteristic of infidelity, may be led to adopt
some trite form of Godliness; having found it necessary
for their existence in the world; or to cover their enormities; or to propagate their sentiments with more fatal
effect. Or this trait of character here given may peculiarly relate to some *class* of them; perhaps *that* from
the mouth of the *false prophet;* zealots in religion;
while yet they are propagators of real infidelity. Their
clandestine operations in the propagation of their
sentiments, are strikingly noted, by their creeping into
houses and leading captive the simple and uninformed,
who are under the influence of sensual motives. Their
fair pretences are hinted. *Ever learning.* Yet they
are *never able to come to the knowledge of the truth.*
For their hearts are utterly hostile to the truth, corrupt,
and reprobate.

Peter informs us of the same characters; whom he
calls *scoffers in the last days.* He fills a whole chapter
with the most lively and affecting descriptions of them.
It is evident that the wretched beings, presented in 2 Pet.
ii chapter, are the very characters predicted by Jude.
For Jude evidently has this very chapter, and the beginning of the next, in view, not only when he directs us
to "remember the words, which were spoken before of
the apostles of our Lord Jesus Christ, how they told
you, there should be *mockers in the last time;*" but in
the *whole* of his Epistle. None, who will compare the
two chapters, can doubt of this. The characteristics
given, and the stile, are the same. We are hence assured, that the deceivers described by Peter, are the infidels of the last days.

He says, "But there were false prophets also among
the people, even as there shall be false teachers among
you, who privately shall bring in damnable heresies,
even denying the Lord that bought them, and bring
upon themselves swift destruction." Here is the very
character of Antichrist; "denying the Lord, that bought
them." And as in Jude, they introduce their damnable heresies *privately.* Also, as in the various other
predictions of them, their *destruction comes swiftly.*

They are here *false teachers.* —They are those, who (some under one disguise, and some under another,) undertake to *instruct* mankind, and to *form* the public sentiments. This they will do in *preaching; in gazettes; or in other* communications.

"And many shall follow their pernicious ways; by reason of whom the way of truth shall be evil spoken of." As Paul had before said to Timothy, *For the time will come, when they (the mass of the people) will not endure sound doctrine: but, after their own lusts, shall heap to themselves teachers; having itching ears; and they shall turn away their ears from the truth, and shall be turned unto fables.* Peter proceeds.

"And through covetousness shall they with feigned words make merchandise of you: whose judgment now of a long time lingereth not; and their damnation slumbereth not." With deceptive words, and sordid views, they seduce and ruin the people.

Peter now, as did Jude, in the beginning of his description, relieves the minds of his readers with the idea, that their reign should be *short,* and their ruin *terrible;* by adverting to the destruction of the sinning angels, of the old world, and of Sodom and Gomorrah, as an emblem of what shall shortly befall these wretches of the last days. See verse 4—7, And for the support of the persecuted people of God, at the same period, they are here reminded of God's delivering *"just Lot,* vexed with the filthy conversation of the wicked," and with their unlawful deeds. "For the Lord knoweth how to deliver the Godly out of temptation; and to reserve the unjust unto the day of judgment to be punished." And especially these characters of the last days, who, he tells us, "walk after the flesh, in the lust of uncleanness, and despise government;" i. e. all evangelical and *virtuous* government:—"Presumptuous are they, self willed, they are not afraid to speak evil of dignities. Whereas, Angels, who are greater in power and might, bring not railing accusation against them before the Lord. But these are natural brute beasts, made to be taken and destroyed, speak evil of the things, which they understand not, and shall utterly perish in their own cor-

ruption: And shall receive the reward of unrighteousness, as they that count it pleasure to riot in the day
time. Spots are they and blemishes, sporting themselves with their own deceivings, while they feast with
you." Horrid pictures of depravity! Sporting themselves with the success of their devices; while they are
enjoying, with the deceived, the blessings of life.
"Having eyes full of adultery, and that cannot cease'
from sin; beguiling unstable souls; an heart they have
exercised with covetous practices; *cursed children:*
Who have forsaken the right way, and are gone astray,
following the way of Balaam the son of Bosor; who lov-
ed the wages of unrighteousness, but was rebuked for
his iniquity; the dumb ass speaking with man's voice,
forbode the madness of the prophet. These are wells
without water; clouds that are carried with the tempest;
to whom the mist of darkness is reserved forever. For
when they speak great swelling words of vanity, they
allure, (through the lusts of the flesh through much
wantonness,) those, who were clean (wholly) escaped
from them who live in error. While they promise them
liberty, they themselves are the servants of corruption:
For of whom a man is overcome, of the same he is
brought into bondage." Amazing and most interesting
catalogue of the mischievous characteristics of the horrid deceivers of the last days, who will desolate the civilized world! Liberty and the rights of man are their
first theme: While corruption the most *diabolical,* is
the origin, and bondage and ruin the sure result, to all
who are overcome by their delusions. Beguiling the
unstable. Their greatest success is with the unprincipled and fluctuating parts of communities. And by
swelling words of vanity, they present the most depraved motives in such an enticing light, as to *allure* many
into ruin, who were thought to have *wholly escaped*
from those, who live in error; or, were thought to be
verily good people. Through the abounding of this iniquity, *the love of many* (even of this class) *will wax
cold;* and, to the surprise and grief of the Godly, they
will be found among the enemy. The chapter closes
with solemn remarks, relative to *such apostates,* who

were introduced, in verse 18, as being *allured,* after
they were thought to have *escaped;* "For if, after they
have escaped the pollutions of the world through the
knowledge of the Lord and Savior Jesus Christ, they
are again entangled therein, and overcome, the latter
end is worse with them, than the beginning. For it
had been better for them not to have known the way
of righteousness, than after they have known it, to turn
from the holy commandment delivered unto them 'But
it is happened unto them according to the true proverb,
The dog is turned to his own vomit again: and the sow
that was washed to her wallowing in the mire." We
have here a most solemn and express warning to *professors* of *Religion,* when those last days shall arrive!
They will be tried to the uttermost.' Many of them
will *fall.* The love of many of such will *wax cold.*
"But he, that shall endure to the end, the same shall be
saved."

Peter, in the next chapter, pursues the same subject.
He informs his *pious readers* (whom in the introduction of this Epistle he had called, "*elect,* according to
the foreknowledge of God the Father, through sanctification of the spirit unto obedience, and sprinkling of
the blood of Jesus Christ;" and "who have obtained like
precious faith with us,") that this second Epistle he
now writes, in which to stir up their pure minds by way
of rememberance; "That ye may be mindful of the
words, which were spoken before by the holy prophets, and of the commandment of us the apostles of the
Lord and Savior; knowing *this first,* that there shall
come, *in the last days, scoffers,* walking after their own
lusts; and saying, Where is the promise of his coming?
for since the fathers fell asleep, all things continue as
they were from the beginning of creation. For this
they are willingly ignorant of, that by the word of God
the heavens were of old, and the earth standing out of
the water, and in the water: Whereby the world that
then was, being overflowed with water, perished. But
the heavens and the earth, which are now, by the same
word are kept in store, reserved unto fire against the
day of judgment and perdition of ungodly men."

9

There have been some perhaps, in all ages, of this *in-fidel cast*. But in the *last days*, there is to arise a *generation* of them, whose audacity and awful wickedness are to be such, that they are spoken of, as though such men *never before existed*. They deny the coming of Christ; and insultingly challenge, the people of God upon the subject.' Their wilful unbelief concerning the *deluge*, and the future judgment is noted; also the falsehood of the premises, on which they rest; and the sophistry of their reasonings. To give plausibility to their denial of any future coming of Christ, they say; "For since the fathers fell asleep, all things continue as they were, from the beginning of creation." But this is not true. All things have *not* continued as they were, from the beginning. God *once* (notwithstanding that the habitable earth was raised *above the water*, and the laws of nature seemed to ensure that it should safely continue thus verse 5,) controlled the laws of nature, and deluged the world, in fatal judgment to an impious generation. Though these scoffers of the last days may deny it, and may ransack the bowels of the earth, and may exert all their impious sophistry, in hopes of giving plausibility to the denial, yet the fact is *incontestible*. But what if all things *had* continued as they were, from the beginning? Would *this* render it certain that they always *will* so continue? and that Christ will never punish his enemies? Here is a specimen of the boasted reasonings of scoffers! But their ignorance of the coming of God, in the judgment of the flood, is a *wilful* ignorance. And it is *wilful* ignorance, that scoffers do not infer from the judgment of the flood, the certainty of the future destruction of scoffers, and of all the enemies of Christ. For the same word of God, which predicted the judgment of the deluge, has predicted the coming of Christ to judge and destroy his enemies, and save his friends. And as the former was fulfilled, so the latter will, at the appointed day be fulfilled. But such reasoning, and to believe and obey the word of God, is far beyond all the moral ingenuity of the scoffers of the last days:—

This the apostle clearly ascertains in the passage which has been given. '

Thus, four of the apostles have in their Epistles strikingly ascertained the rise of the terrible Power, and influence of infidelity in the last days.

SECTION V.

Antichrist predicted in Revelation XIIth Chapter.

In this chapter the church of Christ is symbolized by a *woman* away in the aerial *heavens, clothed with the sun; the moon under her feet; and on her head a crown of twelve stars.* The desires and exertions of the Church for the propagation of the Gospel and the salvation of men, are represented by *the woman's travailing in child-birth, and being pained to be delivered.* The devil is symbolized by *a great red dragon, having seven heads and ten horns, and seven crowns on his heads;* and *his tail drawing a third part of the stars, and casting them to the ground.* And his rage against the cause of Christ is represented by his *standing before the woman, to devour her son as soon as it was born.** The eventual safety of the succession of the Church, is represented by the *child's being born;* and being *caught up to the throne of God.* The devil now persecutes the church; upon which she flies into the wilderness for 1260 years. From what follows in the chapter, we learn, as it is thought, that the war of the devil against Christ was carried on, through the dark ages of Popery, in the symbolical heaven of the Papal church. The devil fought under the standard of Religion, in the corruptions and persecutions in that wicked system. But at the time of the reformation under Luther, the devil was cast out of this symbolical heaven, by the exposure of the abominations of Popery, to the symbolical earth; or where he commenced a system of Infidelity, and of direct opposition to the Protestant cause. This new system of opposition the devil is represented as instigating with

---

* This may be in allusion to Pharaoh's destroying the male infants in Israel. Exod. i, 22; Isa. li, 9; and Ezek. xxix, 2, 3.

great rage. *Woe to the inhabiters of the earth and of
the sea: for the devil is come down unto you having great
wrath, because he knoweth that he hath but a short
time.* The inhabiters of the earth and of the sea, being contrasted with the heaven of the Church, or a
zealous profession of Religion, must mean the great
mass of Infidels, scoffers, and non-professors. For
these bear a similar relation to the church of Christ,
to that which the earth bears to the heavens. And they
are likewise denominated inhabiters of the sea. The
great mass of the people of this character are said to be
*like the troubled sea, when it cannot rest, whose waters
cast up mire and dirt.** The sea is repeatedly used to
symbolize the mass of God's enemies, who are marked
out for judgment.† And their peculiar state of revolution and effervescence, at the time of the devil's coming down to them, may well entitle them to the appellation of *the inhabiters of the sea.* In Luke xxi, 25, *The
sea and the waves roaring*, are expressions of similar
import, and relate to the same period. The infernal
Power will now bring into the most furious operation his new and master-engine against the
Church, because he learns that the Kingdom of Christ
is *at the doors.* The Church is therefore represented
as *again* fleeing into the wilderness. And floods of delusions, of wicked agents and impostors, of falsehoods
and abuse, of national rage, armies, and bloody violence, *will be excited*, as though belched forth against
the cause of Christ out of the mouth of the old serpent, like an overwhelming torrent: Insomuch, that
nothing can save the cause of Christ from destruction,
but signal interpositions of Providence, in counteracting those violent measures, and confounding the
enemy; like the earth's opening her mouth, and swallow-
ing up floods of water. All this implies the rise of a
terrible Antichristian Power, at that period; who by
himself and his agents, shall be the instruments of these
tremendous operations. For though the devil is represented as being the mover of these scenes of oppo-

* Isa. lvii, 20.   † See Rev. viii, 8, and xvi, 3; also xvii, 1; 15.

sition and violence; yet his being symbolized by a great
red dragon, of seven heads and ten horns, and seven
crowns upon his heads; indicates that his operations
will be through a Power of this description. By the
dragon, (says, an expositor) "we understand the devil
in the heathen emperors of Rome."*   Satan's operations against the Christian church, when she was *first*
travailing in birth for the propagation of the Gospel
through his dominions in heathen lands, was by the
instrumentality of bloody *Pagan Rome.*   And his last,
violent operations against the Church, previous to the
Millennium, and while she is again peculiarly strug-
gling to propagate the Gospel through heathen lands,†
will be through the instrumentality of *Infidel Rome*, under her *last head.*   And both these states of Rome, (or
Rome Pagan, and Rome Infidel, under her last head,)
are unitedly symbolized, Rev. xiii, 1—11, by a beast
of seven heads and ten horns.   And Rome Infidel, under her last head, is symbolized, Rev. 17th chapter,
by a scarlet Beast of seven heads, and ten horns.   The
devil therefore, the malignant manager of these beasts,
and who gives to them *his power, and seat, and great
authority*, though he be an invisible agent, is represented as having the body of a great red dragon, with
seven heads and ten horns, and seven crowns on his
heads.   The reason of which no doubt is, that his most
violent, and mischievous operations were to be
through a Power of this symbolical description; the
revival, and last reign of which, were to fulfil the predictions concerning the Antichrist of the last times.

This Power of the last days, we learn in this chapter, is to receive great providential checks.   The earth
is to open her mouth, and swallow up his floods.
The same thing we find in various other figures.   In
Dan. ii, the *feet* and *toes* of the great image, (symbolizing the last part of the Roman Power, and that part
which is destroyed by the coming of Christ, at the battle of the great day,) are part of *iron*, and part of *clay:*
Or, that furious kingdom of the last days "shall be

---

* Pool on Rev. xiii, 1.   † See Rev. xiv, 6, 7, 8.

partly *strong*, and partly *broken*." The prophet upon
the same event informs, that "the Lord shall create
upon mount Zion and upon all her assemblies, a cloud
and smoke by day; and the shining of a flaming fire by
night; for upon all the glory shall be a *defence*."
Another prophet represents God *as camping round
about his house*, (the church) *because of the coming and
going of the enemy.* And the psalmist expresses the
same idea, when he says, of God's coming down to
save the meek of the earth, "Surely, the wrath of man
shall praise thee, and the *remainder of that wrath shalt
thou restrain.*" All this implies an *annoying Power, a
terrible enemy to the Church,* at that day: The same,
that is implied in this twelfth chapter of the Revelation.

SECTION VI.

The Roman, Papal, and Antichristian Beasts.

In order to find the terrible Power under consideration
among the prophetic Beasts, we will examine three portions of Scripture, in which those Beasts, which relate
to Rome, are found. Although references are repeatedly had to some of these Beasts, we find a full
description of them given only in three passages; Dan.
vii, and Rev. xiii, and xvii. In each of these passages,
it is remarkable, that we find two distinct powers given;
the Roman empire; and the Papal hierarchy. The *two*
are not blended; but *given* and *kept distinct*, in each
passage.
  In Dan. vii, 7, we find the Roman empire symbolized by *a great Beast strong and terrible, (rising out of
the sea,* verse 2,) *with great iron teeth; and with ten
horns.* The explanation is given, verses 23 and 24.
None doubt of its application to the Roman empire.
In a little horn of this Beast is symbolized the Papal
hierarchy. (verse 8.) And it is to be noted, that this
Beast, as distinct from the little horn, is in existence,
when the Ancient of days appears; or the battle of the
great day commences. This Roman Beast is the great
dominant power then destroyed. Verse 11, *I beheld*

*then, because of the voice of the great words, which
the horn spake; I beheld even till the beast was slain,
and his body destroyed, and given to the burning
flame.* Here is in existence the Roman, Beast, as distinct from Popery, and predominant, when they are
destroyed. Let this idea be remembered. It will aid
our forming a correct view of Antichrist. In the 13th
of Rev. we find this subject resumed; and the same
two powers, the *empire,* and the *hierarchy,* distinctly
given in a still clearer view. In verse 1, the empire is
presented under the same symbol, as in Daniel; *a Beast
rising out of the sea;* but with some additional append-
ages; and more particularly described. The description
of this Beast given in Daniel relates more peculiarly
to the deeds and circumstances of the Beast in the
former part of his existence. And the description
given in Rev, xiii, may relate especially to those of the
last part of his existence; or just before his destruction.
The genera of the different parts of the Beast are now
given. His body is like a *leopard;* or like the Macedonian empire. His feet are as the feet of a *bear;* or
like the Medo-Persian empire. And his mouth is as
the mouth of a *lion;* or like the Babylonian empire.
The meaning is, all the terrors of the preceding empires concentre in this one. This beast has seven
heads, and ten horns. On his horns are ten crowns;
and on his heads the name of plasphemy. And he received from the dragon, (the devil) his power, and
seat, and great authority. *And I saw one of his heads
as is were wounded to death; and his deadly wound was
healed.* His sixth, or his imperial head was wounded
to death A. D. 320, in the revolution from Rome Pagan, to Rome Christian, under the reign of Constantine.* But this imperial, deadly wounded head is,

---

*As a beast, in the symbolic language of prophecy, is a great
power, *hostile to the cause of Christ;* so the wounding to death
of such a beast may be effected by a revolution in such an empire, from Paganism to Christianity; as well as by its being utterly destroyed Such a revolution took place in Rome, in 320;
or, according to some, in 323; and others 317. Soon after the
tenth most bloody persecution in Pagan Rome, under Dioclesian, Constantine, upon the death of his father Constantius, be-

before the battle of the great day, healed; the sense of which healing we shall learn by and by, in chapter xvii; where this *newly healed head* is distinctly symbolized by a new beast, that *ascendeth out of the bottomless pit, and goeth into perdition.* After this imperial head is healed, so great and terrible is the event, that we read, chap. xiii, 3, *And all the world wondered*

came emperor of his part of the western branch of the Roman empire. Galerius, who had succeeded Diocletian, was emperor of the other part of the western branch; who carried on persecution against the Christians. Galerius was smitten with a loathsome, tormenting, and incurable disease After he had raged under its torments for a considerable time, he became conscious, that it was the hand of God upon him, for his cruelty to the Christians. He therefore put an end to his persecutions, by a public edict; and desired the Christians to pray for his restoration to health. But his disease soon terminated his life! Maxentius had got himself declared emperor at Rome; and a large faction followed him. Constantine became friendly to the Christians; and determined to favor their cause. He marched against Maxentius; who met him with an army of 170,000 foot, and 18,000 horse. After a bloody battle, Maxentius was defeated; and Constantine became sole emperor of the west. In the eastern wing of the empire, Maximin, and Licinius were emperors. The former made war upon the latter; but was defeated with great slaughter of his numerous army. Upon this, Maximin put to death many of his Pagan priests and soothsayers, as impostors, for their false flatteries. Soon after, as he was meditating another battle with Licinius, he was smitten with a violent disease of intolerable torments, became blind, and died raging in despair; confessing the just judgment of God upon him, for his spite and violence against Christ and his religion. Licinius was now the only emperor in the east, as was Constantine in the west. The former yet violently persecuted the Christians A war broke out between Constantine and Licinius. Licinius was worsted, and forced to flee. But recovering, he gave Constantine another most furious battle. Licinius was again defeated; 100,000 men are reported to have been slain. Licinius was taken prisoner. And not long after, for an attempt against the life of Constantine, he was put to death.

Thus Constantine became emperor of the whole eastern and western empire. He soon after removed the seat of his empire from Rome to Byzantium; which he named Constantinople He new modelled the government of the empire; put the administration into the hands of four prætorian præfects; abolished all the power of Paganism; and established the Christian Religion throughout the empire. And all the power of the persecutors was totally destroyed.

after the beast. And they worshipped the dragon, which gave power unto the beast; and they worshipped the beast, saying, Who is like unto the beast? Who is able to make war with him? By worship here is not meant religious homage; but admiration, and perhaps subjection. The days of superstition are then chiefly over; and the days of Infidelity will be found to have commenced. *And there was given unto him a mouth speaking great things, and blasphemies; and power was given unto him to continue forty and two months.* This latter passage has perplexed, and I believe misled, expositors. It has induced them to think, that a power is here intended, different from that, symbolized by the Beast in Dan. vii, 7; which has been noted, as representing the *Roman empire.* In short, it has induced them to believe this first Beast, in Rev. xiii, 1, to be the *Papal hierarchy;* because its chronology is supposed to agree with that of the latter; but not with Daniel's Roman Beast.

Bishop Newton upon the event says, "The great lights of the heathen world, the powers civil and ecclesiastical, were all eclipsed and obscured. The heathen emperors and Cesars were slain; the heathen priests and augurs were extirpated. The heathen officers and magistrates were removed. The heathen temples were demolished; and their revenues were appropriated to better uses."

Here we have the wounding to death of the sixth head of the old Pagan Roman Beast. He now ceased to be a Beast, in the language of prophecy; the empire became friendly to Christianity. Now was fulfilled the judgment of the sixth seal; Rev. vi, 12, to the end. *And I beheld when he had opened the sixth seal; and lo, there was a great earthquake, and the sun became black as sackcloth of hair, and the moon became blood. And the stars of heaven fell unto the earth, even as a fig-tree casteth her untimely figs, when she is shaken of a mighty wind. And the heaven departed as a scroll, when it is rolled together; and every mountain and island were moved out of their places. And the kings of the earth, and the great men, and the rich men, and the chief captains, and the mighty men, and every bondman, and every freeman, hid themselves in the dens, and in the rocks of the mountains, and said to the mountains and rocks, Fall on us, and hide us from the face of Him that sitteth on the throne, and from the wrath of the Lamb. For the great day of his wrath is come; and who shall be able to stand.*

10

But their opinion on this subject I believe to be a mistake; and that this is the *very Roman Beast*, presented
in Daniel, symbolizing the idolatrous empire, from
the time it captivated the Church of God, sometime
before Christ, till its final destruction at the battle of
the great day. The passage relative to his continuance forty and two months, forms no serious objection
to this idea. It does not say, the whole term of his
existence is forty and two months; as in the objection
is taken for granted. But it relates only to the time
of his *end*. When this terrible Beast is presented, as
an event most interesting to the Church, the question
naturally occurs, How long is this terrible adversary to
continue? The correct reply is, *The forty and two
months;* or to the end of that well known term of the
residence of the Church in the wilderness. The passage
must be viewed as elliptical; not designed to inform
relative to the origin of the Beast; nor the whole term
of his continuance; but *when* the Church shall be re-
leased from his tyranny. This was the interesting point.
And it should be at the end of the *forty and two months.*

A similar passage we find Rev. xii, 14; which to me
confirms the sense of the passage here given. In the
former part of this xiith chapter, after the man-child is
caught up to the throne of God, and at the commencement of the war between Michael and the dragon, in
the mystical heaven of the Roman Church, the true
Church flies into the wilderness, there to remain 1260
years; the exact period given in Dan. vii, 25, for the
giving of the saints into the hands of the little horn.
After the war in heaven closes, and the dragon, upon
the reformation under Luther, was cast out into the
earth, he again persecutes the woman. Upon this she
again flies into the wilderness, *into her place, where
she is nourished for a time, and times, and an half time,*
(or 1260 years) from the face of the serpent. Now,
can this mean that she was to continue in the wilderness *from this time of her second flight,* 1260 years?
This cannot be. It would confound all chronological
calculations upon the subject. The 1260 years were
the *whole term* of her continuance in the wilderness.

This term commenced many centuries before; at the commencement of Popery; at the time of her *first flight;* and it was now nearly expired. Yet she is represented as again flying into the wilderness *for* 1260 *years.* The sense must be, she flies back into the wilderness, to remain there *the residue* of her 1260 years; or to the *end of that well known term.*

So in the passage under consideration. The Roman Beast, with his head, which had once been wounded to death, now healed, was to *continue forty and two months;* i. e. to the *end* of that well known period. He drives the Church, in her second flight, into the wilderness, for 1260 years; i. e. for the short residue of this noted term; and his own continuance is represented as being for the *same term; forty and two months;* i. e. for the *short residue* of this noted term. Then the Church is to obtain relief; and he, with his false prophet, the wretched remains of the Papal hierarchy, and his vassal kings, is to go into perdition.

To me it appears a very evident point, that this first Beast in Rev. xiii, and the Beast in Dan. vii, 7, symbolizing the Roman empire, as distinct from the Papal horn, are *one* and the *same.* They have the same origin. Both rise out of the sea; or the convulsed state of the world, before the time of the coming of Christ in the flesh; and both terminate at the same period. As the Beast in Daniel exhibits the Roman empire, from its rise, to its going into perdition; so we should surely expect to find something in the Revelation answering to this symbol. Shall the Papal hierarchy be represented in the Revelation by a number of different Beasts; and the Roman empire, which in Daniel is symbolized by the Beast, that arose out of the sea, be represented exclusively by none? Such an idea cannot be admitted. As the empire and the hierarchy are, in Daniel, kept distinct, even to their end; so when we find in both the passages in Revelation, where the Beasts are noted, (chapters xiii and xvii) two distinct powers, why should we blend them? Why shall we not naturally conclude, that the one answers to the Beast in Daniel; and the other to his little horn? We must

so conclude. Every objection against it is capable of a
fair solution. And the arguments in favor of it are in-
vincible.*

The consideration of the remaining part of the account given of this first Beast, Revelation xiii, will be
deferred, till I come to remark upon the Beast in chapter xvii; which is the same with the *healed head* of the
Beast just considered; or which is the Roman empire
revived under-its last head. For the characteristics in
both are essentially the same.

A second Beast appears, in Rev. xiii, from the 11th
verse to the end; symbolizing the Romish hierarchy;
and answering to the little horn of the Roman Beast,
Dan. vii, 8. Upon the wounding to death of the sixth,
the imperial head of the Roman Beast by Constantine,
and while this Beast lay dead, an intermediate Beast,
after some centuries, rose out of the earth; or out of
the earthly views of the Romish Christians. *He had*

---

* Some may deem it an objection to the idea of this first
Beast in Rev. xiii, being precisely the same with that of Daniel;
that the rise of the civil Roman Beast was an event long *past*,
when John had his vision; whereas the vision of John purported to be of things *future*. This objection has no weight. It
fully accords with the usual imagery of prophetic writings, for
the revealing Angels to present to John as a preparatory scene,
the *origin* of the Beast then in existence; when his object was,
to unfold the most interesting character and deeds of the same
Beast, at a period *then far future*. Such a preparatory scene
was necessary, in order to ascertain who this Beast was, whose
future deeds were to be predicted; or to identify him with the
Roman Beast in Daniel.

The Antichristian Beast, in Rev. xvii, rising out of the bottomless pit, in the last days, is presented with his *seven heads*,
symbolizing so many forms of government in the Roman empire. Not because he is personally possessed of them, or that
those different forms of government are then *future*. So far is
the fact from this, that *five* of them had *fallen*, when John had
his vision, seventeen centuries before the Antichristian Beast
rises into existence. Yet the whole seven are represented as
possessed by this Beast, when he rises out of the bottomless
pit in the last days; in order to ascertain, that this is not a fifth
monarchy upon earth; but is mystically the old Roman Beast
revived. In like manner, John beholds the *rise* of the Beast
from the sea, whose far future deeds he was about to predict,
though that *rise* was actually past, when he had the vision.

two horns like a lamb: He gored Christ's witnesses with
his two horns; or his vile, superstitious management
of *ecclesiastical* and *civil* tyranny: But *he spake as a
dragon.* Or, his denomination was *Christian;* but his
spirit and views the same, that governed *Pagan Rome.*
The same infernal agent, that managed the one, managed the other. And this Beast grew, till he came *to
exercise all the power of the first Beast before him,* now
dead, or of Pagan Rome. The lucrative establishments
of Constantine in the Church, (it is said by some,)
proved a source of corruption to the bishops of Rome.
The city of Rome, under their Gothic kingdom, was
suffered to maintain the shadow of her own government. The citizens fell into contentions and factions;
and often found it convenient to apply to the bishop
of Rome for a decision of their quarrels. This gave
him great importance; which he ambitiously improved;
till Boniface III. was by the emperor Phocas constituted *Universal Bishop.*

This haughty, aspiring *prelacy,* either then, or in after
days, obtained the characteristic of the little horn in
Daniel, into whose hands the saints were to be delivered
for 1260 years. This Pontifical establishment was utterly hostile to the Church of Christ. She now flees
into the wilderness. The Romish bishopric now becomes a new Beast, which was to continue to annoy
the followers of Christ, during the death of the Roman
Beast. But this system of annoyance and hostility was
to be veiled under the most sanctimonious Christian
profession. So different was it to be from an open
avowal of Paganism; while yet in essence it was no better than the preceding Roman Paganism. This system is therefore represented as an *image* of the first
Beast, caused by the Papal Beast to be made, and wholly
under his management. A solution of the representation
may be given by a simple history of facts. The Romish
hierarch, in time, procured the establishment of a system
of idolatry and superstition, essentially of the same
nature with that antecedently practised in Pagan Rome.
One essential feature of the idolatry of Pagan Rome
was, paying adoration to deceased heroes and great men;

constituting them their mediators with the superior gods; and venerating their statues and images. And the essence of this idolatry the Papal Beast caused to be revived. "In the eighth century the worshipping of saints was established by law."* The names of deceased favorites were not selected, as before, from the names of the princes and heroes of Pagan Rome; but from those of the Apostles, and of other eminent Christians. But the nature of the idolatry was essentially the same; viz. constituting those deceased Christians, mediators in heaven; and venerating their statues and images; together with establishing many arbitrary rites and doctrines of *human invention.* This newfangled system of idolatry, under the Christian name, and supported under pretence of obedience to Christ, and of his authority, is strikingly represented by an *image made to the first Beast*, or Pagan Rome, and directed by the *Papal Beast.* The latter gave life to this image, and procured obedience to it, by false miracles, decrees, bulls and canon-laws. The Papal Beast is represented as *having power to make this image speak; and to cause, that as many as would not worship the image of the Beast should be killed.* This he verified by excommunicating, and delivering over to the civil sword all, who would not comply with every order of his superstition. The civil powers throughout his dominions, the German empire especially, the Papal Beast came, in a course of time to manage, chiefly by his sanctimonious influence, as a puppet in his own hands, to enforce his laws and dogmas."† And thus he *reigned over the kings of the earth;* and caused the Roman earth to worship the first Beast, or Pagan Rome, by worshipping his image in the hands of the Papal hierarchy.‡

---

* Scott. The worship of images was established by the second council of Nice in A. D. 787. See Faber, vol. ii, p. 163, 164, 165.

† Rob. Hist. Charles V. vol. iii, p. 185.

‡ As to the number of this Beast, and of his name, see in section i, chapter ii, of this dissertation. The Papal Beast caused all his subjects to receive a mark, in their right hands, or in their

Several passages occur in the description of this second Beast, which relate to the first Beast, and need

foreheads: And that none might buy, or sell, if destitute of this *mark*, and of the *name* of the Beast, and of the *number* of his name. Repeatedly, in this mystical book, reference is had to this characteristic, chap. xiii, 9. "If any man worship the Beast, and his image, and receive his mark in his forehead, or in his hand; the same shall drink of the wine of the wrath of God." Verse 11, "And they have no rest, day nor night, who worship the Beast, and his image, and whosoever receiveth the mark of his name." In chap. xv, 2— the triumphant saints are described as they, "that had gotten the victory over the Beast; and over his image, and over his mark, and over the number of his name." And in chap. xx, 4, the victorious followers of Christ are again described as those, "who had not worshipped the Beast, neither his image, neither had received his mark upon their foreheads, nor in their hands." Though these descriptions are deeply enigmatical; yet being repeatedly used to distinguish the two great classes from each other, (the righteous and the wicked,) and at a period, which is still *future;* it is of importance to form some correct views of their import.

· ·This receiving of a *mark*, is supposed to be expressed in allusion to an ancient custom, of masters *marking* their servants, in their foreheads, or in their hands with some *characters*, according to their pleasure; either with the initials of the masters' name; or of their god; or what they pleased. Thus the subjects of the Roman Beast are represented, as designated by a *mark.* Certain things were, *in fact*, demanded of Roman Catholics, as essential to their exemption from persecution, and to their peaceable enjoyment of the rights of citizens. They must receive and use the *sign of the cross.* They must cautiously submit to all the superstitious rites of men's invention, attached to that system; a constant round of real idolatry! The members were strictly watched. And if any absented themselves from mass, or any of their idolatrous rites, they were exposed; and if they persevered in the neglect, they were outlawed, and persecuted. Particularly, they had to perform all their devotions in *Latin.* This was a distinctive badge of their order. In the catholic church, every thing was done in Latin; mass, prayers, hymns, litanies, canons, decretals, Papal bulls, results of counsels, canon laws, reading the scriptures, preaching, and all the concerns of the church, were transacted in *Latin.* It was peculiarly the *Latin church.* The ancient Romans were called the Latins. Latinos was their real, or fictitious founder. This name, in numerals, (as will be shown in another section,) forms in Greek, (the language in which the New Testament was first written) the number 666. And the word Rumiit, the name of the Roman empire, in Hebrew, (in which the Old Testament

explanation. Verses 12 and 14; *whose deadly wound was healed;—and which had the wound by the sword*

was originally written,) in numerals makes 666. So that the *name* of the Beast denotes the *Roman*, and the *Latin* church. Submitting then, to the catholic superstition , of performing all their devotions in *Latin* . (a language different from their mother tongues,) may be viewed as *one mark* of the Beast, or of having the number of his name. It was a point with the true witnesses, that they *would not* conform, in those catholic superstitions, to the Romish church. And hence they were grievously persecuted.

The descriptions, in the above texts, are given with an express view to the people of the old Roman earth. But people beyond those local bounds will be found interested in them. As those, who worshipped the *image* of the Beast, were as criminal, as those who worshipped the Beast himself; and as all, who shall partake of Babylon's sins, shall, as well as Babylon herself, receive of her plagues; so the people of whatever nation, under gospel light, who shall be found subjects of *fatal superstition*, of *will worship*, of *hypocrisy*, or *false religion*, will probably be viewed and treated as having virtually the *mark of the Beast*. They have the *very spirit*, and essential character, for which the literal subjects of the Papal Beast were condemned. They all essentially belong to one class; and will *sink* together.

The denunciations in the word of God against certain defined characters, will prove equally true and dreadful against all, who shall be found possessed of charcters essentially the same; whatever circumstantial differences (of time, place, or manner,) may attend. They all have the *mark* of the same class. There are certain characteristic marks which are not affected by minor circumstantial differences.

In this sense *multitudes*, beyond the bounds of the old Roman earth; *multitudes* among us, will be found subjects of the essential mark of the old Papal Beast;—fatally deceived; real idolaters under Gospel light; hypocrites, no better than Roman Catholics, Here let me further note, that the subjects of the Papal Beast were, *in fact*, in the last days, to assume a *new mark*, of *characteristic infidelity*. The mummery of their false religion was to be exposed: And they were, to exchange it for *atheism*. Their system was to be exhibited as a system of blasphemy; as a habitation of devils; a hold of every foul spirit; and a cage of every unclean and hateful bird. The rod of iron, for the dashing to pieces of the wicked nations, was to be forged in the infernal furnace of the Papacy; the Beast from the bottomless pit, was to arise; the tremendous and blasphemous Power of the last days, who was to deny the Father and the Son; and to collect a vast coalition against Zion,—against Heaven! Here was to appear a *mark* of the Beast, abundantly predicted, and most notorious.

and did live. These passages cannot mean,. that the Roman Beast *then*, in the time of the Papal Beast, was *actually alive*; that his deadly wound was *then actually healed.* They are simple references to the description given of the first Beast, in the former part of the chapter. There we have a description of the Beast, symbolizing the civil Roman empire, from its origin, to

The *Papal* Beast was to bring forth the *Antichristian*, as her own executioner; and was fatally to fall under his iron grasp.

He was to be distinguished by the *mark* of blasphemy, and atheism; and also by a mummery of Papal superstition, as a cloak of wickedness. He was to be distinguished by the *mark* of a most efficacious system of falsehood, imposition and delusion; which was to spread over the face of the earth; and to collect the wicked world to the battle of that great day of God Almighty. Here was to be a *mark* of the Beast, to be set upon the *foreheads*, or *hands*, of millions who would be seduced with delusive influences and hopes; and ingulfed in ruin. This was to be a *mark* discerned and distinguished by the Godly; but probably denied by the notoriously wicked. "None of the wicked shall understand: but the wise shall understand." ·

The *Beast* is the great predominant power upon the ground. Mystical *Babylon* is the same. While Popery was predominant, *this* was the *Beast*, and *Babylon*. But when this was succeeded by a greater and predominant power, the latter became the Beast, and Babylon. These two powers have their characteristic *marks;* which, either in the forehead, or in the hand (more evidently, or more covertly) designate their subjects. Those passages which speak of the *mark of the Beast*, in relation to the time of the Papal supremacy, relate to the *Papal mark;* which has been noted. And those which speak of the mark of the Beast, in relation to the time of the *Antichristian* reign, must be viewed as relating to the *Antichristian mark*. And some passages may have reference to both the marks, or characteristics of these fatal systems. The passage Rev. xiv, 9,— seems evidently to relate to the *Antichristian mark*. The missionary Angel had begun his flight. A second Angel announced the fall of *Papal Babylon*, as accomplished. And a third Angel announces the terrors of God against all, who worship the Beast, and *receive his mark*. The *Beast* and *his mark now*, (after the Papal Babylon is *fallen*,) must relate to the *succeeding* Power, the *Antichristian*. His characteristic is *atheism*, including perfidy, disorganization, military disposition, and bitterness against Zion. And each distinguishing manifestation of *this his characteristic*, under whatever *name*, must be viewed as going to constitute his *mark;* over which the Church must obtain the victory, or of which she must be kept clear.

11

the battle of the great day. And among other descriptions, this Beast is represented as having a deadly wounded head healed; or as having a wound
by a sword, yet afterwards living. And this trait
of his character is *referred* to, in the above verses, in
the course of the description of the second Beast:
The reason of which is this; the pagan Beast's having
been wounded to death in the *head*, yet afterwards *living*, was his most *remarkable* characteristic. By this
therefore, he would naturally be spoken of, when allusion was had to him. But this *reference* was not designed to indicate, that this healing of the wounded
head was then *already effected*, nor to indicate any
thing relative to the *time*, when the Roman Beast was
to recover life. The fact, I believe, will appear to be,
that this recovery of life was then *far future*, and that
the Roman Beast lived, through all the ages of the
prosperity of the Papal Beast, only by *his image* in the
management of that officious Pontificate. But that he
himself, all that time, lay dead. The idea of two Beasts
prevailing at the same time, and on the same ground,
for 1260 years; or existing at *all* collaterally; is a sole-
cism, an absurdity never to be admitted. Each one of
two things cannot be the greatest. A Beast, as a predominant power, a dynasty, and the sum of an empire, may
have a number of collateral horns. But he cannot admit
another *Beast* on the same ground; and both continue.
There cannot be in any body, at the same time, more
than one supreme power. Symbolical language cannot
admit of two Beasts in Christendom at the same period.
When the last head of the Roman Beast arises, and takes
Popery into its possession, the latter then ceases *to be*,
or to be *called*, a Beast. It is henceforward called *the
false prophet*,* the mother of harlots;† and the horn of
the Beast.‡ But it is never after this called a *Beast.*§

---

* Rev. xix, 20, and xvi, 13. † Rev. xvii, 5. ‡ Dan. vii, 11.
  § I am aware it *may* here be objected to my proposition, that
we read in Dan, vii, 12; *As concerning the rest of the Beasts,
they had their dominion taken away; yet their lives were prolonged for a season and time*: as though they all existed, *as
Beasts,* at one and the same time. But this cannot be the mean-

The only remaining passage, which seems to militate against the explanations given, is in verse 14th, on the

ing of the prophet. When the real sense of the passage is ascertained, I think it will afford no objection to my proposition, that two Beasts cannot exist on the same ground, at the same time. The pasage, it seems, was designed to note the *contrast* between the manner, in which the Antichristian Beast shall be destroyed; and the manner, in which the preceding ancient Beasts were overthrown. The former loses not only his dominion as a Beast, but his existence on earth, at the time of his overthrow; being not subjugated by a human conqueror, as were the others, but utterly destroyed by the Lord from heaven, in the battle of that great day of God Almighty: when not only the Beast is slain, but his *body is destroyed and given to the burning flame;* as in the preceding verse. But *so it was not* with the former and ancient Beasts, when they lost their dominant power. How many soever of their soldiers were in fact slain in battle, nothing took place, which was like the bodies of those Beasts (the multitudes, who had constituted them) being destroyed, and given to the burning flame; as is to be the case with Antichrist. The powers symbolized by those Beasts, instead of being utterly destroyed, were only subjected, each in his turn, to the dominion of the succeeding power; and there received tolerable treatment as subjects. And to express this difference of treatment, in the immediate view of the body of the Antichristian Beast, *being destroyed, and given to the burning flame*, at the same time, in which the *Beast is slain*, as in the preceding verse; it is said, of the *rest of the Beasts*, they had *their dominion taken away; yet their lives were prolonged for a season and time.* This elliptical mode of expression was most naturally adopted, instead of expressing the whole evident sense, as follows: Concerning the rest of the Beasts, they had their dominion taken away; yet the multitude who had constituted their body, instead of being destroyed and given to the burning flame, as shall be the case with Antichrist, were chiefly spared, and received tolerable treatment under their new masters. But the prophet could not mean to teach us, that all these Beasts had existed, *as Beasts*, at one and the same time! Nothing could be more unnatural; or untrue. When the Macedonian he-goat, for instance, *stamped* upon, and *slew* the Persian ram, this ram is never represented to be in existence, *as a Beast*, afterwards; although the people of Persia still existed *for a season and time;* and to the present day.

The *opinion*, that the two Beasts, in Rev. xiii, were co-existent for 1260 years, must be an absurdity. A universal or a great empire, disposed to persecute the Church, is in prophetic style a *Beast;* whether the empire be of *secular* dominion; or a *hierarchy*. But when did two such independent, persecuting

subject of the Papal Beast, *And deceiveth them that dwell on the earth, by the means of those miracles, which he had power to do in the sight of the Beast.* Here it seems to be suggested, that the Papal Beast wrought miracles *in the sight of the Pagan Beast;* as though the latter were already revived. But if he were already revived, what need of an image being made to him? And it has been noted that two Beasts cannot exist on the same ground, at the same time. It cannot mean then, that the *Pagan Beast* was already revived. The clause, *in the sight of the Beast,* must therefore

powers co-exist on the Roman earth; or in the world? Were it possible for two vast empires to be found independent of each other, and acting in no concert, yet both persecuting the cause of Christ; possibly they might be symbolized by two co-existent Beasts. But two such powers never co-existed on the Roman earth. *Popery* fully answered to such a power. But no *civil* power, within the Papal influence, did at the same time exist, which could answer to such a power. However independent of the Pope the emperors of Germany, or any other civil powers within the Roman earth, might have been, as to their civil jurisdictions during the Papal supremacy; yet those civil powers never persecuted the cause of Christ, only at the *Papal instigation.* The hierarchy was the system, during its supreme power, that persecuted the witnesses. The civil authorities were only its *executioners.* "The fourth council of Lateran (says Bishop Burnet) decreed that all heretics should be delivered to the secular power, to be extirpated.". In the time of Pope Innocent the third, false accusations were raised against the Waldenses and Albigenses;—upon which, the Pope decreed a crusade against them. And he sent his emissaries into the west, enjoining it on sovereign princes, and other Christian people, to extirpate those heretics. Upon this Vitringa observes, that in France alone, a *million* were destroyed. The persecution (though executed by the civil powers) originated in the *Papal* Beast. The same is true of all the persecutions during the Papal supremacy. In this thing the hierarchy was "that great city, which reigned over the *kings* of the (Roman) earth." The *reign* was not *theirs;* but *hers.* The imperial authority, co-existent with Popery, was nothing more (as a persecuting power) than one of the *two horns* of the Papal Beast. This Beast is presented with *two horns.* And his *clergy,* and the *civil powers* under his superstition, were most fitly symbolized by these two Papal horns:—As was his system of real idolatry, under the Christian name by an *image* made to the old Pagan Beast.

mean, either in the sight of the *image* of the Beast;
putting by a metonymy, the prototype for the copy; or,
in *admiration*, or imitation of the Pagan Beast; i. e. that
the Papal hierarch wrought his deceptive miracles with
a view to confirm a system no better, than the old Pagan system.   This he actually did, in what was called
the image of the Beast, before described. "In the sight
of the beast; i. e. to his honor, and to gain him a reputation!" (Pool on the passage.) And what follows the
above clause, as an explanation of it, appears to confirm this as being the true sense; *saying to them, who
dwell on the earth, that they should make an image to the
Beast.* As the Papal Beast caused the earth to worship
the Pagan Beast, (v. 12) by causing them to worship his
image; (v. 14) so the miracles wrought by the Papal Beast
were done *in the presence* of the Pagan Beast, by being
done in the presence of his *image.*   Mistaking the
sense of these several passages, and the one before explained, relative to the continuance of the first Beast
forty and two months, I conceive, has been the occasion of perplexing commentators, and of leading them
erroneously to blend and confound the Roman and Papal Beasts.   I have shown that the two powers in
Daniel are given as distinct; also in Revelation xiii,
just noted.   And they are thus presented, in Revelation xvii; to which I shall now attend.   In this passage, the   terrible Power of the last days is strikingly
exhibited.

One of the Angels, who in the xvith chapter had
poured out the vials of the wrath of God, proposes to
show to the evangelist the *judgment*, or destruction, of
the Papal harlot.   John is carried into the wilderness.
The harlot in her turn is in trouble: She is bewildered.   John beholds a woman in lewd attire; with the
superscription of her abominable character upon her
forehead; indicating, that she, as the worst of criminals, is presented for speedy execution. , Bishop Pear-
son and Doctor Lardner, upon the superscription over
the head of our Savior, have shown, that it was a custom among the ancient Romans to place on, or over,
the foreheads of the worst of criminals, the superscrip-

tion of their guilt, at the time of their execution.
The superscription upon the cross of our Savior was
upon the same principle. The great harlot is presented with this her superscription upon her forehead, in-
scribed in capitals; *MYSTERY, BABYLON THE
GREAT, THE MOTHER OF HARLOTS, AND
ABOMINATIONS OF THE EARTH.* And she
has also upon her the symbols of her past magnificence, and of her allurements, and crimes; in order to
shew her to be the *Papal hierarchy.* She is mounted
on a Beast, that may be said to be bearing her to her
judgment or execution.* This Beast is of a scarlet
color, to denote his cruel and bloody character. He
is full of the names of blasphemy, to denote his Infidelity and wickedness. And he has seven heads, as
well as ten horns, to identify in him the old heathen
Roman empire now revived.

The Angel, in explaining the mystery of the Beast,
informs, that he *was, and is not; and shall ascend out
of the bottomless pit, and go into perdition; and they,
who dwell on the earth, shall wonder (whose names were
not written in the book of life from the foundation of the
world) when they behold the Beast, that was, and is not,
and yet is.* The seven heads, the Angel informs, (in
addition to their being seven mountains, on which the
woman sitteth, or on which Rome was built,) *are sev-
en kings,* or forms of government, in the different periods of the Roman empire. "*Five are fallen,*" those of
Kings, Consuls, Tribunes, Decemvirs, and *Dictators,*
were past, when John had his vision. "One is;" the
then present form *was Imperial,* and was the *sixth head,*
or form of government, "*And the other is not yet come,
and when he cometh, he must continue a short space.*"
Concerning this seventh head, or form of government,
then future, which when it should come should continue a *short space,* expositors have been divided and
perplexed. Every scheme, which they have adopted, appears attended with unanswerable objections. The reason I think is obvious. Nothing had taken place, to

---

* This is not a woman directing and governing an empire;
but just the reverse.

which the description was applicable: Or, the event was still future. The sixth head continued, till the days of Constantine. Then it received its wound, and died. There was now no Beast, till the Papal hierarchy arose. But this was not the revival of the Roman Beast, as has been shown. Whenever the Roman Beast revives in his seventh head, which continues a short space, it must be in his *heathen* or *Infidel* nature of *avowed*, as well as *real* opposition to the cause of Christ. Otherwise he is not the real Roman Beast. For whatever wickedness, cruelty, or real idolatry was attached to the Papal imposture, that was only the *image* of the Roman Beast, but not the Beast himself. Whenever this Beast himself shall revive, it must be with the characteristic of *direct* opposition to the cause of Christ. And that he *was* thus to revive, as distinct from Popery, is evident from the passages relative to the Roman Beast, which have been noted;* and from what we shall find in this xviith chapter. Also that his revival was to be but a *short space* before the battle of the great day, is clearly ascertained, as will appear. This revival of the Roman Beast, in his seventh head, has I believe never taken place, till of late. And, if I am not deceived, this head has recently appeared under an Atheistico-democratic form of government; reducing the principal nations of the old western Roman empire under its power; and continuing the *short space* of several years; which was longer than some of the former heads of this Beast continued. The seventh head then gave way to the eighth; which is symbolized in this chapter by a new Beast, ascending out of the bottomless pit, great and terrible. Verse 11, *And the Beast, which was, and is not, even he is the eighth, and is of the seven, and goeth into perdition.*

Here we find that the Beast in this chapter, who is bearing the Papal harlot to her execution, is the *eighth* head of the old Roman Beast. This last head of the old Beast is symbolized by a *new Beast* of peculiar, and terrible features. And yet there is a *uniting* of this

*See Dan. vii, 11; and Rev. xiii, 3, and onward; and xiv, 8, 9.

symbol with that of the old Roman empire, to evince, that it is mystically the *same Power.* "*The Beast, which was.*" He *was* in his ancient heathen form. "*And is not.*" He was slain; his sixth head was wounded to death, in the revolution under the reign of Constantine; and has *ever since* lain dead, only as he has existed in his *image* in the hands of the Romish hierarchy; till he began to recover his life in his seventh head; which was to continue a short space; and has his deadly wound completely healed in the eighth. As the changing of the government in the Roman empire, under Constantine, from *Pagan* to *Christian,* was the wounding to death of the Pagan Beast, in his sixth head; so the *reversing* of this scene, or changing the government from being professedly Christian, to a government of atheism, is, on the same principle, the recovery of that Beast to life. Now he recovers his *own nature,* independently of an officious, ecclesiastical hierarch. And this new Power, in his turn, takes the Papal hierarchy into his grasp, and makes it a mere tool of his own ambitious policy; and he is, in the course of Divine providence, bearing this Mother of harlots to her execution.

This Roman Beast revives under the immediate agency of the devil. "*And shall ascend out of the bottomless pit.*" The same idea, which we have seen in Rev. xiith chapter; and in chapter xiii, 4; where the dragon gave power to the Beast, after his deadly wound was healed. And the event is but just before the battle of the great day:—*and goeth into perdition.*—Twice expressed in the same words. His exit is thus as it were immediately connected with his rise, in verses 8, and 11: As says the Apostle, of this very Power, *And shall bring upon themselves swift destruction:** And, *Whose damnation slumbereth not.*

But how is this new Beast the *eighth* head; and *of the seven?* The Roman Beast has but seven heads!

Answer. He is the *eighth numerically;* and in point of chronology. The Imperial form of government,

---

* 2 Pet. ii, 1.

existing when John had his vision, was the sixth. *Five are fallen; and one is;* (verse 10.) This was Imperial. The Atheistico-Republican form was the *seventh;* which, when John had his vision, had not yet come, or was far future: And which when he should come, would continue a little time. After a *short space*, this gave way to the *last* head under consideration. This came under an *Imperial* form. And this Imperial head, now healed from its deadly wound, is chronologically and numerically the *eighth*. It is the next after the seventh. But still it must be *of the seven;* or must belong to *one* of the seven. For the Beast has but seven specifically different heads. It *must* be specifically the same with one of the *former* heads. And it *is* specifically the same with the *sixth,* the *Imperial*. It is then mystically the sixth, the Imperial head, recovered from its deadly wound, given in the reign of Constantine.

The greatness of this event is hinted, both in the xviith, and in the xiiith chapters, after the deadly wounded head is healed. I will give the two passages relative to this idea, collaterally. This view of the two passages will at the same time evince, that they both describe one and the same Power.

Chapter xiii. *The Revived Head.*	Chapter xvii. *The Antichristian Beast.*
V. 3—"And I saw one of his heads as it were wounded to death; and his deadly wound was healed: And all the world wondered after the Beast.	V. 8.—"The Beast, that thou sawest, was, and is not; and shall ascend out of the bottomless pit, and go into perdition.
And there was given unto him a mouth speaking great things, and blasphemies.—And he opened his mouth in blasphemy against God; to blaspheme	And I saw a woman sitting upon a scarlet colored Beast, full of the names of blasphemy.

12

The Revived Head.   *The Antichristian Beast.*

his name, and his tabernacle, and them that dwell
in heaven.

And it was given unto
him to make war with the
saints.

These (the horns of the
Beast) shall make war with
the Lamb.

And power was given
him over all kindreds, and
tongues, and nations. And
they worshipped the dra-
gon which gave power un-
to the Beast; and they worshipped the Beast, saying,
Who is like unto the
Beast? who is able to
make war with him?

These have one mind,
and shall give their power
and strength unto the
Beast.—For God hath put
in their hearts to fulfil his
will, and to agree, and
give their kingdom unto
the Beast, until the words
of God shall be fulfilled.

And all the world won-
dered after the Beast. And
all that dwell upon the
earth shall worship him,
whose names are not writ-
ten in the book of life of
the Lamb slain, from the
foundation of the world.
If any man have an ear,
let him hear.

And they that dwell on
the earth shall wonder,
whose names were not
written in the book of life,
from the foundation of the
world, when they behold
the Beast, that *was*, and *is
not*, and yet *is.*

He, that leadeth into
captivity, shall go into captivity: he that killeth with
the sword must be killed
with the sword." (i. e. As
the Papal power has
sought to destroy the
saints; so this power, in
turn, is destroyed.)

And the ten horns,
which thou sawest upon
the Beast, these shall hate
the whore, and shall make
her desolate and naked,
and shall eat her flesh, and
burn her with fire."

Thus we find, that the accounts given of the healed head of the Roman Beast, and those given of the Beast from the bottomless pit, which is also the *eighth* head, and *of* the seven, are essentially the same. The two passages describe one and the same subject. The symbol, or the first Beast, in chapter xiii, contains the Beast in chapter xvii. The latter is that head of the former, which had been wounded to death, and was healed. In chapter xvii, this head is symbolized by a new Beast; which yet, to shew that it is but the healed head of the old Roman Beast in chapter xiii, is described with *seven heads*, as well as ten horns. It is called both the *Beast;* and a *head* of the Beast. It is a *new* Beast; and at the same time it is a *head* of the old Roman Beast; as verse 11; "And the Beast that was, and is not, even he is the eighth (head) and is of the seven (heads.)"

It is remarkable that the Imperial head of the Roman Beast, *that,* under which the greatest mischief has been done to the Church of Christ, is thus represented as twice existing; and its two reigns, which mystically constitute *but one,* are represented as existing at *distant periods.* Under the first reign of this head, and before it received its deadly wound, Jesus Christ was crucified. Under the second reign of the same head, Christ will terribly destroy this Beast. In the first reign, the head persecuted the primitive Christians in *ten* bloody persecutions. The great object of the Beast, in the second reign, is, *war* against the same cause. *These shall make war with the Lamb.** *And it was given unto him to make war with the saints.*† In the first reign, this imperial head destroyed the Jews, according to the prediction of Christ with respect to his coming in judgment upon that generation: And it thus furnished a lively type of the destruction of Antichrist, at the battle of the great day. At the close of the second reign, the same imperial head will experience all the terrors of this latter event. At the close of the first reign, this head experienced the tremendous scene of the *great day of God's wrath,* under the sixth seal,

* Rev. xvii, 14,   † Rev. xiii, 7.

(Rev. vi, from the 12th verse to the end,) in the revolution under Constantine; when the sixth head received its deadly wound. And the same head, at the close of his last reign, will sink into perdition, under that awful appearing of the day of the Lord, to which that former event may be viewed but as a prelude. These reigns of the sixth head of the Roman Beast are numerically two. In this sense the last is the *eighth head*. But they are specifically one; and mystically represented *as one*. In this sense the last head is *of the seven;* being the sixth, healed of its deadly wound.*

* The idea of the late author, that the last head of the Roman Beast arose in Charlemagne, or was in a measure fulfilled in the subsequent German emperors, appears to me *incorrect*, for the following reasons.

1. The Carlovingian dynasty was destitute of the first essential characteristic of the last head of the Roman Beast, *Atheism*. I think there is conclusive evidence that the last head of the Roman Beast and Antichrist are the same. At least, it *is* evident that the last head of the Roman Beast is an *Atheist*. But was Charlemagne an Atheist? So far was he from this, that he was even a *zealot* for the cause of the Catholic religion. In 772 he turned his arms against the powerful nation of the Saxons, in the confines of Germany, in order to abolish their idoltry, and lead them to embrace the Christian Religion. Perhaps his motives were not evangelical. But this piece of history shows that he had not the character of an Atheist. In 775, 776, and 780, he pursued his wars upon the same ferocious people; in hopes of bringing them into the pale of the Christian Church.†

This mighty emperor, called by Guthrie, (p. 427,) "the glory of those dark ages," having Spain, France, Germany, and part of Italy, under his dominion, confirmed to the Popes the grant made by his father Pepin, king of France, of the Exarchate of Ravenna; and he enlarged the donation. And he was, in 800, crowned by the Pope, *king of the Romans*. Mr. Lowman observes,‡ "Charles the Great, like another Constantine, seemed to have laid the foundation of—a state of great outward prosperity for the Church." Dr. Mosheim says, "The reign of Charlemagne had been singularly auspicious to the Christian cause. The life of that great Prince was principally employed in the most zealous efforts to propagate and establish the religion of Jesus among the Huns, Saxons, Frieslanders, and other unenlightened nations." Vol. II. p. 162.

* See Mosheim, vol. ii, p. 47, 48.   † On Rev. xvi, 2.

· The old Roman Beast had ten horns. And this re-, vived new head of the same Beast has ten horns. The Angel informs, verse 12, *And the· ten horns which*

Surely these things do not appear like the Atheistical charac- teristic of Antichrist, or the last head of the Roman Beast.

And the succeeding emperors of Germany were far from having the character of Atheists. Indeed the same objection lies against the Carlovingian dynasty's constituting the Beast from ·the bottomless pit, or Antichrist, that lies against the Papal *hierarchy's* constituting Antichrist. For both alike were firm supporters of the Catholic Religion. And I can conceive of no more propriety in representing Charlemagne as instituting the system, which the French Emperor has perfect- ed, than in supposing that *Peter the Great* did the same; or than in saying, the image of the Beast (Rev. xiii, 14,) is the Beast himself. The powers are wholly distinct. Indeed the family of ·Charlemagne was expelled from the government of Germany in the year 880.

·. 2. The last head of the Roman Beast has *ten horns;* ten vas- sal kingdoms; as we shall see in the chapter under considera- tion. ·But the Carlovingian dynasty did not possess vassal kingdoms, which were sufficient to accord with this representa- tion.

3. It has already been noted, that two Beasts cannot exist on the same ground, at the same period. It is as great a sol- ecism, as to say, there are two captain generals in an army; or that *each one* of two things is the *greatest.* A Beast sym- bolizes a great ruling power of opposition to the cause of Christ. . And surely there can be but *one* such power on the same ground, at the same time. Every subordinate ·branch is but a *horn* of the dominant Beast. The Papal Beast had two horns. He managed two systems of influence, *ecclesiasti- cal* and *civil.* These by their Christian profession were ren- dered horns, of the *lamb.* But neither of them could form a separate *Beast.* The Beast to which they belonged, was but *one*, the *Papal* Beast, the Hierarchy. But· the Papal Beast *was* in existence many centuries after the reign of Char- lemagne; yea, till the revolution in, France. Then his throne was overturned; his whole kingdom was for the first time, fill- ed with darkness, and he ceased to be a Beast. After this the Papal hierarchy is called, *the false prophet;* because another power, hostile-to the Church, becomes predominant. But all this·clearly implies, that the last head of the Roman Beast was not in existence in the days of Charlemagne: Nor can his ori- gin be carried back to this early date, as will be noted. The two Beasts could not exist collaterally. This is the force of the argument used by Paul, 2 Thes. ii, 6, 7, 8; *And now ye*

thou sawest, are ten kings, which have received no kingdom as yet, but receive power as kings, one hour with the beast. These have one mind, and shall.

know what withholdeth that he (the man of sin, or the Papal Beast) *might be revealed in his time. For the mystery of iniquity doth already work; only he, who now letteth, will let, until he be taken out of the way. And then shall that wicked be revealed, whom the Lord shall consume with the spirit of his mouth, and shall destroy with the brightness of his coming.* The spirit of this apostacy had a long previous existence. But it could not prevail to constitute *the man of sin,* or the *Papal Beast,* so long as the Roman empire, which *let* or *hindered,* was in existence. The Roman emperors would not suffer ecclesiastical power to grow to such an height, while they held their authority: Or, the two powers could not each predominate at the same time. And in like manner the last head of the Roman Beast could not exist, during the predominance of the Romish hierarchy, the Papal Beast. The latter in his turn must cease to exist as a Beast, or a dominant power, when the former rises into existence. But the Papal Beast did exist, till his throne was subverted, and his kingdom filled with darkness, upon the rise of Antichrist in France. Consequently the last head of the Roman Beast did not rise till then.

4. It is a characteristic of the last head of the Roman Beast, that he is bearing the Papal harlot to her judgment, or execution, as has been shown.* Popery is borne, or managed, by the Antichristian Beast, as a mere tool of an ambitious policy; and is going to be plunged by his agency into total destruction, as we learn, Rev. xvii, 16. But this thing cannot have been said of the Carlovingian government. For this was a firm supporter of Popery. Notwithstanding the ruptures sometimes existing between the Popes and the Emperors, yet the latter were firm supporters of the Papal religion. And the German empire was not the executioner of the Papal harlot. The Carlovingian dynasty was destitute then, of this essential feature of the last head of the Roman Beast, that he is bearing the harlot (presented for execution) to the scaffold; and that his horns *are to hate her, and burn her with fire.* But the present French Empire has this, as well as every other feature of the last head of the Roman Beast. And this is not the German empire continued; but is of a *new,* and *characteristic* origin.

5. The last head of the Roman Beast was not to exist for *so long a term,* as to admit that Charlemagne was the origin of it. The predictions concerning this terrible infidel Power all go to evince, that his existence was to be but *short.* He was to arise, not in the *latter* days with Popery:† but in the *last* days, *This*

---

* See what is said on Rev. xvii, p. 57. † See 1 Tim iv, 1.

give their power and strength unto the beast. These shall make war with the Lamb, and the Lamb shall overcome them; for he is Lord of lords, and King

know also, that in the last days, *perilous times shall come.** He was not to continue a long course of centuries. But his existeace was to be short; his ruin, at his origin, was to be. *even at* *the doors.* Peter, predicting the agents of this power, says, *Denying the Lord who bought them; and bringing upon themselves swift destruction.* Their judgment, he informs, *lingereth not;* and their *damnation slumbereth not.* This is the Beast, that *ascendeth out of the bottomless pit, and goeth into perdition.* —*He is the eighth, and is of the seven, and goeth into perdition.* This latter clause is thus repeatedly added, as though his destruction were united *with his very origin.* This is a prominent idea in the predictions of this Power. Soon after this development he meets his fatal overthrow. But was this verified in the Carlovingian dynasty? Or, are these predictions consistent with the prosperous existence of *this last head,* for more than a thousand years; i. e. for 1050 years at least? Impossible! The origin of this Power *must have been* of *recent date.* Or, if it have not appeared in France, it must be still future. We find nothing of the Roman Beast, after his deadly wound inflicted by Constantine, till the revolution in France; excepting his *image* in the management of the Papal Beast. The latter held the ground, till his kingdom was *filled with darkness,* at the rise of Antichrist. But this Papal was not the great Roman Beast.

Should it appear to any difficult to admit, that the Roman Beast should lie dead for so long a time; let them remember, that such an event does accord with the tenor of the prophetic writings. Elias lay dead many centuries, before he lived again in John the Baptist. Many of *those,* Rev. xx, 4, who had been *beheaded for the witness of Jesus,* had lain dead for a *longer term,* than did the Roman Beast, before they rose, *in their successors,* to live and reign with Christ, at the commencement of the Millennium. And *the rest of the dead,* (the wicked; Gog and Magog, slain at the battle of the great day) remain extinct through the Millennium. Then *they* rise again, in their successors at the close of the Millennium; *Gog and Magog upon* *the four quarters of the earth,* Rev. xx, 5—8. Here we find the same Power mystically, rising again, or living a third time. Antichrist goes into perdition, at the battle of the great day, under the denomination of *Gog, the land of Magog* Ezek. xxxviii, and xxxix. And after lying dead through the Millennium, he mytically rises again under the same denomination; *Gog and Magog. The rest of the dead* (Rev. xx, 5,) now live again for a

* 2 Tim. iii, 1, et alia.

of kings; and they that are with him, are called, and chosen, and faithful. And the ten horns, which thou sawest upon the beast, these shall hate the whore, and shall make her desolate and naked, and shall eat her flesh, and burn her with fire. For God hath put in their hearts to fulfil his will, and to agree and give their kingdom unto the beast, until the words of God shall be fulfilled. These ten horns have been supposed to be the same with the ten horns of the ancient Roman Beast. But this must be a mistake. Expositors have met with insuperable difficulties, in their attempts to find, in the ancient horns of

short space, to prepare the way for Christ's final coming.* The idea is the same, with that of type and antitype. And these are often at a greater distance) from each other, than were the days of Constantine from the French revolution. There were upwards of 1800 years intervening between the events in Dan. xl, 35, and those in the verse succeeding. The former verse relates to Antiochus; and the latter to the antitype of Antiochus. Yet the reading seems to indicate an uninterrupted series of events. In Psalm lxxii, two systems of events are predicted as one, in an uninterrupted series; which events were yet 3000 years apart; *the reign of Solomon; and the reign of Christ, in the Millennium.* Numerous are the Scripture instances of this kind. Antichrist is *Babylon* raised up again, Rev. xvi, 19. But we find a longer time between the fall of ancient Babylon, and the rise of Antichrist, than between the revolution under Constantine, and the French revolution. It therefore fully accords with the usual imagery of prophetic writings, to represent the ancient Pagan Roman empire, and the present French empire, by one Beast with as many heads, as the Roman empire has had forms of government; with one of these heads wounded to death; but now healed; and the world wondering after him; even though the last head had lain wounded to death for many centuries. We have special notice of this long death. The Beast *was, and is not, and yet is.* This clause, *and is not,* shews that for a long time he had not actual existence; *and yet is;* he had a mystical existence; or he was again to rise: As it is again expressed, *The Beast, that thou sawest, was, and is not, and shall ascend out of the bottomless pit, and go into perdition.* Here he was to be in a state of non-existence, till he should, in the last days, ascend out of the bottomless pit, to go into perdition. His rise under diabolical agency was to be but a *short time* before his fatal overthrow.

* See sect. iii, chap. iii, of this dissertation.

the Roman Beast, the things here ascribed to the horns of the Antichristian Beast. Insomuch, that in Pool's Annotations upon the passage, we read, "But who these ten monarchs be, or what these ten kingdoms are, I must confess myself at a loss to determine. I am much inclined to think the prophecy to concern some kings nearer the end of Antichrist's reign." Even this acknowledgment was made, while under the mistake, of supposing the Beast, that wore these horns, to be the Papal hierarchy; a sentiment attended with inexplicable difficulties! Had the pious expositor viewed the Beast wearing these horns in the character, in which he has just been exhibited, I trust he would have been still *more* inclined to view the prophecy, as respecting events still future; when his annotations were written.

These ten horns are kingdoms under the Antichristian empire. We find the great Power noted in Dan. xi, 36, and onward, subduing neighboring nations, and distributing their principalities to his favorites.* He is thus forming to himself horns. We find in various passages relating to this terrific Beast of the last days, that he has a group of kings at command. Here then are the horns of the Antichristian Beast. *And I saw the Beast, and the kings of the earth and their armies gathered together to make war against him, that sat on the horse, and against his army.*† Whether the number of these horns will be precisely ten; or whether a certain number is put for an uncertain, time will decide. But as the number of the seven heads is definite, I apprehend the number of the ten horns is likewise definite; that ten will be the precise number of the vassal kingdoms of the Antichristian empire.‡

*See Sec. ii, chap. i, of this dissertation.
†Rev. xix, 19. See also Rev. xvi, 13; and sec. 2, chap. iii, of this dissertation, relative to Gog and his bands.
‡"The following arrangement of titles and of dislocations and creations of kings is reported in letters from Germany to have been determined on between the Emperors of France and Austria.

Their servility, as well as the shortness of their existence, is hinted. *Which have received no kingdom as yet; but have received power* as kings, *one hour with the Beast.* The word in the original, made in our translation to import *not yet,* I think is designed here to express only an emphatical *negative.* It is not ουκ ετι; but ουπω prefixed to the verb ελαϐον, from ου not, and πω by any means. *Which have not by any means* received a kingdom. They have not the *independence* of a kingdom. But they have received power *as kings,* one hour with the Beast. Each has only the *resemblance* of a kingdom; or the *name,* without the thing; and this but for a short space, like an hour, under his imperial master.

Their object is noted. *These shall make war with the Lamb.* The final event is given. *And the Lamb shall overcome them.* The unanimity of these horns, and the government of God in it for judgment, are strongly expressed. *These have one mind, and shall give their power and strength unto the Beast. For God hath put in their hearts to fulfil his will, and to agree and give their kingdom unto the Beast, until the words of God*

Napoleon I, Emperor of France, &c. King of the Romans.

Francis II, Emperor of Austria and Franconia, and co-protector of the confederation of the Rhine.

The Archduke Charles King of Spain, and of the Indies.

Joseph Napoleon to be King of Italy.

Ferdinand IV to be restored to the throne of the two Sicilies.

Joachim to be King of Poland.

Eugene to be King of Macedonia.

Louis Napoleon to be King of Bavaria.

The hereditary prince of Bavaria to be King of Holland and. Berg.

Jerome Napoleon to be King of Wirtemberg.

The King of Wirtemberg to be King of Westphalia.

The grand duke of Baden to be King of Switzerland.

The King of Prussia to cede Silesia to Austria."

(Gazette of July 3, 1810.)

This evinces the inclination of the French Empire to create vassal kingdoms, which may answer to the horns of the Antichristian Beast. What vassal kingdoms may eventually be found to answer to the ten horns of this Beast, those who may live at the time of the battle of the great day, will be better able to decide, than we can do at this period.

shall be fulfilled; as in the forecited passage, Dan. xi,
36; *and shall prosper, till the indignation be accomplished; for that, which is determined, shall be done.** And

*The above passages *admit*, and parallel prophecies *teach*, as
was noted in the last section, that the Antichristian Empire
will exhibit a striking mixture of *strength* and *weakness*. It
will, at times, appear, as though it were going to speedy destruction. And yet the Providence of God will signally uphold
it, beyond the limits of human calculations.

The above ten horns have one mind to give their power and
strength unto the Beast. There was not to be found among
them a strange yielding to this their fate, contrary to what might
have been expected. And the reason of so strange an event
is given. "For God hath put in their hearts to fulfil his will,
and to agree and give their kingdom unto the Beast, until the
words of God shall be fulfilled." God signally governs the
event for judgment, to fulfil his own word and purposes.
The strange obsequiousness of those kingdoms to a most despotic dynasty, is hence accounted for. This seems to imply,
that, aside from this special divine superintendence, for judgment, the submission of those states and kingdoms, would be
unaccountable, and contrary to human probability.

This Power, (though with great reverses,) we are assured
on the whole, "shall prosper, (or exist) till the indignation shall
be accomplished; for that, which is determined shall be done;
Dan. xi, 36. This implies, that while this Power may seem
to be on the eve of ruin; and the world are rising on *tiptoe*, to
hail the destruction of their destroyer; yet they will be in a
measure disappointed. The existence of the rod of iron, the
battle axe of the nations, is still *upheld*, till the work of divine
indignation is accomplished.

In the description of the *feet* and *toes* of the great image,
Dan. ii, the idea under consideration is clearly given. The
legs of iron, (verse 33,) were immensely strong: as was indeed
the old Roman Empire. But the feet and toes, or the last part
of the same Empire, with its ten vassal kingdoms, are, for a
season before the coming of Christ to destroy them, presented
to the world as *part of iron, and part of clay*. The sense is
given; verse 41, 42, 43; "And whereas thou sawest the feet and
toes part of potter's clay, and part of iron; the kingdoms shall
be divided; but there shall be in it of the strength of the iron;
forasmuch as thou sawest the iron mixed with the miry clay.
And as the toes of the feet were part of iron, and part of clay; so
the kingdom shall be partly strong, and partly broken. They
shall not cleave one to another, even as iron is not mixed with
clay. And in the days of those kings shall the God of heaven
set up a kingdom." Here is the finishing dynasty of the Roman empire, with its vassal kingdoms, when Christ comes and

the final destruction of the Romish hierarchy by these horns, is predicted. *These shall hate the whore, and shall make her desolate, and naked, and shall, eat her flesh, and burn her with fire.* And thus the Papal power, which has *led into captivity, now goes into captivity.* *He, that has killed with the sword, is now killed with the sword.* *Here is the patience and faith of the saints;* either that righteous vindication, for which the martyrs have been represented as patiently waiting and expecting;* or new trials to the saints under Anti-

dashes them to pieces, to set up his own kingdom. And this dynasty is composed of *iron* and *clay:*—"Partly strong, and partly broken."

Great battles, and vast enterprises may be lost. Men may say, Now this Empire is going to ruin at once! But they will find their mistake. "The end is not by and by." "The time is not yet; but in the days of the seventh angel, when he shall begin to sound, the mystery of God shall be finished." An emperor may be hurled from his throne. For the Antichristian Empire depends on *no one man.* Emperors were hurled from their thrones, and others succeeded them, in the first reign, of the imperial head of the Roman Beast, even in the time of the legs of iron. And similar events may again take place, under the Antichristian reign. But whatever great commotions may take place; this kingdom will stand, till the time arrives for the Stone to grind it to powder.

In Rev. xii, 16, is the same idea. The infernal dragon, by his *new instrument of persecution,* pours out floods of armies, falsehoods, mischief, rage and terrors, to cause the Church to be swept away. But the earth helps the Church, and opens her mouth, and swallows up these floods. Earthly views and motives will induce *some* to counteract the strength and violence of this *great instrument of Satan;* so that, while it is partly *strong;* it will also be partly *broken.* While it has much iron, it will possess much clay. But its strength will prevail, till the indignation is accomplished: or the word of God is fulfilled. While a mixture of iron and clay will be exhibited, which will keep the nations in a tremendous uproar; the iron will prevail, till the period arrives for the Stone, cut out without hands, to smite the feet and toes, and all the materials of the image, to dust, and to set up his own millennial kingdom. But this will not be so immediately, upon the appearing of the Antichristian Power to be *partly broken,* as many may imagine. (See remarks on Rev. x, and Matt. xxiv, in the sequel of this work, under the fifth vial.)

*Rev. vi, 9, 10, 11.

christian tyranny. The Papal harlot appears, in the beginning of the chapter; dressed out and presented, for execution; as has been noted. The Beast is, under the direction of Divine providence, bearing her to her judgment, or execution. *I will show thee the judgment of the whore.* And now the event takes place, under the agency of the ten horns of the Beast, as her executioners. Whether this execution of the Papal harlot will be finished in the mutinies, and bloody havoc, which are to take place among the combined powers, under the Antichristian Beast, gathered in Palestine against the Jews;* or in some preceding events, time will determine. To me the former appears probable. For the false prophet is represented as present, in union with the Antichristian Beast, and going into perdition with him, at the battle of that great day.† By the false prophet here, must be understood Popery, after it ceases to be a Beast, its throne being subverted, and its kingdom being filled with darkness, upon the rise of the Antichristian Beast. This is evident from Dan. vii, 11, compared with Rev. xix, 19, 20. In the former, it is "because of the voice of the great words, which the *horn* (Popery) spake, that the *Beast* (the last head of the Roman Beast) is slain, and his body is destroyed and given to the burning flame." In the latter passage, (which clearly relates to the same period and event,) we find the *Beast* and his kings and their armies, gathered to battle against Christ. "And the *Beast* was taken, and with him the *false prophet,* that wrought miracles before him, and—both were cast alive into the lake of fire." Here we learn, that the *horn,* in the former passage, or Popery, is the *false prophet* in the latter passage. The false prophet in the Revelation then, is *Popery,* in that subjugated form, in which it goes into perdition. This subjected relict of Popery must have some *new name.* And, as it is a scheme of *false religion,* found in the most mischievous connexion with the Antichristian Beast, as his nominal *form of Godliness,* it is rational, that the term *false prophet* should be given.

---

* See Sec. ii and iii, chap. iii. † See Rev. xix, 20.

The destruction of the vast confederacy, at the battle of the great day, is represented as being partly, if not chiefly effected by the swords of each other. The great city, probably meaning the empire of the Antichristian Beast, is then said to be divided into three parts. (Rev. xvi, 19.) The part of the coalition which is more attached to Popery, or the false prophet, may be one of these three parts, rising in mutiny against the Beast their master, and falling first by the swords of his vassal kings: And thus the execution of the mother of harlots be completely fulfilled. An incipient fulfilment it receives, in events, which were to precede the battle of that great day; as appears in the next section.

I shall close this section with some remarks concerning the ancient horns of the Roman Beast. Expositors have, I believe, generally agreed, that the ancient ten horns of the Roman Beast symbolized ten kingdoms, into which the Roman empire was divided, when the western branch of it was overrun by the northern barbarians, in the fifth and sixth centuries. Sir Isaac Newton, Bp. Newton, Machiavel, and others, have undertaken to find these ten horns. But their catalogues have differed. And they have found it no easy task to present one, which has even *plausibility* on its side. For those petty barbarian kingdoms were fluctuating and changing like the waves of the sea. It has never been pretended that the number *ten*, could be found but for a short time among them; and indeed several successive kingdoms on the same ground have sometimes been reckoned to make out the ten.

Is it not possible, that the venerable expositors have been under a mistake upon this point? And that the ten ancient horns of the Roman Beast were designed to represent the different kingdoms or countries existing under the old Roman empire, in its most flourishing state? That empire in the zenith of its power, had indeed its *many*, if not precisely *ten* horns, or governments, united under its imperial dynasty. We may probably count the number ten of the vassal kingdoms, under the sixth head of ancient Rome. Italy, Greece,

Macedon, Syria, Egypt, Ethiopia, Charthage, Spain, Gaul, and Britain, were at once under the dominion of Cesar. Should it be said that Greece and Macedon *may* be reckoned as one kingdom; we *may* reckon *Pontus*, bordering on mount Caucasus, early subjugated by the Roman arms, a distinct kingdom from Syria. Or if this reckoning be deemed incorrect, I do not doubt, but that by further reflection and examination into Roman history, we may be able to find precisely *ten* in the nations, which were under, and which constituted the strength of, the ancient Roman empire. I ask then, why were not these vassal powers to be reckoned the ten horns of the ancient sixth and imperial head of the Roman Beast? That they were to be thus accounted, I apprehend is a truth for the following reasons:

1. A horn is an emblem of power. The seven horns of the Lamb, are emblems of his omnipotence. And the ten horns of the Roman Beast appear to be most proper emblems of ten collateral kingdoms, which constituted *his power.* His power *did indeed* consist in such a number of kingdoms at once under his command. But,

2. To say that the ten horns of the Roman Beast were the ten parts, into which the empire was divided, in the fifth and sixth centuries, after it was subverted by terrible Divine judgments, and by legions of victorious barbarian invaders, seems to give a most lively representation of the *weakness* instead of the power of the Roman Beast. To represent the scattered fragments of a once powerful empire, by so many *horns* of that empire, one would be apt to construe as *ironical!* The notable horn, between the eyes of the Macedonian he-goat was an emblem of his *then present* power in Alexander. And though four horns, which arise after this is broken, symbolize the division of Alexander's empire to his four generals, yet full notice is given that they were to be *subsequent*, and inferior to the first notable horn. But we could hardly construe the one notable horn, even had we not been informed it was the *first king*, as being some king to arise a number of cen-

turies after the period of the greatest strength of the
he-goat, and even after he was destroyed. When the
prophet informs us of the Most High having horns coming out of his hands, and there was the hiding of his
power, we naturally construe this as a symbol of the
present Divine omnipotence, as well as of some certain
act of judgment against his enemies. And when we
read, Dan. vii, 7, of the *fourth Beast, dreadful and*
terrible, and strong exceedingly, having great iron teeth,
devouring and breaking in pieces, stamping the residue
with his 'feet, and having ten horns; we should not
naturally believe, that these ten horns were designed to
symbolize the broken fragments of the empire of this
Beast, after the period of his power was *long past,* and
his dominions had fallen under the ravages of succeeding barbarous nations.

3. The Roman Beast was *dead* of his wound given
by Constantine, long before the division of his empire
took place. The sixth, the imperial, the most mischievous head of this Beast, was wounded to death, in
the revolution from Paganism to Christianity. The Roman empire then ceased to be a Beast. This Beast *had*
been; but now *was not;* Rev. xvii, 11. Nothing more
was to be seen of him, except in his image in the power
of the' Papal Beast, Rev. xiii, 14, till he should revive
in his own *avowed,* as well as *real* Pagan nature, under
his seventh head, and should have his deadly wound
completely healed under his eighth head, which is *of*
the seven, being specifically the sixth revived; *ascend-*
ing, in the last days, from the bottomless pit; and going
into perdition. How then can we conceive that some
kingdoms, which should rise out of the broken mass of
the empire, some centuries after it became Christian,
and the old Beast was dead, should be represented as
his horns? The Papal horn might be represented as a
horn of this Beast, though he rose after the Beast was
dead. For notice is given that his rising was to be
afterward: And another shall rise after them, and he
shall be diverse from the first; Dan. vii, 24. But can
we infer from this representation, that *all the ten* horns
were to rise into existence long after the death of the

Beast? Let us examine the propriety of such a representation. We find the *Antichristian* Beast of the last
days has *his ten horns;* Rev. xvii, 12. Now, could it
be proper to view the ten horns of the Antichristian
Beast as symbolizing some future kingdoms, to arise
on the ground, and out of the broken mass of the Antichristian empire, some centuries after Antichrist is
no more? Are they not designed to symbolize the
vassal kingdoms under the very *dominion*, and which
constitute the *strength* of Antichrist? The latter no
doubt is the fact. And why did not the same thing
hold true of the ten horns of his precursor, the ancient
sixth head of the Roman Beast, which is mystically
revived in Antichrist? Why is it more proper to view
the ancient ten horns as coming into existence long
after the power, and even the actual existence of the
Roman Beast became extinct, than to view the ten horns
of Antichrist as coming into existence long after Antichrist himself shall have gone into perdition? If the
vassal kingdoms, *actually* under the power of Antichrist, be *his ten horns;* why were not the vassal kingdoms *actually* under the power of the ancient Imperial
head of the Roman Beast, *the ten horns of that Beast?*
Another argument in favor of this opinion is found
in Dan. ii, 44; *And in the days of those kings shall
the God of heaven set up a kingdom, which shall
never be destroyed; and—it shall break in pieces and
consume all those kingdoms; and it shall stand for
ever.* In the days of *what* kings? Those represented
by the preceding *ten toes* of the great image; which
must have been the same with the ancient *ten horns* of
the Roman Beast. In *their days* the God of heaven
was to set up his kingdom. This must, at least primarily, refer to the coming of Christ in the flesh, to
set up his Gospel kingdom. But if this was to be
in the *days of those kings*, which constituted the ten
toes of the image, and these were the ten horns of the
Roman Beast, then the vassal kings under Imperial
Rome, at the commencement of the Gospel dispensation, *were indeed* those ten horns. Consequently they
could not have been the kingdoms, into which the Ro-

14

man empire was divided in after ages. It was so far
from being in the days of the latter, that the God of
heaven set up his kingdom, in any peculiar sense;
that it may rather be said to have been in *their days*,
that *Satan* was suffered to erect the Papal and Mohammedan pillars of his kindgom; and the Church of
Christ fled into the wilderness for 1260 years.

This passage in Dan. ii, 44, is one of those predictions, which are constructed with a view to receive a
twofold accomplishment. Its first accomplishment has
been just noted. But its ultimate one is still future,
and will be fulfilled in the destruction of Antichrist,
with his *ten horns;* and the introduction of the Millennium. The latter event is clearly connected with the
passage. The Stone cut out of the mountain without
hands, is to smite the image upon the feet; (the parts of
it *then in power)* upon which the iron, the clay, the
brass, the silver, and the gold, are dashed in pieces, and
like chaff are blown away; and the Stone becomes a
great mountain, and fills the world. This will be fulfilled in the battle of that great day of God Almighty,
and the subsequent Millennium. But though this be
the *ultimate* fulfilment of the passage, it had a *primary*
fulfilment in the apostolic age; in which we learn that
the primitive ten horns of the Roman Beast were *then*
in existence.

There is one passage which at first view may seem
to militate against this interpretation; viz. Dan. vii, 24,
And the ten horns out of this kingdom are ten kings,
which shall rise; and another shall rise after them,
and he shall be diverse from the first, and he shall
subdue three kings. This may seem to indicate, that
these ten kingdoms were to be at some period *subse-*
quent to the Roman empire; or were to *rise* from its ruins. But the text does not necessarily convey such an
idea. If the arguments in favor of the forementioned
scheme, be conclusive, and this text be fairly capable
of receiving a construction, which accords with it, such
a construction must obtain. The ten horns, according to the scheme above given, did indeed rise *out of*
the Roman empire. The Roman government was first.

And those kingdoms rose into view, under this new relation of the *horns of the Roman Beast*, one after another, as the Romans formed new conquests, in ages far future to the period of the prophet Daniel. Might not the expounding Angel then say, of those vassal kingdoms of the Roman empire, *The ten horns out of this kingdom are ten kingdoms which shall rise?* Ten kingdoms *did* rise *from, by* or *through* the power of the Roman dynasty, and both rendered *terrible*, and *characterized* the old Roman Beast. The clause in verse 8, *And behold there came up among them another little horn*, may have induced some to suppose, that the ten, must have been collateral with the Papal horn, or in existence at the same time with it. But no such thing is implied. The clause is only a description of the *symbol*. The horns *there* must have been beheld by the prophet *all at once*. But this did not indicate, that the actual existence of the events symbolized should be *all at once*. The expositors upon the old scheme make the origin of some of the horns some centuries before that of others. And my exposition does only the same. But the explanatory text, verse 24th, decides that the Papal horn, and the ten horns were *not* collateral. *And another shall rise* after them; *and he shall be diverse from the first*. Here the Papal horn was to be *posterior* to the other horns. And nothing is indicated but that this posteriority was to be *as long*, as was the rise of Popery after the death of the Pagan Beast, in the year 320.

There is one more passage, which has led to the supposition, that the horns of the ancient Beast were the kingdoms, into which the European branch of the Roman empire was divided; viz. Rev. xvii, 16, which relates to the ten horns of the Beast from the bottomless pit hating and destroying the Papal harlot. But these are the ten horns of the *Antichristian* Beast of the last days; and not the ten horns of the ancient Roman Beast; as has appeared in the preceding section.

5. Another argument in favor of the view given of the ancient ten horns, I think may be derived from the account of *three* of them being plucked up before the

Papal horn, if we consider this account in the light of its fulfilment. Verse 8, *I considered the horns, and behold there came up among them another little horn, before whom there were three of the first horns plucked up by the roots.* Verse 20, *And of the ten horns; —and of the other, which came up, and before whom three fell.* Verse 24, *And another shall rise after them; and he shall be diverse from the first, and he shall subdue three kings.* Concerning these three kingdoms plucked up by the Papal power, authors have been much divided, and much perplexed. Some have supposed they were Lombardy, Ravenna, and the neighborhood of Rome. Some have conjectured them to have been the exarchate of Ravenna, the senate and people of Rome, and the German empire. And others have formed other, and contradictory conjectures. But one difficulty is, those places, on which expositors have hit, could not be called *kingdoms* among the kingdoms, into which the Roman empire was divided. Or, over those places which might be called kingdoms, the Pope never obtained civil jurisdiction. For expositors have taken for granted, that the Pope's obtaining civil jurisdiction over these three kingdoms, was the true idea of their being plucked up before him. And there never have been three places found, which might be properly said to have been three kingdoms rising out of the old empire, over which the Pope did obtain civil jurisdiction. No wonder then, that authors have been divided and perplexed upon this point. To perceive the difficulties, which attend their schemes, let us concisely examine them. Lombardy has been often mentioned as one of these three kingdoms. The Lombards did indeed set up a kingdom in Italy, after the subversion of the old empire. And they were afterwards subdued; but not by the Pope. And but a part of their kingdom fell afterward under the civil jurisdiction of the Pope. Could so small a circumstance then constitute the plucking up by the roots of one of those three kingdoms noted in that ancient prophecy? Ravenna has been supposed to be one of these three kingdoms. Ravenna was an ancient city in Italy, the capital of Romagna. Of this, and of some provinces in its vicinity, it is ac.t knowledged the Pope obtained civil jurisdiction, by the donation of Pepin, king of France. But could that petty territory be recognized in ancient prophecy as a kingdom, a horn of the Roman Beast? It never was a kingdom! An if every such section, having once belonged to the Roman empire, may be called a *horn* of that empire, we should be furnished with not only *ten*, but perhaps *ten times ten* horns of that ancient Beast. When Theodoric, king of the Ostrogoths took Italy, in 493, he made Ravenna the *capital* of his kingdom. But did this constitute *it a kingdom?* In the reign of Justinian, emperor of Constantinople, Belisarius and Narses, his generals, overturned the kingdom of the Ostrogoths in Italy; and Narses was constituted governor of Italy with the title of duke. He made Ravenna his capital; and not long after it became an exarchate. But could this constitute it a *kingdom*, a horn of the Roman Beast? And with no more propriety could the city of Rome, with her *"senate, people and neighborhood,"* be represented as one of those kingdoms. When Theodoric established Ravenna as his capital, he suffered Rome to retain under him some appearance of her former government. But still it was in fact but one city in his kingdom; and that inferior to his capital. And under the succeeding dukedom of Narses, Rome was stripped of every appearance of her ancient form of government, and reduced to a mere duchy; and this long before it fell under the civil jurisdiction of the Pope. Rome was besieged and taken five times in twenty years; and was reduced to a miserable condition. A sorry kingdom indeed, to be supposed one of Daniel's ten Roman horns; and one of the three, which fell before the Papal hierarchy! But even supposing these, (viz. Ravenna, and Rome with its neighborhood) to be two of the three horns; where shall we find the third? We must leave Italy. And where else did the Pope obtain civil jurisdiction? Some have tried to find one of these three horns in Germany. But surely the Pope had no civil kingdom there. It is true we find there were in Germany spiritual princes with civil jurisdiction. Some time after Pepin gave to the 'Pope the exharchate of Ravenna, and constituted him a civil prince in some of the Italian states, Charlemagne, 'Pepin's son and successor, endowed some of the bishops in Germany, with temporal dominions, and annexed to their bishoprics the civil jurisdiction of their dioceses. These ecclesiastico-civil princes obtained the enlargement of their civil dominions, till some of them came to rank with the highest sovereign princes; were even electors; and not inferior to kings. But these sovereignties were not under the civil jurisdiction of the Pope. So fully disconnected were their civil jurisdictions from his, that Dr. Lowman imagined, (though I think incorrectly) that those German establishments collectively constituted the second Beast in Rev. xiii; while the Roman hierarchy constituted the first.* The sovereign ecclesiastics in Germany constituted but a minority of the German empire. How then could Germany be one of these three kingdoms which fell before the Pope? The long contentions between the Popes and the German emperors concerning the right of investitures, were far from indicating, that Germany had been plucked up by the Papal horn, in point of civil jurisdiction. But even if Germany *had* been under the civil jurisdiction of the Pope, it would fail of answering to the prediction in Daniel concerning any one of the three horns. For the primitive Germans never belonged to the ancient Roman empire. The ancient Germans, a fierce warlike people, though they trembled at the Cesars, and lost bloody battles with the Romans, were never subdued by the Roman arms. Charlemagne was the first, who subdued them, in the beginning of the ninth century. Surely then Germany could not be one of those three horns.

A late celebrated writer on the prophecies, feeling as it is presumed, the difficulties attending the old schemes of exposition upon this point, gives a new one of the following tenor. The first kingdom, he tells us, to be

---

* Lowman on Rev. p. 139.

plucked up, was that of Odoacer, king of the Heruli, who took Italy in 476, put an end to the western Roman empire, and caused himself to be proclaimed king of Italy. But his kingdom was plucked up in 493, by Theodoric, king of the Ostrogoths, when he established his Gothic kingdom in Italy, which I before noted. This latter was plucked up by Belisarius and Narses, generals of the eastern emperor, by the aid of the Lombards, who were auxiliaries under them. Italy now, after being thus twice plucked up, (not by the Pope indeed, nor in his presence; for he was not yet in existence!) was made a province of the eastern emperor, under the dukedom of Narses. Italy now not being an independent kingdom, its next revolution was not to be reckoned. This next, which was not to be reckoned, took place sometime after, by the invasion of the Lombards, who under Alboin set up a kingdom in Italy, about the year 568. In 752, they, under Aistulphus, took Ravenna; and threatened Rome; upon which the Pope applied to Pepin king of France, for protection. Pepin came with an army; subdued the Lombards; and gave the exharchate of Ravenna, as the patrimony of St. Peter, to the Pope. This was the third kingdom plucked up before the Pope. Here is the plucking up of the three kingdoms before the Papal horn. But I think not less difficulties attend this scheme, than those, which attend the others.

First: These three kingdoms are in fact but *one* and the same nation, Italy. If one nation, by successive revolutions, may make the three horns; why not by ten revolutions, make the ten horns? Perhaps there have been revolutions enough in Italy to amount to the ten horns! This would prevent the necessity of looking abroad from Italy to find the ten horns of the Roman Beast: We should have only to ascertain ten revolutions there.

Secondly: But a small part of this *threefold kingdom of Italy* fell under the civil jurisdiction of the Pope. The exarchate of Ravenna, and in after days some other provinces, did in this sense fall before him. But with what propriety could that part of the Lombardic kingdom, which fell into the Papal hands, be reckoned even *one*, and much less the *three* of those kingdoms so long foretold by Daniel?

Thirdly: The above scheme as really makes four horns falling before the Papal horn, as three. The revolution under Belisarius and Narses, was as *real* and *great*, as any of the others. And a vast dukedom under a great empire, may as properly constitute a horn, as a short lived, barbarian kingdom, which embraces only the same territory.

Fourthly: The prophecy says of the Papal horn, *And he shall subdue three kings.** But according to the scheme of this author, the Popes subdued but a part of *one* kingdom; *and not that neither!* for the king of France subdued it for him. And with the preceding conquests of Italy, the Papal horn had nothing to do. For they took place long before his existence! Upon this scheme it appears, that instead of the Pope's subduing three kingdoms, he never subdued one. And if those successive revolutions in Italy, which preceded the rise of the Papal horn, were to be noted in ancient prophecy, as kingdoms subdued by the Pope; why should not all the revolutions in Italy, from the days of Romulus, be thus noted?

The above scheme appears to me untenable; as do indeed all the schemes I have ever seen upon the subject. And I cannot but apprehend, that the lameness, which appears to attend the old expositions on this subject, affords a strong argument, that the old scheme, relative to the ten horns of the old Roman Beast, is incorrect.

To find the fulfilment of the three horns falling before the Papal horn, I think we must find *three* great sections of the primitive Roman empire, falling peculiarly under the fatal delusion of the Papal imposture. This fatal influence, appropriate to Popery, is something, in which the Papal power is indeed *diverse* from all other powers, which had been noted in prophecy. *And another shall rise after them, and he shall be* diverse *from*

* Dan. vii, 24.

the first; and he shall subdue three kings. This *diverse* characteristic seems to have been overlooked. If his subduing three kings mean his obtaining civil juris- diction over them, then he was not in this respect *di- verse* from other civil powers. But the Papal charac- teristic of being *diverse*, is a circumstance, which seems to indicate, that the influence, with which he sub- dues three kings, is of a kind *diverse* from civil gov- ernment. It must mean his filling them with his own *characteristic influence, Popery.* And do we not find this thing fulfilled? Behold *Italy, France,* and *Spain,* (which were indeed horns of the empire of the ancient Cesars,) the chief theatre of Papal delusion; and eventually plucked up by the roots by the consequences of that wicked system! This is an event interesting to the Church; and might be expected to have been a sub- ject of ancient prophecy, when the Papal imposture was predicted. But the old view of the subject appears to be on *too small a scale;* and the events scarcely interest- ing to the Church at all. By Italy, France, and Spain, I mean all that was formerly included in them: Italy con- taining all that country south of the Alps: France, the ancient transalpine Gaul, including all the old Roman dominions between the Alps and the Pyrenees, the Hel- vetii, or Switzerland, and a considerable part of the modern German empire:† And Spain including all west and south of the Pyrenees: For the ancient kingdoms of Spain and Lusitania, or Portugal, were but one horn of the ancient Roman empire. Britain, though it was under the empire of the Cesars; and though it was in the dark ages much perverted with Papal delusion for centuries; yet considering its early renunciation of that pestilent error, its different lot at the end of the scene, and its being reserved as a cradle of the Church of Christ, it would not be represented as plucked up by the roots, or subdued by the Papal horn. The British were the most loath to submit to the impositions of

---

* Dan. vii, 24.   † See Guthrie's Geog. p. 452.

15

Popery. Says Mosheim, vol. ii, p. 16, The ancient
Britains and Scotts persisted long in the maintainance of
their religious liberty; and neither the threats nor promises of the legates of Rome could engage them to submit to the decrees and authority of the ambitious pontiff." This long opposition to the corrupting ambition
of the Papal tyrant; and the very early renunciation of
Popery, in the British isle, we might expect would be
followed with special tokens of the divine benignity.
The evils of Popery were to be of so much longer duration, and its events so much more fatal, in Italy,
France, and Spain, that it appears rational that they
should be thus designated, in that ancient prophecy concerning the Papal delusion, as the principal theatre,
(among the horns of the ancient Beast,) of its fatal operations. The other nations, which constituted the other
horns of the Beast, were not so conspicuously to be
the theatre of Papal delusion and ruin. And we accordingly find *they were not.* The horns in Africa,
Asia, and even Greece, escaped this deadly influence.
Ancient Germany, and the more northern nations of
Prussia, Poland, Denmark, and Sweden, though they
were long enveloped in Papal delusion, and share in the
judgments of Papal nations, yet they did not belong to
the old Roman empire; and therefore could not be represented as horns of that Beast falling before the Papal
horn. The descriptions, of belonging to the horns of
the old Roman Beast, and being subdued by the characteristic influence of the Papal horn, (its false religion),
meet, in a peculiar and equal degree, only in those three
notable, ancient horns, *Italy, France,* and *Spain.* These
three great territories did indeed fatally fall before the
Papal horn. They from first to last formed the principal seat of his delusion; and appear to be forming the
principal theatre of the judgments of Heaven upon that
wicked system.

  If the view given, of the plucking up by the roots of
the three horns before the Papal horn, be correct; it
shows that the horns of the ancient Beast were the kingdoms, which constituted the old Roman empire in its
zenith, and were in existence, when *the God of*

heaven set up his kingdom at the commencement of the Gospel day; and were not the kingdoms into which the old empire crumbled to pieces. For Italy, France, and Spain, including the places above noted, cannot be said to be three of ten different kingdoms, into which the Roman empire was by the northern barbarians divided. And as the old Imperial head of the Roman Beast had its ten horns; so the same head mystically revived from the bottomless pit, in the last days, has its ten horns.

SECTION VII.

Antichrist predicted in the XVIIIth chapter of Revelation.

IN this chapter, a further view is given of the judgments of God upon Papal Rome.

1. *An angel descends from heaven, having great power; and the earth is lightened with his glory:* Indications of some great event now to be accomplished! An event, which should be noted through the whole earth!

2. *And he cried mightily, with a strong voice, saying, Babylon the great is fallen, is fallen.* Here is the *sum* of the event. And the greatness and terrors of it are strikingly indicated by the Angel's having great power; the earth being lightened with his glory, his repeating the event, and doing it mightily with a strong voice. In the preceding chapter, Papal Rome, as distinct from the Antichristian Beast, is symbolized by a harlot, borne or managed by this Beast, and is called, *Mystery, Babylon the great. Babylon the great,* in this xviiith chapter, must be the same power, the Papal hierarchy, as distinct from the Antichristian Beast. In the preceding chapter this harlot is presented for execution, as we have seen. And in this xviiith chapter, we have the commencement and process of her execution. But this Divine judgment upon her implies an *instrument,* by which it is inflicted. Therefore,

3. The origin of the instrument of the fall of Popery is hinted: *And is become the habitation of devils, and the hold of every foul spirit, and a cage of every unclean and*

hateful bird. Some capital revolution in her territories is here indicated, in which her own dominions are
exhibited to the world, as a habitation of devils; the
disgorgings of the infernal world; and a pandæmonium
of every species of licentiousness and abomination.
Here is the origin of the Beast, that ascendeth out of
the bottomless pit, or Antichrist. This is the furnishing of the executioner of Papal Babylon. Here was to
be forged the *rod of iron*, which is fully implied in the
subsequent predictions of her judgments in this chapter. The instrument of the Divine vengeance was to
rise out of her own territories, and corruptions. Here
were to be exhibited the habitation of devils, the hold
of every foul spirit, and the cage of every unclean and
hateful bird. The egg of Papal Babylon was thus to
break out into a viper, which should become a fiery
flying serpent. She was thus to be fatally stung with
her own scorpions; yea, gored to death with the *horns*
rising from her own corruptions. It was a remark of
Sir Isaac Newton, that "the tyranny of the Papal power,
which has so long corrupted Christianity, and enslaved
the Christian world, must be brought to an end, and
broken to pieces, by the prevalence of infidelity."

4. The fulness of the measure of Papal Babylon's
sins, and her consequent judgments, are noted in the
following verses. *And I heard a great voice from
heaven, saying, Come out of her, my people, that ye be
not partakers of her sins, and that ye receive not of her
plagues. For her sins have reached unto heaven, and
God hath remembered her iniquities.* The account proceeds, in which judgments are *doubled to her according
to her works;* her cup of indignation is filled twice as
full as that, which she had filled for the saints. *Torment and sorrow* are given in proportion as *she has glorified herself,* and counted upon prosperity. *Her
plagues shall come* as it were *in one day, death, mourning, famine, and fire,* under the strong hand of God, who
judgeth her. Decisive events are here indicated. Papal Babylon is taken into the grasp of Antichrist, for her
execution. And in the struggles and scenes of blood,
which attend the rise, and the forming of the horns of

the Antichristian Beast, the Mother of harlots finds the execution of the judgments of God upon her in dreadful succession. The scenes of judgment become tremendous on one Papal nation, and on another. All in their turn have blood to drink. And Babylon the great sinks as a mighty millstone into the depth of the sea of revolution, tumult and blood, never to rise again.

5. The kings of the Papal earth, who have revelled in the idolatrous embraces of the harlot, lament and bewail her fall and miseries: At the sight of the smoke of her torments, which rises and is seen to the ends of the earth; or at the sight and hearing of her judgments and miseries, they cry, *Alas, alas!* In her distress they realize their own.

6. The merchants of the Papal earth likewise, (the dignitaries, and various orders of the Popish clergy) who have been literally made rich in her infamous and ungodly traffic, in superstitious rites, *and the souls of men,* now cry, *Alas, alas!* They weep and mourn over the ruins of their beloved hierarchy. Wailings and lamentation are heard through the nations of Papal superstition; while the judgments proceed with tremendous roar, and echo from land to land! These admirers of the harlot, *standing afar off,* some as fugitives in foreign lands, and others inclined to be as far distant as possible, for fear of her torments, lament her fall, crying, *Alas, alas! that great city Babylon! For in one hour is her judgment come! Yea, the ship masters, ship companies,* (it may be in a literal sense) *traders and sailors,* interrupted in their mercantile pursuits, by the perils of the times, are represented as standing afar off, in consternation at the view of the burnings of Babylon, or at hearing of the judgments on Papal nations, and bewailing the loss of their livings.

7. *The blood of prophets and of saints, and of all that were slain upon the earth,* is found here; and it no longer cries for retribution in vain. The God of judgment hears, and rises up out of his holy habitation. A tremendous scene of Divine wrath is opened, which overturns the seat of the Papal kingdom, and fills it *with darkness, so that they gnaw their tongues*

for pain. · The horns of the Antichristian Beast, in this chapter, are beginning to perform the execution of the Mother of harlots; though the scene will not be completed, till the battle at Armageddon. There in due time, the false prophet, (the remaining skeleton of Popery) and the Antichristian Beast himself, *will sink into perdition.*

All the events of this chapter imply the rise of a terrible instrument of judgment on Papal Babylon. This instrument, no doubt, is the Antichristian Beast. His horns were *to hate the whore, to make her desolate and naked, to eat her flesh, and burn her with fire.* These are judgments which *may* be as long a time in execution, as from the time of the fifth vial, to that of the seventh. But they commence at the rise of Antichrist.

8. The judgments in this chapter, cannot be the same with the seventh vial, in the destruction of Antichrist, and all the enemies of the Church. For in the latter case, there will be no Antichristian kings, nor mystical merchants of the Papal earth left, to bewail the fall of Babylon; as is the case in this chapter. For then they will all, far and near, sink together. So the predictions of that event clearly decide. *The whole earth shall be devoured with the fire of my jealousy.* The view of the whole of this xviiith chapter, in the light of the chapter preceding, evinces, that it is *Papal* Babylon, and not *Artichrist,* whose fall is here predicted. It is that Babylon, whose kings and mystical merchants had long been enriched with her delicacies and superstitious traffic. This is a trait of character, which cannot be applied to Antichrist; but which perfectly applies to Popery. The events of this chapter then cannot be the *seventh,* but must be the *fifth* vial.* In this, the Papal Beast is destroyed by the rise of the Antichristian Beast. The events of this chapter are the first capital judgment, which falls on Papal Babylon. *Babylon the great is fallen, is fallen.* However she had before experienced a number of judgments, even

---

* See Treatise on the fifth vial.

four vials of the wrath of God; yet she never *fell* be-. fore. And she is never found standing *on her own foundation*, afterward. This particular appears clearly to identify the event, with that of the fifth vial. For the Papal Beast has a seat (throne) and a kingdom, till the fifth vial; but afterward he has none. His seat is overturned and his kingdom filled with darkness. I apprehend then, that this xviiith of Revelation, and the fifth vial, predict the same event, the subversion of the predominant power of Popery, by the rise of Antichrist; although the events of this chapter may extend further, than those of the fifth vial, even to the time of the *seventh*, when Antichrist himself, as well as the remains of the Papal hierarchy, shall be totally destroyed.

9. This chapter, as well as the one preceding, presents a Babylon, distinct from Antichrist. While the Papal hierarchy was predominant, it was *Babylon the great.* But when it ceased to be predominant, having fallen under the power of Antichrist, the *latter* becomes the mystical Babylon, or Babylon the great. The appellation applies to the great *dominant Power* upon the ground, be it Papal, or Antichristian. Accordingly we find a *Babylon the great* falling in this xviiith chapter of Revelation, which, I conceive, predicts the same event with the fifth vial: and yet we also find a *great Babylon* coming into remembrance before God, when he gives unto her the cup of the wine of the fierceness of his wrath, in after days, Rev. xvi, 19, under the *seventh vial.* The collateral prophecies of this latter event, decide, that by great Babylon here, Antichrist, or the last head of the Roman Beast, is primarily intended, although Popery, as a subordinate power, may be included. While the Papal hierarchy was predominant, this was the *Beast;* and the old Roman Beast lay *dead.* But when the latter revived, and took the ground, the *Papal* Beast died. Popery is not thenceforward called a *Beast,* but *the false prophet,* under the dominion of the new Beast: And as the Papal Beast dies, on the rise of the Antichristian; so in like manner *Papal Babylon* sinks under the fifth vial, and in this xviiith of Revelation, upon the rise of the Anti-

christian Babylon. And the latter is the Babylon;
whose destruction was announced by the ancient prophets in Israel; as an event just to precede the Millennium. Various of those ancient predictions of the destruction of ancient Babylon, will meet their ultimate
accomplishment in the destruction of Antichrist, under
the seventh vial. He is the Babylon to be destroyed
at the battle of the great day.

This view may help to explain Rev. xiv, 8;* *And
there followed another angel, saying, Babylon is fallen;*

* This xivth chapter of Revelation I apprehend will be found
to contain events, which exactly synchronize with the events of
the *seven vials:* Or, events from the opening of the reformation
from Popery, till the close of the battle of the great day, which
is to precede the Millennium. Verse 1; *And I looked, and lo,
a Lamb stood on the mount Zion; and with him an hundred and
forty and four thousand, having his Father's name written in their
foreheads.* This follows a description of the Papal Beast.
Some time in the course of his dismal tyranny, the event here
introduced might be looked for. It was an event some time to
precede the fall of Papal Babylon, by the rise of the terrible
Power of the last days; as the announcing of this fall of Papal
Babylon is found in the 8th verse of this chapter. This appearing of the Lamb on Mount Zion, indicates a remarkable
appearing of Christ in his Church, for the enlargement, purity,
and protection, of his followers. His having with him
144,000, *who have his Father's name written in their foreheads,*
indicates a vast accession to the number of his witnesses. In
Rev. vii, 1; we find four angels holding the four winds, or stay-
ing impending judgments, till the people of God should be
sealed in their foreheads. The number of 144,000 are sealed.
Expositors inform us, that this description related to the prosperous state of the Church, in the Roman empire, after the
revolution under Constantine, from Paganism to Christianity;
and before the awful judgments of the northern invasions commenced. The Church then enjoyed a sealing time, a season of
great enlargement. Vast multitudes, represented as 12 times
12,000 (12 being the number of the apostles, and also of the
patriarchs) were sealed; 144,000, or a vast multitude, a certain
number put for an uncertain. In this verse (chapter xiv, 1) we
have a similar representation; as if it had been said, Christ
again, after a dismal reign of darkness and Papal tyranny, appears in his Church. Another remarkable sealing time commences. Another 144,000 (or class of countless multitudes)
are set apart for God's pure worship. To what event could
this relate, but to the reformation under Luther? The events

is fallen, that great city, because she made all nations drink of the wine of the wrath of her fornication. After wonderful missionary exertions to propagate the

of that day perfectly. answer to the figure. And no events of any preceding period do appear to answer to it. The succeeding verses accord with the events of the reformation. Verse 2; *And I heard a voice from heaven, as the voice of many waters, and as the voice of a great thunder; and I heard the voice of harpers harping with their harps.* 3; *And they sung as it were a new song before the throne, and before the four beasts, and the elders; and no man could learn that song, but the hundred and forty and four thousand, who were redeemed from the earth.* 4; *These are they, who were not defiled with women; for they are virgins. These are they who follow the Lamb withersoever he goeth. These were redeemed from among men, being the first fruits unto God, and to the Lamb.* 5; *And in their mouth was found no guile; for they are without fault before the throne of God.* Here the scene enlarges, as the doctrines of the reformation progress through Protestant lands. The heavenly hosts on the occasion sing, Rev. xii, 10; *Now is come salvation and strength, and the kingdom of our God, and the power of his Christ; for the accuser of our brethren is cast down.* The voice of the Protestant worshippers becomes like the roaring of great waters; yea of mighty thunder. It is the voice of *harpers*, or of those engaged in the sublime worship of God. Their song is *new*, and known by none, but those, who are taught it by the Spirit of grace. The purity of their doctrines and worship from the filthy idolatries of the Papal harlot, is strikingly noted. Idolatry is spiritual whoredom. And the Protestants, having renounced the idolatries of the Papal see, and become correct and holy in their doctrines and modes of worship, are represented *as above*, and as *being spotless before the throne of God.* Freedom from idolatry was the perfection of Job, of David, and of Asa. And this was the perfection of the Protestant multitudes here described. They are *the first fruits unto God and to the Lamb;* a resemblance of the dawn of the Millennium, and an earnest of it. The Church now seemed to be fast coming forth from her long exile in the wilderness.

In process of time, after the doctrines of the reformation are extensively and well established, and the scene of judgments on Papal nations has commenced; the eyes of Protestant multitudes are opened, and their hearts united and enlarged, to attempt great things toward evangelizing the heathen world. Verse 6; *And I saw another angel,* (or the first of several angels) *fly in the midst of heaven, having the everlasting Gospel to preach to them that dwell on the earth, and to every nation, and kindred, and tongue, and people;* 7,

16

Gospel through the world, as we find indicated in the preceding verse, it becomes a matter of public noto-

Saying with a loud voice, Fear God, and give glory to him; for the hour of his judgment is come: and worship him, who made heaven and earth, and the sea, and the fountains of water. A spirit of Missions wakes up, and diffuses itself through the Protestant nations. Much is shortly done toward disseminating the knowledge of Gospel salvation through heathen lands. The Missionaries introduce their message, as they must do to Pagans, by unfolding first the volume of nature: We have come to teach you who made yonder heavens; this great earth; the sea; and the fountains of water; and how you must worship and serve him. Their argument evinces, that the preaching of the Gospel, here predicted, is an advance made from the preaching of the Protestant doctrines to the Papal nations, at, and soon after the commencement of the reformation. It was to be an event *subsequent* to that period. We find it was to be in the *same hour* with the more signal judgments of God on the Papal see. "*For the hour of his judgment is come.*" And the next verse informs of the *object* of this divine judgment, that it was the *fall of Babylon;*—the subversion of the Papal Power. The flight of the Angel to preach the Gospel, is an event collateral with this, or in the same hour with it.

Some exertions have been made, for the propagation of the Gospel among Pagans, for many ages. But they did by no means amount to a fulfilment of the sublime figure under consideration. Here is represented one great and general *exertion* for this object; and the *unity* of the undertakers: The Angel *is* one. And his object is to evangelize *every nation, kindred, tongue and people.* Great engagedness in the object is indicated: The angel cries *with a loud voice.* Great facility and perseverance are implied: The angel flies directly on, over mountains, lakes, and seas. Nothing obstructs his course or progress. Obstacles impassable to footmen, are nothing to him. An event is predicted which God would undertake, by inclining the hearts of the children of Zion to undertake it; by removing obstacles; causing provision to be unexpectedly made; preparing instruments; opening effectual doors; thus sending out his word, and unfolding his glorious grace: Not to convert the heathen world at once. For the millennial morn is still future—But to light up Gospel fires in heathen lands; to call in some; to fulfil his own counsels; and to prepare the way for the Kingdom of Christ. *The Gospel of the Kingdom must first be preached to all nations, for a testimony unto them.* We have lived to see the commencement of this flight of the Angel.

Soon it is ascertained what the unprecedented judgments of God, in the same hour with the flight of the Angel, have effected, Verse 8; *And there followed another angel, saying Babylon is*

riety, that *Babylon is fallen, is fallen.* And it is *that* Babylon, which made all nations drink of the wine

fallen, is fallen, that great city, because she made all nations drink of the wine of the wrath of her fornication. It must be *Papal* Babylon, and not *Antichristian* Babylon, whose fall is here ascertained. For it is the Papal, and not the Antichristian Babylon, who has made all nations drink of the wine of the wrath of her fornication. And the *Antichristian* Babylon does not *fall*, till the close of this chapter, under the tremendous scene of the *harvest*, and the *vintage*.

The clear perception of the fall of Papal Babylon, excites another proclamation through the Church, of solemn *caution* and *warning.* Verse 9; *And the third angel followed them, saying with a loud voice, If any man worship the beast, and his image, and receive his mark in his forehead, or in his hand; 10, the same shall drink of the wine of the wrath of God.* Here note, that a Beast is in existence, which the world is in danger of worshipping, after Papal Babylon is fallen. Terrible denunciations of judgment are here expressed, and follow upon all, who are contaminated with the spirit of the Beast than on the ground.

This bold and powerful warning probably will provoke the then dominant Beast, and the minions of his order, to invade the rights of conscience in the kingdom of Christ. And it follows; verse 12; *Here is the patience of the saints; here are they who keep the commandments of God, and the faith of Jesus.* Here the patience of Christians must be tried, that it may be known who truly have his faith, and keep his commands. Verse 13; *And I heard a voice from heaven, saying unto me, Write, Blessed are the dead, who die in the Lord from henceforth; yea, saith the Spirit, that they may rest from their labors, and their works do follow them.* Here are indicated peculiar trials then to be endured by the Church. But the Captain of her salvation soon interposes. The next verse, and the following verses to the end of the chapter, describe the scenes of consequent judgments to be inflicted on Antichrist, and on all the active enemies of the Church. An Angel, like the Son of man, with a golden crown, and a sharp sickle, appears upon a white cloud. And he soon reaps the harvest of the earth, which is then fully ripe. His ministers of Providence soon collect the vine of the Infidel world, with its grapes then fully matured, and cast it into the great wine-press of the wrath of God; which is trodden; and which emits a river of blood for 200 miles. Here is a double figure to represent the terribleness of the scene of the battle of the great day of God. The *harvest*, and the *vintage*, both unite in that event. For both are subsequent to the depression of the Church under the reign of Antichrist. But

of the wrath of her fornication.   This was the *Papal harlot.*   But this her fall is not the last scene at Armageddon.   For the saints are to be *tried* by the influence of some *other power*, after this announced fall of Babylon; which other power must be Antichrist.   Verses 12, 13; *Here is the patience of the saints: here are they, that keep the commandments of God, and the faith of Jesus Christ.   And I heard a voice from heaven saying unto me, Write, Blessed are the dead, who die in the Lord from henceforth: yea, saith the Spirit, that they may rest from their labors, and their works do follow them.*   And scenes of awful judgment succeed, some time after this fall of Babylon; represented by the Angel on the white cloud, with his sharp sickle, reaping the vine of the earth:— And by another Angel, who has also a sharp sickle:— And by a third, who has power over fire; who directs the second Angel, with the sharp sickle, to thrust in his sharp sickle, and gather the clusters of the vine of the earth, whose grapes are fully ripe.   The latter obeys.   The vine of the earth is gathered, and cast into the great wine-press of the wrath of God; which is trodden; and which discharges a river of blood, as high as the horse bridles, for the space of two hundred miles.   These are the finishing scenes of judgment. And they are subsequent to the above fall of the harlot, Babylon: Which shews, that she, and the subsequent Power finally to be destroyed, are two distinct Powers; and their falls are at different periods.   One is at the *rise* of Antichrist.   The other is at his *destruction.*

There is a striking affinity between these two Powers, the Papal and the Antichristian Babylon.   The latter rose on the ground, and from the corruptions of the former.   It supplanted and took the place of the

no vial of wrath on Antichrist, except the *seventh*, is subsequent to that depression.

Thus the events of the xivth chapter occupy the *same period* with the vials in the two succeeding chapters;—the period of the seven *last plagues* upon the enemies of the Church.   That appearance of Christ on mount Zion introduced enlargement and salvation to his Church; and destruction to her enemies.

former. And in the judgments finally executed upon
Antichristian Babylon, those threatened to Papal Babylon, (as to her *ultimate ruin)* will be fulfilled. But
the two Babylons are spoken of as two distinct Powers.
One of them falls under the fifth vial; the other under
the seventh.

The sense, which has been given in this section, of
the fall of Papal Babylon by the rise of Antichrist, is
not destitute of countenance in Old Testament prophecies. I shall note one passage, Dan. vii, 26. *But the*
judgment shall set, and they shall take away his do-
minion, to consume and to destroy it unto the end.
This is spoken of the *Papal horn;* and of the time and
manner of his overthrow. *The judgment shall set.*
It shall open a new era of Divine judgment. *And* they
shall take away his (the Papal) *dominion. Who* shall
take it away? The antecedent is not expressed. But
the pronoun *they* implies an antecedent. It implies
instruments sufficiently powerful raised up to overturn
Popery, and to execute vengeance on Papal nations,
to take away the Papal dominion, and to consume and
to destroy it. In Rev. xvii, we learn who this instrument is;—*the Beast, that ascendeth out of the bottom-*
less pit. The horns of this Beast *hate the whore, and*
eat her flesh, and burn her with fire. The vengeance
begins to be executed *before* the time of the end; as is
implied in its *continuance till that time;—to consume*
and to destroy it unto the end. This scene, I apprehend, opens in a new and fatal vial of Divine wrath,
which overturns Popery; and which will ere long (or
after the Turks shall be overthrown, and the Jews returned) issue in the seventh vial, the battle of that
great day of God Almighty.

SECTION VIII.

The closing part of the 1260 *years occupied by Anti-*
christ. Paul's *Man of Sin.*

The prophet Daniel informs,* that the saints were to
be given into the hands of the little horn, 1260 years.

*Dan. vii, 25.

But if a portion of the last part of this term were to be occupied by the tyranny of Antichrist, how is this prediction of Daniel fulfilled? Answer. Antichrist originates in the corruptions of Popery. He was to arise directly out of the putrefactions of that abominable collection of filth and impurity. And after his development, and his establishing his *characteristic mark of Infidelity*, he was to re-establish Popery, as his *form of godliness*, and a convenient engine of his ambition. It is not unnatural then, that the Papal horn should be represented, in that concise stroke of ancient prophecy, as having possession of the saints 1260 years, notwithstanding that a small portion of the last part of the term should be occupied by the terrible Antichristian Power. For the latter was to be produced, and the whole wilderness state of the Church occasioned, by the corruptions of that Papal horn. In that ancient concise sketch then, it is no wonder that the saints should be spoken of, as being under the power of the *Papal horn* for 1260 years; even though for a short term, in the closing part of that period, the horn itself, and the saints should be under the tyranny of a superior Power, which rose directly from the nature, and corruptions of the Papal horn.

This solution may aid us in forming a correct idea of the predictions of Paul, relative to the *Man of Sin*, 2 Thess. ii, 3—12; *Let no man deceive you by any means; for that day* (the day of Christ) *shall not come, except there come a falling away first, and that man of sin be revealed, the son of perdition, who opposeth and exalteth himself above all, that is called God, or worshipped; so that he, as God, sitteth in the temple of God, shewing himself that he is God. Remember ye not, that when I was yet with you, I told you these things? And now ye know what withholdeth that he might be revealed in his time. For the mystery of iniquity doth already work; only he, who now letteth, will let, until he be taken out of the way. And then shall that wicked be revealed, whom the Lord shall consume with the spirit of his mouth, and destroy with the brightness of his coming: Even him, whose*

*coming is after the working of Satan, with all power,
and signs, and lying wonders. And with all deceivableness of unrighteousness in them that perish, because they received not the love of the truth, that they
might be saved. And for this cause God shall send
them strong delusion, that they should believe a lie;
that they all might be damned, who believed not the
truth, but had pleasure in unrighteousness.* The apostasy of the Papal hierarchy is here predicted. Yet the
Power here predicted is to be destroyed with the brightness of Christ's coming, at the battle of the great day.
And one would be apt to conclude, from reading the
passage, that the Power spoken of is to be the great
dominant Power of that day. And we are naturally
strengthened in this conclusion, from the allusion the
essential parts of the description appear to have, to the
noted passage in Dan. xi, 36—, which relates to Antichrist. These considerations seem to make the Romish hierarchy, and Antichrist *one* and the same. I
apprehend the fact to be, that the passage presents a
complex view of Popery and Antichrist; the former
rising after the subversion of Pagan Rome; and the
latter rising from the corruptions of the former, in the
last days. The passage, I conceive, contains a prophetic glance at the whole apostasy, both in its *Papal*,
and *Antichristian* form; saying some things peculiarly
applicable to the *one;* some to the *other;* and some to
both. Had no other Scriptures predicted the rise of
the Infidel Power subsequent to Popery, we should
naturally have taken this prediction of the Apostle, as
relating only to the Papal hierarchy; and should not
learn from it the rise of the Infidel Power. But as we
are furnished with such a variety of predictions, which
evidently relate to a vast Infidel Power, subsequent to
Popery; we cannot suppose this short passage of Paul
designed to contradict those passages; or to indicate,
that they were to receive their accomplishment in simply the Papal Power. This passage then, must be
viewed as a general description, or rather *glance*, of the
whole apostasy, Papal and Antichristian, viewing them

in their natural connexion; although other prophecies present them, (as we have seen) as two distinct Powers.

The *Man of Sin* then, *primarily*, is the Papal hierarchy; and *ultimately*, the Infidel Power of the last days, which originated in the corruptions of that hierarchy, and in which the dominant power of the hierarchy was to terminate. Paul's *Man of Sin* properly comprises *both* these Powers, viewed in their connexion. Although they are *two*, when they go into perdition, the *Beast*, and the *false prophet;* yet they both unitedly go to constitute Paul's *Man of Sin*, and that *son of perdition*, whom *the Lord will consume with the spirit of his mouth, and destroy with the brightness of his coming.* That description from the Apostle, which has been recited, viewed in the light of the *other* numerous and more distinguishing predictions, both concerning the Papal hierarchy, and the subsequent Infidel Power, seems necessarily to evince, that the *Man of Sin* was of the complex character above presented;—that he comprised both the hierarchy, and the atheistical Antichrist. For he rises with the *former*, after the Roman empire that let or hindered, was taken out of the way; and sinks with the *latter;* or, the last head of the Roman Beast; and has the characteristics of *both*. He is, in that prophetic glance, presented as *one Power;* though other more definite predictions present him as *two*. He represents the whole Romish apostasy, both in its *Papal* and *Atheistical* form:

Thus we are taught, in the prophetic parts of the sacred Scriptures, to expect the rise of a terrible atheistical Power, and a vast influence of Infidelity, in the last days, or just before the Millennium.

I do not pretend that I have adduced all the prophecies of this event. Various other predictions of it, especially in the Old Testament, will be noted in the future pages of this dissertation, where the way will be better prepared for them to be understood. I shall here add a comment on the words of our blessed Lord;* *And shall not God avenge his own elect, who cry unto*

*Luke xviii, 7, 8.

him day and night, though he bear long with them?
I tell you that he will avenge them speedily. Never-
theless. when the Son' of man' cometh, shall he find
faith on the earth? Here we read of the coming of
Christ to avenge his elect. His coming at the destruction of Jerusalem, probably was primarily intended.' ' But his coming at the battle of the great day, as
well as at the end of the world, must be viewed as
included in the prediction. And the question in the
last verse implies, that what has been called the Christian world will then be found overrun with gross. Infidelity. Our Lord again says of the same period, "And
because iniquity shall abound, the love of many shall
wax cold." This is equal to saying, that what of faith
those may have had, shall *fail:* Infidelity will take its
place.

But so great an effect implies an adequate cause, or
a systematic propagation of Infidelity. And the coming of Christ, at the battle of the great day's being to
avenge his elect, implies, that this Power of Infidelity
will then be found violently directed against his elect,
or his cause. The operations of Infidels, previous to
the rise of Antichrist, or beside that combination,
which gave him birth, did not amount to that systematic propagation of Infidelity necessarily implied in the
rise of Antichrist; although they had their influence in
preparing the way for it. There was a want of unity
and efficiency in their operations. The British Infidels, Hobbes, Tindal, Chubb, Morgan, Woolston,
Collins, Shaftesbury, Herbert, Hume and Bolingbroke,
were *Antichristian* indeed. Yet their operations and
writings did not mark the rise of Antichrist. They
were destitute of that *unity* and *efficiency of operation.*
Many of their first principles counteracted each other.
And they matured no powerful, systematic opposition
to the cause, which they individually hated. It remained for Infidels within the region of Popery to remedy
this *happy* defect. The latter were not only to propagate real Infidelity in a far more energetic system; but
were to furnish a fatal plan of uniting their minions and
sophists of impiety against the cause of Christ; and to

secretly inure their hearts to cruelty, and deeds of violence; till they should be prepared to burst upon the Christian and civilized world, like a torrent of burning lava from a volcano! The uniting of their rivulets of Infidelity into a powerful current; swelling the latter, by the confluence of numberless streams, into an overwhelming flood; and directing this mighty deluge against the principles of the Christian religion, and of all virtuous civil government; this was to be the development of the Infidel Power under consideration; this the Antichrist of the last times.

CHAP. II.

*The last days have arrived; and an incipient fulfil-
ment of the predictions concerning* ANTICHRIST, *is
now fulfilling before our eyes.*

THIS I shall endeavor to evince in the following sections.

SECTION I.

Chronological Remarks.

THE Church of Christ was to remain in the wilderness, after being given into the hands of the Papal power, 1260 years.* Mr. Faber is of the opinion, that this
giving of the saints into the hands of the Papal power
took place in the year 606, when Phocas constituted
the bishop of Rome universal bishop. A former English writer, by the name of Stephens, (noted with approbation in the Annotations of Pool,) was of the
same opinion. And some plausible things may be
said in favor of it. As the saints were to be given into the power of Popery 1260 years, so the committing
of them to this power, may mark the commencement
of the 1260 years. And the *act* of constituting the
bishop of Rome universal bishop, has some appearance
of being the act of giving the saints into his hands. And
if it be thus, then the year 606 of the Christian era may
commence the noted 1260 years; which accordingly
will terminate A. D. 1866.

Some writers have conceived, that the noted number
666, (Rev. xiii, last,) has a two fold application, as the
number of the *Beast;* (Rev. xiii, 18;) and the number
of his *name;* (Rev. xv, 2.) As to the number of his
name, it is ascertained, that the numerical letters in
Greek, which form the name *Lateinos,* contains just
the number 666. Latinus, (or as the name was anciently written, Lateinos) king of Latium, was before Ro-

*Dan. vii, 25. Rev. xii, 6.

mulus; and was the first founder of Rome, either real or fictitous. Hence the ancient Romans were called *Latins;* and their language was denominated *Latin.* And this has been the noted appellation, by which the inhabitants of the south west of Europe have been known in the east, the *Latins;* particularly the Italians, French and Spaniards, have been so denominated. And the Papal Church is there known by the appellation of the *Latin Church.* And in this Church every thing indeed is latinized; mass, prayers, hymns, litanies, canons, decretals, Papal bulls, all have been in *Latin.* This was an essential point in their code. The results of the Papal councils, as well as all their proceedings, must be in this language. And in no other language might their scriptures be read.

And the name Lateinos contains the number 666, thus:

$$
\begin{aligned}
&\text{L} — 30 \\
&\text{A} — 1 \\
&\text{T} — 300 \\
&\text{E} — 5 \\
&\text{I} — 10 \\
&\text{N} — 50 \\
&\text{O} — 70 \\
&\text{S} — 200 \\
&\overline{} \\
&666
\end{aligned}
$$

Also the Hebrew word Rumiit, which denoted the same Roman power, contains the same number 666 thus:

$$
\begin{aligned}
&\text{ר} — 200 \\
&\text{ו} — 6 \\
&\text{מ} — 40 \\
&\text{י} — 10 \\
&\text{י} — 10 \\
&\text{ת} — 400 \\
&\overline{} \\
&666
\end{aligned}
$$

Thus the *Latin Church*, the Roman power, is shown to be that second Beast, in Rev. xiii, 11—; the number of his name being found in the numerals, which

form Lateinos, in the Greek language, in which the
New Testament was written; and also in the numerals,
which form the word Rumiit, denoting the Roman nation, in the Hebrew, in which the Old Testament was
written.

And with respect to the *number of the Beast*, the author by the name of Stephens, before mentioned in
Pool, has attempted to show, that A. D. 606, when
the bishop of Rome was constituted universal bishop,
was, according to the chronology in Daniel, the year
666; or was the year 665 from the time when the Romans first captivated the people of God in Judea. This
he states to have been, when Cicero and Antonius were
consuls, 60 years before Christ. These 60 years added to A. D. 606, makes 666. The number of the
Beast then, according to this author, is the number of
years, from the time that the Church fell into the
hands of the Romans, till that Beast arose A. D. 606.
This *may* give the true solution. But I am not confident of it. There is much enigma or darkness attending this part of the subject, even while some information God has graciously given concerning it. It hence
becomes man to be very *cautious*, and *modest* in his
inquiries.

I conceive it to be very *possible*, after all, that the old
opinion, of the Millennium's commencing about the
year 2000, *may prove correct.*

Let the following scheme be examined.

The number of the Beast, 666, means the year of
the Christian era 666;—*the number of man;*—the reckoning of time in Christendom. This mode of reckoning was so far unknown, when John had his vision, that
it was sufficiently enigmatical for the language of prophecy. If the year 666 of the Christian era be the first
year of the Papal Beast, and of course the commencement of the noted 1260 years of the wilderness state of
the Church, then we are brought, by the addition of
these two numbers, to A. D. 1925, for the battle of
that great day of God. And the two additional numbers of 30 and 45, (making 75,) in the last chapter of

Daniel, bring to the close of A. D. 2000 for the full rising of the millennial sun.

In this last chapter, Daniel was notified of the 1260 years of the depressed state of the church. He pleads for a further understanding relative to the end of that term. But he was informed, that "the words were closed up, and sealed, till the time of the end." Some tokens of the arrival of that *time of the end*, are, however, ascertained to Daniel. "Many shall run to and fro, and knowledge shall be increased." And "many shall be purified, and made white and tried; but the wicked shall do wickedly; and none of the wicked shall understand; but the wise shall understand." These are noted, as striking tokens of that period, called *the time of the end;* till which time, the true sense of the words was *sealed.* The tokens given of the time of the end, were *these;*—a signal flight of missionaries; an increase of Christian light; the signal purifying of many; the trying of good people; and the peculiar perverseness and blindness of the wicked. It is added; "And from the time that the daily sacrifice shall be taken away, and the abomination, that maketh desolate, set up, there shall be a thousand, two hundred and ninety days. Blessed is he that waiteth, and cometh to the thousand three hundred and five and thirty days." Here we find two numbers added to the first 1260 years, in verse 7, concerning which Daniel inquired; viz. 30 years, and 45 years. The *events* of these two additional periods, are not expressed. But it is implied, that they shall be *signal* and *interesting*. The commencement of these numbers, 1290, and 1335 years, must be the same with that of the 1260 years in verse 7. For this is the number, concerning which the inquiry, and the remarks were made. The commencement of these long periods is said to be, when the daily sacrifice is taken away, and the abomination that maketh desolate is set up. This cannot be the same with the taking away of the daily sacrifice, and the setting up of the desolating abomination, by Antiochus, Dan. xi, 31, which was 168 years before Christ. Nor can it be the same with the causing of the sacrifice and oblation to

cease, and the overspreading of abomination that was
to make desolate,. by the Romans, in Dan. ix, 27;
which was 40 years after Christ. For if it were the same
with *either* of them, the whole chronology of the events
of the chapter, would be confounded; and nothing
could be found, in either case, to answer to the fulfilment. The *taking away the daily sacrifice, and setting
up a desolating abomination*, is a noted prophetic phrase,
to import a new and dreadful attack of a notorious' enemy, upon the professed people of God. And the
phrase in this passage, Dan. xii, 11, must relate to the
commencement of the noted 1260 years; the time of
the invasion of the Church by the Papal and Mohammedan impostures; and of the flight of the Church into
her wilderness state. Hence the 1290 years must relate, to some signal additional event, 30 years after the
battle of that great day of God, at the close of the
1260 years;—perhaps, the gathering in of the remnant
of the Jews and of Israel, who will not have been gathered before the battle of the great day; (Isa. xliii, 6.)
And the following number of 1335 years, (giving
another addition of 45 years,) *may* relate to the *coming
in* of the fulness of the Gentile nations, that are to come
in, after the full restoration of the Jews; Rom. xi, 12,
15, 25. "Blessed is he that waiteth and cometh to this
period." Here he shall find the full morning sun of
the Millennium, as risen upon the earth.

Now, it is curious to find, that these additional numbers in Daniel, making 75 years, added to 1925, (the
time for the battle of the great day, made by adding the
1260 years to A. D. 666,) bring to the end of the year
2000, for that period, to which "blessed is he that waiteth and cometh." Add 1335 years to 666, (allowing
the last year of the latter for the first year of the former,
as must be allowed, if the Beast be viewed as having
risen in the year 666,) and we have 2000 years, under
the Gospel, to prepare the way for the full introduction
of the millennial Kingdom of Christ. This scheme
affords a longer season for the accomplishment of the
vast events, that must take place between this, and the
Millennium. And this scheme seems well to accord

with the analogy of the natural week; six days for labor; and the seventh for rest and devotion.

In favor of the preceding remarks, let the following things be also considered.

It is an old opinion, that the seventh thousand years of the world (which is the third thousand under the gospel) is to be the blessed Millennium. And that two thousand years under the gospel (or *about* two thousand) were to be occupied by the reign of sin. This long period appears to be divided by a number of subordinate periods; and among the rest by *three* signal periods and events called *woes*. It would seem natural and striking, should we find the periods of these woes to accord with the *three thirds* of this long period, the two thousand years of the reign of sin. Let us see if this is not *exactly* or *nearly* the case. But here let it be noted, that each wo, instead of being placed at the *beginning* of its corresponding third of the two thousand years, is placed at or *near* the *close* of it. Let us inquire for the time of the commencement of the two first of the woes fulfilled; (as it is agreed) by the Mohammedan delusion, and the rise and ravages of the Turks. When may the *first* of these be said to have commenced? Mohammed retired to his cave, to form his system of delusion, A. D. 606. In A. D. 622, he was driven from Mecca, (where he first propagated his delusion,) to Medina. Here the Mohammedan reckoning of time (the Hegira) begins. In A. D. 629, he mustered an army of 10,000 men, to propagate his religion by force. In A. D. 631 all Arabia were in subjection. In about 30 years more, all the dominions of the Greek emperor in Africa and Asia, as far as Persia, were overrun by these Saracenic locusts. A cessation of conquests then commenced, of about 50 years, in the contentions concerning the Mohammedan *succession*. Soon after the year 700, the western kingdoms of Europe were invaded by these armies. Spain was overrun. And an army of 400,000 men entered France. In A. D. 734, Charles Martel vanquished them in battle. And in a few years they were wholly driven from France and Spain.

Thus from the time the Mohammedan delusion was first propagated, till the Saracenic armies were driven out from the western kingdoms of Europe, was about 120 years. Let a medium then, between these extremes be assumed, as the time for the *fair manifesta-tions* of the first wo. The medium is 60 years. This added to A. D. 606, (the year in which Mohammed retired to his cave, as noted above) makes 666. The year of the Christian era 666 then, or the close of the year 665, may be viewed as the time, when the *first wo* was *fairly manifest.*

And it may be striking to note, that the number 666 is the largest whole number, which multiplied by *three* (the number of the woes,) will fall within the 2,000 years of the reign of sin. 666 multiplied by 3, gives 1998.

This number 666 is the noted number of the Papal *Beast*; as we have seen, Rev. xiii, last. The number of his *name* has been explained. The two systems of delusion, the Papal and Mohammedan, were to be synchronical, or were to occupy the same period. The development of the Papal apostacy was *gradual.* It will, by and by, be noted, that much was done by Justinian, the eastern emperor, as early as A. D. 534, toward the establishment of Popery. But it was 222 years after this, before the Pope was invested with the civil government of the exarchate of Ravenna, by Pepin King of France, A. D. 756. A medium, between these periods may well be assumed as the proper time of the *manifestation* of the Papal power. And no period has a better claim, as being this medium, than A. D. 666, the above noted time of the first wo. This then, may be the true sense of the number of the *Papal Beast*, (Rev. xiii, last,) which is 666. At that period of the Christian era, the judgment by the Papal Beast, and that of the first wo, were *manifest,* as fully introduced, and fairly under way. And the nearest whole number expressing one third of the time previous to the year 2000, was then expired.

The double of the 666, for the time of the second wo, gives A. D. 1332. And *in fact,* at that very time, the second wo, by the rise and ravages of the Turks, was just *fairly manifest* to the world! In the year 1300 the Turks collected their strength under Othoman, their first chief; freed themselves from the yoke of the Tartars; and began to extend their conquests.. In the year 1363 they crossed the Hellespont into Europe; and threatened Constantinople. The medium between these two periods, appears the most proper time to be taken, as the time of the fair development of the second wo. This medium is A. D. 1332; the very number made by the double of the 666. Here is the close of the second third of the 2000 years.

The 666 multiplied by *three*, for the *analogical* time of the third wo, (or the time when it would be natural to expect it, from the analogy of the two preceding woes,) gives the year 1998; just time enough, as it would seem, to have the field of the wicked world cleared, for the introduction of the Millennium, at the close of the year 2000. Analogy from the natural week, (six days for labor, and the seventh for rest,) and the number seven being of so great use in the sacred writings, seem to point out the above time for the introduction of the Millennium.

But relative to the actual taking place of the third wo in the year 1998, it may be remarked, that such is to be the terribleness of the scenes, which are just to precede the third wo, that Christ says, "Except those days shall be shortened, no flesh could be saved. But for the elect's sake, those days *shall* be shortened." The third wo then, must something *anticipate* its analogical period, or the time, in which, from the analogy of the two former woes, it might naturally be expected.

But how long shall be this shortening of the days? Or when *will* the third wo commence? Let the following be examined for a reply. The third wo may be expected in the year made by the addition of the noted 1260 years, to the aforementioned 666. This bring to the close of the year 1925. Then add to this the additional numbers (Dan. xii, 11, 12,) of 30 and 45, making 75 years, (perhaps for the establishing in

Christianity of the remnant of the Jews and Israel, Zech. xii, 9, to end; and for the gathering in of those who shall be left of the *fulness of the gentiles,)* and we are brought to the close of the year 2000, for the full introduction of that period, to which, Daniel says, chap. xii, 12, "Blessed is he that *waiteth* and *cometh.*"

Should this scheme prove correct, we then have the sense of the noted 666, as it is the number of the *Papal Beast.* It is that year of the *Christian era;* being the time for the full manifestation of this Beast to the world; and also of the first wo, which was collateral with the Papal Beast; being the period of the first third of the 2000 years of the reign of sin under the gospel; and the double of which gives the time of the second wo. And also being the time for the commencement of the noted 1260 years, or the time of the mourning state of the witnesses, or the wilderness state of the Church.

According to this view of the subject, the third wo, for the sudden and utter destruction of Antichrist, and of all the persecuting enemies of the Church, is still 113 years future. This 113 years will afford an interesting period, for that power of the last days, that is "part of iron and part of clay, partly strong and partly broken," to perform the things which he is yet to accomplish; and for the Church to do and to suffer the things spoken of her, in the last days.

It appears rational to expect, (according to opinion of some authors,) that as the rise of the Papal Beast was *gradual,* and the judgments of the last days, inflicted on the Papacy, were to be *gradual;* so the 1260 years will be found to measure the times between the *events* of equal magnitude in the *rise,* and in the *fall* of the Papacy. For instance, that just 1260 years before the catastrophe of the Papacy, in the French revolution, some great corresponding event must have taken place, toward the *establishment* of the Papacy. That 1260 years from the further establishment of the Papacy by Phocas, in constituting the bishop of Rome universal Bishop, A. D. 606, may be expected to bring some corresponding event, in the execution of the judgments on God on Papal nations. And according to the same rule, if the preceding view given of the number 666 be correct, 1260 years, from *that period*, may be expected to bring the *last fatal blow* to the Antichristian nations in the battle of the great day.

It is striking to find, that just 1260 years before the filling of the Papal kingdom with darkness in the French revolution, a notable corresponding event *did in fact* take place toward the establishment of Popery. The emperor Justinian, having got possession of Italy, greatly promoted the bishop of Rome, as is ascertained by Fleming, Bicheno, and an author quoted by Bp. Newton. He published what is called, *The Code of Justinian;* "by which (says Bicheno) those powers, privileges, and immunities, were secured to the clergy; that union perfected between things civil and ecclesiastical, and those laws imposed on the Church, which have proved so injurious to Christianity, and so calamitous to mankind." This Code of Justinian has been called, "the strong hold of clerical tyranny." It no doubt formed a strong feature in the visage of Papal corruption.

Relative to the same event, an author quoted by bishop Newton informs,* that in the year 534, Justinian declared him; (i. e. the bishop of Rome) head of all the churches, and judge of all; but himself to be judged by none; he was held in such obsequious awe and veneration, even by the emperors themselves, and he sometimes reproved them with such authority, and anon anathematized them with such force, that he might be said to reign over the emperors, both in spiritual and in temporal things; even while he boasted, that he was all submission, and was a servant of all servants." Mr. Fleming, upon the same event, observes, "I find the

* Nam ex quo anno Domini 534, cum ecclesiasticum omnium caput declaravit Justinianus, aliis omnium judicem, ipsum a nullo judicandum, tanta reverentia et obsequio ab imperatoribus ipsis, cultus est, tauta auctoritate, ipsos subinde reprehendit, interdum etiam anathemate perculit, ut non minus dicendum sit regnasse in spiritualibus, quamvis se subditum semper servum que servorum diceret, quam in temporalibus, imperatores." Vol. ii, p. 321, 10th Edit. Ebing.

Pope, got a new foundation of exaltation, when Justinian, upon his conquest, of Italy, left it in a great measure to the Pope's managment, being willing to eclipse
his own authorty, to advance that of this haughty
prelate."

The above authors differ a little as to the *date* of this
Code of Justinian. Bicheno says, it was A. D. 529
The 1260 years from that time *end*, A. D. 1789; the
very year in which the French revolution commenced.
The quotation in Bp. Newton says it was A. D. 534,
The 1260 years, from this date, end in A. D. 1794.
Granting this latter date to be correct, events accord
with it with no less precision. For in the first stages
of the French revolution, the hostility was not apparent-
ly so direct against the Papal see. The first new constitution, adopted under the National Assembly, gave
toleration to religion. But after this was abolished,
and another adopted under the *Convention*, no further
toleration was given to religion, or conscience. The
reign of terror then commenced. The royal family
were destroyed in 1793. And 1794 opened with unprecedented terrors to the Papal system, and the Papal
kingdom was soon filled with darkness. This was
just 1260 years after the promulgation of the above
Code of Justinian, according to the date found in Bp.
Newton. Mosheim, speaking of events of the same
period, says, "In this apology, (by Ennodius bishop of
Pavia in behalf of Symmachus) the reader will perceive
that the foundations of that enormous power, which the
Popes of Rome afterward acquired, were now laid."
And in a following page, speaking of the same Ennodius as a noted author, at that period, Mosheim adds;
"Though he disgraced his talents and dishonored his
eloquence, by his infamous adulation of the Roman
pontiff, whom he exalted so high above all mortals, as
to maintain, that he was answerable to none upon earth
for his conduct, and subject to no human tribunal."
(Vol. i, p. 446, 450.) And it is ascertained, in Mosheim
vol. i, p. 447, that in the year 529, just 1260 years before the opening of the French revolution) the order of
the Benedictine monks was established. This order

in a measure absorbed all the other orders of monks. They became immensely rich, and vicious. They found their way into the courts of princes, where they acquired vast influence. They augmented the number of superstitious rites; and did much toward enlarging, as well as confirming the power and authority of the Pope. Thus the period found by measuring back 1260 years from the time of the French revolution, was a period of note in the establishment of the Papal system. The vial of wrath executed upon the Papal system and nations, in our day, may be viewed as an event corresponding with it.

These remarks are not to insinuate that the 1260 years are already finally expired. They probably are not; and will not be, till the battle of the great day. But these remarks are made in favor of the opinion, that the 1260 years have *several* fulfilments. Or, they mark the distances between several *grades* in the perverse *exaltation* of the bishop of Rome, and corresponding degrees in his destruction; till in his total perdition, in the battle of that great day, the 1260 years (from some most notable period in his rise) will *finally* terminate. And, at present, I cannot but think it highly probable, that this notable period (1260 years previous to the battle of that great day,) was A. D. 666. If the Pope were not, at that time, a temporal prince, he was completely a *Papal Beast* of two horns, on account of the vast influence, he exercised, in temporal as well as spiritual concerns, over the princes of the empire. His characteristic was *"diverse"* from other powers; (Dan. vii, 24.) Theirs was *temporal;* his *spiritual.* But the saints were given into the hands of the Pope long before the king of France gave him the civil dominion of the exarchate of Ravenna, A. D. 756. This was far from being the act of giving the saints into his hands; and far from being the tenure, by which he held them. It was a mere circumstance, or some *addition only* to his *temporal* aggrandizement.

Should the foregoing remarks relative to the Code of Justinian, and its being 1260 years before the filling of the Papal kingdom with darkness under the French revolution, prove correct; one point seems herein to be decided; viz. the *prophetic* year, and the *civil* year, under the Gospel, are the *same.* Or no deduction is to be made from our civil reckoning, (in finding the periods of predicted events,) on account of the fact, that the Jews allowed but 360 days to a year. For the period from the time of the Code of Justinian, till its recent corresponding event, above noted, was 1260 of our *civil* years.*

---

* It has been a question with some, how prophetic years are to be reckoned? Whether 365 days and about a third are to be allowed to each year? or whether but 360 days are to be allowed? Our mode of reckoning time differs from that of the ancient Jews. Our reckoning nearly accords with that of the Romans. It has not been without difficulty that men have ascertained what number of days belong to a natural year. Julius Cesar, just before the commencement of the Christian era, reformed the Roman calendar. He allowed 365 days, and six hours to constitute a year. These six odd hours in four years made one day. This day he ordered to be added, on each fourth year, to the end of February. And it is called leap year. This reckoning has been found to include in its year about eleven minutes too much. These odd minutes, in 30 years, amount to one day. This excess had run our reckonig forward of the true time, since the commencement of the Christian era, about eleven days. These eleven days were in the 18th century, thrown out of account, by the adoption of what was called the *new stile.* Time was dated *back* eleven days, to meet the true time. It is found that the sun passes through all the signs of the zodiac, or the earth completes her revolution round the sun, in 365 days, 5 hours, and about 49 minutes.

But the Jews had not attained to this accuracy of computation. They allowed 360 days to a year. Hence the prophetic numbers are expressed on this scale. The "forty and two months" of the depressed state of the witnesses, are called one thousand two hundred and threescore days; which is on the scale of the Jewish reckoning, allowing 30 days to each month; and 360 to a year. The same term is also representedly noted, as three years and a half; which is on the scale of allowing 360 days to a year. Hence it has been a question with some, why is not a deduction to be made from our true year of the Christian era, in finding the time of the close of the noted 1260 years, in proportion to the excess of days in our year, compared with the year of the ancient Jews, used in prophetic numbers? This would bring the termination of that period nearly 30 years sooner, than according to our true reckoning.

Reply. The *natural* and *true* year *must* be the year designed in prophetic time. This is founded in the nature of things.

I am much inclined to think, that the way will not be found fully prepared for the Millennium, till the close of the year. 2000.   There were 2000 years before the calling of Abraham. And 2000 from that time to the coming Christ. ; It seems analagous with these facts; that the close of 2000 years, under the Gospel, will introduce the Millennium.

Solomon dedicated his temple at Jerusalem, (a lively type of the introduction of the millennial Church) on the opening of the fourth millenniary from the creation. ˙ (See index to the great Bible upon this.) Just at the close of the third millenniary, the temple was in forwardness and preparation. And on the opening of the fourth, it was finished and dedicated. Let analogy then, number another three thousand years, from the time of that dedication, and it brings to the close of the year of our Lord 2000, for the dedication of the *millennial tem-*

The whole of the natural year is what the Jews designed to express by their year; whatever incorrectness attended their mode of computing the year by days. They found they were incorrect, and that the natural year overrun their 360 days. And they adopted a remedy; which was to *intercalate*, on every third year, the odd time, by which the natural year was found to exceed the year in their reckoning. The last month of their year they called Adar. At the close of this, on every third year, they allowed their intercalated time, and called it Veadar, or second Adar. So that in reality their year, like ours, contained the whole of the *natural year*. For during their intercalated time, their prophetic time, as well as the introduction of their new year, was suspended, till the natural year was fulfilled. A year in prophecy then, is a *natural year*, by whatever different numbers of days different nations have calculated it. By a *year* the Holy Spirit could not have meant, a *term*, as much shorter than a natural year, as the time of 360 days in short of 365 days and a third. The *Jews* meant no such thing. And the calculation would be unnatural and absurd. This mode of reckoning would have run the close of the year, in a continual variation of about five days and a third, through all the seasons of the year, nearly thirty times, since the commencement of the Christian era. The 1260 years then, in the prophecies, are 1260 *natural* years, or according to our reckoning of time. But a *year of years*, we find, in this noted number of 1260, is 360 years, (taken from the Jews mode of reckoning,) and not 365 years and a third, according to the true reckoning of the natural year.

ple. · Just at the close of this latter term, or during the last 75 years, (as before noted from Daniel last chapter,) this temple may be found in a state of peculiar and rapid preparation. This will be a blessed mitigation of the terrors of the scenes preceding the Millennium; expressed by *"those days being shortened."* The millennial day will have *dawned*, in the gathering of the scattered remnants of the natural seed of Abraham; and the gospelizing of the fulness of the gentile nations, (who will survive the battle of the great day) during these 75 years after the battle of the great day. But the millennial *sun* will not rise, till the close of Daniel's 75 years, added to the noted 1260. Blessed is he that waiteth, and cometh to this period.

Whether these remarks will prove correct, or not, time will decide. But it is agreed by all evangelical people, that we are drawing near to the close of the wicked ages of the world; and that the Millennium cannot be far distant. The prophecies relative to the last days, and the signs of the times, clearly conspire to evince the truth of this remark.

Have we not then, reason to believe, that the rise of the terrible Antichristian Empire, the last head of the Roman Beast, which ascends from the bottomless pit, must at the present time, be clearly discernible upon the stage of the world? The affirmitive seems unavoidable, both from a view of the prophecies of that event, and chronological observation.

And what have the eyes of the present generation beheld? We have seen a mighty terrible Power, bursting suddenly into existence; evidently ascending from the bottomless pit; and possessing the very characteristics, noted in prophecy, as descriptive of the origin, and first stages of that Antichristian Empire.

SECTION II.

Enormities of the French Revolution.

WE have recently seen a most powerful Papal nation, whose monarch was styled the eldest son of the Church; a nation of more than twenty seven millions of people,

19

breaking every restraint; beheading their king; pro-
claiming war against all kings; and decreeing fraternity
with all in every nation, who are in rebellion against
their governments.

Revolutionary France, by national authority, not only denied the Christian Religion, but the existence of
God. A piece was written by Anacharsis Cloots, a
member of their national convention, and the reporter
of their committee, and was accepted by the convention,
and printed and circulated by their order, in which are
the following sentiments; "Man when free, wants no
other divinity, than himself. Reason dethrones both
the kings of the earth, and the King of heaven. No
monarchy above, if we wish to preserve our republic below. Volumes have been written to determine whether a
republic of Atheists could exist. I maintain that every
other republic is a chimera. If you admit the existence of a heavenly sovereign, you introduce the wooden
horse within your walls; what you adore by day, will be
your destruction by night."* This Infidel Power virtually abolished the Christian Sabbath; substituting in
it's stead their decades, or the celebration of every tenth
day for political or idolatrous purposes. They virtually abolished the covenant of marriage, by rendering
the support of it optional with the parties. As a fruit
of which national order, 1800 divorces took place in
Paris in the year 1793. They decreed that the promiscuous intercourse of the sexes is no crime.† They
fixed the inscription in their burying-ground, "*Death is
an eternal sleep.*" The Bible was burnt in a public
square, by the hands of the common hangman. They
shut up their houses of public worship, and made only the expression of a desire that they might be opened, a great if not a capital crime. "The sacramental
vessels were mounted upon an ass, and paraded through
the streets; to insult him, who died, that men might
live." They assumed the characteristic of *disregarding
the God of their fathers,*‡ by rejecting the Pope, and all

---

* Barruel's Memoirs, vol. ii, p. 245. † Kett, vol. ii, p. 253.
‡ Dan. xi, 37.

his clergy. And in contemptuously abjuring the Christian Religion, they disregarded Him, who was the ancient desire of women. They *denied the Father, and the Son; denied the Lord, who bought them; denied the only Lord God, and our Lord Jesus Christ.*

"Revolutionary France, in the phrenzy of democratic enthusiasm, established atheism and anarchy by law. They hold out the right hand of fellowship to the insurgents of every nation. They commenced a tremendous massacre of their enslaved citizens. They proclaimed the Son of God an imposter, and his Gospel a forgery. They swore to exterminate *Christianity* and *royalty* from the face of the earth, as they had done from their own dominions. And they madly unsheathed the sword against every regularly established government." During the French revolution a comedian, dressed as a priest of the Illuminati, publicly appeared, and personally attacking the Almighty, said, *No, thou dost not exist! If thou hast power over the thunderbolts, grasp them, aim them at the man, who dares set thee at defience in the face of thine altars. But no! I blaspheme thee; and I still live. No, thou dost not exist.*

Yet they; *in their estate*, or after they viewed their revolution established, honored their *god of forces*, their *Mozim;* whether we translate it *fancied gods,* or *military munitions.* With respect to the former, the French converted the magnificent temple of St. Genevieve at Paris, into a Pagan pantheon.* To this they conveyed, in solemn procession, the bones of the arch-infidel Voltaire, and of Rousseau. The bones of the former they placed upon a high altar, and offered incense to them; while the multitude bowed down in silent adoration.

A female, dressed in fantastic hue as a goddess, to personate Human Reason, was borne upon a carriage on men's shoulders, and escorted by the national guards, and all the constituted authorities. She was

---

* The pantheon was a temple in ancient Rome, dedicated, as its name imports, to *all the gods,*

placed upon a high altar, and worshipped with various religous ceremonies. She was then conveyed to the principal church, where these idolatrous services were repeated. A priest was then brought in, who abjured the Christian faith, and avowed the whole of Christianity to be an imposture. The scene closed with the burning of their religious books, and their various apparatus for public worship; multitudes dancing round the flames in savage mirth. And an account of this whole scene was published in their national Bulletin; an official paper distributed at the expense of government.*

The images of reason and liberty were placed in a temple. Festivals were instituted to the virtues, such as reason and labor. Thus they adopted and honored *the gods of their fancy.*

And the French have honored *military munitions;* should any prefer this rendering of the term *Mozim.* Their unprecedented improvements in the arts of war, afford them a most distinguishing feature in this particular.

A train of other enormities are related in authentic histories and memoirs of the French revolution, too numerous to be cited in this dissertation. "It appears, (says a writer on this subject†) that there have been two millions of persons murdered in France, since it called

---

* See Residence in France, N. Y. edition, p. 270.

† Kett, vol. ii, p. 252. See also Faber, vol. ii, p. 43, 46 where it is ascertained, that the clergy were commanded, by the revolutionary government in France, to quit the realm in fourteen days. And then, instead of giving them liberty even to do this, this whole period was employed, by the Jacobins, in their most wanton destruction:—That a Jacobin miscreant caused an oath to be taken by all the members of the National Assembly, that as a *Committee of insurrection* (as they were pleased to style themselves) against all the kings of the universe, they would use every exertion to purge the earth of royalty. And the purpose was deliberately contemplated, of privately destroying by pistol, sword, or poison, all the sovereigns of the earth. Nothing but fear of reprisals prevented their proceeding to attempt to carry them into the most effectual execution. And many other enormities are there noted.

itself a republic; among whom were 250 thousand woman; 230 thousand children, beside those murdered in the womb; and 24 thousand priests, many of whom were Protestants." Marat, that great professed *friend of the people*, scrupled not to assert, that in order to cement liberty, the national club ought to strike off 200,000 heads. "As for the privilege of extending mercy to the condemned, it was contemptuously disclaimed; and all applications for pardon were rejected with the declaration, that the enlightened government of Republican France possessed no such power. By one vast and cruel act of confiscation, it is supposed more than 800,000,000, of dollars were seized by the hands of the public. It was esteemed indeed a sufficient crime to be suspected of being a suspicious person."† The pupils of their new republican school appearing at the bar, and declaring that all religious worship had been suppressed in their section; and that they *detested God;* and horrible to relate! their establishing a tan-yard, under the auspices of government, to manufacture into leather the skins of their murdered fellow-citizens; their drowning, under guards of soldiers, their new-born infants, born of women kept by the officers in Gen. Jourdan's army, as related by Count Sodin, who was present; and numerous other enormities, which exclusively characterize the annals of modern France;—these are things well known. And they strikingly corroborate the evidence exhibited, that we behold in that nation the rise of the Antichrist of the last time.

The succeeding predictions (Dan. xi, 38,) the French nation have precisely fulfilled. They soon fell under a military despotism; and have become a great and ter-, rible empire. The people who magnified themselves above God, and all legitimate authorities, received their foreign god, their *emperor,* from an origin, which *their fathers knew not;* and have honored him *with gold, and silver, and precious stones, and pleasant things;* or with Imperial magnificence. A Corsican youth was admit-

† Faber, vol. ii, p. 205,

ted to an under office in a company of artillery, in the republican French army. His activity at the siege of Toulon, in 1793, excited the attention of the national agents; and he was advanced. His subsequent rise was rapid. Within a few years the French received him, and honored him, as their First Consul. And his subsequent magnificence, his victories, and his distributions of the nominal crowns of his conquered nations to his kindred and favorites, appear fully to accord with the forecited passage, Dan. xi, 38, 39. *And a god, whom his fathers knew not, shall he honor with gold and silver and precious stones and pleasant things. Thus shall he do in the most strong holds, with a strange god, whom he shall acknowledge and increase with glory And he shall cause them to rule over many, and shall divide the land (earth) for gain.* In the whole of the passage aforecited from this chapter, relative to the Infidel Power, we find a train of particulars, which have been fulfilled in their order in France; but which, I believe, have never been fulfilled in this order in any other nation; and there now appears no probability that they can ever be fulfilled in any other nation.

Have we then any reason to doubt of the correctness of applying the passage to the French nation? And especially considering the origin of their revolution, which will by and by be noted. When this is considered, we shall find also that in the French, as far as they have proceeded, we behold an inceptive fulfilment of the prophecy in Rev. xii, concerning *the devil's coming down to the earth in great wrath;* and of the prophecy in Rev. xvii, concerning *the Beast, that ascendeth out of the bottomless pit, and is bearing the Papal harlot to her execution.* The gross Infidel system, instigated by *the great dragon,* in the former of these passages, has most strikingly appeared in France; and appears to be fulfilling in what has been called the Christian world. And the features of the Beast in Rev. xvii, are conspicuously prominent in that nation, so far as they have proceeded. Examine the prophetic picture. Then look at the French nation. And you will be constrain-

ed to say, the picture there has its original; the prediction, its accomplishment. The seventh head of the
old Roman Beast, continuing *a short space,* has been
verified in the *Terrible Republic.* The succeeding
head, numerically the eighth, but yet *of the seven;* being the sixth healed from its deadly wound, is now
presented before our eyes. This new *Beast from the
bottomless pit, of scarlet color, covered with the deeds of
blasphemy,* forming to himself *his ten horns,* bearing
the Papal harlot to her execution, with the *world wondering after him,* has appeared upon the stage, mani-
fested with dreadful precision. And the events of Rev.
xviii, are fulfilled, or fulfilling. Some of the most
important parts of the dominion of Papal Babylon have
indeed been exhibited to the world, as the *habitations
of devils; the hold of every foul spirit; and the cage
of every unclean and hateful bird.* The *rod of iron,*
for the work of judgment there implied, is presented
before the nations. Papal *Babylon is fallen;* and the
judgments of God on Papal nations are in the most
conspicuous train of fulfilment.

The above ideas will be corroborated, when we come
to ascertain the real origin of the late unprecedented
commotions in Europe. This origin stands clearly exposed in the writings of Dr. John Robison, Professor
of Natural Philosophy in the University of Edinburgh,
in a volume published in 1797, entitled, *"Proofs of a
Conspiracy,* &c." And in the volumes of the Abbe
Barruel, a French Catholic, who wrote Memoirs on the
French revolution. In both these works, although the
plans of the authors are very different, and the writers
were of different kingdoms, and different religious edu-
cations, and unacquainted with the object of each other;
yet the same points are clearly ascertained. They give
the same original letters, mottos, and watch words; and
in short, disclose the same systematic plot, laid to introduce anarchy and Atheism, under the notion of
enlightening mankind.

As much of the evidence concerning the fatal scheme
of Illuminism, was first given in this country by these

writers, it may be suitable to make some remarks upon
their characters.

SECTION , III.

The Characters of Dr. Robison, and the Abbe Bar-
ruel.

MUCH pains have been taken to abate the force of the
testimony of these authors; particularly of the former.
This perfectly agrees with the well known arts of Illuminism.   Men who have adopted such maxims as the
following; "*The goodness of the end sanctifies the
means; We must gain our opposers, or ruin them;
Hurl the javelin; strike deep; but conceal the hand
that gives the blow;*" might be expected to assail, with
the weapons of false accusation, the characters of those,
who should attempt to unveil their wickedness.   Accordingly as soon as Professor Robison's Proofs were
circulated in this country, and excited alarm, scandalous accounts were propagated in the newspapers a-
gainst his character.   These accounts have been proved,
from authentic documents, to have been *utter falsehoods.*
In the process of these proofs, the excellency of Professor Robison's character has been incontestably substantiated.   The history of his life has been made public; which exhibits him as a man of distinguished use-
fulness; of the first degree of erudition; and of the most
unimpeachable veracity and integrity.*   From youth
he has been in public life.   In 1774 he was invited by
the Magistrates of Edinburgh to the Professorship of
Natural Philosophy, in the University of that city;
which ranks very high among the literary institutions
of this age.   In 1786 he was elected a member of the
Philosophical Society in Philadelphia, of which Mr.
Jefferson is the President.   In 1797, he was elected a
member of the Royal Society of Manchester.   In 1799,
the University of Glasgow, where he had received his
education, conferred on him the honorary degree of
Doctor of Laws; at which time, contrary to their usual

*See Payson's Modern Antichrist.

custom, they gave a very particular and flattering account of his nine years study in that University. He was Secretary to the Royal Society of Edinburgh. And in 1800 he was unanimously elected a foreign member (of which they admit but six) of the Imperial Academy of Sciences at Petersburgh; which is one of the three highest in reputation in Europe. These facts evince that Dr. Robison was one of the most eminent literary characters in Europe. Would he then have risked his reputation in giving such a publication to the world, if he were not, from the most authentic documents, sure of its correctness? It is incredible! As to Dr. Robison's moral character, it is established beyond doubt. The following is an extract from a letter written by one of the most respectable literary men in Scotland. Leave was not obtained to give his name; though it is presumed he would not have made objection. "Professor Robison's character is so well established among those, who know him best, that it would be ridiculous, at Edinburgh, to call in question his veracity or abilities. I had read many of his authorities in German originals, before his book was published. And the first notice I received of his book was in the preface to Dr. Erskine's Sketches of Ecclesiastical History, where you will see the honorable testimony, that he gave to Mr. Robison, and the great expectation that he had from its publication."

The Rev. Dr. Erskine, so celebrated in America, and neighbor to Dr. Robison, in a letter dated Edinburgh, Sept. 25, 1800, says, "I think highly of Professor Robison's book. Some of the most shocking facts it contains, I knew, before its publication, from a periodical account of the Church history of the times, by Professor Koester, at Glessen, of which I lent to Professor Robison all the numbers, relating to that subject. In a subsequent letter of June 13th, 1801, Dr. Erskine, having heard of some of the aspersions of Dr. Robison's character circulating in America, says, "Had these reports been sent to Edinburgh, for their *papable falsehood*, they would have been despised and detested." Mr. J. Walker, a reputable inhabitant

20

of Great Britain, wrote an attestation to the excellent character of Dr. Robison, to Professor Boetiger of Germany, who had written some aspersions on Dr. Robison's character; upon which Boetiger honorably retracted those aspersions. Mr. Walker, after giving Dr. Robison's character, says, "Nor is this the exaggerated praise of a friend. No one, who knows Mr. Robison, as I know him, (and he is almost universally known in Britain,) will dare to call it in question." Thus, notwithstanding these mischievous aspersions, Dr. Robison's character is fully established. And the information given in his book is entitled to every degree of credit.

As to the character of the Abbe Barruel, I know not that it was ever materially impeached. His volumes, while they contain the errors of the Roman Catholic religion, and indicate the indignation of their author against the enormities of the French; they likewise indicate, to an uncommon degree, his strict veracity, in the relation of facts. He would never relate the substance of any account, but with the document before his eyes. And when the enormity of its contents appeared almost incredible, he would subjoin the originals verbatim, that the reader might translate for himself.

These two authors, of different nations, religions, and habits, writing their books at the same time; unacquainted with each other's object; and pursuing their inquiries through very different arrangements, arrive at the same points; and unitedly develop the same diabolical scheme of Illuminism. The evidence therefore, which they afford upon the subject, must by the judicious be deemed irresistible.

SECTION IV.

Origin of the French Revolution:—And a further description of that Revolution.

It has been fully ascertained, that the French revolution was not that virtuous struggle for liberty, which Americans at first apprehended. Nor were its enormities the accidental frenzy of an infuriated mob. But the revolution, and those enormities, were under the direction of a system of wickedness, matured by men of the first talents; and most subtly propagated by multitudes, in hidden concert, for nearly half a century, before its first ripe fruits appeared in that revolution. This we learn from the aforementioned writings of Robison and Barruel; and from numerous other authentic sources. They unfold at large the most diabolical scheme, with its ample evidence. In this I cannot follow them, in a short dissertation. I can only sketch the outlines of the dismal plot.

Voltaire, the great French philosopher, who was born at Paris, Feb. 20, 1694, and who died not long before the French revolution, conceived a design in his early days to overturn the Christian Religion. This was his avowed object. And such were his genius, and early turn of mind, for the impious object of his undertaking, that while he was but a youth, he received the following reprimand from his professor; "Unfortunate young man! you will one day come to be the standard bearer of Infidelity." So he proved in fact; and to a far greater degree, than his professor, or any other man could have conceived. Voltaire was wont to say; "I am weary of hearing people repeat, that twelve men have been sufficient to establish Christianity. I will prove, that *one* may suffice to overthrow it."* And would add; "Christianity yields none but poisonous weeds." And to the object of overturning the Christian Religion, he vowed to dedicate his life. To *"crush the wretch,"* (as he would express it) meaning Jesus Christ, was henceforth to be the object of all his exertions. And this impious phrase became the watch word of his order, "Crush the wretch then, crush the wretch!"

Voltaire associated with himself for his horrid purpose, a group of Infidel philosophers; Diderot, D'Alembert, Rosseau, and Frederic, king of Prussia; and shortly after he subtly found means to unite with him five or six of the crowned heads in Europe, in an im-

* Life of Voltaire.

pious conspiracy to destroy the religion of the Gospel.
The numbers and influence of the conspirators rapidly
increased. Their success was astonishing, even to
themselves, as some of them exultingly acknowledged:
So that they would often speak of the amazing power
of *secret societies;* and of the facility with which they
might *bind the world with invisible hands.*

Such was the preparedness of the mass of the Roman
Catholics for Infidelity, and such the influence of the
infernal dragon, who was now furiously intent on erecting this new standard against the cause of Christ, that
the scheme of Voltaire took effect, like fire in a field
of dry stubble, with a strong wind to accelerate its
fury. "Circumstances were favorable. He did not
foresee all that he has done. But he has done all that
we now see." Voltaire boasted, that from Geneva to
Berne, not a Christian was to be found; and that if
things went on at this rate, *in twenty years God would
be in a pretty plight."*

This plan was prosecuted with incredible vigor, and
success. Secrecy was the soul of their order. "Strike
deep, but hide the hand that gives the blow," and similar phrases, were with them watch words of great sig-
nificancy. Their leaders received fictitious names; and
they transacted their business in a language newly invented for the purpose. They prevailed to poison the
sources of education. The highest of the French literary Societies, they, after much intrigue and management, filled with their members; and finally rendered
the institution wholly subservient to their views.

Although the subversion of the Christian Religion
was their first object, as has been noted; yet the subversion of civil government was after a while united
with it, by these propagators of impiety and licentiousness. It became a principle of their order, that all the
restraints of religion, and of civil government, were
but an intolerable imposition; and that the goodness of
the end sanctifies whatever means may be adopted to
abolish such restraints.

Free masonry was insidiously perverted, and made a
medium and covert of this mischief, in a manner con-

trary to its principles, or original design.* Many of
the lodges in France and Germany, and other Popish
countries, were corrupted, and became subservient to
the views of Illuminism. Upon the discovery of this,
an honorable mason in Europe thus bewails it, in an
oration to his associates; "Brethren and companions,
give free vent to your sorrow. The days of innocent
equality are gone by. However holy our mysteries
may have been, the lodges are now profaned and sullied.
Let your tears flow. Attired in your mourning robes,
attend, and let us seal up the gates of our temples; for
the profane have found means to penetrate into them.
They have converted them into retreats for their impiety, and dens of conspirators. Within the sacred
walls they have planned their horrid deeds, and the ruin
of nations. Let us weep over our legions, whom they
have seduced. Lodges, that may serve as hiding places
for these conspirators, must for ever remain shut, both
to us, and to every good citizen."†

Thousands became leagued in secret concert, to en-
lighten mankind with the wonderful doctrine of *Liberty*
and *Equality;* liberty from all the restraints of religion;
and equality from all the subordinations of civil government. Their highest secret was, that there is no
God; and no future state; and that every restraint on

---

* I hope none of the Masonic Fraternity will admit the idea,
that any thing in this dissertation is designed to reflect upon
their order. We know there is no institution among men, which
is not capable of being abused to perverse purposes. And if
simply this circumstance were to decide against the merit of institutions, perhaps every institution would be reprobated. The
advocates of the most important institutions will readily hear the
conduct of the base perverters of their respective orders exposed; and will by no means wish to keep concealed such per-
versions. The honor and patriotism of the *honorable* masons of
this day will not permit them to wish, that the modern innovations made in their order, and in the institutions of religion and
government, by Infidels, should be kept out of sight. For
many, and those among the most honorable of the Masonic
Fraternity, have themselves sounded the alarm, and given notice
of this horrid abuse of their order. And the thing itself is most
notorious.

Barruel's Memoirs, vol. iv, p. 63.

the appetites and passions of man, is an abridgment of his rights, and ought to be abolished. These senti-ments it was the business of the adepts of their order to instil into the minds of mankind, and especially of the rising generation; and to do it without giving alarm. Their methods of effecting this were systematic, and subtile, almost beyond description, or detection. They allured their young candidates, whom they had marked out for their prey, with seemingly accidental hints of the amazing power and great benefits of secret societies; that there *were* such societies, embracing the greatest of characters, who were able to govern the world. These youth were seduced into the most positive engagements of obedience to unknown leaders in those societies, of whom they were led to form the most exalted opinion, as being great and wise men, devoted to the reforma-tion of mankind; and to the good of the world. The attention of these pupils was allured with the idea of there being various grades in these secret societies; and of new and wonderful discoveries to be made, or secret things to be revealed, at each advance. Thus all the principles of ignorant ambition, and the love of novelty, were addressed and fatally arrested; while the adepts were insidiously engaged in erasing from the mind of the candidate every impression of any past religious instruc-tions; and in preparing him for a higher grade of In-fidelity. To this higher grade he was admitted, with various ceremonies, so soon as it was discovered by the instructor, that he was prepared to receive it with-out alarm. In this gradual process thousands were led on to their highest secrets, of *Atheism, Anarchy*, and *Licentiousness.*

Books were written by the most subtile of their or-der, calculated to unhinge the mind from the truths of Revelation, and to bring the Gospel into contempt. A learned Encyclopædia was devised and written *for this very purpose*, that the poison of Infidelity might be imperceptibly diffused. And other books innumerable, even down to the lowest tracts, teeming with the most artful suggestions of Infidelity, were profusely scattered through the whole mass of society. Printers and booksellers were artfully enlisted into the same cause. And funds were raised to indemnify them, in suppressing every evangelical publication. So that few or no *good books* could circulate in society; or even be found. Reading societies were formed by the agents of this fatal scheme, in order that their impious publications might be read, and thus take the more sure effect. The direction of schools the leaders of Illuminism found means to get into their own hands; and to furnish them with instructors of their own order. A celebrated character in our nation, writing upon this horrid combination, says, "They ultimately spread the design throughout a great part of Europe: and embarked in it individuals, at little distances, over almost the whole of that continent. Their adherents inserted themselves into every place, office and employment, in which their agency might become efficacious; and which furnished an opportunity of spreading their corruptions. They were found in every literary institution, from a-b-cdarian school, to the academy of sciences; and in every civil office, from that of the bailiff, to that of the monarch. They swarmed in the palace: they haunted the Church. Wherever mischief was to be done, they were found. And wherever they were found, mischief was done. Of books they controlled the publication, the sale, and the character. An immense number they formed; an immense number they forged; prefixed to them the names of reputable writers, and sent them into the world, to be sold for a song; and when that could not be done, to be given away.—They possessed themselves, to a great extent, of a control nearly absolute, of the literary, religious, and political state of Europe.— They penetrated into every corner of human society. Scarcely a man, woman or child, was left unassailed, wherever there was a single hope, that the attack might be successful. Books were written and published, in innumerable multitudes, in which infidelity was brought down to the level of peasants, and even of children; and poured with immense assiduity into the cottage, and the school. Others of a superior kind crept into the shop, and the farm house; and others of a still higher

class found their way to the drawing rooms, the university and the palace."

Said the chief of the Illuminati; "All the. German
schools, and the benevolent society, are at last under
our direction. Lately we have got possession of the
Bartholomew Institution for young clergymen; having
secured all their supporters. Through this, we shall be
able to supply Bavaria with *fit priests*. We must acquire the direction of education, of church management, of the professional chair, and of the pulpit. We
must preach the warmest concern for humanity, and
make people indifferent to all other relations. We must
gain the reviewers, and journalists, and the booksellers."* See an instance of their impious hypocrisy:—
A president of their society, in an initiatory discourse,
said, "Jesus Christ, our grand and ever celebrated
master, appeared in an age, when corruption was universal. He supported his doctrines by an innocent life, and
sealed them with his blood." Yet Christ was the *wretch*,
whom their order had *sworn to crush!* And the following
sentiments we read in their own language. "All ideas of
justice and injustice, of virtue and vice, of glory and
infamy, are purely arbitrary, and dependent on custom.
The man, who is above law, can commit without remorse the dishonest act, that may serve his purpose.
The fear of God, so far from being the beginning of
wisdom, would be the beginning of folly. Modesty is
only an invention of refined voluptuousness. Virtue
and honesty are no more than the habit of actions personally advantageous."† "The supreme king," (says
their code) "the God of philosophers, Jews, and Christians, is but a chimera, a phantom. Jesus Christ is an
impostor.".

It was one of the hidden maxims of their philosophy,
first to gain a firm footing by fraud, and afterwards to
propagate their scheme by force; adopting the words
reason, toleration, and *humanity,* as a *quietus,* till they
could *call to arms.* The following instructions were

---

* Faber, vol. i, p. 251.   † Barruel, vol. iii, p. 164; and
Kett, vol. ii, p. 178.

accordingly given to their initiated brethren, by the hierophant of their order. "Serve, assist, and mutually support each other; augment our numbers; render yourselves at least independent; and leave to time and posterity the care of doing the rest. When your numbers shall be augmented to a certain degree, and you shall have acquired strength by your union, hesitate no longer, but begin to render yourselves powerful and formidable to the wicked," (i. e. all your opposers.)— "You will soon acquire sufficient force to bind the hands of your opponents, and subjugate them. · Extend and multiply the children of light, till force and numbers shall throw power into our hands."—"*Nations must be brought back*—by whatever means—peacably if it can be done; if not, then by *force*. For all subordination must be made to vanish from the earth."*

No iniquity, perfidy, or hypocrisy was too bad to be adopted, provided they could but keep it concealed. *Lying*, and a *stubborn perseverance in false assertions*, either to conceal, or to accomplish their plots; or to ruin characters or interests, that stood in their way, were among the most powerful principles of their system in *crushing the wretch.*

This fatal scheme spread in Germany under the direction of its arch-agent Dr. Adam Weishaupt, (professor of the Canon Law in the university of Ingoldstadt, in Bavaria, a learned, subtile Jesuit;) and others. It became powerful in other Roman Catholic countries. In France it wrought wonders, and prepared the way for the dismal scenes there of modern date.

By a train of the most apposite ceremonies and operations, men were taught and hardened to become murderers, and capable of every cruel and perverse thing without remorse. Let one instance suffice to illustrate this remark. "A candidate for reception into one of the higher orders of Illuminism, after having heard many threatenings denounced against all, who should betray the secrets of the order, was conducted to a place, where he saw the dead bodies of several, who were said

* Barruel.

to have suffered for their treachery. He then saw his own brother tied hand and foot, begging his mercy and intercession. He was informed, that this person was about to suffer the punishment due for this offence; and that it was reserved for him (the candidate) to be the instrument of this just vengeance; and that this gave him opportunity of manifesting that he was completely devoted to the order. It being observed that his countenance gave signs of inward horror, he was told, that in order to spare his feelings, a bandage should be put over his eyes. A dagger was then put into his hand; and his left hand was laid upon the palpitating heart of the supposed criminal; and he was ordered to *strike*. He instantly obeyed. And when the bandage was taken from his eyes, he saw that it was a lamb he had stabbed."*

No combination ever "united within its pale such a mass of talents, or employed such a succession of vigorous efforts." The grand sentiments of the scheme were the following, "that God is nothing; that government is a curse; and authority a usurpation; that civil society is the only apostasy of man; that the possession of property is robbery; that chastity and natural affection, are mere prejudices; and that adultery, assassinations, poisoning, and other crimes of a similar nature, are lawful, and even virtuous."

Says President Dwight, "Under these circumstances were founded the societies of Illuminism. They spread of course with a rapidity, which nothing but fact could have induced any sober mind to believe. Before the year 1786, they were established, in great numbers, throughout Germany, in Sweden, Russia, Poland, Austria, Holland, France, Switzerland, Italy, England, Scotland, and even *America*. In all these was taught the grand sweeping principle of corruption, that the *end* sanctifies the *means*."

It was this scheme of Illuminism in France, which took the lead of their revolution. This was the origin of those events, which have deluged Europe with blood;

* Robison's Proofs, p. 299.

and filled a great part of the civilized world with terror! The plan, which came into operation in the French revolution, was previously matured; and legions of illuminees were at their respective posts, to manage the fatal operations.

The subterranean fire, which had long been kindling in dark recesses, now burst like a volcano from its dire caverns; terrifying the nations with its portentous discharge. And in the *terrible Atheistical nation* appeared the *rise*, instead of the *fall* of Antichrist.

It is to be confessed, that the French nation needed a redress of their grievances. For a long season they had been under the yoke of despotic authority. And though Lewis XVI was a mild king, his ministers of finance had much oppressed the people. M. Neckar, who had almost retrieved the miseries of their financial system, was, through the jealousy of interested courtiers, ejected from this department; and M. de Calonne appointed in his stead. This step proved fatal to the government. For the king found his affairs so embarrassed, that he thought it adviseable to convene his *notables*, in hope of availing himself of their influence with the people in the imposition of such taxes, as he thought his affairs now required. The notables, after using an unaccustomed freedom in examining their financial concerns, shrunk from the task assigned them, of sanctioning an enormous stamp act; and proposed the calling of an Assembly of the States. The States General had never been called but twice, since the revolution, in the days of Lewis XI, from a feudal aristocracy, to absolute monarchy. They once met in the reign of Henry IV; and again in the year 1617; but to very little prupose. But their next meeting, in 1789, was followed with scenes infinitely more interesting. Upon the above proposal, Lewis XVI dismissed his notables, and established a council of finance. *They* complied with the royal order. But the parliament of Paris refused to *register* this order; and agreed with the opinion of the notables, that the States General ought to decide the point. Whether the Jacobinic club, (so called) the leaders of the Illuminati, were at the bottom of this proposal, or not, it, completely answered their purpose; and afforded a noble opportunity, in the event, for them to put in execution the scheme, which they had long been concerting; and, which was now just ready to burst into operation. After various manœuvres on the part of the king, the deputies of the States were convened. The *"Jacobinic club"** had previously been exceedingly busy in their correspondence through different parts of the nation, to give a direction to the public opinion, and to form the people to that unity of sentiment, which afterward appeared in their popular councils. The deputies of the people being convened, and finding themselves supported by public opinion, which had been formed, both by the real injuries inflicted by the government; and by artful management for the purpose, proceeded on the 17th of June, 1789, to assume to themselves the legislative government, under the name of the *National Assembly*.

The nobility complained to the king of this usurpation, that "the deputies of the *Third Estate* had attempted to concentrate in their own persons the whole authority of the States General, without waiting for the concurrence of the other orders, or the sanction of his majesty; that they had attempted to convert their decrees into laws; and had ordered them to be printed, published, and distributed to the provinces; had repealed, and reenacted laws, relative to the taxes; and that they seemed to attribute to themselves the united rights of the monarch and the three great orders, who compose the States General."

The king sent his soldiers over night, and took possession of their hall. But the assembly met in another place, and proceeded to business. Upon this the king convened the other branches of the States General, the *nobles* and the *clergy*, and held a royal session. In this, his keeper of the seals read a concession to his subjects of 35 articles, in which the grievous points in his government were given up; and the States General

---

* Of these there were 300,000 adepts, supported by 2,000,000 of men, scattered through France, armed with the implements of revolution. See Faber, vol. ii, p. 43.

might evidently have had his consent to manage the affairs of the nation as they pleased. But after the king, and those of his nobles and clergy, who pleased, had retired, the commons (who had formed themselves into the *National Assembly)* remained, and proceeded in their business. The duke of Orleans, 40 of the nobility, and 200 of the clergy, now joined them. Deputies were received from the different parts of the nation, assuring the *Assembly* of the approbation of the people of the revolution which had begun. Orders were received from the king commanding them to disperse; but in vain. The soldiers were then commanded to disperse them. But the commander in chief informed the king, that he could not answer for the safety of his *royal person,* if these orders were enforced. In short the king soon lost all his authority; a new constitution was formed; and a revolution was completed. The king, upon his submission to the Assembly, retained a shadow of executive authority. But upon his attending an entertainment of a new regiment of troops at Versailles, who trampled on the national cockade, and assumed a black one in its stead, he was brought to Paris under guard, and lodged in the old ruined palace of Thuilleries. The Assembly gave toleration to religion; and their constitution had in it many good things. They continued their sessions two years and four months; and on the 30th of Sept. 1791, the Assembly dissolved itself.

A new assembly soon met, under the name of the *National Convention.* Under *their* government, the designs of the leading men in the revolution appeared. War having broken out between France and Austria, the Convention issued a decree, of which the following is an extract: "The National Convention, faithful to the principles of the sovereignty of the people, which will not permit them to acknowledge any of the institutions against it, and, willing to fix the regulations to be observed by the generals of the armies of the republic, in those countries, to which they may carry their arms, decree;

That in those countries, which shall be occupied by the armies of the French republic, the generals shall immediately proclaim the abolition of all the existing customs, and rights; of all nobility, and generally all privileges; they shall declare to the people, that they bring them *peace, succor, fraternity, liberty* and *equality.*

The French nation declare, that it will treat as enemies the people, who, refusing or renouncing liberty and equality, are desirous of preserving their *prince,* and privileged casts, or of entering into an accommodation with them. The nation promises and engages not to lay down its arms, until the sovereignty and liberty of the people, on whose territory the French armies shall have entered, shall be established "

Here the real object of the French revolution is clearly ascertained. Or, it is here clearly evident, that, how many soever forwarded that revolution from better views, the Jacobins took the whole direction of it, and found in it the very opportunity, which they had long wished and desired, to give their plan its full effect. Some moderation, at first, appeared under the National Assembly. But their scheme now, under the *Convention,* was soon unfolded. Even the French nation were not prepared to behold Illuminism in all its extent, at first view. For some time therefore, the French revolution was pleasing to many of the friends of virtuous liberty. But after the meeting of the National Convention, their views were rapidly unfolded. On the midnight preceding the 10th of August 1792, all the bells of Paris rang an alarm; the drums beat; the citizens flew to arms; the old palace, where the members of the royal family were, was attacked. The Swiss guards fired upon the populace. But they, with the national guards, were cut to pieces by bodies of soldiers, brought by the Jacobins from Brest and Marseilles. The gates of the palace were broken, after about 800 men had been killed. The king some time after was brought to trial before the Convention, and was beheaded, Jan. 21, 1793. The queen was beheaded, on the 16th of the Oct. ensuing. Roy-

alty was abolished by the Convention; and a new constitution was by them formed and published; and it
was accepted by the people, in the stead of the first,
formed by the National Assembly. The moderate
principles of the first constitution were abandoned.
No further toleration was given to religion or conscience. On the 26th of August, 1792, "an open profession of Atheism was made by a whole nation, once
zealously devoted to the Papal superstition. Corresponding societies and Atheistical clubs were every where
held, fearless and undisguised."

Massacres and the reign of terror succeeded; to hint
the particulars of which would fill a volume. It it a
prominent idea in prophecies relative to this horrid
Power of the last days, that his destruction is nearly
connected with his origin; that he ascends from the
bottomless pit, to *go into perdition;* and his *damnation slumbers not.* Many events, which took place
soon after the revolution, may be viewed as an earnest
of this truth; as a first fruit or pledge of the fulfilment
of it. It appeared in facts that infidelity has the heart
of a demon; the ferocity of a tiger; the fangs of a pan-
ther; and the fury of a lion. Its delicious food is
blood. It flies with the winds of a fiend, to the field of
carnage; and sucks the blood of its own brotherhood.

This was verified in France. About 100 of the
prime leaders in the revolution, soon fell by the hand
of violence. Being enemies to heaven and earth, they
were, of course, enemies to each other. And being
inured to murder and blood, they were prepared to cut
each other's throats. The righteous God thus far
blessed the world, by letting those infernal lions loose
upon each other. They, and hundreds of thousands
of their deluded followers, soon found for each other a
premature grave; and thus presented the world with a
miniature of the tremendous exit, which, at but little
distance, awaits the body of that Antichristian Beast.

Something of the feats of the French arms abroad,
soon after their revolution, may be learned from the
following report of Dubois Crance, to the convention,

Jan. 30th, 1795. He says; "Last year you maintain-ed. nearly eleven hundred thousand fighting .men. France stood armed on one side, Europe on the other; and victory constantly followed the three colored stand-ard. Holland is conquered; and England trembles. Twenty three regular sieges terminated; six pitched battles gained; 2000 cannon taken; 200 towns submit-ted. Such is the glorious result of the last campaign. The next campaign promises, if possible, still more surprising successes."

The loss of men sustained by the armies of France from 1791, to 1796, was calculated at twelve hundred thousand. And beside this loss, the number of mur-dered citizens, including men, women, and children, during the reign of terror, is said to have been two millions.

This account is confirmed by Gen. Danican, a French officer, who declared, that three millions of Frenchmen perished within the first four or five years of the French revolution.

Such a series of events could not have been without some deep and most mischievous plot. And such a plot the history of Illuminism unfolds.

SECTION V.

The re-establishment of Popery by Bonaparte not inconsistent with Atheism's being the characteris-tic of the French Empire.

THE present French Emperor has evinced, by his proclamation in Egypt, and by other documents, that, in point of sentiment, he was not unprepared to be-come a prime leader of the Antichristian Empire.*

---

* The object of Bonaparte's expedition into Egypt, in 1798, is expressed in the following extract from an intercepted letter, written by a major in his army; dated Grand Cairo, July 28th, 1798. "The government have turned their eyes toward Egypt and Syria; countries, which by their climate, goodness, and fer-tility of soil, may become the granaries of the French com-merce, her magazines of abundance, and in course of time the depository of the riches of India. It is most indubitable, that, when possessed of, and regularly organized in, these countries,

Bonaparte's re-establishment of Popery forms no objection to his being an Atheist; nor to Atheism's being

we may throw our views still farther, and in the end destroy the English commerce in the Indies, turn it to our own profit, and render ourselves the sovereigns also of these parts of Africa and Asia. All these considerations united have induced our government to attempt the expedition to Egypt. That part of the *Roman power* has been governed, for many ages, by a species of men called Mamalukes, who have Beys at the head of each district. They deny the authority of the Grand Seignor; governing tyrannically, and despotically, a people and a country, that in the hand of a polished nation, would become a source of wealth and profit." Kett. vol. ii, p. 268.

But Bonaparte had the subtilty to disguise this object, by the following proclamation in Egypt; in which his own sentiments may be learned; his turn for the work of deception; and his flatteries of those, who are marked out for his prey. "In the name of God, gracious and merciful. There is no God but one; he has no son, or associate in his kingdom." Here is an express and designed denial of Christ, and of the Christian Religion. One God must be acknowledged. For the Mohammedan Egyptians acknowledge him: And Bonaparte was now courting them! He proceeds; "The present moment, which is destined for the punishment of the Beys, has been long anxiously expected. The Beys coming from the mountains of Georgia and Bajars, have desolated this beautiful country. Bonaparte, the general of the French republic, according to the principles of liberty, is now arrived; and the Almighty, the Lord of both worlds, has sealed the destruction of the Beys. Inhabitants of Egypt! when the Beys tell you, the French are come to destroy your religion, believe them not, it is an absolute falsehood. Answer those deceivers, that they are only come to *rescue the rights of the poor from the hands of their tyrants*; and that the French adore the Supreme Being, *and* honor the prophet, (Mohammed) and his holy Koran; (the Mohammedan Bible.) All men are equal in the eyes of God; understanding, ingenuity, and science alone, make the difference between them. As the Beys therefore do not possess any of these qualities, they cannot be worthy to govern the country. The Supreme Being, who is just and merciful toward all mankind, wills that in future none of the inhabitants of Egypt shall be prevented from attaining to the first employments, and the highest honors. The administration, which shall be conducted by persons of intelligence, talents, and foresight, will be productive of happiness and security. The tyranny and avarice of the Beys have laid wast Egypt, which was formerly so populous and well cultivated. *The French are true Musselmens;* (disciples of Mohammed) They have at all times been

22

the characteristic of the French Empire. For this characteristic the French nation clearly and officially assumed, and for years retained. And they have not since
taken a single step to change this national characteristic,
nor to evince, that Atheism is not their real sentiment as a nation. It has been ascertained, that the
French *as a nation* are Atheists. In support of this,
let Dr. Priestly testify: And no one will suspect the
Doctor to have been *greatly prejudiced against them!*
He relates the following; "When I was myself in
France, in 1774, I saw sufficient reason to believe, that
hardly any person of eminence, in church or state, and
especially in a great degree eminent in philosophy or
literature, (whose opinions in all countries are sooner
or later adopted by others) were believers in Christianity. And no person will suppose, that there has been
any change in favor of Christianity, in the last twenty
years. A person, I believe now living, and one of the
best informed men in the country, assured me very
gravely, that (paying me a compliment) I was the
first person he had ever met with, of whose understanding he had any opinion, who pretended to believe
in Christianity. To this, all the company assented.

the true and sincere friends of Ottoman emperors; and the enemies of their enemies. May the empire of the Sultan therefore be eternal. But may the Beys of Egypt, our opposers,
whose insatiable avarice has continually excited disobedience
and insubordination, be trodden in the dust and annihilated!
Our friendship shall be extended to those of the inhabitants of
Egypt, who shall join us; as also to those, who shall remain in
their dwellings, and observe a strict neutrality, and when they
have seen our conduct with their own eyes, shall hasten to submit to us. But the dreadful punishment of death awaits those
who shall take up arms for the Beys, and against us. For them
there shall be no deliverance; nor shall any trace of them remain. All the inhabitants of Egypt shall offer up thanks to
the Supreme Being, and put up public prayers for the destruction of the Beys. May the Supreme God make the glory of
the Sultan of the Ottomans eternal; pour forth his wrath on
the Mamalukes; and render glorious the destiny of the Egyptian nation." (Kett, vol. ii. p 258—261)

The hypocrisy and Atheism exposed in this siren chant,
need no comment. They exhibit the *heart* of the man, who
was raised up to scorge a wicked world, and to be the first
bloody leader of the Antichristian Empire.

And not only were the philosophers, and other leading men in France at that time, unbelievers in Christianity, or, Deists; but they were *Atheists; denying the being of God.*" (Priestley's Fast Sermon. 1794.)

The French are to be denominated, in the language of prophecy, from the characteristic of Atheism, which they did, in their revolution, by national authority, and undisguisedly assume. The remarks of authors, relative to the ancient ten horns of the Roman Beast, (whether they were correct in their application of those horns, or not,) illustrate my present idea. They, tell us, it is sufficient to answer to the prophetic characteristic of the Beast's having ten horns, if we can find precisely *ten kingdoms at any one time*, into which the old empire was divided For it is not supposed, they add, *that the precise number ten continued.* New conquests, subdivisions, or unions, soon deranged and altered their number from being precisely ten. But it it sufficient, that it *once* was *precisely ten.* So in the present case. It is enough to affix to Antichrist the characteristic of *Atheism*, that he *officially assumed this characteristic*; maintained it for years; and has never discovered the least *real* disapprobation of Atheism! His character then, is Atheism, notwithstanding that political views, and a kind of *necessity*, have induced the tyrant of France to re-establish Popery as his nominal *form of godliness.* The nation derives its characteristic, in the language of prophecy, not from this circumstance, but from its antecedent, undisguised profession of Atheism. Popery is re-established by the French emperor, merely as a tool of ambitious policy.* After the French nation had been torn for years by factions, and drenched in the blood of two millions of its murdered citizens, beside the seas of blood shed in war, it was there clearly ascertained by woeful experience, that subordination and civil government could never be maintained, without adopting some kind of religion. The Papal sys-

* Cicero said of Cataline, "Had he not possessed some apparent virtues, he would not have been able to form so great a design; nor to have proved so formidable an adversary."

tem, the tyrant of France found most subservient to his views. This he therefore nominally adopted, instead of Mohammedism, as when in Egypt. But this manœuvre did by no means obliterate the national feature of Atheism, which they had officially assumed. They had adopted, and in the language of prophecy *still possess*, this essential characteristic of Antichrist.

The following is the finishing of a description, given by Mr. Yorke (who was present) of the celebration of the re-establishment of Popery by Bonaparte. "These are the principal incidents, which occurred at Notre Dame. I leave you to form a just idea of the emotions of those present, whether they be considered as Christians or not. The far greater part of the Senate, the legislative Body, the Tribunate, and the generals, being *avowed Atheists*, and notorious for the murders, thefts, and atrocities, which they had perpetrated; with their chief Magistrate, who had worshipped at the altar of Atheism, some years before in Paris; who afterwards knelt down before the Pope at Rome; and embraced the religion of Mohammed in Africa; assembled together in one place to adore a God, in whom they had no faith; and to profess a religion which they despised; *merely*, that they might be enabled to preserve their usurped authority over the people, and to retain their places: this is an occurrence in the history of pious fraud, not to be met with since the days of Judas Iscariot. I may safely venture to affirm, that with the exception of the bishops (if they may be excepted) there was not a single person in the cathedral, who quitted this religious mockery with a sentiment of piety excited in his breast; nor one, who did not perfectly see through the whole object of the ceremony."*

The re-establishment of Popery in France is so far from furnishing an argument against the nation's bearing the character of Antichrist, as has been stated; that it furnishes the decisive argument in favor of it. The Beast from the bottomless pit, (Rev. xvii,) is *bearing*

---

* Letters from France in 1802, vol. i, p. 269.

the Papal harlot to her execution, as has been shown. This implies that the Power symbolized by the Beast has, for some sinister purposes, taken the Papal power into his arms. This same Beast is presented in Rev. xvi, 13; and xix, 20, in this *very connexion with Popery;* which is now (since its subjection to the Antichristian Beast) denominated *the false prophet.* The Beast and the false prophet are there found unitedly instigating the coalition for the battle of the great day; and, in that battle, going together into perdition. The Beast and the false prophet, *who wrought wonders before him*, were taken, *and cast into the lake of fire burning with brimstone.* In chap. xx, 10, after the devil is loosed from his confinement, where he has been, during the Millennium, and is again taken, he is said to be now *cast into the lake of fire and brimstone, where the Beast and the false prophet*, (or Antichrist and the Papal power) *are.* Here is the third passage in the Revelation, where the two Powers are spoken of in this *very connexion; the Beast and the false prophet.* And these three passages accord with Dan. vii, 11; *I beheld then, because of the voice of the great words, which the horn spake, I beheld even till the Beast* (the Roman Beast under his last head, which goeth into perdition) *was slain, and his body destroyed, and given to the burning flame.* In all these passages, Antichrist and Popery are found *in this very connexion.* Accordingly Paul, in sketching the character of Antichrist,* closes the description in these words, *having a form of godliness, but denying the power thereof.* Thus the present nominal religion of the French Empire is so far from furnishing an objection to that Empire's being the *Antichrist of the last time*, that this very circumstance is essential to its sustaining this character; and presents an unanswerable argument in favor of its being the *very* Antichrist.

And no other Power, beside the French Empire, can now possibly be expected to arise on the ground of the old Roman empire, which can answer to the

---

* 2 Thes. iii, 1—5,

predictions of the last terrible Beast; and which can be found in this connexion with the false prophet; and can with him go into perdition, in the battle of the great day. This argument then, in my opinion, approaches near to demonstration, that the French Empire is *that last and terrible head of the Roman Beast; and is the very Antichrist of the last time.*

SECTION VI.

Antichristian Influence in the United States.

WE are not without evidence, that the systematic operations of the Infidelity of the last days, have found their way to this our highly favored nation. It could not be expected, that so fair a portion of the Christian world, as the United States, would escape the insidious attempts of modern Infidels. And we are furnished both with distressing indications, and *direct evidence*, that we have *not* escaped! It may be an unpleasant task to collect and exhibit this evidence. It may excite both ridicule and censure. But these are small considerations, compared with the reproaches of conscience for unfaithfulness in the watchmen. If the latter see evil approaching, and do not sound the alarm, they can never answer it to their fellow men, nor to their own consciences; and much less to their Divine Lord. If Antichristian agency be lurking among us, surely it ought to be detected. No objection can be made against this, unless it be suggested by the enemies themselves, who are using every artifice to effect their own concealment.

Should any say, Where are these wicked agents? Let us see them pointed out to us! Such ought to consider, that the strength of this Infidel order lies in concealment. All their long improvements in the knowledge of human nature, and in the most subtle arts of their order, are exerted to the uttermost to escape detection, as well as to effect their object. We cannot suppose them to have yet forgotten to "*hide the hand, that gives the blow;*" nor to have abandoned their object, which was to "*bind the world with invisi-*

ble hands." No doubt they, with their other refined sub-
tleties, have learnt to suit themselves to their climate;
or to adapt their operations to the times, and to the
genius of the government, and of the people, where
they are making their innovations. Weishaupt himself
has unintentionally disclosed this item of their character. Writing to Plato (Diderot) he says; "I have fore-
seen every thing, I have prepared every thing. Let
my whole order go to wreck and ruin; in three years,
I will answer to restore it; and that to a more perfect
state, than it was before. Obstacles only stimulate my
activity."* No doubt his followers have imbibed the
same sentiment.

Doubtless this order is not now known in America,
by any alarming appellation. But that there *have been*
men and societies in the heart of this nation, in close
connexion with the Illuminees of France, and most
subtly propagating the same designs, is very evident.
And it is a thought distressing to many of the warmest friends of religion, and of their country. That the
same baneful influence is now managed by the dynasty of the French Empire, is not by any means to be
doubted. And to sleep under such danger, will be
death. "There are seasons of infatuation (says an author) when a people, for their sins are permitted to
slumber, and to make no effectual resistance, till *invaders*
(at first *contemptible*) become *fatal.*" Hearken to
this, O civilized nations!

Upon the list of Societies of Illuminism, furnished
by Professor Robison,† several are mentioned as existing in America, before the year 1786. The Abbe Bar-
ruel‡ makes mention of a lodge of this order in Portsmouth, in Virginia; and that two lodges had descended
from it; one in Virginia; and the other in St. Domingo.
In 1785, four Professors of Marianen Academy,
viz. Utschnider, Cosandy, Remer, and Greenberger,
who had withdrawn from the order of Illuminism, and
exposed the wickedness of the scheme, were summoned before a court of inquiry. Their depositions

*Barruel, vol. iv, p. 130.   †Proofs, p. 159.
‡Memoirs, vol. iv, p. 213.

given separately,, under oath, and with their names subscribed, on comparing, appeared perfectly harmonious, in detecting the abominations of the order. And three of these witnesses declared, that while connected with that order, they were repeatedly informed, that Illuminism had extended to Italy, to Venice, to Austria, to Holland, to Saxony on the Rhine, and to *America.** In the original writings of that order, several lodges in America were found on their lists. In a report of a provincial meeting in Randolstown, in Ireland, August 14, 1797, relative to the spark of Illuminism; which caught in Ireland, and threatened a universal blaze, under the denomination of United Irishmen; it is stated, that *a number of these societies were formed in North America; from which, in the then last eight days, a certain sum of money had been received.*

A letter from a man of the first respectability in New England,† written in 1798, says; "Illuminism exists in this country. And the impious mockery of the sacramental Supper, described by Mr. Robison,‡ has been acted here." The writer proceeds to state that his informant, a respectable mason, and a principal officer of that brotherhood, declares, that among the higher orders of masons in this country, this piece of Illuminism (the mockery of the holy Supper) is at times practised. And that this was decisive proof of Illuminism in America; as the celebration of the holy Supper was not, in any sense, a part of the rites of original masonry.

A long official communication was intercepted, from the illuminated lodge Wisdom, in Portsmouth in Virginia, to the illuminated lodge the Union of New York; in which were all the names of the officers and members of the lodge Wisdom; together with their horrid seal, in which were emblems of carnage and death.‖ In this intercepted official document it is ascertained, that the lodge Wisdom in Portsmouth was a branch of

---

*Payson's Mod. Anti. p. 116, 127.
†President Dwight.   ‡Page 138, 139.
‖See Dr. Morse's Fast Sermon, of April 1799.

the Grand Orient of Paris, which was a kind of parliament of all the lodges of the Illuminees in France; that the lodge Wisdom was the 2660th descendant from the Grand Orient; that it consisted chiefly of French emigrants; being then one hundred in number. And there is no room to doubt, but that their object was to revolutionize this country, after the manner of the French revolution. The letter also mentions another lodge of this order, *the Grand Orient of New York,* which had instituted (probably in the heart of our country) at least fourteen other lodges; as the lodge *Union,* to which the intercepted letter was addressed, was the fourteenth branch, instituted by the Grand Orient of New York. How many more than fourteen, the Grand Orient of New York had instituted, was not ascertained. It appears in the letter, that the lodge Wisdom of Portsmouth kept their agent in France, to communicate from their mother lodge, (the Grand Orient of Paris) all needed instruction. Their motto accompanying their seal is significant; the literal rendering of which is this; "Men believe their eyes further than their ears. The way by precept is long; but short and efficacious by example." Here is cautiously hinted the first object of Illuminism; to revolutionize mankind (as to religion and politics) by efficacious craft. Their plan was not for *amusement;* but for *activity,* in objects the most serious.

A very respectable mason, who has been master of all the masonic lodges in the state, in which he resides, has informed, that he was prepared to believe the above account, relative to the lodge Wisdom; having once, by a very natural mistake, while Grand Master, as above hinted, had a communication made to him, but which was designed for that lodge in Virginia; *in which were things wholly above his comprehension.* The communication, by some means, went out of his hands. This was before he had heard of Illuminism.

These lodges of Illuminism were utterly disowned by reputable free masons. And some of their dignitaries, their seal, and their motto, were declared by free masons not to be masonic. In a printed oration de-

23

livered before the Grand Royal Arch Chapter of New York, Feb. 3, A. L. 5801, by Rev. John Ernst, Grand Chaplain of the lodge, and reputable among the masons, is the following; "The unrivalled and deep designs of modern masons, called the Illuminati, who have almost inundated Europe, *and are fast gaining ground in America,* have clearly demonstrated the abuse untyled mason lodges have met with; and how they, when not presided over and guarded by men of genuine masonic principles, can be overthrown, revolutionized, and moulded at pleasure."

A gentleman of high respectability, who belonged to a lodge of the order of ancient masons, in a letter to a friend in New England, dated March 23, 1800, says; "The lodge in Portsmouth, to which you allude, called the French lodge, was considered by me as under the modern term of masonry, (Illuminism.) Its members, in 1789, were mostly French." In a subsequent letter he says; "That you had good grounds to suspect the designs of the French lodge of Portsmouth in Virginia, I have no reason, nor *ever* had, to doubt. And at a time it is evident to me, that their work was to effect the plans of France in this country; and that the bulk of the members, who composed the lodge in 1797, were ready to further any designs, which the French government may have had on this country; and to give their aid, to carry them into effect."

A member of the above mentioned lodge, at the time when Americans thought well of the French revolution, boasted, that he belonged to a lodge in Germany, in which *that revolution was planned!*

The societies of United Irishmen, which have appeared in some of the southern states, have evinced the progress of French Illuminism in this country. The constitution of the American society of United Irishmen, was discovered and published in Philadelphia, in May, 1798; in which it is evident, that their object was to enlist and organize the factious and malecontents, especially foreigners, in the different parts of the United States, into the very scheme of Illuminism. *Equality and Liberty to all men* were held forth in their declar-

ation, and in their test. Each member pledged himself, that he would direct all his efforts to the attainment
of *"Liberty* and *Equality.* to *mankind,* in whatever
country, he may reside." And, "that the test of this
society, and *the intention of this institution,* in all other
respects, than; as a social body attached to freedom,
be considered as *secret and inviolable* in all cases, but
between members, and in the body of the society."
Such a constitution in our states, from such characters,
needs no comment. But its members need the vigilant and jealous eye of every friend of our nation.

A worthy gentleman in Pennsylvania thus writes to
his correspondent in New England; "On the occasion
of the election of citizen McKean, an altar was erected
on the commons, on which the statues of liberty and
peace were placed. Large libations were poured on the
altar by the priests of liberty, who were clothed in white,
with red caps, stuck round with sprigs of laurel: After
which, an ox was sacrificed before the altar, and his
flesh divided among a thousand citizens; while many
republican toasts were drunk by the company. The
ox was likewise adorned with garlands, according to
the Pagan ritual." Christian Americans, did you ever
expect things like these in this nation, so highly favored of Heaven?

The times of ancient Pagan "ignorance God then
winked at." Ancient Pagans had no revelation. Though
the volume of nature was such, as to leave them without
excuse; yet they were infinitely less criminal, than present *Gospel Pagans.* For people under all our light and
privilges to turn *Pagans,* and observe Pagan *rituals,*
is only a specious cover of *wilful, determined Atheism!*
They like not to retain God in their knowledge. Men
cannot turn from Gospel light to heathen gods, with
any real belief in the latter. If they believe not in the
true God, they *cannot* now believe in *Jupiter.* They
are destitute of the honesty and simplicity therefore, of
ancient Pagans. Such are *wilful* and most *criminal
Atheists!* And no wonder the terrors of the battle of
the great day of God will be directed against all such;

while it will be infinitely less terrible *to* (if it reach at
all) nations never favored with the Gospel!

A sect of enthusiasts called New Lights, a few years
ago, appeared in Nova Scotia, whose religious and political sentiments were pernicious; and indicated, that
their instigators were of the order of Illuminism. Vol-
ney *on the Ruins of Empires,* a noted instrument of
French Atheism; Paine's Age of Reason; and a flattering account of the French revolution, were read and
privately circulated by these New Lights.

It would be a task indeed to exhibit but a sketch of
all the items of most credible evidence, relative to this
subject.

I lately received the following information from a
respectable man of my acquaintance, and his wife, both
of whom are professors of religion. They inform, that
about ten years ago, their son had occasion to reside for some months in **********, a capital town
in one of the middle states: And that when he returned, to their great astonishment and grief, he returned
an *Atheist;* as he has ever since remained; neglecting
and despising all religious order. They learnt from
him, that while he was in that capital, he became con-
versant with a society there, instituted under French
agency, with a view to propagate the sentiments which
he had imbibed. He spoke to his parents of his attending an entertainment in that society, at which the guests
were about sixty; and such an entertainment in point
of elegance, as he never before saw; the *plate* being of
immense value. From which we may infer, that the
members of that society were persons of affluence and
rank. After their son returned home, he went and resided for several years in an old town, in a state adjacent to that, in which his parents reside. There a society was instituted (as the parents learnt from their son)
of the same nature with the society, in which he had
imbibed his Atheism; and embracing some very *influential* characters. This society instituted a printing
office in a neighboring town, for the purpose of justify-
ing French measures; and of propagating the sentiments
of their order. This was about the time the envoys of

President Adams were rejected by France. These
parents informed, that their son often suggested, that
such societies were *abundant;* and were going to prevail through our country; and was very confident, that
within twenty years, not a Gospel minister would be
supported, or heard in our nation; but that such ministers would be *pointed at* as they walked the streets.
He asserted also that all religious order was an impo-
'sition, which would soon be abolished. Such were
the impressions, which this man received from the society in that capital of a middle state. The fullest confidence may be placed in the correctness of the above
account. Alas, shall strangers devour a people, and
they know it not! Shall bands of secret enemies prey
upon the heartstrings of our republic, and be unheeded?
These secret machinations have proved deadly to other
nations. Have we nothing to fear from them? Behold Sampson asleep in the lap of the fascinating harlot,
till his locks are shorn, and he is undone! Behold him
mocked for his credulity; and falling a prey to the insulting lords of the Philistines! To have "armies of
principles prevail, where armies of soldiers could not be
admitted;" to be "bound with invisible hands," and
deprived of every right, sacred and civil, must sting the
enslaved with scorpions of torture, when it is too late!
To subvert religion and even civil order, has been the
object of the scheme, which is proved to have been in
full operation in the Christian world, not excepting
these United States.

Girtanner, in his Memoirs on the French revolution,*
has the following remarks; "The active members of
the club of Propagandists were, in 1791, fifty thousand.
And their general fund for the promotion of their object, was thirty millions of livres, (six millions of dollars.) The Propagandists are extended over the face
of the *world;* having for their object *the promotion of
revolutions and the doctrines of Atheism.* And it is a
maxim in their Code, that it is better to defer their attempts for fifty years, than to fail of success through

* Barruel, vol. ii, p. 245.

too much precipitancy." Let the friends of Zion and of order pause at this, and consider! Fifty thousand, eighteen years ago, of the most sagacious adepts in the wiles of Illuminism! that master-piece of Infidelity, and of infernal artifice, spread over the Christian world, in impious concert, to undermine religion, and every virtuous institution! "For the purpose of overturning, the throne and the altar, they let loose at once those two dogs of hell, *anarchy* and *atheism*." Would so fair a field as America be shunned or overlooked by these agents of darkness? Would not a large portion of their attention be turned to this western hemisphere, which has been the envy of the old nations? None can doubt it. Recollect their object! "the promotion of revolutions, and the doctrines of Atheism." Their means are powerful; "*bundles of lies;*" as a chief of their own order described them;* subtility and all the craft, which party interest and local circumstances can suggest; or which the infernal dragon can devise; together with a fund of six millions of dollars, nineteen years ago, (and doubtless a sufficiency of millions since added) to *bribe* and to *corrupt!* If one sinner can "destroy much good," as inspiration asserts, what may not these united legions effect? Behold their caution, and their perseverance; creeping in disguise; urging on, or withdrawing, as circumstances may direct; and this for fifty years; rather than fail of success through too much precipitancy. Need we wonder, that Infidelity and *other* evils have unitedly increased? The effects of these agents of wickedness, and of disorganization, have been very visible: and they have placed in jeopardy our dearest interests.

No doubt since the exposure of the object and wiles of the Voltaire system of Infidelity, the exertion of its agents for concealment have been redoubled. But can we suppose their societies in our nation to have been annihilated? We have no *reason* thus to believe. It is *far* more probable, that their numbers are greatly increased; that their exertions have been stimulated by

---

* See Robison's Proofs, p. 135.

their successes; and that their expectations are sanguine.

Antecedently to the development of the system of
Illuminism; and while its agents were less on their
guard, how evident and disgusting were the interfer-
ences of French agents, in the affairs of our nation? We
have not forgotten the conduct of Genet, their agent at
Philadelphia, who appealed from our venerable Wash-,
ington, then in the chair of the nation, to the people;
representing him in a hateful light, as intriguing to deprive the people of their liberties. So impudent was
his attempt to alienate the Americans from their own
government, even from the first political father of the
nation himself! Genet had previously at Geneva pursued the same detestable policy; which proved fatal to
that incautious people. And the same abominable kind
of agency has destroyed every republic, on the eastern
side of the Atlantic; that of Lucca, Pisa, Venice, the
thirteen republics of Switzerland, that of the Seven
Isles, of St. Marino, of Genoa, of the Netherlands, and
all the free cities of Germany. But one republic, *our
own*, remains on earth! Robespierre, in his rivalship
with the Brissotine faction, exposed the *real object* of
Genet's commission to America, in the following charge;
"Genet, their minister at Philadelphia, made himself
chief of a club there, and never ceased to make and
to excite commotions, equally injurious to the government." For this conduct of Genet, his recall was procured by the firm patriotism of Washington. But this
French Illuminee took up his residence in America.
And we must naturally conjecture that his subsequent
exertions were abundant; though conducted with greater caution.

The French became sensible, that greater caution
was necessary in carrying on their schemes in America.
But their object was not relinquished; as was evident
from many things; particularly from Fauchet's intercepted letter, in 1795. In this that French minister,
speaking on the insurrection in the western counties
of Pennsylvania, says of those insurgents; "Republicans
by principle, independent by character and situation,

they could not but accede with enthusiasm to the criminations, which *we had sketched for them.*" Here
we learn, from the French minister *himself*, that the
western insurrection, which under the Washington ad-
minstration disturbed and endangered the peace of our
states, and cost the nation a million of dollars, originated in French agency; in the "criminations," which
(says Fauchet) we had sketched for them." Will
Americans forget this? Here is hinted the origin of
our calamities. ... Could we at once see all, that the same
agency, and the minions of their order have *sketched*
with the same general design, it would no doubt give a
striking view of the depravity of the human heart, and
of the manner, in which Satan deceives the nations.

President Washington saw and lamented the prevalence of this hateful influence; as is evident from many
things; particularly from the following extracts from
his letters. In a letter of 1794, addressed to one of the
first characters of our nation, (Mr. Jefferson,) he says;
"As you have mentioned the subject yourself, it would
not be frank, candid, or friendly (in me) to conceal, that
your conduct has been represented as derogating from
that opinion, which I conceived you entertained of me;
that to your particular friends—*you* have described (me)
and they have denounced me, as a person under a dangerous influence; and that if I would listen more to
some other opinions, all would be well. Until the last
year or two, I had no conception, that parties would,
or even *could* go the lengths I have been witness to.
Nor did I believe, until lately, that it was within the
bounds of probability, hardly within those of possibility,
that, while I was using my utmost exertions to establish a national character of our own, independent, as far
as our obligations and justice would permit, of every
nation on earth; and wished by steering a steady course
to preserve this country from the horrors of desolating
war, I should be accused of being an enemy to one nation, and subject to the influence of another. And to
prove it, that every act of my administration would be
tortured; and the grossest and most insidious misrepresentations of them would be made, by giving one

side only of a subject, and that too in such exaggerated
and indecent terms, as could scarcely be applied to a
Nero, to a notorious defaulter—or even to a common
pickpocket. But enough of this. I have—gone
further in the expression of my feelings, than I intended."

In a letter to the Hon. Charles Carrol, in 1798, he
says; "Although I highly approve of the measures taken
by government, to place this country in a posture of
defence, and even wish they had been more energetic;
and shall be ready to obey its call, whenever it is made;
yet I am not without hope, mad and intoxicated as the
French are, that they will pause, before they take the
last step. That they have been deceived in their calculations on the division of the people, and the powerful support from *their party*, is reduced to a certainty; though it is somewhat equivocal still, whether
that party, who have been the *curse of this country!*—
may not be able to *continue their delusion.*" Alas,
they have continued it! Upon the Jay treaty, (under
the operation of which, the country enjoyed the greatest prosperity; but which was most violently opposed
by the opposition under the Washington administration, who have since been the ruling party in our
country;) President Washington thus wrote, in a letter
to the secretary of State; "There is too much reason
to believe, from the pains that have been taken *before,*
at, and *since* the advice of the Senate, respecting the
treaty, that the prejudices against it are more general,
than has been imagined. How should it be otherwise?
when no stone has been left unturned, that could im-
press on the minds of the people the most *arrant mis-*
representations of facts: that their rights have not only
been neglected, but absolutely *sold:*—that the benefits
(of the treaty) are all on the side of Great Britain;
and what seems to have more weight with them, (the
opposition party) than all the rest, and has been more
pressed, that the treaty was made with the design to
oppress the French republic, and is contrary to every
principle of *gratitude* and sound policy. If the treaty
is ratified, the *partizans of the French,* or rather of *war*

24

and confusion," (Mark these words of the venerable Washington, O reader! uttered so many years since; and while he was in the chair of state, relative to the leaders of those, who styled themselves *Republicans;* and relative to their great hostility to the *Jay treaty,* which was found to be so advantageous to these States; and which prevented a rupture then with Britain, and a consequent alliance with France! Mark the words of our political Father.) "If the treaty is ratified, the *partizans of the French, or rather, of war and confusion,* will excite them to hostile measures." President Washington made no stick here, and in other letters, at calling the leaders of democracy, *"partizans of the French:"* And he even adds, *"of war and confusion!"* Had he not seen full evidence that they *were* thus, he never would have risked such suggestions. President Washington proceeds in his letter. "It is not to be inferred from hence, that I *am* or *shall* be disposed to quit the ground I have taken. (i. e. of peace with England, and strict neutrality.) For there is but one straight course; and that is to seek truth, and to pursue it steadily. But these things are mentioned to shew, that a close investigation, of the subject is more than ever necessary; and that there are strong evidences of the necessity of the most circumspect conduct, in carrying the determinations of government into effect with prudence, as respects our own people."

In a letter to Mr. Jay, President Washington, (relative to *those societies,* which at first appeared very *bold,* and were set up in imitation of the *French Jacobinic societies;* and even took this name; but afterward became far more cautious,) that venerable patriot says, "That the self created societies, who have *spread themselves over this country,* have been laboring incessantly to sow the seeds of distrust, jealousy and of course, discontent; hoping thereby to effect some *revolution in the government,* is not unknown to you. That they have been the fomenters of the western insurrection, admits of no doubt." This was the rebellion, of which our present Secretary of the treasury was at the head; and to suppress which, President Washington raised fifteen thousand men. President Washington in his next speech to Congress, says; "When in the calm moments of reflection the citizens shall have retraced the origin and progress of this insurrection, let them determine whether it has not been fomented by combinations of men, who have disseminated, (from ignorance, or perversion of facts,) suspicions, jealousies, and accusations of the whole government." That great man, then at the head of his country, clearly saw the *danger*, that was rising, and the *origin* of it. And he did not scruple at all to call them *a French party, the curse of this country, spread in societies over the nation, incessantly laboring to sow the seeds of distrust, jealousy and discontent; hoping to effect some revolution in the government!* He himself by them was called a *traitor;* and held up in the most hateful light. How is it possible the eyes of the people could be so blinded, relative to things so evident, the origin of our national calamities? How strange and interesting was the fact, that after *that* influence prevailed in this nation, the very man, (a very suspicious foreigner, from the countries, where the Voltaire principles had corrupted the heart of the community,) the very *man*, who had headed the above insurrection in the western counties, was selected, above all other men in America, to be the Secretary of our national treasury, and one of the first in the cabinet council!

In the noted paper, the *Aurora*, published under the eye of Mr. Jefferson, there was shamelessly given to the public the following, on the retirement of President Washington from office; "Lord now lettest thou thy servant depart in peace: for mine eyes have seen thy salvation," was the pious ejaculation of a man, who beheld a flood of happiness rushing in upon mankind. If there ever was a time, that would license the reiteration of the exclamation, *that time is now arrived.* For the man, who is the source of all the *misfortunes of our country*, is this day reduced to a level with his fellow-citizens—is no longer possessed of power to *multiply evils* upon the United States. If ever there was a period for rejoicing, this is the moment. Every heart in

unison with the freedom and happiness of the people,
ought to beat high with exultation, that the name of
Washington from this day ceases to give currency to
political iniquity, and to legalize corruption! A new
era is now opening upon us; and an era, that promises
much to the people. For public measures now stand
upon their own merits; and nefarious projects can no
longer be supported by a *name.* When a retrospect is
taken of the Washington administration, for eight
years, it is a subject of the greatest astonishment, that
a single individual could have cankered the principles
of republicanism in an enlightened people, and should
have carried his designs against the public liberty so
far, as to have put in jeopardy its very existence. Such
however are the facts. And with these staring us in
the face; this day ought to be a *jubilee* in the United
States."

The language of the French, when the envoys of
President Adams were rejected in France, evinces how
much they calculated on the success of their agents and
influence in this nation. They insolently boasted, that
they well knew their strength in America; and that let
them do what they would, they could turn all the odi-
um of it here upon those who favored not their designs. These things all accord with the arts of Illuminism. And they indicate how firm a footing was
then obtained in this land, by that diabolical system.

Subsequent events in our States, which well accord
with all, that has been noted in this section, are fresh
in every memory, and need not be mentioned. But
what has been passing may well remind us of the following prophetic traits in the character of Antichrist,
and of his agents, viz. *False accusers, fierce; despisers of them that are good; traitors; heady, high-
minded; crept in unawares; despising government;
having men's persons in admiration because of advantage; presumptuous, selfwilled; not afraid to
speak evil of dignities; beguiling unstable souls;
promising liberty, while they themselves are the servants of corruption; filthy dreamers; murmurers,
complainers; speaking evil of things, which they*

know not; ungodly men, walking after their own lusts; these be they that separate themselves.

Much has been seen in modern times, on more than one side of the Atlantic, which appears like an inchoative fulfilment of these prophetic strokes. The rise of Antichrist is from *the bottomless pit.** The devil gives him his power, and seat, and great authority. But the devil is a liar from the beginning. *Falsehood* then, is to be an essential mean of the propagation of the principles of Antichrist. Of the events of this period we accordingly read;† *In transgressing and lying against the Lord, and departing away from our God, speaking oppression and revolt, conceiving and uttering from the heart words of falsehood; and judgment is turned away backward, and justice standeth afar off; for truth is fallen in the streets, and equity cannot enter. Yea, truth faileth; and he that departeth from evil maketh himself a prey.* What follows this passage, being a prediction of the battle of the great day, and of the commencement of the Millennium, decides, that the above prophetic picture relates to the rise and wickedness of Antichrist. And the *lying spirit* of that day is no less than *four times* expressly noted in that concise prophetic description. *Lying against the Lord—conceiving and uttering from the heart words of falsehood—truth is fallen in the streets —yea, truth faileth.* Perfectly does the scheme of Illuminism accord with this description. And too perfectly does much, which our ears have heard, accord with it. We may expect when the above predictions are fulfilled, those, who propagate falsehoods, will by no means acknowledge this their wickedness, but will deny it, and highly resent every imputation of it. Their object is to fasten the falsehood upon others; and to propagate their own schemes under fair pretences.

But the Holy Ghost says, *they lie against the Lord; they conceive and utter from the heart words of falsehood; that with them truth is fallen in the streets; yea, truth faileth!* And charity itself is by no means at-

* Rev. xvii.   † Isa. lix, 13.

liberty to disbelieve this distressing account! It will be found to be verified.

The prophecies relative to the last days are such, as may well lead us to expect, that this great nation of ours will not escape the Infidelity, dissensions and judgments of that period. Old corrupt, Popish countries no doubt, will share more largely in the tremendous scenes of the last days. But we have no ground to believe our nation will escape. Some of the last of the vials, no doubt, will reach us, as having the mark of the Beast. All, who partake of Babylon's sins, shall receive of her plagues. Though the fatal judgments of the battle of the great day may open in Palestine, the scenes will roll through the Antichristian empire; and to the ends of the world. *A whirlwind shall be raised up from the ends of the earth. The evil shall run from nation to nation. All, who partake of Babylon's sins, shall receive of her plagues. The whole earth shall be devoured with the fire of my jealousy. He shall destroy the sinners thereof out of it. And the slain of the Lord shall be many, from one end of the earth, even to the other end of the earth. According to their deeds, accordingly he will repay, fury to his adversaries, recompense to his enemies, to the isles he will repay recompense. So shall they fear the name of the Lord from the west, and his glory from the rising of the sun; when the enemy shall come in like a flood, the Spirit of the Lord shall lift up a standard against him. For behold the day cometh, that shall burn as an oven, and all the proud, yea, and all that do wickedly shall be as stubble, and that day that cometh shall burn them up, saith the Lord of hosts, that it shall leave them neither root nor branch.* And many other predictions there are, of the judgments of that day, which seem evidently to give them a far greater extent than the Roman earth.

Such being the tenor of the predictions, relative to the battle of that great day of God Almighty, America can by no means expect to escape its terrors.

The wicked agency and seductions of Antichrist then, must here be experienced. We shall, to a greater or less degree, be partakers of his sins, and receive of his plagues. And we have reason, from these considerations, and from the general language of the prophecies relative to Antichrist and the last days, to believe that *that* licentious, and Atheistical influence must be *at this time* in full operation in this land.

Let none then deceive you, by treating lightly the warnings relative to this subject; or insinuating that they are chimerical. People, who are *inclined* to Infidelity, as well as the real agents of Antichrist, will no doubt discredit every such warning. *If ye were of the world, the world would love his own.* There will be a strange blindness in the wicked world, relative to the agency and seductions of Antichrist. *None of the wicked shall understand; but the wise shall understand.* When any therefore despise the warnings given upon this subject; consider well their characters, to what class they belong, and what connexions, or influence may induce them to wish to keep concealed the iniquity of the system, which is so manifest in the world. And *take heed that no man deceive you.*

SECTION VII.

The views and conduct of the French Government.

I HAVE had no doubt but the essence of that profound scheme, which produced the French revolution, is now by the Imperial government of France employed with the most fatal success, in nations marked out for conquest. It was a system calculated to assume new colors and shapes, with the occurrence of new circumstances; and to become an engine of mischief in the hands of any successive dominant power, that is wicked enough to flatter it, and adopt the use of it. Though for a time it had the subversion of all *civil subordination*, as well as of *religion*, for its object; yet when France fell under a military despotism, her great *principal* and his minions well knew how to take this powerful engine into their hands, and to accommodate it to their purposes of universal dominion. Since finishing the writing of this volume, I have found evidence directly in point upon this particular in a late publication, "On the Genius and Disposition of the French Government," by an American recently returned from Europe. On perusing the book, I have been induced to insert this section, in order to exhibit some thoughts contained in it, interesting to the nations, particularly to our own; and corroborating the sentiments stated in the preceding section relative to that diabolical, secret French agency. The author of that book undertakes to disclose the truth, the result of his long inquisitive investigations as a *traveller.* He appears to be a man of first rate abilities and information; and a man of candor. He acknowledges that he had been greatly prepossessed against the British politics. He travelled for a course of years in Europe, on purpose to gain correct information. For a considerable time he resided in Paris; and had access to, and gained the confidence of, men of the first information there. And his communications carry with them great evidence.

In this book, are the following sentiments, concerning the views and conduct of the French government. The writer describes it as being "a power, which, circumscribed by no law, and checked by no scruple, meditates the subjugation of *this,* as well as of every other country." He further says, that "it is a sytematic plan of the government of France to grasp at universal dominion;" that "*we* not only share with the British in the hatred, which is cherished against them by the cabinet of St. Cloud; but are equally marked out for destruction." "Gentz in his *Fragment on the balance of power,* enumerates three traits in the present constitution of France, which according to his idea, must render her irresistible. 1, The unlimited form of her government. 2, The decisive influence of the military character over the whole system. 3, Their successful employment of *revolutionary instruments and means!* Add to these the federal strength, which she has acquired by the extension of her limits; the torpor, which seizes almost every nation, even at the name of France; the subtlety of her statesmen; and the skill of her commanders; and it will be at once apparent that she may bid de-

fiance to the united efforts of Europe. It was long predicted by a great writer, who had studied the affairs of
modern Europe, "that the continent would be speedily
enslaved, should a nation, with the resources of France,
break through the forms and trammels of the civil institutions of the period, turn her attention to military affairs, and organize a regular plan of universal
empire." Gen. Jourdan exultingly exclaimed to the
French Convention, when about to enact their law of
the *requisition;* "The moment you announce the com-
pulsory *levy en masse* to be permanent, you decree the
power of the republic to be imperishable." The determination of France for universal empire, is "the result
of a deliberate project—framed and acted upon, even
before the reign of the Directory!" This conclusion
was "sanctioned by the acknowledgment of all the actors in the scene of the revolution, with whom I had
occasion to converse (says the writer) in Paris." The
archives of antiquity have been ransacked by the French,
to collect the arts of fraud, terror and seduction, that
they might combine cunning with force, to deceive,
overwhelm, and confound mankind: "Combining the
subtlety of the Roman senate, and the ferocity of the
Goth;—the wildest passions with the most deliberate perfidy;—they have far exceeded all the examples furnished by the records of antiquity."* "From the commencement of the revolution, emissaries have been scattered
over Europe, in order to study and delineate its geographical face. The harvest of their labors, deposited
at Paris, has furnished their government with a knowledge of the territory of the other powers, much more
minute and accurate, than what the latter themselves
possess." Several hundreds of clerks are employed at
Paris in this business, of collecting these details, trac-
ing maps, and aiding the accomplishment of this great
plan. Spain was thus marked out before her invasion.
And England has been thus partitioned. The designs
of France upon Spain were all previously matured.
The writer heard it much conversed upon in the me-

* See Rev. xiii, 2, where all the terrors of the ancient empires are combined in this Roman Beast.

25

tropolis, that the Bourbons were to be dethroned in Spain, and a Bonaparte placed in their stead. And for years before the seizure of the royal family, Spain was deluged with French *emissaries*, to prepare the way for the event. The universal empire of the French is the popular song at Paris, and in different parts of the nation. *Paris, the metropolis of the world,* is the great idea with which the people not only of Paris, but of the provincial cities, and of the country, are enamored, when they can so far forget their own wretchedness, as to turn their attention to it.

Upon Russia the writer remarks; "The divisions of the Russian cabinet, and the preponderancy of a French faction at St. Petersburgh, *which now sways their national council,* constitute another and great source of weakness. The French partizans have subdued the spirit of Alexander, by an exposition of the impotency of his means; and have debauched his principles by specious statements of the benefits he is to derive from French alliance."

With respect to the old Jacobinic agency being successfully employed by the present French government, the writer remarks as follows; "But there is another species of hostility preliminary to open violence, and scarcely less efficacious in the end, which they are now indefatigably waging against *this country* (America.) They are in fact at war with us, to the utmost extent of their means of annoyance. What the sword fails to reach may be almost as destructively assailed by the subtile poison of corrupt doctrines, by domestic intrigue, by the diffusion of falsehood, and by the arts of intimidation. The world has not more to dread from their comprehensive scheme of military usurpation, than from the *co-extensive* system of seduction and *espionage,* which they prosecute with a view, either to supersede the necessity, or to insure the success, *of conquest by arms.* Upon the model of their domestic policy in this respect, they have established a secret inquisition into the manageable vices and prejudices, into the vulnerable points, as well as the strong holds, of every country, obnoxious to their ambition. As they station a spy in every dwelling of the French empire, so they plant traitors every where abroad, to corrupt by bribes, to delude by promises, to overawe by threats, to inflame the passions, and to exasperate the leading antipathies, *of every people.* As they maintain by their domestic police an intestine war in France herself, so by their foreign missions they sow every where abroad the seeds of division and discontent. They foment the animosities of faction, and prepare the train for the explosion, which, by disuniting and dissipating the *single*, as well as *federative* strength of a nation, lays her completely at their mercy."

The writer proceeds to give a striking account of the perfection, to which the art of *espionage* is wrought in France; every family and even individual being watched by some secret spy; so that none can with safety communicate his sentiments to another, unless they be such as the government would approve. He states an account given by one, who had been a chief clerk in one of the offices of this diabolical machination. The clerk informs, that when the revolution in France was accomplished, he thought the object of this business was obtained and finished; and that great was his surprise, when he found it *continued!* And concerning the *extent* of this secret agency, he proceeds; "By means equally profligate they exercise a supervision over *other countries*, and improve to their own advantage whatever principles of corruption and disunion may be interwoven with their social or political constitutions. These French agents never loiter in the discharge of their functions, nor sleep on their watch. No means nor instruments, however contemptible in appearance, are neglected in the prosecution of their plans. It is notorious, that even the foreigners employed in the theatres and opera houses *of Europe*, to minister to the public amusements, are marshalled in the service of the French government, for the purpose either of collecting information themselves, or of facilitating the labors of more intelligent agents. The Gazettes of every part of the continent of Europe are debauched by *largesses*, or driven by *force*, to war against humanity, by propagat-

ing the misrepresentations of this horrible despotism.
During the peace of 1802, an attempt was made to enlist the principal Gazettes of England in the same cause.
A person of the name of Fievee, who has since officia-
ted as editor of the *Journal de l' Empire*, was deputed
to England on what he boastingly styled, *un voyage de
corruption.* He returned however unsuccessful; and
vented his own spleen, as well as that of his government, in a libellous book on the British nation.

This foreign police (adds the writer) was propagated
under the old *regime.* During the reign of Jacobin-
ism the number of its agents was multiplied, and its
activity greatly increased. *Those means, he says,
which were employed by—the Jacobins, to subvert all
governments, are now, under the military despotism of
Bonaparte, levelled upon a more enlarged plan, and
with more active industry, against the liberties and morals of every people!* That we ourselves are vigorously
assailed, no reflecting man, as it appears to me (says
the writer) can for a moment doubt. Inaccessible as
we are at this moment, to any other mode of aggres-
sion, this engine of subjection is used against us with
redoubled force and adroitness. In this way we are
perhaps more vulnerable than any other people. There
are none, whose party feuds may be more quickly inflamed into the worst disorders of faction. The simplicity and purity of character, by which we are, when
viewed in the aggregate, so advantageously distinguished above the nations of Europe, is almost as favorable
to the designs of France, as the corruption or venality of
her neighbors. *A backwardness to suspect treachery
may entail all the consequences of a willingness to abet
it.* One, who has had an opportunity of observing the
workings of the French influence elsewhere, cannot
possibly mistake the source, from which the politics
of some of our own Gazettes are drawn. The most un-
wearied industry to disseminate falsehoods on the
subjects of Great Britain; a watchful alacrity to make
even her most innocent or laudable acts the subject of
clamor; a steady, laborious vindication of all the measures of France; and a system of denunciation against

those, who pursue an opposite course, are the *distin-guishing features* of the venal presses of Europe; and the symptoms, by which those of our own country may be known. The distance, at which we are placed from the immediate range of the power of France, opens to her 'missionaries here a wide field for invention and exaggeration.' What is by them wickedly fabricated, is innocently believed, and propagated by the multitude of well meaning persons, whose antipathies against England blind them both to the atrocious character, and to the hostile designs of our real and most formidable enemy."*

' With respect to the burdens of the people in France; also with respect to the most perfect organization of the military despotism there, this author gives a most striking view. Their revenue in one year was 402 millions of dollars. But this was something extraordinary. The annual amount of their public burdens, at a moderate calculation, exclusive of a 20 per cent cost of collection, is 240 millions of dollars. The annual expense of the Imperial household is five millions, six hundred thousand dollars. The collectors of the revenue form a complete machine of despotism. Every village and commune has a taxgatherer. He pays to a *particular receiver* of a district. The latter pays to a *general receiver* of a department. Thence it goes into the treasury. But besides these, there are inspectors, verificators, controllers, directors, sub-directors, inspectors, sub-inspectors, clerks, visitors, receivers, excisemen, and a variety of others, all appointed by the emperor, all perfect tools of his ambition, and who serve as a host of spies and of petty tyrants, to devour, to watch, and to manage the people; who are deceived and blinded by duplicity and perfidy. If a man refuse to pay all, that is demanded of him, a file of soldiers are immediately quartered upon him, till his tyrants are satisfied.

' The post-office establishment is of the same complexion. Every communication is examined; and noth-

ing passes, but what accords with the views of the emperor. In Paris only, thirty clerks are constantly employed in opening and copying letters in the post-offices.
"The feudal vassalage (says the writer) never exerted
an influence half so pernicious," as the present influence of the French despotism. "The anarchy of the
revolution relaxed the springs of industry, and destroyed the influence, and banished the consolations of religion. And the present government have neither strengthened the *one*, nor restored the *other*." The writer ascertains the violent enmity of the emperor against commerce in general, as inconsistent with that universal
military despotism which he designs. Yet Bonaparte
studiously dissembles this enmity. "The assurances of
his unremitting solicitude (for commerce) are loud and
solemn, just in the degree, that they are insincere and
unproductive." At times his enmity bursts forth.
"He told a deputation of merchants from Hamburgh,
that he *detested commerce and all its concerns*." And on
various occasions he has expressed the same sentiment.
And all his regulations tend to annihilate commerce.
*Such is the genius and state of the Power, which has ris-
en in the world!*

The writer set himself to find the feelings and views
of the French government with respect to our United
States. He for ten months was much in the company,
and had the confidence of persons, "whose contiguity to
the throne, and whose political stations and connexions
opened to them the sources of correct information."
Many of the facts and reasons, on which their opinions
were founded, were confidential, and may not be exposed. But general information is given by this writer,
that the French are not wanting in the keenest hostility
to America. On their official communications, dependence is not to be placed.

The writer ascertains, that ever since the revolution in France, their views have been hostile to this country. And that nothing since has occurred to allay their
enmity and contempt; but that these passions are much
augmented. We are identified with the British. Our
refusing hitherto to unite with France against England,

also our liberties and popular institutions; these are *unpardonable offences with the emperor.* The general language of all in France, in office, and out, is *hatred* and *contempt* of America:—"That we are a nation of fraudulent *shopkeepers;* British in prejudices and predilections; and equally objects of aversion to the emperor; *who had taken a fixed determination to bring us to reason, in due time.*" "The British he hates, dreads, and respects. The people of this country he detests, and despises." This latter idea is there universally understood; and that we are finally to feel the *whole weight of the emperor's resentment!* Every act of humiliation on our part increases the evil. And notwithstanding the tumultuous affairs of France, "we are followed with an acute and malignant eye.—Our Gazettes are diligently searched at the instigation of the emperor himself; and such parts as relate to his character and views, extracted and submitted to his inspection. The invectives, with which many of them abound, are read with the bitterest resentment, and uniformly with denunciations of vengeance." Bonaparte said to several foreign ministers, in 1807, *I have sworn the destruction of England, and will accomplish it: And thenceforward. I will trample under foot all the principles of neutrality.*

These and many more of the same character, are the communications of this traveller, lately from France; and they appear worthy of every degree of confidence. Thus (as this writer expressly informs us) the fatal engine framed in the school of Voltaire, which managed the French revolution, and which planted its emissaries through the civilized world, is "*now under the military despotism of Bonaparte, levelled upon an enlarged plan, and with more active industry, against the liberties and morals of every people.*" And "*we are vigorously assailed with this engine of subjection, —with redouble force and adroitness.* *

* Thus much from the late publication.
I shall here subjoin a *royal Spanish Order,* of August, 1810. It will throw some light on this subject. The council and re-

Thus most evident and extensive is this system of French espionage, and secret mischievous agency. The United States are stocked and poisoned with them! Here they range without fear! Here is their place of rendezvous for this western continent! says the Spanish proclamation, in the note below. *"His majesty being assured that those emissaries are assembled in the United States of America!"* Americans; if you have

gency of Spain and the Indies, in the name of Ferdinand VII, issued the following order. "Having received information that the universal disturber of Europe, Napolean Bonaparte, is about sending *emissaries* and *spies*, from various quarters, to the Spanish transatlantic possessions, and that he has already sent some with the base design of destroying their tranquillity, and introducing sedition and anarchy, since he cannot reach those remote regions with his forces; and his majesty being assured that those emissaries (among whom there are some unnatural Spaniards) are *assembled in the United States of America,* from whence they endeavor by artifice and deceit to penetrate by land into the Province of Texas, or embark for other Spanish possessions; his majesty is resolved, that no Spaniard, under any pretence whatever, shall be permitted to land in any of the ports of said dominions without presenting authentic documents and passports, granted by the legitimate authorities resident in the places from whence they may proceed, in the name of our king and master, Ferdinand the VIIth, proving, in a manner beyond all doubt, the legitimacy of their persons, and the object of their coming:—That the Viceroys and other military and civil authorities observe and execute this royal determination with the utmost exactness, and cause it to be observed:—That if, through any of those incidents, which cannot always be avoided, one of the said emissaries or French spies effect his introduction in said country, by sea or land, he be brought immediately and without delay, to trial, sentenced to capital punishment, and executed:—And lastly, that they proceed to the seizure and confiscation of the vessel, in which such spy may come, together with the cargo; which last regulation is to be equally observed with regard to the vessels of all nations, for the single act of introducing persons not furnished with the proper licences given by legitimate authorities in the name of Ferdinand the VIIth, even should they be natives of these dominions."

Signed, JUAN STOUGHTON, *Consul of Spain.*

Consulate Office,
Boston, Aug. 17, 1810. }
Made public.

any regard to the land of your fathers, and of your nativity, remember this; and improve the hint! Are emissaries assembled here, with a view to subvert the dominions of Spanish America; and yet no designs formed, and no exertions made against the United States? And what are those exertions from the agents of a system, which depends on the *"prevalence of armies of sentiments, where armies of soldiers cannot be introduced?"* The intelligent and judicious cannot be at a loss, if they but attend to the subject.

I shall here subjoin some extracts from M. Faber, (not the *British* Faber, but the *German*,) as they are found in the *"American Review,"* printed at Philadelphia, No. II, April, 1811; page 259.

M. Faber, at the time of the French revolution, flew from Germany to France, to aid in what he deemed the work of rendering mankind happy. He was cordially received. And being a man of great erudition, he obtained some important posts in the civil administration. He continued there a number of years. But finding the character of the French to be most abandoned, and their wickedness to exceed all bounds, his conscience roared upon him; and he fled from that abandoned Sodom. He took refuge in Russia. There he wrote his "Sketches of the internal State of France." This work is entitled to full confidence. Bonaparte himself was so alarmed at this correct development of French abominations, that he exerted his power, by flatteries and threats, with Alexander, emperor of Russia, to have the work suppressed.

From this very able and interesting production large quotations are given, in the above named *American Review.* The pictures drawn are most horrible. It is believed, that the enormities exceed all the fruits of human depravity, ever before known on earth. A few samples here exhibited must suffice for multitudes of the same complexion.

The author says; "The most extraordinary phenomenon ever known, a prodigy unexampled in the history of mankind, is now exhibited in France: I mean, the regular, systematic, elaborate organization of *false-*

26

hood, as the basis of the government, and the soul of all its acts; a total abnegation, (renunciation or denial) in favor of the military Ruler, of all individual feeling, of all personal character, and almost of all private thought. The public functionaries *universally,* who perform the parts, and speak the language assigned them by their master, give up all moral liberty, and sacrifice totally and without reserve, *truth, conviction, conscience, honor,* and *principle.* When the senators, counsellors of state, or any of the chief dignitaries of the empire, *speak,* we know that they do of course but repeat the words of their master, and ply their trade with servility." Again M. Faber says, "In France falsehood is proclaimed as truth under the warrant of every possible official form, and attested as such in the face of those, who know the fact to be otherwise. You find every public functionary asserting, before the universe, that, which he does not believe, and discarding all pretentions to good faith in the opinion of those, who are about him. Every day, every hour is marked by some gross falsehood, which, passing from mouth to mouth, begins at length to wear the guise of truth, in consequence of the unanimity, with which it is rehearsed." He adds, "all the proceedings of their public functionaries, all their official papers, contradict their private convictions, and the opinions, which they are known secretly to entertain, and which most of them have heretofore openly and ostentatiously expressed."

This author proceeds to give in detail many particulars of this most infernal system of iniquity, and falsehood. And for years he had every advantage to know this system; having the most intimate connexion with it.

To people of our habits, these things appear strange, if not utterly incredible. But the word of God positively and abundantly predicts the rise of just such a Power in the last days; rising from the bottomless pit, under the immediate agency of the father of lies; and the devil giving him his power and seat and great authority:—Being in *covenant with death and at an*

*agreement with hell, and under falsehood hiding them-
selves; conceiving and uttering from the heart words of
falsehood, so that truth is fallen in the streets and equity cannot enter.* (See Isa. xxviii, 15, 17, 18, and lix,
13—15.) And with most incontestible evidence we
are assured, that these things are exactly fulfilled in
the French Empire; if not fulfilling in *other places!.*

M. Faber remarks, that when we hear those, who
pretend to be the organs of the people, eagerly and
with every artifice of rhetoric, propagating the insidious
falsehoods of their masters, "we feel the most lively
sentiments of contempt and indignation." "It is from
this class of men (he adds) that the system of imposture receive its strongest support. Their baseness is
infectious, and it contaminates the world. Their official testimonies, reechoed on all sides, and translated
from language to language, every where tend to viti-
ate and pervert the public opinion."

In this author we learn, that despotism imposes dejection; and dejection silence. That its victims have
no other consolation, than to mourn in secret. But
that Bonaparte "has robbed his slaves of this last resource; and has not left them even the enjoyment of
their own solitary reflections. He has pursued them to
this their last retreat; and has forced them to break silence, and to celebrate without intermission, and against
the dictates of their own conscience, the *praises of
their oppressor.* He compels them to feign admiration
and zeal for all his proceedings. The public functionaries are *forced* in their reports, to give those expressions, in glowing colors, *of the public felicity,* which
crowd the columns of the *Moniteur,* (Bonaparte's
official paper.) The miserable people are forcibly
taught and made to speak that language of adulation,
which is poured forth on every side. They are obliged
to violate their consciences in celebrating the praises of
their destroyer.

"To *take* and never to *give;* to demand contribu-
tions of money and of men; but to grant no substantial
favors, is the whole amount of the administrative sci-

ence in France." Yet "when the French government takes, it affects to *give*, and makes a merit of it."

The people, in a *circular*, were informed, that "his Majesty, who is incessantly occupied in consulting the happiness of his people, has not failed to remark, the progress of *industry* and *commerce* and has thought it advisable to advance the interest of both, by enabling them to offer a new resource to the state." This outrage upon truth and insult upon their understandings, was contained in an introduction to the most oppressive and vexatious of all taxes, *the droits ruinis*, when the people were already crushed under the weight of taxes of every description, and commerce and industry were almost totally annihilated.

The following was added, which is here given as a specimen of French deception. "The spring, which commerce and all branches of industry is now taking. requires a correspondent, or proportionate charge of the post-offices.

Nothing can be more just, than a small increase in the rates of postages, when the greater activity of business gives extent to correspondence. The tender solicitude, which his Majesty has uniformly displayed, in favor of commerce, and the encouragement, which he has always labored to give it, vouch for the justice of the measure now adopted."

This was from the man, who had said to a deputation of merchants from abroad, that *he detested, commerce in all its parts;* and who had done every thing in his power to destroy it.

"France now, (says this author) exhibits the extraordinary spectacle of a nation, in which not only is there no individual, who dares utter what he thinks; but in which almost every individual is habitually employed in circulating sentiments, which he knows to be false."

The same spirit of intrigue and falsehood, the author informs, uniformly operates through France, and in their foreign countries. Their military despotism treats with the same perfidy, and rapacious violence, their own cities, and their conquered cities abroad.

The same kind -of- insulting irony, is offered to both, when stripping them of their property; telling them of their *happiness* under the care of him, who feels the most tender concern for their welfare; when they are writhing under the iron gripe of their merciless tyrant.

A part of a city was destroyed in the course of the war. Bonaparte passing through it, issued a decree, that it should be built at the public expense. The inhabitants were then instructed to eulogize him in the following language. "You know how to triumph in war; but your most satisfactory triumph is that of dry-ing up the tears, which war causes to be shed. The sensibilities of your heart are co-extensive with your heroism. You have but to look upon ruins, and they cease to be such; they are instantaneously converted into asylums for the wretched." This was blazed abroad in the public papers. But not the least thing was ever done toward repairing the city. Passing it again, some years after, Bonaparte issued a second de-cree, "for accelerating the labors of the re-construc-tion!!" The part of the city however continued in ruins, He had no revenues to spare for such a work. But his Moniteur again informed the public, of the *lively joy and gratitude, which penetrated the hearts of those citizens toward the hero, who rebuilds their asylums!*

This author observes, that he should never finish, if he undertook to narrate the instances, which daily oc-cur, of the *fraud, cunning, hypocrisy, avarice,* and *ra-pacity,* of the French government; and all under the mask of *generosity* and *clemency.* And not a soul, un-der all the insult, dares to open his mouth. "With respect to that kind of public opinion (he says) which consists in the free manifestation, by a people, of their real feelings and sentiments, there is not a glimmering of it in France." The object of Bonaparte is, that none shall *speak,* or *think,* but in conformity to his object. Gazettes are employed for carrying his sys-tem into effect. "It is his object, that the kind of opinion, of which the Moniteur is now the representa-tive in France, should prevail throughout the world." It is his object, that men shall every where speak alike, in abject servility to him. "He has succeeded (says the writer) in establishing, throughout the greater part of Europe, *the reign of terror.*"

The accounts, which this author gives of the conscription in France, is enough to rend a heart of stone. For parents to see their sons thus dragged to butchery, is a wretchedness, which exceeds all description. But it would exceed my limits to detail the particulars. "Here then (says M. Faber, after describing the conscription, and showing that men of all ages in France are soldiers at command) is the appalling spectacle of a whole nation, the most populous, enterprising and ambitious of Europe, formed into one military mass.— The levy *en masse*, attempted in the revolution, is now calmly and systematically organized, and, grafted permanently on social institutions, industriously shaped, so, as to give it stability; and is made to embrace all conditions and all periods of life, from childhood to old age. A whole people with all their resources, both physical and intellectual, is thus transformed into an instrument of destruction. All France is, in the hands of Bonaparte, but an engine for the subjugation of the world; and one which he wields with the most arbitrary and absolute authority. So it is, by some incomprehensible fatality, that so great a part of the continent of Europe is prostrate before an individual; who nevertheless, is held in universal execration."

SECTION VIII.

Some other causes, which facilitate the spread of Infidelity in our nation, considered.

The American revolutionary war was on our part just and necessary. And the revolution, which gave the Americans a national existence, was among the great events of Providence, which were to prepare the way for the millennial glory of the Church. Yet such is human nature, that this event was attended with sad consequences to our morals. Antecedently to that war, and especially before the war of 1755, the people of this land, particularly of New England, were famous for their purity of morals; and their support and practice of religion. But war and armies, are the bane of morals. Generally a larger portion of the dregs of society, than of men of regular habits, at such a time become soldiers. In the camp the wickedness of the former is augmented, like the glowing of fire, when brands are thrown together. And the moral infection is with facility communicated through the whole army, with few exceptions. Young men thus situated usually soon become vicious; and many to a dreadful degree. The soldier thus corrupted by and by returns home to mingle in society. He must now exhibit what he has learned in the army. His profaneness and vice strongly tend to contaminate his listening associates, and to diffuse a baneful influence, especially through the youthful part of the community. In this way, the morals of our country experienced a sad depression, in the revolution, which gave us national independence. Vice and irreligion soon gained an ascendency. Educational restraints were relaxed and much impaired. And it became with too many an object of ambition to free themselves from the impressions of a religious education, under the notion of a noble independence of thought. The seeds of licentiousness thus extensively sown, became prolific; and the baneful fruit has been produced an hundred fold.

The suspension for a time, in the American provinces, of the restrains and operations of civil law, diffused among a large class of people a spirit of licentious liberty, which could not be without extreme difficulty reduced to proper civil subordination. The operations of this spirit were visible in the course of our revolutionary struggle. And under the subsequent confederation it became in some instances very alarming. And this spirit was prepared to open a distressing avenue to the innovations of modern licentiousness.

The corrupt manners of foreign nations have been copied and adopted in the United States. Our connexions abroad have introduced the vices of old corrupt countries, and have furnished both the knowledge and the means of refined luxury.. These things have gradually prepared the minds of thousands to become unhinged from the principles of the religion of Christ. And Infidelity is the natural result of this process; as fact has lamentably evinced.

And it must be here noted, that our peculiar acquaintance, and connexion formed, in the time of our revolution, with that nation, which was destined in Providence to give birth to Antichrist, or to form the terrible atheistical Power of the last days, have given a great facility to the dissemination of sentiments of licentiousness and Infidelity in this country. That nation, under its monarchy, was induced to aid us; and fought by our side. This circumstance has of course, opened a distressing avenue to intrigues and Infidelity in America.

In viewing the causes of the mischief under consideration in the United States, we find striking evidence, that irreligion, fanaticism and Infidelity, are nearly allied.

Skepticism has occasioned a flood of irreligion; and the latter has been followed by a torrent of systematic Infidelity. The great neglect of religious education, and the means of Christian knowledge in our land, has opened the door to religious imposture; and this powerfully aids the cause of Antichrist. It leads its subjects in the way to Infidelity. The Christian religion in this depraved world demands assiduous cultivation. Youth must be piously restrained. And they must be taught with *line upon line,* and *precept upon precept.* The things of God must be often unfolded and pressed upon them. *Thou shalt teach them diligently unto thy children, thou shalt talk of them when thou sittest in thine house, and when thou walkest by the way, when thou liest down, and when thou risest up.* Family religion, holy precepts and examples, a pious family government, the sanctification of the Sabbath, and the vigilant cultivation of all regular habits; these are means, which God has appointed for the salvation of the rising generation: These are means, which the God of nature has kindly adapted to the support of the Christian faith in families. These means are essential barriers against Infidelity.

But how notorious has been the neglect of these means, in our nation, in late years? How few houses are houses of God? How lamentably has family religion gone to decay? How few of the hundreds of thousands of the American youth, are favored with a strictly religious education? The Sabbath is profaned by many thousands in our land. And the evil has long been rapidly increasing. The public worship of God has, with a great portion of the people, grown into disuse. The means of supporting the Gospel ministry, are covetously withholden by a large part of the community; who thus prefer the darkness of Paganism, to the light of salvation. In short, the doctrines of the Gospel have been perverted; and the main pillars of the Christian system have been attempted to be overthrown.

Yet man has a conscience; and guilty beings under its lashes dread the judgment. *Who among us can dwell with devouring fire? Who can inherit everlasting burnings?* These are questions not instantly disposed of. The conscience is not seared as with a hot iron at once. This is usually a work of time. And some kind of religion in the mean time must be had, to quiet the alarms of guilt. But to embrace the humbling doctrines of the cross; uniformly to endure the restraints, and perform the duties of the pure religion of Christ, is intolerable to the proud heart, to the ignorant and the perverse. Some substitute then, must be adopted; some kind of religion invented, more consonant with the feelings of the wicked; which yet may sooth their consciences. How perfectly are such people prepared to fall a sacrifice to the wiles of some subtile imposture. They have become habituated to despise the genuine doctrines, and the regular order of Christ. And yet not having quite reached gross Infidelity, they seem to want some religion. The fanatic preacher arrives. And there are multitudes of them at this day! He declaims against those doctrines of

27

grace, which are most offensive to the carnal heart; and harrangues upon imaginary doctrines, which are much more pleasing. He proposes a cheap and easy religion; one which allows to man much of that independence and importance, which he claims; a religion, which saves man the labor of diligently searching and comparing the word of God, and of studying his own heart. All is done, both by preacher and hearer, by—*immediate inspiration!* Proselytes become at once first rate Christians; yea, fit for teachers; being admitted to a high and peculiar intimacy with God! They reach at once the top of the mount. Every passion is addressed, and wrought up to the highest pitch. These new fangled Christians are confident, dogmatical, and above the reach of salutary instruction. The regular teachers of religion are by them accounted hirelings, and ignorant of spiritual things. The improvements of such people usually are, to learn the most common cavils against the doctrines of grace. In this they often make great proficiency. And they become a prey to enthusiasm and error, of one denomination or another, according to the notions of their teachers.

Such people are in the high road to Infidelity. Their religion is no better than a dream. Their God is only a fiction; a creature of their own imagination; and no better than an idol. The essential glories of the true God are by them denied, and often with bitterness. Such fanaticism is often followed by Infidelity, at a period not far distant. The human passions are not capable of long retaining such an elevated tone. The feelings will by and by vibrate to the opposite extreme. Such characters, after a series of heats and colds, become tired of their religion. Its novelty is gone. Their former attachment to it sickens into disgust. They find much plain Scripture against their tenets. Yet they will not renounce their scheme for that which is correct. They thus form a habit of perverting the word of God. This conduct prepares them to doubt of the Divine authority of those offensive passages; and they are gradually prepared to doubt of the inspiration of the whole Bible. They become conscious that there is no goodness in *their* religion; and they hence infer, that there is none in that of *other people*. For they readily imagine their own religion, to have been as good as that of others. Often have such persons asserted, that they have been through the *whole* of religion, and have found that there is nothing in it all. Thus their progress of error and fanaticism has carried them to the dreary regions of Infidelity. Such characters will readily become the tools and agents of Antichrist. They have the very *spirit* of Antichrist. And they will act, as far as they find opportunity, essentially the same part of opposition to the Christian cause, with the terrible infidel Power of the last days, even should they not be politically united, or should they not have opportunity to act in immediate concert with that terrible Power. Perhaps national politics may not suffer, that all, who have the *spirit* of Antichrist in the last days, shall be found *politically united with Antichrist*. Many may not be of his armies, or allies, who yet will possess his essential characteristic, *a violent Infidelity;* which will engage them in the same cause of opposition to the kingdom of Christ.

Much has appeared of late, in some parts of our land, *in revivals of Religion*, answering to the blessed prediction, *When the enemy shall come in like a flood, the Spirit of the Lord shall lift up a standard against him.* And this Divine grace will still be fulfilled, to the eventual salvation of Zion. But let not Zion's friends hence lose sight of their dangers, by indulging hopes, which exceed their prospects. God engaged, with ample promises, to restore the Jews from their seventy years captivity in Babylon; and that Jerusalem and the temple should be rebuilt. "Not by might, nor by power; but by my *Spirit*, saith the Lord of hosts." And the event was accomplished. But the walls were built "in troublous times." Though that work had been patronized by such vast authority as the express edict of Cyrus; yet, by the clamor and rage of persecuting enemies, it was wholly suspended for a time. Malicious accusers, round about the Church, sanctioned by the authority of their distant monarch, with force and arms for a season, caused the blessed work to cease. (See Ezra 1—6 chapter.) The *antitype* of this event *may* be experienced in the Church of Christ, just before the introduction of her millennial glory. And the church in this nation may share in the depression. When we consider the small proportion of the people of our nation, who graciously embrace the Christian faith; and the very great numbers, who are subjects of fatal errors, of Infidelity, or of real heathenism; our prospects cannot be otherwise than gloomy. Think of whole sections of our vast territories at but a small remove from heathenism, and that of the worst kind; a heathenism chosen in preference to the Christian religion, by those who had been accustomed to despise the Gospel. The Roman Catholic religion, so offensive to God, and so favorable to the rise of Antichrist, occupies some portion of our country. Its followers in years past, before the acquisition of Louisiana, have been calculated at 50,000. In Louisiana nearly all, that exists of the Christian religion, is of this corrupted kind. And what a vast wilderness of error and heathenism is *there* united to our nation! A great contiguous territory also to the *north* of us is chiefly of the Roman Catholic religion. And too much of the religion now propagated in many of our States, is but too favorable to the growth of Infidelity, and may be expected to land many of its followers on that fatal ground.

In the view of the preceding remarks, and of the dangerous process of fanaticism and false religion, we must believe that many false teachers are among the agents of Antichrist, and are the most successful promoters of Infidelity. Open propagators of Atheism would not be so successful. People would be more likely to be alarmed, and would shun them. But let the same principles be *really* taught in gradual process; and let it be done under the notion of religion, and a pious zeal, and it is far more fatal. People imbibe the poison imperceptibly, and under the belief of its being something salutary. In this way Infidelity is now making rapid progress. We accordingly find, 'that many of the inspired warnings, relative to these last days, are against the seductions of *false teachers.* Says the apostle Peter, when introducing his prediction of Antichrist; *But there were false prophets also among the people, even as there shall be false teach. ers among you, who privily shall bring in damnable heresies, even denying the Lord that bought them; and bring upon themselves swift destruction. And many shall follow their pernicious ways, by reason of whom the way of truth shall be evil spoken of.* Here is one of the modes, and probably the most powerful one, of propagating Infidelity in Protestant countries in the last days. Much of it is done under the guise of religion. False teachers pervert Gospel sentiments. *For the time will come, when they will not endure sound doctrine; but after their own lusts will heap to themselves teachers; having itching ears; and they shall turn away their ears from the truth, and shall be turned unto fables.** When Paul warns of the perilous times of the last days, and notes the wicked characters of men at that period, he adds; *For of this sort are they who creep into houses, and lead captive silly women laden with sins, led away with diverse lusts.*† And repeatedly does Jesus Christ, when speaking of that period, warn against false teachers. *Take heed that no man deceive you; for many shall come in my name,—and shall deceive many.— When they shall say, Lo here is Christ; or lo there; believe them not.* Our Lord forewarns of false teachers at that period, who if it were possible *should deceive the very elect.* False teachers then, in such a land as this, will be among the apostles of Infidelity. Their heresies and schisms tend to bring the Word of God and the Gospel ministry into contempt. The feelings if not the remarks of heedless souls will be, *The preachers cannot agree among themselves; and there is nothing in all their religion!* False teachers unhinge the minds of people from religious habits and instructions; throw them into parties; and prevent both the

---

* 2 Tim. iv, 3.   † 2 Tim. iii, 6.

support, and the improvement, of the regular administration of the Gospel. And among many of their followers, who never come to *profess* gross Infidelity, the
following text is fulfilled; *And with all deceivableness
of unrighteousness in them that perish, because they
received not the love of the truth, that they might be
saved. And for this cause shall God send them
strong delusion, that they should believe a lie; that
they all might be damned, who believed not the truth,
but had pleasure in unrighteousness.*

Let none take an occasion from these remarks on
false teachers and fanaticism, to think unfavorably of
true religious awakenings. Blessed be God, the Holy
Spirit is sent down, as *rain upon the mown grass, and
as showers, that water the earth*, to regenerate dead
souls. This the arch tempter well knows. Hence he
transforms himself into an angel of light; and labors to
discredit these works of grace, and to ruin the souls
of men, by counterfeiting these Divine operations. Fanaticism is but the counterfeit of true religion. But
counterfeits suppose the existence of *true coin*. Learn
then the weight of the following caution; *Believe not
every spirit; but try the spirits, whether they be of God;
because many false prophets are gone out into the world.*

Before I close this section, let several things be noted. Antichrist must be viewed as comprising not
only the Infidel *Empire* of the last days; but also the
spirit and *prevalance* of the *Infidelity* of the same period, where the Gospel has been enjoyed; whether the
people there be or be not subjected to the Infidel Empire.

The system and influence of French Infidelity *may*
extend and prevail where their arms cannot reach
The event alone will decide, whether their *arms* will be
co-extensive with the system of their *Infidelity*. The
latter is their Antichristian characteristic. And *this*
is essentially the same, even where a people may find
themselves exempt from the military despotism of
France. To become contaminated with the *spirit* of
Antichrist, is to be fatally *one* with him. We read of
Antichrist; and of those who have the *spirit* of Anti-

christ. We read of the *Beast;* and of those, who have
the *mark* of the Beast. We are informed of *Babylon;*
and of those, who *partake* of her sins, and shall *receive*
of her plagues. Should not political subjection to
France be effected by Gallic intrigue or violence, for
instance, in America; yet should *that Infidelity* here
prevail, which the old serpent, in his rage of these last
days, is laboring to propagate; which French agents
have introduced; and to which the depraved heart of
man is too readily inclined;—it must then be said, that
Antichrist *here exists!* Should the *political* designs of
France be here disappointed; yet should her system of
Infidelity here predominate; we should be an *Antichristian* nation. The cause of Christ then, might *here* be
attacked, and his *witnesses slain;* even though the event
should be planned in an *American,* and not in a *French*
cabinet.

In some of the preceding pages it has appeared, that
two kinds of influence have concurred in this nation to
bring on the events of the last days; *the agents of
French Infidelity and disorganization; and the propaga-
ters of false religion.* It is not suggested, that these
two classes of persons knowingly act in concert.
Doubtless no express agreement has been made between them. But their affinity is *real.* Their invisible instigators have a system: But multitudes who are
made the instruments of it, know not the nature or the
tendency of what they propagate.

Some of the prophecies, it is thought, indicate a *third*
influence or agency, uniting to advance the same wicked cause. *And I saw three unclean spirits like frogs
come out of the mouth of the dragon, and out of the
mouth of the Beast, and out of the mouth of the false
prophet. For they are the spirits of devils working
miracles, (wonders) which go forth unto the kings of
the earth, and of the whole world, to gather them to
the battle of that great day of God Almighty.* Although this prediction relates to the period after the
sixth vial, and is to prepare the way for the *seventh,* both

* Rev. xvi, 13, 14.

of which are now future; yet the height to which this three-fold agency will *then* have risen, seems clearly to indicate, that its origin must have been of *long stand-ing*, or from earlier date. The text does not say that their *origin* is subsequent to the sixth vial; although it gives notice of them at that period. Their exist-ence, no doubt will prove to have been coeval with that of Antichrist. And no doubt some, if not all of them are accordingly *now operating in the world,* and in this nation. The dragon in this text is the devil.*
The Beast is Antichrist. And the false prophet is *Pa-pal religion;* and it may be viewed as including the whole spirit of *false* religion, under whatever form. What particular influence will be found to be rep-resented by the frog out of the mouth of the drag-on, as distinct from the other two; or what shades of difference the two former of these modes of dia-bolical agency will be found to have assumed, it may be difficult now to ascertain. I have no doubt but Illuminism is one of these three unclean spirits; and that re-established Popery, including all fanaticism and fatal religious error, wherever it be found, is the last. And with respect to *a third,* time and events will no doubt cast light upon the subject. Let it be *what* it may, it will prove to have been of *diabolical produc-tion. For they are spirits of devils.* The devil will have peculiar power among men to instigate things favorable to disorganization and Infidelity; and by his satanic influence to prepare men to unite in his cause. He has ever been said to *work in the children of diso-bedience, and to lead them captive at his will.* But in the fulfilment of *this* prophecy, having come down *with great wrath, because he knoweth he hath but a short time,* the devil will be suffered to exercise an un-usual influence among men, in exciting their corrup-tions, of pride, lusts, covetousness, enmity, rage, and all the malignant passions. Satan will then be able to instigate the wicked to overleap usual restraints; to *break such bands asunder,* and to *cast such cords from them.*† Whether any thing more than this, in a land

* Rev. xii. † Psalm ii, 3.

so distant from the seat of the Antichristian Beast as ours, will be observable, as fulfilling the other system of diabolical influence; or whether it will not appear, that the old dragon has long been preparing *some engine,* which will then be brought into operation against the cause of Christ, *the event must decide.* The latter seems much to accord with the deep policy of that old serpent who deceives the world. His plans extend far beyond the apprehensions of the multitudes, who are involved in them; and who, with different motives, prove instruments of their fulfilment. People may be led, by trifling and seemingly harmless views, into con-nexions, which Satan *may* eventually manage to ac-complish his malignant designs; and perhaps to sub-serve one of the three systems of influence under con-sideration.

———

Thus I have endeavored to make it appear, in this chapter, that the last days have arrived; and that an in-ceptive fulfilment of the predictions concerning Anti-christ is now manifest before our eyes. Chronological remarks, and the events and signs of the times, appear to unite, and to present the present age, as the period of the rise of Antichrist.

Various other tokens of this event are suggested in the word of God; such as, *Signs in the heavens and in the earth, blood and fire, and pillars of smoke:—Wars and rumors of wars:—Pestilence, famines, and earthquakes in divers places:—And an angel flying through the midst of heaven having the everlasting Gospel to preach to them who dwell on the earth, to every nation, kindred, tongue and people;* or a most remarkable missionary spirit in the Christian world, *in the same hour* with the fall of Papal Babylon. These signs of the last days, serious and judicious people be-lieve they have seen fulfilling, or fulfilled, with amazing evidence and precision.

Concerning the reign of Antichrist, and the prev-alence of Infidelity, if John could say to his Jewish brethren, in relation to the continuance of their national polity; *It is the last time; and as ye have heard that Antichrist shall come, even now are there many anti-christs, whereby we know it is the last time;* truly we may adopt his inference with an *emphasis.* If the Infidelity of the impenitent Jews indicated that *wrath to the uttermost* was just ready to be poured upon their nation; truly the present extensive, systematic, and prevalent agency and Infidelity of the real Antichrist of the last time, does evince, with more emphatical decision, that the battle of the great day is not far distant. For the deduction of the Apostle rested on this ground, that the destruction of Antichrist, at the time of his first appearance, should be *even at the doors.* Zion will be redeemed with judgment, and her converts with right-eousness. The vintage will commence; the wine-press will be trodden. *The Lord will roar out of Zion, and utter his voice from Jerusalem; and the heavens and the earth shall shake.* The wicked powers of his enemies will be swept from his presence. *And the meek shall inherit the earth, and delight themselves in abundance of peace.*

*Some other Particulars relative to the Subject under
consideration.*

SECTION I.

The Trials of the Church under the reign of Antichrist.

In this section I shall remark upon some of the prophecies, which are thought to relate to the trials of the
people of God under the prevalence of Antichristian
tyranny. But previous to the consideration of the
prophecies, relative to those days, let it be noted, that
the denominating of the infidel Power of the last days
Antichrist; his being also represented as the old *Roman
Beast* revived, and as the sixth, or Imperial *head*, recovered from its deadly wound; these things alone por-
tend solemn things to the Church. Why is this Power
called *Antichrist?* Why was his existence in the last
days so long, and so abundantly and solemnly predicted to the Church under this, and various other terrific
appellations? Will he not verify the *hostility* indicated
in his very *name?* Can the appellation of *Antichrist*
be unmeaning? Why is he represented, in addition to
this, as the last head of the old *Roman Beast?* And the
sixth, the most persecuting head, recovered from his
deadly wound? The best expositors agree, that a
Beast, in the symbolic language of prophecy, means a
great power *hostile* to the Church of Christ. Powers
ever so great, not hostile to the Church, are not symbolized by Beasts. And when a great power, that has
been hostile to the Church, and has been symbolized
by a Beast, ceases to be hostile to the Church, that
Beast is represented as dying, - or being wounded to
death: As in the case of the old Pagan Roman empire,
when, in the revolution under Constantine, its government was changed from Pagan to Christian. And when
the same Beast is represented as *reviving*, the indica-

tion can be nothing less, than that a similar Power equally hostile to the Church, and mystically the same, has come into existence. If this trait of character be not verified by the hostility of such a Power to the Church, there can be no meaning in the representation, that the old Beast is revived.

And the representation of the *sixth*, the *Imperial* head of the old Beast being recovered from its deadly wound, and this under the immediate agency of the *devil*, in his *rage* of the last days, because he knoweth that he has but a short time, *must* indicate *alarming hostility* to the cause of Christ! This was the head, which in ancient days was the most terrible of all the heads of the Roman Beast. Under *this*, Christ was crucified. Under *this*, the Apostles were put to death. And under *this*, the greatest exertions were made, in ten bloody persecutions, to eradicate primitive Christianity from the earth. If this head then, be symbolically represented as rising out of the bottomless pit, being revived under the agency of the devil, in his last rage before the Millennium, and all this under the additional name of *Antichrist*, who the Christians in the days of John had heard *was to come;* we need not wonder, that solemn admonitions are given to the Church relative to the event. And if amazing hostility be not exerted by this Power against the Church, why is Jesus Christ abundantly represented as coming from heaven, with all his armies and equipage of a most mighty conqueror, to carry on a war against him, and to vanquish him in the *battle of that great day of God Almighty?* Does not all this indicate the most violent hostilities to be undertaken by the terrible Power of the last days against the true Church of Christ?

In Rev. xvii, 14, we read, concerning the horns of the last head of the Roman Beast, *These shall make war with the Lamb.* Here we learn, that one real object of Antichrist is, *War with the Lamb.*

In Rev. xiii, 6, 7, 8, it is said of the *healed head* of the Roman Beast; (which is the same that is symbolized by a new Beast in chap. xvii;) *And he opened his mouth in blasphemy against God, to blaspheme his name, and his tabernacle* (or church) *and them, that dwell in heaven,* (live in Gospel order.) *And it was given unto him to make war with the saints, and to overcome them; and power was given him over all kindreds, and tongues, and nations. And all, that dwell upon the earth, shall worship him, whose names are not written in the book of life of the Lamb slain from the foundation of the world.* Here is the *extent* of his power. God grant it may mean only the old *Roman earth!* Here is his *object,* as in chap. xvii, 14, just noted; *war with the saints.* Here is his fatal success against the saints for a time;—*and to overcome them.* But how does this agree with the other prediction of the same event, chap. xvii, 14; *These shall make war with the Lamb; and the* Lamb *shall overcome them.* Reply. These passages, which seem to contradict each other, relate to different parts of the scene. Antichrist will prevail for a season; as did the Egyptian tyrant, when he had the tribes of the Lord shut up in Pihahiroth; (the straits of Hiroth;) and every thing external indicated that they were given into his hands. But at the close of the scene, the *Lamb* shall overcome; as in *that case,* when the people of God were by and by safely standing on the eastern bank of the Red Sea; and the terrible enemy sunk like lead in the mighty waters. This we may view as a prophetic miniature of the destruction of Antichrist. On the occasion of the latter, the saints sing the song of *Moses,* and of the *Lamb;* which indicates, that the song of Israel on the eastern bank of the Red sea, and its occasion, were a type of the victory and the song of the followers of the Lamb, at the close of the period of the vials.

In Rev. xii, we find the depression of the Church under the reign of Antichrist. After a long season of warfare in the symbolic heaven of the corrupt Church of Rome, the dragon was, at the reformation, cast out unto the earth. For a space of time the Church of Christ now rises, like the spouse coming up out of the wilderness, leaning on her Beloved. She doubtless hopes her days of tribulation are at an end; and that she is going uninterruptedly to ascend into her millennial glory.

But alas, it is there added, (verse 13,) *And when the dragon saw that he was cast out unto the earth, he persecuted the woman, who brought forth the man child. And to the woman were given two wings of a great eagle, that she might fly into the wilderness, into her place, where she is nourished for a time, and times, and half a time from the face of the serpent. And the serpent cast out of his mouth water, as a flood, after the woman, that he might cause her to be carried away of the flood. And the earth helped the woman; and the earth opened her mouth and swallowed up the flood, which the dragon cast out of his mouth. And the dragon was wroth with the woman, and went to make war with the remnant of her seed, who kept the commandments of God, and have the testimony of Jesus Christ.* Mr. Faber supposes, and I think it is very evident, that the casting out of the dragon from heaven to earth, was fulfilled at the time of the reformation under Luther. Consequently, the new attack of the dragon upon the Church must be sometime subsequent to the reformation; viz. after his prime instrument, the Imperial head of the Roman Beast, is revived. But this new attack produces a *second flight* of the Church into the wilderness. She had fled into the wilderness at the commencement of the war in heaven, verse 6; or upon her being delivered into the hands of the Papal Power, for 1260 years. But after the reformation, and the devil was thus cast out of the Papal heaven, by the discovery of the abominations of that system, and before he had prepared his new engine of persecution, the Church had in some good degree returned from her wilderness state. The Lamb had appeared on mount Zion, or in the Protestant Church, and with him vast multitudes, with their Father's names on their foreheads; worshipping God in the purity of the Protestant religion, in opposition to the idolatries of Papal Rome. When lo! the woman is again driven into the wilderness, by the new attack of the dragon in Antichrist, *for a time, times and half a time;* i. e. for the short *residue* of this noted term: It cannot now mean for the *whole* of this term. For 1260 years were the term of her depression, at the time of her *first flight*, many centuries before. Her being *now* to remain in the wilderness 1260 years, must of course mean; *the short remaining part of the* 1260 *years*. And the days of this remaining part, Christ will *for the elect's sake* cause to be short: Otherwise, no flesh could be saved. He will alleviate the distress, by causing the earth to *help* the woman. *When they shall fall, they shall be holpen with a little help.* The extreme sufferings of the Church may not continue more than *three days and an half;* i. e. three years and an half. The Captain of her salvation will interpose, and lighten the rest of the way with the cloud of his gracious presence, the wonders of his Providence, till her deliverance shall be complete. Floods of rage, mischief and violence, poured forth against the Church, as from the mouth of the old serpent, will be providentially *swallowed up.* Unexpected events, probably from earthly, or political views, will counteract the mischief aimed against the cause of Christ. And the Spirit of the Lord will lift up a standard against the flood of the enemy. Upon this the dragon, in vexation and rage, goes to make war with the *remnant of the woman's seed;* or with some distant branch of the Church. Some new and powerful attack is undertaken. Probably this will be fulfilled in the furious coalition led by Antichrist against the converted Jews in the Holy Land; which will prepare the way for the battle of the great day. Thus in the xiith chapter of Revelation, appear to be clearly predicted great trials to the Church, under the reign of Antichrist.

Do the preceding passages furnish a clew to the events in Rev. xi, 7, relative to the *slaying of the two witnesses?* The striking coincidence, between the former and the latter, has forced a conviction on my mind, which I cannot relate without sensible concern. Alas! I had long hoped, that the slaying of the witnesses was a past event. I well knew that some good men are of opinion that it is still future. But others have in this differed from them; and have indulged the pleasing hope, that all the peculiarly fiery trials of the Church are past; and that she is henceforth to enjoy greater and greater degrees of prosperity, till she reaches her millennial glory. I had fondly embraced this opinion; and was pleased when I found arguments adduced in favor of it. May the king of Zion mercifully grant, (if it accord with his holy plan,) that this may yet prove to be the case! But attention to the subject has constrained me to doubt of the correctness of the sentiment, that the slay- ing of the witnesses is a past event.   I have turned to the arguments of those, who view it thus; and I cannot on the whole feel satisfied with them, or deem them conclusive.   May the friends of Zion examine the sub- ject with *devout attention!*

. *And when they* (the two witnesses) *shall have. fin- ished their testimony, the Beast that ascendeth out of the bottomless pit, shall make war against them, and shall overcome them, and kill them.   And their dead bodies shall lie in the street of the great city, which spiritually is called Sodom and Egypt, where also our Lord was crucified.   And they of the people and kindreds and tongues and nations shall see their dead bodies, three days and an half, and shall not suffer their dead bodies to be put in graves.*   And they, that dwell upon the earth shall rejoice over them, and make merry, and shall send gifts one to another; because these two prophets tormented them that dwell on the earth.   And after three days and an half, the spirit of life from God entered into them; and they stood upon their feet; and great fear fell upon them, who saw them.   And they heard a great voice from heaven, saying unto them, Come up hither.   And they ascended up to heaven in a cloud; and their enemies beheld them.*

'Upon the question, Who are the witnesses? much has been said.. Some have supposed them to be the

---

* The witnesses lie dead three days and an half, probably meaning three years and an half. Was not this event prefigured by the *abominable desolation* made upon the Jewish Church by the typical Antiochus? Bp. Newton observes, that "the desola- tion of the temple and the taking away of the daily sacrifice by Appollonius (the commissioner of Antiochus) continued three years and an half." Vol i, p. 310.

two Testaments. This appears irrational. We find
no other instance, in which either of the Testaments is
personified, or represented as God's witness. Bp.
Newton thought the two witnesses to represent the few
faithful followers of Christ through the 1260 years.
Mr. Faber thinks them to mean the twofold Church of
the Old and New Testaments. Some have supposed
them to mean a Christian magistracy and ministry.
Pool's continuators understood by them the faithful
Gospel ministry. They observe that Christ first sent
out his ministers *two and two;* and note, that the embassadors of Christ are called *witnesses,* in many sacred
passages. *"And ye are* witnesses *of these things."*
"And ye shall be witnesses *unto me, both in Jerusa-*
lem, and in all Judea,—and unto the uttermost parts
of the earth." These were the last words spoken, by
Christ on earth. Addressing his ministers, (after having told them before, *Lo, I am with you always, even*
unto the end of the world,) he now, the moment he ascended, tells them, *they shall be his witnesses unto the*
uttermost parts of the earth. Accordingly we abundantly find them afterward so denominated. *"One must*
be ordained to be a witness *with us of the resurrec-*
tion." *"This Jesus hath God raised up, whereof we*
are all witnesses." *"Not to all the people, but unto*
witnesses *chosen before of God, even to us."** Does not
the clause, *"I will give power unto my two witnesses,"*
imply that they are persons known by this appellation?
But who are so well known by this appellation, as the
true ministers of Christ? The prophesying of the witnesses, Dr. Lowman observes, "signifies persons full
of the Spirit of God; preaching God's word, and bearing witness to the truth."† The witnesses are called,
the two prophets who tormented them that dwell on
the earth.‡ But who else answer so well to this description, as do the faithful preachers of the Gospel?
"These (says the Revelator) are the *two olive trees."*

---

* See also Acts iii, 15, and iv, 33, and v, 32, and x, 39, and
xxii, 15, and xxvi, 16; 1 Peter v, 1.
† On Rev. p. 109. ‡ Rev. xi, 10.

This relates to Zech. iv, 3, 11, 14. The two olive trees *there* (one on each side of the candlestick) are supposed to have been Joshua and Zerubbabel, who unitedly prefigured Christ; and who Pool supposes prefigured also the embassadors of Christ. *These* (said the angel to Zechariah) *are the two anointed ones* (sons of oil, Heb.) *that stand by the Lord of the whole earth.* The gifts and graces of the Holy Spirit are represented by an anointing with oil. And the ascension-gifts of Christ to his embassadors, *for the work of the ministry, and for the edifying of the body of Christ*, render it fit for them to be called, *olive trees*, or *sons of oil.* Thus reference appears to be had, in the witnesses, more immediately to the ministers of Christ.

. But the witnesses are also the *two candlesticks.* A candlestick is a noted emblem of the Church. *The seven candlesticks which thou sawest, are the seven Churches.** Doubtless the true members of Christ are not to be excluded from constituting the witnesses. They are cordially united in the same cause with their pastors. And though special reference is had *to the latter*, in the description of the witnesses, yet all the true Church are to be viewed as *included.*

But why are the witnesses said to be *two?* Reply. Two witnesses constitute a complete testimony. *At the mouth of two or three witnesses shall every word be established.* Two were essential to the scriptural validity of a testimony. See Deut. xix, 15; and Matt. xviii, 16. And God never left himself without a competent testimony from his followers among men. In the darkest times his number of witnesses was indeed small, but always competent. Our Lord first sent out his disciples *two* and *two.* Many are of the opinion, that two elders were ordained over each primitive Church. Under the Old Testament Moses and Aaron were sent for the deliverance of Israel from Egypt. Zerubbabel and Joshua were found united in after days. The prophets Elijah and Elisha were found in company.

* Rev. i, 20.

In the darkest times under Papal tyranny, and in after days, there appears something remarkable in the duality of signal instruments of salvation. We find Luther and Calvin; Cranmer and Ridley; John Huse and Jerome of Prague; yea, and the Waldenses and Albigenses. No doubt it is a fact, as Mr. Faber observes, that in this small number of the true followers of Christ, was *in a sense* contained the essence of the Church of the Old and New Testaments. Whether some reference be not had to this circumstance, in the dual number of the witnesses, I would not decide.

Concerning the *slaying* of the witnesses, authors have been much divided. It would be tedious, and needless to hint their different schemes, and the proper objections to them. See the schemes given in Bishop Newton, vol. ii, p. 226, 7, 8, 9. But after all, the good Bishop deemed the event still future. He says;— "The greater part of this prophecy, relating to the witnesses, *remains yet to be fulfilled.*"

I will mention the scheme of a late celebrated author upon the point, and my objections to it. His scheme is this; that the witnesses were slain in Germany, in 1547; when the two German princes, the Elector of Saxony, and the Landgrave of Hesse, sometime after the commencement of the reformation, were overcome at Mulhberg, in a battle with the emperor of Germany, and were forced to submit at discretion. Several years before this event, these German princes, and some others, espoused the cause of the reformation. They by an association, called the league of Smalkalde, gave a kind of *political life* to the Protestants in Germany; which at the defeat above noted, was taken from them; and the cause of the reformation in Germany, seemed to be lost. But the reformers again stood upon their feet in 1550, by defeating the duke of Mecklenburg; and in 1552 a peace was ratified at Passau, and confirmed at Augsburg, in 1555, by which the Protestants in Germany were allowed the free exercise of their religion. And the Church, according to this author, then 'ascended to her political heaven.'

Against this scheme, the following objections appear to me of weight;

1. Those events were *inadequate* to a fulfilment of the prediction; and in some things *contrary* to it.

One would think so much importance could not be attached to the political privileges obtained, and for some years enjoyed by the Protestants in Germany, as that the interruption of those privileges, for several years should be represented, in ancient prophecy, as the *slaying* of God's witnesses? The witnesses had *lived* and *prophesied*, without those privileges, through all the preceding ages of their testimony, till within a few years of their defeat at Mulhberg. And if they were alive before those privileges were obtained, why not equally alive, after they were taken from them? Indeed if the throwing of the Protestant Churches *now*, in the vast Christian world, into a similar situation with that of the reformers in Germany, after the battle of Mulhberg, might amply amount to what was designed in ancient prophecy by the slaying of the witnesses; it does not hence follow, that the above event in Germany was adequate to a fulfilment of that prophecy.

It is evident that the slaying, the lying dead, and the resurrection, of the witnesses, are represented in the prophecy as events of extensive and great moment. *And they of the people, and kindreds, and tongues, and nations, shall see their dead bodies three days and an half, and shall not suffer their dead bodies to be put in graves. And they, that dwell upon the earth, shall rejoice over them, and make merry, and shall send gifts one to another, because these two prophets tormented them, that dwell on the earth.* What kindreds, and tongues, and nations took so great delight in the defeat of the German Protestants at Mulhberg? Wherein did they rejoice, and make merry, and send gifts one to another? How long had the people, who dwelt on the earth, the *kindreds,* and *nations* and *tongues,* been tormented by the German Protestants? What were the emotions *in fact* excited among the catholic nations on that occasion? They were the very *reverse* of the joy and triumph indicated in the prophe-

cy, upon the slaying of the witnesses.* Upon the dispersion of the army of the Protestants, combined under the Smalkalde league,and the submission of all to the
Emperor, except the Elector of Saxony, and the Landgrave of Hesse; and when the prospect'appeared certain,
that these two princes *would* be overcome, as they afterward were; a general spirit of *jealousy* arose among the
Catholic powers, in fear of the unrestrained dominion
about to be obtained by Charles. He had professed,
this his war against the confederate princes was not
undertaken on account of *their religion;* (though this
was evidently the Pope's motive in aiding this war) bu
to vanquish a political combination. The real motive
of the Emperor no doubt was, the extension of his own
power, at the expense of the liberties of Germany; and
the eventual re-establishment of the Catholic religion
through Germany, as being more favorable to his ambitious views. But in the terms of the submission of
those Protestant states to Charles, not a word was said
concerning any abridgment of their religious rights,
nor even *concerning* religion. But as the Smalkalde
league had been viewed, even by other Papal powers,
as a salutary check to the thirst of the Emperor for universal power, and as the Catholic nations dreaded his
ambition; so upon the dispersion of the Protestant army,
and the prospect that the Elector and the Landgrave
would soon be subdued, the Papal powers became
alarmed. The Pope himself trembled for the fate of
the Italian states. And he immediately sent and recalled his troops from the Imperial army. This greatly perplexed the Emperor. For he had depended on
the aid of these troops, for the reduction of the two
princes yet in arms. Charles entreated, and threatened; but all in vain. The Pope was inflexible; and his
armies were recalled to Italy.

The Pope also at the same time revoked the license,
which he had given to Charles, of taking to himself certain Church lands in Spain, as an inducement to suppress those, whom he called heretics. Francis also,

---

* See vol. iii, p. 368, of Robertson's Hist. of Charles V.

the French monarch, was distressed at the thought of
the reduction of the Protestant German princes. Not
that he favored the reformation; but rejoiced in the
check of his rival. He sent his embassadors, and labored to revive the Smalkalde league; and to prevent
the submission of the Elector and the Landgrave to
Charles. And he sent them large sums of money,
to enable them to withstand the Emperor. The Pope
expressed great joy upon hearing of the total defeat of
Albert, marquis of Brandenburg, whom Charles had
sent forward with a detachment, to aid Maurice against
the Elector, but whom the Elector had intercepted, and
cut off. And great exertions were made to form a coalition, to consist of the Pope, the Italian states, France,
England, and Denmark, against the Emperor on this occasion. The Emperor, after he had subdued the two
princes, published his system called the *Interim*, a
kind of bungling attempt to reconcile the Catholics
and Protestants. This was disgusting to all parties.
The Pope and the Catholics execrated it. And the
Protestants despised it. In short, the feeling and conduct of all, on that occasion, formed a *striking contrast*
with the events in the prophecy, of all nations, tongues
and languages *rejoicing*, and sending gifts one to another.

The compact obtained by the Protestants, in the
peace of Augsburg, respected only the Protestants in
Germany; and those only, who adhered to the confession of Augsburg. The *others*, who thought this confession was too lenient to the catholics, the followers of
Calvin and Zuinglius, and all the Protestants in other
countries, *were left by this peace unprotected.*

2. A difficulty attends the scheme of this author, in
point of *chronology*. The slaying of the witnesses is
said to be *when they shall have finished their testimony.*
I am sensible that some critics are of opinion, that the
verb τελεσωσι, being found in the first aorist, subjunc-
tive, may admit the rendering, When they shall be
about to finish If the word *may* bear this construction, it is not the most *natural* one. Had that *been* the
meaning of the writer, he might have adopted words

to have expressed it *precisely.* But the literal render-ing of the words οταν τελεσωσι, is *when they shall fin-ish*, or *have finished.* It is the same *verb, mode* and *time*, found in the following verse, Matt. x, 23, which is rendered thus, "Ye *shall* not *have finished* the cities of Israel." But admitting the rendering in the criticism referred to; with what propriety could the witnesses be said to have been even *about* to finish their testimony, at the time of the defeat at Mulhberg? That defeat was in 1547; 319 years before they will *actually* have fin-ished their testimony, according to the above au-thor's calculations; making the 1260 years terminate in 1866. Should they terminate at a *later* period, the difficulty would be proportionably increased. There was *then*, according to this scheme, at the time of the slaying of the witnesses, more than one quarter of the *whole* long time of their prophesying still before them. Surely they were not, at that time, even *about* to finish their testimony. They were to prophecy 1260 years; Rev. xi, 3. But according to the above scheme, they prophesied but 941 years.

3. We should conceive, from reading the account of the resurrection of the witnesses, and of their ascen-sion to heaven, that their days of sore trial were chiefly over. I cannot but think this idea, upon perusing that prediction, would *at first* be impressed *without a doubt* upon every impartial reader. But some of the most dismal persecutions ever experienced by the Church, under Papal tyranny, have taken place, in various Cath-olic countries, since the peace of Augsburg. Recol-lect the massacre of the Protestants in France, on the evening of St Bartholomew, in 1572 under Charles IX, when 30,000 were destroyed; the slaughter of them in Ireland, in the reign of Charles I; and in Poland, in after days. Recollect the persecutions under Louis XIV, who repealed the edict of Nantz, in 1685, and murdered and banished nearly two millions of his Protestant subjects in one year; the persecutions of the Piedmontese by the duke of Savoy, toward the close of the seventeenth century; when one million in France were murdered; and many other bloody scenes, expe-

rienced by the followers of Christ, in Popish countries, since the aforementioned peace of Augsburg.‖‸ And read the prophecies of the trials, which the Church is to experience under the reign of Infidelity, just before the battle of the great day, whether the witnesses be then to be slain, or not. These things do not appear to accord with the representation given of the witnesses, after their resurrection, and their ascension to heaven.

' 4. *In the same hour* with the ascension of the witnesses to heaven, *there was a great earthquake, in which a tenth part of the city fell.* There was no event within a prophetical hour of the peace of Augsburg in 1555, which can answer to this prediction. No event is by the aforementioned author supposed to have answered to it, till the revolution in France, in 1789. But this was 234 years after the supposed resurrection of the witnesses.' And to say that two disconnected and different events, 234 years apart, may yet be said to take place in the *same hour,* would be extraordinary indeed. It would be unprecedented in the Bible, and in all common conversation.

5.   The agent, by whom the witnesses are said to be slain, was not in existence, till centuries after those events in Germany. The *first* apocalyptic Beast *rose* (as did the same Beast in Dan. vii, 2, symbolizing the heathen Roman Empire) *from the sea.** The *second* apocalyptic Beast (answering to the little horn of the Roman Beast in Daniel, and symbolizing the Romish hierarchy) *rose from the earth.*† The *third* apocalyptic Beast (numerically the *eighth*, but specifically the *sixth* head of the old Roman Beast, healed of his deadly wound, and at the same time symbolized by a *new Beast*, in Rev. xvii) *rose from the bottomless pit. This* is expressly said to be the agent, that slays the witnesses. Twice in the description of this Beast, in Rev. xvii, he is said to ascend out of the *bottomless pit.* And it is said of the witnesses, *And when they shall have finished their testimony,* (or when their 1260 years shall

---

*Rev. xiii, 1. '   †Verse 11.

be closing,) *the Beast that ascendeth out of the bottom-less pit, shall make war against them, and shall overcome them; and kill them.* The rise of this Beast is by far too recent, to have slain the witnesses in Germany in 1547. There can be no plausible pretence, that Charles V. was this Beast, that ascendeth out of the bottomless pit. And it appears most evident, that this last head of the Roman Beast did not rise in Charlemagne, as has been ascertained.

Finally. The Papal Beast had been making war upon the witnesses from the beginning of the 1260 years. No new attacks then, instituted in his dying struggles, could amount to a *new war* against them. But the text, "And when they shall have finished their testimony, the Beast that ascended out of the bottom-less pit, shall *make war against them*, and shall over-come them and kill them," seems clearly to indicate, that a *new war*, by a *new Power*, shall then commence against the witnesses;—a war subsequent to that, which was prosecuted against them by any Papal power.

For these reasons I am constrained to dissent from the aforementioned scheme, relative to the slaying of the witnesses; and to admit the sentiment, that the event is still future. The remarks above stated go equally to refute all the schemes of authors, who have placed the slaying of the witnesses in past centuries.*

The dead bodies of the witnesses are to lie three days and an half in the street (according to Mede and Pool,

*Since the publishing of the first edition of this dissertation, I have for the first time learned the sentiment of the celebrated Mr. *Scott*, upon the above point.

I am strengthened in my opinion, in finding that *his* fully ac-cords with it. He says, "Many private interpretations (for so they appear to me) have been given of this passage, (Rev. xi, 7—12) as if it related to the martyrdom of individuals, or par-tial persecutions, in past times: And some imagine, that it de-notes only the constant persecutions of true Christians through the whole period of 1260 years I cannot, however, but think, that it relates to events *yet future;* and that it will be fulfilled about the time of the sounding of the seventh trumpet!

In the following page he further informs, that, though the *above* was written some time since; and he has, before the pub-

in "*the territories, and jurisdiction*") of the great city,
which spiritually, or mystically, *is called Sodom ,and
Egypt, where also our Lord was crucified.* Our Lord
was crucified under the *sixth head* of the Roman Beast.
A governor of *Imperial* Rome, at the instigation of the
Jews, condemned and crucified him. And under the
same head our Lord was crucified, in his members, in
ten bloody persecutions, before that head received its
deadly wound in the year 320. Must it not then be
in the city, or under the dominion, of this *same head,*
healed of its deadly wound, in order to be in the city
where our Lord was crucified, that the witnesses are to
lie slain and unburied? It is to be in a city mystically
called *Sodom* and *Egypt.* Sodom and Egypt were
Pagan. How much better the Atheism of Antichrist
accords with *their* character, than did the sanctimonious professions of Papal Rome? Our Lord was not literally crucified under Rome.*Papal;* but he *was* under
Rome **Pagan.** And under the latter, revived in the
last days, it is natural to look for the slaying of his
witnesses.

What is to be particularly understood by the witnesses being *slain,* and lying *unburied,* the event will
determine. The predictions of the event may lead us
to expect, that the rights of the Church, and of con-

lication of his last edition, had time to *re-consider* the subject,
and to compare it with the writings of others, and with the
events of Providence; "he still avows his full conviction, that
the transactions (the slaughter and resurrection of the witnesses) have not hitherto taken place." He gives his belief, that
till the testimony against idolatry and Popery, in the ten kingdoms, is *generally suppressed,* the witnesses are not slain. That
"the triumphs of the persecutors, in Germany, Bohemia,
Spain, or Italy, do not amount to *any thing,* which can be called
the slaying of the witnesses; so long as a public testimony—
for the true Gospel, is *born* in any other parts of the western
empire." Again. "Nor is the *term* (the 1260 years) yet expired. The witnesses are not indeed, at present, exposed to
such terrible sufferings, as in former times. But these scenes
will probably be re-acted, before long. And they have abundant cause to prophecy in sackcloth, on account of the state of
religion, even in the Protestant churches." These remarks
of Mr. Scott are indeed of weight.

science, will under some pretence be invaded. And the pretence probably will be, as it was in ancient times, against Christ, and against his persecuted followers; *a pretence of their being bad and dangerous members of civil society, detrimental to national interests; speaking against Cesar; moving seditions; weakening the hands of the men of war; and, We have a law; and by our law he ought to die.*

Perhaps the *process* of the events of that period is hinted in Rev. xiv. Christ there appears on mount Zion; or comes powerfully into his Church, in the *reformation* under Luther. The Church enjoys a sealing time, as she did after the revolution under Constantine, Rev. vii, 1—8. Vast numbers, as at *that* period, are sealed to the day of redemption. A description of the enlargement of the Protestant churches, and of their purity from the defilements of the Papal harlot, follows. In process of time a missionary spirit is excited, and pervades the Church; the Angel, having the everlasting' Gospel to preach to heathen lands, begins his flight. This, he gives us to understand, is in the *same hour* with the judgment of God on the Papal see.† A *sec-*

* That great man, the late President Witherspoon, published a very able sermon entitled, "The Charge of Sedition and Faction against good Men, especially faithful Ministers, considered and accounted for." The preacher concludes one part of his subject by saying, "That worldly men have been always disposed first to oppress the children of God, and then to complain of injury from them; that by slander they might vindicate their oppression. Their slander too hath still run in the same strain; troublers of Israel, deceivers of the people, enemies to Cesar, and turners of the world upside down, have been the opprobrious titles generally give to the most upright and most faithful men, in every age and country."

In accounting for this fact, he says, "True religion does indeed, give trouble and uneasiness to wicked men, while they continue such; and it cannot be supposed, but they will deeply resent it."

See Witherspoon's Works, vol. ii, p. 415, Woodward's edition.

† As this flight of the missionary Angel, is a very interesting event; I shall here adduce some of the other prophecies, which foretell the same thing. So signal an event we might expect to find in other prophecies. And it is there found.

ond Angel announces, *Babylon is fallen, is fallen.* The signs of the times become *notorious.* The fall of Papal Babylon, by the rise of Antichrist, *is ascertained.*

Christ, when predicting to his disciples his *coming,* Matt. xxiv, Mark xiii, Luke xxi, informs, that *"this Gospel of the kingdom must first be preached to all nations, for a witness unto them; and then shall the end come."* It is, by and by in this section, shown, that while this coming of Christ, with which this passage stands connected, had a primary reference to the destruction of Jerusalem, it had a more signal reference to the battle of that great day, immediately preceding the Millennium. Though the above prediction had a primary fulfilment in the propagation of the Gospel by the apostles through the Roman world, before the destruction of the Jews; yet it is to have a more extensive fulfilment just before the ruins of Antichrist; or in the flight of the missionary Angel, above noted.

We might expect that the prophet *Isaiah* would give some intimation of this great event. And repeatedly *does* he give sublime hints of it.

In Isa. xl, the chapter begins with a prediction of the final restoration of the Jews; that their long dispersion is accomplished; and they have received of the Lord's hand double for all their sins. An account then follows of the same event with that of the missionary Angel, Verse 3. "The voice of him that crieth in the wilderness; Prepare ye the way of the Lord; make straight in the desert a high way for our God. Every valley shall be exalted; and every mountain and hill shall be made low; and the crooked shall be made straight; and the rough places plain; and the glory of the Lord shall be revealed; and all flesh shall see it together; for the mouth of the Lord hath spoken it."

This passage had a primary and typical fulfilment in the preaching of John the Baptist, in the wilderness of Judea, to introduce the advent of the Messiah. He accordingly says, John i, 23, "I am the voice of one crying in the wilderness, Make straight the way of the Lord; as said the prophet Isaias." But we are no more taught in this, that the passage had then its *ultimate* fulfilment, than we are taught, that the predictions concerning the kingdoms of Christ on earth had their final accomplishment in the primitive Christian Church; or the introduction of the Gospel dispensation. They had only a primary, incoative fulfilment in those days.

The above prediction in Isaiah is one of those, which are to receive a primary, and an ultimate fulfilment. Mr. Faber informs of such; which, "instead of being incapable of a double fulfilment, we perpetually find such evidently constructed with the express design of receiving a double accomplishment. They are first fulfilled in an inchoate manner; and afterward

The warning flies through the Church. Upon this, a third Angel follows; warning of the sins of God's enemies; and of the judgments of Heaven now just ready

will be fulfilled more amply at a period, to which they ultimately and principally refer." Many great authorities he quotes to support this opinion.

At the time of the ministry of John in the wilderness of Judea, the "warfare," or dispersion, of the Jews was so far from' being accomplished, that the introduction of their long dispersion of at least 18 centuries, was then at some distance future. Certainly then, the ultimate and most important fulfilment of that voice in the wilderness, just at the period of their final restitution, must have been *far future*, in the days of John. And his ministry in the wilderness of Judea was but a *type* of it; and, as to a type of it, he was led to apply the prophecy to, himself.

It is to prepare the way for the millennial glory of the Lord to be revealed, when all flesh shall see it together, that the voice of missionaries is to be heard in the wilderness of the Pagan world; saying, "Prepare the way of the Lord! Make straight in the desert a highway for our God." It is *then*, that God's "highway" is to be exalted; where the unclean shall not pass; in which the way-faring man, though a fool, shall not err; and where the redeemed of the Lord shall walk, and shall return and come to Zion with songs and everlasting joys.

After the voice in the wilderness adds, that all the nations, *then* are like a field of *grass* just about to be cut off, (as the missionary Angel announces, that "the hour of his judgment is come") this most animating direction follows; "O Zion, that bringest good tidings, get thee up into the high mountain. O Jerusalem, that bringest good tidings, lift up thy voice with strength; lift it up; be not afraid: Say unto the cities of Judah, Behold your God! Behold the Lord God will come with a strong hand, and his arm shall rule for him: Behold his reward is with him, and his work before him." This and what follows indicate the introduction of the Millennium. Hence the final fulfilment of the voice in the wilderness is at that period.

In Isa. xxvii, 1—7, is a prophecy of the destruction of Antichrist; and of the dawn of the Millennium. The prophet informs, that God will, *"in that day,"* (viz. when he shall have come out of his place to punish the inhabitants of the earth for their iniquity, as in the preceding verse,) punish, with his great and strong sword, leviathan, the piercing and crooked serpent; or the Antichristian dynasty; and will be about to water his vineyard of red wine, and to keep it, night and day. He now, (as is usual,) notes the event of its dawn. Verse 13. "And it shall come to pass, in that day, that the great trumpet shall be blown; and they shall come, who are ready to perish, in the

to fall upon all, who have the mark of the Beast, and plunge them into endless burnings. The trumpet is now blown in Zion; the alarm is sounded in God's

land of Assyria, and the outcasts of the land of Egypt, and shall worship the Lord in the holy mount at Jerusalem." The great trumpet of Gospel grace is then to sound through Pagan lands: And many of the miserable *outcasts* of the heathen are to be brought to the worship of God, in the order of his kingdom.

In Daniel xii, 4, (found in close connexion with the battle of the great day, as you may see, by turning to the passage) it is predicted, as one token of the time of the end, that "many shall run to and fro; and knowledge shall be increased." This is the same event, at the same period, with that of the missionary Angel, Rev xiv; and with that of the voice in the wilderness, Isa. xl.

The prophet Joel predicts this event. Chap. ii, 1, "Blow ye the trumpet in Zion; sound an alarm in my holy mountain, let all the inhabitants of the land (earth) tremble: for the day of the Lord cometh, for it is nigh at hand." Here, when the great day of the Lord is nigh at hand, the trumpet is to be blown from Zion, or the church, that all the inhabitants of the earth may hear and tremble. That day of the Lord is described; and then it follows chap. iii, 1, "For behold in those days and in that time, when I shall bring again the captivity of Judah and Jerusalem, I will gather all nations, and will bring them down into the valley of Jehoshaphat." This decides, that the time, when the trumpet is to be blown, that all the inhabitants of the earth my tremble, is *about* the period of the return of Judah and Jerusalem from their long dispersion. The Gospel must then first be preached to all nations.

I shall note one passage more upon this point; which is in the last chapter of the Old Testament. With a primary reference to the destruction of Jerusalem, but with much more important reference to the great battle, at the fall of Antichrist, the prophet introduces the chapter: "Behold the day cometh, that shall burn as an oven; and all the proud, yea all that do wickedly shall be as stubble; and that day that cometh shall burn them up, saith the Lord of hosts, and it shall leave them neither root nor branch. But unto you, who fear my name shall the sun of righteousness arise with healing in his wings; and ye shall go forth and grow up as calves of the stall. And ye shall tread down the wicked; and they shall be as ashes under the soles of your feet, in the day that I shall do this, saith the Lord of hosts." It is certain that this passage is not yet, more than in a typical sense, fulfilled. Doctor Hopkins refers it to the battle of that great day of God. And the great and dreadful day of the Lord, in the next verse but one, and in the last but one in the chapter, *must* relate to the same event. The prophet now, as

holy mountain.* Warning is given concerning all, who worship the *Beast*, or receive his *mark.* This bold warning through the Church must be very *offensive* to

is usual in such cases, proceeds to note an important event, which introduces the scene. "Behold I will send you Elijah the prophet, before the coming of the great and dreadful day of the Lord." As the prediction of judgment in this chapter had a primary fulfilment in the destruction of Jerusalem, but is to have an ultimate one still future; so this prediction of the coming of Elijah had a primary fulfilment in John the Baptist; but is to have an ultimate fulfilment in the flight of the missionary Angel, just before the battle of the great day. In relation to that primary fulfilment, our Lord applied the passage to John. Matt. xi, 14, "This is Elias, who was for to come." But Christ no more teaches, that the passage received its *highest* and *final* accomplishment in John, than he taught, when he predicted his *coming*, in Matt xxiv, Mark xiii, and Luke xvi, and said it should take place upon *that generation*, that his *coming*, in the ruin of the Jews *finally* accomplished that awful *coming* in those chapters predicted. Those terrible predictions received only a *typical* fulfilment in the subversion of the Jews, (as is shown in this section) In like manner the passage in Malachi, concerning the coming of Elijah, received only a *typical* fulfilment in the ministry of John. His preaching in the wilderness of Judea, just before the *coming* of Christ in his public ministry, was a beautiful *emblem* of the ministry of the missionary Angel, just before the battle of that great day.

Bp. Hurd remarks, More than one sense was purposely inclosed in some of the prophecies. We find in fact that the writings of the New Testament give to many of the old prophecies an interpretation very different and remote from that, which may be reasonably thought the primary and immediate view of the prophets themselves. This (he says) is what divines call, the double sense of prophecy; by which they mean an accomplishment of it in more events than one,—at distant intervals." (Introduction to the study of prophecy, p. 55) This remark is exactly fulfilled in the application, which Christ makes, of that prediction of the coming of Elias before the great and notable day of the Lord, to John the Baptist This may account for the apparent contradiction between Christ and John, upon this point. When the priests and Levites interrogated John who he was? and whether he was Elias? or that prophet predicted? John i, 21, "He saith, I am not " Yet our Lord, in the afore noted passage, said, he *was* Elias. The sense appears to be this. John was instructed to say, he was *not* Elias: i. e. in the final and most important sense of the prediction. But Christ said he *was* that Elias: i. e. in a primary and typical sense.

* Joel ii, 1.

those who are implicated. Infidel powers, or Antichristian Babylon, and those, who partake of her *sins*,
and are now *notified* of it, and that they are about to
receive of her *plagues*, will be far from taking this in
good part from the witnesses of Christ. And *God only
knows what the former will now be enraged to attempt
against the latter!* The texts, which follow, are indicative of evil to the Church. Verses 12 and 13; *Here
is the patience of the saints: here are they, that keep
the commandments of God, and the faith of Jesus.
And I heard a voice from heaven, saying unto me,
Write, Blessed are the dead, who die in the Lord from
henceforth; yea, saith the Spirit, that they may rest
from their labors, and their works do follow them.*
Here the *patience* of the saints is to be tried. Now
it is to be known, *who* keep the commands of God,
and have the faith of Christ. Now the voice from

Viewing the two passages in this light there is no contradiction.

This then, is the sense of that passage in Malachi. Behold
I will send you *one* in the spirit of Elijah, about half a century
before the great and dreadful day of the Lord upon the Jewish
nation. And this shall be a type of a similar event, upon a far
greater scale, in the last days. For the spirit of Elijah shall
diffuse itself among the sons of the churches, not long before
the battle of that great and notable day of the Lord, which shall
burn as an oven, and consume all who shall be found in array
against the Church. A wonderful missionary spirit, a spirit of
zeal and of power from God, (such as Elijah possessed, in the
days of the wicked, idolatrous, and persecuting Ahab,) shall
be excited among the ministers and people of God. Though
Elijah had to flee into the wilderness, under that persecution;
yet thence he returned, confounded the persecuting idolaters,
and vindicated the cause of the God of Israel. Then, after a
distressing drought of three years and six months, the cloud
like a man's hand soon overspread the heavens, and a plentiful
rain ensued.

Various events in this history of Elijah may prove to have
been emblematical of things still future, relative to the Church.
"Elijah must first come." This coming of his had a primary
fulfilment in John the Baptist. John for his faithfulness was
imprisoned and beheaded. But the most important sense of
the coming of Elijah, before the great and notable day of the
Lord is still to be fulfilled, or is fulfilling.

Trials of the Church under Antichrist.   241

heaven announces, that *from henceforth*, and while the
troubles then overwhelming the Church shall continue,
peculiarly blessed are the pious, who find rest in their
graves.   The cruelties of the enemies of the Church,
here indicated, soon demand the presence of the Captain of her salvation.   The next verse, accordingly,
presents him upon the *white cloud*, with his *sharp sickle*.
The harvest of the earth is reaped; the vine of the earth,
with her grapes now fully ripe, is gathered; and the
wine-press trodden: striking emblems of the judgments
of the *last vial;* or the destruction of Antichrist, and
of all the contending enemies of the Church.   In this
striking portrait of the affairs of the Church, from the
days of *Luther,* till the close of the battle of the great
day, reference appears to be had, to that depression of
the Church, under consideration; and perhaps we find
also, a hint of the immediate occasion of it; the *faithfulness* of God's witnesses, in ascertaining the signs of
the times; warning the wicked of that day; and announcing the impending judgments of Heaven.   But
the particulars of the event, the day will unfold.
  Our blessed Lord gave to his disciples a description
of an *awful coming of his* in judgment against his enemies; and of scenes, which should both indicate its
approach, and prepare the way for it: See Matt. xxiv,
Mark xiii, and Luke xxi. These are parallel accounts
of the same predictions.   We are here presented with
several instances of the coming of Christ.   Chronological predictions, Mr. Faber informs us, can receive
but one accomplishment.   But this prediction of
Christ is not of that description; but is to be ranked a-
mong those prophecies, which are constructed to receive a twofold accomplishment; and involve both type
and antitype.   There are many predictions of this ten-
or, as Dr. Hopkins, and other judicious writers on
the prophecies, inform us.   Mr. Faber upon this
point observes, "But an unchronological prophecy,—
instead of being incapable of a double fulfilment, we
perpetually find such evidently constructed with the express design of receiving a double accomplishment.
They are at first fulfilled in an inchoate manner;

and afterward will be fulfilled more amply at a period, to which they ultimately and principally refer."* Many of the predictions of the battle of the great day, in the Old Testament, are of this description. They had a primary and literal fulfilment in ancient events; but are to receive their ultimate fulfilment in events still future. This is the case with the above noted prediction of our Lord. It had a primary and typical fulfilment in the destruction of Jerusalem. But it will receive a much more interesting fulfilment in the battle of the great day: And a still more important fulfilment at the great judgment day. In relation to the former, Christ gave assurance, that it should take place upon *that generation.* But in relation to the latter, he informed his disciples, *that as a snare shall it come on all them, that dwell on the face of the whole earth.* This could not be said of the destruction of Jerusalem. For that event came as a snare on but a very *small part* of the earth. It was predicted of our Savior, that he should proclaim the acceptable year of the Lord, and *the day of vengeance of our God.*† But surely if the copious and affecting predictions of Christ, recorded in Mat. xxiv, Mark xiii, and Luke xxi, related only to the destruction of Jerusalem, he did but in a very partial sense indeed proclaim the *day of vengeance of our God.* But Christ decides this point. *Then shall be great tribulation, such as was not since the beginning of the world to this time, no, nor ever shall be.*‡

* Faber on the Jews, p. 46.

Mr. Faber quotes, in favor of this opinion, Archdeacon Woodhouse, Bp. Lowth, Jortin, Sir I. Newton, Bp Hurd, Bp. Sherlock, Bp. Warburton, Bp. Horne, Jones, and Nares.

Bp. Hurd informs us, (Introduction to the Study of the Prophecies, p. 55,) "There is reason to believe that more than one sense was purposely inclosed in some of the prophecies. And we find in fact that the writers of the New Testament give to many of the old prophecies an interpretation very different and remote from that, which may be reasonably thought the primary and immediate view of the prophets themselves. This is what divines call the *double sense* of prophecy; by which they mean an accomplishment of it in more events than one; in the same system indeed; but at distant intervals, and under different parts of that system."

† Isa. lxi, 2.   ‡ Mat. xxiv, 22; and Mark xii, 10.

Compare this with Dan. xii, 1, which relates to the war
between Antichrist, and the great head of the Church,
just before the Millennium. After having described
the terrible infidel Power of the last days, and brought
him into Palestine against the Church there, the Angel
says; *And at that time shall Michael stand up, the
great Prince, who standeth for the children of thy people;
and there shall be a time of trouble, such as never was,
since there was a nation, even to that same time.* Now
if the words of Christ, in the former of these passages,
had exclusive reference to the destruction of Jerusalem,
then the above passage in Daniel is untrue. For our
Lord declares there never shall be such trouble on
earth again, as that, which he then predicts. Certainly
both the passages are not true, if they relate to different events. For each of two different scenes of distress cannot be the greatest, that ever was, or ever shall
be. This argument evinces, that the event predicted
by Christ, is the same with that in Dan. xii, 1. And
the words of Christ it is thought evidently allude to
that very passage. But the latter is the battle of
that great day of God. Consequently these predictions
of Christ must relate to the same. Although they
received a primary fulfilment in the days of the Apostles; yet they also related to events then far future.
This point is still more clearly decided, in 1 Thes. ii,
1—9. Paul there exhorts the Church to which he
wrote, not to be shaken in mind, nor troubled, from an
opinion, that the *day of the Lord* was at hand. For
that day, he assured them, should not come, till after
the great Papal apostacy, and the rise of the man of
sin; "whom the Lord will consume with the Spirit of
his mouth, and destroy with the brightness of his coming." The Thessalonians, reading those predictions
of Christ relative to his *coming;* and finding it stated,
that it should take place upon *that* generation, were
trembling in immediate expectation of the event. Paul
instructs them on the subject. q. d. It was only as the
prediction of Christ's coming related to a primary, typical fulfilment on the *Jews,* that it was to take place
on *that generation.* As it relates to the Antichristian

world, it is not to be accomplished, till after the 1260 years of the Papal delusion. It is then to have a dreadful accomplishment in the overthrow of that Power. Here it is decided by divine authority, that a more important instance of that predicted *coming of Christ,* was to be fulfilled in the destruction of Antichrist in the last days. The same thing is again decided, in Rev. xvi, 15. Between the sixth and seventh vials, Christ gives the warning; "Behold I come as a thief—" q. d. The time is now just at hand, (the effusion of the seventh vial,) when my *coming as a thief,* of which I gave notice, in the days of my humiliation, shall be accomplished. It is no longer then, a matter of doubt, whether those solemn prophecies uttered by Christ, in Matt. xxiv, Mark xiii, and Luke xxi, have a special reference to his coming in the battle of that great day of God Almighty; or the seventh vial. The above two passages *decide in the affirmative.*

Our Lord says,[*] *And when ye shall hear of wars, and rumors of wars, see that ye be not troubled; for all these things must come to pass; but the end is not yet. For nation shall rise against nation, and kingdom against kingdom, and there shall be famines, and pestilences, and earthquakes in divers places. All these are the beginning of sorrows.* Here I apprehend we have predicted the wars and commotions, which were to attend the rise of the Antichristian Beast, and the formation of his horns. The latter events must of course occasion as great wars and commotions, as are here predicted; as great as are indicated of the same period, in Rev. x, 3, by the *seven thunders uttering their voices.* But as the Angel there affirms, that *the time shall not be yet,* as in the original, verse 6; or the time shall not be prolonged; so our Lord informs, with respect to the wars and rumors of wars; *But the end is not yet.* A season is to intervene, though not long, between the rise of Antichrist, and his overthrow. And Christ proceeds to foretell some of the events of this intermediate space. Some of these predictions I will now adduce, as they are collected in harmony from the evangelists, by Dr. Doddridge.

[*]Matt. xxiv, 6—.

: "And fearful sights and great signs shall there be
"from heaven. All these are the beginning of sorrows.
"But take heed to yourselves. For they shall lay their
"hands on you, and persecute you, and shall deliver
"you up to councils, and into prisons, to be beaten and
"afflicted, and shall kill you; and ye shall be hated of
"all nations; and shall be brought before rulers and
"kings for my name's sake, for a testimony against
"them.   And it shall turn to you for a testimony. And
"the Gospel must be first published among all nations.
"But when they shall lead you, and deliver you up,
"settle it in your hearts not to meditate before what ye
"shall answer; and take no thought beforehand what
"ye shall speak; but whatsoever shall be given you in
"that hour, that speak ye.   For it is not ye that speak,
"but the Holy Ghost.   For I will give you a mouth
"and wisdom, which all your adversaries shall not be
"able to gainsay, nor resist. And then shall many be
"offended, and shall betray one another, and shall hate
"one another. Now the brother shall betray the broth.
"er to death; and the father the son; the children shall
"rise up against the parents, and shall cause them to be
"put to death.   And ye shall be hated of all men for
"my name's sake.   But there shall not an hair of your
"head perish.   In your patience possess ye your souls.
"And many false prophets shall rise, and shall deceive
"many.   And because iniquity shall abound, the love
"of many shall wax cold.   But he that shall endure
"unto the end, the same shall be saved.—In those days
"there shall be great tribulation, and distress in the
"land, such as was not from the beginning of the cre-
"ation unto this time; no, nor ever shall be.   And ex-
"cept that the Lord had shortened those days, no flesh
"should be saved; but for the elect's sake, whom he
"hath chosen, those days shall be shortened.—And
"there shall be signs in the sun, and in the moon, and
"in the stars; and upon the earth distress of nations
"with perplexity, the sea and the waves roaring; men's
"hearts failing them for fear, and for looking after those
"things which are coming upon the earth.   Immedi-
"ately after the tribulation of those days shall the sun

"be darkened; and the moon shall not give her light;
"and the stars shall fall from heaven; and the powers
"of the heavens shall be shaken. And then shall ap-
"pear the sign of the Son of man in heaven; and then
"shall the tribes of the earth, mourn; and they shall
"see the Son of man coming in the clouds of heaven
"with power and great glory. And when these things
"begin to come to pass, then look up, and lift up your
"heads; for your redemption draweth nigh."

No events of the Apostle's days are to be viewed as
more than a primary and typical fulfilment of these
sublime and interesting predictions. The last clause,
which seems to relate to much that precedes, *Then look
up, and lift up your heads; for your redemption draweth nigh,* had no relation to the days of the Apostles.
It can relate to no period short of that which is connected with the dawn of the Millennium. Does not
this clause then decide, that these predictions relate
to scenes, which shall just precede the Millennium?
And do they not indicate most solemn things to the
Church, at this period?

The battle array of the last head of the Roman Beast,
and his false prophet, and the kings of the earth, against
Jesus Christ and his armies, Rev. xix, 19, confirms
the sentiment, that the Church is to be sorely tried under the reign of Antichrist. For although this passage
relates to the last attack, the expedition in Palestine
against the church of Judah and Israel, yet it shews,
that war with Christ is the object of Antichrist. And
such a Power will be able greatly to afflict the people
of God.

Our Lord gave his disciples a signal, when they
should flee out of Jerusalem.* *When ye therefore
shall see the abomination of desolation spoken of by
Daniel, stand in the holy place, (whoso readeth let
him understand) then let them who be in Judea flee
into the mountains. Let him who is on the house-
top not come down to take any thing out of his house:
neither let him who is in the field return back to take
his clothes.*

* Matt. xxiv. 15.

Daniel had spoken of the abomination of desolation in *three* passages, and in relation to *three* different events. The *first* is Dan. ix, 27; *And in the midst of the week, he shall cause the sacrifice and the oblation to cease, and for the overspreading of abominations he shall make it desolate, even until the consummation, and that determined shall be poured upon the desolate.* This related to the armies of the Romans in array against Jerusalem, with their eagles and other images, which they worshipped; which were an abomination to the Jews; and which (when seen around the walls) indicated the speedy destruction of Jerusalem. The *second* is Dan. xi, 31; *And arms shall stand on his part, and they sall pollute the sanctuary of strength, and shall take away the daily sacrifice, and they shall place the abomination, that maketh desolate.* This relates to the invasions and garrisons of Antiochus, the noted type of Antichrist, in order to compel the Jews to renounce their religion; to eat swine's flesh, and to violate their consciences. Upon this occasion many of the Jews suffered martyrdom, and underwent the most cruel torments.*

This conduct is here predicted by the Angel, when he was preparing the way to give a prophetic description of Antichrist, and was first presenting him by his *type*, Antiochus. The *third* passage, in which Daniel speaks of the *abomination of desolation*, is in chap. xii, 11; *And from the time the daily sacrifice shall be taken away, and the abomination that maketh desolate, set up, there shall be a thousand two hundred and ninety days.* This relates to the impious establishment of Popery, or Mohammedism, or both, in the year 606, or whenever Popery was established.

The question then occurs; To which of these three passages in Daniel did our Lord refer, when he spoke of the abomination of desolation, as the token to his

---

* The particulars of this persecution are given in the 5th, 6th, and 7th chapters of the second book of the Maccabees. The material parts of the account are copied by Polybius and Josephus; and are found in Rollin's Ancient History. Book xviii, Art. 2.

people to flee into the mountains? Answer. As the direction applied to the Apostles and Church at Jerusalem, we must conclude he referred to that which relates to the Roman eagles and idolatry, when the Romans were besieging Jerusalem; Dan. ix, 27. As the direction applied to the Christian Church at the commencement of Popery, or Mohammedism, the direction must be viewed as referring to the passage, which relates to *that* period; Dan. xii, 11. And as the direction respects the Church in the days of Antichrist, we must view our Lord as referring to that passage, Dan. xi, 31, which relates to the *type* of Antichrist, or to Antiochus; and was given, when the Angel was undertaking to give a description of the infidel Power of the last days. When that shall take place under Antichrist, which was prefigured when his type Antiochus set up the abomination, that made desolate, in the holy place, then this token to the Church at that period will be fulfilled. Violating the rights of the Church, making a direct attack upon them, *may prove* to be this abomination, that maketh desolate. Setting up a desolating abomination, seems to be a prophetic figure to express a violent attack upon the people of God. As the persecutions of Antiochus are noted by the Angel, when his object was to predict the rise, character, and overthrow of *Antichrist*, this seems to indicate, that events may be expected under the reign of Antichrist, corresponding with those cruel deeds of Antiochus. It becomes interesting then, to examine those predictions concerning the cruelties of Antiochus, and their fulfilment. The Angel says;* *And arms shall stand on his part, and they shall pollute the sanctuary of strength, and shall take away the daily sacrifice, and they shall place the abomination, that maketh desolate. And such as do wickedly against the covenant shall he corrupt by flatteries;* i. e. hypocrites and apostates will be found to be fit tools of his intrigue and malice against the Church; *but the people that do know their God shall be strong, and do exploits. And*

* Dan. xi, 31.

they that understand among the people, shall instruct many, yet they shall fall by the sword, and by flame, by captivity, and by spoil, days. This was a sore persecution under Antiochus. Now it was, that the events took place, narrated in Heb. xi, 35—38: *And others were tortured not accepting deliverance,* (i. e. on wicked terms) *that they might obtain a better resurrection. And others had trial of cruel mockings and scourgings; yea, moreover of bonds and imprisonments. They were stoned, they were sawn asunder, were tempted, were slain with the sword. They wandered about in sheep skins, and goat-skins, being destitute, afflicted, tormented; of whom the world was not worthy; they wandered in deserts, and in mountains, and in dens, and caves of the earth.* Antiochus at this time plundered and defiled the temple at Jerusalem; calling it, The temple of *Jupiter Olympus;* and erecting there, upon the sacred altar, the image of this heathen God. This, with the attendant evils, of *defiling* the Jewish altars, forbidding their sacrifices, and compelling the Jews to conform to the rites and manners of the heathen, *was the abomination of desolation standing in the holy place.* Upon this, multitudes of the pious Jews fled to the mountains, as is noted in the above passage in Heb. xi, 35—; an event, to which probably our Lord *alludes,* when he gave the direction to his disciples, to *flee to the mountains,* at the destruction of Jerusalem. A powerful army was sent by Antiochus, with a command to destroy Jerusalem; to put to death all the men, and to sell for slaves the women and children. The commander, after arriving at Jerusalem, concealed his object; till on the sabbath, when the Jews were assembled for Divine worship, he undertook to execute his orders. The massacres and horrible scenes, which followed, were dismal. The city was plundered, set on fire, and some of the walls demolished. The temple was spared. But a fortress was built, to prevent any worshipper approaching it. The impious monarch resolved utterly to extirpate the Jewish religion. He issued a decree, enforced with the severest penalties, that no God should be worship-

32

·ped, within his dominions, but his own gods. And he adopted the most rigorous measures to carry the edict into full execution Athenias, an old and ferocious minister, skilled in the Grecian idolatry, was sent to enforce the edict among the Jews: For the suppression of *their* religion was the great object of the decree. He dedicated the temple to Jupiter Olympus; and erected on the altar the image of this god. All, who refused to worship this idol; he either put to death, or put them to dismal tortures. Altars, groves and statues were established throughout Syria. And all the Jews were commanded to worship them, under the severest penalties. Another edict was issued by Antiochus, making it instant death to sacrifice to the God of the Jews, to observe the sabbath, or any Mosaic rite. Strenuous attempts were made to destroy every copy of the law; which the king commanded to be given up, under pain of death. After great numbers had fled to the wilderness, some had apostatized, and many had most firmly sealed their testimony with their blood; Antiochus, in person, came to Jerusalem, to see his edicts enforced with greater violence. He had recourse to the stake, the rack, and to various modes of execution the most horrid. The constancy of the sufferers filled him with surprise and madness.

After a season of such cruel sufferings, the Jews armed in defence of their religion, and their rights. And God enabled them to do wonders, in the time of the Maccabees, in destroying their idolatrous enemies, and freeing themselves from their horrid oppressions. "This desolation of the temple, and the taking away of the daily sacrifice under Antiochus, continued *three years and a half;*"[*] the *very term* given for the slaughtered state of the witnesses![†]

It is striking to observe the coincidence of the following events. When the tribes of Israel, just redeemed from Egypt, fell under the Divine displeasure, they were doomed to wander forty years in the *wilder-*

---

[*] Newton on the Prophecies, vol. i, p. 310.   [†] Rev. xi, 9.

ness. When Jezebel persecuted the prophets of the Lord, Elijah fled into the wilderness.. When Antiochus was suffered to invade the rights of the Jewish Church, and set up his abomination in the temple of Jerusalem; some of the pious Jews fled into the wilderness, and *wandered about in sheep-skins and goat-skins,—in deserts, mountains, dens and caves of the earth.* When the Roman abomination of desolation was found in array against Jerusalem, the disciples were directed to flee, in the utmost haste, over the tops of their flat-roofed houses, and from their fields, out of Jerusalem, into the mountains. When Popery and Mohammedism were suffered to invade the rights of conscience, and thus set up their abomination of desolation in the holy place, the true Church fled into the wilderness, (or into a situation mystically so represented) for 1260 years. And when Antichrist appears, and the dragon commences his last furious attack upon the woman, previous to her millennial glory, she is represented as again flying into the wilderness, the residue of her 1260 years;* indicating, that she had previously in a measure come forth from her wilderness state; but is again driven back to it. What particular kind of fulfilment this prediction of the woman's *second* flight into the wilderness, will receive, time will disclose. But the predictions which relate to that event, give it a very interesting complexion.

In Isa. xxvi, the introduction of the Millennium, and the tremendous events preceding it, are prophetically described. And the chapter closes with the following address to the saints; *Come my people, enter into thy chambers, and shut thy doors about thee; hide thyself as it were for a little moment, until the indignation be overpast. For, behold, the Lord cometh out of his place to punish the inhabitants of the earth for their iniquity: the earth also shall disclose her blood, and shall no longer cover her slain.* The former of these texts has been supposed to import only the flying of God's people to *Him,* in that day of

---

* Rev. xii, 14.

distress.   And this, no doubt, is a blessed idea involved in the words. *The name of the Lord is a strong tower; the righteous runneth into it, and is safe.*   But in
the light of the predictions already noted, relative, to
that period, it appears natural to view this text as a
brief description of the *state* of the Church, during the
little moment, or the three prophetic days and a half, of
the severest trials of the witnesses; that for this short
term, they will, through the violence of the tempest, in
some way resemble persons, who are driven from their
business, and hid in their inner chambers.   This idea
has countenance as has been noted, in Ezra iv.   The
return of the Jews from Babylon, and the rebuilding of
Jerusalem, were a *type* of the introduction of the Millennium.   But the walls of *that* new Jerusalem were
built in *troublous times.*   And the builders, through the
falsehood and violence of their enemies, were forced to
discontinue the work, for a time.   The antitype of this
event may be experienced in a time still future, through
the instigation of vile Samaritans, and by persecuting
authorities.

Is it not analogous with God's usual dispensations
toward his people, that the Church should endure her
most severe conflict with her enemies, just before the
dawn of her millennial glory? What has given rise to
the well-known maxim, *The darkest time is just before
day?*   No doubt this has abundantly been found to be
true, in its figurative import.   The Church and individuals have often found it true in their trials.   The
severest struggle is often just before relief comes.   Recollect the oppressed state of the Church in Egypt;
and in the subsequent captivities of Israel.   The truth
of the above remark was there very manifest.   The
events, which have been supposed to be emblematical
of the relief of the Church, at the dawn of the Millennium, favor this idea; for instance, the scene at the
Red Sea; and the passing of Israel over Jordan, into
the promised land, when that river was overflowing all
its banks, in the time of wheat harvest.   Relative to
the former, the Egyptians seemed to have been vanquished; and Israel, saved from their power, had com-

menoed their march.   But the most frightful scene of all was still before the Church of God;—the scene at the Red Sea, which was but a *type* of that which will occasion the song of Moses and of the Lamb.   Gideon with his three hundred men wrought a great deliverance in Israel from the vast combined hosts of the Midianites, Amalekites, and children of the east, whose camels and numbers were as the sand of the sea. (Judges vii, 12,—)   This deliverance was preceded by the *breaking* of the *pitchers,* which contained the lights, in the little army of Gideon.   How fit an emblem were those pitchers of the *followers,* particularly of the *ministers* of Christ!   Paul said to the Corinthians, *But we have this treasure in earthen vessels, that the excellency of the power may be of God, and not of us;* alluding probably to that very passage in the history of Gideon.   How far Christ's earthen vessels are to be *broken,* before the armies of Antichrist shall be vanquished, God only knows.   But the severest trials often just precede the greatest deliverances.   This idea has been found *true* in the greatest and in smaller events.   When the devil found he was about to be cast out of the youth brought to Christ, (Matt. ix, 20,) he exerted all his violence upon the unhappy subject. He threw him down, cried out, tore him, yea rent him sore, and left him as dead.   The reason is evident; *it was his last opportunity.*   And how natural is the import of the solemn notice from Heaven, *Woe to the inhabiters of the earth and of the sea; for the devil is come down unto you having great wrath, because he knoweth he hath but a short time.*   Here Satan's rage *increases,* as his time to persecute *diminishes.*   Does not the above text decide, what analogy forcibly suggests, that the Church will see most trying scenes, just before her millennial salvation?   Or will the analogy of God's usual dealings with his people fail on that occasion?*

* Possibly all the predictions, which indicate the fiery trials of Christ's witnesses, may relate only to his witnesses on the *old Roman earth,* or within the present compass of the Empire of the last head of the Beast.   For that seems to be the theatre of the events of many of the predictions of the Apocalypse.   And

Scripture and analogy seem unitedly to teach, that it may be said of the Church general, at the opening of the Millennium, *These are they who came out of great tribulation.* And the same thing is indicated in their *song of Moses and of the Lamb.* The Church will just have been delivered, under the Captain of her salvation, from the most violent assaults of the enemy; as were Israel on the eastern bank of the Red Sea, under the direction of Moses, when they uttered their song of praise.†

It is not to be expected, that the Church will again see *such depression*, as she saw in the worst times in the dark ages; *such smallness of numbers; and involved in such clouds of ignorance!* It does not seem probable that she will be forced to return to *this state.* The present numbers of the Church, and the light which has dawned upon her, seem to forbid it. Perhaps the numbers of true Christians, and the light enjoyed in the Church, will never be less than at present; nay, will *increase.* But can we hope a majority of the people of the Christian world will become gracious, before the battle of that great day? No doubt a *very great* majority of them will continue to reject Christ. This is gathered from the predictions, which relate to that period. What then may we expect this *very great* majority of people, rejectors of Christ, will be found to be doing, under all the artful and powerful attacks of Infidelity and licentiousness? and under the attack of that three-fold agency, of the dragon, of Antichrist,

no doubt some of Christ's true witnesses are there, notwithstanding that those regions are so enveloped in Atheism. Whether the predictions of the depressions of the people of God in the last days, under the reign of Antichrist, will principally be fulfilled upon the few followers of Christ who may be found in the old Popish countries, the event will decide. God in mercy grant, that the calamities may be no more extensive! But I do not feel satisfied, that the prophecies do not give them a far wider extent. The Church of the restored Jews in Palestine is surely included in the last struggle. And we have much reason to apprehend that the great body of the Christian Church will be involved in trials under the reign of Antichrist.

† Exodus xv.

and of false religion;* which *if it were possible, would deceive even the very elect?* They will be gathered to the battle of that great day of God Almighty! They will be found rapidly filling up the measure of their sins. Usual restraints will be taken off. *Let us break their bands asunder; and cast away their cords from us.* The abounding of iniquity will cause the love of many to wax cold, and to indulge violent hatred. Their opposition will *rise* in proportion to the evangelical light, which they reject; as did that of the crucifiers of Christ. This principle of human depravity, of hating the more, the more clearly the light shines, will then be found operating to an unprecedented degree; as restraints will be taken off, and things will be found ripening to an unprecedented crisis. This may cause the Jordan of Antichristian violence to overflow all its banks; and to roll its turbid billows, even in the time of wheat harvest, between the tribes of the Lord, and their millennial Canaan *then in view!* In this way the impenitent under the Gospel will be prepared for the awful scenes of judgment, which will burst forth upon them, and accomplish the designs of the battle of the great day. The slain of the Lord, at that period, are to be *many, from one end of the earth, even to the other end of the earth.* And they will prove to be *the slain of the Lord,* in consequence of being found in battle array against the Lord. And this their battle array will be *threatening,* as the subsequent judgments will be *decisive* and awful.

———

Ye friends of the kingdom of Christ; how interesting are the times, into which it has been our lot to fall? We behold the last head of the Pagan Roman Beast; the deadly wounded head healed; and the Beast, that ascendeth out of the bottomless pit, presented before our eyes! This is mystically the head, that crucified our Lord; and in ten bloody persecutions, endeavored to banish primitive Christianity from the world! And his eventual object now will be, *war with the Lamb;*

* Rev. xvi, 13, 14.

(Rev. xvii, 14;) *war with the saints;* (Rev. xiii, 7;) *persecution of the woman;* (Rev. xii, 13;) *to make war against him who sitteth on the horse;* (Rev. xix, 19;) to fulfil the deeds of the antitype of Antiochus; (Dan. xi, 31—35;) to make war against the witnesses; (Rev. xi, 7;) and to fulfil the distressing things against the Church, predicted by Christ in Matt. xxiv, Mark xiii, and Luke xxi, as noted in this section. This *may* not be the present motive of Antichrist. While forming his vassal kingdoms, his object will appear to be more political. But the above are objects predicted to be *eventually* accomplished by him, and by men of *his spirit.* These things are interesting to us. We *may* have peace in our day; and we *may* see the *reverse.* Let us not be greatly disappointed, if we are called to meet *sore trials!*

When these days are found opening upon us, are not the following sacred injunctions emphatically applicable?

"Watch ye; stand fast in the faith; quit you like "men; be strong. Be strong in the Lord, and in the "power of his might. Put on the whole armor of God, "that ye may be able to stand against the wiles of the "devil.—Take unto you the whole armor of God, that "ye may be able to withstand in the evil day; and having "done all, *to stand.* Stand therefore having your loins "girt about with truth; and having on the breastplate "of righteousness; and your feet shod with the pre- "paration of the Gospel of peace. Above all, taking "the shield of faith, wherewith ye shall be able to "quench all the fiery darts of the wicked. And take "the helmet of salvation, and the sword of the Spirit, "which is the word of God: Praying always, with all "prayer and supplication in the Spirit; and watching "thereunto with all perseverance, and supplication "for all saints. Seek the Lord all ye meek of the "earth,—seek righteousness, seek meekness; it may "be ye may be hid in the day of the Lord's anger. "For as a snare shall it come on all who dwell on the "face of the earth. Ye are not in darkness, that that "day should overtake you unawares. Exhort one an-

"other, and so much the more as ye see the day
"approaching. Take heed that no man deceive you.
"Watch ye therefore, and pray always; that ye may
"be accounted worthy to escape all these things, that
"shall come to pass; and to stand before the Son of
"man."

What matter of gratitude and joy, that we are not
left in darkness relative to the termination of the trials
of the Church under the tyranny of Antichrist! Though
she may for a season be depressed; yet God will be
near, and will regard her as the apple of his eye. And
she will eventually *rise;* and the enemy will *sink.* The
first reign of the Imperial head of the Roman Beast
closed in his being wounded to death. And the *second,*
his present reign, will close in his *going into perdition.*
This will be inconceivably more terrible and decisive,
than the *first* catastrophe. Concerning the *first,* in the
revolution under Constantine, we read, (Rev. vi, 12, to
the end,) *And I beheld, when he had opened the sixth
seal, and lo, there was a great earthquake; and the
sun became black as sackcloth of hair, and the moon
became as blood; and the stars of heaven fell unto the
earth, even as a figtree casteth her untimely figs when
she is shaken of a mighty wind. And the heavens
departed as a scroll, when it is rolled together; and
every mountain and island were moved out of their
places. And the kings of the earth, and the great
men, and the rich men, and the chief captains, and
the mighty men, and every bond man, and every free
man, hid themselves in the dens, and in the rocks of
the mountains; and said to the mountains and rocks,
Fall on us, and hide us from the face of him that sitteth on the throne, and from the wrath of the Lamb.
For the great day of his wrath is come, and who shall
be able to stand?* This exhibition of divine wrath, at
the wounding to death of the Imperial head of the Roman Beast, was terrible. How much *more* terrible
will be the exhibition, when Antichrist, who is represented as *this same head revived,* and renewing his war
with Christ, shall be utterly destroyed under the most
signal judgments of heaven? This latter event will an-

swer to that description, in a far more extensive and terrible sense, than did the revolution in Rome, in the year
320, to which the passage, in its chronological order
relates.

Ye learn then, O Christians, who may live in the
days of Antichristian violence, the happy termination
of your struggles with Antichrist. Your afflictions
will for a time abound; and your consolations may also
abound. Hear the animating words of your Almighty
Captain, when the terrors of the battle shall be perceived.

"Fear not, for I am with thee; be not dismayed, for
"I am thy God. When thou walkest through the wa-
"ters, they shall not overflow thee; and through the
"fire thou shalt not be burnt. I am with thee, to de-
"liver thee, saith the Lord. I, even I am he, that
"comforteth you. Who art thou, that thou shouldst
"be afraid of a man, that shall die, and of the son of
"man, that shall be made as grass; and forgettest the
"Lord thy Maker, who hath stretched forth the heav-
"ens, and laid the foundations of the earth; and hast
"feared continually every day, because of the fury of
"the oppressor, as though he were ready to destroy?
"And where is the fury of the oppressor? When these
"things begin to come to pass, then look up, and lift
"up your heads; for your redemption draweth nigh.
"Fear ye not the reproach of men, neither be afraid of
"their revilings. Fear not them, who kill the body;
"and after that have no more that they can do. But
"fear him, who is able to destroy both soul and body
"in hell. Are not two sparrows sold for a farthing?
"and one of them shall not fall to the ground, without
"your Father. But the very hairs of your head are all
"numbered. Fear ye not therefore, ye are of more
"value than many sparrows! Whosoever, therefore,
"shall confess me before men, him will I confess also
"before my Father, who is in heaven. But whosoever
"shall deny me before men, him will I also deny before
"my Father, who is in heaven. Awake, awake, put
"on strength, O arm of the Lord; awake, as in the
"ancient days, in the generations of old. Art thou
"not it, that hath cut Rahab, and wounded the dragon?

"Art thou not it, that hath dried the sea, the waters of
"the great deep; that hath made the depth of the sea a
"way for the ransomed to pass over? Therefore the
"redeemed of the Lord shall return, and come with
"singing unto Zion; and everlasting joy shall be upon
"their head: they shall obtain gladness and joy; and
"sorrow and mourning shall flee away."

SECTION II.

*Gog and his Bands: Or the final expedition and over-
throw of Antichrist, in Palestine.*

It may be fairly collected from various predictions,
noted in the preceding pages, that Antichrist is the
Power, who is to lead the attack upon the ancient people of God, after their return from their long dispersion, to the land of their fathers. The noted pasage in
Dan. xi, 36, to the end, clearly favors this opinion.
Says the Angel, in his preparatory remarks; *Now I am
come to make thee understand what shall befall thy
people in the latter days; for yet the vision is for
many days.** And the Power, whom he proceeds to
predict, is found, at the time of the end, in the Holy
Land, and there meets his overthrow! The prediction,
relative to the coalition and destruction at Armageddon; Rev. xvi, 13—; *that* relative to the Beast from
the bottomless pit; Rev. xvii; *that* relative to the last
battle of the Beast, and his vassal kings, with Christ;
Rev. xix, 19—; and that relative to the Roman Beast,
as distinct from the Papal horn, being slain at the battle
of the great day, and his body destroyed, and given to
the burning flame; Dan. vii, 11; all unite to evince,
that Antichrist is to lead in this attack upon the Church
of Judah and Israel in Palestine.

We have then a clew, by which to understand the
predictions in the xxxviiith, and xxxixth, chapters of
Ezekiel, concerning *Gog* and his *bands.* The Angel said
to Daniel, when about to predict Antichrist;† *But I
will show thee that which is noted in the Scripture of
truth.* Antichrist then, was before *noted in the Scrip-*

* Dan. x, 14. † Dan. x, 21.

ture of truth. We may believe he here refers to these very chapters of Ezekiel. For in no other part of the Old Testament had Antichrist been more clearly predicted.

In Ezekiel xxxvi and xxxvii, we have very express predictions of the return, re-union, and conversion of the *house of Israel;* meaning not only the Jews, Levites and the tribe of Benjamin; but also the other ten tribes. In chapter xxxvi, 16—; God relates the criminal cause of their dispersion; the great dishonor they had done to his name among the heathen, where they had resided; and that for his own name's sake he would gather them.* God says; *For I will take you from among the heathen, and will gather you out of all countries, and will bring you into your own land. Then will I sprinkle clean water upon you, and ye shall be clean; from all your filthiness, and from all your idols will I cleanse you. A new heart also will I give you, and a new spirit will I put within you; and I will take away the stony heart out of your flesh, and I will give you a heart of flesh. And I will put my Spirit within you, and cause you to walk in my statutes; and ye shall keep my judgments and do them. And ye shall dwell in the land, that I gave to your fathers; and ye shall be my people, and I will be your God.* In chapter xxxvii, the subject is resumed; and their restoration and conversion are predicted under a figure of the resurrection of a valley full of dry bones. The vision is applied, verse 11; *These bones are the whole house of Israel;* i. e. the Jews, and all the other tribes. *Therefore prophesy, and say unto them, Thus saith the Lord God, Behold, O my people, I will open your graves, and cause you to come out of your graves, and bring you into the land of Israel. And ye shall know that I am the Lord, when I have opened your graves, O my people, and brought you up out of your graves, and shall put my Spirit in you, and ye shall live, and I*

* The following texts predict God's treatment of the Jews in their dispersion; and their return. Hos. iii, 4; Deut. xxix, 64; Numb. xxiii, 9; Deut. xxviii, 37, 65; Hos. iii, 5.

will place you in your own land. Then shall ye know that I the Lord have spoken it, and performed it saith the Lord.

A striking representation follows of the re-union of the Jews and the ten tribes. The prophet by Divine direction takes two sticks. Upon the one he writes, *For Judah, and for the children of Israel his companions;* i. e. For the Jews, and such of the other tribes, as returned with them from Babylon. On the other stick he writes, *For Joseph, the stick of Ephraim, and for all the house of Israel, his companions;* i. e. For the ten tribes of Israel, who revolted in the days of Rehoboam, and have ever since been separate from the Jews. These two sticks miraculously become one in the prophet's hand. And this miracle God explains, by the two nations, the Jews and Israel, becoming permanently *united* in one nation, in the land of their fathers, and remaining holy and happy thenceforward under the reign of Christ, their spiritual David.

And now, in the two following chapters, we have a description of a terrible event, which is to take place upon this their re-union and re-settlement in the Holy Land. Lest Israel should expect to regain their ancient inheritance, and enter upon their millennial bliss, without any signal danger; or lest, when they should find an extensive and furious coalition formed against them, not long after their return, they should deem this event inconsistent with the promises of God; and also that the Church of God might be forewarned of so signal an event, as what was now to follow; *an account is given of a most extensive and terrible combination against the Jews and Israel in Palestine.*

As the ancient deliverance of Israel from Egypt was attended with signal judgments on the Egyptians; as their entrance on the possession of the promised land was succeeded by the destruction of the Canaanites; and as their deliverance from Babylon was attended with the total destruction of that Pagan empire; so the re-settlement of that people of God in the promised land, after their long dispersion, must be succeeded by scenes of *destruction* to the surrounding enemies of the Church.

And these scenes of destruction are to be as much more *terrible*, than were those of old, as the importance of this restoration of Israel shall exceed those former restorations. God will now suffer the devil, and his legions of followers on earth, to do their *worst*, and make their most *desperate* effort, in order to exhibit a new *momento* of what is in the human heart; to occasion to the Church of Israel their last and most *fiery* trial, previous to their millennial glory; and to afford the great Head of the Church an opportunity to make an exhibition of his power and faithfulness, in the most signal vindication of his cause; and in the destruction of the kingdom of the devil.

This last and most terrible effort is to be directed by a Power, called *Gog, the land of Magog, the chief prince of Meshech and Tubal.**

The prophet begins; *And the word of the Lord came unto me saying, Son of man, set thy face against Gog, the land of Magog, the chief prince of Meshech and Tubal, and prophecy against him, and say, Behold I am against thee, O Gog, the chief prince of Meshech and Tubal.* The Power here addressed is veiled with a mystic appellation; as is usual in prophecy. Different things have been conjectured concerning this name. Some have supposed it derived from Gyges, an ancient king of Lydia, a country in Asia Minor, which fell un-

* Some expositors read the above passage; *Gog, the land of Magog, the prince of Rosh, Meshech and Tubal.* This I think is *incorrect.* We find the names of Magog, Meshech and Tubal, in ancient sacred record; but not the name *Rosh,* or *Ros;* excepting a son of Benjamin of this name, (Gen. xlvi, 21) who could not have been reckoned among the re-settlers of the earth after the flood. Why this Hebrew word *ros,* found in connexion with *prince* in the text under consideration, should be construed as a *proper name,* I cannot comprehend. *Ros* in Pike's Lexicon, signifies *head, chief, top, captain, principal, first.* This word then, when found among the names, who were known to be among the ancient re-settlers of the earth, and united with the word, which imports *prince,* is well rendered by our translators, *the chief prince;* or prince of the chief, as rendered by Pool. But to render it a proper name, *fetters* the text with the needless difficulty of having to ascertain who can be meant by *Ros,* and what connexion Gog has with him. To ascertain which, no data can be found.

der the dominion of Antiochus; and that the address was to Antiochus. Possibly this may account for the name, as Antiochus was a designed type of Antichrist. But whether it account for it, or not, there appears full evidence, as I shall attempt to shew, that the address was designed for *Antichrist.* The name Gog appears a natural abbreviation of *Magog;* and is doubtless designed to signify a noted dynasty or government of the descendants of *Magog.* It signifies a *roof* or *covering;* and would be naturally applied to the most noted sovereignty of the descendants of Magog, at the time of the restoration of Israel.

The dominions of Gog are called, *the land of Magog.* Magog was a son of Japhet, and grandson of Noah. His descendants peopled ancient Scythia, which lay east and north of the Euxine and Caspian seas, north of Syria. Thence they spread, and peopled the vast regions of the present Tartary. They are said to have peopled a large tract in the north of Asia and Europe, 5000 miles in length, from east to west; and of great breadth, from north to south. "There can be no doubt (says Mr. Guthrie, Geo. p. 89,) that the Scandinavians" (the inhabitants of Denmark, Norway and Sweden,) "were Scythians by their origin." The descendants of ancients Magog, under the various names of Scythians, Tartar, Moguls, Turks, Goths, Vandals, Huns, Franks and others, have made the most terrible ravages in the earth. Various clans of them, in early ages, overran, and peopled a considerble part of Asia and Europe. "A little before the Christian era, (says a geographer,*) Sigge, afterward called Odin, from the north east of Asia," (where Magog settled) "conquered and then inhabited part of Sweden." There we accordingly find a *Gothland,* whose ancient inhabitants were thus of the descendants of Magog. Hordes of these northern barbarians were ravaging various kingdoms in the south of Europe, in the early days of Christianity. In the reign of Gallus, "an almost innumerable company (says Dr. Lowman†) of Scythians

* Morse, Geog. p. 64.　†On Rev. p. 49.

fell upon Italy; and ravaged Macedonia, Thessaly and Greece; a part of them, from the Palus Mœotis, broke through the Bosphorus into the Euxine sea, and laid waste many provinces." And abundantly are we informed of the terrible ravages made in the Roman empire, or in the kingdoms in the southwest of Europe, in the former ages of the Christian era, by floods of these invading northern barbarians. "These fierce tribes were scattered (says Mr. Guthrie*) over the vast countries of the north of Europe, and northwest of Asia, which are now inhabited by the Danes, the Swedes, the Poles, the subjects of the Russian empire, and the Tartars.—Great bodies of armed men, with their wives and children,—issued forth, like regular colonies, in quest of new settlements. New adventurers followed them. The lands, which they deserted, were occupied by more remote tribes of barbarians. These, in their turn, pushed forward into more fertile countries; and, like a torrent continually increasing, rolled on, and swept away every thing before them.—The *scourge* of God, and the *destroyer* of nations, are the dreadful epithets, by which the most noted of the barbarian leaders were known." These barbarians, it is well known, overran, and settled in the south of Europe, particularly in the western branch of the old Roman empire. The Suevi and Alans settled in Spain in the year 409. They were afterward overran by the Goths. In 410 the Goths took Rome; and settled in Italy. The Franks about the year 420 overran the ancient *Gauls*, and settled in *France*. The Huns took up their abode in Hungary, in 460; some say at earlier date. The Gapidæ and Lombards established a kingdom in Italy, in 568. The Vandals, who had before settled in Gallicia in Spain, crossed the straits of Gibraltar, under the command of Genseric, and invaded the seven northern, rich and fertile provinces of Africa, where they established a kingdom. Thence *they*, in 455, invaded and plundered Rome, which they possessed for nearly a century, till they were subdued by Justinian. Thus

* Geo. p. 56, 57.

these floods of barbarians, the descendants of Magog, left their own countries in the regions of the north; and for several centuries rendered the fairest parts of Europe a field of blood; and they took up their residence there; they divided the Roman empire into various kingdoms. Well may these territories then, be called, *the land of Magog.* They perfectly answer that prophetic and mystical appellation.

Gog is called also *the chief prince of Meshech and Tubal.* Meshech and Tubal were brethren of Magog: And no doubt their descendants were mingled. The posterity of Meshech peopled Cappadocia, and Armenia. Thence they sent colonies to the north, who were called the Moschi, or Moscovites. The posterity of Tubal, Josephus informs, peopled Iberia on the Black Sea. According to Bochart, Tubal was the father of the Tibarenes, on the north of Armenia the Less. And Martin (in his Philological Library) informs, that Tubal was the father of the Russians. All these may have been different branches of the desendants of Tubal. We must naturally suppose, that in the rage of invasion, which excited the numerous clans of the northern barbarians in the fifth and sixth centuries, the descendants of Meshech and Tubal united with their neighbors and brethren in these incursions upon the Roman empire. No doubt so many of the ancient posterity of Meshech and Tubal intermingled with their neighboring brethren, the posterity of Magog, and became *one* with them, that it was proper, in a prophetic hint, to add the names of *Meshesh* and *Tubal* to that of *Magog,* to designate a distant and most interesting *Empire* of their descendants.

Other reasons *may,* in the course of Providence, occur, to evince the propriety of the addition of these two names. Should the influence of the French dynasty be found to be extended over regions in the *north east,* evidenly peopled in ancient times by the descendants of *Meshech* and *Tubal,* it might afford an additional reason why their names were added in the prophetic description of their sovereignty, of the last days. This we are led to suspect *may* be the case, after the judg-

34

ment of the sixth vial; or the subversion of the Turkish empire by the arms of the infidel Power. And this
appears to be hinted in the course of these descriptions
of Gog, where he forms various of *those nations* into
his vast confederacy, and directs their operations against
the house of Israel.

A terrible Power rising on the ground of the old
Roman empire answers with as *real precision* to the description of Ezekiel's Gog, as would a Power rising in
the north of Europe, or Asia, should such an event
take place, where the posterity of Magog, Meshech,
and Tubal, had their *primary* residence. Indeed, the
description given, as it respects these three names,
affords an almost boundless range, in which to look
for the dynasty represented by Gog. We have the vast
field, of the old Roman empire; especially its western
branch; the present Russian empire; and the north and
western parts *at least* of the Ottoman empire. Pool
informs, that Syria, and Asia Minor have been supposed to belong to *the land of Magog.* And he was of
opinion that the Scythians or Tartars, the Turks, and
the Roman *Antichrist,* (by which he meant the *Papal
Power*) would be found, *at some time* to unite in the
confederacy predicted in this chapter concerning Gog.
He was of opinion, that in the last times some active,
daring prince would be found to unite these numerous nations, and lead them against the Church of Israel re-settled in Palestine. But this must be done under the last head of the *Roman* empire. For if another
Power should rise to do it, it would be a *fifth* monarchy upon earth: Which the prophetic scriptures forbid.
See Dan. ii, and vii, chapters.

In looking over this vast range of nations, to find the
Power designated by Gog, are we not constrained to
fix our attention on the terrible Power, which has risen
on the ground of the old Roman empire; and which
exhibits every characteristic of the last head of the
Roman Beast; the Imperial head, recovered from its
deadly wound; the Antichrist of the last times? Here
we find a Power, which bids fair to be of equal magnitude with Gog; which with sufficient precision *is in the*

land of Magog, is the *chief prince of Meshech and Tubal*, and which goeth into perdition on the same ground, at the same period, and on the same expedition, with the *Gog* and his bands, under consideration. Do we need further evidence then, that Antichrist and Gog are the same? The numerous points of coincidence between them leave no room to doubt of the affirmative.*

* As some have doubted whether the Gog of Ezekiel, and the last head of the Roman Beast are the same Power, the following is subjoined to prove the affirmative.

The Roman Beast is clearly and repeatedly represented as the *last* great Power in hostile array against the Church; in the times just preceding the Millennium. And the prophecies relative to that period do not admit of a *fifth* monarchy arising on earth, before the Millennium. The succession of the great eastern monarchies, symbolized by the different parts of the great image, Dan. ii, 31—35, is to close with the *fourth*, the *Roman* monarchy; denoted by the legs of iron, and the feet and toes, part of iron, and part of clay.

This is the part of the image, that is last destroyed, to prepare the way for the Millennium. The Stone (Christ) cut out without hands, smites these feet and toes, and grinds them, with the remaining materials of the image, to powder; upon which the Stone becomes a great mountain, and fills the world. Inspiration explains it, verse 44, that in the days of *these kings* (the ten toes of the image, under a dynasty partly strong and partly broken, the last head of the Roman Beast) the God of heaven shall set up his millennial Kingdom. Surely then, it cannot be admitted, that so notable a Power as Gog, shall rise after the destruction of the Roman Beast, and before the Millennium.

The same thing we find in the parallel prophecy, Dan. vii, 11. "I beheld then, because of the voice of the great words which the horn spake, I beheld even till the Beast was slain, and his body destroyed, and given to the burning flame." Here is the destruction of the secular Roman Beast, at the battle of the great day. And the millennial Kingdom is represented as the *next* event. Verse 17, 18; "These great Beasts, which are four, are four kings which shall arise out of the earth. But the saints of the Most High shall take the kingdom, and possess the kingdom forever." Here no dynasty or Power rises between the destruction of the fourth Beast, and the reign of the saints. In Rev. xvii, it is the last head of the secular Roman Beast, that ascends in the last days from the bottomless pit, and goes into perdition, to prepare the way for the Kingdom of Christ. And in chap. xix, the same thing is evident. There it is the *Beast*, (clearly the last head of the secular Roman Beast,) with his false prophet, (Popery in its reduc-

The reasons why Antichrist may properly receive the appellation of *Gog, the land of Magog, the chief prince of Meshech and Tubal*, may be *summoned up* as follows.

ed form;) and with his kings of the earth, that is found in array against Christ, and that is destroyed, and cast into the lake of fire, in order immediately to prepare the way for the Millennium, which there follows. And it appears evident that this Beast is the Gog of Ezekiel. The destruction of each is found in the same connexion with the Millennium. And descriptions essentially the same are given of both. Take one instance: In Ezek. xxxviii, 17—20, is a call from the Most High (relative to the slaughtered bands of Gog) to the carnivorous fowls and beasts, to gather themselves together, to eat the flesh, and drink the blood of the mighty, of the princes of the earth, and to be filled at the table of God with slaughtered armies. And in the account of the destruction of the last head of the Roman Beast, Rev. xix, 17—19, is the *same thing;* and it rests on that very passage in Ezekiel. An Angel, standing in the sun, calls on the *fowls*, to gather themselves together to the supper of the great God, to eat the flesh of kings, and captains, and mighty men, and their hosts. This, and the various descriptions in the two chapters clearly relate to the same Power, and period. And they appear evidently the same with the forenoted text, Dan. vii, 11, where the Beast and his subordinate horn are destroyed and given to the burning flame. Surely then, Gog cannot be a Power rising in Turkey, or among some of the eastern nations, after the destruction of the Roman Beast, and before the Millennium.

To ascertain this point still further, consider what address is made to Gog; Ezek. xxxviii, 17; "Thus saith the Lord God, Art thou he, of whom I have spoken in old times by my servants the prophets of Israel, who prophecied in those days, many years, that I would bring thee against them?" Here we learn, that Gog is a great and notable dynasty; and not a mere accidental rising of some nations; and of so small account, as not to be reckoned a monarchy on earth. We learn here, that Gog is the very Power so abundantly predicted of old by the prophets in Israel; and who is to collect the nations, in the last days, to the battle of that great day of the Lord, in an expedition against the Jews;—"that I would bring thee against them." But this great Power, so much noted in the prophets, was clearly the *Roman Beast* of the last days; and not a Power subsequent to the Roman Beast.

To prepare the way for the striking prediction of the last head of the Roman Beast, in Dan. xi, 36—to the end; the Angel says; chap. x, 14, 21; "Now I am come to make thee understand what shall befal thy people in the latter days; for yet the vision is for many days.; I will shew thee that which

1. Gog is a natural abbreviation of Magog, and may naturally be taken as a mystic appellation of a terrible *dynasty* or *government* of some important empire of the descendants of Magog.

2. The French, and the nations, which do or will constitute the French empire, may properly be said to have been the natural descendants of Magog, Meshech and Tubal, since the northern barbarians overran, and settled in those nations, in the fifth and sixth centuries.

3. These appellations are *striking*, on account of the similarity between Antichrist, and those northern barbarians; in point of real *heathenism, conquests*, and *cruelty*; both alike overwhelming the Roman empire, and nations marked out for a prey, like a sweeping flood; pulling down and setting up kingdoms at pleasure, in

-is noted in the scripture of truth." Here the last head of the Roman Beast is the power that was "noted in the scripture of truth;" or much predicted of old; just as Gog was "*he* of whom God spake of old times by the prophets;" as before noted. Also here the last head of the Roman Beast is to occasion what shall befal the Jews, in the last days; just as Gog is to be brought against them; Ezek. xxxviii, 17.

In the view of the above scriptures, compared with what is said of the seventh trumpet, and the seventh vial, we learn that Gog, and the last head of the Roman Beast, are the same. Rev. x, 7; But in the days of the seventh angel, when he shall begin to sound, the mystery of God shall be finished, *as he hath declared to his servants the prophets.*" Here the Power that *falls*, under the third wo, is that Power noted and destined to this destruction, in the prophets. Rev. xvi, 14;—"to gather them to the battle of THAT great day of God Almighty." The seventh vial then, is *that* great day, so well known in the prophets, as destroying the last enemy of the Church, before the Millennium.

If Gog be not the *same*, with the last head of the Roman Beast; but be some subsequent eastern Power; then he is a *fifth monarchy upon earth.* For the Gog of Ezekiel is a great and most noted Power; as is evident from the afore noted address of the Most High to him; and from the wonderful exploits to be done by him, of collecting so great a part of the world, and leading them against Palestine. But it has been shown that the prophecies do not admit of a *fifth monarchy.* Hence Gog and the last head of the Roman Beast *must be the same*—the great Kingdom of the last days, partly strong, and partly broken.

defiance of all justice, and the laws of nations. Antichrist has thus exhibited a character similar to the *chief princes* of those barbarous invaders, who were called *The scourge of God; and the destroyers of man.* And

4. The future conquests and influence of Antichrist in the *east,* and *north,* may add a still further emphasis to the propriety of these appellations. *Thus much for his description.*

The prophet proceeds in recording the words of the Most High to Gog, in Ezek. xxxviii: *And I will turn thee back, and put hooks into thy jaws, and will bring thee forth, and all thine army, horses and horsemen, all of them clothed with all sorts of armor, even a great company with bucklers and shields, all of them handling swords.* This text suggests not only the entire control, which God will exercise over Gog, but also the greatness of the numbers of the mixed multitudes under him. Other passages of Scripture speak of them as being *the kings of the earth, and of the whole world.* For behold in those days, and in that time, when I shall bring again the captivity of Judah and Jerusalem, I will also gather all nations, and will bring them down unto the valley of Jehoshaphat.†*

The prophet proceeds to give a summary list of the nations in this coalition under Gog:—*Persia, Ethiopia, and Libya with them; all of them with shields and helmets: Gomer and all his bands; the house of Togarmah of the north quarters, and all his bands, and many people with thee.* Vast mixed multitude! Let us trace them. Persia is at the head of the catalogue. Persia is situated on the east of the Ottoman empire; and is of the same religion, the Mohammedan. And as it is of late thought that the Afghans in Persia are the ten tribes of Israel, who will then have quitted their Persian territories, and gone to the land of their fathers, the Persians will readily be induced to unite in the coalition against Israel in Palestine. Perhaps they will claim them as their subjects; as the

---

* Rev. xvi, 14, and xix, 19.　　† Joel iii, 1, 2.

ancient Egyptian monarch did the tribes of Israel, when they were fleeing from his territories.

Ethiopia and Libya: These names are noted, as in connexion with the infidel Power, in his preceding expedition into the east; Dan. xi, 43; *And the Libyans and Ethiopians shall be at his steps.* It is natural then, to expect them to be in *this final coalition.* But who are the Ethiopians here mentioned? A considerable part of Africa is comprised under the name of Ethiopia;—Upper and Lower. The former including Nubia, and Abyssinia. The latter all the kingdoms south of the equinoctial line. But it is not probable that this vast territory, so far to the south, can be the Ethiopia in the coalition under Gog. The original Ethiopia, or Cush, was in the northwestern parts of Arabia. *Here*, east of the northern parts of the Red Sea, Cush, the son of Ham, took up his residence. From him those regions, in the Stony Arabia, were called the land of Cush, or Ethiopia. Here Moses married his Ethiopian wife.* This is nearly in the line pursued by the infidel Power in his preceding expedition.† These northwestern Arabs, it is natural then to suppose, will be the Ethiopians in the coalition under Gog. Probably they will be induced to unite, in hopes of rich plunder.

Libya comprises the *States of Barbary.* The Hebrew word for Libya here, is *Phut.* But *Phut*, the son of Ham, (Martin in his Phiollogical Library informs,) took up his residence in the western parts of Africa, on the Mediterranean, in the country of Mauritania, now Morocco and Algiers, where we find a city Putea, and a river Put. Pool on this passage informs, that Libya here means "a people of Africa, either now subjects of, or confederate with the Turks." As the Libyans are said to be at the steps of the Infidel Power, at the time of the overthrow of the *Turks;* as the States of Barbary are now subject to the Turks, and are the only powers of any note west of Egypt; and as the Libyans in the prophecy under consideration must

---

* Numb. xii, 1.   † Dan. xi, 40—43.

be supposed to be of some note, to have been predicted three or four and twenty centuries ago, to be in the
coalition under Gog; *the Barbary powers must have
been designed by the Libya or Phut in this place.*

Gomer and all his bands. Gomer, the oldest son of
Japhet, peopled Galatia, Phrygia, and some regions
round about the Euxine Sea. Thence his descendants
penetrated into Europe; and according to Brown they
peopled Hungary, Germany, Switzerland, France,
Spain, Portugal and Britain. Some of the Scots and
Irish, the Picts particularly, are supposed to have been
of the same origin. Martin is not so full upon the descendants of Gomer. But *he* informs that the ancient
Gomerites and the Galatians were the *same:* That from
Galatia they sent colonies into Europe, and settled
Germany; from which they spread themselves into
France, where they were called by the Greeks Galatæ,
or Gomerites, by the Latins Celtæ, and by the Britons
Gauls. Thus the name Gauls is derived from Gomer. And from Germany, or France, Martin informs,
came the first inhabitants of Great Britain. France,
being the only people of importance, who retain the
name of their primitive ancestor, or an evident derivation from it, must be the people meant by *Gomer.*
Gomer, and all his bands: i. e. The *Gauls* and all their
Empire. It was the *original* inhabitants of France, and
some of her neighboring nations, who descended from
Gomer. They in process of time became mixed with
their barbarous invaders from the north, the descendants of Magog, as has been shown. They now therefore, answer to *both* the names. The two names of the
French illustrate this idea; *Gauls*, or *Gomerites;* French,
or Franks, a clan of the descendants of Magog. Brown
informs,* that the ancient Gomerites in France and
Switzerland were long a terror to the Romans; but
were conquered by them; *and were finally swallowed
up by the descendants of Magog;* meaning the floods of
the northern barbarians.

*Dictionary of the Bible.

But some may inquire, whether *more* is not included in the clause, *Gomer and all his bands*, than the nations included in the present French empire? The original inhabitants of *Britain*, after the flood, were from *Gomer's line.** The Welsh in Britain call themselves Cumri, Cymro, or Comeri. These also are ancient Britons, who upon the invasion of England by the Saxons, from the north of Germany, in the sixth century, (in the fifth century, according to Milner, or in A. D. 447, vol. iii, p. 109) were driven into Wales. It is evident then, that the first inhabitants of Britain were Gomerites. If therefore France is included in *Gomer and all his bands*, notwithstanding her being overrun by the northern invaders, because her original inhabitants were *Gomerites;* why must not Great Britain, and consequently the United States, be likewise included, notwithstanding that Britain, after it was settled by the Gomerites, was afterward overrun by the Saxons, and then by the Normans; and the present English have descended from some of them? Reply. *Should* Britain and the United States fall under the French Empire, they *would* answer, with sufficient precision, to the description of Gomer, and all his bands, both a s being, in their primitive ancestors, the descendants of ancient Gomerites; and as belonging at last to the *bands* of the Gallic Empire. But we devoutly trust, that gracious Heaven does not design the subjugation

*The present *Gaelic* multitudes, in the Highlands and Islands of Scotland, are a remnant of this people. The above denomination of their dialect is, no doubt, a derivation from the name Gomer. This people are descendants from the ancient *Celtæ*, or Gomerites. Says the Secretary of the Society in Scotland for propagating Christian knowledge, relative to a new edition of the Bible in the Gaelic language,—"I will not enter into the question, how far the preservation of that ancient dialect of the Celtic, the language of our forefathers, the primitive inhabitants of this island, is an object of *just* desire.—Surely while the *Celtic*, whether in the *Irish*, *Welsh*, or *Gaelic* dialects, is the existing language of great bodies of remote and ignorant people, no wise and good man will refuse to give them the means of instruction in the only language, in which they are capable of receiving it." See the Panoplist for Sept. 1805, p. 167.

35

of our land, nor of that of our ancestors, to that devouring Power. We may hope for exceptions under
this general prediction. The great body of the Church
of Christ is now found in these two nations, the distant
ramifications of Gomer's line. And

"Oft has the Lord whole nations blest,
"For his own Church's sake."

But how many nations will eventually be found included in the *bands of Gomer,* time alone will disclose.

The house of Togarmah. Togarmah, a grandson of
Japhet, peopled Phrygia, Cappadocia, Turcomania,
some parts of Armenia and Paphlagonia. No doubt
Asia Minor is here included, and probably the chief of
the countries of the present Turkish or Ottoman empire. *Of the north quarters and all his bands.* This
may be read in *apposition* with the house of Togarmah; and leave out the *of: The house of Tagarmah; the
north quarters; and all the bands of the north:* Many of
the Tartars, and perhaps the Russians. *And many
people with thee.* Many others promiscuously united.

Here is a traversing round Palestine, from Persia on
the east, to Arabia on the south; and to the west,
through the north of Africa; then to the north, through
the southern and middle nations of Europe; then
round to the east, through Asia Minor, and the Turkish empire; then away indefinitely to the vast regions
of the north. Amazing combination, collected from
at least three of the quarters of the globe, to destroy
and plunder the Hebrews, recovered from their long
dispersion; a combination excited by the threefold
agency of the dragon, the Beast, and the false prophet;
and prepared for the *battle of that great day of God
Almighty.** This is indeed *gathering the nations
and assembling the kingdoms, to pour out upon them
the Divine indignation.*† *I will gather all nations
and tongues, and they shall come and see my glory.*‡
For I will gather all nations against Jerusalem to

---

* Rev. xvi, 13, 14.   † Zech. ii, 8.   ‡ Isai. lxvi, 18.

battle.* *And I saw the Beast, and the kings of the earth, and their armies gathered together to make war, against him that sat on the horse, and against his army.*†

Various motives no doubt will be found operating among the various nations and tribes thus uniting; such as enmity against the Christian religion; rage at the restoration of the Hebrews; rage at their conversion to Christianity; *rage against some rival nation, who will have been aiding in their restoration or conversion, and may be ready to afford them further assistance;* a desire among the fragments of different denominations, (as Papists and Mohammedans,) to meliorate their own broken cause; and an expectation of *rich plunder.* The latter will be a prime motive among many of these confederates; as we learn in the course of this chapter. The Jews and Israel having gone in great numbers from different parts of the world to Palestine, and transported with them vast sums of property; *their silver, and their gold with them unto the name of the Lord;*‡ this will naturally turn the attention of the multitudes, among whom they have resided, *after them.* No doubt some will feel as though they have a right to pursue and recover them, as their subjects; or to plunder them, as having conveyed off vast wealth from their territories. They may hence be excited to pursue them, like Pharaoh of old, rallying his army to pursue Israel, when leaving his dominions. And all the mighty movements will fall under the direction of Gog, or Antichrist.

The Most High addresses him. *Be thou prepared, and prepare for thyself, thou and all thy company, that are assembled unto thee; and be thou a guard unto them.* Most significant, ironical admonition! *After many days thou shalt be visited; in the latter years thou, shalt come into the land, that is brought back from the sword, and is gathered out of many people, against the mountains of Israel, which have been always waste; but*

---

* Zech. xiv, 2.   † Rev. xix, 19.   ‡ Isai. lx, 9.

it is brought forth out of the nations, and they shall dwell safely all of them. In the last days God will fulfil these things by you against his people, just recovered from their long dispersion, and dwelling heedlessly; or, they shall be built up, notwithstanding all your rage against them. *Thou shalt ascend, and come like a storm; thou shalt be like a cloud to cover the land, thou and all thy bands, and many people with thee.* Your attack shall be like a terrible *shower*, which ascends from the horizon, rises, approaches, roars, darkens the hemisphere, extends its wings beyond sight, becomes terrific with its lightning, thunder and wild commotion, till it overwhelms all, and seems about to blend the heavens and earth in ruin. *Thus saith the Lord God, it shall also come to pass, that at the same time shall things come into thy mind, and thou shalt think an evil thought. And thou shalt say, I will go up to the land of unwalled villages. I will go to them who are at rest, and dwell safely, all of them dwelling without walls, and having neither bars nor gates, to take a spoil, and to take a prey, to turn thine hand upon the desolate places, that are now inhabited, and upon the people, that are gathered out of the nations, who have gotten cattle and goods, and dwell in the midst of the land.* Here one motive of the vast movement is exposed, *which is plunder.* They will expect to make an easy prey of the rich and defenceless. The Hebrews will return with much riches, of *cattle and goods: Their silver and their gold with them unto the name of the Lord.*[*] They will have no city walls, nor gates; will have made no effectual arrangements for defence; but will appear an easy prey. This text clearly indicates, that the attack will be made not long after Israel's return: And yet that it will be a season; probably a number of years.

Mark what follows! *Sheba, and Dedan, and the merchants of Tarshish, with all the young lions thereof, shall say unto thee, Art thou come to take a spoil? Hast thou gathered thy company to take a prey? To*

---

[*] Isa. lx. 9.

carry away silver, and gold; to take away cattle and goods; to take a great spoil? Who are these? Is this an additional account of the nations in the confederacy under Gog? Or does it present a coalition in opposition to him? In favor of the *latter,* it may be observed, that the nations in a coalition under Gog, from every point of the compass, were before enumerated. And it does not seem probable, that the Holy Spirit would resume this subject, as though several powers had been forgotten or passed over. We must conjecture, that Gog had anticipated a powerful opposition in this enterprise. Else why had he collected so vast an army? The motive of the Most High, is to destroy *his enemies;* and that the nations should be collected, to see his justice and glorious power. But this is no part of the motive of Gog. And he too must have a *motive,* or reason, for collecting so vast an army. Do such sagacious generals make such vast collections of forces, to beat the air? Or to take a city, where they expect little or no opposition? No verily! The movements of Gog indicate, that he expects powerful opposition. The earth had previously helped the woman, and swallowed up *his* floods cast forth for her destruction. And *he,* in vexation and rage, undertakes this new expedition.* Tidings out of the east and out of the north trouble him. Some rival power assisting in the restoration of the Hebrews, or the conversion of the latter, fills him with wrath: *Therefore he shall go forth with great fury to destroy, and utterly to make away many.*† This text, and the vast collection, which he makes of forces, clearly indicate an expectation of vastly more opposition than he can expect from the Jews and Israel in Palestine. It is evident in this chapter that he expects little or none from the latter. His expectations of opposition must be from another quarter beside the Jews. Palestine is at that time chosen as the seat of contest with a more formidable power; although the affairs of the Jews and Israel afford a pretext for the expedition. A most desperate effort Antichrist

---

* Rev. xii, 17.　　　† Dan. xi, 44.

now makes, to destroy and utterly to *make away
many;* Dan. xi, 44, to *exterminate* the forces of some
rival enemy. Hence the *vastness* of his movements.

And this rival enemy is here presented, under the
name of *Sheba, and Dedan, and the merchants of Tarshish with all the young lions thereof.* Their language
is not that of friendship, but of opposition. *Art thou
come to take a spoil? Hast thou gathered thy company
to take a prey? To carry away silver and gold; to take
away cattle and goods; to take a great spoil?* Here
then is a voice, that dares to interrogate Gog in the
height of his glory; at the head of his countless legions;
in those days of revolution, and of blood!

But who are they, that constitute this coalition? *Sheba, and Dedan, and the merchants of Tarshish, with
all the young lions thereof!* God can either raise up, or
strengthen an opposition to Gog, from nations, that may
now appear the most unlikely. Some noted power may
be, aided by others now insignificant. Who are these
merchants of Tarshish, with all the young lions thereof?
Tarshish was a grandson of Shem. He peopled Ci-
licia. And from him the city Tarshish, or Tarsus,
there (the birth place of St. Paul) had its name. Its
inhabitants became the most expert seamen; built the
best ships;* and many of them became merchants.†
The Mediterranean in their vicinity came to be called
the sea of Tarshish. This name was given to a city
in Spain, Tartossus, or Tarshish. The west end of
the Mediterranean came to bear the same name. And
finally, authors inform us, *Tarshish* came to be a name
for the *sea* in general. Accordingly, the *ships of Tarshish* (Psalm xlviii, 7, and other places) mean *the ships
of the sea.* (See Pool on this passage.) Nothing is
more common, than for names in prophetic language
to be thus extended, and transmitted from one place,
and even nation, to another. When we read therefore,
of the *merchants of Tarshish,* at the time of the restoration of Israel, we must understand, not the descendants
of any of those ancient cities of that name; but the

* 1 Kings x, 22.   † Ezek. xxvii, 25; and Jer. x, 9.

merchants of the sea; or some great mercantile, maritime power. And their ships of war, we may suppose, are designed by *all the young lions thereof.* The *lion* may be the sign of their navy; or their coat of arms; as Castor and Pollux was the sign of the ship, in which Paul sailed to Rome. Acts xxviii, 11.

This naval, mercantile power will appear interested for the Jews; and will dare to interrogate the leader of the coalition against them. This idea receives countenance from collateral prophecies. In Isaiah lx, the return of the Jews is predicted in lively colors; *flying as clouds, and as doves to their windows.* In verse 9th, we are informed of an agency employed in their restoration. *Surely the isles shall wait for me, and the ships of Tarshish first, to bring thy sons from far, their silver and their gold with them, unto the name of the Lord thy God.* Here we find the same power; *the isles, and the ships of Tarshish first,* officiating in the return of the ancient people of God, *with their treasures,* to Palestine. And as this naval power of the isles will be found with ability to do this, in those days of revolution and of terror; so we must naturally expect they would do what is indicated by the above interrogations to Gog, when he shall be about to plunder the Jews of their treasures, and to seek their ruin. The isles and ships of Tarshish first bring back the people of Israel, and their *silver and gold* with them unto the name of the Lord. Gog rises to plunder and ruin them. And the merchants of Tarshish, with all their young lions, and with others upon this occasion, interrogate Gog; *Art thou come to take a spoil? Hast thou gathered thy company to take a prey? To carry away silver and gold; to take away cattle and goods; to take a great spoil?* Surely then, the isles, and the ships of Tarshish, in Isa. lx, 9; and the merchants of Tarshish, and all the young lions thereof, in the passage under consideration, *must be the same.*

In Psalm lxxii, we find the same thing. To predict the Millennium is the object of the Psalm. And in verse 10 we read, *The kings of Tarshish and of the isles shall bring presents.* In the light of the preced-

ing texts, we must naturally conceive, that this bringing of presents, by the powers of *Tarshish* and of the
isles, must refer to the *restoration* of the house of Israel;
which is a most prominent event in the prophecies of
the introduction of the Millennium. Then that ancient
people of God will need just such services; but probably not afterward. In Zeph. iii, 10, we read, *From beyond the rivers of Ethiopia, my suppliants, the daughter
of my dispersed, shall bring mine offering.* Or, *From beyond the rivers of Ethiopia,* (away in the western hemisphere,) *my worshippers shall bring mine offering, viz.
the children of my dispersed, or of Israel.* It is natural
then to expect, that this mercantile naval power, (be it
who it may,) with all its lions of naval strength, will be
found, with whatever nations they may find to unite with
them, in opposition to Gog, in his expedition against
the house of Israel in Palestine.

But who are the Sheba and Dedan connected with
them in this passage. We find several of the name
of Sheba; as Sheba, a grandson of Cush;* Sheba, the
son of Joktan of the line of Shem;† and Sheba, son of
Joksham, and grandson of Abraham.‡ These all settled in Arabia; "and perhaps most of them in the southern parts of it."§ *There* was a country of this name.
Thence it is supposed some of their descendants crossed the Red Sea, and peopled Abyssinia.‖ Here I apprehend is the place designed by the Sheba under consideration. The queen of Sheba came to hear the wisdom of Solomon. Solomon's reign was a type of the
Millennium. And his visit from the queen of Sheba may
be viewed as a kind of prelude to the early aid Sheba
is to afford to the house of Israel at, or after, their restoration. In Psalm lxxii, where the reign of Solomon
and the Millennium are unitedly predicted, (one as
type, and the other as antitype,) we read, verse 10;
*The kings of Tarshish and of the isles shall bring pres-
ents; the kings of Sheba and Seba shall offer gifts.*

---

* Gen. x, 7.   † Gen. x, 27.   ‡ Gen. xxv, 3.   § Brown.
‖ See Pool on Joel iii, 8; and Brown on the word Sheba.

Here are Tarshish and Sheba connected; as in the text under consideration. In the afore noted prediction of the restoration and conversion of the house of Israel, Isa. lx, where the isles and ships of Tarshish are first to wait on God, *to bring thy sons from far, their silver and their gold with them unto the name of the Lord;* it is predicted, verse 6; *All they from Sheba shall come; they shall bring gold and incense.* Where then is this Sheba? Whence did the queen of Sheba come to hear the wisdom of Solomon? Brown says it is not agreed whether she came from Sheba in Arabia Felix, or from a place of this name in Abyssinia. In favor of its being the latter, he observes, that Abyssinia abounds with just such kind of treasures as that queen brought to king Solomon. And she is said to have come from the uttermost parts of the earth; i. e. the uttermost parts then known to the Jews. But Abyssinia was then known to the Jews, and was the southernmost nation then known by them. Sheba in Arabia was not so far distant. In Abyssinia their language and religion are similar to those of the Jews. And that people have a tradition, that a queen of theirs in ancient times visited king Solomon. And they fondly relate a number of things relative to this event. These things render it most highly probable, that the Sheba sought was in Abyssinia. The Sheba in the text no doubt denotes the *country*, in which it was situated; under whatever name it may now be known. And it must appear highly probable, that Abyssinia is the place designed. This is a large country in Africa, south of Egypt; bounded east by the Red Sea; 900 miles in length; 840 in breadth; and is an important part of Ethiopia. "This spacious empire (says a historian) contains a great mixture of people, of various religions; Pagans, Jews, and Mohammedans; but the main body of the natives are professed Christians, who hold the Scriptures to be the sole rule of faith. Their emperor is supreme, as well in ecclesiastical, as in civil matters. The patriarch is the highest ecclesiastical dignitary in this empire. This patriarch is by his clergy called *Abuna*, the Hebrew word for *our father.*

36

The next order of ecclesiastics—is a kind of Jewish Levites, who assist in all public offices in the Church. They boast that they are of Jewish extraction; and pretend to imitate the service of the Jewish temple.— They have other priests of various orders. They use different forms of baptism; and keep both Saturday and the first day of the week, as a Sabbath. They are circumcised, and abstain from swine's flesh.—Their Divine service consists in reading the Scriptures, administering the Eucharist, and hearing some homilies of the fathers."*

It was from this country, it is believed, that the pious eunuch came to Jerusalem to worship, to whose chariot Philip was commanded by the Holy Ghost to join himself.† Milner upon this event observes; "This Ethiopia seems to be that part of the country whose metropolis is called Meroe, situated in a large island encompassed by the Nile, and the rivers Astapus and Astabora. For in these parts, as the elder Pliny informs, queens had a long time governed under the title of Candace."‡

This eunuch was said to be a man of great authority under Candace, queen of Ethiopia. And his coming up to Jerusalem to worship indicates, that some peculiar acquaintance then subsisted between his nation and the Jews. This was probably the case ever after the visit of their queen to king Solomon. How many of the Jews might flee thither, after their dispersion by the Romans, we know not. But multitudes of Jews now reside there. Accordingly we read, of the time of their restoration, (Isa. xi, 11,) *And it shall come to pass in that day, that the Lord shall set his hand again the second time to recover the remnant of his people, which shall be left, from Assyria, and from Egypt, and from Pathros, and from* CUSH (Ethiopia) *and from Elam, and from Shinar, and from Hamath, and from the isles of the sea.* The Cush or Ethiopia here mentioned, is among the places, from

* H. Adams's View of Religion, p. 363,—
† Acts viii, 26—   ‡ Church Hist. vol. i, p. 54.

which God will set himself to recover his people, the Jews. And it seems the Ethiopians will be so far from being disposed to pursue after them, or unite in a coalition against them, that they will be found operating in a coalition of powers in their behalf; and will early share in the blessings of the Millennium. *Ethiopia shall soon stretch out her hands unto God.* *From beyond the rivers of Ethiopia my suppliants shall bring mine offering even the daughter of my dispersed.† All they from Sheba shall come.‡ And he shall live; and to him shall be given the gold of* Sheba.§ These predictions seem to indicate, that *Sheba*, or Abyssinia, will be of some note in favor of the Jews upon their return to Palestine. Sheba is mentioned first in the coalition, in the text under consideration; *Sheba and Dedan and the merchants of Tarshish.* And the repeated mentioning of the latter as *beyond* the rivers of Ethiopia, seems to indicate some connexion between the Ethiopians, and this mercantile, naval power, in aid of the Jews.

Dedan is another power in this coalition. We find two of this name among the early settlers of the world; Dedan a brother of Sheba, and grandson of Cush;‖ and Dedan a brother to another Sheba, and grandson of Abraham.¶ These both settled in Arabia; the former on the west side of the Persian gulph, in Arabia Felix, where there is a city Dedan.†† The other Dedan probably gave name to the city Dedan on the frontiers of Idumea. The Dedanites were formerly of some note as merchants, trading in the fairs of Tyre.‡‡ But probably no correct genealogy is now to be found of their posterity. No doubt they mingled with the other tribes of Arabia. The Dedan in the text will probably be found to mean some people inhabiting Arabia Felix, and the southeastern parts of Arabia; and is the same with *Seba*, found in connexion with the kings of Tarshish and Sheba, who are engaged in favor of the

---

* Ps. lxviii, 31.   † Zech. iii, 10.   ‡ Isa. lx, 6,
  § Ps. lxxii, 15.   ‖ Gen. x, 7.   ¶ Gen. xxv, 3.
†† Brown on the word Dedan.   ‡‡ Ezek. xxvii, 15, 20.

Jews, at the time of their restoration. *The kings* (or powers) *of Tarshish, and of the isles, shall bring presents; the kings of Sheba and Seba shall offer gifts.** Here are *three* powers, connected in the same object, at the same period, with the three powers in the text under consideration. Must not the *powers* then, be the *same?* Two of them are of the *same name.* And we must suppose the third to be the same with the Dedan in the text. A rational account can be given for this changing of names. It has been noted, that several by the same of Sheba settled early in Arabia; and some of them in the southern parts of it; whose descendants emigrated, and peopled Abyssinia. Those who remained were known by the name of Sabeans, or Seba. Dedan, it has been observed, settled in the *same region.* And no doubt his descendants intermixed, and became one people with the Sabeans. And the subsequent inhabitants of that country were called Sabeans, or Seba; and Dedanites, or Dedan. They were *travelling companies;* Isa. 21, 13; "O ye travelling companies of Dedanim." A tribe of the Sabeans in the time of Job, infested Arabia Deserta, and robbed him of his cattle.† But most of the Sabeans probably dwelt farther southeast.‡ These Sabeans are mentioned in Joel iii, 8, in a sublime prediction of the battle of the great day; which seems to indicate that the Sabeans will then be present in some kind of opposition to the enemies of the Jews on that occasion. The Most High announces to the nations to be convened to the valley of Jehoshaphat, that their children shall be sold *to the Sabeans, a people far off.* Repeatedly we find in the predictions of the salvation of the Jews, in the last days, Sheba and Seba connected in their behalf. *I gave Ethiopia and Seba for thee:§* The same with *Sheba* and *Seba,* as shown before. *The merchandise of Ethiopia and of the Sabeans, men of stature, shall come over unto thee.‖* Here then, are *Sheba* and *Seba,* connected with the kings of Tarshish and of the isles, Psalm

---

* Ps. lxxii, 10. † Job i, 15. ‡ See Pool on Joel iii, 8.
§ Isa. xliii, 3. ‖ Isa. xlv, 14.

lxxii, 10, in aid of the Jews, after there restoration:
And the *Sheba* and *Dedan,* in the same connexion
with the merchants of Tarshish, with their lions, must
be the *same.*

*The merchandise of the Sabeans shall come over unto
thee.* The people of the southeast of Arabia, as well
as in Mecca, have been famed for trading with the
Turkish caravans, in balm, manna, myrrh, cassia, aloes,
frankincense, spikenard, cinnamon, pepper, cadamum,
oranges, lemons, pomegranates, figs, honey, wax and
other articles. The city of Bassora, at the head of the
Persian gulf, in Irac Arabia, is one centre of this trade.
"Here are many Jews."[*] Probably there are Jews in
Arabia Felix, as well as in Abyssinia. In the enume-
ration of nations, from which devout men were at Jerusalem, on the day of Pentecost; (Acts ii, 5—11,) are
mentioned *Arabians.* And more went thither in after
days. A writer remarks; "Egypt and Arabia were
filled with Jews, who had fled into these corners of
the world from the persecution of the emperor Adrian."[†] And when God shall bring the seed of Israel
from the east, and gather them from the west; shall
say to the north, Give up; and to the *south,* Keep not
back; these Jews in Arabia, as well as in Abyssinia,
will fly as clouds, and as doves to their windows.[‡]

And the friendly interest, which the Dedanites, or
Seba, will be excited to take on the occasion, in connexion with the two other powers noted, *time will disclose.* It is remarkable, that these three powers are so
repeatedly found in this connexion, in the prophecies,
as aiding the people of God in Palestine, after their return thither.

This Dedan, or Seba, most probably, is the people
meant by the *Edom, Moab, and the chief of the children of Ammon,* in Dan. xi, 41; who are to escape out
of the hands of the infidel Power, in his *first* expedition into the east. The ancient nations under these
names have long since been *extinct,* or been swallowed up among the Arabian tribes. When these names

* Morse's Gaz.   † Morse's Geo. p. 578.   ‡ Isa. lx, 8.

therefore are said to escape out of the hands of Antichrist, in his first excursion into the east, in distinction from the Ethiopians in the northwest of Arabia,
who shall *be at his steps;** they must mean the people
of Arabia Felix, and those in the east of Arabia. And
why are they expressly excepted from the conquests of
Antichrist, in his first expedition; unless to indicate,
that they are to be of some note *in opposition to him,* in
his *subsequent operations?* The name of Edom is in
prophecy mystically applied to the greatest enemies of
the Church. Christ, in the battle of the great day, is
said to come *from Edom with died garments.†* The
Edom *here* is Antichrist. But when it is applied to
some people in Arabia, who shall escape the domination of Antichrist, it is not thus *mystically,* but is more
literally applied: And it may denote a people there,
whom God will excite to aid his cause in the re-establishment of the Jews in Palestine. And probably this
Edom, and Moab, and chief of the children of Ammon,
and Dedan, and Seba, all denote the *same power.‡*

* Dan. xi, 43.   † Isa lxiii, 1.

‡ The agency of the *naval power* in this coalition, in the return of the Jews to the land of their fathers, we find predicted in
Isa. xviii, as well as in other passages. I will quote this chapter, with some small variations from our translation, but which
are according to Bp. Lowth, in his Isaiah, or other able translators.

"Ho land shadowing with wings, which is beyond the rivers
"of Ethiopia: 2 That sendeth messengers on the sea in vessels
"of bulrushes, on the face of the waters. Go ye swift sailors,
"to a nation scattered, and with their hair plucked off; to a peo-
"ple remarkable from the beginning and hitherto; a nation of
"*line, line;*" (or, "the people looking for, and expecting one to
"come;" so some Jews in the east have translated the passage;) "and trodden under foot; whose lands the rivers have
"spoiled. 3 All ye inhabitants of the world, when the standard
"is lifted up on the mountains, behold ye; and when the trum-
"pet is sounded, hear ye. 4 For thus hath the Lord said to me,
"I will take my rest, and will regard my fixed habitation, like
"the clear heat after rain, and like a cloud of dew in the days of
"harvest. 5 Surely before the vintage, when the bud is perfect,
"and the blossom is becoming a swelled grape, he shall cut off
"the shoots with the pruning hooks, and shall cut down and take
"away the branches. 6 They shall be left together to the ra-
"pacious fowls of the mountains, and to the wild beasts of the

· The prophet proceeds. *Therefore son of man, prophesy and say unto Gog, Thus saith the Lord, in the day when my people dwell safely, shalt thou not know it?*

"earth; and the fowls shall summer upon them; and the beasts "shall winter upon them. 7 At that time shall the present be "brought unto the Lord of hosts, of a people scattered, and with "their hair plucked off; of a people remarkable from the begin-"ning and hitherto; the people looking *for,* and expecting *one* "*to come;* who are trodden under foot; whose lands the rivers "have spoiled, to the place of the name of the Lord of hosts, "the mount Zion."

Paraphrased thus:

1 Ho nation, darkening with thy sails, or thou great *maritime* power of the last days, when this address shall become applicable; thou land beheld in vision as though in *a line* with Ethiopia, (or the Sheba, who shall aid my people) but away beyond her rivers; how far, and in what particular direction, the event shall unfold: 2 Thou land, whose embassadors and mis-'sionaries are conveyed by sea to distant climes seemingly with as great facility as that nation, beyond which thou art in vision beheld, used to navigate its rivers in light vessels made of the rind of Papyrus:* Come thou naval power; I have a business for thee to perform. Thy art and power in navigation shall now be found to answer a new and important purpose. Go ye swift seamen; collect my ancient people: That people, who have long been scattered over the face of the earth; who have long been insulted and abused: That people, whose history has been so remarkable from ancient date: That people long looking for and expecting another Messiah, beside Jesus of Nazareth; but in vain: Who have been trodden under foot among the nations: Whose ancient inheritance in Palestine, the mystic rivers of invading nations, (the Romans, the Persians, Saracens, Turks, Egyptians, and Ottomans in turn) have overflown and ravaged. But the Ottoman Euphrates being dried up, and the way for the return of my people being prepared, *go ye now, and aid their return.* Thus it is predicted, *Surely the isles shall wait for me, and the ships of Tarshish first, to bring my sons from far, their silver and their gold with them, unto the name of the Lord.* (Isa. lx, 9.) 3 All ye inhabitants of the world, now behold the standard of salvation, which I am about to erect! Hear ye the great trumpet, which shall now be blown. (Isa. xxvii, 13.) 4 For thus saith the Lord, I am going to regard and renew my ancient resting place; I will again have a fixed habitation in Canaan, as I have declared by the prophets; especially in Zech. i, 16; *Therefore thus saith the Lord, I am returned to Jerusalem*

---

* The bulrush vessel, in ancient date, contained a scourge for the tyrannical oppressor of God's people, and the deliverer of the chosen tribes. Exodus ii, 3.

Thou wilt hear of their defenceless state, and wilt attempt their ruin. *And thou shalt come from thy place
out of the north parts, thou and many people with thee,*

with mercies; my house shall be built in it. And viii, 3, *Thus
saith the Lord, I am returned unto Zion, and will dwell in the
midst of Jerusalem.* This event shall be as life from the dead
to the Gentiles: Therefore ye nations behold: I will now be to
mine heritage like the genial heat of the sun after rain, and like
the cooling dew after the sultry heat of harvest; as I have repeatedly predicted, Israel shall be *as the tender grass springing
out of the earth, by the clear shining after rain.* (2 Sam. xxiii, 4.)
*I will be as the dew unto Israel; he shall grow as the lily; and
cast forth his roots as Lebanon.* (Hos. xiv, 5.) 5 But, connected
with the introduction of this event, is a scene which awaits mine
enemies, as I have always given notice, in the many predictions
which relate to that period; *ruin to mine enemies, and salvation
to my cause!* The seventh vial, the vintage of wrath, must be
fulfilled. And at the time of the return of the house of Israel,
this event will be *even at the doors.* As in the natural vineyard,
when the blossom is succeeded by the swelled pulp, which soon
arrives to the size of the grape, indicating that the vintage is
near; so at the time of the return of the Jews, wickedness will
have blossomed, pride will have budded: The sour grapes will
have obtained their bigness; and the time for casting the vine of
the earth into the great wine-press of the wrath of God, will be
at hand. (Isa. lxiii, 2—6; Joel iii, 13; Rev. xiv, 8—20.) 6 Soon
the most prominent branches of this vine shall be *scattered upon the mountains of Israel,* at Armageddon; and the fowls of
heaven, and the beasts of the earth, shall feast upon them.
(Ezek. xxxix, 4, 17—21; and Rev. xix, 17, 18.) 7 To prepare
the way for this event, the present, which I now claim of you,
must be brought unto the Lord of hosts, of the people long scattered over the earth, and long insulted and abused; that people,
whose history has been so remarkable from ancient date; that
people long expecting another Messiah beside Jesus of Nazareth, but in vain; who have been trodden under foot among the
nations; whose ancient inheritance in Palestine invading nations
have long occupied; the present shall be brought consisting of
this people, unto the Lord of hosts, to the literal mount Zion.*

The naval power here addressed, being described in relation
to the *rivers of Ethiopia,* both in the first verse of this chapter,

* Since writing the preceding comment on this chapter, I have, for the first
time, seen Bp. Horsley's comment upon it; published in Mr. Faber's volume upon
the return of the Jews; and am pleased to find my opinion on the great points of
this prophecy confirmed by so distinguished an authority. In some particulars his
exposition differs from the one, which I have given. But in those differences I
think my interpretation as well accords with the text, and better with collateral
prophecies.

all of them riding upon horses, a great company, a mighty army. Ancient Babylon was called, *the land of the north,** because most of the Assyrian empire

and in Zeph. iii, 10, before noted, which rivers may mean the *Nile,* and according to Pool, the *Red Sea,* which lies upon the eastern bound of Ethiopia, and resembles a great river; also the skill of this naval power in navigation being described by the bulrush navigation of the Nile and the shores of the Red Sea, seems to indicate some connexion of this naval power with these Ethiopians (Abyssinians, or people of Sheba) in this service, to which they are called. If the meaning be simply, that this naval power is *away* somewhere *westward* of the mouths of the Nile, why are these called the rivers of Ethiopia? perhaps the true solution may be, this power is beheld in vision, in a line with Ethiopia, or Sheba, to denote some connexion between them, in the friendly aid to be afforded to the Jews. This power's being *beyond the rivers of Ethiopia,* does not decide relative to the particular point of compass, or the distance, at which the power is to be found. It decides only, that it will be in the *western hemisphere* from Jerusalem: But whether in the west of Europe, or in America, the event will decide.

Other predictions seem to favor this coalition against Gog. Obad. 21; *And saviors shall come upon mount Zion to judge the mount of Esau; and the kingdom shall be the Lord's.* By the mount of Esau here must be meant, that terrible enemy of the Church, prefigured by ancient Edom, (Isa. lxiii, 1.) The event is to take place when the *kingdom becomes the Lord's,* or at the introduction of the Millennium. And *saviors* are then to come to mount Zion, to aid the destruction of the great enemy. Though *Christ* fights *that battle,* yet he may make use of some human instruments. And this prediction hints that *he will.*

Micah v, 5—9. "For now shall he be great unto the ends of "the earth. And this shall be the peace, when the Assyrian shall "come into our land, and when he shall tread on our palaces, "then we shall raise against him seven shepherds, and eight "principal men. And they shall waste the land of Assyria with "the sword, and the land of Nimrod in the entrances thereof: "thus shall he deliver us from the Assyrian, when he cometh "into our land, and when he treadeth within our borders. And "the remnant of Jacob shall be among the Gentiles, in the midst "of many people, as a lion among the beasts of the forest, as a "young lion among the flocks of sheep; who, if he go through, "both treadeth down, and teareth in pieces, and none can de- "liver. Thine hand shall be lift up upon thine adversaries, and "all thine enemies shall be cut off."

*Jer. iv, 6; and xlvi, 20; and iii, 12.
37

lay in a latitude north of Jerusalem. But *France* lies in a latitude much *farther* north, than did the Assyrian empire. It extends almost twenty degrees north of

"Some imagine, (says Dr. Gray, Key to the Old Test. p. 465,) that Micah foretells in this prophecy the victories obtained by the leaders of the Medes and Babylonians, who took Ninevah. Others suppose him to speak of the seven Maccabean leaders, with their eight royal successors, from Aristobulus to Antigonus." But the Doctor goes on to give his opinion, that it refers to some *higher triumph* still future, and refers us to the scene of *Ezekiel's Gog* for its accomplishment. The prediction might receive a primary and typical accomplishment at the time of the Maccabees. For Antiochus then afflicting the Jews, was a type of Antichrist. But it will probably receive its great fulfilment in the antitype of the wars of Antiochus upon the Jews, or at the time of the last expedition of Antichrist into the east. And if so, it teaches, that God will then make some use of human instruments in the destruction of the Antichristian confederacy against the Jews in Palestine, beside their *own swords. I will call for a sword against him.* (Ezek. xxxviii, 21.)

Zech. ix, 11—14. "As for thee also, by the blood of thy "covenant, I have sent forth thy prisoners out of the pit, where- "in is no water. Turn you to the strong hold, ye prisoners of "hope; even to-day do I declare that I will render double unto "thee: When I have bent Judah for me, filled my bow with "Ephraim, and raised up thy sons, O Zion, against thy sons, O "Greece, and made thee as the sword of a mighty man. And "the Lord shall be seen over them, and his arrows shall go forth "as the lightning; and the Lord God shall blow the trumpet, "and shall go with whirlwinds of the south."

Here is the return of Judah and Ephraim (the Jews and the ten tribes) at the latter day. The passage received but a very *partial*, if any degree of accomplishment, in the return of the Jews from Babylon. For but a few, *if any* of Ephraim then returned. God did not then *fill his bow with Ephraim.* The event *must* be *still future:* And by the blood of the covenant, (the entail of the covenant with Abraham,) it will ere long be fulfilled. The Jews and Israel are indeed like prisoners in a dry pit. But they are prisoners of *hope.* God has promised to recover them. And he will fulfil his promise. And at that period God will find occasion to raise up the sons of Zion against the sons of Greece; and he will make the former like the sword of a *mighty man.* Grotius gives this paraphrase to this part of the passage, "I will animate the Jews against the troops of Antiochus." But those scenes of warfare were but a type of the scene still future between Antichrist and the Jews, as has been noted. Accordingly Bishop Newcome, upon the

Jerusalem; and may well therefore be called *the north parts. And thou shalt come up against my people Israel as a cloud to cover the land; it shall be in the latter days; and I will bring thee against my land, that the heathen may know me, when I shall be sanctified in thee, O Gog, before their eyes. Thus saith the Lord God, Art thou he, of whom I have spoken of old times by my servants the prophets of Israel, who prophesied in those days, many years, that I would bring thee against them?* As though the Most High comes out to view the combined armies; and address their chief; Art thou that mighty being, so long foretold by the various prophets in Israel, to do such wonderful things in the last days? Most portentous address!

"And it shall come to pass at the same time, when "Gog shall come against the land of Israel, saith the "Lord God, that my fury shall come up into my face. "For in my jealousy, and in the fire of my wrath, "have I spoken. Surely in that day there shall be a "great shaking in the land of Israel; so that the fishes "of the sea, and the fowls of heaven, and the beasts of "the field, and all the creeping things, that creep upon "the earth, shall shake at my presence, and the moun- "tains shall be thrown down, and the steep places shall

above passage of Grotius, observes, "It is true, that Judas Maccabæus gained some advantages over the Syrians. But the language of this prophecy seems too strong for *these* events; and may remain to be fulfilled against the present possessors of the countries called Javan, or Greece." When we consider that Antiochus, in his wars against the Jews after their restoration from Babylon, was a lively type of Antichrist, in his attack upon the Jews to take place after their final restoration; and when we consider that the armies of Antiochus were considerably composed of Grecians, and that the nations of Greece, or of Asia Minor, are to be in the final coalition of Antichrist against the Jews and Israel, we shall discover that the prophecy quoted had a primary and typical fulfilment in the success of the Maccabees against Antiochus; but it is to receive its *great fulfilment* in some *power* to be raised up against Antichrist in his final expedition against the Jews in Palestine. And this probably will prove to be the coalition indicated in Ezek. xxxviii, 13, by *Sheba, Dedan, and the merchants of Tarshish, with all the young lions thereof.*

"fall, and every wall shall fall to the ground. And I
"will call for a sword upon him throughout all my
"mountains, saith the Lord God; every man's sword
"shall be against his brother. And I will plead
"against him with pestilence, and with blood; and I will
"reign upon him and upon his bands, and upon the ma-
"ny people, that are with him, an overflowing rain,
"and great hail-stones, fire and brimstone. Thus will
"I magnify myself, and sanctify myself; and I will be
"known in the eyes of many nations; and they shall
"know that I am the Lord."

Here we have the tremendous scene of the *vintage**
on Gog, and his vast armies. The judgments, at the
same time, will be executed on the cities of the nations, and on the enemies of the cause of Christ
through the Christian world. Here is the battle of that
great day of God Almighty, the seventh vial.

The next chapter, Ezek. xxxix, is taken up in repeating and enlarging on the predictions of this destruction of Gog and his bands. In verse 6, the judgment is extended. *And I will send a fire on Magog,
and among them that dwell carelessly in the isles.* The
empire of Gog, the nations of his government, will be
burnt in the same fire. And the wicked and careless
people of distant lands will perish. As in other prophecies; *The cities of the nations fell. To the isles he
will repay recompence.* This slaughter is not to be confined to the literal armies of Gog. Nor will it probably
be effected at once. But the fatal evil will progress
through the nations. The slain of the Lord are to be
from one end of the earth to the other.

In this xxxixth chapter, the beasts and fowls are in-
vited to come and partake of the supper of the great
God, the sacrifice, about to be made for them; as in
Rev. xix, 17; where the same figure is used upon the
same occasion; being borrowed from this passage.
The stench of the unburied carcasses of the bands of
Gog fills various parts of the land. Seven months are

† Isa. lxiii, 1,— Rev. xiv, last part.

occupied in burying their carcasses, and cleansing the country.

The military apparatus of these slaughtered hosts fur-nishes the nation of Israel with a sufficiency of fuel for seven years. And the account closes thus: *Then shall they* (the Church of Israel;) *know that I am the Lord their God, who caused them to go into cativity among the heathen: But I have gathered them into their own land, and have left none of them any more there;* (in heathen lands;) *neither will I hide my face any more from them; for I have poured out my Spirit upon the house of Israel, saith the Lord God.*

Thus ends the infidel Power of the last days. Af-ter he shall have filled a considerable part of the world, for a course of years, with carnage and terror, *he shall come to his end, and none shall help him.** He is thus *slain, and his body destroyed, and given to the burning flame.*† The Beast, *that ascendeth out of the bottomless pit,* thus *goeth into perdition.*‡ *And the beast was taken, and with him the false prophet, that wrought miracles before him—these both were cast alive into the lake of fire, burning with brimstone.*§

The nine succeeding chapters of this prophet, which close the book of Ezekiel, present a description of the Church of God in the Millennium, under the similitude of a vast capacious temple and city, whose name thenceforth shall be, THE LORD IS THERE.

SECTION III.

Mr. Faber's Opinion concerning Gog and Magog considered.

SINCE the writing of the preceding section, I have learned that Mr. Faber supposes the Gog in Ezekiel not to be the same with Antichrist; but to be the power that is to rise at the close of the Millennium, or the Gog and Magog in Rev. xx, 8. To evince this point he has labored for nearly twenty pages. I have

---

* Dan. xi, last part.　　† Dan. vii, 11.
‡ Rev. xvii, 8, 11　　§ Rev. xix, 20, 21.

endeavored to weigh his arguments; and I think them *inconclusive.* I will state my reasons for disbelieving his scheme upon this point; and make some remarks upon his arguments. My reasons for disbelieving his scheme, are the following:

1. The attack made by Gog and his bands upon the land of Judah and Israel, is evidently an event intimately connected with their return from their long dispersion. *In the latter years thou shalt come into the land, that is brought back from the sword, and gathered out of many people, against the mountains of Israel, which have been always waste; but it is brought forth out of the nations, and they shall dwell safely all of them.* * Could the bringing back of Israel, here spoken of, have been a *thousand years* before this invasion of Gog, which occasioned the address? Again Gog attacks Israel, *to take a spoil and to take a prey, to turn thine hand upon the desolate places, that are now inhabited, and upon the people gathered out of the nations.*† Surely this *gathering* of Israel must have been of *recent date,* when Gog arrives; and those places having been desolate, a *recent event;* and not an event of a *thousand years* before; and an event as it were *unknown* to them; as must have been the case, if the address be to a power at the close of the Millennium.

2. One object of the judgments upon Gog is stated to be, that the nations may know that Israel had been dispersed for their wickedness. *And the heathen shall know that the house of Israel went into captivity for their iniquity; because they trespassed against me; therefore I hid my face from them, and gave them unto the hand of their enemies.*‡ Can this apply, as the reason for gathering the Gog and Magog at the close of the Millennium and of the world? *that the heathen may know* that God *some thousands of years before,* had dispersed Israel for their sins? The reason perfectly applies at the time of the overthrow of Antichrist. Israel then will have recently returned from their long

* Ezek. xxxviii, 8.   † Verse 12.
‡ Chap. xxxix, 23. See also verse 8—21.

dispersion for their sins. But it does not apply at all at the time of the overthrow of the apocalyptic Gog and Magog.

3. This Gog in Ezékiel is the very power long predicted by the prophets in Israel, to' make this attack. *Thus saith the Lord God, Art thou he, of whom I have spoken of old times by my servants the prophets of Israel, who prophecied in those days, many years that I would bring thee against them?** But Mr. Faber has, in his last volume, clearly shown, that it is *Antichrist* before the Millennium, who is so abundantly predicted in the prophets, to attack the Jews, upon their restoration. But the apocalyptic Gog and Magog were *never* expressly predicted in the prophets.

4. The destruction of Gog in Ezekiel is said to be, that the house of Israel may know God is their God. *So the house of Israel shall know that I am the Lord their God from that day and forward.†* Can this apply to the destruction of the Gog and Magog, at the end of the world? Will the Church of Israel, after all their millennial glory, have to learn, that the Lord is their God? To Israel at the beginning of the Millennium the remark perfectly applies; but in no sense at the close of it.

5. The destruction of Ezekiel's Gog is said to be, that God may be known and magnified among the nations. *Then will I magnify myself, and sanctify myself; and I will be known in the eyes of many nations.‡* This fitly applies to the destruction of Antichrist in Palestine. But we cannot think it so fitly applies to the scene at the end of the world.

6. The calling of the fowls of heaven to feast on the slaughtered carcasses of the bands of Gog, in chap. xxxix, 17, fully accords with the prediction of the same event, in Rev. xix, 17, relative to the slaughter of the bands of Antichrist. The latter passage appears to be copied from the former, and evidently to relate to the same period and event. But how absurd to apply it to the scene at the end of the world, which is suc-

* Chap. xxxviii, 17.   † Chap. xxxix, 22.
‡ Chap. xxxviii, 23.

ceeded by the general resurrection, and the final judgment!

7. The Israelites being seven months, burying the
slain of Gog, and cleansing the land; and seven years
burning for fuel their implements of war, (chap. xxxix,
9,) is a very different account from that of the final
judgment, which succeeds the overthrow of the apocalyptic Gog and Magog.

8. All that is said in these chapters of Ezekiel, upon
events subsequent to the overthrow of Gog, clearly indicates the re-establishment of Israel in the land of their
fathers, and their quietly dwelling there from that time
forward. *But I have gathered them* (Israel) *into their
own land, and have left none of them any more there*
(among the heathen.) *Neither will I hide my face any
more from them; for I have poured out my Spirit upon
the house of Israel, saith the Lord God.** How *utterly
irrelevant* is this to the time of the overthrow of the
Gog and Magog of the Revelation!

9. The two passages are very different in point of
the *extent* of their objects. The Gog and Magog at
the end of the world inhabit the face of the earth, upon
the *four* quarters of the world. Their *number is as the
sand of the sea;* and their going up against the saints is
upon the breadth of the earth. But the bands of Ezekiel's Gog are not so extensive. And their fall is upon
the *mountains of Israel.* We might as well speak of
all the people of New England's being seated at once in
the state house at Boston; as of the apocalyptic Gog
and Magog's falling upon the *mountains of Israel.* And
were the latter possible, and even were they to be
slain and buried, instead of going to the judgment
(which is represented as immediately succeeding their
overthrow) neither seven months, nor seven times
seven, could suffice for the cleansing of the land of them,
by the saints in Palestine.

10. The whole description of the expedition and
overthrow of Gog and his bands, in Ezekiel, accords
with the expedition and overthrow of Antichrist in

* Chap, xxxix, 28, 29.

Palestine: But I think it agrees not at all with those of
Gog and Magog at the end of the world. Some of
these points of coincidence were hinted in the first part
of the preceding section. I shall not now repeat them;
but only remark, that the connexion of the xxxvith,
xxxviith, xxxviiith, and xxxixth chapters of Ezekiel,
decides that Gog and Antichrist are the same. And
this point has been ascertained in a note in the preceding section.

The powers constituting the coalition under Gog,
are *just such*, as we must suppose Antichrist will collect in his last expedition against the Church in Palestine. The coalition of Antichrist, on that occasion,
extends beyond his vassal European kings. In Rev.
xvi, 13, 14, after the sixth vial, and to prepare the way
for the seventh, we find a subtle, powerful agency, exerted by the devil, Antichrist, and the false prophet,
going forth unto the kings of the earth, *and of the whole
world,* to gather them to the battle of that great day of
God Almighty. Here the coalition of Antichrist is to
extend not only to the kings of the European earth, *but
of the whole world;* which must mean, *at least* some parts
of the Asiatic and African world. And what can be
more natural than to suppose these kings of Asia will
be those very nations round about Palestine, in addition
to those in Africa, which are mentioned in the coalition
of Gog? Antichrist will have formed some powerful
influence in those eastern parts, in his first expedition,
at the pouring out of the sixth vial, in the subversion
of the Turks. And now he will send his diabolical
agency among the remains of those Mohammedan nations in Asia and Africa, and among the Persians, and
the Northern Tartars, to unite them against the Church
of Israel in Palestine. This extent of the coalition under Antichrist, we find in various passages of the Old
Testament. I will note but two. In Zech. xiv, 2, this
event is evidently predicted. God says, *For I will
gather all nations against Jerusalem to battle. Then
shall the Lord go forth; and fight against those na-*

tions as when he fought in the day of battle.* Joel iii,
1, 2. *For behold, in those days, and in that time,*

* Since the publication of the first edition of this work, the
following sentence has appeared in public. The author, speaking of the seventh vial, the battle of that great day, as now receiving its fulfilment, says; "This battle has been *erroneously*
supposed to be the same with that mentioned, Zech. xiv;
3—5, 14."

I am still, and truly of opinion, that the battle under the seventh vial, and the battle in the above passage in Zechariah, are
one and the same. I admit that the passage in Zechariah
might receive a primary or typical fulfilment in the destruction
of Jerusalem by the Romans. But its ultimate reference is to
the battle of the great day, introductory to the Millennium. And
no event, after the battle under the seventh vial, and before the
Millennium, can be admitted, as fulfilling the passage in Zechariah. The following remarks are submitted.

1. That battle in Zech. xiv, is the *same* that is known through
the prophets, as the great and notable day of the Lord, which is
to take place soon after the restoration of the Jews, and introductory to the Millennium. To see this, compare the passage
with some other passages. The following is the passage in
Zechariah. "Behold, the day of the Lord cometh, and thy spoil
shall be divided in the midst of thee, (the Jews.) For I will
gather all nations against Jerusalem to battle; and the city shall
be taken, and the houses rifled, and the women ravished; and
half of the city shall go forth into captivity; (or be taken as
though going to be led off) and the residue of the people shall
not be cut off from the city. Then shall the Lord go forth and
fight against those nations, as when he fought in the day of battle;" or as in his most signal interpositions for his people in
former days. The whole connexion of this passage decides,
that it is the introduction of the last tremendous scene of judgments before the Millennium. Compare it with Joel iii, 1,
"For behold, in those days, and at that time, when I shall bring
again the captivity of Judah and Jerusalem, I will also gather all
nations, and will bring them down into the valley of Jehoshaphat." The decisive scenes of judgment, and the Millennium
follow. Compare it with Zeph. iii, 8, 9, "Therefore wait ye
upon me, saith the Lord, until the day that I rise up to the prey;
for my determination is to gather the nations, that I may assemble the kingdoms, to pour upon them mine indignation,
even all my fierce anger; for all the earth shall be devoured
with the fire of my jealousy. For then will I turn to the people a pure language, that they may all call upon the name of the
Lord, to serve him with one consent." Compare it with the
descriptions of Gog and his bands, in Ezek. xxxviii, and xxxix,
noted in the preceding section. And Mal. last chapter, where
we have predicted the day that shall burn as an oven; and all

when I shall bring again the captivity of Judah and
Jerusalem, I will also gather all nations, and will

the proud and wicked shall be burnt up; but upon the Church
shall the Sun of righteousness rise with healing and salvation;
and he will cause that the enemy shall afflict them no more.
This burning day is there called, "the great and dreadful day
of the Lord." And abundantly is it described through the
prophets. Various of them expressly decide that this terrible day is soon after the restoration of the Jews to Palestine;
that it opens in the destruction of a vast coalition formed
against the Jews there. Is not this clearly the same with that
battle in Zechariah?

2. The battle of that great day, under the seventh vial, Rev.
xvi, 14—21, is the last great scene of judgment, preparatory
to the happy thousand years. It is the same with the event,
chap. xiv, last part,—the Angel upon the white cloud, gathering the harvest, and the vintage. And the same with chap.
xix, 11, to the end—the battle between Christ, and the Beast.
And none of these passages admit, that a scene of judgments,
later than that of the seventh vial, can fulfil the description of
that battle in Zechariah.

3. These descriptions in the Revelation of the destruction
of the last head of the Roman Beast, manifestly allude to the
prophecies in the Old Testament, concerning that great and
notable day of the Lord, subsequent to the restoration of the
Jews, Rev. x, 7; "But in the days of the seventh angel, when he
shall begin to sound, the mystery of God shall be finished; *as he*
hath declared to his servants the prophets." And the scene under the last vial is called "the battle of T.HAT great day of God
Almighty;" alluding to the ancient prophecies of the great and
notable day of the Lord, after the restoration of the Jews.

If a doubt remain relative to this point, in the mind of any,
let him please to turn to the note in the preceding section,
showing that Gog and the last head of the Roman Beast are the
same. Or let him please to compare Rev. xix, 17—19, with
Ezek. xxxix, 4, 17—20; Rev. xix, 19, 20, with Dan. vii, 11;
also Rev. xiv, 14, to the end, with Isa. lxiii, 1—6; and Joel
iii, 13.

We hence learn the great impropriety of separating the last
battle in the Revelation from the great day of the Lord in the
prophets. They are *one* and the *same.*

4. It has been shown, in a note in the preceding section, that
if the Gog of Ezekiel, in whose destruction the great day of the
Lord in the Old Testament opens, be a different Power from
the last head of the Roman Beast, destroyed under the seventh
vial; then Gog is a fifth monarchy upon earth, contrary to the
repeated and express decisions of Old Testament prophecy.

Thus the battle in Zech. xiv, and the battle under the seventh
vial are the same.

bring them down into the valley of Jehoshaphat.
Must not the *all nations* in these passages mean more
than the *European vassal kings of Antichrist?* Will
God have no enemies but *them*, at that time, to be destroyed? Are none of the millions under the *Mohammedan* delusion to be destroyed at the same period, in
the same expedition?

11. The names *Gog* and *Magog* in Rev. xx, 8, *suppose* the existence of Ezekiel's Gog and Magog, at the
battle of the great day preceding the Millennium. For
the former are but the latter mystically raised from the
dead. Hence it is, that the same *name* is given them.
Mark the connexions, and this will appear. The battle
of the great day, in which Antichrist, or Ezekiel's Gog
and his bands, had been destroyed, was described in
the latter part of the preceding chapter, (Rev. xix, 11,
to the end.) In the xxth chapter an Angel binds the
devil, and confines him in the bottomless pit, from de-
ceiving the nations any more, for a thousand years.
The Millennium is now introduced. *And I saw the
souls of them, that were beheaded for the witness of
Jesus, and for the word of God, and which had not
worshipped the beast, neither his image, neither had
received his mark upon their foreheads, nor in their
hands; and they lived and reigned with Christ a
thousand years.* This cannot mean a *literal* resurrection. The chapter is mostly *figurative* and *not* literal.
We are not to conceive that there will be a mixture of
glorified saints, and imperfect beings, on earth, during
the Millennium. It is not said to be the *bodies*, but the
souls of the martyrs and saints, that are raised at that
time. They will live in the *saints* of the Millennium,
just as Elias lived in John the Baptist. This accords
with the most common prophetic language. One person, people, or nation, is said to live in another. Thus
the Papal hierarchy *was Babylon.* And Antichrist is
the Roman Beast; and is *Edom, Bozrah;* and many other names of the ancient enemies of God. It is only in
the *mystical* sense, that the souls of the martyrs and the
other saints are raised in the Millennium. Mark what
follows. *But the rest of the dead lived not again, until*

the thousand years were finished. *This is the first resurrection.* But this first mystical resurrection supposes a *second.* And the whole sentence implies a second, when the *rest of the dead shall live again.* This must be a resurrection of the *wicked,* at the close of the Millennium. *The rest of the dead lived not again, till the thousands years were finished.* Then they will mystically rise again, *in kindred souls;* as the martyrs and saints had done. But who are *the rest of the dead,* the revival of whose cause will constitute the *second* mystical resurrection, which is implied in the prediction of the first? They are the enemies of the Church, *who fell in the battle of the great day of God Almighty!* They are Antichrist! They are Gog, *the land of Magog, and all his bands.* These are the *rest of the dead who shall live again, when the thousand years are finished.* Accordingly when Satan is loosed from the bottomless pit, and goes out to deceive the nations, that are in the four quarters of the earth, the figure is carried forward; and in raising up *the rest of the dead,* he raises up *Gog* and *Magog,* who were slain a thousand years before, in the *battle of that great day of God Almighty.* The world of apostates, and a generation, who know not the Lord, then over the face of the globe, receive these appellations, because they rise in the spirit of that *then ancient* Power. Thus the prediction concerning the apocalyptic Gog and Magog, is so far from indicating, that Ezekiel's Gog, and Antichrist, are two distinct powers, that it *rests on the very ground* of their being one and the same. The Gog and Magog, at the close of the Millennium, are only Antichrist mystically raised again; who went into perdition, before the Millennium, under the denomination of Gog, the land of Magog.

I will now make some remarks upon Mr. Faber's arguments in favor of Ezekiel's Gog and Antichrist being different powers.

His most weighty argument is, that one *third part* of the bands of Antichrist are to be spared; Zech. xiii, 8, 9. But to Gog it is said, *And I will leave but a sixth part of thee.** Upon this argument, I remark,

---

* Ezek. xxxix, 2.

1. I am not convinced, that the passage in Zechariah, relative to leaving a *third part*, relates to the bands of Antichrist. The whole connexion, and the language of the sentence, seem rather to indicate, that it relates to the Jews. *And it shall come to pass, that in all the land, saith the Lord, two parts therein shall be cut off and die; but the third shall be left therein. And I will bring the third part through the fire, and will refine them as silver is refined, and will try them as gold is tried: they shall call on my name, and I will hear them: I will say, It is my people; and they shall say, the Lord is my God.* I think this must refer to the *Jews*, at the time of the attack of Antichrist upon them, rather than to the bands of Antichrist. But however this may be, I think Mr. Faber's argument fails; For

2. The clause in Ezek. xxxix, 2, *I will leave but a sixth part of thee*, is an incorrect translation. The Hebrew word *sesa*, from *ses*, six, is rendered differently from our translation by critics. The Septuagint, the Vulgate, the Targum, Buxtorf, Kimchi, and Pool, dissent from our translation in this sentence. Pool's margin reads it thus, *I will strike thee with six plagues, or draw thee back with a hook of six teeth;* as chap. xxxviii, 4. In the verse here referred to, we read, *I will turn thee back, and put hooks into thy jaws, and will bring thee forth.* Some part of chap. xxxix, is but a repetition of various passages in chap. xxxviii. In chap. xxxviii, 3, 4, we read, *Thus saith the Lord God, Behold, I am against thee, O Gog, the chief prince of Meshech and Tubal: And I will turn thee back, and put hooks into thy jaws, and will bring thee forth.* In chap. xxxix, 1, 2, we read, *Thus saith the Lord God, Behold I am against thee, O Gog, the chief prince of Meshech and Tubal: and I will turn thee back, and* (sesa) *will drag thee with a six pronged hook*, as Buxtorf renders it: or, according to Pool, *I will strike thee with six plagues; or draw thee back with a hook of six teeth.* This fully agrees with its parallel text; *I will turn thee back and put hooks in thy jaws.* This might refer to the six judgments threatened to Gog, in

chap. xxxviii, 21, 22;—*the sword, pestilence, blood, rain, hail, and fire.*

Another argument Mr. Faber adduces from Ezek. xxxviii, 11, where the Most High says to Gog, *And thou shalt say, I will go up to the land of unwalled villages, I will go to them, that are at rest, that dwell safely, all of them, dwelling without walls, and having neither bars nor gates.* The state here described, Mr. Faber thinks Israel cannot reach, short of *all*, or a considerable *part* of the Millennium: And therefore it cannot relate to the attack of Antichrist upon the Jews. But I think we may suppose the Jews, after their return to Jerusalem, may arrive at the situation here described in a *few years*. Nothing forbids this.

Another argument Mr. Faber derives from a persuasion, which he has, that Antichrist is to attack the Jews, before the return of the *ten tribes*. But it is evident, he allows, that the ten tribes, as well as the Jews, return before the attack upon them to be made by Gog and his bands. (See Ezek. xxxvii.) In answer to this, I must say, I have never been able to discover, in the scriptures adduced for the purpose, any evidence that the final attack of Antichrist upon Palestine, is before the return of *a body* of the ten tribes. And I think there is no such indication. The subversion of the Turkish empire, under the sixth vial, is said to take place, *that the way of the kings of the east may be prepared.* Mr. Faber admits, that these kings of the east, probably mean the ten tribes, under the name of the Afghans, now in Persia; who call themselves Melchim, *kings.* And if the way be prepared under the sixth vial for *their return*, surely it cannot be strange, that they *should* return before the seventh vial; for this event appears clearly implied. Otherwise why is the event of the sixth vial said to be, to *prepare the way* for it? I am sensible there are various predictions of the gathering of God's ancient covenant people from the various nations, after the battle of the great day. But such predictions do not teach, nor imply, that *a body* of the ten tribes are not returned to Jerusalem *before* the battle of the great day; any more than they

304 Mr. Faber's Opinion of Gog considered.

imply, that a body of the *Jews* are not returned, before
the battle of the great day. No doubt there will be vast
gleanings, both of Israelites and of Jews, after the destruction of Antichrist. (Isa. xliii, 5, 6.) But a body
of each will be previously restored. The dry bones
of the house of Israel are raised; and the sticks, of
Ephraim and Judah, are united in one, before the attack of Gog.*

Another argument of Mr. Faber is;—that Antichrist
invades Jerusalem from the *north;* but Gog and his
bands come from *all points.* But I find as much said
of *Gog's* coming from the north, as of *Antichrist's* coming from the north. *And thou shalt come from thy place
out of the north parts, thou and many people with thee.*†
And I will cause thee to come up from thy north parts.‡
It is true the auxiliaries of Gog come to Jerusalem
from every point of the compass from that place. And
this is not inconsistent with any thing said of the hosts
of Antichrist. The latter are said to be *the kings of
the earth, and of the whole world.*§

Mr. Faber's last argument, on which I shall remark,
is derived from Dan. vii, 12; *As concerning the rest of
the Beasts, they had their dominion taken away; yet
their lives were prolonged for a season and a time.*
This text, Mr. Faber thinks, relates to the time of the
destruction of Antichrist; and teaches that though the
preceding Babylonian, Persian, and Grecian Beasts
have their dominion, at the time of the fall of Antichrist, taken from them; yet their existence will be
prolonged after the battle of the great day: they may
exist through the Millennium; and may at the close of
it constitute the Gog and Magog, then to arise. But
Persia is expressly said to be among the bands of Ezekiel's Gog, who perish in his expedition. (Ezek.
xxxviii, 5.) Therefore this Gog, and Antichrist *cannot be the same.* To this argument I submit the following remarks.

---

* See Ezek. xxxviith and xxxviiith chapters. See also Isa.
xi, 11, to the end.

† Ezek. xxxviii, 15. ‡ Chap. xxxix, 2. § Rev. xvi, 14.

1. ,We find that those nations signified by *the rest
of the Beasts*, are to be destroyed at the time of the fall
of Antichrist; and are not *prolonged for a season and a
time*, after that event. In Dan. ii, 35, concerning *those
very nations*, which had been symbolized by the golden
head, the silver breast and arms, and the belly and
thighs of brass, as well as concerning the feet and toes
of the Roman empire, it is said, (upon the smiting of
the stone upon them,) *Then was the iron, the clay, the
brass, the silver, and the gold, broken to pieces* together,
*and became like the chaff of the summer threshing floor,
and the wind carried them away, and no place was found
for them.* Certainly we here learn that those Beasts had
not their lives prolonged for a season and a time, after
the battle of the great day of God Almighty. *This*
therefore, could not be the period referred to in that
text.

2. It cannot accord with the predictions of the battle
of the great day, that the nations which formerly constituted the Babylonian, the Persian, and the Grecian empires, should be all exempt from the terrors of that day;
and should be *prolonged for a season and a time*, after
Antichrist falls, and the whole earth is devoured with
the fire of God's jealousy.

3. The seclusion of those vast sections of the earth
from the blessings of the Gospel, during the Millennium, does not accord with the predictions concerning
the kingdom of Christ, at that period. In that case,
how is the *earth filled with the knowledge of the Lord,
as the waters cover the seas?* How shall *all flesh come
and see God's glory; and the kingdom and dominion,
and the greatness of the kingdom, under the whole
heaven, be given to the saints;* and the *stone become a
great mountain, and fill the whole world;* if the people of those *vast territories* of the ancient Babylonian,
Persian, and Grecian empires continue of the nature of
the Beast through the Millennium? Very numerous
are the predictions of the extent of Christ's kingdom,
at that period; which appear utterly inconsistent, with
Mr. Faber's scheme, of those vast nations remaining in
heathenism through the Millennium.

4. The prolongation of the lives of those Beasts then, must have related to the *very time*, when their dominion was taken away; and not to the time of the destruction of Antichrist. Their dominion was taken away, when each in his turn fell under the victorious arms of his successor: But their lives were *then* prolonged for a time. It was not with them, as it will be with the Antichristian Beast. They did not, as he will, lose their dominion, and their existence on earth together. When their power was taken from them; (each in his turn) their multitudes still lived, that they might unite in the last coalition under Antichrist, and with him go into perdition. Thus, though Persia be expressed in the coalition of Gog; we cannot infer from this, in connexion with Dan. vii, 12, relative to the lives of the rest of the Beasts being prolonged, that Gog is a different power from Antichrist. For Persia, as well as Antichrist, will feel the terrors of the day of God. I now submit it to the reader, if it has not been made clearly to appear, that Gog and Antichrist are one and the same.

I shall close this section with several remarks.

1. From the comments made on Rev. xx, relative to the resurrections there mentioned, we may perhaps learn the true sense of several passages in the Old Testament. In Isa. xxvi, 19, we read; *Thy dead men shall live; together with my dead body shall they arise. Awake and sing, ye that dwell in dust; for thy dew is as the dew of herbs; and the earth shall cast out the dead.* The connexion of this text decides, that it relates to the return of the Jews, and the Millennium. The whole chapter is a prediction of these events. The chapter closes with this address, which follows the above text: *Come my people, enter thou into thy chambers, and shut thy doors about thee; hide thyself as it were for a little moment, until the indignation be overpast. For behold, the Lord cometh out of his place, to punish the inhabitants of the earth for their iniquity: the earth shall also disclose her blood, and shall no more cover her slain.* Some have supposed this passage, in verse 19, to predict a *literal* resurrection. This is in a sense

true: For a *mystical* resurrection implies a *literal* one. A thing never to exist, would not, in this case, be adopted as a metaphor. The doctrine of the resurrection was hence learned from the above text. But that it did *not* predict a *literal* resurrection, to take place at the time, to which it relates, is evident from various considerations. 1. We find no use made of this text, to prove the resurrection of the body. Our Savior when he would prove to the Sadducees the doctrine of the resurrection, did not note this text; but referred to what God said to Moses at the bush.* 2. Mystical resurrections are common in the prophetic writings. John the Baptist was Elijah risen. And it is on the same principle, that the enemies of the Church, in the latter days, *have* ascribed to them the names of her *ancient enemies.* The restoration of Israel, at the time referred to in the text, is predicted by this very metaphor of a resurrection, in Ezekiel xxxvii. In explaining the vision of the valley of dry bones there, the Most High says, (verse 12) *Behold, O my people, I will open your graves, and cause you to come up out of your graves, and bring you into the land of Israel.* Here we have the true sense of the text under consideration, by another, which relates to the same time, and event, under the same metaphor. 3. Able expositors view this text as containing a *mystical* resurrection. See Pool on the passage. Its sense is this; Israel shall again live: They shall be gathered, and live to God in Palestine. *Together with my dead body shall they rise.* Isaiah was inspired to predict his own mystical resurrection; together with that of his people, at the time of the restoration. 4. The tenor of the Scriptures teach us to look for the literal resurrection at the *end of the world;* and never till then. It is *then,* that *All who are in their graves shall hear his voice and come forth.* It is then, that *Death and hell shall deliver up the dead that are in them.* (Rev. xx, 13.)

Awake, and sing, ye who dwell in dust. Entertain hopes, ye, who are dispersed, like bodies dissolved in

---

* Matt. xxii, 31, 32.

the grave. *For thy dew is as the dew of herbs.* God
will shed down his influence, and cause your restoration, *as rain upon the mown grass, and as showers that
water the earth:*—As a kind shower to revive plants,
which appear dry. "For so the Lord said unto me, I
"will take my rest, and I will consider in my dwelling
"place, like a clear heat upon herbs; and like a cloud
"of dew in the heat of harvest."* "I will be as the dew
"to Israel; he shall grow as the lily; and cast forth his
"roots as Lebanon:"†—"As the tender grass springing
"out of the earth by the clear shining after rain."‡

And the earth shall cast out her dead. Upon this
passage Pool remarks,—"The verb here used doth not
signify to *cast out,* but to *cast down.*" These words
(he says) may be, and *are,* both by ancient and later
interpreters rendered—*And thou wilt cast down the
land of the giants,* or *of the violent ones,* of the proud
and potent tyrants of the world. For the word here
rendered *dead,* is elsewhere rendered *giants;* as 2 Sam.
xxi, 16, 18, (and many other texts.) But the words
(he tells us) seem to be better rendered, *And thou
wilt cast the giant down to the ground.* A striking
prediction of the destruction of the great enemies of the
Church, soon after the restoration of the Jews; or in
the battle of the great day, which immediately follows
the passage. The wicked cause will then fall and be lost.

Another passage, which predicts a resurrection at
the same period, is in Dan. xii, 2. *And many of them,
that sleep in the dust of the earth, shall awake, some
to everlasting life; and some to shame and everlasting
contempt.* This prediction is found connected with
the same events with the other above noted; as is evident from consulting the connexion of the passage.§
The same difficulties attend the viewing of this as a literal resurrection, which attend viewing the passage
just considered as a literal resurrection. The passage
in Rev. xx. 4, (noted in this section,) may unfold the
true sense of these predictions. For John is the best
expositor of Daniel. There we find, at the same peri-

---

* Isa xviii, 4.   † Hosea xiv, 5.   ‡ 2 Sam. xxiii, 4.
§ See the close of Sec. ii, chap. i, of this dissertation.

od, a *resurrection.* And, says the passage, *This is the first resurrection;* as though it were an event predicted and thus known. It does not say, this is *a* first resurrection; or an event, which *may* be so called: But, *This is the first resurrection;* seeming to indicate, that we may find this *very event* predicted under this metaphor. And we do find it thus, in the above noted passages in the prophets.

But Daniel speaks of some raised *to shame and everlasting contempt.* To whom, and to what period, does this relate? Let John, who was Daniel's interpreter, decide it. He tells us, when treating of the same period and events, of a *first* resurrection; which must be *mystical,* consisting of the saints. This implies a *second* mystical resurrection. And he informs of one, of Gog and Magog. The subjects of the first resurrection live and reign with Christ, a thousand years. *But the rest of the dead,* (he tells us,) *lived not again until the thousand years were finished.* This thousand-year-resurrection is the *first* resurrection. That of Gog and Magog, therefore, a name of Antichrist, is the *second.* This may be Daniel's mystical resurrection, *to shame and everlasting contempt.* Upon the latter event the *literal* resurrection soon follows, when "All who are in "their graves shall hear his voice, and shall come "forth; they that have done good to the resurrection of "life; and they that have done evil, to the resurrection "of damnation."

Says the Revelator, "Blessed and holy is he, that "hath part in the first resurrection; on such the second "death hath no power; but they shall be priests of God "and of Christ; and shall reign with him a thousand "years."* Here we learn, that *all the Church,* all the elect are included in the first mystical resurrection; all, on whom the second death shall have no power. And indeed this idea is clearly taught in the preceding verses. Though the martyrs are there set in the front of those, who are said to be raised, yet they do not comprise the *whole,* as has been by some supposed. But we find added to them those, "who had not wor-"shipped the beast, neither his image, neither had re-

* Rev. xx, 6.

"ceived his mark in their foreheads, nor in their hands:"
Descriptions, which comprise all the true people of
God. And, that all were designed to be comprised, is
evident from their being contrasted (verse 5) with the
rest of the dead, who comprise all the wicked; and contrasted (verse 6) with those, on whom the second death
hath power. These two mystical resurrections then, are
designed to comprise all the race of man; or *the cause
of Christianity; and the cause of wickedness*. In the Millennium, the former is raised: And in the apostasy at
the close of it, the latter.

We hence learn the true sense of Rev. xi, 18;
where the elders, upon the commencement of the Millennium, give thanks to God; "Because thou hast ta-
"ken to thee thy great power, and hast reigned: And
"the nations were angry; and thy wrath is come; and
"the time of the dead, that they should be judged,
"*(avenged)* and that thou shouldst give reward unto
"thy servants the prophets, and to the saints, and them,
"that fear thy name, small and great; and shouldst destroy them, that destroy the earth." Here the cause
of wickedness is *destroyed;* and all the people of God
have *reward*. What is the additional reward now giv-
en to all the saints, who have long been in *glory?* It is
this;—to see their cause revived universally on earth;
represented by their *own* resurrection for a thousand
years. If there is new *joy in heaven over one sinner,
that repenteth;* how great will be the additional joy
there, when the *whole earth* shall be filled with peni-
tence and salvation, for a thousand years, as the waters
cover the seas! This is their *new,* their *additional* reward.

2. We are furnished, in the preceding pages, with a
clew, by which to understand some predictions of the
coming of Christ. I am induced to make this remark,
from a consideration, that some authors, and especially
a late *one*, have seemed to suppose, that the final judgment commences at the battle of the great day of God
Almighty: An idea, which I think very erroneous.
Gog and his bands, or the enemies of the Church, will
sink in the judgment of the seventh vial, under a *coming of Christ*. In Rev. xvi, 15, after the sixth vial, and

just before the seventh, Christ says, *Behold I come as a thief.* And abundantly that event is predicted as the *coming of Christ.* After the Millennium, and 'Gog and Magog, are resuscitated, Christ *comes to judgment.* Hence, we learn, that the predictions of the *coming of Christ* are fulfilled in *different periods, and events.* And nothing is more evident than this.

In the destruction of the infidel Jews, Christ *came* to judgment. "Verily I say unto you, There be some "standing here, who shall not taste of death, till they "see the Son of man *coming* in his kingdom." (Matt. "xvi, 28.) "This generation shall not pass, till all these "things be fulfilled;" (Matt. xxiv, 34,) i. e. have a *primary* fulfilment in the destruction of Jerusalem. In the wounding to death of the Imperial head of the Roman Beast in the days of Constantine, Christ *came* to judgment: See Rev. vi, 12, to the end, under the sixth seal; where all nature is convulsed, and the great and the wicked are in consternation, because, *the great day of his wrath is come; and who shall be able to stand.* And the *coming* of Christ, at the battle of the great day of God, and *that* at the end of the world, I have before noted. We observe here a gradual rising, in point of importance, in the fulfilments of the *coming of Christ.* *That coming,* in the destruction of the Jews, was terrible. *That* in the revolution at Rome, was in some respects more important. *That* at the destruction of Antichrist, will be still *more extensive,* and terrible by far. And the *coming* at the end of the world will infinitely exceed all the preceding instances of his coming. There are many texts, which predict the *final coming of Christ,* at the end of the world, and which can admit of no primary fulfilment. They relate to that event only: Such as the following: Psal. l, 1—. Matt. xxv, 31—46. John v, 28, 29. Acts i, 11. 1 Cor. xv, 52. 1 Thess. iv, 16, 17. 1 Tim. vi, 14. 2 Tim. iv, 1, 8. Titus ii, 13. Heb. ix, 28. 1 Pet. i, 7, and v, 4. 2 Pet. iii, 10, 11, 12. Rev. xx, 11, 12. But there are other passages, which predict this same event only as their *final* fulfilment;—passages, which announce a *coming* of Christ, which were to be fulfilled in *successive* events; the last of which is his literal appearing to judge the world.

These different fulfilments of the *coming of Christ*, are to be viewed as *distinct;* are not to be blended together. We are not to apply things to one of them, which exclusively belong to another. Should we apply the literal resurrection; the personal appearance of Christ, the commencement of the final judgment, or the conflagration of the world, to the *coming* of Christ at the destruction of Jerusalem; or to his *coming* in the revolution at Rome; we should *greatly err.* And why not as *really err*, to apply them, or any of them, to the coming of Christ in the destruction of Antichrist? It is true, the figures used to predict this latter event, are *strong.* And so were those used to predict *the coming* of Christ in the revolution at Rome; and in the destruction of the Jews. They appeared to predict his last coming, at the end of the world; and will *then* receive their final accomplishment. It is true, the prediction of the destruction of Antichrist, under the seventh vial, as given in Dan. vii, 9, 10, 11, appears like a prediction of the end of the world; and may perhaps be viewed as "*the mother text*" from which some of the apostles' descriptions of the end of the world are borrowed. But we can no more infer from *this*, that the final judgment then commences; than we can infer from the predictions of the above noted ancient instances of the *coming* of Christ, that every event of the final judgment *then* commenced. "And I beheld till the thrones were cast "down, and the Ancient of days did sit, whose gar- "ment was white as snow, and the hair of his head "like the pure wool; his throne was like the fiery flame, "and his wheels as burning fire. A fiery stream issued "and came forth from before him: thousand thousands "ministered unto him; and ten thousand times ten thou- "sand stood before him. The judgment was set, and "the books were opened. And I beheld then, because "of the voice of the great words, which the horn spake, "I beheld even till the beast was slain, and his body "destroyed, and given to the burning flame." The last verse here decides, that this *coming of Christ* is at the destruction of the last head of the Roman Beast with his Papal false prophet, at Armageddon, just before the Millennium. But none of the numerous predictions of the same event gave an idea, that the *final judgmemt* commences at that period. Daniel speaks of the *books* being opened. But St. John, Daniel's best interpreter, tells us when the books shall be opened *for the final judgment;* that it shall be *after* the thousand years of the reign of Christ; and *after* the destruction of the final, mystical Gog and Magog. Rev. xx, 11, 12. Then, and never till then, the great white throne of judgment is erected; and the dead, small and great, stand before God. This will be immediately preceded by a literal resurrection of all, good and bad. Here the predictions of the coming of Christ will meet their ultimate accomplishment. This is called the *second* coming of Christ; called thus in relation to his *first* coming in the flesh. "So Christ once suffer- "ed to bear the sins of many; and unto them, that look "for him, shall he appear the second time, without sin "unto salvation." (Heb. ix, 28.) "This same Jesus, "who is taken up from you into heaven, shall so come "in like manner as ye have seen him go into heaven." Acts i, 11. Here is the literal, and personal, the *second* coming of Christ. But to imagine, *as some have done,* that there will be a personal appearing of Christ, and a commencement of the final judgment, at the battle of that great day of God Almighty, which precedes the Millennium; I think is *very incorrect*; and involves the subject in great obscurity and error.

3. We are presented, in some of the predictions noted in the preceding pages, with the *sameness* of the characters and judgments of the most notorious enemies of the Church, in the different ages of the Gospel day. For they are designated by the same appellations, and are spoken of as though the same things were *again and again* repeated. The infidel Jews were *antichrists,* because they were of the same spirit of the great *Antichrist* of the last time. (1 John ii, 18.) And they were destroyed under a *coming* of Christ. The primitive Pagan Rome, laboring to destroy the Church of Christ,

40

was symbolized by a great and terrible Beast. The infernal agent, who managed this Beast was symbolized by a *great red dragon, of seven heads and ten horns, and seven crowns upon his heads,* laboring to destroy the Church. The revolution in the Roman empire from Paganism to Christianity, is represented not only by the wounding to death of the sixth, the Imperial head of the Roman Beast; but by a *coming of Christ,* as before noted. The new system of Papal corruption and opposition, which rose upon the same ground, under the Christian name, was symbolized by another *Beast* of two horns like a lamb, but who spake like a *dragon;* i. e. was really under the influence of the same infernal agent, with the preceding empire; and accordingly was said to exercise all the power of the *first,* the *Pagan Beast;* and to make an *image* to him; because the essence of the same idolatry was established; though under the Christian name. And the judgments of God upon *Papal Rome* consequently, were to be no less terrible, than those on *Pagan Rome.* Her seat' or throne was to be subverted, and her kingdom filled with darkness, under the rise of Antichrist; and her broken remains, under the name of the *false prophet,* are to go into perdition with him.

The infidel French Empire is symbolized by the *last head* of the old Pagan Beast; the *eighth* numerically; but specifically one *of the seven,* viz. the *sixth,* the *Imperial,* recovered from its deadly wound given under Constantine. It is represented as this sixth head thus recovered, as well as by a new Beast of seven heads and ten horns, from the bottomless pit; (Rev. xvii,) on account of the similarity of the character and object, of the French Empire, with those of ancient Pagan Rome, in its persecuting Imperial form.' And they are represented as under the management of the same great red dragon, of seven heads and ten horns, and seven crowns upon his heads, laboring to destroy the Church, and who gives to this newly healed head, *his power, and seat, and great authority.* And the destruction of this last head of the Beast, under the seventh vial, is represented as an awful *coming of Christ to judgment.*

Also the apostasy over the face of the world, at the close of the Millennium, and the new attack then to be made on the cause of Christ, are represented as the resurrection of these former wicked powers, the kingdom of darkness on earth; particularly Antichrist under his appellation of *Gog and Magog;* in whose fall the cause of the kingdom of darkness is lost. Under these same names the wicked cause is represented as *rising again*, at that period, on account of the *similarity* of the character and conduct of the world of Infidels, who will then arise, with the character and conduct of Ezekiel's Gog, or Antichrist preceding the Millennium.

Thus powers of Infidelity and of heathenism, of different ages and nations, are represented as essentially *one and the same power*, raised up from time to time, and falling under the same judgment, the *coming of Christ*. This strikingly indicates the *similarity* of their characters. To the same point it might here be noted, that the great infidel Power of the last days is mystically identified with the notorious enemies of the Church under the Old Testament. He is *Edom, Bozrah*, and *Babylon*. And many of the judgments denounced against these ancient enemies, are to have an ultimate accomplishment in the destruction of Antichrist.

And for the same reason, all mankind, of whatever place or nation, who are of the same infidel spirit, belong to the same family; and may expect similar judgments from God. Should they not belong *politically* to Antichrist; if they belong to him spiritually; partake of his sins; they may expect to receive of his plagues. In this sense, the class of the children of perdition is vast. Their characters are fast maturing; and their prospects are dreadful! *O my soul, come not thou unto their secrets! Unto their assembly, mine honor, be not thou united!*

The Chambers of Imigary.

THE Jews, for their idolatry and wickedness, were un.
der divine judgments. A part of them were carried
captive to Babylon. And the other part were in a fee.
ble state in Judea. Ezekiel was among the captives
in Babylon. After he had been there, probably in
private life, for several years, he was called to the work
of a prophet.

In the viiith and ixth chapters of his prophecy, we
find things singularly interesting;—*a description of
wickedness in the chambers of imigary; God's setting a mark upon those, who sighed and cried for
this wickedness; and destroying the rest.*

The vision of the chambers of imigary may be viewed as both *historical,* and *prophetical.* The Jews, then
in Babylon, were here furnished with a symbolic representation of their own wickedness while in Judea,
which had occasioned their captivity. In the picture
was figuratively exhibited likewise the wickedness of
the Jews *then* at Jerusalem, for which they should be
destroyed. And the passage also predicts events *then
far future.*

In these chapters we no doubt have representations,
interesting to *all men,* at *all times;* and peculiarly to the
wicked. In the chambers of imigary is given a portrait of the *depraved human heart,* in its *vain, covetous,
impure, subtile* and *wicked* imaginations. This part of
the word of God, as well as others, "is a discerner of
the thoughts and intents of the heart." It is designed
to "cast down *imagination,* and every high thing."
"For, as in water face answereth to face, so the heart of
man to man." And the ixth chapter gives a lively
representation of the Most High's setting apart the
Godly for himself; sealing his chosen to the day of redemption; of their being thus secure against the sword
of divine justice; of all others being cut off in their
sins, and lost; and that divine judgment will be peculiarly severe against *hypocrites.* These are solemn
truths, applicable at all times.

But though these chapters contain such general instruction; yet they evidently contain *particular* instruction; and were to be emphatically applicable at *particular* times. They were designed to predict signal events, at different periods.

It is a common thing for prophecies to have a primary relation to events then near at hand: And also to have a more interesting relation to events far future of those primary events; and which are but *typified* by the events, to which the passage more literally refers. The contents of these two chapters are clearly of this description; as I trust will appear, in the course of this section. They have a special reference to the last stages of the Jewish polity about the time of the commencement of the Christian era; as Peter expressly decides; 1 Pet. iv, 19; which passage will be noted. And they have a more signal reference to the terrible scenes of the last days;—the abominations of Antichrist;—and the utter destruction of all the enemies of the Church.

The prophet begins; "And it came to pass in the sixth year, in the sixth month, in the fifth day of the month, as I sat in mine house, and the elders of Judah sat before me, that the hand of the Lord God fell upon me." These elders, in their captivity and despondency, came to the prophet's abode, probably to hear what he had to communicate. They seemed now more candid, than when in their own land they could persecute the true prophets for faithfully delivering the warnings of God; and could flatter the false prophets, and believe *their* falsehoods. Heavy judgments sometimes bring wicked people to their senses. The prophet was now in a sense snatched from them. "Then I beheld, and lo, a *likeness*, as the appearance of fire; from the appearance of his loins downward, fire; and from his loins even upward, as the appearance of brightness, as the colour of amber." A Person of this divine description appeared present before him. This we may believe was *Christ*. "And he put forth the form of an hand, and took me by the lock of mine head; and the Spirit lifted me up between the earth and the heavens, and brought me, in the visions of God, to Jerusalem,

to the door of the inner gate, that looketh toward the
north; where was the seat of the image of jealousy."
The prophet fell into a trance; and he related things
as they were impressed on his mind by the Holy Ghost.
He seemed to himself to be carried swiftly through the
air, to the temple at Jerusalem, where scenes of wickedness were to be presented in such figures, as accord
with prophetic language. He viewed himself brought
to the door of the inner gate on the north side of the
temple, the court of the priests. This court had four
gates; one toward each cardinal point of the compass.
At the north gate, where the prophet was now set, was
a "seat of the image of jealousy." Ahaz had here set
up an idolatrous altar, after the manner of the idolatry
of *Damascus,* the capital of Syria:—(2 Kings, xvi,
10—16.) Manassah had also placed images here. Josiah destroyed them. And succeeding idolatrous kings
had again set them up. This altar, and these images
were calculated and designed to entice the people off,
gradually, to idolatry. And they thus provoked God
to *jealousy;* as idolatry is spiritual whoredom. "And
behold the glory of the God of Israel was there, according to the vision, that I saw in the plain. Then
said he unto me, Son of man, lift up thine eyes now
the way toward the north, and behold northward, at the
gate of the altar, this image of jealousy in the *entry.*"
This insnaring apparatus of idolatry, after the manner,
of a favorite, foreign nation, was placed in the *entry*
to the temple, to entice those, who came to the worship of God. Innovators and corrupters are *sly* and
subtile, to steal imperceptibly upon those, whom they
have marked out for their prey.

"He said furthermore unto me, Son of man, seest
thou what they do? even the great abominations that
the house of Israel commit here, that I should go far
from my sanctuary. But turn thee yet again, and thou
shalt see greater abominations." q. d. You see how
those impious rulers of my people tempt their Maker
to forsake his people and temple, by laboring, in a
subtile indirect way, to introduce the customs and the
wickedness of a foreign nation, hostile to my religion,

But still deeper abominations are before you. "And he brought me to the door of the court; and when I looked, beheld a *hole* in the wall:" He came now to a *second door*, on the north side of the temple, round about which were the chambers of the priests, the ministers of the temple. Here he discovered a small *aperture*, or a blind window, looking into some of the apartments, where the priests, the ministers of the temple, resided, and transacted their business. Through this, *something* could be seen, though with difficulty, what was done in those apartments. The abominable iniquity began to appear:—Yet but little of it could be seen. "Then said he unto me, Son of man, dig now in the wall:"—Take away the materials round the aperture.—Make it larger:—So that you may behold their conduct; yea, that you may *go in*, and make a full discovery. "And when I had digged in the wall, behold a door." When he had obeyed the direction, and cleared the way for discovery, he found a private *back door*, by which the idolaters entered into their chambers, to pursue their favorite wickedness, in a way hidden from the public eye. Those men of the temple, who were indeed the subordinate rulers of the people, had their apartments, which had been assigned for their official duties, converted into the hidden retreats of idolatry, and secret receptacles of mischief; in violation of the law of God, and of their own official duties. And they had their *back door* prepared, by which to pass and repass, concealed from public view. "And he said unto me, Go in, and behold the wicked abominations, which they do here." Do not close your eyes upon such wickedness. Never connive at it. Explore it, and bring it out to light. Go boldly into their apartments:—Nor fear the violence, or rage, which such base characters will discover against those, who detect them in their wickedness. Investigate all their abominations; that you may be prepared to expose them; to warn others; and to denounce the judgments of God against them. "So I went in, and saw and behold, every form of creeping things, and abominable beasts, and all the idols of the house of Israel, portray

ed upon the walls round about." Here, it seems, was
an imitation of a heathen pantheon, or idol's temple,
decorated with the representations of their gods, in the
forms of beasts and reptiles: As Stephen accused the
Jews; "Ye took up the tabernacle of Moloch, and the
star of your god Ramphan, *figures*, which ye made to
worship them; and I will carry you away *beyond Babylon.*" And as Paul remarks upon the mythology of
idolaters; "And changing the glory of the incorrupti-
ble God into an image made like to corruptible man,
and to birds, and to four footed beasts, and creeping
things." A representation of this wickedness Ezekiel
found in that chamber of imigary;—exposing the wicked hearts of the rulers of the Jews, and others, in for-
saking God, the institutions of his Church, and manners of their own nation; and privately adopting *those*
of some beloved, foreign, idolatrous nation: Doing all
this through private avenues; or in a subtile, hidden
manner. This is the most usual way to introduce dangerous innovations; as the apostle expresses it, "—*privately* bringing in damnable heresies; denying the
Lord, who bought them."

The prophet proceeds. "And there stood before
them seventy men, the ancients of the house of Israel;
and in the midst of them stood Jaazaniah, the son of
Shaphan; with every man his censer in his hand; and
a thick cloud of incense went up." *What, alas, do we
here behold? The seventy! The Sanhedrim! The grand
council of the nation! They* had left their high calling,
of governing a nation for God; and were cloistered in
the chambers of imigary, uniting in all the intrigues
there practised; with Jaazaniah, their prefect, at their
head. Horrid abuse of their trust! These principalities,
this *wickedness in high places*, had crept in through a
hidden aperture, and were plotting their deeds of
abomination in the dark. They had "every man his
censer in his hand. And a cloud of incense went up."
Idolatry was at that time the *rage;* as the virtual denial
of *all* true religion was to be, in the last days. The
seventy were here, in a two-fold sense, invading the
order of God. Burning incense was the work of the

priests. But the seventy had, with impious hands, in vaded this rite. And their incense was burned to *foreign* and *false* gods. And the token of their united wickedness ascended in a cloud.

In how wretched a plight is such a nation here represented! Their first rulers, all their constituted authorities, plotting together, in secret conclave, to subvert the religion of God, and the ancient establishments of their nation! And, in admiration of a foreign idolatrous people, intriguing to introduce their spirits and manners!

"Then said he unto me, Son of man, hast thou seen what the *ancients* of the house of Israel do in the *dark*, every man in the chamber of his imagery? For they say, The Lord seeth us not; the Lord hath forsaken the earth." Here all their vile imaginations in the dark, their wild schemes, were founded in real *atheism*. "The Lord seeth us not; the Lord hath forsaken the earth." What a language for *rulers!* No wonder such can trifle with their oaths, and official duties; and intrigue in the *dark*, to introduce the gods and the manners of some distant favorite people, agreeable to their atheistical hearts.

"He said also unto me, Turn thee yet again, and thou shalt see greater abominations, that they do. Then he brought me to the door of the gate of the Lord's house, which was toward the *north;* and behold there sat women weeping for Tammuz."* Tammuz was a heathen god of *prostitution.* And here were his female votaries, in a cloister of the temple, forming a part of the mystery of iniquity, in the chambers of imagery. All parts of their *impure mysteries* are here to be understood, in the *modest* expression of their *weeping* for their idol. Idolatry, infidelity and *lewdness* are intimately connected. When God, or the purity of his religion, is denied; a decree like the following (expressly or implicitly) might be expected; that "the promiscuous intercourse of the sexes is no crime." This is one

---

* These visions are chiefly on the *north* side of the temple. The evils of the Jews came from the *north.* And the ultimate fulfilment of the abominations predicted, was to be in *northern* regions from Jerusalem.

41

capital *object* of idolatry and infidelity. And hence it is furnished, in the picture of the infidels of the last days; *Having eyes full of adultery, that cannot cease from sin; beguiling unstable souls; hearts exercised with covetous practices; cursed children.*

"Then said he unto me, Hast thou seen this, O son of man? Turn thee yet again, and thou shalt see greater abominations than these. And he brought me into the inner court of the Lord's house; and behold at the door of the temple of the Lord, between the porch and the altar, were about five and twenty men, with their backs toward the temple of the Lord, and their faces toward the east; and they worshipped the sun toward the east." This part of the description is attended with much mystery. The scene is drawn in the inner court, the court of the *priests;* and between the porch and the altar, where the priests were to *intercede* and *worship;* Joel ii, 17. The number twenty five, is probably taken for an *indefinite* but *large* number. Their *position* is striking. They have their backs to God, and his temple, and to their own country; and their faces toward the *east,* worshipping the sun; in imitation of the eastern idolaters, who worshipped the morning sun.

The Jewish priests, no doubt, led the people off to idolatry. But *this* seems to have been represented in the *beginning* of these scenes, in the first chambers. The utter defection of the sanhedrim then followed: And then the abandoned *lewdness* of their idolatry. And after all, greater abominations still, were to be unfolded, in the vision concerning these twenty five men. It is probable that this part of the scene was *wholly prophetical;* and related entirely to events then *far future.* This greatest of all the abominations in the chambers of imagery, was probably to be fulfilled in the last days by men, in the *inner temples* of their deep mysteries of iniquity, operating in concert to subvert the religion of Christ; and to substitute the boasted *illuminism* of their own impious and bewildered imaginations in its stead.

It is a notorious and most interesting *fact,* as has proved in event, that men of the *very character* here described, were to introduce the terrible, exterminating scenes of the last days, under the fond conceit of a deep, wonderful, philosophic *illumination.—Priests* of the light of nature! And most aptly and strikingly represented by the symbolic and prophetic description under consideration. Men in the inner temple of the priests, with their backs toward *God* in his temple, and their faces toward the *east;* worshipping the morning sun; rejecting revealed religion and its Author; boasting of the light of nature, as sufficient for the perfection and happiness of man. Boasting of their wonderful *light.* And propagating their scheme, in hidden concert, with the subtilty of demons, and with a success, which was to astonish, and subvert the world! Whatever kind of primary fulfilment this part of the representations *might* have, in jewish apostates, in the days of Ezekiel, or in any *Jewish Sects*, at the time of the commencement of the Christian era; it was probably, to have its *most interesting* fulfilment in the *last days.*

"Then said he unto me, hast thou seen this, O son of man? Is it a light thing to the house of Judah, that they commit the abominations, which they commit here? For they have filled the land with violence, and have returned to provoke me to anger; and lo, they have put the branch to their nose." As though he had said; They have done all this wickedness in the dark, in their chambers of imagery, in secret conclave. Yet they make very light of it; and are much *offended*, if any *reprove*, or think ill of them. By their subtile means, the land is filled with *violence.* They despise and destroy men. "And have returned to provoke me to anger." They introduce not only oppression and violence among men; but also horrid impiety and outrage toward God, and the Redeemer. "And lo, they put the branch to their nose." Some expositors think this may relate to a custom among ancient idolaters, of holding some branch, or sprig, with which they have touched their idol, and which they put to their nose. But it rather appears to relate to their system of *provoking* their fellow men, or their Maker, or both. Anger among the Hebrews was represented by an unnatur-

al appearance of the nose; and by its breathing out fire.
In allusion this Hebraism, the poet, speaking of the
anger of God, says,

"His nostrils breathe out fiery flames."

Putting a branch to the nose, is then, a striking symbol of a *system of irritating conduct;* provoking and en-
flaming men. Some have rendered it, "lo, they put a
branch to *my* nose." Or, they are provoking their
Maker; treasuring up wrath against the day of wrath;
like one putting a dry branch to a flame of fire.

It is probable *both* the above scenes are included
in the phrase. "*Lo they put the branch to the nose.*"
They provoke God; and irritate one another. The
phrase, of putting the branch to the nose, probably
was *proverbial,* and the sense of it *forcible,* and fully understood by all, at that day, as indicating a most *impious* and *irritating* line of conduct.

A denunciation of their ruin accordingly follows.
"Therefore will I deal in fury; mine eye shall not spare;
neither will I have pity: And though they cry in mine
ears, with a loud cry, yet will I not hear them." Such
characters, whether *rulers, subjects, teachers,* or be they
what they may, God will utterly destroy, without re-
prieve or pity.

A symbolic prediction of the fulfilment of this judgment then follows, in the ixth chapter. "He cried also,
in mine ears, with a loud voice, saying, Cause them
that have the charge over the city to draw near, every
man with his destroying weapon in his hand." When
God cries aloud, the indication is dreadful. This is
often found in symbolic language; and it always indicates the introduction of a terrible scene of judgments.
Isa. xlii, 13, 14; "The Lord shall go forth as a mighty man: he shall stir up jealousy like a man of war; he
shall *cry,* yea *roar;* he shall prevail against his enemies.
I have long time holden my peace;—now will *I cry,*
like a travailing woman; I will destroy and devour at
once." (See also Jer. xxv, 30; Hos. xii, 10; Joel iii,
16. Amos i, 2; Rev. x, 1—3; xviii, 1, 2.)

"And behold, Six men came forth the way of the higher gate, which looketh toward the north; and every man a slaughter weapon in his hand." Here were six *armed executioners* from the *north.* It is said that the Assyrian army against the Jews were composed of *six nations.* And they were from regions in the northern latitude from Jerusalem. *Rome* also, the executioner of the Jews in after days, (or forty years after Christ,) was to the *north.* And Antichrist under the name of Gog, at the time of the end, is to be destroyed with *six plagues:* See Pool's marginal reading of Ezek. xxxix, 2. "*I will strike thee with six plagues; or, will draw thee back with a hook of six teeth;*" as predicted in chap. xxxviii, 21, 22;—*the sword, pestilence, blood, rain, hail and fire.*

"And one man among them was clothed with linen, with a writers inkhorn by his side. And they went in, and stood by the *brazen altar.*" Yes, the anger of God will blaze against those *impious beings*, who shall dare to pour contempt upon his altar! "And the glory of the God of Israel was gone up from the cherub to the threshold of the house." The Shekinah had left its usual place, and was *retiring*, to leave the temple.. "And he called to the man, clothed with linen, who had the writers inkhorn by his side; and the Lord said unto him, Go through the midst of the city, through the midst of Jerusalem, and set a mark upon the foreheads of the men, that sigh and that cry for all the abominations that be done in the midst thereof. And to the others (the armed men) he said in mine hearing, Go ye after him, through the city, and *smite;* let not your eye spare; neither have pity. Slay utterly old and young, both maids and little children, and women! But come not near any man, upon whom is the mark; and begin at my sanctuary.. Then they began at the ancient men, who were before the house. And he said unto them, Defile the house, and fill the courts with the slain: Go ye forth. And they went forth and slew in the city."

None can pretend, that this representation received more than a *partial*, and *typical* fulfilment in Jerusa-

lem. A partial fulfilment it received in the destruction
of the Jews by the Romans. Peter applies the passage
to that event; 1 Pet. iv, 17. "For the time is come,
when judgment must begin at the house of God."
God directed the armed men, to *begin at his house.*—
"And they began at the ancient men, who were before'
the house.". From *this*, Peter infers, that "judgment
must begin at the house of God." It should begin
with those, who bore the name of God's people. Such
were the *Jews.* And such were the *Papal nations*, on
which the judgments of the last days were to begin.
The remark of Peter, that *"the time was come,* when
judgment must begin at the house of God," carries
the event of the prophecy in Ezek. ix, far future of
the days of Ezekiel, even to the destruction of Jerusalem. From this we may infer, that the predictions,
in the chambers of imagery, related ultimately to things
far future of the days of Ezekiel. For the wickedness
there described, and the judgments in the succeeding
chapter, are nearly allied. The latter are but the punishment of the former. And if the one predicted
events then far future; the other likewise did. And
Peter, in his above passage, does not suggest, that the
prediction in Ezek. ix, was to receive its *final* accomplishment in his day; any more than the denunciation
of Christ, that the predictions of his *coming*, in Matt.
xxiv, should be fulfilled upon *that generation*, decided,
that his coming, in the destruction of Jerusalem, was
the *ultimate* fulfilment of those predictions of his coming. The destruction of the Jews was only a *primary*
and *typical* fulfilment of that coming of Christ. Its
more important fulfilment was then far future. (See 2
Thes. ii, 1—8, and Rev. xvi, 15.) In like manner
that ruin of the Jews was only a typical fulfilment of the
scene in Ezek. ix. The above prophecies no doubt
relate to one and the same event;—*the desolating judgments of the last days.*

The descriptions in the chambers of imagery then,
were to have their most important fulfilment in the peculiar abominations, which *bring on* the judgments of
the last days. They *may* have had a very considerable

relation to the abominable system of *Popery. That* was indeed a system of *abomination* in the *temple of God.* It has introduced all the more gross abominations of the last days, which now are opening the flood-gates of divine vengeance. But the gross abominations of the last days, we may believe, are forming a most signal fulfilment of the descriptions in the chambers of imagery. These descriptions give the very same characteristics, which are found in the various predictions, that do evidently relate to the *wicked* of the last days. And these various predictions appear to be, in some instances, expressed in manifest allusion to the descriptions of the wickedness in the chambers of imagery. I shall now note some instances of coincidence between the characters, in the chambers of imagery, and the characters of the last days.

The horrid atheistical influence of the last days, goes out *unto the kings of the earth,* and of the whole world, to gather them to battle against God. (Rev. xvi; 13, 14.) It insinuates itself *into,* and *corrupts,* the *cabinets* of nations; and causes them to lead the way to destruction. The kings of the earth are made to agree, and give their kingdom unto the Beast. And in the chambers of imagery are found, in clandestine concert, the *seventy,* with their prefect;—or, the grand council of the nation organized.

The wicked characters of the last days are *"privately* to bring in their damnable heresies"—"crept in unawares." And the vile beings in the chambers of imagery, were intriguing there in hidden conclave, having crept in at a *back door,* concealed from public view.

The vile characters of the last days are called *filthy dreamers.* Their *schemes* are like romantic dreams; visionary; at war with common sense, and with every maxim of wisdom and prudence. And God said to Ezekiel, "Seest thou what the ancients of the house of Israel do in the *dark,* every man in the *chambers of his imagery?"* As Jude says of the same; "These be they that *separate* themselves." All is done in the *dark;* and by a *back door* influence.

Peter says of them; "Having eyes full of adultery, that cannot cease from sin." And Ezekiel presents them, as having *one cloister* in their temples devoted to women, weeping for Tammuz; or devoted to lewdness.

In various prophecies these men are represented as *atheists*: "Denying the Lord, who bought them." "Denying the Father and the Son." And in the chambers of imagery, "they say, The Lord seeth us not; the Lord hath forsaken the earth."

Other prophecies present them as *traitors*, as well as heady, high minded, and lovers of pleasure, more than lovers of God. And this trait of character is implied in all the descriptions of them in the chambers of imagery; especially in those, where their *backs* are toward the temple, and interest of their own nation; their faces toward the east; and they are enamored with the abominations of a foreign, favorite nation.

Paul says of them; "Having a form of Godliness, but denying the power thereof; from such turn away." And in the chambers of imagery, the seventy have, every man his *censer;* and a cloud of incense went up:" While yet they say "The Lord seeth us not; the Lord hath forsaken the earth." Strange absurdity! God they said did not behold them! Yet each must have a *censer;* and must furnish his part of a cloud of incense! Some shreds of religion may serve as a convenient cloak of covetousness, a vail to their enormities. Hence even Antichrist and his followers must have, (at least at times) some "form of Godliness."

Paul describes them as *heady, high minded, fierce, false accusers, despisers of the good.* And in the chambers of imagery, "they put the branch to the nose." They irritate and provoke mankind.

Paul informs, that "in the last days perilous times shall come. For men shall be lovers of their own selves—truce breakers, false accusers." Isaiah says of the *same;* "Truth is fallen in the streets, and equity cannot enter." And of the men in the chambers of imagery, it is said; "They have filled the land with violence."

And the last class of men in those chambers, who are represented as the *most abominable* of all with their backs, toward God, and worshippers of the *sun*, or the *light*, present a striking emblem of the *order of illuminees;*—the hidden, atheistical agents of the innovations and terrible scenes of the last days; who go forth, as spirits of devils, and like hateful obtrusive frogs, to the kings of the earth, and of the whole world, to gather them to the battle.

Events of modern date afford a solemn comment upon this vision of Ezekiel. After the visible temple of the catholic church had long become a sink of abominable wickedness and idolatry, under the Christian name;—and had long been exhibited to the people of God, as a collection of filth and wickedness; France became deluged with the infernal influence of the Voltaire system of atheism. This influence flew, almost with the rapidity of lightning, into other catholic countries; and prepared the way for the terrible scenes, which have followed.

This scheme managed the French revolution. And being planted in other Popish nations, it prepared the way there for the quick and fatal success of the French arms. On this intriguing influence the *French* (in revolutionizing the Roman world) made their chief reliance. They either bribed and seduced the governments of those nations to betray their territories into their hands; or they seduced other leading characters, and found means to divide the people from their government. And thus those nations became a prey to the devouring grasp of *the bloody nation*. It is said, Bonaparte complained, when subduing Italy, that his hosts of spies and secret agents then in Germany, cost him more than all his army in Italy.

By such means the French tyrant found himself able to corrupt the vitals of the Papal nations, marked out for his prey; and to make an easy conquest of them; or to seduce them into an alliance with him; which invariably proved their destruction. All the republics in Europe have, in this way, been blotted out from un-

42

der heaven. The intrigues of the chambers of imagery have *destroyed them.*

The French at first pledged their faith to the wold,
for the three following principles: That they wold
make no *conquests:* That they would make war oly
upon *tyrants:* And that they would give *liberty* nd
equality to all people, wherever their arms cme.
With these sentiments proclaimed to the world, nd
privately propagated, by their insidious agents, throgh
the nations, (with other intriguing flatteries, which pe-
pared the way for the quick success of their arms,)
they subverted and enslaved every European repubc:
That of Lucca, Pisa, Venice, St. Marino, Genva,
the Netherlands, the thirteen republics of Switzerlad,
and that of the Seven Isles; as well as the *great kig-
doms* of Papal Europe. With all their soft infernal at-
teries, conquest and a universal military despotism, e-
came their *sole object.*

The same abominable influence of the modern chm-
bers of imagery, has made insidious attempts upon
England, Scotland, Ireland and Russia, upon the gv-
ernment of Persia, in the East Indies, and (it is sp-
posed) upon China. Tippo Saib was by this influece
seduced, and ruined. These emissaries of mischef,
have labored to embroil in their cause the Sieks ad
Mahrattas. And they have set on fire the Sparsh
America.

Thus the French have disseminated (or attemped
to disseminate) through all Europe, into Asia, nd
at least into the Spanish part of America, the abomia-
tions of the chambers of imagery.

Tremendous scenes of judgment have followd!
Where these sentiments, have been embraced, the le-
luded people have found, to their cost, that their *jug-
ment has not lingered, nor their damnation slumberd.*
Scenes of slaughter and divine vengeance have followd.

What then shall we say of *our own nation?* If ve
have escaped the fatal abominations of the chamber of
imagery, it must be deemed a *miracle!* That thse
diabolical intrigues have been, with the greatest assiu-
ity practised upon the vital parts of this natin,

we may infr, *for certainty,* from the word of God, and from aalogy and the nature of things. This influence of ital systematic intrigue, was to *go* into *all the earth;* to teir *kings,* and *cabinets.* It *has* gone to all the *rest* of the civilized earth. What could induce its instigatcs to avoid this great nation, this *envied republic?* Nthing! But every consideration would induce them o make this a *principal point* of attack.

And the *successes* in *other* parts of the world have been almot *miraculous.* Britain and Scotland have come the rarest to being full proof against them. And the late dissters of the French in Russia; it is hoped, have shake their influence in that empire. But the voice of aspiration represents these three unclean spirits like frogs, not only as spirits of *devils,* but as *working mracles* of success, in their going out unto the kings or coinets of the earth, and of the whole world, to gather tem into a coalition against heaven; Rev. xvi, 13—6.

The question (interesting to us,) then occurs. Have the first chracters of these United States had the deep, wise, and virtuous *sagacity,* to discern the nature and the designof these pointed and most subtile intrigues, which hav wrought such wonders in other nations, and betrayd and enslaved unnumbered millions of the human rac? And have our first characters possessed the singulr firmness, to *withstand,* and expose those fatal intriges, which, (we are divinely assured,) if it were possile, would deceive even the very elect? Is it, or is it not, the official duty of such a government as ours, *expose* such dark attempts when made? and to wan their nation of its dangers from them.

When in insidious communication was made to Hezekiah, king of Judah, from a foreign, intriguing, ambitiousower, Hezekiah forthwith laid it before the public; ye before the Lord; Isa. xxxvii, 14—. "And Hezekiahreceived the letter, from the hand of the messenge; and read it. And Hezekiah went up into the houseof the Lord, and spread it before the Lord. And Hezkiah prayed unto the Lord, saying, O Lord of hosts, God of Israel, that dwellest between the cher-

der heaven. The intrigues of the chambers of imagery have *destroyed them.*

The French at first pledged their faith' to the world, for the three following principles: That they would make no *conquests.* That they would make war only upon *tyrants.* And that they would give *liberty* and *equality* to all people, wherever their arms came. With these sentiments proclaimed to the world, and privately propagated, by their insidious agents, through the nations, (with other intriguing flatteries, which prepared the way for the quick success of their arms,) *they subverted and enslaved* every European republic: That of Lucca, Pisa, Venice, St. Marino, Geneva, the Netherlands, the thirteen republics of Switzerland, and that of the Seven Isles; as well as the *great kingdoms* of Papal Europe. With all their soft infernal flatteries, conquest and a universal military despotism, became their *sole object.*

The same abominable influence of the modern chambers of imagery, has made insidious attempts upon England, Scotland, Ireland and Russia, upon the government of Persia, in the East Indies, and (it is supposed) upon China. Tippo Saib was by this influence seduced, and ruined. These emissaries of mischief, have labored to embroil in their cause the Sieks and Mahrattas. And they have set on fire the Spanish America.

Thus the French have disseminated (or attempted to disseminate) through all Europe, into Asia, and at least into the Spanish part of America, the abominations of the chambers of imagery.

Tremendous scenes of judgment have followed! Where these sentiments, have been embraced, the deluded people have found, to their cost, that their *judgment has not lingered, nor their damnation slumbered.* Scenes of slaughter and divine vengeance have followed.

What then shall we say of *our own nation?* If we have escaped the fatal abominations of the chambers of imagery, it must be deemed a *miracle!* That those diabolical intrigues have been, with the greatest assiduity practised upon the vital parts of this nation, we may infer, for certainty, from the word of God, and from analogy, and the nature of things. This influence of fatal systematic intrigue, was to *go* into *all the earth;* to their *kings,* and *cabinets.* It *has* gone to all the *rest* of the civilized earth. What could induce its instigators to avoid this great nation, this *envied republic?* Nothing! But every consideration would induce them to make this a *principal point* of attack. And their *successes* in *other* parts of the world have been almost *miraculous.* Britain and Scotland have come the nearest to being full proof against them. And the late disasters of the French in Russia, it is hoped, have shaken their influence in that empire. But the voice of Inspiration represents these three unclean spirits like frogs, not only as spirits of *devils,* but as *working miracles* of success, in their going out unto the kings or cabinets of the earth, and of the whole world, to gather them into a coalition against heaven; Rev. xvi, 13—16.

The question (interesting to us,) then occurs. Have the first characters of these United States had the deep, wise, and virtuous *sagacity,* to discern the nature and the design of these pointed and most subtile intrigues, which have wrought such wonders in other nations, and betrayed and enslaved unnumbered millions of the human race? And have our first characters possessed the singular firmness, to *withstand,* and expose those fatal intrigues, which, (we are divinely assured,) if it were possible, would deceive even the very elect? Is it, or is it not, the official duty of such a government as ours, to *expose* such dark attempts when made? and to warn their nation of its dangers from them.

When an insidious communication was made to Hezekiah, king of Judah, from a foreign, intriguing, ambitious power, Hezekiah forthwith laid it before the public; yea, before the Lord; Isa. xxxvii, 14—. "And Hezekiah received the letter, from the hand of the messengers; and read it. And Hezekiah went up into the house of the Lord, and spread it before the Lord. And Hezekiah prayed unto the Lord, saying, O Lord of hosts, God of Israel, that dwellest between the cher-

ubims; thou art the God, even thou alone of all the
kingdoms of the earth. Thou hast made heaven and
earth. Incline thine ear, O Lord, and see and hear all
the words of Sennacherib, which are sent to reproach
the living God. Of a truth Lord, the kings of Assyria
have laid waste all the nations, and their countries; and
have cast their gods into the fire; for they were no gods
but the work of men's hands, wood and stone; therefore they have destroyed them. Now therefore, O
Lord our God, save us from his hand; that all the
kingdoms of the earth may know, that thou art the
Lord, even thou only."

Here is an example, worthy of the government of a
great, enlightened people, who believe in the *being and
government of God,* when an intriguing foreigner, a
haughty Babylonian (either of *ancient* or *modern* date)
is making mischievous communications. Has our nation had opportunity to witness any event of this kind?
If not, is it because no mischievous communications
have reached this side of the Atlantic? Can we rely on
this inference, and say, that no such communications
have been made? Is it possible, that the fatal influence
of the chambers of modern imagery, having reached the
cabinet of this nation, has there been connived at;
or concealed; yea, and has taken its designed effect?
Should this prove to be the case, wo be to our nation.
"Wo unto us; for the day goeth away; for the shadows
of the evening are stretched out."

Ancient Babylon was destroyed. Modern Babylon
is to be destroyed, with a far more dreadful destruction.
The Jews, when they became idolatrous, were most
deeply chastised. And when they became *antichristian,*
they were by the Romans *destroyed.* Just so far, as
they partook of the abominations portrayed in the chambers of imagery; so far they shared in the judgments
symbolized in the ninth chapter there following. The
time is, no doubt, drawing near, when the exterminating scenes in that chapter shall be *finished.* The Holy
Spirit has been, and still is, sitting his mark on the men,
who sigh and cry for the abominations done in the
midst of them. The subjects of this mark will be

safe. But the command will be executed, to *slay utterly all*, destitute of this mark.

And not only is mystical Babylon to be destroyed; but also *all*, who participate in her abominations. There are those, who constitute this Babylon. And we read of those, who partake of her sins; and shall receive of her plagues. We are informed of *Antichrist*; and of those, who have the *spirit* of Antichrist. We read of the *Beast*; and of those, who have the *mark* of the Beast; who worship his image; and shall share with him the cup of divine indignation, in the battle of that great day of God Almighty.

The voice from heaven then, proclaims to *us*; "Ho; ho, come forth and flee from the land of the north. Deliver thyself, O Zion, that dwellest with the daughters of Babylon." "Come out of her, my people, that ye be not partakers of her sins; and that ye receive not of her plagues." "And a third angel followed, saying, If any man worship the Beast, and his image, and receive his mark in his forehead, or in his hand, the same shall drink of the wine of the wrath of God, which is poured out without mixture into the cup of his indignation; and he shall be tormented with fire and brimstone in the presence of the holy angel, and in the presence of the Lamb. And the smoke of their torment ascendeth up forever and ever; and they have no rest, day nor night, who worship the Beast and his image, and whosoever receiveth the mark of his name." Rev. xvi, 8—11. These are pointed warnings from heaven against all affinity with the Beast of the last days. It is worthy of note, that the above warning is given by a third Angel, after the first was flying through heaven, having the Gospel to preach to every nation, and announcing the arrival of the hour of God's judgment; and a second Angel had announced the *fall of Papal Babylon*. After the fall of Papal Babylon then, it seems a great *Beast*, (the Roman Beast of the last days) *is on the ground;* with the world worshipping him; and men in the utmost danger of being caught in his toils. Such a Beast has appeared before the eyes of the world. And the above warning voice is addressed to the people of *this very period*, from the throne of God.

Let men peruse and reperuse the above passages, and similar warnings; and learn to obey the heavenly messages. Look into the graves of the republics, and kingdoms, who have fallen under the iron grasp of the tyrant of the age. Behold their fields, white with the bones of their citizens, and fattened with their blood! Their liberties annihilated! Their pomp brought down to the grave, and the noise of their vials! The worms are spread under them; and the worms cover them. The terrible of the nations has cut them off. The earth has shaken at the sound of their fall. God has spoken concerning them, to pull down, to pluck up, and to destroy. And the dreadful event has been seen in tremendous execution.

What has yet appeared, is but the *beginning of sorrows;* yet sorrows they *are*, indeed. So sudden and great a crash of nations probably never before tortured the human ear; or wrent the heart of man. And the scenes must be yet far more dreadful, in the closing parts of the most tremendous and exterminating judgments of the last days.

Must *these States* share in the terrors of that day? *We must;* so certainly as the Heavens bear rule; if we partake of Babylon's sins; if we unite in that blasphemy; if we are caught in those snares. Unless our nation disarm and withstand the abominations depicted in the chambers of imagery, or the diabolical influence, which has already desolated a vast section of the earth, and sent at least *ten* if not *twelve* millions of souls to their long home, this nation must unavoidably share the exterminating terrors of the battle of the great and terrible day of the Lord.

SECTION V.

The Bastard of Ashdod: Or, the illegitimate Antichristian government.

WE find various names of the ancient noted enemies of the Church, mystically applied to the Papal hierarchy, and to the great hostile Power of the last days. They are called *Babylon*, after the name of the capital of Chaldea:—Also *Edom*, *Bozrah*, and other names of ancient hostile cities and nations. We might then, rationally expect to find the name of the *capital* of *Syria*, and the names of other noted cities in Palestine, that were most hostile to the ancient people of God, applied to the notorious enemies of the Church, in the last day. Had not this been the case, we should not be able to account for the omission. For many of the most vexing and bloody wars against God's ancient people, were from the Philistines, and from nations and people in the land of Syria. We might then, expect to find the names of ancient noted *cities* in *Syria*; and among the hostile *Philistines*, mystically applied to the terrible enemies of the last days. And we might expect, that denunciations would be uttered of divine judgments against *those cities*, which, after receiving a primary accomplishment upon those cities, were to receive their ultimate fulfilment upon the destructive enemies of the last days.

And such prophecies *are found.* I shall now note one of this description. In Zech. ix, we have predictions of judgments upon hostile cities round about Judea; a promise of protection to the Church; of the coming of Christ; of the restoration of the Jews; the ruin of their enemies; and the commencement of the Millennium. "The burden of the word of the Lord in the land of Hadrach, and Damascus shall be the rest thereof; when the eyes of man, as of all the tribes of Israel, shall be toward the Lord." By the *burden* of the word of the Lord here, is meant, (says Pool,) "the heavy, sad, grievous, menacing prediction of future evils," upon Hadrach; and upon Damascus shall it *rest.* Hadrach was a great city near Damascus; hostile to the Jews. And Damascus, on which the burden of this prophecy *should rest*, was the capital of Syria. Those names ultimately represent the *Papal nations.* Hadrach imports *joy of tenderness:* And Damascus, *a sack of blood; or the blood of a righteous man;* and was supposed by the ancients, to be the place where *Abel* was murdered; and that it hence derived its name. And the nations of the Papal harlot are represented as *joy-, ful and delicate*; and yet *drunk with blood, the blood of martyrs;* Rev. xvii, 4, 6; and xviii, 7—10, 24. And the fulfilment of this prophecy is to be, "when the eyes of man, as of the tribes of Israel, shall be towards the Lord.", A striking representation of the state of the true Church, and of the tribes of the Jews, about the time of their *restoration.*

The judgments that follow, in the fulfilment of this *burden,* are represented as executed on the cities round about Hadrach and Damascus;—as Hamah, Tyre, Zidon; and the more southern cities of the Philistines;. —viz. Ashkelon, Gaza, Ekron, and *Ashdod.* These are here to be viewed as mystical names of the modern nations in the Papal delusion. The judgments, threatened in this passage to those nations, are these; verse 4, 5; *that behold, God would cast them out, and smite their power; and devour them with fire. Ashkelon shall see it and fear. Gaza also shall see it, and be sorrowful. For her expectation shall be ashamed; and the king shall perish from Gaza. And Ashkelon shall not be inhabited.* This prediction well accords with Rev. xviii; where, in the fall of Papal Babylon, the different kingdoms of her communion bewail her burnings; and cry Alas, alas. This prophecy, in Zech. ix, no doubt had a partial, typical fulfilment upon those cities in Palestine, when Alexander subdued them; and swept across that region, in his victorious flight into the *east.* Also, when his generals, in after days, scoured those countries, in their furious invasions of each other, in Syria, and Egypt. But it is acknowledged, that this prophecy is not *yet* finally fulfilled. What follows in the chapter shows, that its most interesting import, or ultimate fulfilment, was to be in days far future of the time of Alexander; and was to introduce the period, when (as verse 10,) God "will cut off the chariot from Ephraim, the horse from Jerusalem, and the battle-bow shall be cut off, and he shall speak unto the heathen, and his dominion shall be from sea even to sea, and from the river even to the ends of the earth." All that follows in the chapter decides, that the ultimate fulfilment of its contents was to be in the *last days.*

The celebrated Mr. Scott, in his notes upon verse 8th, where God promises the Church, that *no oppressor shall pass through her any more;* (a promise, which clearly relates to the Millennium,) says; "But the passage, no doubt, refers to events *yet future;* which will more signally accomplish it."

In this chapter, we find the following interesting prediction. Verse 6. *"And a bastard shall dwell in Ashdod; and I will cut off the pride of the Philistines."* *Ashdod* was a great and capital *city* of the Philistines. Here was their temple of Dagon, to which the ark of God was carried, when it was taken by the Philistines in the days of the advanced age of Eli; 1 Sam. iv, and v. Here God plagued the Ashdodites, on account of the ark, till they were obliged to send it out of their country. Here Dagon fell before the ark, and broke off his head and hands. And here Samson, after a scene of captivity to the lords of the Philistines, and being brought forth to make sport for them, on the day of a great festival to Dagon, overturned their temple, and slew thousands of the enemies of the Church. Those things were not without mystical import, relative to the salvation of the gospel Church. *Ashdod* then, is a striking name given to some *leading nation* in the Papal communion, at the time when God is about to *cut off the pride of the Papal Philistines,* or of *Mystery Babylon.*

A *bastard* dwelling there, must denote some great and very unusual character, or dynasty, there set up; one out of the line of legal succession. Nothing is known to have taken place, in the ancient literal Ashdod, which even afforded a *typical* fulfilment of this part of the burden of the prophecy. Upon this bastard of Ashdod, expositors have been sparing. One, upon the passage, says, "Jonathan, one of the Maccabees, took it and destroyed many of the Philistines." But what then? Jonathan did not dwell in Ashdod. And it is a singular compliment paid to him, to intimate, that he was the *bastard of that place.* Pool observes,

43

"Some say, Alexander was, by Olimpia's confession, declared to be a bastard; and that he is here pointed at." But there are objections to this exposition. The passage is no doubt *mystical*, and not literal;—even if it were a given point that Alexander was not the son of Philip of Macedon, but was of illegitimate issue;—a point, however, which I apprehend is *not conceded*. But Alexander did not *dwell in Ashdod* He merely *swept* across this, as he did the other cities of Palestine, in his victorious flight into the east. Pool dissented from the opinion of its being Alexander; and rather thought it meant strangers dwelling there, with no right of inheritance. But he hint no instance of such an event. And such an event, even if we could ascertain that some men had dwelt *there*, without much if any right of inheritance, could not be expected to be a subject of solemn prophecy, nor to be noted under such an appellation. The fulfilment of this prediction, I apprehend, was *still future* when Pool wrote his annotations; and that it has recently begun to be fulfilled in the *new French dynasty*, in the infidel Empire; the *god whom their fathers knew not*, Dan. xi, 38, 39; the strange god, whom they should acknowledge, and increase with glory; and who should cause them to rule over many, and divide the earth for gain. Such a dynasty, of *foreign extraction*, is most strikingly represented by the prophetic appellation of *bastard;* though it should be continued in a *succession* of men, upon the imperial throne: And still more strikingly, (if possible,) should succeeding emperors be from different families; according to the rank of generals; or the length of their swords.

We may then, with some confidence pronounce, that we have seen the event of a *bastard's dwelling in Ashdod*, in the assumed imperial government, in a most noted *capital* of the land of the *Papal Philistines;* or in France. And the event has operated, according to the text, to *cut off the pride of the Papal Philistines!* This *illegitimate dynasty*, perched on the ruins of the Capits, has indeed humbled the pride of the modern Philistines, or of *Papal Europe.*

The prophet proceeds. "And I will take away his blood out of his mouth, and his abominations from between his teeth. But he, that remaineth, even he shall be for our God; and he shall be as a governor in Judah; and Ekron as a Jebusite." The first of this verse may apply either to the *bastard;* or to *Ashdod;* and is strikingly applicable in either case. Both may be represented as *fed on human blood.*

The Papal Ashdod has been "drunken with the blood of the saints." And the *bastard,* in his turn, may be said to have fed on blood and carnage, in wantonly spilling the blood of millions. And all this blood is, by righteous Heaven, to be avenged. When the Lord comes out of his place, to punish the world for their iniquity, *the earth shall disclose her blood, and no longer cover her slain.* Then "he that remaineth shall be for our God." God will then "turn to the remnant of the people, a pure language, that they may all call upon the name of the Lord, and serve him with one consent." And they shall be as *governors,* yea, as *kings* and *priests* unto God. "And Ekron shall be as a Jebusite." A *remnant,* even among the most hostile nations, shall be *left,* shall be converted, and shall unite in the true Church; even as a remnant of the Jebusites (a tribe of the Canaanites near Jerusalem) was spared, and incorporated with the Jews. The pious Araunah, who offered David his threshing floor for a place to build an altar, was one of these natives of the land.

"And I will encamp about mine house, because of the army, because of him that passeth by, and because of him, that returneth; and no oppressors shall pass through them any more: For now have I seen with mine eyes." The Lord, as a Man of war, in the time of this battle of that great day of God Almighty, will *camp* about his Church, because of the perils of the times. He will destroy every oppressor; representing himself after the manner of men, as having personally *come;* and as having *seen,* and *avenged* the injuries of his people.

A new paragraph, in the chapter, begins. Christ in his humiliation comes to the daughter of Zion, riding upon an ass. This was literally fulfilled, when Christ rode into Jerusalem. And it is to be mystically fulfilled, in his people, when they shall be *left*, in the midst of the earth, *an afflicted and poor people*, as the prophet expresses it, at the close of the battle of the great day; with whom the Millennium will begin; and the *meek* shall inherit the earth. Then, as the next verse informs, Christ will have cut off the chariot, the horse, and the battlebow; and he will speak peace to the heathen; and his dominion shall be from sea to sea; and from the river to the ends of the earth. The Jews, as it then follows, will have come forth, as prisoners of hope, from the pit, in which is no water of salvation. God will have *bent* Judah for him; and filled his *bow* with Ephraim; or the Jews and the ten tribes will be recovered, and united. At which time he will raise up the sons of Zion against the sons of Greece; and make the former as the sword of a mighty man. (See remarks on Zech. ix, 11—14, in the last part of the note, page 286.) The Lord will now be *seen* over the tribes of the people of his ancient covenant. He will be seen as their Protector against the vast coalition formed against them. His arrow shall go forth as the lightning; he shall blow the trumpet; and go as whirl- winds of the south. "And the Lord their God shall save them in that day, as the flock of his people; for they shall be as stones of a crown, lifted up, as an en- sign upon his land;" or as most rich gems in the crown of Christ, rendered most conspicuous to the na- tions. The blessedness of the Millennium follows, and closes the chapter. "For how great is his goodness, and how great is his beauty? Corn shall make the young men cheerful; and new wine the maids." Bless- ings, spiritual and temporal, shall fill the world.

Thus we have a modern Hadrach, and a Damascus, —on which the burden of the word of the Lord, or the heavy judgment of his word, *rests*. We have beheld a *modern Ashdod*, with its *illegitimate dynasty;* a mean of cutting off the pride of the Papal enemies of the Church. But the *Dagon* of Ashdod will be found prostrate in ruin, with his hands and head broken off, before the ark of the Lord. Should the lords of the Philistines for a short season even captivate the *ark* of the God of Israel, they will find it too *mighty* for them; and it will soon rise out of their hands. And Sampson will eventually subvert the pillars of their *boasted temple;* and *crush* and *bury* them under its ruins.

SECTION VI.

Some other Prophecies in the Old Testament, relative to the last expedition, and the overthrow of Antichrist; and the ruin of the enemies of the Church.

THE Most High addresses Gog, *Art thou he, of whom I have spoken in old times by my servants the prophets of Israel, who prophesied in those days many years, that I would bring thee against them?* (Ezek. xxxviii, 17.) This terrible Power of the last days then, was much predicted by the ancient prophets in Israel. The same idea we find in Rev. x, 7. After the seven thunders had uttered their voices, and the Angel had sworn that the *time should not be yet*, or should not be *prolonged*, he adds; *But in the days of the voice of the seventh angel, when he shall begin to sound, the mystery of God shall be finished, as he hath declared to his servants the prophets.* This finishing of the mystery of iniquity, at the beginning of the seventh trumpet, involves the destruction of Antichrist. And this is what God had *revealed to the ancient prophets.* The phrase relative to the preparing of the enemies of the Church for the seventh vial, Rev. xvi, 14, *To gather them to the battle of that great day of God Almighty*, implies that it is a *day well known*, as being much predicted in the prophets. We may then open the books of the prophets with an assurance that we may there find the overthrow of Antichrist. I shall now note a few of the passages which relate to this event.

The prophet Joel describes a terrible scene, which he calls, *The day of the Lord; a day of darkness and*

gloominess, of clouds and thick darkness. He directs
the people to fast and cry mightily to God; and promises, that thereupon God would remove from them the
northern army, which he represents as *innumerable,*
and most *ruinous;* and that the stench of their ruined
hosts should come up, because they had done great
things. Upon this he predicts the outpouring of the
Spirit of God upon all flesh. This received an incipient fulfilment on the day of Pentecost, Acts ii, 16—,
But it is to have its ultimate fulfilment in the introduction of the Millennium. Then, in chapter iii, he
gives a more particular account of the terrible scene of
judgment, and identifies it with the destruction of Antichrist, which has been described. "For behold, in
"those days, and in that time, when I shall bring again
"the captivity of Judah and Jerusalem, I will also gath-
"er all nations, and will bring them down into the val-
"ley of Jehoshaphat." The battle of the great day
follows, verse 9,—"Proclaim ye this among the *Gen-*
"*tiles;* prepare war; wake up the mighty men; let all
"the men of war draw near, let them come up. Beat
"your ploughshares into swords, and your pruning-
"hooks into spears; let the weak say, I am strong.
"Assemble yourselves and come, all ye heathen,
"and gather yourselves together round about: thither
"cause thy mighty ones to come down, O Lord. Let
"the heathen be wakened and come up to the val-
"ley of Jehoshaphat; for there will I sit to judge all the
"heathen round about." The bringing of this vast army
to the valley of Jehoshaphat, is supposed to be expressed in allusion to the account in 2 Chron. xx, of the
vast combined army, that came against the Jews, in the
reign of Jehoshaphat. This pious king, upon this occasion, convened the people to the house of God, and
prayed for deliverance. The Lord by his prophet engaged to fight the battle. A spirit of mutiny was excited in the combined hosts. They fought among
themselves; and all were destroyed together. The Jews
collected the spoils, and blessed God for the deliverance. In allusion to this event the vast armies of An-

tichrist against the Jews are to be collected to the
valley of Jehoshaphat, where the Lord will sit to judge
the heathen round about.' The prophet proceeds.
"Put ye in the sickle, for the harvest is ripe: come
"get ye down; for the press is full; the fats overflow;
"for their wickedness is great. Multitudes, multi-
"tudes in the valley of decision; for the day of the
"Lord is near in the valley of decision. The sun and
"the moon shall be darkened; and the stars shall with-
"draw their shining. The Lord also shall roar out of
"Zion, and utter his voice from Jerusalem; and the
"heavens and the earth shall shake: but the Lord shall
"be the hope of his people, and the strength of the
"children of Israel. So shall they know that I am the
"Lord your God dwelling in Zion, my holy moun-
"tain. Then shall Jerusalem be holy, and there shall
"no stranger pass through her any more." Here is
the overthrow of Antichrist in the valley of *decision.*
Here God *decides* the controversy between the Church
and her enemies. From this chapter some part of the
representation of the same event, in Rev. xiv, is borrowed. The Angel upon the white cloud, with his
sharp sickle, reaps the harvest of the earth, which is
fully ripe; he gathers the vine of the earth, with its
ripe grapes, and casts it into the great wine-press of
the wrath of God, in allusion to this passage in Joel.
And the application of the passage there decides, that
it is fulfilled in the battle of the great day, which just
precedes the Millennium, or the destruction of Antichrist.

In Isa. lxiii, 1—6, is the same event under a similar figure. Jesus Christ appears as a conqueror, coming away from the slaughter of Edom, and from
Bozrah its capital, glorious in his apparel, travelling in
the greatness of his strength, mighty to save; his garments red with the blood of his enemies, whom he
had trampled in his fury in the great wine-press of the
wrath of God. The ancient Edomites were noted
enemies of Israel. And the names of their nation and
capital are here taken to represent Antichrist in the
last time.

. In Zech. xiith, xiiith, and xivth chapters, we find this expedition and overthrow of Antichrist in Palestine. Chap. xiv, 1—5; "Behold the day of the Lord "cometh, and thy spoil shall be divided in the midst "of thee. For I will gather all nations against Jerusa"lem to battle; and the city shall be taken, and the "houses rifled, and the women ravished; and half of the "city shall go forth into captivity, (or be taken captives) "and the residue of the people shall not be cut off from "the city.* Then shall the Lord go forth and fight "against those nations, as when he fought in the day of "battle;" i. e. as in the ancient most signal instances of his fighting for his Church against her enemies. "And "his feet shall stand in that day upon the mount of "Olives, which is before Jerusalem on the east; and the "mount of Olives shall cleave in the midst thereof to"ward the east, and toward the west, and there shall be "a very great valley; and half of the mountain shall re"move toward the north, and half of it toward the "south.. And ye shall flee toward the valley of the "mountains." i. e. So great will be the commotion and terror attendant on this coming of Christ to destroy your enemies, that you his people will be terrified, and set out to flee. "Yea, ye shall flee, like as ye fled from "before the earthquake, in the days of Uzziah, king of "Judah.† And the Lord my God shall come, and all "the saints with thee." Or, as Pool renders this last

---

* Here is fulfilled the prediction in Ezek. xx, 38, upon the same period and event. *And I will purge out from among you the rebels, and them that transgress against me: I will bring them forth out of the country, where they sojourn, and they shall not enter into the land of Israel; and ye shall know that I am the Lord.* Numbers of the Jews, more obstinate and perverse, shall, after they have returned to Jerusalem, be cut off by Antichrist, and not be suffered to dwell in Jerusalem after the battle of the great day. Multitudes more shall be taken captive. But the speedy destruction of Antichrist will afford them release.

· † The prophet Amos speaks of this earthquake, (chap. i, 1,) informing, that his prophecy was two years after it. Josephus speaks of this earthquake, and informs, that the mount of Olives was by it cleft asunder on the west; and the part, which was broken off, was removed to the distance of half a mile.

sentence; *Yet O Lord my God come; and all the saints with thee;* as Rev: xxii, 20, *Even so, come, Lord Jesus.* Here is a figurative, but terrible representation of the coming of Christ to destroy Antichrist in Palestine, after the latter shall have grasped his prey. Let the manner of this appearance of Christ be what it may, whether supernatural; or only a terrible direction of the motives and passions of men, and of the laws of nature, arming them against the wicked; the scene will be terrible and fatal to the enemies of the Church. Verse 13; *And it shall come to pass in that day, that a great tumult from the Lord shall be among them; and they shall lay hold every one on the hand of his neighbor, and his hand shall rise up against the hand of his neighbor.* As in the forecited passage, Ezek. xxxviii, 21; *Every man's sword shall be against his brother.* This was the manner of the destruction of the vast army combined against Israel, in the days of Gideon;* and of the vast confederate army that perished in the reign of Jehoshaphat.† To these, and similar instances of signal judgments against the ancient enemies of the Church, allusion is often had, in the predictions of the battle of the great day.‡ The predictions of these judgments of the Lord upon Antichrist in these three chapters, (the xiith, xiiith, and xivth of Zech.) are too long to be here quoted. They inform, (as chap. xii, 9,) that the Lord will *destroy all the nations that come against Jerusalem.* And predictions of the millennial glory of the Church succeed these scenes of the battle.§

In many instances in the writings of the prophets, predictions of the same event are found; and also of the general ruin of the enemies of the Church, in Gospel lands, at the same period.

Zeph. iii, 8.—"Therefore wait ye upon me, saith the "Lord, until the day that I rise up to the prey; for my "determination is to gather the nations, that I may

---

* Judges vii, 22.   † 2 Chron. xx, 22, 23, 24.
‡ See Isa. xxviii, 21, with 2 Sam. v, 20,—and Josh. x, 12,—
§ Zech. x, 10, to the end, and xiv, 16, to the end.

44

"assemble the kingdoms, and pour upon them mine
"indignation, even all my fierce anger; and all the earth
"shall be devoured with the fire of my jealousy. For
"then will I turn to the people a pure language, that
"they may all call upon the name of the Lord, and
"serve him with one consent. From beyond the riv-
"ers of Ethiopia my suppliants shall bring mine offer-
"ing, even the daughter of my dispersed."

The battle which begins at Palestine, will proceed
in all its desolation to the open enemies of the Gospel,
through the nations. The slaughter is by no means to
be confined to Palestine. It will be extended through
all Antichristian nations, whether on the eastern or the
western continent. It may be a work of years. But
it will be a short and decisive work. All who have
been *partakers of Babylon's sins, will now receive of
her plagues.* God having taken the sword in hand,
*he will make an utter end: affliction shall not rise a
second time.* Neither their silver nor their gold
shall be able to deliver them, in the day of the Lord's
wrath; but the whole earth shall be devoured with the
fire of his jealousy.* A speedy riddance will now be
made of all who have the mark of the Beast, whether
they shall have been politically united with him, cr not;
or wherever they shall be found. "A noise shall come
"from the ends of the earth; for the Lord hath a con-
"troversy with the nations; he will plead with all flesh;
"he will give them that are wicked to the sword, saith
"the Lord. Thus saith the Lord of hosts, behold, evil
"shall go forth from nation to nation; and a great whirl-
"wind shall be raised up from the coasts of the earth;
"and the slain of the Lord shall be at that day from one
"end of the earth, even to the other end of the earth;
"they shall not be lamented, neither gathered, nor
"buried; they shall be dung upon the ground.† And
"the hand of the Lord shall be known toward his ser-
"vants; and his indignation toward his enemies. For
"behold the Lord will come with fire, and with his
"chariots, like a whirlwind to render his anger with

* Nahum i, 9.   † Jer. xxv, 31—33.

"fury, and his rebuke with flames of fire. For by fire
"and by sword will the Lord plead with all flesh; and the
"slain of the Lord shall be many.* For behold the day
"cometh that shall burn as an oven; and all the proud,
"yea all that do wickedly, shall be as stubble; and the
"day that cometh shall burn them up, saith the Lord of
"hosts, and it shall leave them neither root nor branch.
"But unto you that fear my name, shall the Sun of
"righteousness arise with healing in his wings; and ye
"shall go forth, and grow up, as calves of the stall."†
The two events, the battle of the great day, and the introduction of the Millennium, are abundantly predicted
in connexion, through the prophets. The former is
Christ's *ruling the nations with his rod of iron, and
dashing them in pieces like a potter's vessel.‡* · This
is the smiting of the *stone, cut out without hands, upon
the feet of the image; so that the iron, the clay, the
brass, the silver, and the gold, are broken to pieces
together, and become like the chaff of the summer
threshing floor, and the wind carries them away, that
no place is found for them.§ And the stone that
smote them, becomes a great mountain, and fills the
world.*‖ Thus *evil doers shall be cut off; but those
that wait upon the Lord, they shall inherit the earth.
The wicked shall perish, and the enemies of the Lord
shall be as the fat of lambs;* (offered in sacrifice:)
*they shall consume; into smoke they shall consume
away.—But the meek shall inherit the earth, and shall
delight themselves in abundance of peace.*¶

A Babylonian and Assyrian of the last days.

SOME prophecies, relative to ancient Babylon, are evidently to have their ultimate fulfilment upon Antichrist,
in the last days; who is accordingly, in the Revelation,
repeatedly called *Babylon.* And things are said, rela-

---

* Isa. lxvi, 14.   † Mal. iv, 1,—
‡ Psalm ii, 9; Rev. ii, 27, and xix, 15.   § See also Isa. xli, 15, 16.
‖ Dan. ii, 34,—   ¶ Psalm xxxvii, 9, 11, 20.

tive to the apocalyptic Babylon, in evident allusion to things said of the ancient literal Babylon; and in such a way, as to evince, those ancient prophecies related *ultimately to Antichrist.* In Jer. l, and li, we have predictions relative to Babylon; which Mr. Scott observes, from Bp. Lowth, "comprises the fall of mystical Babylon." Bp. Lowth adds, that this is the case *"here, and in the parallel passages of Isaiah, and the Revelation."* The passages then, in the Revelation, in Isaiah, and in the list. chapter of Jeremiah, Bp. Lowth views *"parallel passages"* comprising, *the fall of Antichrist.* And in the latter passage, we read;—"The violence done to me and to my flesh, be upon Babylon, shall the inhabitant of Zion say; and my blood, upon the inhabitants of Chaldea, shall Jerusalem say." "Babylon shall become heaps, a dwelling place for dragons, an astonishment and a hissing, without an inhabitant." "A rumor shall both come one year, and after that in another year, shall come a rumor, and violence in the land, ruler against ruler:" (as our Lord predicted; "wars and rumors of wars.") "I will bring them down like lambs to the slaughter, like rams with he-goats." "My people, go ye out of the midst of her, and deliver ye every man his soul from the fierce anger of the Lord." As Babylon hath caused the slain of Israel to fall, so at Babylon shall fall the slain of all the earth.

In Isa. xiv, is one of these passages, which Dr. Lowth calls *"parallel passages; comprising the fall of mystical Babylon."* After announcing, in the preceding chapter, that Babylon shall be as when God overthrew Sodom and Gomorrah; the fourteenth chapter is introduced with a promise of Israel's restoration; which was partially fulfilled in their ancient restoration from Babylon; but which is to receive a more important accomplishment in their final restoration, which is still future. "For the Lord will have mercy on Jacob, and will yet choose Israel, and set them in their own land." The prophet then goes on to describe the destruction of Babylon, their oppressor. This description will be most emphatically fulfilled in the destruction of Gog and his bands, in the battle of that great day of God,

"Thou shalt take up this proverb against the king of Babylon, and say, 'How hath the oppressor ceased! the golden city ceased! The Lord hath broken the staff of the wicked, the sceptre of the rulers. The whole earth is at rest and is quiet; they break forth into singing." This clause has never been fulfilled. But it *will* be,—after the battle of that great day. "Yea, the fir-trees rejoice at thee, and the cedars of Lebanon; saying, 'Since thou art laid down, no *feller* (or cutter of wood) is come up against us." i. e. Wars, upon the fall of the antichristian Babylon, shall cease, to the ends of the earth; as predicted Psalm xlvi, 8, 9. The prophet proceeds; "Hell from beneath is moved for thee, to meet thee at thy coming!" The inhabitants of the regions of the dead are, by a figure, represented as in vast commotion, at the approach of this Power (called Babylon) among them. Kings and chieftains address him; "Art thou also become weak as we? Art thou become like unto us? Thy pomp is brought down to the grave, and the noise of thy vials. The worm is spread under thee; and the worms cover thee. How art thou fallen from heaven, O Lucifer, son of the morning! How art thou cut down to the ground, who didst weaken the nations. For thou hast said in thine heart, I will ascend into heaven; I will exalt my throne above the throne of God. Yet thou shalt be brought down to hell—They that see thee shall narrowly look upon thee, and consider thee, saying, Is this the man, who made the earth to tremble, and did shake the kingdoms? that made the world as a wilderness, and destroyed the cities thereof? All the kings of the nations lie in glory, every one in his own house." i. e. Their bodies, when they died, were laid in *superb tombs*, under lofty monuments. But so it shall not be with this *hateful Babylon.* "But thou art cast out of thy grave, like an abominable branch, and as the raiment of those, who are slain, thrust through with the sword, that go down to the stones of the pit, as a carcass trodden under feet. Prepare slaughter for his children, for the iniquity of their fathers. For I will rise up against

them, saith the Lord of hosts, and cut off from Babylon the name and the remnant, and son and nephew,
saith the Lord." Exactly this all agrees with the predicted destruction of Antichrist; beginning with his coalition against the Jews in Palestine, and thence rolling
through antichristian nations. The tremendous scene
opens, upon the mountains of Israel; and thence proceeds
through the wicked world. The prophet proceeds: "The
Lord of hosts hath sworn, saying, Surely as I have thought,
so shall it come to pass; and as I have purposed, so shall it
stand: That I will *break the Assyrian in my land, and
upon my mountains tread him under foot.*"   Here it is
decided, that the prediction has a special relation to
the destruction of Antichrist in the last days, under
the name of Gog, Ezek. xxxix. For the slaughter is
to be in *God's land, upon the mountains in the land of
Israel,* the very place where, and at the very time when
Gog and his bands fall. But there ancient Babylon did
not fall. "Then shall his yoke depart from off them
(the Jews returned) and his burden depart from off
their shoulders. This is the purpose that is purposed
upon the whole earth; and this is the hand, that is
stretched out upon all the nations."

Babylon is here, verse 25, called the *Assyrian.* The
Babylonian monarchy was *subsequent* to the Assyrian
monarchy. Yet in the above prophecy the name of
the *Assyrian* is given to *Babylon:* Or rather, the names
Babylon, and the *Assyrian,* as though one and the
same, are applied to *Antichrist.*

This may lead us to understand the tenth chapter of
Isaiah. Here is another of those parallel passages,
which Dr. Lowth informs comprise the mystical Babylon. This tenth of Isaiah had an awful fulfilment upon the ancient people of God; and in the literal destruction of the Assyrian, who captivated them. But it was
to have a much more awful fulfilment in the events
of the last days.

Verse 5—"O Assyrian, the rod of mine anger, and
the staff in their hand is mine indignation. I will send
him against an hypocritical nation, and against the people of my wrath will I give him a charge, to take the

spoil, and to take the prey, and to tread them down
like the mire of the streets." I shall show, by and by,
from subsequent passages in this chapter, that these
events clearly relate (as to their most interesting fulfilment) to the events of the last days, about the time
of the restoration of the Jews. At *that* time was to appear a terrible *Assyrian*, a Rod of God's anger, commissioned *against the hypocritical nation, the people of
God's wrath:* Names, which perfectly apply to *Papal
Babylon;* or the body of nations of the Papal delusion.
He has a *providential charge* against them, to plunder
them; and to tread them down as mire. All his power against them originates in God's indignation against
them, and determination to cut them off. This Assyrian is the *rod of God's anger*, his *saw*, his *axe*,
(verse 15.) But notice is given of the different and
wicked motive of this *horrible agent.* "Howbeit he
meaneth not so, neither doth his heart think
so: But it is in his heart to destroy and cut
off nations not a few. For he saith, Are not my *princes* altogether *kings*?" He has no view of fulfilling
the righteous judgments of God; but to destroy and
rule the nations. He boasts that his vassal princes
are *fully kings.* The Revelator says, *they have received no real kingdom; but have received power as kings,
one hour with the beast.* (Rev. xvii, 12.) The prophecy proceeds to announce, that when God shall have
performed his *work upon the hypocritical nation,* (the
perfidious people, that have borne his name,) that God
will punish the fruit of the stout heart of this kingdom
of *Assyria,* and the glory of their high looks. This
enormous Power shall be utterly destroyed. He is
represented, verse 16—19, as being burnt up, 'like
thorns, *in one day.* And those who shall be left of him,'
shall be few, *that a child may write them.* Verse 20—
24. "And it shall come to pass, in that day, that the
remnant of Israel, and such as are escaped of the house
of Jacob, shall no more again stay upon him, that smote
them, but shall stay upon the Lord, the Holy one of
Israel, in truth. The remnant shall return, even the
remnant of Jacob, unto the mighty God. For though

thy people Israel be as the sand of the sea, yet a remnant of them shall return; the consumption decreed
shall overflow with righteousness. For the Lord God
of hosts shall make a consumption even determined in
the midst of the land;" or *earth.*

Here a remnant of the Jews are to return, in the last
days, and are to stay themselves thenceforth upon God
in truth. And the event is to be nearly connected with
the above destruction of that Power, called the *Assyrian.* The Lord of hosts will make, at that time, a
consumption even determined, (or that work of desolation,
well known in prophecy) in the wicked world. About
the time of this return of the remnant of Israel to God,
"the consumption decreed shall overflow with righteousness." Paul (Rom. ix, 27, 28,) notes this remnant of Israel, who shall be saved, when they shall be
turned to the Lord, in the *last days.* And relative to
the consumption decreed, which God will cause to overflow in the midst of all the earth, Paul there says,
"For he will finish the work and cut it short in righteousness; because a short work will the Lord make upon the earth." That consumption determined, which
is to overflow with righteousness, and to be a short
and decisive work of judgment, was far future in the
days of Paul. It was to be at the time, when the remnant of Israel shall turn to the Lord; or be grafted into
their own olive tree. That is an event now still future.
Consequently the destruction of that *Assyrian,* in Isa.
x. 5—(as to its ultimate and most interesting fulfilment) is still future. The present generation have
seen an incipient fulfilment of his commission,against
the *hypocritical nation, the people of God's wrath, or Papal Babylon.*

But his own destruction is to be a subsequent event.
When God shall have performed his work of judgment
upon the people, who have borne his name, that Assyrian will, in his turn, be utterly destroyed.

The character and destruction of this Babylon of the
last days, and of the minions of his order, we find in
Isa. xxviii, 15—"Because ye have said, We have made
a covenant with death, and with hell are we at an agree-

ment; when the overflowing scourge shall pass through, it shall not come nigh unto us; for we have made *lies* our *refuge*, and under falsehood have we hid ourselves: Therefore thus saith the Lord God,—Judgment also will I lay to the line and righteousness to the plummet, and the hail shall sweep away the refuge of lies, and the waters shall overflow the hiding place. And your covenant with death shall be disannulled; and your agreement with hell shall not stand; when the overflowing scourge shall pass through, then ye shall be trodden down by it. From the time that it goeth forth it shall take you: for morning by morning shall it pass over, by day and by night; and it shall be a vexation only to understand the report. For the bed is shorter than that a man can stretch himself upon it; and the covering narrower than that he can wrap himself in it. For the Lord shall rise up, as in mount Perazim (where God miraculously destroyed the Philistines before David; 2 Sam. v, 20) he shall be wroth as in the valley of Gibeon: (where the sun and moon stood still for a day, that Joshua and Israel might destroy the army of the five kings of Canaan; Joshua x, 12)—For I have heard, from the Lord of hosts, a consumption even determined upon the whole earth." How striking is the picture drawn, of these wretched characters of the last days! Being at an agreement with hell—making *lies* their refuge—and under *falsehood* hiding themselves! Here is the lying spirit of the last days—*conceiving and uttering from the heart words of falsehood;* as the same prophet expresses it, (Isa. lix, 13—) *lying against the Lord—yea, truth faileth—truth is fallen in the streets! Lies* are resorted to, as a cover of the most perfidious designs! *Hear, ye scornful men, that rule this people: Because ye have said—(not that they do actually profess this. No! Their professions are smoother than oil! But the meaning is, this is in fact their character, and the language of their conduct;) We have made a covenant with death; and with hell are we at an agreement—We shall escape—for we have made lies our refuge—and under falsehood have we hid ourselves!* Verily, the thing is certain, and the inter-

45

pretation sure! The word of God is indeed a discerner of the thoughts; and explains the dark events of the age in which we live.

It is most evident that these predictions describe the scenes of this day; and are to receive their ultimate fulfilment in the battle of that great day of God Almighty. *Then* it is, that the Assyrian is to fall upon the mountains of Israel; and the consumption determined, or predicted, is to overflow with righteousness, through all Antichristian nations. Paul refers the passage to the time of the final restoration of the Jews, when a short work will the Lord make upon the earth; or the controversy of Zion shall be soon and effectually decided.

I shall quote and remark upon one passage more relative to this period and event. Isa. xxvii, 1, *In that day, the Lord, with his sore and great and strong sword; shall punish Leviathan, that piercing serpent, even Leviathan that crooked serpent, and he shall slay the dragon that is in the sea.*

1. Upon this text I shall first note the time here referred to: *In that day;* which is predicted in the preceding verse. *For behold the Lord cometh out of his place to punish the inhabitants of the earth for their iniquity; the earth also shall disclose her blood, and shall no longer cover her slain.* The whole connexion of the text evinces, that *the day* referred to is *the battle of that great day of God Almighty;* or the destruction of Antichrist.

2. Let us note the *subject* of the fatal operation in the text: *Leviathan, that piercing serpent, even Leviathan that crooked serpent, the dragon that is in the sea.* For an account of *Leviathan,* see Job xli. This appellation is given to Antichrist; and it is repeated in the text, to indicate most emphatically that the Power designed will be most terrible. The accumulation of names, and of the qualities of *piercing* and *crooked,* is a forcible expression of the subtile, furious, potent, and terrible nature of this enemy of the Church at that day. Pharaoh of old was called the *dragon,* doubtless mean-

ing the crocodile in the river of Egypt, because he cast
the offspring of Israel into this river; and persecuted the
people of God.* And the Power in the text is called
the *dragon*, because he is the antitype, of which Pharaoh was the type; and like Pharaoh will labor to destroy the people of God.

3. He *lieth in the sea.* This part of the symbol de-
notes the, *multitudes*, and the *tumultuous* state of his
subjects. *Woe to the inhabiters of the earth, and of
the* sea; *for the devil is come down unto you having
great wrath, because he knoweth that he hath but a short
time.*† Among the events of that day, our Lord says;
*The sea and the waves roaring; men's hearts failing
them for fear, and for looking after those things which
are coming on the earth.*‡ The events of that day, the
perplexity and distress of nations, are repeatedly predicted under this similitude. *And in that day they
shall roar against them like the roaring of the sea;
and if one look unto the land, behold darkness and
sorrow, and the light is darkness in the heavens
thereof.* The state of the nations will be like a sea in
a tempest. And those who *look to the land,* or where
stability used to be found, and long to find it again,
shall see nothing but *sorrow;* and darkness will be instead of light. *Woe to the multitude of many people,
who make a noise like the* noise *of the seas, and to the
rushing of nations, that make a rushing like the rushing
of mighty waters. The nations shall rush, like the rushing of many waters* § This relates to the scenes of the
last days. In the xlvith Psalm, relative to the same period, we find the same similitude. *Therefore will we
not fear, though the earth be removed, and though the
mountains be carried into the midst of the sea. Though
the waters thereof roar and be troubled, though the
mountains shake with the swelling thereof.* What follows shows it to be a description of the battle of the
great day of God:—The Most High making *desolation*

* Exod. i, 22; Psalm lxxiv, 13; Isa. li, 9, and Ezek. xxix, 3.
† Rev. xii, 12.　‡ Luke xxi, 25.　§ Isa. xvii, 12, 13.

in the earth;—making wars to cease to the ends of the world;—breaking the bow, cutting the spear in sunder, and burning the chariot in the fire. And relative to the preparatory scenes, in the above verses, it is as though the speaker had said; Seeing God is our refuge, we will not fear, though the political earth be dissolved; and though the first nations, which have long stood like *mountains,* be thrown into the *sea of revolution;* though their inhabitants are tossed, like the ocean in a tempest; and the national establishments tremble with the swelling thereof. In Psalm xciii, 3, 4, the floods are lifting up their voice and their waves: But the Lord on high is mightier than the noise of many waters, or than the mighty waves of the sea. In the Revelation, a great people, in a tumultuous or revolutionary state, are repeatedly symbolized by the sea.[*]

Thus we learn the true sense of the great Leviathan and dragon of the last days being described as lying in the sea. He lies in the sea of revolution and tumult. The ten toes of the image, Dan. ii, 41,—are part of iron, and part of clay. The Antichristian Empire will be partly strong, and partly broken. The strength of iron will appear. And the mixture of clay will also discover itself. The component parts will not adhere one to the other. Some vassal kingdom, or kingdoms will revolt. Great battles and expeditions may be lost. The symbolic earth will open her mouth and swallow up the floods of the dragon. And these things will occasion a sea of tumult, a roaring among the nations.

4. This power is destroyed with *dreadful ruin.* It is with the *sore, and great, and strong sword* of the Most High. It is terrible to be slain with the *sword of the Lord.* But when the slaughter is with God's *sore,* and *great,* and *strong* sword, the *terrible* things may

[*] See Chap. viii, 8, and xiii, 1, and xvi, 3; Dan. vii, 2, et alia.

be expected, which are abundantly predicted of the destruction of Antichrist.*

* Any, who may wish to consult other prophetic passages, which are thought to relate to the battle of the great day, may turn to the following Scriptures. 2 Sam. xxiii, 6, 7; Psalm xxi, 8—12; and xxxvii, and cx; Isa. i, 24,—end, and ii, 10,—end; and xi, 4, and xiii, 6—11, and xxiv, and xxviii, 16—22, and xxxiv, 1—8, and xli, 10—16, and lix, 9,—end, and lxiii, 1—6; and other passages noted by Dr. Hopkins, in his Treatise on the Millennium, sec. iv.

CHAP. IV.

On the Seven Apocalyptic Vials.

THAT the way may be prepared to note the prophecies relative to Antichrist, in some of the *last* of the vials, I shall endeavor to give an explanation of the *whole* of them.

We are informed, Rev. xv, 1; *And I saw another sign in heaven, great and marvellous, seven angels having the seven last plagues; for in them is filled up the wrath of God.* Verse 7; *And one of the four beasts gave unto the seven angels seven golden vials full of the wrath of God, who liveth for ever and ever.* Chap. xvi, 1; *And I heard a great voice out of the temple, saying to the seven angels, Go your ways, and pour out the vials of the wrath of God upon the earth.*

The vial here mentioned is a plain cup, out of which to drink. (Φιαλη from πιειν, to drink.) We read, Psalm lxxv, 8. *In the hand of the Lord there is a cup, and the wine is red; it is full of mixture; and he poureth out of the same; but the dregs thereof all the wicked of the earth shall wring them out and drink them.* Also Psalm xi, 6, "Upon the wicked he shall rain snares, fire and brimstone, and an horrible tempest: This shall be the portion of their cup." A cup is often used in sacred Writ, to signify a portion from God, either of blessing, or of judgment.* The seven golden vials full of the wrath of God, poured out from heaven to earth, are symbols of a series of peculiar judgments, which were to be inflicted upon the most notorious enemies of God on earth. Each vial being poured out by an Angel, indicates that Angels are the ministers of Divine Providence, to inflict the judgments of heaven on the enemies of the Church. The apocalyptic vials are seven. The number seven is much used in the word of God; and especially in this mystical book.

* See Psalm xi, 6; Jer. xxv, 15, 17, 28; Exek. xxiii, 32 Mark xiv, 36, and x, 38; Psalm cxvi, 13, and many others.

Here are the seven seals; the seven trumpets; the seven spirits of God; and the seven vials. There were to be seven signal scenes of judgment, probably in a kind of systematic connexion, which were to destroy the enemies of the Churh, and to prepare the way for her millennial glory: And these are the seven *last plagues*, in which is filled up the wrath of God, which is to finish the scene with the most notorious enemies of the cause of Christ. God had been inflicting judgments on his enemies, who had attacked his Church, for many ages under the Gospel. There were the seals of judgments upon Pagan Rome; four trumpets of judgments upon Christian Rome; and two woe trumpets of judgments on more eastern nations, as well as on Rome, in the rise of Mohammedism, and of the Ottoman empire; or in the ravages of the Saracens, and of the Turks. But these were not God's *last plagues;* were not comprised in the vials. The vials were to be subsequent to them, and were to finish the scene of judgments preparatory to the Millennium. The Papal and Mohammedan enemies of the Church were to have an existence of 1260 years; and then they were to be destroyed. Accordingly, toward the close of the 1260 years, the direction is given from the temple in heaven to the seven Angels, *Go your ways, and pour out the vials of the wrath of God upon the earth.*

It has been the opinion of some, that the seventh trumpet, or third woe, comprises all the vials; even as the seventh seal comprises all the trumpets. Whatever plausible things may be said in favor of this, I think there are unanswerable objections against it; and that the *old* opinion, that the commencement of the vials was antecedent to the commencement of the seventh trumpet, will be found correct. For there can be no plausible pretence, that the third woe commenced, previously to the French Revolution. But the supposition, that the seven vials were at that period all future; that four or five of them were accomplished on the French nation, and some neighboring nations, in less than twenty years, according to the scheme of Mr. Faber; and that none of the preceding judgments, which had been regularly bringing down the Papal hierarchy, for several centuries, were yet to be reckoned as any part of the vials, must appear *very extraordinary.* Some of those preceding judgments appear to have an incontestable claim to be reckoned among the events, which were to fulfil the vials. The opinion, that none of the vials were poured out, till the revolution in France, appears, as real an extreme, as that of most of the old expositors, that the vials have been poured out through all the ages of Popery. The old scheme of the vials is as follows: That the *first* vial, inflicting a noisome and grievous *sore*, began to be poured out in the early part of the ninth century, in the contentions between the Popes and the emperors of Germany, relative to power. That the *second*, poured upon the sea, and turning it to blood, was fulfilled in the fanatical crusades to the Holy Land, in the eleventh and twelfth centuries. That the *third*, upon the rivers and fountains of water, was fulfilled in the persecuting crusades against the Albigenses in the vallies of Piedmont; and in the quarrels between the ecclesiastical, and the civil powers, and their respective parties, the Guelphs and Gebelins, concerning the right of investitures: That the *fourth*, poured upon the sun, was fulfilled in the rivalships of different Popes, in the last of the fourteenth and the former part of the fifteenth centuries; there being *two*, and at one time *three* Popes set up at once, to the vexation of their different parties in Christendom: That the *fifth*, poured upon the seat of the Beast, was fulfilled in the events of the reformation under Luther: That the *sixth*, upon the river Euphrates, was fulfilled in the subsequent failing of the sources of Papal wealth: And that the seventh, poured into the air, *is to be* fulfilled in the total destruction of the Papal nations, and the enemies of the Church. But according to this scheme, why were the vials called the *seven last plagues?* For the first of them was fulfilled five or six hundred years before the second woe-trumpet! And indeed three or four of them preceded the second woe! If the old scheme be correct, the vials are so far from being God's *last* judgments on the Papal apostasy, that they were indeed his *first*. They attended the very rise, progress, and highest state of the Papal power. Such a power as the Papal hierarchy, could not be expected to rise, and continue 1260 years, without some contentions and bloody scenes. But shall those contentions, which were yet consistent with the rise and zenith of the Papal power, be supposed to be the four first of the *vials of the seven last plagues*, which are to sweep the enemies of the Church from the face of the earth? It is incredible! It must appear unnatural, on the one hand, to apply the vials of the last judgments of God, to events, which attended the rise, and the highest state of Papal Rome; and unnatural, on the other hand, to *exclude* from the vials those events, which have been evidently destroying the Papal power, in a new and regular series of judgments, till we come down to the French revolution; and then to suppose a number of the vials to have been poured out almost at once.

A series of events, which were accomplished, some of them long before the French revolution, and which were fatally disastrous to the Papal power, appear fully to answer to the description of some of the vials: While yet the events, which were consistent with the rise and zenith of that power, must be excluded from these judgments. The vials appear to contain a series of judgments, which were to commence after the second woe, peculiarly calculated to destroy the most noted enemies of the Church.

THE FIRST VIAL.

And the first went and poured out his vial upon the earth; and there fell a noisome and grievous sore upon the men, who had the mark of the Beast, and upon them who worshipped his Image. (Rev. xvi, 2.)

THE Papal Beast rose out of the earth; (Rev. xiii, 11;) out of the earthly views of the Roman Christians. The *earth*, in distinction from *heaven*, is, in symbolic language, a fit representation of an earthly, corrupt sys-

46

tem. A star falling from heaven to earth, is a striking emblem of apostasy. The *earth,* the seat of the discharge of this vial, then, must mean a most notable, corrupt, earthly system. And as it must relate to the system of this description, which was most injurious to the Church of Christ; so it must have related to that Beast, which rose out of the earth, or to the Papal apostasy. By the men, who had the mark of the Beast, and who worshipped his image, must be understood the members and supporters of the Papal see; who adhered to that system of idolatry, under the Christian name, which is but a real substitute for the gross idolatry of ancient Pagan Rome.

A sore, in symbolic language, signifies some distressing calamity; but the symbol does not decide what *kind* of calamity. David says, Psalm lxxvii, 2, "In the day of my trouble I sought the Lord: *my sore ran in the night, and ceased not;* my soul refused to be comforted." His *sore* here was some heavy affliction. Solomon, at the dedication of the temple prayed,— *When every one shall know his own* sore, *and his own grief, and shall spread forth his hands in this house; then hear thou from heaven.* (2 Chron. vi, 29.) Here every man's own *sore* is his own *grief;* and his *grief* is his *sore.* The following are familiar phrases in our language; *sorely pained; sorely afflicted; sorely amazed.* The use even of this adverb, originates in the idea, that a great calamity is a *sore.* Whatever be the *cause* of the calamity; still it is a sore. Yet some calamities may more fitly be represented by a sore, than others; as may appear in attending to this vial.

To find the noisome and grievous *sore* inflicted in the first vial; look for the first signal event, which began the downfall of the Papal hierarchy. For this was the enemy first to be attacked. This power had its rise; its zenith; and its fall. And the first capital step toward its fall, must have been the first vial. This clew appears infallible. And what was the first capital event toward the destruction of Popery? Few need to be informed, that it was the reformation under Luther and others, early in the sixteenth century. This was

a fatal stroke, and the *first* fatal stroke, to that wicked
power. It gave Popery its death wound. And it was
the introduction of a series of events, which in their
issue were to terminate the existence of the Papal imposture. Until the reformation, Popery may be said
to have flourished. Notwithstanding those various
calamities attendant on Popery from its origin, and in
which authors have imagined the four first vials received their fulfilment; and notwithstanding the judgment
of the second woe, in the invasion of the Turks upon
the eastern wing of the Roman dominions, and their
taking Constantinople in 1453, and making it the seat
of their empire; yet till the reformation, Popery. remained in its *zenith;* it felt superior to all danger, and
seemed to bid defiance to the world. This is evident
from the whole history of the hierarchy at that period;
from their extravagant claims; unbounded insolence;
and from the scandalous traffic of Leo X, and the minions of his order, in the vending of indulgences to commit sin; which wickedness, overleaping all former
bounds, opened the eyes, and excited the zeal of Martin Luther; and facilitated the exposure of the abominations of the whole scheme. How fitly then might
the events of that day be represented, in symbolic language, by the *falling of a noisome and grievous sore
upon the men who had the mark of the Beast, and who
worshipped his image?* The reformation with its consequences, has indeed operated like an incurable wound
upon the body of the man of sin. All his applications
and exertions to effect a healing, by the skill and intrigues of the Jesuits, and other means, have proved
utterly ineffectual. Large portions of the Papal dominions soon fell off. England, Scotland, Sweden,
Denmark, about half the states of Germany, a number
of cantons in Switzerland, and vast numbers of people
in France, Hungary, and Bohemia, received the doctrines of the reformation; separated from the communion of the church of Rome; and utterly renounced the
Papal authority. This was a *sore* indeed, and has already issued.in the death of the Papal Beast. As a *false
prophet,* in the grasp of Antichrist, the phantom of the

Papal power is dragging out a miserable existence; or rather, is on his way to execution. But as the Papal Beast, or a predominant power on the Roman earth; he *is no more!* The light of truth and grace, which broke out and shone at the time of the reformation, was indeed an event most excellent in its nature and consequences. But it was both noisome and grievous to the men, who had the mark of the Beast; peculiarly so to the Pope, and all his clergy; and indeed to all the millions of zealous Catholics; as is reproof to the scorner; and salutary rebuke to the irreclaimable son of Belial. It was most vexing and distressing, as is a fretting and incurable sore upon the human body.

Or shall we not a little vary the figure, and say, the light of the reformation, the art of printing (not long before invented) and the revival of learning in Europe, uncovered and presented to view the deep, filthy, and fatal *ulcer,* formed in the body of the Papal church? They evinced to the world, that *that* body, instead of being the temple of Christ; was but a mass of corruption, like a great filthy ulcer! That the church of Rome, so long and so highly venerated, was *Mystery, Babylon the great, the mother of harlots and abominations of the earth:* That with all her high pretensions, she was but a corrupt, filthy system, like a noisome and fatal sore upon the human body, by which the vitals are gradually destroyed. Such a figure is perfectly in point to represent such a case. We find it so used in sacred Writ, beside in the passage containing the first vial. To represent the very corrupt state of the Jewish church, in the days of Isaiah, God inspired that prophet to tell them, that *from the sole of the foot, even unto the head, there is no soundness in it; but wounds, and bruises, and putrifying sores.* Isa. i, 6. The same, only with an amazing emphasis, the Most High caused to be proclaimed to the world, relative to the church of Rome at the reformation. How fitly then might this exposure of the "putrifying sores" of that system be predicted in the mystical language of the first vial?

The event under consideration is so far from being incapable of being fitly represented by the figurative sore of the first vial; that it seems capable, in a two-fold sense, of such a representation. This event may be said both to have *inflicted*, and *discovered* a noisome, grievous sore upon the men, who had the mark of the Beast. Perhaps both these senses were designed to be included, as united in one. An *application* to a large, infected tumor, on the human body, which application would produce no injury on healthful flesh; but which *would* produce a speedy and fatal eruption on such a tumor, though it had before occasioned but little attention, may be said both to *inflict*, and to *discover* a noisome, grievous, and deadly sore. The effect of the first vial in the discovery, which produced the Reformation, may be viewed in this twofold light, both as *inflicting*, and *discovering* a noisome and grievous sore upon the men, who had the mark of the Beast, and who worshipped his image.

The events, which produced the reformation, were not only the first signal step toward the overthrow of Popery; but were just such events, as might be expected to begin its ruin. A beam of light was let into the dark recess; or the concealment was taken off from that blasphemous system. Were a magistrate about to put an end to a scene of wickedness in operation behind a curtain; after having made his arrangements to seize the actors; and after having silently presented himself, with proper aids, by the side of the guilty apartment; what would be his *first step* in the process? Surely to raise the curtain, or draw it aside. Then the way is prepared to arrest the criminals, and to bring them to condign punishment. If the Most High were about to take vengeance on a corrupt establishment, which is disguised under the most artful pretences; we might expect his first step would be, to strip off those false covers, and exhibit the system in its own corrupt nature. Then the propriety of his subsequent judgments will appear. This was the very thing done with the corrupt and disguised Papal system, at the time of the reformation. The process of the final judgment seems to confirm the correctness of this view. Refuges of lies will be swept away. And then the condign punishment inflicted. An argument is hence furnished in favor of the idea, that the reformation was the commencement of the period of the vials.

The ministrations of Luther, and of the other reformers, with the benefit of the art of printing, and the revival of learning in Europe, after the dark ages, stripped the vail from Popery, and discovered the deadly corruption of that system. And what symbolic figure could more correctly depict the operation, than the one given, as the effect of the discharge of the first vial; viz. *the falling of a noisome and grievous sore upon the men, who had the mark of the Beast; and who worshipped his image.* Here was a new scene opened. And it was the *first*, and a most natural step in that process of judgments, upon which a holy God was then entering with the man of sin. A sore was made; a deadly wound given, in a system, which was itself shown to be but a great and filthy excrescence, like a fatal abscess upon the body of a man.

As the above explanation of this vial, and that of the second, third, fourth, and fifth vials, which is to follow, *is new;* it may be expedient to adduce here some further proofs and illustrations, to shew that the time of the reformation was the commencement of the period of the vials; and that the reformation itself was the first vial. And as my track is wholly unbeaten, and the scheme, if correct, involves consequences very interesting to this age of the world, I shall take liberty to dwell somewhat largely upon this vial, and to show that the sixteenth century opened the period of the vials.

Let any one read the history of Europe in the dark ages, and through the sixteenth and seventeenth centuries, and he must be convinced that Popery continued entire, till the commencement of the sixteenth century; and that then it began to experience a fatal reverse of circumstances. Such a reader must clearly perceive, that all the affairs of the nations of Europe had been preparing the way for the commencement of just such events, as seem to be indicated in the vials, till Luther arose, and Charles V came to the Imperial throne of Germany; and that then the drama, tremendous to the Papal see, *opened.* It has already been observed, that the commencement of the vials must have been the opening of a new and fatal series of judgments on the Papal system. But no such event took place till the above period; notwithstanding the judgment of the second woe, and other calamities.

The fanatical crusades to the Holy land, in the eleventh and twelfth centuries, in which it has been supposed the second vial was poured out, though they were in themselves bloody and dismal, yet tended to the confirming of the Papal domination. Upon those crusades, Dr. Lowman has the following sentence; "In effect no policy could have so well served the Pope's ambition, nor any mean be better suited to render his authority supreme and absolute."* Was this then a vial of wrath upon the Papacy? Those events gave the Pope the management of the alms, legacies and revenues, poured in, in vast profusion, for the support of those wars. He had in effect the supreme control of all those operations; which vastly established his influence. At the same time those wild expeditions laid a foundation to meliorate the state of Europe; and to cause light to dawn upon the barbarous ages. The travelling of such multitudes of ignorant beings abroad from their own cells, into other regions, and particularly through Constantinople, that city of knowledge and refinement, gave them new ideas of the world, of what man is capable, and of the benefits of civilization. This had a beneficial effect upon those, who lived to return; and they communicated it to others. The crusades tended to the establishment of civilized governments, instead of the anarchy of the feudal times, by drawing away contentious barons, who perished in the expeditions, and whose fiefs reverted to their kings. And the kings of the west of Europe had been enabled to purchase vast tracts of territory from the chiefs of the wild adventurers, who calculated on new possessions in the east. This did considerable towards retrieving

* On Rev. p. 181.

the miseries of the dark and feudal ages. Commerce also received a spring from the crusades. The procuring of supplies for the thousands, and hundreds of thousands, who embarked in those expeditions, suggested the idea of barter and trade, especially in Italy. And rapid advances were made in this most gainful and civilizing art, by the Lombards and others; till the spirit of commerce spread through most of Europe. Light in the art of civil government soon increased; and *Charters of Communities* under the crown; or *towns*, with incorporate privileges, were established in Italy and France, and finally through Europe, and took the place of the wretched petty baronies of the feudal ages.* Chivalry, or the order of knighthood, which followed, and aided the melioration of those days;—having "valor, humanity, courtesy, justice, and honor," for its professed characteristics; and the redress of the oppressed, under the feudal barons, for its professed object,—operated as a favorable mean of refinement and civilization from the barbarity of the dark ages. Men were trained to this order by an appropriate discipline, and admitted with solemn forms. Its honors were sought as of high importance; and monarchs were proud to receive them from the hands of private gentlemen. And on the taking of Constantinople by the Turks, in 1453, many of its inhabitants fled, with their books and literature, to the more western parts of Europe; and happily aided there the revival of learning.

These things fast prepared the way to overturn the impositions of Popery; and to strip from the eyes of men, the bandages of delusion and superstition. At the same time these approaches toward light and civilization, brought forward a system of preparations for the most desolating scenes of Divine judgment on Papal nations; as will appear under the succeeding vials. Standing armies, disciplined troops, were not known in Europe, after the days of the Cæsars, and the northern invasions, till this period. Charles II, king of France, now introduced the practice. This, while it confounded the aris-

---

* Robertson's Hist. Ch. V, vol. i, p. 31—40.

tocracies of the feudal barons, opened the door for new scenes of extensive and desolating wars. The idea of the balance of power, for the mutual interest of the European nations, was conceived at this period; a principle, which however necessary, often, in after days, involved the nations of Europe in a general blaze of war.* Tactics and the arts of war were from this period studied. Gunpowder and firearms had not long before been invented:—Refined instruments for a new period of judgments! The art of printing also, to facilitate their progress in the arts of war, as well as in arts more beneficial to society, was now considerably improved; having been invented about a century before. Every thing had been conspiring to prepare the way for a new and most interesting era of events. And every thing indicated that, with all its rich advantages of increasing light and civilization, that era was to open a period of terror and devastation to the *Papal see.* Great generals were raised up. Most ambitious rivals came to the thrones of the most powerful nations. Charles V, king of Spain, was elected to fill the Imperial throne of Germany. And he was formed with powers and ambition, and accommodated with dominions and opportunity, to be a *scourge to man!* Francis I, who had been a violent competitor with Charles for the Imperial crown, and was his powerful rival, was on the throne of France. Henry VIII, ready to unite in any object of enterprise and ambition, was king of England. And Solyman, formed for war and enterprise, was emperor of the Turks. Such a preparation of executioners of the Divine judgments, could not have risen, and been placed in their posts, without vast design in Providence. And it is allowed that a new era of most important affairs commenced with the sixteenth century, after the long reign of darkness and Papal superstition. Dr. Robertson remarks, "Accordingly the sixteenth century opened with the certain prospect of its abounding with great and interesting events."† And such events

* Robertson's Hist. Ch. V, vol. i, p. 107.
† Hist. Ch. V. vol. i, p. 145.
47

did in fact take place. The Pope himself, (till now unshaken,) in the view of these preparations, trembled, and predicted the approaching ruin of the Papal see! as will be noted under the next vial. To this period then, we must look for the commencement of the vials of Divine wrath on the Papal Beast.

And when this apparatus, which has been hinted, and will more fully appear under the next vial, was prepared, the first most natural and necessary step would be, to draw the curtain, to *expose* the wicked delusions of the system now destined to ruin; and that God's elect might be called out of that sinking Sodom. This must have been the design of the first vial.

Accordingly this scene opened. Martin Luther, a pious Augustine monk, a man of prime natural and acquired abilities; remarkably fitted by Providence for the purpose, and a professor of philosophy in the university at Wittemberg, became disgusted and alarmed at the impious sale of indulgences; and openly preached against it, in 1517. This was a few years before Charles V came to the Imperial throne. This most licentious and abominable practice of Pope Leo X, of vending pardons for all past sins, and liberties to commit any sins in future, for certain sums of money, and conveying official diplomas, sealing the pardon and indulgences in the name of Christ, was the occasion of, opening that series of evils to the Papal see, which was to issue in its total ruin. Luther raised his warning voice against this wickedness; and was led on, to discover and expose all the abominations of the Papal system. Others followed him. And their success was astonishing. I cannot in this short work, and *need* not, give the history of the reformation. I shall only hint some things, in which it will appear, that the man of sin now received a deadly wound, in the exposure of the abominations of his system; which was now presented to the nations as a noisome, grievous ulcer.

Great attention was soon paid to the preaching of Luther. Some of the first characters in Germany had been inwardly vexed, that such vast sums of property were collected from among their people, for indulgences; that the people were thus drained of their money, at such expense of their morals; and all under the cloak of religion. And the intrigues, oppressions and licentiousness of many of the ecclesiastical German princes, and of the Papal clergy, had been a source of vexation. These things prepared people to listen to the preaching of Luther. And his proselytes became numerous. After some fruitless attempts of the Papal party to silence Luther, and to extinguish his light, the Pope published against him a bull of excommunication; and demanded, that the law against heretics should be executed upon him. Upon this Luther declared the Pope to be the *man of sin;* and publicly burnt the Pope's bull against him, and his own Papal books. At the diet of German princes, at Worms, called to suppress the new religious commotions, the emperor Charles labored to procure the destruction of Luther. Upon this, Luther retired for a season from public view, and translated the Bible into the German language; which was of infinite service to the reformation. The wars which soon broke out between the emperor and the king of France, of which Italy was the bloody theatre, for a long course of years, (as will be noted in the next vial) prevented both the Pope and the emperor from being able to crush the reformation. Providence designed that the Pope should have other business to engage his attention; being placed between two fires; warring and intriguing; sometimes on the one side, and sometimes on the other, of the two great rival champions of Europe, Charles and Francis; and in continual scenes of danger and vexation. The same cause prevented the emperor from being able to oppose the reformation to any effect. So urgent and precarious were the affairs of Charles abroad, that he viewed it bad policy, if not dangerous, to provoke those German princes, who had favored the cause of the reformation. And indeed Charles himself, being often embroiled with the intrigues and power of the Pope uniting with the king of France against him, as often secretly rejoiced to see the abominations of the Pope exposed, and his influence thereby curtailed. And at

times Charles himself (as great a catholic bigot as he
was to the last) was not wanting to put a helping hand
to expose the Pope's duplicities and wickedness.   As
an instance of this;—upon the Pope's publishing an
angry brief against Charles, as a reason why the former
had united with the king of France against him; Charles
published a long reply; in which he enumerates many
instances of the Pope's ingratitude, deceit, and ambition.   He at the same time wrote to the college of cardinals, complaining of the Pope's partiality and injustice; and requiring of them, that if the Pope still refused to call a council to attend to the affairs of the reformation, (which he had hitherto refused to do; choosing
rather to attempt to crush it by dint of power) they
should show their concern for the peace of the Christian church, "*so shamefully neglected by its chief Pas-
tor,*" by summoning a council in their own names.
This manifesto (but little inferior to Luther's charges
against the Pope) flew over Germany, and did much
toward confirming the charges of the reformers against
the Papal corruptions.   Many great and free cities of
the first rank openly embraced the reformed religion.

   Great advantages were on the side of the reformers.
"Erudition, industry, accuracy of sentiment, purity of
composition, even wit and raillery, were almost wholly
on the side of the reformers, and triumphed with ease
over illiterate monks, whose rude arguments, expressed
in a perplexed and barbarous style, were found insuffi-
cient for the defence of a system of errors, for which
all the arts and ingenuity of later and more learned advocates, have not been able to palliate."*   Erasmus of
Rotterdam, a great wit, and of the first rate attainments
in the literature of that day, was educated for the
Church.   But discovering the abominations of the Papal system, he turned all the torrent of his popular sa-
tirical acumen against those abominations.   The landgrave of Hesse, the electors of Saxony and Brandenburg, the dukes of Brunswick and Lunenburg, and
the prince of Anhalt, embraced and patronized the

* Hist. Ch. V. vol. ii, p. 155.

reformed religion. The Pope demanded a diet, to destroy Luther, and crush the reformation. But the princes informed him, that they could not comply with his order; *for a reformation was absolutely necessary;* and so many had embraced the reformed religion, that it would be dangerous to use any violence against them. This diet of the princes, assembled at Nuremberg, now drew up a remonstrance of an *hundred* articles, against the corruptions and abominations of the Papal see. The Pope's nuncio, perceiving what the diet were doing, and finding himself unable to prevent it, fled abruptly from the city, even without taking leave of the diet, lest he should have to be the bearer of a message, which would be so painful to the court of Rome. The ecclesiastical princes also withdrew from a business, in which they, as well as their whole system of Papal corruption, were so deeply implicated. The secular princes united in their remonstrance of an hundred charges. They are two long to be enumerated. "They complained of the sums exacted for dispensations, absolutions, and indulgences; of the expense arising from law-suits, carried on by appeals to Rome; of the innumerable abuses-occasioned by reservations, commendams, and annates; of the exemption from civil jurisdiction, which the clergy had obtained; of the art, by which they brought all secular causes under the cognizance of the ecclesiastical judges; of the indecent and profligate lives, which not a few of the clergy led;"— and of many other particulars, which had long tortured the people of Germany, and had prepared the way for the quick reception and progress of the doctrines of the reformers. And the diet concluded their remonstrance by announcing, "that if the holy see did not speedily deliver them from these intolerable burdens, they had determined to endure them no longer; and would employ the power and authority, with which God had entrusted them, in order to procure relief."* Thus the Pope was utterly defeated. The diet, instead of *destroying* Luther, and *crushing* the reformation, took a

* Hist. Ch. V. vol. ii, p. 273.

most effectual step to widen the *sore* upon the men, who had the mark of the Beast, and who worshipped his image, by exposing the *intolerable wickedness* of their system; and doing it with such authority, as to add an amazing weight to the event.

These things opened the eyes of the people with a rapidity, which might be expected in such a case. And hundreds of thousands were astonished to behold the *filthy depravity* of the system, which had so long been held in the highest veneration. To add to the grievousness of the *sore*, and to give the most deadly force to the exposure of Papal corruption, Pope Adrian, who succeeded Leo X, most frankly acknowledged and bewailed these corruptions; and engaged to do all in his power to reform them: Upon which his clergy at Rome were highly offended, and complained that he was betraying their interest. Adrian suddenly died. And there was boldly fixed to the door of his chief physician in capitals, *"To the deliverer of his country."* Thus acknowledging, and rejoicing, that the Pope, who was betraying the corruptions of the Romish see, was hurried out of the world, with murderous design! These things added to the horror already excited at Papal corruption.

Most of the princes of Germany, who had favored the reformation, established that worship of God in their territories, which they approved; and suppressed the rites of the Papal church. Almost half the Germanic body revolted from the Papal see. And in the cities, which followed not this example, the Papal authority was much weakened. The emperor was troubled at the prevalence of the reformation. He viewed it unfavorable to that plan of dominion over the princes of Germany, which he had secretly in view. And the tolerance, which the urgency of his affairs abroad had obliged him to give to it, had offended the Papal powers. Charles therefore assembled the diet at Spires in 1529, and demanded of them an order, that the innovations of religion should spread no further among those, who were now Papists, till a meeting of a general council. After much debate, a majority of votes was obtained in the diet for this purpose. Upon this, the elector of Saxony, the margrave of Brandenburg, the landgrave of Hesse, the duke of Lunenburg, the prince of Anhalt, with the deputies of fourteen Imperial and free cities, entered their solemn *protest* against the decree, as unjust and impious; and they hence obtained the name of *Protestants*.

The Pope and Charles, upon making a temporary peace, agreed to exert themselves to suppress the reformation. The diet of Augsburg was accordingly called. Melancthon there drew up a confession of religion as soft and inoffensive as was possibly consistent with the views of the reformers. But the Popish clergy objected to it. And the divines in the reformation would come no lower. Charles turned from them to the *princes* of the reformation. But *they* were no less zealous, than were the divines. The emperor then obtained a vote of the majority of the diet, (there being many ecclesiastical princes in it) condemning the tenets of the reformers; and containing things of a threatening aspect. The Protestant states upon this were alarmed; and they assembled at Smalkalde, and formed a solemn league of defence. They also formed an alliance with Francis, king of France, and Henry, king of England; who confederated with them; not indeed to favor the reformation; but to cramp their great rival Charles. Upon this the emperor was alarmed, and became more moderate. And as the Turks were now threatening him, he formed terms of pacification with the Protestants at Nuremberg, which were ratified at the diet of Ratisbon, agreeing, that the laws in force against the Protestants should be void; and all should enjoy liberty of conscience, until a general council; which Charles engaged should be called if possible within six months. The emperor had often proposed to the Pope to call a council to sit in Germany, to settle their religious disputes. But the Pope had ever been reluctant. He doubtless understood, better than did the emperor, that his affairs could not endure such an investigation; and especially of a council sitting in *Germany*, where all the Protestant divines had a right to attend and act.' The Pope wished rather to crush the reformation by dint of power. And the Protestants had good reason to believe that Charles designed to attempt the same, if more peaceful means proved ineffectual. They therefore renewed their league of Smalkalde in 1535; and it was signed by the elector of Saxony, the duke of Brunswick, the landgrave of Hesse, the duke of Wurtemburg, the dukes of Pomerania, the princes of Anhalt, the counts of Mansfield, the count of Nassau, and by the deputies of twenty four free cities. We here learn to how great a degree the *sore*, on the men, who had the mark of the Beast, became offensive; and to how great a degree, the abomination of the Papal system was unfolded.

The Pope, that he might crush the reformation with a better grace, set about a reformation in his own system. He deputed a number of cardinals and bishops, to inquire into the abuses and corruptions of the Romish court; and to propose the best method of correcting them. In this duty they were reluctant, slow, and remiss. Defects they touched with a gentle hand, afraid of probing too deep into the dismal *sore.* But many enormities they could not but expose; while the remedies suggested were wholly inadequate; or were never applied. The report of these deputies was designed to be kept a secret in the court of Rome. But it got air. It reached Germany. It was made public. And it afforded the Protestants ample matter for reflection and triumph. This added weight to the remonstrances of the reformers. And it evinced, that it was in vain to expect a reformation from the Catholics; who (as Luther on this occasion expressed it) "piddled at curing warts; while they overlooked, or confirmed *Ulcers.*" How *striking*, that Luther himself, in expressing what was discovered in the Papal see, should, without any view of the language of the first vial, use the *very word* there used! The word there translated *sore,* in the original is ἑλκος, from which the English word *ulcer* is derived. Luther discovered a noisome and grievous *sore* on the men, who had the mark of the Beast.

The depth and rankling nature of this *sore* upon the men, who had the mark of the Beast, appeared in the attempts made by the Pope and the German emperor, to crush the Smalkalde league. However long Charles had dissembled his designs, and however long his wars abroad had prevented his being able to use violent means to crush the reformation; he still carried the purpose in his heart, if other means should prove ineffectual. And, as he found a cessation of his wars abroad, about the year 1547, he made his arrangements to carry his purpose into effect. But his designs being perceived by the vigilant Protestants, they with incredible celerity made their arrangements to meet him. And notwithstanding Charles, by his fair protestations of having no design against the Protestant religion, but only to crush a political faction, had caused many Protestant cities to remain neutral, and some even to join with him; he in a short time found 70,000 foot, and 15,000 horse, in arms against him; with 120 cannon, 8,000 beasts of burden, and 6,000 pioneers. The emperor was astonished at their numbers and force! But for want of experienced generals, and through the treachery of Maurice, to whom the elector of Saxony had committed the care of his dominions in his absence, as well as through the superior generalship of Charles, this army of the reformers was soon dispersed. And Charles for a time thought he was going to effect his purposes, both of crushing the reformation, and of destroying the liberties of Germany. But such were the numbers and zeal of the reformers, and such their view of the abomination of Popery, that his attempts proved vain. Maurice, who had deserted the Protestants, now became alarmed for the liberties of Germany; and in a plan of deep policy he out-generaled Charles;—rescued both the cause of the Protestants, and the liberties of Germany, out of his hands;—and brought about the peace of Passa..., in 1552, which was confirmed in the diet of Augsburg, in 1555; and which formed the basis of the religious peace in Germany. The following are chief articles of this recess: "That such princes and cities, as have declared their approbation of the con-

48

fession of Augsburg, shall be permitted to profess the doctrines, and exercise the worship, which it author-izes, without interruption or molestation from the emperor, or the king of the Romans, or any power or person whatsoever: That the Protestant powers, on their part, shall give no disquiet to the princes and states, who adhere to the tenets and rites of the church of Rome: That for the future no attempt shall be made toward terminating religious differences, but by the gentle and pacific methods of persuasion and confer-ences: That the Popish ecclesiastics shall claim no spiritual jurisdiction in such states, as receive the con-fession of Augsburg: That such as had seized the benefices or revenues of the church, previous to the treaty of Passau, shall retain possession of them, and be liable to no prosecution in the Imperial chamber on that account: That the supreme civil power in every state shall have right to establish what form of doctrine and worship it shall deem proper; and if any of its sub-jects refuse to conform to these, the government shall permit them to remove, with all their effects, whither-soever they shall please: That if any prelate or eccle-siastic shall hereafter abandon the Romish religion, he shall instantly relinquish his diocese or benefice; and it shall be lawful for those, in whom the right of nomina-tion is vested, to proceed immediately to an election; as if the office were vacant by death or translation, and to appoint a successor of undoubted attachment to the ancient system."* If there be defects in this instru-ment, in point of religious liberty; when we consider *when, where, by whom,* and *in favor of whom* it was confirmed, we see in it the death wound of the Papal Beast, and a discovery of the rottenness of the Romish system, which must have issued in its ruin. The above articles extended only to those of the re-formers, who embraced the confession of Augsburg. Consequently the followers of Zuinglius, and of Calvin, who viewed that confession as too soft toward the Cath-olic interest, remained without any legal protection

* Hist. Ch. V, vol. iii, p. 181.

from the rigor of the law against heretics, till the treaty of Westphalia; nearly a century after that of Augsburg. And in France, and other Papal countries, that compact afforded no protection to the Protestants.

But the reformation spread into other countries with amazing rapidity. The Pope himself, now felt the fatal nature of his wound; and he languished under it. Of the council of Bologna, called to deliberate on their wretched affairs; after a broken, unavailing session, Dr. Robertson remarks; "The Pope had no choice, but to dissolve an assembly, which had become the object of contempt; and exhibited to all Christendom a most glaring proof of the impotence of the Romish see."* The emperor Charles himself took an occasion from the above incident to stigmatize the Pope, and to endeavor to render him odious, even to all zealous Catholics. And various things occurred, which did in fact render him odious to the Papal, as well as Protestant world; particularly the following incident. Pope Julian bestowed the cardinal's hat (the most sacred official gift in his power) on one *Innocent*, an obscure youth of about 16 years of age, known by the name of the *ape;* because he took the care of an ape in his master's family. Upon this strange occurrence a writer observes, "In an enlightened age, when by the progress of knowledge and philosophy, the obligations of duty, and decency were better understood, when a blind veneration for the Pontifical character was every where abated, and one half of Christendom in open rebellion against the Papal see, *this action was viewed with horror.*" Libels filled even Rome itself, satirizing the Pope upon this conduct; and imputing it to a nameless, horrible passion, which the Pope was supposed to have indulged toward this youth.

Pope Julius III brought indelible disgrace on the Pontifical chair. While his nuncio Morono was laboring by his direction at the diet of Augsburg, to set aside the peace of Passau, which has been noted

* Hist. Ch. V, vol. iii, p. 457.

as in favor of the Protestants; the Pope was at the
same time wallowing in *licentiousness* in his capital
at Rome. Through excessive indulgence he had become averse to all serious business. An application
which required attention to business was made to him,
which he wished to avoid; for which purpose he feigned himself sick. And to give plausibility to his pretence, he *retired*, and altered his *diet*. This course was
in fact followed by sickness, of which in a few days he
died! Thus while the Protestants were trembling at the
intrigues of his nuncio, in the diet of Augsburg, the
Pope was suddenly snatched out of time by his own
mean artifice: Upon which his nuncio left the diet, and
hastened to Rome, to be present at the election of a
new Pope; and the peace of Passau was confirmed.
What an exposure of the deadly corruption of that system! No wonder, indeed, that hundreds of thousands
hastened to flee out of it, as from a house infected with
the plague! For the exposures of this Papal corruption,
flew like lightning over Europe; and suddenly broke
the enchantments of superstition, in which millions
had been miserably enslaved. Upon this, a historian
remarks; "The charm, which had bound mankind for
so many ages, was broken at once. The human mind,
which had continued long as tame and passive, as if it
had been formed to believe whatever was taught, and to
bear whatever was imposed, roused of a sudden, and became inquisitive, mutinous, and disdainful of the yoke,
to which it had hitherto submitted. The wonderful
ferment and agitation of mind (which at this distance
of time appears unaccountable, or is condemned as
extravagant) was so general, that it must have been
excited by causes, which were *natural*, and of *powerful efficacy*. The kingdoms of Denmark, Sweden,
England, Scotland, and almost one half of Germany,
threw off their allegiance to the Pope; abolished his
jurisdiction within their territories; and gave the sanction of law to, modes of discipline and systems of doctrine, which were not only independent of Papal power, but hostile to it. Nor was this spirit of innovation
confined to those countries, which openly revolted from

the Pope. It spread through all Europe, and broke out in every part of it with various degrees of violence. It penetrated early into France, and made quick progress there. In that kingdom the number of converts to the opinions of the reformers, was so great, their zeal so enterprising, and the abilities of their leaders so distinguished, that they soon ventured to contend for superiority with the established church; and were sometimes on the point of obtaining it. In all the provinces of Germany, which continued to acknowledge the Papal supremacy, as well as in the low countries, the Protestant doctrines were secretly taught; and had gained so many proselytes, that they were ripe for revolt, and were restrained merely by the dread of their rulers from imitating the examples of their neighbors, and asserting their independence. Even in Spain and in Italy symptoms of the same disposition to shake off the yoke, appeared. The pretensions of the Pope to infallible knowledge and supreme power, were treated by many persons of eminent learning and abilities, with such scorn, or attacked with such vehemence; that the most vigilant attention of the civil magistrate, the highest strain of Pontifical authority, and all the rigor of inquisitorial jurisdiction, were requisite to check and extinguish it."

Who then can doubt but this fatal wound given to the Papal power, this sudden and most astonishing exhibition of the filthy abomination of the Papal see, fulfilled a vial of the wrath of God on that corrupt system? And who can doubt but this was the *first vial,* which was to operate as a noisome, grievous sore upon the men who had the mark of the Beast, and who worshipped his image? With such a rankling, deadly *sore* they *indeed did languish,* under the development of the abominations of their system, and under the progress of the doctrines of the reformation, *The Lamb now appeared on mount Zion;* (Rev. xiv, 1;) or Christ appeared in his Church, for the salvation of his cause; and for the confusion of his enemies. This his appearance marked the commencement of a new era of judgments upon the wicked. And they have never found any thing like a healing. The total filthiness of their system stands exposed before the nations, as in the light of the meridian sun. And this event was the first fatal stroke toward their destruction!

THE SECOND VIAL.

And the second Angel poured out his vial upon the sea; and it became as the blood of a dead man: and every living soul died in the sea. (Rev. xvi, 3.)

As by the earth, on which the contents of the first vial were discharged, is to be understood the corrupt system of the Papal hierarchy; by the sea, in the second vial, we are to understand the multitudes of people in the most central parts of the Papal dominions. *I will show thee the judgment of the great whore, that sitteth upon many waters. The waters, which thou sawest, where the whore sitteth, are people and multitudes, and nations and tongues.** Here probably, we are presented both with the sea in the second vial; and the rivers and fountains of water, in the third. The two vials (the second and third) divide them into sea, and rivers and fountains of water. By the sea then, in this second vial, we are naturally led to understand the most central parts of the Papal delusion. *Italy* first presents itself, as entitled to this symbolic appellation. And probably the great Papal nations bordering upon it, Germany, France, and possibly Spain, are to be viewed in a sense included in this sea, as the *instruments* of the judgment of this vial. There appears a fitness in symbolizing Italy by *the sea.* At the commencement of the sixteenth century it was a great collection of different states and governments, of jarring and contending interests. This remark indeed held true of the great Papal nations bordering upon Italy, which were in a sense included in the sea in this vial, as the *instruments* of the judgment. Those great Papal nations, locally united, may be viewed as being at that time a

---

* Rev. xvii, 1, 15.

vast collection of contending interests, both as great
nations, in relation to each other; and as containing
partial, discordant interests, in each nation, which grew
out of the peculiar circumstances of the feudal times.
These jarring, internal interests, without any common
principle of strength sufficient to unite them, much re-
sembled the tempestuous sea. "In the German empire (says a noted author) which was a confederacy of
princes, of ecclesiastics, and of free cities, it was impossible that they should incorporate thoroughly."
In Germany and Italy the education of ecclesiastics,
and their genius and connexion with the court of Rome,
rendered them so different from the other princes, that
it was a source of jealousy and discord. Consult the
hundred articles of grievance, presented to the Pope by
the diet of Nuremburg, and the discordant nature of
these national materials strikingly appears. There is
then, a fitness in their being symbolized by the sea.
And another more general reason why they should be
thus represented, was the tumultuous state into which
they were thrown, in consequence of the judgments of
this vial. Great nations in the effervescence occasioned
by wars and judgments, are abundantly represented in
sacred Writ, by the *sea.**

　It has been supposed that the turning of this sea to
blood, by the contents of the second vial, and the turning of the rivers and fountains of water to blood by
the third vial, are expressed in allusion to that plague
on Egypt, in which the rivers and fountains of water
were turned to blood; so that every thing in them died. And the events were to be fulfilled, no doubt, by
desolating wars.

　It has already been stated, that a long train of providential circumstances had been preparing the way for

* Whether in the symbols, which represent Italy by the *sea;*
and the distant Papal nations by *rivers* and *fountains of water*,
any reference may be had to the geographical *fact*, that Italy
lies, like the shape of a boot in the Mediteranean, and is
mostly surrounded by the seas;—and that the inland Papal nations do abound with fountains, and are intersected with vast
rivers; readers will judge for themselves.

the sixteenth century to commence with the certain prospect of its abounding with most interesting events. The invention of gunpowder, and of fire-arms; the keeping of regular standing armies; and extending the prerogatives of the crown, or the better organization of national governments, so that the force of a nation might be brought into action at the pleasure of an ambitious sovereign; these things, together with a number of the most powerful and ambitious potentates coming to the thrones of the great nations, bordering upon Italy, indicated the most bloody and dismal events as about to commence.

Charles V was born in 1500. Upon the death of his father Philip, archduke of Austria, he became heir to the crown of Spain. And upon the death of his grandfather Maximilian, emperor of Germany, Charles and Francis I, the powerful monarch of France, became competitors for the Imperial crown. Upon which Dr. Robertson remarks; "Pope Leo X trembled at the prospect of beholding the Imperial crown placed on the head of the king of Spain and of Naples; and foretold, that the election of either *Charles* or *Francis*, would be fatal to the independence of the holy see, to the peace of Italy, and perhaps to the liberties of Europe."* The Pope himself saw an apparatus of fatal judgments; and he trembled! And events soon showed, that he did not tremble in vain. Charles was elected to the Imperial dignity; at which Francis felt all the chagrin and rage of a haughty, disappointed rival. These two haughty potentates soon commenced tremendous preparations for war; and "Italy soon became the theatre, on which the greatest powers of Europe contended for superiority:" And, till about the year 1559, its fairest provinces were turned into fields of carnage and blood. In but little short of *twenty* successive campaigns in Italy, (contending for Milan, Naples, and for *one* Italian state and *another,)* Charles and Francis, those mightiest potentates of Europe, exerted themselves to the utmost for victory. Sometimes success crowned the arms of *one;* and sometimes of the

* Hist. Ch. V, vol. i, p. 70, 71.

other. The Pope was found intriguing between them, sometimes in alliance with the one; sometimes with the other; but generally between two fires; and in danger, vexation and distress!

Here it may be proper to remark, that the second vial was not deferred till the first was finished. The events of the *first* had but fairly commenced, when the second began to be poured out. A celebrated modern author observes; "It is no where said, that each vial is emptied, before its successor begins to be poured out. Hence it is not unreasonable to conclude, that two or more of the vials may be pouring out at the same time; though the effusion of one commences before that of the other."* Although the two first vials be of natures wholly different; yet the second soon commenced, to aid the effects of the first. Here the wisdom and mercy of God appeared. By the events of the second vial, God furnished employment for the powerful enemies of the reformation; and thus prevented their being able to withstand the effects of the first vial. Although the first vial began to be poured out for a course of years before the second; yet the two were to be poured out for the most part collaterally. The discovery of the surprising impositions of the Papal see, was to be made, and was to progress. While at the same time a train of sore judgments, from causes entirely foreign for the most part, from those of the reformation, were to attend; both to exhibit the wrath of Heaven against the man of sin; and to protect the reformers and the reformed from his fury, till their cause should be established. There can be no rational objection against this opinion, of the two vials being poured out at the same time. The reformation was not of a nature to come to a close, before the effusion of the succeeding vial should commence. It was to progress for centuries, till Popery should be no more. Other vials then, if they are poured out at all, must be poured out collaterally with it. And if so, what objection can be made to the effusion of its successor commencing *soon* after

* Faber vol. ii, p. 199.

the effusion of the first? The nature of the case shows the necessity of such an event, and the goodness of God in it.   Were a man to order his son to throw off the cover from a nest of vipers; would he not be ready, at the same time, with his proper implements, to begin their destruction; and thus to prevent their destroying his son? We find the *times* of the seals; and of the trumpets. But we do not think it necessary to find all the effects of one to have *ceased*, before the succeeding one commences; nor to find equal distances of time between them. Their distances were *unequal;* and their effects often collateral.

We find in history, that after Charles V was elected to the Imperial crown, he was urged to repair speedily to Germany, on account of the innovations in religion, which were progressing there. "Unknown opinions concerning religion (says the historian) had been published, such as had thrown the minds of men into an universal agitation, and threatened the most violent effects." And "the new opinions concerning religion made such rapid progress, as required the most serious consideration." Accordingly, as soon as Charles arrived at Germany, he called a diet of the princes at Worms, we are informed, "to concert the most proper measures for checking the progress of those new and dangerous opinions, which threatened to disturb the peace of Germany, and to overturn the religion of their ancestors." Now, had not Charles and the Pope been diverted from this object, by the tremendous scenes of war, which soon opened upon them in Italy, and kept them employed, till the work of the reformation became established; *the reformers must soon have been crushed.* Humanly speaking, the events of the first vial could not have produced their designed effect, without the concurring aid of the judgment of the second. For which reason, as we may believe, the second vial was not deferred for that proportionable length of time, which might otherwise have been expected, when the whole seven were to occupy the space of several centuries. When these things are considered, I trust no objection will arise to the explanation given of these two vials, from the partial synchronism of their events.

To trace in order the events, which I apprehend relate to the second vial, would be to write a long history. I shall mention only a few of those events. Let any one peruse the history of that period; and he will not doubt whether the events were of sufficient *magnitude* to answer to the second vial. For but little short of 40 years we find an almost continual series of wars, of which Italy was chiefly the bloody theatre. The powers engaged were, the emperor of Germany, (who was at the same time king of Spain and of Naples,) the king of France, the Pope, the emperor of the Turks, the king of the Romans, of Hungary and Bohemia, and more than once the king of England. Terrible battles were fought. And all the calamities of sieges and captivities, and all those evils usually attendant on furious wars, were experienced in Italy. The Pope himself met with rough treatment. He was more than once a prisoner; and his capital was plundered. Cardinal Pompeo Colona, a disappointed rival of Pope Clement, instigated by the Imperial ambassador, while the Pope was engaged with Francis in war against the emperor, seized the gates of the Pope, at the head of an army, and dispersed his guards. The Pope fled to the castle of St. Angelo; which was immediately besieged. The palace of the Vatican, the church of St. Peter, and the houses of the Pope's ministers and servants, were plundered. The Pope capitulated; being forced to agree to grant his cardinal a full pardon for all this conduct; and to withdraw his troops from the confederate army then at Lombardy. Not long after, Bourbon, who had fled disgusted from the king of France to the emperor, and had been made general of the Imperial army in Italy, and duke of Milan, marched at the head of 25,000 veteran troops toward Rome. They had been rendered desperate by want of money and provisions. And without the knowledge of Charles their emperor, they engaged in this expedition. The Pope, then at war with the emperor, became alarmed, and speedily formed a treaty with Lannoy, another Imperial general; in which he agreed to a suspension of arms, for eight months; and to pay 60,000 crowns toward the support of the Imperial army. Upon this, the Pope thought all was safe; and disbanded his troops. This credulous conduct his generals imputed to infatuation. Be it so; it was designed to aid his unprecedented calamity! *Quem Deus vult perdere, prius dementat. Whom God designs for ruin, he often first infatuates.* Lannoy informed Bourbon of the armistice, which he had concluded with the Pope; and desired him to turn his arms against Venice. But Bourbon's hungry and half naked troops, elated with the idea of plundering Rome, would not be diverted from their object. And Bourbon himself discovered little or no inclination to control them. They continued their march. The walls of Rome were scaled. Bourbon fell by a ball from the ramparts. His soldiers took the city. The Pope with thirteen cardinals and others, fled to the castle of St. Angelo. On his way thither, the Pope "saw his troops flying before the enemy, who gave them no quarter; and heard the cries and lamentations of the citizens of Rome." It is impossible to describe the horrors of the scene, which followed. Whatever a city, taken by storm, can dread from military rage, unrestrained by any leader; "whatever excesses the ferocity of the Germans, the avarice of the Spaniards, or the licentiousness of the Italians could commit; these wretched inhabitants were obliged to suffer." Churches, palaces, and the houses of private persons, were plundered without distinction. No age, character, or sex, was exempt from injury. Cardinals, nobles, priests, matrons, virgins, all were a prey to a brutal, enraged soldiery, deaf to every call of humanity. Nor did these outrages cease, as is usual in places taken by storm, when the first rage is over. Those 25,000 armed plunderers had the undisturbed possession of that vast wealthy city for several months; in which time their brutality scarcely abated. Their booty in ready money amounted to a million of ducats.*

---

* Ducat, a coin struck by dukes; in silver $0,75; in gold 9s.6d, sterling.

And what they raised by ransoms and exactions, far exceeded that sum. Dr. Robertson observes, that though Rome had been taken at several different times, by the northern barbarians in the fifth and sixth centuries, it was never treated with so much cruelty by the Huns, Vandals, and Goths, as it experienced at this time. Here let the reader be reminded, that expositors suppose the first and second trumpets, (the fiery hailstorm upon the earth, and the burning mountain cast into the sea,*) to have been fulfilled by those former sackings of Rome, to which Dr. Robertson here refers. And if Rome experienced greater severity under the ravages of Bourbon's army, than in those ancient calamities, which fulfilled the first and second trumpets; surely this scene under Bourbon's army, together with those furious wars, which for nearly half a century, shook Italy, Germany, and France, cannot be esteemed too *diminutive* to have fulfilled the second vial.

While the Pope and his cardinals were confined in the castle of St. Angelo, and Bourbon's army were plundering Rome, the duke of Urbino advanced with an army of Venetians, Florentines, and Swiss, in the pay of France, sufficient to have relieved the Pope, and to have driven the army of plunderers out of Rome. The Pope, from the ramparts of his castle, beheld the advance of those troops at a distance; and leaped for joy, imaging relief was now at hand. But the duke of Urbino, having a private pique against the Pope, on coming in sight of Rome, pronounced the attempt to rescue the city too hazardous; and he wheeled his army, and retired; and thus left the Pope and Rome in all their wretchedness.

The Florentines rose in insurrection against the government of the Pope, declared themselves a free people, broke in pieces the statues of Leo X, and of Clement, the then present Pope; and established their ancient popular government. The Venetians also seized Ravenna, and other places belonging to the church. And the dukes of Urbino and Ferrari seized property be-

* Rev. viii, 7, 8.

longing to the Pope, whom they now considered as irretrievably ruined! Also Lannoy, Moncada, and the marquis del Guesto, three Imperial generals then in Italy, at the head of all the troops they could assemble in Naples, marched to Rome; not to relieve, but to add to its distresses. This army, envying the wealth of their companions, who had plundered the city, imitated their conduct; and, with the utmost rapacity, gathered the gleanings, which had escaped the avarice of Bourbon's army. The Pope in the castle of St. Angelo, after being reduced by famine, and feeding on asses' flesh, capitulated; agreeing to pay his besiegers 400,000 ducats; to surrender to the emperor all the places of strength belonging to the church; and to give hostages; and himself to remain a prisoner, till the articles of capitulation should be fulfilled. The Pope was accordingly delivered to the care of Alarcon, who had some years before been the keeper of Francis I, the monarch of France, while he was a prisoner to the emperor. After an imprisonment of six months, the Pope procured his liberty, by the additional sum of 350,000 crowns.

The emperor, when he came to hear of these things, feigned deep mourning and sorrow. But he was inwardly *pleased;* because the Pope had excited and headed a coalition against him, consisting of the Pope, the king of France, and the king of England. All Christendom was struck with *horror* at a view of the violence offered to his holiness; and the plundering of Rome. The emperor afterwards came to Rome, restored to the Pope the church lands, and treated him with some apparent respect, that he might seem to make some amends for such indignities.

It has been before hinted that Solyman, the magnificent, on the Ottoman throne, seemed to have been raised up in Providence to aid the same work of judgment, with Francis and Charles. We accordingly find him, with fleets and armies, repeatedly annoying those great Papal nations, at this period. He attacked Hungary with an army of 200,000 men, and a fleet of 400 sail, and took Belgrade and Rhodes. A second time he invaded Hungary, with 300,000 men. An army of 30,000 Hungarians and Bohemians undertook to meet him, led by the monk, archbishop of Golocza, in his pontifical dress. They fought at Mohacz. The Catholic army was cut in pieces. The flower of the nobility, and more than 20,000 of the Hungarians, fell. Hungary was overrun; and nearly 200,000 persons were by the Turks carried into captivity. Solyman, not long after, laid siege to Vienna with an army of 150,000 men. Naples was ravaged by the Turkish admiral Barbarossa. Rheggio in Italy was plundered and burnt by a Turkish fleet of 110 gallies. The same fleet the next spring ravaged the coasts of Naples and Tuscany. In Hungary the Turks defeated the Germans in a great battle at Essek on the Drave. And repeatedly was the Turkish emperor in alliance with the king of France, against the emperor.

The civil wars, which broke out in Italy and Germany, were far from being of a trifling nature. The events in consequence of Charles's undertaking to destroy the league of Smalkalde, were not without terror and blood. The subsequent war of Maurice, in which he out-generaled Charles, and wrested the rights of the German Protestants, and the liberties of the empire, out of his hands, was a heavy judgment upon the Papal see. Maurice and the landgrave of Hesse, had before had a civil war with Henry of Brunswick, in which the latter was subdued. Albert of Brandenburg, one of the confederates under Maurice for humbling the emperor, conceived the wicked design of forming for himself an empire. And after the emperor and Maurice had made peace, Albert continued in arms, and made awful ravages in the empire. He turned his army of veteran desperadoes against the ecclesiastical states; which, with various cities on the Rhine, he ravaged and plundered, with wanton barbarity. A league of princes was formed against him. An army was raised; and Maurice was appointed their general. The two armies, of 24,000 each, met. The battle was obstinate and bloody. Maurice was slain; and many of his first officers. But the vile Albert was defeated. Soon however, he was in the field again, with 15,000 men. Another bloody battle was fought: Albert was vanquished, and his army dispersed.

Two expeditions Charles made into Africa: The first to drive Barbarossa from Tunis, and to restore Muley Hascen; and the second against Algiers. In the latter we see much of the tremendous judgments of this period. In this view I will give a sketch of it. Charles embarked late in the fall of 1541, with a great army and fleet, containing the flower of the Italian youth. He landed at Algiers, and prepared to attack the city. But a most furious storm came on; and the scenes, which followed were dreadful. The powder of the assailing army was wet; their matches were extinguished. The ground became soft, and almost covered with water. They had no shelter from the tempest. The soldiers were wet, numb, and almost dead with the cold rain. In this situation a sally was made upon them from the city. Many of them were killed, and the rest driven back. A dreadful consternation was excited. "But all feeling or remembrance of this loss and danger (says the historian) were quickly obliterated, by a more dreadful as well as affecting spectacle. It was now broad day-light, after a most dismal night. The hurricane had abated nothing of its violence; and the sea appeared agitated with all the rage, of which that destructive element is capable. All the ships, on which alone the army knew their safety and subsistence depended, were seen driven from their anchors; some dashing against each other; some beat to pieces on the rocks; many forced ashore; and not a few sinking in the waves. In less than an hour 15 ships of war, and 140 transports, with 8,000 men, were destroyed. And such of the unhappy crews, as escaped the fury of the sea, were murdered without mercy by the Arabs, as soon as they reached the land. The emperor stood in silent astonishment, beholding this fatal event; which at once blasted all his hopes of success; and buried in the deep the vast stores, which he had provided for the annoyance of the enemy, and for subsisting his own troops."* The admiral with much ado got word to

* Hist. Ch. V, vol. iii, p. 227.

Charles, that he must repair with his remaining forces to cape Metafuz; as, it was impossible to find a harbor for his few remaining vessels short of that place. In this miserable state therefore, his shattered troops had to perform a *three days march.* They had not a moment's time to lose. It seemed impossible for them to reach the destined place. But they had no choice between this, and certain death. They therefore, in the most miserable plight, set forth. They were harassed, day and night, by the Arabs. They were dispirited; subsisting chiefly on roots and berries, with a little horseflesh; wading over brooks to their chin; and their way almost unpassable. Many were killed. Many perished by famine. And many through fatigue *sunk down* and *died* by the way. The few, who reached the place, were taken on board, and returned, to Italy. Doria their admiral declared, that during 50 years of his knowledge of the seas, he had never seen a storm of equal fierceness and horror. This was a small *item,* in those days of vengeance upon the Papal see.

The French nation, a main instrument of the judgments of those days, suffered immensely. Repeatedly was it invaded by powerful armies; and the most distressing ravages were made in their country. Several times France was invaded by the emperor, and the king of England, in alliance against her. And more than once she trembled for her capital.

Charles, in his last war with France, suffered rough treatment. Merely in the siege of Mentz, he lost 30,000 men; and was obliged to raise the siege, and retire in great mortification. And being perplexed with his adverse affairs, he formed a determination to abdicate the Imperial throne; to resign his Spanish crown to his son Philip; and to *retire.* To prepare the way for which, he proposed a peace with the king of France, "that he might have the merit (says the historian) when quitting the world, of re-establishing that tranquillity in Europe, which he had banished out of it, almost from the time that he had assumed the administration of affairs."* Accordingly Charles

* Hist. Ch. V, vol. iii, p. 215.
50

made peace with Henry, king of France, (who succeeded Francis now dead) in 1556; abdicated the Imperial throne; constituted Philip his successor in Spain; and retired to the monastery of St. Justus in Spain; where he spent his time in a rigid attention to the rites of the Catholic religion, till he died.

By the base instigation of the Pope, one more furious and bloody war was undertaken by the king of France, in league with the Pope on the one hand; and Philip, and his queen Mary of England, on the other; which was the finishing scene of this vial. The object of the war was to take Naples from Philip, and annex it to the crown of France. The duke of Guise was sent from France with an army, to join the army of the Pope. Great ravages were committed in Naples and Italy. But Philip and Mary determined to prosecute the war nigher home. Their army therefore invaded France, and invested the city of St. Quintin; which they soon reduced, with the dreadful slaughter of the French army, under the prime minister Montmorency; who came to relieve the city, and who was taken prisoner. Upon this, France was filled with consternation; and preparations were made to defend Paris, in an expected siege. The duke of Guise was recalled out of Italy. This filled the Pope with consternation; as the war was furiously going on there, and his chief dependence was on the army of the duke. But the distresses of France could admit of no attention to the remonstrances and entreaties of the Pope. And the French army fled home with all speed, to defend their own capital. Their arrival in France soon changed the face of things. Calais was besieged and taken from the English; and the latter now lost all their possessions in the kingdom of France. And a peace was concluded among all the contending powers.

Various things indicated, that the terrors and devastations of these scenes of war, unprecedented in Europe since the northern invasions, were dreadful. The French on their part, in the general treaty of peace, gave up 189 fortified places, which they had taken during those contests. And the arguments, which had been used by the Pope, to induce the king of France to break the peace between him and Philip, as before noted, strikingly indicated the devastations of those wars. His arguments were,—"That the flower of the veteran Spanish bands had perished in the wars of Hungary, Germany, and the Low Countries; that the emperor (Charles) had left his son an exhausted treasury, and kingdoms drained of men; and that Henry might drive the Spaniards out of Naples, and add to the crown of France a kingdom, the conquest of which had been the great object of his predecessors for half a century." These arguments imply the terrors of that period of judgments. And, that so great a monarch as Charles V should abdicate the Imperial throne, indicates the terrors of those scenes, in which he had been engaged. And the histories of those times show these terrors to have been extreme.

At the general peace above mentioned, it is apparent, that an important era closed. In the articles between Philip and the Pope, the balance of power among the Italian states was poised with an equality not known before, since the commencement of that period of judgments. Upon which the historian observes, "From this period Italy ceased to be the great theatre, on which the monarchs of Spain, France, and Germany, contended for power and for fame. Their dissentions and hostilities, though as frequent and violent as ever, were excited by new objects; and stained other regions of Europe with blood; and rendered them miserable in their turn, by the devastations of war."* Had this judicious historian been designing to describe the close of the term of the second vial, and the transition from the second to the third; what more could have been said? He adds, "Exhausted by extraordinary efforts, which far exceeded those to which the nations of Europe had been accustomed, before the rivalship between Charles V, and Francis I, both nations longed for repose." We accordingly find, that in the peace established in 1559, great pains were taken, by inter-

---

* Hist. Ch. V, vol. iv, p. 261.

marriages and mutual concessions, to give it a decided permanency. All past transactions were to be buried in oblivion. "The Pope, the emperor of Germany, the kings of Denmark, Sweden, Poland, Portugal, the king of the Scots, and almost every state in Christendom, were comprehended in this pacification, as the allies either of Henry or Philip. Thus by this famous treaty, peace was re-established in Europe. All the causes of discord, which had so long embroiled the powerful monarchs of France and Spain, seemed to be wholly removed or finally terminated." Soon after this, Henry II, king of France, died. Pope Paul, a violent, perfidious Pontiff, died. And his two nephews, most intriguing, mischievous characters in the court of Rome, were put to death for their crimes. "Thus most of the personages, who had long sustained the principal characters on the great theatre of Europe, disappeared about the same time. A more known period of history opens at this era; other actors enter upon the stage, with different views, as well as different passions. New contests arose, and new schemes of ambition occupied and disquieted mankind." This brings us to the consideration of the next vial.

THE THIRD VIAL.

And the third Angel poured out his vial upon the rivers and fountains of water; and they became blood. And I heard the Angel of the waters say, Thou art righteous, O Lord, who art, and wast, and shalt be, because thou hast judged thus: For they have shed the blood of saints and prophets, and thou hast given them blood to drink, for they are worthy. And I heard another out of the altar say, Even so Lord God Almighty, true and righteous are thy ways. (Rev. xiv, 4—7.)

As by the *sea* in the second vial, we are to understand Italy, as the *seat* of the judgment, including the great Papal nations bordering upon it, as the *instruments* of the judgment of that vial; so by the *rivers and foun-tains of water* in the third vial, we are probably to understand the individual Papal nations, as *distinct* from Italy, the seat of the Papal impositions. The rivers and fountains of water run into the sea. And the influence of the Papal nations in Christendom, flowed into Italy, to support the Papal authority there instituted. If Italy, then, be symbolized by the *sea;* we might naturally expect the other Papal nations, as distinct from Italy, would be symbolized by *rivers and fountains of water.** And they, in their turn, to the remotest parts of Christendom, were now to experience terrible scenes of Divine judgment. And we find this vial fulfilled with awful precision. Some of the great Papal nations, which had been instrumental in the judgment of the second vial, and were in a sense included in the *sea* there turned to blood, were likewise included in the judgment of the third vial. But in the latter case their wars had no immediate concern with Italy. They might

* Should any inquire, why it is not more proper to view the sea in the second vial as symbolizing all the Papal nations; and the turning of it to blood, in the second vial, as involving not only the scenes of judgment on Italy, which have been contemplated, but also the scenes of the same nature, on other Papal nations, which are now to be contemplated, as fulfilling the third vial? And whether this might not more properly leave the third vial to be fulfilled in the drying up of the sources of Papal wealth and power; which one might suppose to have been symbolized by rivers and fountains of water? I reply as follows: It is evident that the third vial is of the same *specific* nature with the second, or literally blood. This we learn from the devout acknowledgment of the Angel of the waters. *Thou art righteous, O Lord,—because thou hast judged thus. For they have shed the blood of saints and prophets; and thou hast given them* blood *to drink; for they are worthy.* Here we learn, that the third vial is fulfilled not by *mystical,* but *literal* blood. This devout acknowledgment of the Angel must be viewed as alluding both to the second and the third vials; which indicates them both to be of the same *specific nature,* or fulfilled chiefly by bloody wars. And the judgment, with which they are visited, is of the same kind with that wickedness which occasioned it, *blood.* For a part of the blood which they shed, see Faber, vol. ii, p. 155. And rivers, in symbolic language, when applied to political systems, import *nations,* and not streams of wealth. (See Isa. xviii, last of 2, and xlii, 15; Ezek. xxix, 4, 10, et alia.)

well therefore, in the third vial, be symbolized, among the promiscuous nations of the Catholic religion, by *rivers and fountains of water.* And the peculiar Papal corruption and guilt of those great nations, might well entitle them to a double share in the judgments of these two vials.

I shall now note some of the events of the third vial; which commenced soon after the general peace in 1559. To give a view of the transition of events from the second to the third vial, I will here repeat the account before recited from Dr. Robertson. "From this period Italy ceased to be the great theatre, on which the great monarchs of Spain, France, and Germany, contended for power and for fame. Their dissentions and hostilities, though as frequent and violent as ever, were excited by new objects; and stained other regions of Europe with blood, and rendered them miserable in their turn, by the devastations of war." "The nations of Europe united in the general peace. All causes of discord, which had so long embroiled the powerful monarchs of France and Spain, seemed to be wholly removed, or finally terminated."—"Other actors entered upon the stage, with different views, as well as different passions. New contests arose, and new schemes of ambition occupied and disquieted mankind." What a perfect description does the historian here give, of the finishing of the *second vial,* and the introduction of the *third;* yet without any view of the subject as relating to a fulfilment of those vials. A new era of wars, on the Papal nations *generally,* commenced; wars, prosecuted by different heroes, and undertaken with different views from those of the wars in Italy, in the preceding period. To give a particular account of these, would be to write the history of Europe for two centuries; which would fill a volume. I shall only note a few leading events, in which I believe the third vial was fulfilled.

One great cause of the wars in Europe, subsequent to the peace of 1559, was the growing power of the house of Austria. Extensive territories had descended to Charles V, from his Austrian, Burgundian, and

Spanish ancestors. And the new world in South Amer!
ica had become subject to his command, as the king of
Spain. All these prerogatives and powers, Charles had
transmitted to his son Philip. And he delivered up
his dominions much improved from the state, in which
he had received them, both as to extent of territory, and
extent of the royal prerogatives. His people had become habituated to expenses, efforts and subordination,
unknown in Europe previously to his reign. The
provinces of Overyssel, Friesland, Utrecht and the
duchy of Gueldres, had added a vast weight to the
Burgundian provinces in possession of the first branch
of the house of Austria. These, with the kingdoms
of Spain, which Charles had found means to subject
wholly to his authority, their vast territories and inex-
haustible mines in South America, the kingdom of
Naples, and the populous and fertile duchy of Milan
in Italy, which kingdom and duchy were, in the aforementioned peace, confirmed in quiet possession to the
crown of Spain; these gave an amazing predominance
to the first branch of the house of Austria, and rendered Philip formidable to the other European powers.
The younger, or German branch of the house of Austria, was also formidable. Ferdinand, the younger
brother of Charles V, had by the motion of Charles
himself, in the midst of his Imperial career, been
crowned king of the Romans, as a kind of lieutenant
to Charles, to manage his concerns in Germany in his
absence. Ferdinand soon after, by marriage, acquired
the crown of Hungary and Bohemia. These, added to
his own crown, and to the ancient, hereditary Germanic dominions of the house of Austria, which fell to
Ferdinand, rendered him a powerful monarch. And
to add to his influence, the diet upon Charles's abdi-
cating the throne, conferred the Imperial honor upon
Ferdinand. Happily for Europe, the two branches
of the house of Austria were in a state of alienation from
each other. But in time a regard to their mutual
family interests overcame their alienation, and induced
them to adopt the aggrandizement of the house of Austria for their common object. And the consequences

were most serious. "A family so great and so aspiring, became the general object of *jealousy* and *terror*. And all the power as well as policy of Europe was exerted, during a century, in order to check and humble it." Its ascendancy, and the terror it had inspired, continued, even after its vigor had become chiefly exhausted, by a long series of extraordinary exertions and wars, and the monarchs of Spain especially had sunk into debility. "The nations of Europe (says the historian) had so often felt the superior power of the house of Austria, and had been so constantly employed in guarding against it, that the dread of it became a kind of political habit; the influence of which remained, when the causes, which had formed it, ceased to exist." In the progress of these wars, we are presented with a series of bloody and awful judgments on Papal nations.

· During the wars of Charles V, the European nations had become acquainted with their internal resources and strength for war; and had learned how to put themselves in a formidable attitude. Those nations at the same time became acquainted and connected with each other, like one great political system, the contending interests of whose different parts kept them, in after days, in an almost continual scene of bloody strife.

Soon after the peace of 1559, before noted, "the violent and bigoted maxims of Philip's government being carried into execution in the Netherlands, with unrelenting rigor, by the duke of Alva, the people there became exasperated to such a degree, that they threw off the Spanish yoke, and asserted their ancient liberties and laws. These they defended with a persevering valor; which gave employment to the arms of Spain, during *half a century;* and exhausted the vigor, and ruined the reputation of that monarchy." The Netherlands thus gained their liberties, and became a respectable Protestant power, after long and dismal scenes of blood. In this bloody contest, the English were engaged with the Dutch against the king of Spain; and aided the former in the establishment of their independence. Spain and England had before fallen out. Philip had been the husband of the English queen

Mary. Upon her decease, and the accession of Elizabeth to the crown of Britain, Philip tendered marriage to Elizabeth. And upon receiving a denial, (Elizabeth determining to support the Protestant cause in England, which Mary had labored to destroy,) Philip, a bigoted supporter of Popery, fitted out a most formidable expedition against Elizabeth. He employed the immense wealth which flowed into his coffers from Mexico and Peru, in preparing a fleet of the largest ships, which ever had been built; and with the terrible Armada he undertook a descent upon England. Lord admiral Howe met his fleet; engaged and dispersed the ships; and after chasing them several days, a tempest plunged in the ocean the most of those which were left; so that but few regained a harbor. Eighty one Spanish ships were lost in this catastrophe; and many thousands of their men. The British fleet in their turn attacked Spain; took and plundered Cadiz; and took and destroyed property to the amount of 20 millions of ducats.*

Portugal had been united to the kingdoms of Spain. But being oppressed by viceroys, they rebelled against the crown of Spain, which, after the reign of Philip, fell into the hands of weak princes. Portugal placed the duke of Braganza on the throne; and became an independent nation. The Austrian line of Spanish kings failed in the person of Charles II; and the duke of Anjou, grandson of Lewis XIV, mounted the throne, by the name of Philip V. This occasioned a long and bloody struggle between the house of Austria, and Lewis XIV, in which the French monarch was almost ruined. But he accomplished his object, of transferring the kingdom of Spain, with its enormous wealth, from the house of Austria to that of Bourbon. In these wars, and in those of the Low Countries, *Spain* had a copious share in the vial poured upon the rivers and fountains of the Papal see.

France had her full share in this vial. Some of her wars of this period have already been mentioned. In

* Guthrie, pp. 326, 7.

eight successive civil wars in France, from 1560, to
1605, (the last continuing twenty years) it was 'calculated that she lost more than a million of lives; 9 cities,
400 villages, 2,000 churches, 2,000 monasteries, and
10,000 houses were burnt;' and vast sums of property
were expended.† The judgments in which France
was involved, during the reign of Lewis XIV, were
terrible; to write the history of which, would be to
write the history of Europe during that period. The
ambition of this French monarch embroiled him with
all his neighbors; and rendered Germany a dismal
scene of devastation and blood. He wickedly repealed 'the edict of Nantz;‡ and murdered and banished
nearly two millions of his Protestant subjects in one
year. He made treaties; and perfidiously broke them
at pleasure; till he raised against himself a confederacy of most of the European powers, with William,
(prince of Orange, and afterward king of England,) at
their head. Against this formidable coalition, Lewis
for some time prevailed. But the arms of the English
and of Germany (the former under the duke of Marl-
borough, and the latter under prince Eugene) at last
prevailed: And they rendered the latter part of the
reign of this ambitious monarch miserable. From
1702 to 1711, he was tortured and disgraced with a series of defeats and disasters. Places, which he had
formerly acquired, at the expense of many thousands
of lives, he was now forced to yield up to triumphant
enemies. Reduced and old, Lewis was forming the
desperate purpose of collecting his people, and dying at
their head, in a last effort; when the peace of Utrecht
was concluded, in 1713; and the combined armies retired. But in various bloody wars France was afterwards engaged with the house of Austria and others.
Thus the *French* river and fountain of the Papal see
had a dreadful portion of this vial.

† Guthrie, p. 430.
‡ By this edict Henry IV, had granted the Protestants the
free exercise of their religion.

In Germany the wars of this period of the second vial, were terrible. With civil wars, and wars of foreign powers, her fields became fields of blood.* The Turks renewedly invaded Germany. The Hungarians contended with the emperor Randolf; and the Bohemians with his successor Matthias. The Bohemians threw the Imperial commissioners out at the windows at Prague; which brought on a furious war of thirty years. Terrible scenes followed in Germany. Great battles were fought under some of the ablest generals of the age. The Protestant princes had many able generals, who prosecuted their defence with great firmness against the house of Austria. Christian IV, king of Denmark, declared for them. This monarch, at the head of the evangelic league, was defeated by the Imperialists. But the Protestants formed a new confederacy at Leipsic, with the celebrated Gustavus Adolphus, king of Sweden, at their head. The subsequent victories, which attended the Protestant arms, were amazing; till the excellent Gustavus fell at the battle of Lutzen, in 1632. But the brave generals, who had served and learned under him, continued to shake the Austrian power, till the general peace of Munster in 1648. In these scenes, *Germany*, that river and fountain of the Papal see, was turned to blood. Nor did the terrible judgment cease at this time. Wars were rekindled. France and the Turks were again troublesome neighbors. The former took Alsace, and other frontier places of the empire. And the Turks laid siege to Vienna, and had well nigh carried their point; when prince Eugene defeated them. France now threatened to overrun the empire; till the aforementioned confederacy against Lewis XIV checked him. The Hungarians, under protection of the Porte, were in arms. Terrible battles were fought between the Germans and the Turks at Peterwaradin, and at Belgrade; till a peace was concluded between them in 1718. Soon after, a rupture took place between the emperor and George I, king of England.

* See Guthrie, p. 470,—.

"And so unsteady was the system of affairs all over
Europe, at that time, (says Mr. Guthrie,) that the first
powers often changed their old alliances, and concluded
new ones, contrary to their interests." Upon the death
of the emperor Charles VI, 1740, a new blaze of war
broke out, and the pregmatic sanction (so called) a
"concordat of Francis I, which stipulated for the
freedom of the Gallician church" from some of the
usurpations of the Pope, was attacked on all hands.
Spain, France, England, the elector of Bavaria, and
the king of Prussia, (a bigoted Papal kingdom) were
now engaged. The king of Prussia with a powerful
army took Silesia. The French poured their armies
into Bohemia, and took Prague. The Hungarians en-
countered them, and drave them out of Bohemia.
George II gained the battle of Dettingen. The king
of Prussia invaded Bohemia, took Prague, and subdued a great part of the kingdom. Soon after this, the
king of Prussia announced, that he had discovered a
combination between the empress queen, the empress
of Russia, and the king of Poland, (another bigoted
Catholic kingdom) to divide his dominions among them.
Upon which he suddenly attacked the king of Poland,
as elector of Saxony, defeated his armies, drave him out
of his Saxon dominions, and took Dresden. This war
continued in the Low Countries, to the great injury of
the Dutch, and of the Austrians; till the peace of Aix
la Chapelle, in 1748. But the awful judgment of this
vial was not yet finished upon the rivers and fountains
of the Papal see. Soon after, another war blazed in
the empire. The empress queen, the king of France,
the king of Poland, and the empress of Russia were
engaged on one side: And the king of Prussia, and
George II, king of England, on the other. The king
of Prussia broke again into Saxony; defeated the Saxons under general Brown; and caused the king of Poland to flee. Upon this the French and the Russians
poured their armies into Germany, to co-operate against
the king of Prussia. The conduct of the latter was
most astonishing. He rushed, with incredible rapidity, into Bohemia, in order to defeat the Austrian ar-

my, before the combined armies of his enemies should
form a junction; which he accomplished. He defeated
100,000 Austrians; and killed their valiant general
Brown. He besieged Prague. with a tremendous artillery; but was soon after defeated. The war now
raged with increasing fury. The Prussians gained the
battle of Lissa; took Breslau, and other places. The
Russian army advanced to aid the Austrians. They
too were at first defeated. But the king of Prussia
was soon after defeated, and forced to flee from Saxony.
"Few periods of history (says the historian) afford such
matter for reflection, as did this campaign. Six sieges
were raised almost at the same time." Important
events were also transpiring in other places between
the armies of the contending powers. The French
were by the English driven out of Hanover. And Mr.
Guthrie remarks upon the operations on both sides,
that although they were terrible and bloody, they were
"of little importance to history, because nothing was
done, that was decisive." Those events appear to have
been a mere *dashing* among the nations, to execute the
judgments of the third vial. The Russians had taken
possession of the kingdom of Prussia; and had laid
siege to Colberg, the only Prussian port on the Baltic.
And a Russian army of 100,000 men were advancing
to Silesia. In this distress the king of Prussia met them
with desperate fury; but was defeated, with the loss of
20,000 of his men, in the battle near Frankfort. Succeeding defeats seemed to announce his total ruin.
He had lost his great marshal Keith, and 40 brave
generals, beside many wounded and made prisoners.
At Landshut also, his army, on which he had placed
great dependence, was defeated; and thus an avenue
was opened to the Austrians into his favorite Silesia.
It seems as though any general, excepting the king of
Prussia, must in such a situation have given up all for
lost! Berlin his capital was taken, and laid under trib-
ute. But this veteran hero collected his shattered
troops, and gave the Imperialists a defeat at Torgau;
it cost him, however, ten thousand of the flower of his
troops; while he occasioned dreadful carnage to his

enemies. New armies from Russia pressed upon him. Colberg had been taken by the Russians; and Schweidnitz was taken by the Austrians. And his affairs began to appear desperate; when the empress of Russia died; and George III had come to the crown of England. A peace ensued. The combined armies of his enemies were recalled. The German princes, unwilling to annihilate the house of Bradenburg, thus ceased from any further operations. Did not these events amount to a *vial of Divine wrath* on those Papal nations? And do they not perfectly accord with the description of the *third vial?*

England, having been a Papal nation, and defiled in some degree with the blood of the saints, was involved, more or less, in almost all these wars, from the opening of the period of this vial. And the British nation was not destitute of events *at home*, in which some part of her portion of this vial was fulfilled. Mary, queen of Scotland, having assumed the title of the queen of England, was a source of mischief between the English and the Scots, in the days of Elizabeth. The gunpowder plot, in the reign of James I, indicates the perils of those times. Charles I had a turbulent reign; till a civil war broke out. His two ministers, Stafford and Laud, were beheaded. He was hated by his subjects. A rebellion broke out in Ireland, and the massacre of two or three hundred thousand of the Protestants took place there. Charles demanded, in the house of commons, that five of his ministers should be apprehended. This was pronounced high treason against the people. The militia *in*, and *about* London, flew to arms. The king raised an army; the parliament another. The Scots joined the latter. Battles were fought. The independent party arose, with Cromwell at their head. After several battles the king was defeated. Great numbers were killed. The royal interest was lost; and Charles was beheaded. Both the royalists and the Presbyterians hated Cromwell; yet they employed him in the reduction of Ireland, and against the Scots, whom he totally defeated. Cromwell was made generalissimo of the English armies against the Dutch; whom in several battles he defeated. He usurped authority to dissolve the parliament; and to annihilate the council of state; and got himself declared *Lord protector of the commonwealth of England.* But he died in 1658, after an usurpation of nearly five years. Seven bloody battles were fought with the Dutch at sea, in this interregnum. And it was a period of *judgment.* Charles II came to the throne. New troubles arose, not only in a war with Holland, but in commotions at home. Charles II was a base devotee to the court of France. His parliament remonstrated; but in vain.

A judgment of the most terrible kind now fell upon the capital of the English nation. The plague broke out in London, and swept off a great portion of the inhabitants.

It broke out about the beginning of the year 1665, and continued till the next September. As the account of this plague is in many hands, it is not necessary to enter upon a minute description of it. Few calamities, even of that dreadful kind, have surpassed it in circumstances of terror and dismay.*

In a little short of a year, after the plague, or on Sept. 2, 1666, the *dreadful fire* broke out in London, and destroyed the habitations, as the plague had done the inhabitants, of a considerable part of that vast city.

* Possibly the following hint may be worthy of notice, as connected with the plague in London. It has been observed that the 16th century, while it opened a new era of blessings to the cause of Christ, opened also a new era of judgments upon the enemies of the Church. As a small item of this, it is ascertained in medical sketches, that the petechial or spotted fever, (a species of the plague) made its first appearance in Europe, in the beginning of the 16th century. "The first particular account that we have of the petechial (spotted) fever, is by Fracastor, who says, it infested Italy in 1505 and in 1528." Burserius in his chap. x, says, "Since the beginning of the 16th century, the petechial disease has been universally known in Italy, and the whole of Europe." Within several years this terrific disease has made its appearance in New England. To what degree it may prevail, or how far it may be among the means of the desolating judgments of the last days, the event alone will decide.

The following is the inscription on the monument erected in commemoration of this dismal catastrophe: "In the year of Christ 1666, Sept. 2, eastward from hence, at the distance of 202 feet, (the heighth of this column,) a terrible fire broke out about midnight; which, driven by a high wind, not only wasted the adjacent parts, but also very remote places, with incredible crackling and fury. It consumed 89 churches, the city gates, Guildhall, many public structures, hospitals, schools, libraries, a vast number of stately edifices, 13,000 dwelling houses, and 400 streets. Of the 26 wards it utterly destroyed 15; and left 8 others, shattered and half burnt. The ruins of the city were 436 acres, from the Tower, by the Thames side, to the Temple Church; and from the northeast, along the wall by the Holborn bridge. To the estates and fortunes of the citizens, it was merciless; to their lives very favorable; that it might resemble the last conflagration of the world. The destruction was sudden; for in a small space of time the city was seen most flourishing, and reduced to nothing. Three days after it commenced, when this fatal fire had, in the opinion of all, baffled all human counsel and endeavors, it stopped as it were by a command from Heaven, and was on every side extinguished."

This was the city, in which queen Mary had burnt and destroyed many Protestants; and was the capital of a nation which had been one of the rivers and fountains of the Papal see.

James II succeeded Charles II. A rebellion broke out, headed by the duke of Monmouth, who assumed the title of *king*, as being the son of Charles II. He was subdued, and beheaded. James now made an impious attempt to re-establish Popery. He pretended to have power to dispense with laws. He instituted an illegal ecclesiastical court; admitted the Pope's emissaries; and made alarming encroachments on the civil and religious liberties of England. The people were in consternation. Lewis XIV was threatening Europe with his despotic sway. The first characters in England and Scotland sent to William, prince of Orange then in Holland, who had married Mary, eldest daughter of James, (William and Mary being Protestants) to come and take the British crown. He embarked with a fleet and army for England, with the avowed design of restoring to the church and state their rights; which he accordingly did. Here was the noted English *revolution*, so favorable to the Protestant cause. In these events; in the struggles of the *pretender;* and in similar events; as well as in the bloody wars in coalition with other nations, already briefly mentioned, *Britain* had her portion of the vial of wrath upon the rivers and fountains of the Papal see.

The parts which Sweden, Denmark, Prussia, and Poland, shared in the judgments of this vial, have already been partially noted; as these nations were engaged in several of the wars which have been described as raging in Christendom. All these nations *had been,* and some of them *still were* among the Papal rivers and fountains of water. And they had their parts under this vial, of being *turned to blood.* Should we trace their internal histories of that period, together with their bloody connexions with other nations, the truth of this remark would appear.

I must beg the reader's patience, while I make a few remarks more particularly relative to *Poland.* This was a bigoted Roman Catholic country. The reformation made some advances there. And after long struggles, the Protestant cause was legally established by the treaty of Oliva, in 1660; and guaranteed by the principal powers of Europe. But the Poles afterward, disregarding the above treaty, and instigated by the most flagitious Catholic clergy, made a public massacre of the Protestants, under the sanction of law. And it may be instructive to trace, more particularly, *their part* in the judgments, which we are contemplating.

The Poles, soon after the commencement of the period of this vial, had a long and bloody war with Russia and Sweden; and were defeated in their designs. They were "afterward engaged in a variety of unsuc-

52

cessful wars with the Turks and Swedes."* And afterward with the Turks and Russians. A terrible civil
war followed* between the king and the Cossacs, a
hardy race of people upon the frontiers of Poland.
The king treated them perfidiously. And the brave
Cossacs defeated the Poles in two great battles. Soon
after, the Russians again came to a rupture with the
Poles. And they and the Cossacs took Smolensko,
Wilna, and other places, and "committed the most
horrid ravages in Lithuania." The next year Charles
of Sweden overran the great and little Poland, with
dreadful slaughter. Soon afterwards the Poles, aided
by the Tartars, cut the Swedes in pieces. The subsequent tumultuous state of Poland induced Casimir,
their king, to abdicate the throne, and retire to France.
This occasioned a new tempest of rivalship and contention. The weak Michael Wiesnowiski was chosen
king. The Cossacs put themselves under the protection of the Turks, who attacked and "conquered all
the provinces of Podalia; and took Caminiack, till then
deemed impregnable." The greatest part of Poland
was now ravaged; and the Poles became tributary to
the Turks. A train of wars with the Turks now succeeded. Upon the death of Sobieski, new scenes of
distraction occurred. Different confederacies were
now formed. The crown was put up for sale. Conti
of France was the highest bidder. But Augustus of
Saxony, after a kind of sham election, took possession
of Cracow, with a Saxon army, and was crowned king.
A contention between him and Conti ensued. Augustus was afterward driven from the throne by
Charles of Sweden; but was restored again by Peter
of Russia. The Poles perpetually formed plots against
Augustus; and he supported his authority only by
means of his Saxon armies. Upon his death a war
broke out between his son Augustus, and the French
king, who determined to place Stanislaus, his father in
law, upon the Polish throne. The Poles were divided. Augustus with a powerful army obliged his rival

* Guthrie p. 409.

to retreat, and to flee to France. Augustus died; and in the succeeding reign Poland presented a scene of desolation. To add to the miseries of this devoted kingdom, a scene of new disturbances broke out. An attempt was made to establish a principle of religious toleration and equality between the Catholics and Protestants. Upon this the whole nation ran into confederacies, and formed distinct provinces. The Popish clergy raged against religious equality. And the unhappy "country became the theatre of the most complicated wars, partly civil, partly religious, and partly foreign." Some years were filled with blood and devastation; and the country was almost destroyed. Many of the first families fled to foreign lands, and for ever abandoned their native soil. Warsaw the capital had well nigh exhibited a scene of plunder and total massacre. The plague at the same time broke out and carried off 250,000 of the people. Attempts were made to assassinate the king. And, to complete the ruin of Poland, it soon after appeared, that the empress of Russia, the king of Prussia, and the empress queen, had entered into a secret alliance to dismember the kingdom, and to unite it to their own dominions. They agreed upon the portion which each should receive. And they forced the Poles to call a diet, to cede those portions of the kingdom, according to the partition, under penalty that the whole nation should be exposed to military execution, as a conquered people. Some of the Popish nobility protested against this violent tyranny, and fled to other nations. But the king was obliged to sign the treaty, and was followed by his remaining nobility: And thus Poland was erased from the list of independent kingdoms. The oppressions which followed from the king of Prussia, were unprecedented in any civilized nation. Twelve thousand families, in a single year, were torn by him from one province, to people his other dominions. And every town and village were forced to furnish a given number of marriageable females; and with each one a considerable dower, in order to furnish wives for the peasants in distant regions of Prussia. And some of these poor young females were bound hand and foot, and carried off as criminals. And the sums of money otherwise robbed from the Poles, by order of the king of Prussia, were incalculable. These violent proceedings against the Poles, are said to have reduced them in a few years, from fourteen, to nine millions of inhabitants. Thus the *Polish river* and fountain of the Papal see had a full share of the third vial.

Thus I have noted some instances of judgments on Papal nations, in which I apprehend the events of the third vial to have been accomplished. These events constituted a new period of judgments. And they were *long* and *dreadful.* They had not been equalled by any preceding events in those nations. And though their commencement marked a new era, from that of the preceding wars in Italy; yet they were but an *extending abroad* of the same *kind* of judgments; as is purported in the third vial, as related to the second.

The violent dismemberment of Poland was the first capital violation of the modern political system of Europe, or of the law of nations. And the astonishing indifference with which it was beheld, in the courts of Europe, forcibly indicated their fatigues in war, and their imbecility to support their own national principles. All which implies the terribleness of the judgments of war, which they had experienced. Other instances of judgments collateral with, and subsequent to, those noted, might be mentioned. But enough has been said. I apprehend it may be found, that the terrors and severity of those judgments on the Papal nations, were in a sriking proportion to the malignity of their Papal wickedness; and that in them the third vial was accomplished.

THE FOURTH VIAL.

And the fourth angel poured out his vial upon the sun; and power was given unto him to scorch men with fire. And men were scorched with great heat, and blasphemed the name of God, who · had power over these plagues; and they repented not to give him glory. (Rev. xvi, 8, 9.)

"THE sun, (says Sir Isaac Newton) is put in sacred prophecy for the whole species and race of kings, · in the kingdoms of the · world politic." No one doubts but the sun is a · prophetic emblem of *civil authority.* The darkening of the sun is an emblem of the weakening or confounding of civil authority. And the sun's scorching men with fire in this vial, must be designed to represent the producing of some effects, by the civil authorities of Christendom, *fatally injurious* to the interests of the Papal see. And history furnishes events which fully accord with this representation.

Through the dark ages, how fully did the Papal harlot *reign over the kings of the earth?* Such was the influence which the Pope held over the kings of Christendom, that he must be at the head of all their affairs, alliances, and pacifications. Nothing was binding without his sanction. And he gloried that he could depose kings at pleasure. He could dispense with the obligations of the most solemn treaties; could absolve subjects from their oaths of allegiance to their kings; and claimed power to settle, and unhinge the affairs of nations at his nod. "The canonists asserted, that there was no sovereign · power, but in the Pope. And that the Popes have repeatedly maintained, that all regal authority was derived from them. Boniface the eighth, wrote to Philip the Fair, *We will have thee know, that thou art subject to us, both in temporals, and in spirituals.*" Bishop Newton, on Rev. xiii, informs, that the Pope was "the head of the state, as well as of the church; the king of kings; as well as bishop of bishops." · One bishop in the council of Lateran, styled the Pope, "the prince of the world." Another orator styled him, "king of kings, and monarch of the world;" Another prelate said of him, *that he had all power above all powers, both of heaven and earth.* Pope Innocent boasted of the church, as his *spouse,* who brings to him her *dowry* of absolute power, in spirituals, and in *temporals:*—That she brings him his mitre, as priest; and his crown, as king; and constitutes him *his* vicar, who is King of kings, and Lord of lords.

But did this Papal *supremacy continue*, after the events, which have been contemplated, as fulfilling the former vials? How far otherwise was the fact! All the Protestant powers cast off the Papal yoke by *civil authority*. England, Denmark, Sweden, Holland, a great part of the princes of Germany, and other places, established the Protestant cause by law; and stood ready, with all their *civil power and arms*, to support it. Even in France, Henry IV, by his edict of Nantz interposed the authority of his crown to give free toleration to the Protestants. Truly the Pope and the men of the Papal Beast felt a most distressing scorching upon their cause, from the sun of civil authority, even those very authorities which had before shone with kind influence upon them. The Protestant powers took the most direct steps, and did as much as they were able to do, to scorch, dry up, and annihilate, the Papal interest. And in those kingdoms and states, which yet professed the Papal religion, even *their* civil governments lost much of their genial influence in favor of the Pope's supremacy, and the dignity of his clergy. They gradually lost that superstitious veneration for the Papal see; which for many centuries had been uniformly maintained. The Papal kings at first trembled at the idea of any rupture with the Pope. When they, by his perfidy, were forced to carry on war against him, it was with extreme reluctance and hesitation. And they would seize the first opportunity of making peace with him, though much to their own disadvantage. But as the events of the preceding vials progressed, this superstition abated. The Protestant powers despised and renounced the Romish Pontiff; and even the Catholic princes became well able to treat his holiness, especially in their secular concerns, with much neglect. The sun of civil authority in Europe became too hot for the creatures of his order, which had been hatched and fostered in the dark. When it came to shine in upon them, it dried and burnt them up.

Guthrie remarks, (Geog. p. 565,) "I shall not here enter into a detail of the ignorance of the laity, and the other causes, that operated to the aggrandizement of the Papacy, previous to the reformation. Ever since that era, the state of Europe has been such, that the Popes have had, more than once, great weight in its public affairs; chiefly through the weakness and bigotry of temporal princes; *who seem now to be recovering from their religious delusion.* The Papal power is evidently now at a low ebb. The Pope himself is treated by the Roman catholic princes, with very little more ceremony, than is due to him as bishop of Rome, and possessed of a temporal principality. This humiliation, it is reasonable to believe, will terminate in a total separation from the holy see of all its foreign emoluments; which even since the commencement of the 18th century, were immense."

This drying up of the sources of the Papal wealth and power is a natural and necessary consequence of that *scorching*, from the political sun in Europe, denounced in the fourth vial. And the *time*, in which the noted author, in the above quotation, mentions the severe effects against the Papal influence, resulting from the recovery of civil princes from their religious delusions; exactly accords with the effects of the fourth vial, according to the scheme of the vials in this chapter.

The revenues of the Pope, in his highest prosperity, were vast; not less than eight millions of dollars annually. (See Morse's Gaz. under *"Pope's Dominions."*) But this vast source of wealth was scorched and dried up, under the rays of the political sun of Europe, to a very great degree.

The failure of the Pope's revenues indeed *commenced* before the effusion of the fourth vial. As soon as Henry VIII, king of England, had renounced the Papal supremacy, considerable sums were saved to that nation, of which it had been annually drained, for dispensations, indulgences, pilgrimages, annates, first fruits, and other taxes, which a covetous, intriguing Papal court had found means to levy upon the credulity of mankind.

But it was under the *fourth vial*, that this evil on the Papal see became *extreme* and *fatal*. Then it was, that this infamous traffic and source of power, not only wholly failed in protestant nations, but chiefly failed also in catholic nations. The sun of civil authority, after light arose, powerfully burnt and dried up those streams of Papal wealth, and reduced the Romish see to poverty and meanness; like a scorched part of the earth, dried and burnt under the vertical rays of the sun.

A striking instance of the Judgments of this vial on the Papal power, we find in the subversion of the order of the Jesuits, in the great kingdoms of Europe. To see the force of this remark, let us take a view of *that order.* They were called the Janissaries. They were indeed the *life-guard* of the Romish hierarchy. The Jesuits were instituted in 1540, by Ignatius Loyola, a Spaniard; 23 years after the commencement of the reformation. And we find in them a masterpiece of Satan's policy, to support the then sinking Papal cause. The fertile imagination of Loyola suggested to him such an institution; and he obtained the sanction of the Pope for the establishment of it. The Jesuits came under a vow of monastic obedience, and of undertaking, in behalf of the Papal interest, in any service directed by their general, without any reward from the Papal see. Loyola was commissioned their first general. They were trained for, and admitted to this order with amazing art. Their constitution and laws were revised and perfected by Laynez and Aquaviva; two most able and subtile generals, who succeeded Loyola. Their object was to gain a decided influence in the *courts* of Europe; and so to manage the civil affairs in the nations, as to support the Papal see. The other orders of monks were devoted to mortification and seclusion from the world. But the Jesuits were designed for *activity* in all things, which might tend to the support of Popery. They studied human nature, and the dispositions of rulers. They flattered the great; and became prodigies of intrigue and of enterprize. In less than half a century they were, established in every Catholic country. And their numbers, wealth and influence became vast, and made rapid progress. They were "celebrated by the friends, and dreaded by the enemies of the Romish faith."* Their government was purely monarchical; consisting of a general, chosen for life by deputies from the Jesuits in the different nations. His power was supreme and independent. He appointed his provincials, rectors, and every officer; and employed and removed them at pleasure. The revenues and funds of the order he held in his hands. Under this direction every member of the vast community was passive, as clay in the hands of the potter. They were taught to be incapable of resistance to their general, as they would be to their Maker. The profound subtilty of their system, for learning the dispositions of their members, and of mankind, and for holding the perfect control of their order, exceeds all that was ever known among men; excepting the more modern system of Illuminism, which appears to have been copied from it, with improvements. The general of the Jesuits (according to M. de Chalotais) was furnished annually with 6584 registers and reports from his 37 provinces through the kingdoms; beside numberless letters from spies. In these communications all the affairs of their order, and of the states and nations of Christendom, were ascertained. All was done in cyphers invented for the purpose; so as to defy detection. The general could thus see at once what needed to be done; and who were the proper instruments of doing it; and his orders were remitted accordingly, and with the most irresistible effect. To manage the education of youth, was a prime object with the Jesuits. They aimed at the control of all instruction and religion. They preached much. They sent their missionaries every where. And they found numerous admirers and patrons. They in fact obtained the chief direction of the means of education in every Catholic country. They

* Hist, Ch. V, vol. iv, p. 191.

became the confessors and controllers of kings; and the spiritual guides of almost all people of rank. And they "possessed in the highest degree the confidence and interest of the court of Rome, as the most zealous and able champions of its authority."* And finally, "they possessed the direction of the most considerable courts in Europe." "They took part in every intrigue and revolution;" and managed all things to their mind with amazing efficacy. They formed vast possessions in every Catholic country. The numbers and magnificence of their public buildings, were immense. They obtained license from the Pope to trade wherever they resided. And they were engaged in an extensive and lucrative commerce, both in the East and West Indies. They opened warehouses in different parts of Europe; vied with commercial societies in obtaining settlements; and they obtained vast fertile provinces in Paraguay in South America; and reigned *there* as sovereign princes, over some hundreds of thousands of subjects. Their influence among men became *vast*. And their attachment to their order and object was *inviolable*. Their professions were such as to steal upon the confidence of the Catholic multitudes; while yet their morality was pliant, and suited to the passions of every person, upon whom they wished to operate. Their object was, imperceptibly to restore the Papal prerogatives of the dark ages, or heal and support that wounded cause. Many of the Jesuits were most learned. They produced more works of genius than all the other Catholic orders. They claimed it as their prerogative to combat the Protestants: And they labored to excite against them all the rage of civil and ecclesiastical power. They were the authors (says Dr. Robertson) of "most of the pernicious effects arising from that corrupt and dangerous *casuistry* of the times; from those extraordinary tenets concerning ecclesiastical power, and from the intolerant spirit, which has been the disgrace of the church of Rome throughout that period; and which have brought so many calamities upon civil society." Moshiem observes of the Jesuits, that they were "the very soul of the hierarchy,

* Hist. Ch. V, vol. iv, p. 198.

the engines of the state, the secret springs of the motion of the one, and of the other; and the authors and directors of every great and important event, both in the religious and political world." (Vol. iii, p. 195.)

For two centuries Europe beheld this powerful order, and felt its dismal effects: But not having discovered the deep internal policy of the system, they knew not to what to impute its amazing success. The internal policy of the order was designed to be kept concealed in impenetrable mystery. They refused even in courts of justice to expose it; and they were long connived at in this particular.

But this mysterious system was at length developed; which excited *disgust* and *alarm*. And the Jesuits having been found guilty of many dangerous intrigues, and even *assassinations* of monarchs, and statesmen; the civil authorities of Europe were awakened; and the order was suppressed. And the suppression of them in France, Spain, Portugal, Naples, and other nations; the shutting up of their schools, the confiscation of their revenues, and the banishing of them from these kingdoms, operated as a deadly stroke toward the ruin of the Papal see. Dr. Langdon, on the Revelation, (page 229) viewed this event as an effectual step, taken by the European governments, toward the overthrow of the Papal interest. He says, "The banishment of the Jesuits from all the nations of Europe, and the dissolution of the order, as guilty of treasons, rebellions, and assassinations of monarchs, *is the most remarkable event in Providence.*" Dr. Trumbull, in his sermon at the close of the 18th century, remarks, "In the last half century the order of the Jesuits, who constituted the most deceitful, intriguing, and formidable branch of the Romish hierarchy, were abolished. They made rapid and astonishing progress through all the Roman Catholic countries, till they were supressed in 1773."*

Events so great, and so fatal to Popery, as the parts, which the civil goverments of Christendom thus act-

---

* No doubt the more modern system of Illuminism was copied from that of the Jesuits; the great affinity between the two systems, warrants the conclusion.

ed, in throwing off their superstitious veneration for the
Papal authority, many of them protecting the Protestant cause, and abolishing the rites of Popery; and even
the others despising the arrogant pretensions of the
Roman Pontiff; and at last determinately abolishing
the order of the Jesuits, on whom the Papal see was
making its chief dependence, *must be viewed* as having
a place among the essential steps taken in Providence
toward the ruin of the Papal cause. The connexion
of this conduct of the civil European governments with
the events of the three vials already noted, seems to
give it a claim to be reckoned as the fourth vial. And
the nature of the event appears fully to accord with the
symbolic representation, of *power being given to the
sun to scorch men* (the men of the Papal interest) *with
his fire and great heat.*

And the events, which in fact have followed those
effects of the political sun, in the great nations of Europe, have been just such, as were predicted under this
vial;—*And men blasphemed the name of God, who had
power over these plagues; and they repented not to give
him glory.* Most completely have the impenitence and
blasphemy, here foretold, been fulfilled in the greatest
Catholic nations, in the scheme of Illuminism, or the
Voltaire system of Infidelity; which, at this very time,
went into operation. So far were those nations from
repenting, and giving glory to God, under those plagues;
that they *blasphemed his name,* by adopting another
latent system of darkness, which aimed at the total subversion of all religion, and of the belief of the being of
God. We read nothing, in the vials, of men's *blasphem-
ing* the name of God, till the close of the fourth vial.
And we find in fact no systematic attempt to introduce
Atheism, till just at the close of the fourth vial, as just
explained. And then we do find such an attempt in
fatal operation. This furnishes an argument in favor
of the explanation given of the fourth vial. It can be
no objection to the view given of this vial, that it began its operation before the effects of the third vial, on
the rivers and fountains of water, had ceased. Let
me here repeat the remark, before noted, of a celebrated

author; "It is no where said, that each vial is emptied before its successor begins to be poured out. Hence it is not unreasonable to conclude, that two or more of the vials may be poured out at the same time; though the effusion of one commences, before that of the other." As the two first vials were of a nature to be partially collateral; so were the third and fourth.

Should any suggest, that events in France under the tyranny of Bonaparte, may seem strikingly to fulfil the judgment of the fourth vial; I answer; those events may also strikingly fulfil *another* vial, as may appear. And it must be incorrect to construe one event in the place of another, on account of a coincidence in *some point.* Many a tyrant has scorched his subjects with the fire of his lawless despotism. But all such events cannot, on this account, be viewed as the fulfilment of the *fourth vial.*

THE FIFTH VIAL.

And the fifth angel poured out his vial upon the seat of the beast; and his kingdom was full of darkness; and they gnawed their tongues for pain, and blasphemed the God of heaven, because of their pains and their sores, and repented not of their deeds. (Rev. xvi, 10, 11.

THE last capital scene of the fourth vial was some time after the middle of the 18th century. And it was to have this effect, as we have seen, to cause the men, who had the mark of the Beast, to blaspheme God, and to persevere in their impenitence. This might be expected soon to bring on the events of the fifth vial, in the utter destruction of the *Papal Beast.* The Beast; on whose seat (throne) this vial is discharged, must be the *Papal.* For he is the great power, on which all the preceding vials were poured out. He was the enemy, with which the Church of Christ had the most immediate concern; and therefore was first to be attacked and destroyed. The preceding vials were preparing the way for his *ruin.* The fifth completes his

ruin as a Beast, or predominant Power. The Papacy
was the *only* Beast on the Roman earth, till the Antichristian Beast arose. The Beast in the fifth vial therefore, must have been the *Papal Beast.* Whether his
seat (throne) and kingdom mean his temporal principality; or his influence in Papal delusion, or both;
may be a question. *Both* in fact were to be subverted.
Accordingly in the year 1789, sixteen years after the
last most signal event of the fourth vial, in the subversion of the order of the. Jesuits, the revolution
in France commenced. This opened a new and most
interesting era, and did in its progress overturn the
throne of the Papal Beast, in both the senses afore
hinted. It has filled the Papal kingdom with gross
darkness; and has exhibited scenes probably the most
terrific and bloody, which ever blackened the historic
page. The rise of Antichrist will be found, I apprehend, to have opened the scene of the *fifth vial.* The
events of the four preceding vials greatly perplexed the
Papal Beast. But they were not to subvert his throne,
nor fill his kingdom with darkness. He still had light;
hoped to continue his existence; yea, hoped to regain
something of his former glory. But the fifth vial was
to overturn his seat; and for the first time to fill his
kingdom with darkness! And the French revolution
has *done both,* in relation to the Papal see.

No light, no rational hope of a restoration remained
to the Pope. His clergy in France were destroyed.
His dominions in Italy were overrun. His authority,
and the Christian religion itself, were rejected. The
person of "the Pope was seized. He was divested of
his temporal dominions; restricted to a certain pension;
and exiled from his royal city." The events, which
have followed, are so well known to the people of this
generation, and the impressions made by them are so
deep, that they need not here be recited. The Papal
power has ceased to be a Beast; having fallen wholly
under the power of the *Antichristian Beast,* newly risen.
The remains of the Papal power (now, and henceforth,
till he shall be utterly destroyed with the Antichristian
Beast) constitute the *false prophet,* under the power

and management, of the Roman Beast, under his last, and newly *healed* head. He may now be viewed as the *tail* of this Beast. The governing power, he is the head; "and the prophet that teacheth lies, he is the tail." Isa. ix, 15.

The evidence, that the rise of Antichrist in France opened the period of the fifth vial, with awful precision, I cannot but conceive to be more clear, than what usually attends the fulfilment of ancient prophecies. In addition to the evidence arising from its *period*, in connexion with the preceding vials, the evidence arising from the *events*, in view of the prophetic description of the fifth vial, seems to be conclusive. Until the fifth vial, the Papal Beast had a *throne* and a *kingdom.* After it, he has *none!* For the fifth vial is poured upon his throne; which must indicate its *subversion.* Consequently, his kingdom is filled with darkness. And till the rise of Antichrist in France, the Papal power may be said to have had a *throne* and a *kingdom.* Now he has *neither.* His throne, is destroyed; and his kingdom is filled with darkness. Few, fulfilments of prophecy were ever capable of equal demonstration. And have not the consequent blasphemies and events, predicted in this vial, been fulfilled? The people of the Papal earth may well be said to have *gnawed their tongues for pain.* They have indeed languished under their pains and their sores. Their judgments have *been*, and *are* awful. How abundant have been their atheistical blasphemies! and how obdurate their impenitence!

Since the printing of the first edition of this dissertation, I have found it to be a question, in some writers, whether all seven of the vials have not an exclusive appropriation to the destruction of the Antichristian Beast, or the last head of the secular Roman Beast? They have doubted whether *any* of the vials were to be executed on the Papal Beast: Or whether it be the Papal Beast, that is mentioned in Rev. xvi, 2, 10, on which the five first vials are executed. A piece was hence inserted in the Panoplist, for October, 1811; or vol. iv, (New Series,) page 193, in which it is thought to be shown, that the Beast on which the five first vials are executed, Rev. (xvi, 1—11,) is *most clearly the Papal Beast.* Any, who entertain a doubt upon this subject, are referred to that piece in the Panoplist.

Some have expressed an opinion, on the other hand, and according to the old scheme of the vials, that the late tremendous scenes of judgment in Europe were the commencement of the seventh vial on the Papacy; all the vials having been exclusively appropriated to that corrupt power; and the vials having been running for, a great course of centuries.

Diffidence and caution become writers upon this subject. For it is involved in some mystery. And the greatest and best of men have, in relation to it, had their different opinions. I shall here adduce arguments to show the *great probability,* that the vast events of modern date, or since the French revolution, are not in fulfilment of the *seventh,* but of the *fifth* vial. At the time of writing the first edition of this work, I thought the truth of this opinion was so evident, that but *little* was said upon this vial. I shall now say considerable *more,* to evince the truth of this opinion.

Perhaps the time has not yet arrived for the great events of the last days, predicted by Daniel and John, to be correctly understood. If so, all conjectures concerning them will be found to be premature. Daniel, after he had predicted the great infidel Power of the last days, in chapter xi, and in the first of chapter xii, and had spoken of the time of trouble in those days, pleads for *further information* upon the subject. He receives the following reply; "Go thy way, Daniel; for the words are *closed up* and *sealed, till* the time of the end." It seems to be here *decided,* that the great peculiarities, relative to this terrible Power of the last days, were *not* to be understood, till the time of the end; or till the events were transpiring before the eyes of men. I do not recollect, that any such intimation was ever given, relative to other events of prophecy. *They might* be understood before their fulfilment. But *this* event should *not* be understood, till it *opened* upon the world. *The words were "closed up and sealed, till.*

the time of the end." If the *present* period may not be considered the *time of the end*, then it is in *vain* to conjecture what may be the sense of the prophecy. For we are divinely assured, that it shall not be known, till the time of the end. But these words to Daniel imply, that the sense of the prophecy *may*, at the time of the end, or as the event is unfolding, be known.

John is the best interpreter of Daniel. The most important prophecies of Daniel are noted and enlarged upon, in the Revelation. Should we find the sense of the above passage in Dan. xii, 9, noted in the Revelation, we should have further light upon the subject. This, I conceive, is the case, in Rev. xth. In chapter ixth, the first and second wo-trumpets are described. In chapter xth, instead of going on, to describe the third wo, as would seem natural, and as is done in the xith chapter; we have information of a signal *intervening* event, attended with an express caution not to believe this to be the seventh trumpet; for *that* is then still future. And we there find the *very idea*, of the *sealing up* of the import of the prophecy, (till it should open upon the world,) in the sealing up of the seven thunders. As I conceive this tenth of Revelation to throw light upon some of the last parts of Daniel's prophecy; that it predicts the events of modern date, which have astonished the world; and is a description of the events of the fifth vial;—I shall comment upon the chapter, in order to make this appear, and to compare it with parallel prophecies.

"And I saw another mighty angel come down from heaven." Some great event, after the sixth trumpet in the fourteenth and fifteenth centuries, and before the seventh trumpet (which in verse 7 is declared to be still future) is here indicated. The Angel is a *mighty* Angel. And he is *another* Angel *beside* and *after* the one, who had sounded the sixth trumpet. He is *"clothed with a cloud."* The several comings of Christ are in clouds. *"Behold he cometh in clouds." "The Lord rideth on a cloud." "Clouds and darkness are round about him."* This Angel has "a rainbow upon his head." The rainbow is an emblem of God's cove-

54

nant faithfulness., The great events, to be accomplished by this Angel, were in *faithful fulfilment of God's
word.* "*And his face was as it were the sun; and his
feet as pillars of fire.*" We here find, as we may believe, a *most signal descent* of Christ, the adorable Angel of the covenant; though not his great *coming* in
the third wo; as he himself by and by decides. "*And
he had in his hand a little book open.*" So great is the
event, about to be accomplished, that a *little book* is
appropriated to it; indicating, that it is going to form
a distinct history, or open a new era, in the affairs of
men. The book being *open* may suggest, that at the
fulfilling of the event, the time has arrived for it to be
understood. The Angel "*sets his right foot upon the
sea, and his left foot upon the earth.*" He is Lord of
earth and sea. And the sea, as well as earth, is now
going to be the theatre of astonishing events; as is said
in chapter xii, 12, upon the same period; "Wo to the
inhabiters of the *earth,* and of the *sea;* for the devil is
come down unto you having great wrath." This Angel, "*cried with a loud voice, as when a lion roareth.*"
When God (in prophetic language) *cries* with a loud
voice, the indication is *dreadful:* As God says by the
prophet; *These things hast thou done, and I kept
silence.—Now will I cry like a travailing woman; I
will destroy and devour at once.* "*And when he had
cried, seven thunders uttered their voices.*" Thunder
is a prophetic emblem of *war.* (Isai. xxix, 6.) The
number *seven* is, in this book, a number of *perfection.*
Here we read of the seven Spirits of God: The seven
seals: And various other septenaries.—Seven shocks
of thunder, striking at once, afford a perfect emblem of
an unprecedented scene of wars; such as must attend
the rise and progress of Daniel's wilful king. These
seven thunders were made to communicate to John
some intimation of their import. This intimation John
was about to write. But a voice from heaven forbid:
"*Seal up those things, which the seven thunders uttered, and write them not.*" Here is the same idea,
with that to Daniel, relative to the same event, the period of the reign of the wilful king: "The words are

closed up and sealed, till the time of the end:", †In both the passages, the particular things imported should not be known in the Church, till their commencement should *alarm the world:* John's being directed to seal up the things, which the thunders had uttered, does not intimate, that they shall *never* in this world be known. The passage being left on sacred record, with other sacred passages, indicates, that attempts ought to be made, (especially after we may suppose the period for the fulfilment has arrived) to learn their true sense. At the time of the end, the prophecy may be expected to be understood.

The angel now lifts up his hand to heaven, and decides with an oath of great formality, that *"the time shall not be yet;"* (as literally in the original;) *"but in the days of the seventh angel, when he shall begin to sound, the mystery of God shall be finished; as he hath declared to his servants the prophets."* The same thing we find in the corresponding passage, Dan. xii, 7. There, standing upon the waters, the sacred Messenger, with hands lifted to heaven, *swears by Him who liveth forever and ever, that it* (the period of those wonders, or of the wilful king) *shall be for a time, times, and an half.* This shows the sense of the corresponding passage in the Revelation; or of the oath, that the *time shall not be yet.* The 1260 years (at the time of the seven thunders uttering their voices) are *not quite expired.* The third woe, which will finish the 1260 years, and destroy Antichrist, is then yet future. *The time shall not be yet. But in the days of the seventh angel, when he shall begin to sound, the mystery of God shall be finished;* as the prophets foretold.

It is here made *certain,* that the tremendous era introduced in this chapter, (sometime between the second woe in the fourteenth and fifteenth centuries, and the end of the noted 1260 years,) is, not the seventh vial, nor the third woe. And the oath of the Angel implies, that the terrible scenes, then introduced, would naturally be *mistaken* for the terrors of the third woe, or seventh trumpet. Hence he corrects the mistake; and assures, that the seventh trumpet (the end of the 1260 years) *is not yet;* but is *future* of the terrible scenes of the seven thunders.

Two ends are answered by this oath of the Angel. *One* has been noted above; viz. the correcting of a natural *mistake* at that period. The *other* is *implied,* and is *this; The finishing scene of the seventh trumpet shall not be much longer deferred. A new era of events is introduced, which shall ever long introduce the seventh trumpet.* Though these events are not that actual commencement of it, which many will imagine; yet the Church are implicitly *assured,* and the wicked world *warned,* that the then present terrible scenes of the *seven thunders* shall lead rapidly on to that event; and the mystery of God (in enduring the insolence of his enemies) shall ever long be finished; as the ancient prophets abundantly foretold. The seventh *trumpet* (the battle of *that* great day of God Almighty, so well known in the Old Testament) shall conclude the scenes with the enemies of the Church.

In this tenth chapter of the Revelation, we find events predicted, which seem fully adequate to the events of the present day; and an implication that they would naturally be mistaken for the seventh trumpet; while yet it is ascertained that they are previous to, and distinct from the seventh trumpet. Let us compare this chapter with some of the predictions of Christ, in Matt. xxiv, and Luke xxi, relative to his coming. It is evident, that while these prophecies of Christ had a primary fulfilment upon the Jews of that generation; they were to have a much more important fulfilment in the overthrow of the Antichristian powers of the last days. This I shall here take for granted. Some of the evidences of it are exhibited in the section on the trials of the Church under the reign of Antichrist, in the preceding pages; especially in remarks there on 2 Thes. ii, 1—9; and Rev. xvi, 15. I shall now note some of the passages in those predictions uttered by Christ, in Matthew and Luke, as they relate to the events, which are just to precede the Millennium.

Christ undertook to give some *signs* of his coming. The first sign is thus expressed; "Take heed that no man deceive you." (Matt. xxiv, 5; Mark xiii, 5; Luke xxi, 8.) As though Christ had said; The first capital sign of my approach shall be the institution of a system of most *fatal deception;* such as never before was known. The devil will come with all his intrigue and rage, to deceive the nations. His master-piece of deception will now be set in motion; and will lead on to that noted coming of Christ.

Information is *next* given, that this system of *imposition* will be propagated by *false teachers,* coming in Christ's name to deceive and to ruin; and they, shall deceive many. As the apostle notes, of the same period and event; 2 Pet. ii, 1—; that false teachers in the last days shall privately bring in damnable heresies; and many shall follow their pernicious ways, by reason of whom the way of truth shall be evil spoken of. The next sign noted is this; "And ye shall hear of *wars and rumors of wars:*" In Luke it is, *"wars and commotions."* The Church have heard of wars and commotions, from the beginning: The wars of the Romans; of the northern barbarians; of Charlemagne; of the Saxons, and Normans; the crusades; the wars of Tamerlane, and the Tartars. And Christians have heard of the more modern wars and commotions, occasioned by the Turks; those of Charles V, and Francis I; and the subsequent wars with the house of Austria; and through the nations of Europe. The question occurs; which of all those wars could our Savior mean? *None of them,* I apprehend, could be designed; as the sign related to his coming in the overthrow of Antichrist. He must mean *wars and commotions much more worthy of the name,* than any of them: And such as would seem to suggest, in a comparative view, that there had been *no* wars and commotions before. The implication clearly is, that they should behold a *new train* of wars and commotions, such as never before had been known. He therefore adds; "See that ye be not troubled." In Luke; "Be not *terrified.*" Implying, that the scenes would be *terrifying,* beyond any thing they had before seen. "For these things must first come to pass; but the end is not by and by." In Matthew it is expressed, "But the end is not yet."

Here is the *same*, with the oath of the Angel, in Rev. x, 7; "*The time shall not be yet.*" What are those wars and rumors of wars then, but the seven thunders uttering their voices? Both are found in the same connexion; and at the same period. And both are attended with a declaration from the Most High, that the *end is not yet;* Or the time of the seventh trumpet, the end of the 1260 years, (at the time when the seven thunders are roaring,) is *still future.* These wars, Christ assures are but the *beginning of sorrows;*—Or the introduction of that new era of affairs, which in due time should issue in the battle of that great day of God Almighty. "For nation shall rise against nation; and kingdom against kingdom. And great earthquakes shall be in divers places; and famines; and pestilences; and fearful sights, and great signs shall there be from heaven. All these are the *beginning* of sorrows." These wars, and terrifying tumults, which in the last days open that new era of affairs, peculiarly evidential of the coming of Christ, and is leading on to that event, are so far from belonging to the closing scene, that they are but the *beginning of sorrows.* And the warning is given to correct the opinion, which mankind would then naturally form, that this is the concluding scene of judgment. Assurance is given, that "the end is not by and by." "The time shall not be yet; but in the days of the seventh angel, when he shall begin to sound, *then* it shall be accomplished."

Our blessed Lord proceeds to predict persecutions; that his people shall be betrayed by family connexions; and some of them put to death. "And ye shall be hated of all men for my name sake." And he predicts signs in the sun, moon and stars; distress of nations, with perplexity; the sea and the waves roaring; men's hearts failing them for fear, and looking after those things that are coming upon the earth; for the powers of heaven shall be shaken. Other signs are stated, in the parallel chapters, to follow before the coming of Christ, or the end of the 1260 years;—*tribulation,* such as never was from the beginning, and never shall be again. As in Dan. xii, 1, upon the same period; "And there shall be a time of trouble, such as never was since there was a nation even to that same time." And except those days be shortened (Christ assures,) no flesh could be saved. Another warning is then given of false teachers, who if it were possible would deceive even the very elect.

Another event is then noted, between all these that precede, and the *coming* of Christ in the battle of the great day; *a general collection* (as we may believe) for that great battle, noted in these words; "For wheresoever the carcass is, there will the eagles be gathered together." Where a dead carcass is to be devoured, there eagles and birds of prey will gather round. As this related to the destruction of the Jews; it is as though he had said; Where the seat of the Jews to be destroyed is, there will the *Roman eagles*, as the executioners of wrath, be gathered round. And as the passage relates to the still more dreadful day of the ruin of Antichristian nations, it is as though he had said; Where the tremendous scene of slaughter is to *commence*, there shall the armies of prey (to devour, and to be devoured) be gathered together. How clearly this agrees with the many predictions relating to the same period; that God will then *gather* the nations, and *assemble* the kingdoms, to pour upon them his indignation, even all his fierce anger; and the whole earth shall be devoured with the fire of his jealousy:—That he will gather all nations against Jerusalem to battle:—Will gather all nations to the valley of Jehoshaphat, and there sit to judge and destroy them:—That the three unclean spirits shall *gather* the kings of the earth, and of all the world, to the battle of *that* great day of God Almighty,—the *seventh vial.*

Our Lord proceeds. "Immediately after the tribulation of these days, shall the sun be darkened; and the moon shall not give her light; and the stars shall fall from heaven; and the powers of the heavens shall be shaken. And then shall appear the sign of the Son of man in heaven; and then shall all the tribes of the earth mourn; and they shall see the Son of man coming in the clouds of heaven with power and great glory."

Here is Christ's coming in the *seventh vial;* as he gives warning, between the sixth and seventh vials; (while those spirits of devils were collecting the world in battle array against heaven,) "*Behold I come as a thief.*" Here is that *end,* which Christ assures his people (upon their hearing of the new and dreadful series of wars) *is not yet;* and which upon the seven thunders uttering their voices, the Angel decides with an oath, *shall not be yet;* but which shall arrive "in the days of the seventh Angel, when he shall *begin to sound.*"

It is here to be noted, that these prophecies all unite, to make that *final scene,* which is called the *coming of Christ,* a distinct event from those preparatory and terrible wars and commotions, and those seven thunders uttering their voices, which are the beginning of sorrows. These would terrify men; and be mistaken for the seventh trumpet. But assurances are given, that the seventh trumpet is then still future. These prophecies all unite to make that signal coming of Christ to be at *some distance,* subsequent to those wars and rumors of wars. And they unitedly teach, that trying scenes may be expected to the Church, in this interval of time:—As Christ assures; that his people shall be hated of all men; and some of them shall be *betrayed* and *put to death.* Accordingly, the little book, in the hand of the Angel, when *digested* by the sacred embassador, was *bitter.* He "must again prophecy (or bear witness) before people, and nations, and tongues, and kings."

The same train of successive events we find in *various* of the collateral prophecies in the New Testament. I will note *one;* Rev. xiv. The Lamb had appeared on mount Zion, in the reformation under Luther. A vast multitude came under his standard, with his Father's name upon their foreheads. They learned and sung the new song of salvation, known only to the *gracious.* The purity of these Protestants (in doctrine and worship) from the idolatries of the Papal harlot, is noted by their not being *defiled with women.* In due time a missionary Angel commences his flight through the aerial region flying on, to preach the Gospel to every nation. And to inforce it, he announces, that the *hour of God's judgment is come.* This very event (as we may believe) we have lived to behold, in the missionary-exertions of *our day.* What is the sense of the clause; "for the hour of his judgment is come?" Judgments have been executed in every age. But now (at the same time with these missionary events) is an *hour of God's judgment!* The sense must be this; a new period of judgments, on the Papal world, is commenced. Here (it is natural to conclude) are the wars and rumors of wars, which are the beginning of sorrows; the seven thunders, or the terrific events introduced by the descent of the Angel of the covenant; Rev. x. Another Angel follows; announcing, that Papal Babylon *has fallen.* And a *third* Angel flies, warning against the influence of the Beast; and denouncing the fatal judgments of God against all, who fall under it. Indications follow, of a solemn complexion, relative to the *sufferings,* and the *patience* and *faith,* of the saints. And a voice from heaven announces the peculiar comparative blessedness of all from that time, who died in the Lord. Here are implied trials for the Church. And their *period* appears the same with the trials predicted by Christ, Matt. xxiv. They are between the wars and commotions, which are the beginning of sorrows; and the appearance of the Son of man in the clouds of heaven, in the battle of that great day. And those trials appear to be at the same time also, with the bitterness of the little book, Rev. x, between the seven thunders, and the seventh trumpet; verse 6, 7.

After this warning of the voice from heaven, relative to the dead, who die in the Lord, the *white cloud* is presented; and the Son of man upon it appears with his sharp sickle. In the language of Matt. xxiv, 30, the *sign of the Son of man* now appears in heaven. By a heavenly Messenger it is announced, that the time is come to reap the harvest of the wicked earth; which is fully ripe. The sickle is thrust in; and the earth is reaped. But so vast is the event, that an additional,

55

and most terrible *figure* is appropriated to it. Another heavenly Messenger, who has *power over fire*, with
a loud cry warns of the thrusting in of the sharp sickle,
to gather the clusters of the vine of the earth, which
are fully ripe. The event follows. The great wine
press of divine wrath is trodden; and a river of blood
flows forth, for two hundred miles. Here is the battle
of that great day of God Almighty. *Now*, is not the
hour of God's judgment, which had *come*, at the time
of the flight of the *missionary* Angel, a distinct thing
from, and some time antecedent *to*, that tremendous
coming of Christ in the concluding scene? May the
two events be blended, as one and the same? This
would be to confound the subject. However terrible and
unprecedented the scene is, which is called, "the hour
of judgment," indicating, that nothing like it had been
known; yet it is utterly incorrect, to take an accession
from this greatness of the judgment, to view it as the
final scenes of judgment introductory to the Millennium. For the latter are clearly distinct from that hour
of God's judgment, which had come, and some time
subsequent to it.

In the Old Testament we find those preparatory
scenes of judgment sometime preceding the battle of
that great day.

The prophet Joel treats of this great day of God,
which is to be fulfilled in the seventh vial. He teaches that notice shall be given of it when it is approaching. "Blow ye the trumpet in Zion, and sound an
alarm in my holy mountain; let all the inhabitants of
the land tremble; for the day of the Lord cometh;
for it is nigh at hand; chap. ii, 1. He goes on to give
a most affecting description of the scene. In the beginning of the following chapter he informs *when* this
day of the Lord shall come. "For behold in these
days, and in that time, when I shall bring again the
captivity of Judah and Jerusalem, I will gather all nations, and will bring them down into the valley of Jehoshaphat." A terrible account of the final battle follows; verse 9—17. But in chap. ii, 31, we are informed; "The sun shall be turned into darkness, and

the moon into blood, *before* the great and terrible day of the Lord come." Here it is expressly decided, that *before* the great and terrible day of the Lord (or the battle of that great day of God Almighty) *come*, the sun shall be turned into darkness, and the moon into blood. What can be meant by this turning of the sun into darkness, and the moon into blood, *before* that great day of the Lord? We naturally conclude, that it relates to a tremendous darkening of the civil authorities in the Papal earth, and the turning of their armies into blood, preparatory to the coming of the battle of that great day of God. This darkening of the sun of civil authority, and turning the moon into blood, we may believe, relates to the *darkening fo the kingdom of the Papal Beast in the fifth vial.* The leading feature in the symbol, in both cases, is, the same, *darkness.* Both alike are *before* that great and terrible day. And both may be viewed as introductory to a new scene of events, which shall lead on to it.

The prophecy of Zepheniah has been considered, by great expositors, as having an ultimate and special reference to the battle of that great day. God here announces, that he will utterly destroy all things from off the earth; will search Jerusalem with candles, and punish the men, who are settled on their lees.—That the great day of the Lord is near, and hasteth greatly. —That it is a day of wrath, of distress and trouble, of wasting and desolation, of darkness and gloominess, of clouds and thick darkness; a day of the trumpet and alarm against the fenced cities and high towers.— That God will bring this distress upon men, and they shall walk as blind men, because they have sinned against the Lord; and their blood shall be poured out as dust, and their flesh as dung. This dreadful theme, introduced in the first chapter, is pursued through the second, and the third. At the close of the second it is said; "This is the rejoicing city, that dwelt carelessly, that said in her heart, I am, and there is none beside me. How is she become a desolation?" Exactly the same, with the description of Papal Babylon, Rev. xviiith chapter. Papal Babylon then, was to receive the final and fatal accomplishment of these plagues. In the next verse, and onward, she is described; and her judgments follow. Chap. iii, 1—6, "Woe to her that is filthy and polluted, to the oppressing city. She obeyed not the voice; she received not correction; she trusted not in the Lord; she drew not near to her God. Her princes within her are roaring lions; her judges are ravening wolves.—Her prophets are light and treacherous persons; her priests have polluted the sanctuary; they have done violence to the law. The just Lord is in the midst thereof; he will do no iniquity. Every morning doth he bring his judgment to light; he faileth not: But the unjust know no shame." While this passage *might* have some primary relation to the state of the Jews, just before their seventy years captivity; it had a much more important relation to the corrupt symbolic *city of Papal Babylon.* The latter it describes to the life. And following passages clearly relate to the scenes of the last days; and the introduction of the Millennium. But just before the battle of that great day, which is predicted in verse 8th, we find a series of signal *preparatory* judgments, distinct from that battle; verse 6, 7; (immediately following the description just given of this filthy city.) "I have cut off the nations: Their towers are desolate; I made their streets waste, that none passed by. Their cities are destroyed, so that there is no man, that there is none inhabitant. I said, surely thou wilt fear me; thou wilt receive instruction; so their dwelling should not be cut off, however I punished them. But they rose early and corrupted all their doings." How exactly has this been fulfilled among the nations of the old Papal communion, since the French revolution? Nations have indeed been *cut off; their towers desolated; their streets laid waste; their cities destroyed; and many millions of people cut off.* The language of Providence has tacitly been; surely they must now fear God, and be instructed; so that, however dreadful their calamities are, they should not be *utterly cut off.* But they *have,* as stated in this prophecy above, remained impenitent, and grown worse.—Precisely as it is stated in the description of the fifth vial; Rev. xvi, 11; that while they gnaw their tongues for pain, they blaspheme the God of heaven, and repent not of their deeds. An account of the battle of the great day, the seventh vial accordingly' follows; verse 8, 9: "Therefore wait ye upon me, saith the Lord, until the day that I rise up to the prey: For my determination is, to gather the nations, that I may assemble the kingdoms, to pour upon them mine indignation, even all my fierce anger. For all the earth shall be devoured with the fire of my jealousy. For then will I turn to the people a pure language, that they may all call upon the name of the Lord, to serve him with one consent." It is here decided, that the whole passage relates to the scenes of the *last days.* And we find, after a description of *Papal wickedness,* the fearful 'trains of *preparatory* judgments, answering to the fifth vial; to the wars and commotions; the seven thunders; the hour of God's judgment; the turning of the sun to darkness and the moon to blood; and the beginning of sorrows. The description appears to accord fully with the divine judgments, that we have seen in our day on Papal nations; desolating their towers; cutting off nations; laying waste their streets; destroying their cities! But these scenes are *before,* and distinct from, the fatal gathering and destruction of the nations, in verse 8; as much so, as are the different vials distinct from each other.

The same things are found in other passages of the Old Testament; particularly in Isa. xxvi, 9, 11, 21. But passages enough have been adduced to this point.

We may strongly conjecture, that within half a century we have seen the system of imposition, first noted by Christ, Matt. xxiv, 4, 5, as the first peculiar harbinger of his *coming,* implied in these words; "Take heed that no man deceive you." This warning, we may believe, related to the *Voltaire-system of atheism.* We have heard the consequent wars and rumors of wars; the beginning of the sorrows of the last days. Within twenty-five years, we may believe that we have seen that *descent* of the Angel of the covenant, in Rev. x; his tremendous voice astonishing the nations; and the seven thunders uttering their voices. We may see the propriety of the caution of Christ to his followers; "Be not terrified." For the scenes have appeared enough to terrify all men.

We have seen, that it appears natural and easy to view these passing events, as the commencement of the *third woe*, or the battle of that great day of God Almighty. Such a sentiment has in fact been excited. Yet the sacred passages consulted forbid their being viewed in this light. "The end is not yet." "The end is not by and by." "The time shall not be yet; but in the days of the seventh Angel, when he shall begin to sound, the mystery of God shall be finished; as he hath declared to his servants the prophets." Various events, most interesting to the Church, are still to intervene between the seven thunders, and the seventh trumpet; as has been noted.

It would appear analogous with the events of Providence, should even short seasons of peace, between the contending powers of Europe, intervene between the present scenes of judgment, which are fulfilling the fifth vial, and the judgments of the two following vials. These would more definitely mark the transition from one vial to its successor. These transitions between the three last capital vials, we may conjecture, will be attended with some distinguishing notifications,—either of a short *peace;* or of some new and notable turn given to the events of Providence. Whether these transitions, from the fifth to the sixth vial, and from the sixth to the seventh, will be marked by short cessations of hostilities;—or, by what events the close of the one, and the commencement of another, will be distinguished, time must decide. But a transition from the fifth to the sixth vial may probably be ere long expected. The Ottoman Euphrates must soon be dried up, to prepare the way for the restoration of the Jews to Palestine.

Let it be asked; can there be much doubt then, whether the terrible scenes of the present age of the world, are those wars and commotions, those seven thunders, that hour of divine judgment, which have been noted? These certainly were to be very *signal* *events;* and the beginning of a *new period*, which was to lead on to the great battle. It appears, in Rev. x, compared with the chapter preceding, that the notable descent of the Angel of the covenant, was to be subsequent to the second woe by the Turks in the fourteenth and fifteenth centuries; and sometime before the third woe. Now, what events, since those ravages of the Turks, and before the revolution in France, can be viewed as answering to those prophecies, of the wars and commotions; and the seven thunders? There were none, which appear to answer *by any means* so *clearly* to them, as the events since the French revolution.*

* It is a truth, I apprehend, that the sixteenth century opened a new era of judgments on the Papal earth, and was the commencement of the judgment of the vials.

The following scheme then, has *occurred* to mind, as attended with some *plausibility;* which scheme I think I should adopt, as most probably true, if that in the preceding pages should prove *incorrect.* The scheme is this.

1. That the first warning given by our Savior, (relative to his coming in the battle just before the Millennium,) "Take heed that no man deceive you; for many shall come in my name—and shall deceive many," instead of relating chiefly to the Voltaire scheme of infidelity, related to *Popery:* As the apostle warned the Thessalonians; "For *that day* (the coming of Christ) shall not come, except there come a falling away first, and that man of sin be revealed, the son of perdition—whom the Lord will—destroy with the brightness of his coming."

2. That the subsequent wars and rumors of wars, which should be the beginning of sorrows, were fulfilled in the new period of wars, which opened in the former part of the sixteenth century,—the wars in Italy between the emperor of Germany, and the king of France; in those which followed with the house of Austria; and those that raged through the Papal nations. That as these wars fulfilled the second and third vials, we see in them the notable descent of the Angel of the covenant, in Rev. x; and the fulfilment of the seven thunders uttering their voices. That as the Angel set his right foot upon the sea, and his left upon the earth; so the three first vials were discharged upon the earth, sea, and rivers and fountains of water. And that *that* was the time when the Angel lifted up his hand to heaven, and swore, that the *time shall not be yet.*

3. That the subsequent persecutions, noted by Christ, and those hinted in the bitterness of the little book, were fulfilled in the Papal persecutions of the Protestants, after the reformation, and while the four first vials were running; or in the sixteenth and seventeenth centuries.

Which of the vials has been fulfilled in the late scenes in Europe? Some *one* of them, at least, must certainly have been introduced. Which can it be? Which of

4. That the subsequent warning, that "false Christs and false prophets shall arise, and show signs and wonders, to seduce, if it were possible, even the elect, (Mark xiii, 22; Matt. xxiv, 24) has been fulfilled in the Papal impositions; especially in the Jesuits;—in the Voltaire system of imposition, and the three unclean spirits like frogs. (Rev. xvi, 13, 14)

5. That the warning, "And because iniquity shall abound, the love of many shall wax cold;" and, "Then shall be great tribulation, such as was not since the beginning of the world;" (Matt. xxiv, 12, 21,) are fulfilling in the *present scenes*, in Papal nations, and others.

6. That the notice, "And this Gospel of the kingdom shall be preached in all the world, for a witness unto all nations; and then shall the end come," is receiving its accomplishment in the missionary exertions of the present day. And

7. That the way is prepared for the battle of that great day to be nearer, than has been supposed.

In relation to the *above scheme*, I readily admit, that the 4th, 5th, and 6th particulars in it, relative to the powerful systems of imposition; the abounding of iniquity, and the waxing cold of the love of many; and the preaching of the Gospel to all nations; *are now fulfilling*. In these particulars, this scheme accords with the one in the preceding pages. But the question *is*, whether the beginning of the notices, given by Christ, of his coming, (viz. that notice relative to the signal danger of *deception,*) can be viewed as referring to an event so far *back* of his coming, as the commencement of the Papal delusion? And whether the "wars and commotions," next noted by Christ, as the beginnings of sorrows, could be at so great a *distance* from his actual coming, as were the wars of the sixteenth century? Whether those wars were sufficiently great and peculiar, to answer to the representation given? Whether the persecutions, predicted by Christ, as signs of his coming, could have been so long *before* his coming, as were those under the Papal tyranny? And whether those events of the sixteenth century (which are thought to have introduced the period of the vials) were of sufficient magnitude to answer to the *descent of the Angel, and the seven thunders,* in Rev. xth chapter.

Upon these questions the following things are submitted.

1. Our Lord was not asked by his disciples to inform what events should take place from the then present time, till the end of the world; or till the battle of that great day. And there is no appearance, that *this* was the thing undertaken by Christ. Had this been his object, we should indeed expect, that he would have begun as far back as *Popery*, or farther: And that

the vials was to have been fulfilled by the vast events of the xth chapter of Revelation?—that descent of the Angel; and the seven thunders? Some one of the vials

he would have noted more than that *one* event,—(the Papal delusion,—) in the first fifteen centuries!

But Christ was asked, what should be the *sign* of his *coming?* and of the end of the world? This is what he appears to have undertaken to answer. As it related to the battle of that great day, *we* may view the question as follows: What events shall point out to the world, that this coming is *near?* What are the events, which shall appear intimately *connected with it?* And would Christ, to answer this, have stated things as far back, as the reign of *Popery?* or even as the commencement of the *vials*, in the sixteenth century? Would he not rather have begun at that train of events, more nearly connected *with* his coming; and indicative of its near approach?

2. Did the Church appear to need any special warning, that the wars of the sixteenth century were not the immediate coming of Christ in the seventh trumpet? The wars, of which he speaks, as the beginning of sorrows, Christ warns, are *not* that coming. "The end is not yet." "The end is not by and by." As the Angel also decides with an oath, "The time shall not be yet." These passages imply, (as was before noted,) that those wars predicted would be attended with a current sentiment, that the last trumpet *had sounded.* But did any such sentiment prevail, upon the wars of the sixteenth century, that the battle of that great day of God, was then actually introduced? I apprehend *not;* And that the events of those days were not adequate to the exciting of such an expectation. But the events, which have opened upon the world, in our day, *are* adequate; they are calculated to excite such an expectation; and have *actually excited it*, in the minds of men of eminence!

3. Though the wars of the sixteenth century, were signally terrible, and it is thought to be evident, that a new era, in the events of the Apocalypse, then commenced; as has been noted under the first vial; yet those wars do not appear to have been so much more terrible, than all preceding wars, as to entitle them *exclusively* to the name of *"wars and commotions."* "And ye shall hear of *wars and commotions:*"—Implying, that all *wars* and *commotions*, that had preceded, were as *nothing;* or were unworthy of the *name*, compared with these. The wars of the French appear fully adequate to this representation. But I can hardly think the same can be said of any wars preceding the French revolution. When we view the wars of the northern barbarians, invading the Roman empire; the wars of the Saracens; the crusades; and the wars of the Turks; we can hardly imagine, that the wars of Charles V are entitled to the *exclu-*

was certainly here to have been fulfilled. The events are placed between the sixth and seventh *trumpets;* or the second and third woes; and expressly distin-

sive appellation of "wars and commotions:" Though they were tremendous.

4. Difficulties attend our viewing Christ's predictions of *persecution,* as fulfilled after the commencement of the wars of the sixteenth century; and before the French revolution. For though the Protestants were indeed *persecuted,* in various catholic nations; the true followers of Christ had been persecuted *before,* in catholic countries. And, why should those later persecutions be thus noted, to the exclusion of the former? Wherein was the *one* more peculiarly indicative of Christ's *coming,* than the other?

The *slaying of the witnesses,* in Rev. xi, *no doubt,* is the same event, with the persecutions, noted by Christ among the signs of his coming. But can that slaying of the witnesses have been fulfilled in any of the latter persecutions of the Protestants, by the *declining* Papal authorities. See the objections to this, in the former part of the section upon the trials of the Church under the reign of Antichrist.

Is it probable, that the falling power of the Papacy, after the reformation, (and thus after the Papacy had received its *death wound,* and the Protestant cause was established,) would be able to effect what is called the *slaying of the witnesses?* Shall all the fatal success of Papal Babylon against the witnesses, in her zenith of power and glory, fail of answering to the event of *slaying them?* And shall any success of the dying Papal power against *some branches* of the Protestant multitudes, amount to this event? This looks very improbable.

But it was not the *Papal power* that was to *slay* the witnesses: It is the *Beast, that was to ascend from the bottomless pit;* Rev. xi, 7. But this is a Power subsequent to, and distinct from, Popery. Rev. xvii. And the slaughter of the witnesses is to be, "when they shall have finished their testimony." They were to prophesy in sackcloth 1260 years;—a period not *yet* expired. How then could the slaying of them have been at a considerable time, even centuries, now past? "And when they shall have finished their testimony, the Beast, that ascendeth out of the bottomless pit, shall make war against them, and shall overcome them, and kill them." Happy should I be to find this a *past event!* Might this be made to appear, I would gladly acknowledge my mistake.

5. It has been shown, that the great scenes of Rev. x,—the descent of the Angel, and the seven thunders,—are the same with the events, Dan. xii, 6—9. This vision to St John is an enlargement of that then made to Daniel. And in that to Daniel, it seems evident, that the events of it were to be *at,* or *after,*

guished from *both*. They must then, have been a *vial*. Could they be either of the *four first?* Unanswerable objections, I think, appear against this. They could

the rise of the *wilful king*, or the terrible Empire; whose rise and end had been there just described. It would be difficult indeed, to view the passage as relating to events previous to the rise of that wilful Empire. The whole connexion forbids it. This Empire had been the great object of the two preceding chapters. And this xiith chapter is introduced with a description of the miseries attendant on the closing scenes of this mighty Power.

The communications then, of the Man upon the waters, who lifted up his hands to heaven and swore by him that liveth forever and ever, that the *time*, for the end of *these wonders*, (this *mystery of God*, Rev. x, 7,) shall be at the end of the 1260 years, and when the time for the dispersion of the Jews shall close; (verse 7)—these communications seem clearly to relate to the period *after* the rise of the wilful kingdom. Consequently, the parallel scene, Rev. x, must have been the same; and thus subsequent to the wars of the sixteenth century; and subsequent to the French revolution; which opened the door for the rise of this Empire of the last days.

6. The warning of Christ, (given Rev. xvi, 17, between the sixth and seventh vials, and while the three unclean spirits like frogs, are gathering the nations to the battle of that great day,)—*"Behold I come as a thief,"*—affords an argument to evince, that the warnings given by him, Matt. xxiv, relative to his *coming* in the battle of that great day, began with the scenes of *those last days;* and not with the rise of Popery; nor even the judgments of the sixteenth century.

We may conclude, that this warning of Christ, in Rev. xvii, 17, relates to the same period of judgments, with his warnings in Matt. xxiv. It may be viewed as an *abridgment* of them; or a concise *memento* to them. And this memento is given, not at the *introduction* of the vials; but just at their *close*, or between the sixth and seventh.

The warning seems to be, as though Christ had said; *The infernal influences of these three unclean spirits like frogs, which, after the effusion of the sixth vial, are so notable and fatal over the face of the world, as to occasion the prophetic warning here given of them;* (though their origin was *before* this vial, and even occasioned the judgment of the *fifth* vial;) *these infernal influences of the last days, mark the introduction of the tokens given,* (in Matt. xxiv, Luke xxi, and Mark xiii,) *of my coming like a thief.*

If those tokens given by Christ had related to events as long previous to his coming, as was the rise of Popery, or even the sixteenth century, I must think this warning, *"Behold I come as*

not be the *seventh.*, For the Angel decides, that the seventh *trumpet* was still future. Could they have been the *sixth vial*, poured upon the river *Euphrates?* I trust it is made to appear, in this treatise, (and it has been shown by great authors) that the sixth vial clearly relates to the subversion of the Turkish empire. I venerate the memory of the writers, who have been of opinion, that the sixth vial was to be poured on the Papal see, to dry up its streams of wealth and power; and is in allusion to the mode, in which Cyrus reduced ancient Babylon. But I must say, the application appears a mere assumption, without argument in support of it; and with weighty objections against it; as I think is made to appear under the sixth vial.

But the great events, which have transpired within the last five and twenty years, appear fully to accord with the descriptions given in Rev. x; also with those given of the fifth vial, poured upon the throne of the Papal Beast. And the fifth vial, we may conjecture, will be as far distant from the seventh, as are the wars and rumors of wars, noted by Christ, (as the beginning of sorrows,) from the *end,* which Christ assures

a *thief,* would have been found at the *beginning* of the vials; and would not have been deferred till after the sixth vial, and till the midst of the fatal career of that abominable influence of the last days, which has raised the Antichristian Beast from the bottomless pit; and has introduced the new series of terrors, which do indeed indicate the approach of that day of God. The time or place of the introduction of this warning given by Christ, (being in the midst of the account of the operations of the three unclean spirits, between the sixth and seventh vials,) teaches, that the notices given by him in Matt. xxiv, (as they relate to his coming in the battle of the great day,) are to be viewed as *beginning* with the operations of that infernal influence of the three unclean spirits. But the origin of this influence is of modern date, and began the new scenes of terror, which we have lived to behold. Hence it appears, that when Christ introduced his warnings with, "Take heed that no man deceive you;" his omniscient eye was upon the *Voltaire system of atheism and fatal imposition:* That he did not begin with events so far distant from his coming, as the Papal reign; nor the sixteenth century! But that he began with events nearer the time of his coming; events more peculiarly indicative of his coming; and more intimately connected with the event.

is not by and by:—And as far, as are the seven thunders from the time of the seventh trumpet; which the
Angel decides *"shall not be yet."*

To obtain further light upon this subject, and show
the probability that the vast events of *this period* are
a fulfilment of the *fifth vial* on Papal nations; I will
note the *analogy* there is, between the *trumpets* and the
vials, in the view, which I have given of the fifth vial.

The four first trumpets were *minor* and *preparatory*
events, inflicted on the Roman earth. And the three
last trumpets are capital events, and are called *wo-
trumpets;* (see Rev. viii, 13;) each one of which respects a different power. And the four first *vials,* according to the scheme in this book, are *minor,* and
preparatory events, inflicted on the Papal Roman earth.
And the three last vials are capital events; each one of
which respects a different power; and is *fatal* to that
power.

The *first trumpet* opened a new series of judgments
upon the Roman *"earth;"* Rev. viii, 7. And the *first
vial* was poured upon the Papal Roman *"earth;"* Rev.
xvi, 2.

The *second trumpet* fell upon the *sea,* and turned a
third part of it to blood; Rev. viii, 8. And the *second vial* is poured upon the *sea,* and turns it to blood;
Rev. xvi, 3.

The *third trumpet* fell upon the rivers and fountains
of water; Rev. viii, 10. And the *third vial* is poured upon the rivers and fountains of water; Rev. xvi, 4.

The *fourth trumpet* affects the *sun,* and the heavenly
luminaries; Rev. viii, 12. And the *fourth vial* is poured upon the *sun;* Rev. xvi, 8.

The *fifth trumpet* (the first capital, or wo-trumpet)
unlocked the bottomless pit; from which an infernal
smoke arose, and *darkened* the world; Rev. ix, 1—.
From this smoke countless myriads of mischievous
and horrid locusts swarmed forth, to terrify, and to
destroy mankind. The name of their king, or emperor, is given. It was Apollyon, *the destroyer.* He
revolutionized and tormented unnumbered millions in
three quarters of the world; in defiance of all the rights

of nations, and of the laws of God and man. The Saracenic armies were extremely effeminate and corrupt; while their armor and battle array were efficacious, and most terrible.

Their commission was, to torment men, who had not the seal of God in their foreheads. And they did it to such a degree, that life itself became a burden; and men longed to die; Rev. ix, 6.

These bloody and tremendous armies continued their successful ravages and conquests; and in 120 years they had subjugated (in addition to their own country of Arabia) Palestine, Syria, both the Armenias, the chief of Asia Minor, Persia, India, Egypt, Numidia, Barbary, as far as the River Niger, Portugal, Spain, a considerable part of Italy, Candia, Sicily, Cyprus, and other isles of the Mediterranean; and entered France with an army of 400,000 men. They were the scourge of man; the curse of the earth! Such was the *fifth trumpet.*

And do we behold any thing in its *corresponding vial,* analogous to it? How very *great* is the analogy! The fifth vial has also unlocked the *bottomless pit;* and filled and *darkened the Papal world* with the infernal smoke of atheism. From this dark, infernal vapor, have issued *armies,* millions of armed myrmidons more lecherous, ferocious, bloody and terrible, if possible, than were the saracenic locusts. They have subverted the throne of the Papal Beast, and filled his whole kingdom, *for the first time, full of gross darkness.* By the smoke from the bottomless pit, under the fifth *trumpet,* "the sun and air were darkened." And by the smoke from the bottomless pit, under the fifth *vial,* the *whole Papal region is full of gross darkness.* And all the kingdoms of the *civilized world* have been darkened with terror, falsehood, blasphemy, and every disorganizing principle; rolling forth, like vast columns of infernal smoke, from the French nation.

The *fifth vial,* instead of raising from the bottomless pit the system of Mohammedan delusion and violence, (as did the fifth trumpet, or first woe) has raised, from the same *diabolical region,* the blasphemous Antichrist of the last days;—"the Beast that ascendeth out of the bottomless pit." As the Saracenic armies were symbolized by most destructive *locusts;* so the numerous and bloody armies of the terrible Power of the last time, are, in Joel ist and iid chapters, predicted under the *same symbol;* and that of similar devouring insects; chap. i,4. As under the fifth *trumpet* men sought death, and longed to die; Rev. ix, 6: So under the afflictions, which commence under the fifth *vial*, (according to the above scheme,) it is announced, that "blessed are the dead, who die in the Lord." Under the fifth trumpet, the delusion was propagated with *fire* and *sword*. And the object of French intrigue and ambition has indeed been propagated with *fire* and *sword*. With new improvements in the arts of war, and with intrigue, falsehood, revolutions, and vast carnage, their numerous armies have been intent on propagating an universal military despotism.

The former had their king, or emperor, who was an angel of the bottomless pit, whose name was *Apollyon*, the *destroyer*. And the latter have their king, or emperor, who is no less an angel of the bottomless pit; being the first ruler of the Beast, from the bottomless pit; and he has indeed *been* the *destroyer*. The similarity between the fifth trumpet and the fifth vial is striking:—As is the above resemblance between their kings, or leaders. *Napoleon* has probably been as great a *destroyer*, as was the Saracenic *Apollyon*.

The conquests of the Saracens were rapid and extensive. And thus have been the conquests of the French.

Thus striking is the anology between the *fifth trumpet*, (or first *woe*,) and the *fifth vial*, as explained in this treatise.

The sixth trumpet (or second woe) founded the Turkish empire, (as the best expositors agree) by loosing the four Turkish sultanies, bound or restrained upon, or near, the *river Euphrates;* Rev. ix, 14.—And the sixth vial forms the counterpart of *this*, and dries up the *river Euphrates*, that the way of the kings of the east may be prepared. Rev. xvi, 12.

And the seventh trumpet, or third woe, and the seventh vial, are given in the same language, as to every essential idea; see Rev. xi, 15—19; and xvi, 17—to end. And see the remarks upon this subject, under the seventh vial.

Thus the analogy between the trumpets and the vials appears *perfect.* The language in each vial appears to be adopted in allusion to that of its corresponding trumpet. This is most clearly the case in the four first, and two last. And is it not also the case in the *fifth?* The language of the fifth vial is *short;* but of the most decisive kind. Its great features are, *darkness,* and *subversion.* It is poured upon the Papal *throne; and fills his kingdom with darkness;* so that they gnawed their tongues for pain; and blasphemed God. And the first feature of the fifth trumpet is, a *darkening* of the sun and the air, with a *smoke from hell.* And the correspondent prophecies, which give the events of this period, as well as the evident fulfilment of them before our eyes, *decide,* that there is a notable similarity between the events of the fifth trumpet, and those of the fifth vial, according to the view given of this vial in the preceding pages.

From these considerations, (and the sixth vial, in the subversion of the Turks, being *future)* I cannot but think it *most probable,* that the great events of these days are a fulfilment of the judgment of the *fifth vial.* And that they are the same with the hour of God's judgment, and the fall of Papal Babylon,—Rev. xiv, 7, 8; and chapter xviii: The same with the descent of the Angel, and the seven thunders: Rev. x: The same with the coming of the devil upon the inhabiters of the earth, and of the sea: Rev. xii, 12: The same with the wars and rumors of wars; Matt. xxiv, 6, 7: The same with the healing of the head of the old Roman Beast; and his subsequent ravages: Rev. xiii, 3, 4: And the same with the new Beast from the bottomless pit; Rev. xvii; as well as the same with the many other predictions, noted in the preceding pages, which are now receiving their fulfilment, in the character and, affairs of the French Empire.*

* The following remark, in favor of the opinion, that the terrible events of the present period are the fulfilment of the *seventh vial*, has been made by a writer; viz. "*As this great work* (of the judgments introductory to the Millennial) *is in substance done; the vials, if they be to be poured out hereafter, will have no objects on which their force may be employed.*" Reply. However *terrible*, recent events in the world have been, we cannot certainly conclude, that events far more extensive and terrible are not still in reserve, to intervene between *this*, and the Millennium; and events, which will mark the commencement of *new vials*.

Is not the *Turkish empire* most evidently to be overthrown in this period? Is that empire to remain, and to occupy the land of Palestine, to the end of the world? The Mohammedan delusion, and the Turks (the modern supporters of it) have been of great notoriety, and a most grievous curse to the Church, and to unnumbered millions. Are not that fatal delusion, and the Turkish government, to be *done away*, before the millennial Kingdom of Christ? And would it be unaccountable, if *one* of the seven vials should be reserved for the accomplishment of this object? Here then is an "object, on which the force of *one* vial *may* be employed." The rise of Mohammedism, and the Turks, were objects of sufficient magnitude to employ the force of the *two first wo-trumpets;* Rev. ixth chapter. And these abominable enemies of the Church are *still in existence.* Is their *destruction* too *small an object*, to render it *possible*, that it may employ *one* of the last vials?

The *Jews* are not yet returned. Are *they* not to be restored to the land of their fathers? Is not a *coalition* to be formed against them there? And is not that mighty coalition to be *destroyed*, in a remarkable manifestation of the God of the Jews? Are not these events great and express subjects, in ancient prophecy? Is not this overthrow of the enemies of the Jews, and of all God's enemies, the same event with the seventh *trumpet?* Rev. x, 7; "But in the days of the seventh Angel, when he shall begin to sound, the mystery of God shall be finished, as he hath declared to his servants the prophets." And is it not the same event with the seventh *vial?* which is called, the battle of THAT great day of God Almighty; as an event well known in the prophets? And may not the fatal destruction of this final coalition, and of all the persecuting enemies of the Church, "from one end of the earth even to the other end of the earth," (Jer. xxv, 31—33,) be of sufficient magnitude, to employ *one vial*, the *seventh?* We find it decided in the prophets, that an enormous Power, under the name of Gog, is to be in existence, after the return of the Jews to Palestine. May

I cannot but apprehend, that as the three last *trumpets* were to be most signal and capital events; so the three last of the *vials* were to be most signal and capital events; which should form a new and most interesting era in the history of man. And, that the first of these has been fulfilling in the events of modern date. As the four first of the *trumpets* were *minor* events; and the three last, *capital* events, or wo-trumpets; so it may be with the *vials*. The same things appear to have been true of the *seals*. The four first of them presented *minor* events; and the three last *capital* events. Surely the *seventh* seal unfolded capital events. For it contained *all* the subsequent trumpets. The *six* seal also unfolded a capital scene of events; fulfilled in the revolution in Rome from paganism to Christianity, under Constantine; described in Rev. vi, 12—17, in figures, which seem to describe the final catastrophe at the end of the word. And the *fifth seal*, in like manner, clearly relates to capital events, compared with the four preceding seals, Rev. vi, 9—11; "And when he had opened the *fifth seal*, I saw under the altar the souls of them, that were slain for the word of God, and for the testimony, which they held. And they cried with a loud voice, saying, How long, O Lord, holy and true, dost thou not judge and avenge our blood on them that dwell on the earth? And white robes were given unto every one of them. And it was said unto them, that they should rest yet for a little season, until their fellow servants also, and their brethren, that should be killed, as they were, should be fulfilled." Probably this seal might have a special reference to the horrid persecution (the *tenth*

not the final destruction of this same Power, together with that of all his admirers, and all that is antichristian on earth, be an object on which the force of one vial may be employed?

Can we certainly decide, *before hand*, that the iise, progress, ravages, and the final overthrow, of *this* Power (and the overthrow of *all on earth*, found possessed of his spirit, "partakers of his ruin, and about to receive of his plagues,") shall all be accomplished under *one vial?* Who knows but such complicated, tremendous, and very different events, may afford objects sufficient to employ *more* than *one* of the vials?

and *last)* in the pagan Roman empire, under the emperors Dioclesian and Maximian: And that it looked, in a *special manner*, to the signal judgments of God, which were to *follow*, under the sixth seal. But we have, in this fifth seal, the language of the blood of *all* the martyrs, crying to heaven for avenging justice. And we read in it the infallible divine denunciation, that justice shall awake; and all this blood shall be avenged: As the prophet expresses it, of the battle of the great day; "The earth also shall disclose her blood, and no longer cover her slain." The fifth seal then, may be viewed as a preparatory note to all that inquisition for blood, which God would make. The voice of the blood of the martyrs, in this seal, seems to overlook the preceding seals of judgment, inflicted on persecutors, as though they were beneath notice, compared to those judgments, for which they called. They inquire how long, before the martyrs should be avenged? As though they had not been avenged under the preceding seals. This shows that the fifth seal ultimately related to judgments far more *signal*, than *any* or *all* the judgments under the preceding seals: That it related to new and more tremendous scenes of judgment. The judgments imprecated under the fifth seal were to have their ultimate, and more signal accomplishment in the terrible events of the last days; which are ever represented as a new and signal *inquisition for blood.* Of that event God says, "For I will cleanse their blood, that I have not cleansed; for the Lord dwelleth in Zion;" Joel iii, 21. "For the day of vengeance is in mine heart; and the year of my redeemed, is come;" Isa. lxiii, 4. "And in *her* (i. e. mystical Babylon destroyed in the last days) was found the blood of prophets and of saints, and of *all that were slain upon the earth;*" Rev. xviii, 24. Here is the great fulfilment, of the judgments imprecated under the fifth seal. This seal then, may be called the opening of the most tremendous judgments then future; or it was the *first* seal, that most signally related to them.

And the fifth vial, as has been explained, is the opening of the more tremendous scenes of judgments of the last days; "the beginning of sorrows," or of that more signal inquisition for blood, the blood of the martyrs, which God had engaged to institute.

It has been said by the best expositors, that the judgments of various of the vials are expressed in allusion to the *plagues on Egypt.* It is evident, that the history of those plagues, and of the liberation of the chosen tribes from their Egyptian bondage, was designed to afford instruction, relative to the salvation of the Church, and the judgments of God upon her enemies, *in the last days.* I shall not make *many* remarks by way of attempting to find analogies between the two courses of events. Between the *three last* of these plagues, and the *three last* of the vials, we do find *some manifest analogies.*

The *first* of the three last plagues on Egypt, *filled their kingdoms with gross darkness, darkness which might be felt;* Exod. x, 21—23. And the first of the three last vials, the first *capital* vial, *fills* the Papal kingdom with *darkness;* Rev. xvi, 10; darkness, which indeed is felt. The *second* of the three last plagues, slew the first-born in every family of the Egyptians, and *prepared the way* for the speedy liberation of Israel from their bondage. This judgment made thorough work, in preparing the way for the setting out of the children of Abraham, for the promised land. Fatal obstacles, till now, appeared before them. Now every obstacle fled at once; and the people were immediately *under way.* How great and striking the analogy will prove to be, between that plague on Egypt, with events connected with it, and the last *vial* but one, (the sixth) time will decide. This vial is to dry up the mystic Euphrates, that the way of the kings of the east may be prepared: Or, it is to subvert the Euphratean, or Turkish empire, to prepare the way for the restoration of the children of Abraham from their long bondage, to the Promised Land; Rev. xvi, 12. So far the great analogy, between the two judgments, *is manifest:* Under the sixth vial, (which is still future, and will ere long be effected,) things *may* take place, which were well prefigured by the death, of the first born of the Egyptians; and by the consternation occasioned by that event to the enemies of the Church. It is remarkable, that both the *plague*, and the *vial* immediately *prepares the way* for the setting out of that people of God, for the *promised Canaan.*

The *last plague* on Egypt plunged their king and the flower of his armies, in the Red Sea: So that Moses and Israel sang their song of praise for their final deliverance from Egypt; Exod. xv. And the *last vial* sinks the enemies of the Jews and of the Church in perdition. These enemies will be found laboring to destroy the Jews in Palestine, like Pharaoh pursuing the Israelites. And, like Pharaoh and his armies, they will be destroyed, under the avenging hand of God. And the liberated Church will again sing the song of Moses;—they will all now unite in the *song of Moses and of the Lamb;* Rev. xv, 3. The very sentiment of the song, in Exod. xv, will be there ultimately fulfilled.

Thus the analogy between the three last *plagues* on Egypt, and the three last *vials*, (as well as that between the three last trumpets, and seals, and those vials) *is manifest.* This, if I mistake not, affords an argument of some weight, in favor of the correctness of the view given of the *vials*, in this dissertation. And if this view be correct, the vast events of our day have been in fulfilment of the *fifth vial.* See further remarks, under the seventh vial, to show, that the third *woe* is most probably still future.

THE SIXTH VIAL.

And the sixth Angel poured out his vial upon the great river Euphrates; and the water thereof was dried up, that the way of the kings of the east might be prepared. (Rev. xvi, 12.)

VARIOUS authors have been of opinion, that the sixth vial was to be fulfilled in the failing of the sources of wealth and power, of the Papal see: And that it was expressed in allusion to the mode, in which Cyrus reduced the city of ancient Babylon; turning the waters of the Euphrates from the city; and marching his army into the city, in the night, in the bed of the river. But I apprehend those writers to be correct, who have thought this vial relates to the overthrow of the *Turks,* to prepare the way for the restoration of God's ancient people to the Holy Land. Five of the vials have been fulfilled on the *Papal Beast.* The fifth subverted his throne and kingdom. The sixth then, it seems, cannot relate to the failing of the revenues of the Pope; an event antecedent to the fifth vial. It must relate to another of the great powers found in array against Christ; the *Mohammedan.* Both *this* and Popery have been terrible to the Christian cause. Both were to be destroyed; and probably by the same rod of iron, or Antichrist. And can it be viewed as too much, that one of the seven *last plagues* should have an exclusive reference to the overthrow of the vast Mohammedan imposture?

The old exposition of the vials seems objectionable, as it relates to the *sixth,* as well as to the preceding vials. The *first* vial was to operate as a sore on the subjects of Papal Babylon. The *second* vial was to turn the Papal sea to blood. The *third* was to turn their rivers and fountains to blood. The *fourth* was to scorch them with the *sun* of their civil governments. The *fifth* was to be poured on the throne of the Papal Beast, and was to fill that kingdom with darkness. After this, the sixth vial was, according to the exposition, which I am refuting, to dry up the sources of Papal wealth and power! What sources of wealth and power can be supposed to remain to the Papacy, after the operations of the five preceding vials? Did not each of the four first of these vials do its part in drying up those sources? And does not the fifth, which subverts the Papal throne, and fills that kingdom with darkness, finish what might remain of the sources of Papal wealth and power? Just so much of wealth and power, as might remain to the Pope, after the fifth vial, so much light he still enjoyed. But the fifth vial subverts his throne, and *fills* his kingdom with darkness. We have no right to say, that the darkness here, occasioned by the fifth vial, is only *partial* darkness; and the sixth vial is to aid the completion of it. This darkness is represented as *total.* When a *partial* darkness, under the fourth trumpet, was predicted, the partiality is expressly noted:—A *third part* of the day and night was darkened. See Rev. viii, 12. But the fifth vial *fills* the Papal kingdom with darkness. And being poured upon its *throne*, it must surely subvert it. How unnatural then, after all this, to represent another and subsequent vial, as drying up the sources of Papal wealth and power; and thus but *preparing the way* for the subversion of this throne, and the filling of this kingdom with darkness?

You are informed that *one man* has put another *to death*, in the following manner. 1. He made a *sore* attack upon him. 2. He bruised his breast, till the blood flowed profusely from his mouth. 3. He next bruised his limbs, till they were covered with a gore of blood. 4. The sufferer, after crying to the officers of the peace, who happened to be near, found himself abandoned by them to his fate. They frowned upon him, and gave countenance to his destruction. 5. A fatal blow was then aimed at his *head;* upon which he fell, *deprived of sight*, to the ground. You are next informed that 6. The assailant adopted measures to deprive him of his bodily strength. What would be your conception of this sixth step? Would you deem it natural, or necessary? Is not his bodily strength already destroyed by the preceding steps? What of strength remained, after the *fourth* step, the *fifth* surely had finished.

The sixth vial must relate to a different power, beside the Papal. I conceive there is no weighty argument in favor of its *relating* to the Papal power. This has been assumed, or taken for granted; but never proved. There are other powers to be destroyed, beside the Papal Beast. The empire of the Turks; whose rise fulfilled the *second woe*, and whose Mohammedan delusions fulfilled the *first woe*, are to be destroyed, before the Millennium. Their empire embraces the river Euphrates. The sixth trumpet gave rise to them, by loosing the four Turkish sultanies, *near the river Euphrates;* Rev. ix, 14. The sixth vial is to this a perfect counterpart; a subversion of the same empire. Whether its phraseology alludes to the manner, in which Cyrus reduced ancient Babylon; or to the language of the sixth trumpet; it subverts the power, to which the sixth trumpet gave rise. This trumpet united the four petty Turkish governments, whose capitals were Bagdat, Damascus, Aleppo, and Iconium. Having relieved them from the restraints, which had long circumscribed their power, (the bloody crusades, and the attacks of the Tartars,) it formed them into one powerful empire; and aided their bloody incursions into Europe. This empire is now in existence; but is soon to be no more. The conclusion seems most natural, that the fall of this Euphratean empire will be accomplished under the sixth vial.

We never find the figure of drying up a river used to denote the failing simply of wealth and power. *Rivers,* in symbolic language, are *nations.* Isa. xviii, 2—"whose land the rivers have spoiled." Or, the nations have overrun Palestine. The rivers and fountains of water, on which the third vial was poured, were the Papal *nations.* And the drying up of such rivers, is the subversion of such nations. Isa. xlii, 15; "I will make the rivers islands, and will dry up the pools." i. e. I will destroy Antichristian nations. Ezek. xxx, 12, "I will make the river dry, and sell the land into the hands of the wicked." i. e. Egypt shall be reduced by Nebuchadnezzar. Repeatedly the drying up of rivers symbolizes the subversion of nations. But never does it symbolize simply the failing of wealth and power, unless in the solitary instance of the sixth vial.*

* Relative to the *time* of the overthrow of the Turks, some are of opinion that we have some information. The Euphratean horsemen, at the rise of the Ottoman empire, are said (Rev. ix, 15,) to have been "prepared for an *hour,* and a *day,* and a *month,* and a *year.*" The true length of the time here mentioned, is matter of doubt; as well as from what time it is to be reckoned. It probably marks either the time of the Turks

Relative to the *means* of the overthrow of the Turks, we are informed, of the infidel Power of the last days, Dan. xi, 40,—"And at the time of the end shall the

most mischievous operations; or else the time of their *existence, after* their most mischievous operations, till they shall be destroyed. *If the hour, day, month* and *year* apply to the *latter*, it is natural to suppose it marks the time from the taking of Constantinople by the Turks, A. D. 1453, to the period of their destruction. If the hour, and day, and month, and year be to be *added,* they make, in prophetic calculation, (allowing 360 days to a year,) 391 years, and 15 days. These added to A D. 1453, in which Constantinople was taken, bring us to A. D. 1844 for the overthrow of the Turks. But if we read the passage as President Langdon explains it, the time of their subversion is still *nearer.* He supposed the sums are not to be *added.* According to his sense of the passage, those Turkish sultanies, when loosed, were to make successive incursions into Europe, as of an *hour*, a *day*, a *month* and a *year;* or each incursion was thus to exceed its predecessor, in length, and in terror. The first should be a short expedition for plunder, like the alarm of a prophetic hour, or a few weeks. In the next, the plundering Turks would proceed further, and pillage and waste for a prophetic day, or a year. Their third attack should be still more terrible, and their depredations continue for a prophetic month, or thirty years. And in their last attack they should take Constantinople, make it the seat of their empire, and continue for a prophetic year. The history of the events (all excepting the last, whose termination is still future) is thought to accord with this representation. The Turks did at first brake into Europe for plunder; and soon retired. This was like the alarm of an hour. Bajazet afterward made a longer incursion, and threatened the speedy conquest of Greece. But an attack of the Tartars at home called him away; and the danger appeared to subside. After an interval of rest to Europe, he commenced a new attack; took Adrianople; and a considerable part of Greece now fell before his victorious arms. Constantinople itself was besieged eight years. A French army, which came to its aid, was defeated. But the Turks were called home by another Tartar invasion under Tamarlane. This Turkish invasion of Europe may be called an alarm of a month, or of thirty years. After a season, the Turkish invasion of Europe was renewed; and Mahomet II. took Constantinople, A. D. 1453, and made it the capital of the Turkish empire in Europe, established upon the ruins of the Greeks. If this capital event may be viewed the commencement of the prophetic year of their continuance, 360 years added to the 1453, give A. D. 1813, for the overthrow of the Turks. If 365 years be, *in this case,* to be allowed to the king of the south push at him, and the king of the north shall come against him like a whirlwind, with chariots, and horsemen, and with many ships; and he shall enter into the countries, and shall overflow and pass over. He shall enter also into the glorious land; and many countries shall be overthrown; but these

prophetic year, (according to the true number of days in a year) this brings to A. D. 1818 for their subversion. In favor of the latter time it may be noted, that the 2300 years, in Daniel viii, 14, which should terminate the Mohammedan horn, (if the date of these 2300 years may be viewed as beginning when the emperor of Persia entered into an alliance with the Carthagenians to invade Greece, 482 years before Christ,) *end in the year* 1818. This alliance with the Carthagenians is said to have been formed 482 years before the commencement of the Christian era. (See Bicheno, p. 72.) The next year the Persian emperor marched as far as Sardis; and the spring following he crossed the Hellespont. This was the opening of the next vast eastern revolution, after the days of Daniel; or the preparing of the way for the empire of the *he-goat,* from one of whose horns the Mohammedan horn was to rise; which after the noted 2300 years, (if our reading be the correct one) was to be destroyed, and the sanctuary cleansed; (Dan. viii, 14;) or Palestine to be delivered from the enemies of the Jews; and the way prepared for the Jews' restoration. The 2300 years, whose termination shall introduce these events, (if it be proper to date their commencement at the above period, which began the scene of the revolution, from the Persian to the Macedonian monarchy,) *end in the year* 1818; the year made by the addition of 365 years (for the prophetic year of the continuance of the Turks) to A. D. 1453, the taking of Constantinople.

Whether any of these calculations will prove correct, time will soon decide. Should they prove essentially incorrect, it will indicate that the other alternative is the true reckoning; or the *hour, day, month* and *year,* for which the Turks were prepared, (Rev. ix, 15) are to be added; making 391 years, and 15 days: And that this period marks the time for their most mischievous operations. In that case, history in fact furnishes events, which appear like a fulfilment of the passage. From the Turks conquest of Kutahi, A. D. 1281, to that of Camaniac, A. D. 1672, were 391 years. At the time of the last above named conquest, 48 towns and villages were delivered up to the Turks: Since which time they have gained little or no territory in Europe. Let whichsoever of these senses fulfil the times for which the Turks were prepared, that empire is soon to be subverted. And its subversion, may be expected to fulfil the sixth vial.

shall escape out of his hand, even Edom, and Moab, and the chief of the children of Ammon. He shall stretch forth his hands also upon the countries, and the land of Egypt shall not escape. But he shall have power over the treasures of gold and of silver, and over all the precious things of Egypt; and the Libyans and Ethiopians shall be at his steps." Upon this passage let it be remarked,

1. The time of this expedition of the Infidel Power into the east, may well be supposed to accord with that of the subversion of the Turks, and of the pouring out of the sixth vial;—being not long after his subversion of many of his neighboring nations, and dividing their land for gain. (Verse 39.) After the fulfilment of the fifth vial, in the judgments of God on Papal nations, by the instrumentality of this rod of iron, (the Antichristian Empire,) we naturally ere long, look for the fulfilment of the sixth vial, in the overthrow of the Turkish government.

2. The king of the south, and king of the north, in the preceding parts of this chapter, meant Egypt and Syria. These are now under the dominion of the Turks. These names then, may possibly mean the Turkish empire. If so, by the king of the south, we should naturally understand, the Turkish dominions in Africa, including not only Egypt, but also the states of Barbary. Some other powers *may* at this late period, be meant, by the king (or kingdom) of the south, and the king of the north. The king of the south will make some kind of push, (or *butt*, as in the Hebrew) at the infidel Power: Which will be followed by an attack from the king of the north, and probably a *confederacy* of other powers; as seems to be indicated, by their coming like a whirlwind, with chariots and horsemen; or infantry and cavalry; and with many ships. A general and most furious attack is made, either by the ancient, or by some modern king of the south, and king of the north, with a view to crush this Power at once.

3. Upon this, the infidel Power goes forth, in process of time; he overflows, and passes over; enters Pal-

estine, now subject to the Turks; and many countries
are overthrown by him. But the eastern Arabs, under
the name of Edom, Moab and Ammon, are excepted
from his conquests; which implies, that his conquests
in the east will be extensive. What can all this mean,
but the subversion of the 'Ottoman, or 'Turkish
empire?

4. This Power beats his way round into Egypt,
where he finds access to whatever treasures may be in
their possession, or may have been conveyed thither,
by the fleeing Turks. "And the Libyans and Ethiopians shall be at his steps." All the southern Turkish
provinces shall lie prostrate at his feet. From this expedition he retires; and opportunity is afforded for the
accomplishment of the events, which will intervene between the sixth and seventh vials.

5. As this last empire is raised up for a rod of iron,
to execute the judgments of God upon wicked nations,
it appears most probable, that it will be the instrument of the overthrow of the Turks. Various sacred
passages concerning this Power, represent it as subduing the nations; making the earth to tremble; and
prospering, (so far as to continue to exist, and to execute judgment) till the indignation is accomplished:
For that which is determined shall be done. (Dan. xi,
36.) It is natural to conjecture then, that this Power
will be the means of the ruin of the Ottoman government, (that grand supporter of Mohammedan delusion,) as well as the means of the ruin of the Papal: Or
that it will be the instrument of the fulfilment of the
sixth, as well as of the *fifth* vial.

As the way had been, for some time, preparing,
for the overthrow of the Papal power, before it was effected under the fifth vial; so the way has been preparing, in a series of events, for the ruin of the Turkish empire. Constantinople was eighteen times on
fire, in the course of the last century. In these fires
upwards of 120,000 buildings were destroyed, and
multitudes of the people. In 1750 the plague raged
in that city. In the next year, it was almost destroyed
by an earthquake. Other principal cities in that empire

have been nearly desolated by earthquakes.' In 1752, the city of Adrianople, (the second in opulence and population in the empire) was by an earthquake more than half destroyed. In 1754, Grand Cairo had two thirds of its buildings shaken down by an earthquake, and 40,000 people swallowed up in the earth. In 1755, Fez in Morocco was by an earthquake half destroyed; and 12,000 Arabs were buried in the ruins. But a few years since, those parts of Morocco were almost desolated by the plague. Various other instances of plagues and earthquakes have, at different times of late, ravaged in different sections of that empire. Terrible wars between the Turks and the Russians, in late years, have greatly weakened and impoverished the Turks. And in April, 1810, 8,000 houses were destroyed in Constantinaple by fire, and 80,000 people were driven houseless to the fields. These are some of the preparatory events of Providence, to aid on the terrors of the sixth vial.

It is remarkable that a sect arose in Arabia about the same time, in which Voltaire's scheme of Infidelity was planned, which is as threatening to the *Mohammedan*, as the scheme of Voltaire was to the *Papal* imposture. Abdul Wahab, a native of Aijerene, appeared about the middle of the last century, denying the Mohammedan religion. His followers, called Wahabees, have become numerous and terrible. In 1802, their armed force consisted of from 80, to 90,000. Their expeditions were conducted with the greatest secresy and celerity. They had plundered Tyeef, Mecca, Medina, and Kubula, with terrible slaughter. They had demolished the tomb of Mohammed at Medina; and had destroyed the mosques, after having plundered them of their vast treasures. In short, they had effected a revolution in the government of Arabia. And the Turkish government were forced to purchase their friendship. The founder of this sect received his education under the chief Mohammedan doctors at Bassora, and Bagdat. The Wahabees profess to believe in God: But they deny Jesus Christ, and all revealed religion. Thus the way has been providentially preparing for the subversion of the Mohammedan delusion, and consequently the ruin of the Turkish government, which rests upon it. But the end of that empire will be with a flood of wrath, under the instrumentality of Antichrist, as appears from the forecited passage of Dan. xi, 40,—and the other considerations before mentioned.*

---

* Should any object, that the *drying up* of the mystic Euphrates seems not consistent with a violent subversion of that empire by a foreign power; but seems rather to indicate a gradual decay, and kind of natural death; as the horn of the Macedonian Beast is said (Dan. viii, 25,) to be *broken without hands;* I answer, the drying up of the river Euphrates, by Cyrus, that he might destroy ancient Babylon, was a sudden and violent event, produced by a foreign invading foe. But that event was predicted under the same figure, with the judgment of the sixth vial. *I will dry up her sea, and make her springs dry.* (Jer. li, 36) *that saith to the deep, Be dry, and I will dry up the rivers.* (Isa. xliv, 27) *A drought is upon her waters, and they shall be dried up.* (Jer. l, 38.) These predictions were fulfilled upon Babylon by the violent siege and artificial operations of the Medo-Persian monarch. And the drying up of waters is a common prophetic figure, to signify the violent subversion of one nation by the arms of another. Thus the reduction of Egypt by Nebuchadnezzar was predicted; (Ezek. xxx, 12.) *And I will make the rivers dry, and sell the land into the hands of the wicked.* And the dividing of the waters of the Red Sea by the arm of the Most High, was noted under the same figure, Isa. li, 9, 10. The arm of the Lord is invoked; and the prophet says, *Art thou not it, that hath dried the sea?* I recollect no instance in prophecy, where the drying up of waters, is used to predict the gradual decay, or kind of natural death of any people or nation. The drying up of the mystic Euphrates then, we must naturally conclude, will be fulfilled by the arms of some powerful nation. The horn of the Macedonian Beast's being *broken without hands,* (Dan. viii, 25,) may be found, to mean, that it shall be broken without any *hands to uphold;* as is predicted of Antichrist, (Dan. xi, last)—*yet shall he come to his end, and none shall help him.* Such a clause is often added to the denunciations of Divine wrath upon the wicked; *And there be none to deliver. None can deliver out of mine hands.* But if that passage in Daniel, relative to the Macedonian horn, *truly* mean, that it shall be destroyed *without human aid,* it must mean the gradual decay and death of the *Mohammedan delusion;* but not of the Turkish empire, the last, most powerful supporter of it. It does not accord with the analogy of the judgments of the vials, or the signal judgments of God

The *object* of the judgment of the sixth vial is expressed—*that the way of the kings of the east, may be prepared.* That the way may be prepared for the return of God's ancient covenant people to the land of their fathers. This sense accords with Mede, Moor, Durham, Pool, and others. That people are to be gathered to the Holy land, before the seventh vial, or the battle of that great day of God Almighty. This point is made certain in numerous prophecies.* But they cannot return to the land of their fathers, till the Turkish empire is subverted. For Palestine is in possession of that empire; and the Turks, so long as they are in power, will never suffer Judah and Israel to resettle there.

The ancient prophets, in predicting the restoration of the Jews from their long dispersion, repeatedly annexed the idea of a drying up of water, to prepare the way for that event. To these passages the language of the sixth vial probably has some allusion. Isa. xi, 15. "And the Lord shall utterly destroy the tongue of the Egyptian sea, and with his mighty wind shall he shake his hand over the *river*, and shall smite it in its seven streams, and make men go over dry'shod. And there shall be an high way for the remnant of his people." Chap. x, ii; "And he shall pass through the sea with affliction, and shall smite the waves of the sea, and all the *deeps* of the *river* shall *dry up.*" Here, to prepare the way for Israel's final restoration, the sea, and rivers are to be dried up. In the language of the sixth vial we find what river it is, that is to be dried up. It is the river Euphrates; or the empire nearest to the Eu-

generally, that the sixth vial should be fulfilled without any special, visible instrument of the vengeance. God usually works by means; and usually has visible instruments prepared, adequate to effects, which are to be produced. And we have no reason to believe the signal judgment of the *sixth vial* will be an exception to this general rule; notwithstanding that a writer of celebrity has suggested that this will be the case.

* See Ezek. xxxvi, xxxvii, xxxviii, and xxxix; Joel iii; Zech. xii, xiii, and xiv; Jer. xxxi; Isa. xi, 11—16; Jer. xxiii, 5—8; Hosea i, 10, 11; and iii, 4, 5; and xiv, 4—8.

phrates is to be subverted, to prepare the way for the resettlement of God's ancient people in their own land. The deliverance of that people from Egypt was attended with the literal parting of the Red Sea. Their entrance into Canaan was preceded by the dividing of Jordan. Their deliverance from Babylon was preceded by the drying up, or the turning of the river Euphrates from that city. And the way is to be prepared for their final restoration by a mystical drying up of the same river. "And there shall be an high way for the remnant of his people—like as it was to Israel in the day that he came up out of the land of Egypt. It is striking, that the drying up of the river Euphrates by Cyrus, was the great step, preparatory to the restoration of the Jews from Babylon. And that the drying up of the same river, in the sixth vial, is mystically the *preparatory step* for the final restoration of the Jews, and Israel. Perhaps we need look no further to find the allusion of the sixth vial. And as the drying up, by Cyrus, destroyed the power that had prevented the restoration of the Jews; so the drying up, by the sixth vial, will subvert the power now in the way of the restoration of the Jews,—the *Turks.*

But why are the ancient people of God called *the kings of the east?* Perhaps the signal care, which God has for so many ages taken of that people, and the wonders of Providence still in reserve for them, may entitle them to this mystic appellation. They were formerly called, *a kingdom of priests.** And they are to become the most signal branch of that church, which is to be made *kings and priests unto God.* The phrase may have a special reference to the ten tribes, *now in the east.* In modern writings we are informed of a people in Persia, whither the ten tribes, at the time of their dispersion, were led,† called the Afghans, whose traditions and history seem clearly to evince, that they are the ten tribes of Israel. They entertain this opinion of themselves. And the best Persian historians give

* Exod. xix, 6. † 2 Kings xvii, 6.

this opinion of them. The descendants of the dispersed Israelites may. have emigrated to different and distant regions. Admitting that the scattered descendants of Israel may, after the battle of the great day, be gathered from the east, west, north, and south; from far, even from the ends of the earth;* yet the Afghans in Persia, it appears most highly probable, are that body of the ten tribes, who are to be restored with the Jews to Palestine, before the battle of the great day; or the seventh vial.† These Afghans call themselves *Melchim*, the Hebrew word for *kings*. *These* may prove to be the *kings of the east*, to prepare the way for the return of whom, to the land of their fathers, the mystic Euphrates must be dried up.‡ For this empire extends between the Holy land and Persia, which lies in the east. And the Turks being in possession of the Holy land, and being of a religion' utterly hostile to our holy Revelation, are as fatal an obstacle in the way of the return of Israel, as was the Red Sea, in front of the ancient tribes, when they came out of Egypt, and were

---

* Isa. xliii, 5,6. † See Ezek. xxxvii, 16—21, in connexion with the context, and the succeeding chapter.

· ‡ Possibly the kings of the east here may relate to, or include; the vast eastern kingdoms. They have been chiefly secluded from the blessings of the gospel. But we are led to believe they will be brought to the knowledge of the truth, at the introduction of the Millennium. The Mohammedan delusion is a vast obstacle in the way of their conversion. And the drying up of the mystic Euphrates, will no doubt be an essential step toward preparing the way for the general conversion of the vast kingdoms of the east; whether this event is noted in the language of the sixth vial, or not. I have had some apprehensions that this
 ' language of the sixth vial *may* include such an event. It is striking that in a prediction of the *coming in of the fulness of the Gentiles*, Isa. xlix, 12, as though vast companies of them were then visible, it is said, "Behold, there shall come from *far*; and lo these from the *north*, and from the *west*; and these from the land of *Sinim*." The latter, Dr. Parish has shown, in his Gazetteer of the Bible, most probably is the *vast empire of China*. This is indeed their coming *from far*, and from the point opposite to the *west*; as Sinim clearly is in the text. "The Chinese books speak of their country under the appellation of Sin," of which Sinim is the plural.

in Pihahiroth.* But as the Red Sea in that case was parted, as though it were dried up;† so the mystic Euphrates will be no less effectually removed under the judgment of the sixth vial.

Upon the fulfilment of the sixth vial, we read, *And I saw three unclean spirits like frogs come out of the mouth of the dragon, and out of the mouth of the Beast, and out of the mouth of the false prophet. For they are the spirits of devils, working miracles, which go forth unto the kings of the earth and of the whole world, to gather them to the battle of that great day of God Almighty.*‡ Here we find predicted a complicated, powerful, extensive agency, which will be in a special manner exerted in the period between the sixth and the seventh vials. Upon this prediction a number of things are to be noted. The *greatness* of the event is forcibly indicated by the facts, that it was so long predicted; that the prediction occupied so considerable a part of the description of the vials; and that the event should occasion such a warning from the mouth of Christ, relative to his speedy, subsequent coming.—*Behold I come as a thief: Blessed is he that watcheth, and keepeth his garments, lest he walk naked, and they see his shame.* The *origin* of this agency, is interesting: *Out of the mouth of the dragon, and out of the mouth of the Beast, and out of the mouth of the false prophet.* The dragon here is the devil, as we learn in Rev. xii. The Beast is Antichrist. And the false prophet is the Papal system, after it ceased to be a Beast, at the rise of Antichrist, and was taken into his grasp, as a tool of ambition. "For they are the spirits of devils." The devil will be suffered to exercise a powerful agency among men, *at that period. Woe to the inhabiters of the earth and of the sea! For the devil is come down unto you, having great wrath, because he knoweth that he hath but a short time.* (Rev. xii. 12.) His operations will be multiform, peculiar, and mischievous. The great infidel Power, and his tool, the Papacy, will unite in despatching their agents over the

* Exod. xiv.   † Isa. li, 9, 10.   ‡ Rev. xvi, 13, 14.

world. And so completely under the direction of the wicked one will the whole agency be found to be, that it is said, *For they are the spirits of devils.* Their *subtilty* is indicated;—*like frogs:*—Unclean, hateful reptiles! Sly, out of sight, slippery, *stationary,* or *swift* in their motion, as will best answer their purpose; creeping into every apartment; as was said of the frogs in the Egyptian plague—*which shall go up, and come into thine house, and into thy bed chamber, and upon thy bed, and into the house of thy servants, and upon thy people, and into thine ovens, and into thy kneading troughs.* Sly, yet bold, impudent, and disgusting. Their *power* of deceit is noted. *Working miracles; doing wonders* in the sight of men. The depth of their scheme, the unity of their design, their incredible perseverance, the corruptions of the human heart, and the agency of Satan, will all unite to give the most astonishing force to their operations. Every incident, every corrupt passion, and all the power of sly insinuation, will be pressed into their service. In a word, licentiousness, Infidelity, and false religion, will unite their influence to aid the *same cause.*

So great, complicated, and fatal an agency, from the three kindred systems of licentiousness, of infidelity, and of false religion, as we here find predicted to go forth to the cabinets and nations of the world, after the sixth vial, cannot be expected to have risen *at once.* No verily! Their rise and organization will be found to have been a *work of time.* These very spirits are in fatal operation some time *before* the subversion of the Ottoman empire; though they are not noted in the predictions of the vials, till *after* the sixth vial; and to prepare the way for the *seventh.* The effects of these spirits of devils will then be more peculiarly seen, preparing the world apace for the tremendous harvest. They are hence predicted, as most *notorious* and *fatal,* at that period. But this prediction does not teach that those three systems of influence *originate* after the sixth vial; though the symbol presents them as *then* appearing from the mouths of the dragon, Beast and false prophet. This does not *forbid,* (and the vast deeds ascribed to them do *imply*,) that they will have been in operation *for some time before* the period, at which they are here first noted. For such vast and subtile systems of influence do not spring into existence at once. Their rise and deep organization will be found to have been a *work of time*. These abominable spirits have been in operation from the time of the rise of the infidel Power. The many predictions of the rise and progress of that infidel Power, teach, that this complicated agency, which will be found to be so extensive and fatal, *after the sixth vial,* was prevalent and dreadful, *long before it.* (See section 4, chapter i, of this dissertation;—*Antichrist predicted by the apostles.*) These unclean spirits like frogs have already long been discovered, as operating in the Papal earth; and going forth thence in multitudes over the civilized world. They in fact gave direction to the French revolution; and have been the most mischievous occasion of the terrible scenes of judgment, through the civilized world, of modern date. But their agency and mischievous operations are to be still more *extensive* and *fatal,* after the effusion of the *sixth* vial, and to prepare the way for the *seventh* vial, the battle of that great day of God Almighty. Some great checks they will receive, in the prosecution of their plans, till after the return of the Jews to Palestine. Their kingdom will be "partly *strong* and partly broken." The earth will *swallow up* some of their floods. And the alarms of many may be laid to sleep. But the wicked object is not relinquished. The infernal agents gain strength in dark recesses. And after the restoration of the Jews, they will work *miracles* of success; and will *sink the wicked world,* or introduce the battle of that great day.

The *extent* of this agency is amazing: *Going forth unto the kings of the earth, and of the whole world.* If the whole world literally be *not* here designed, a great part of it surely must be understood. The nations favored with the light of Revelation will be included. The *object* of this combined and vast agency is interesting: *To gather them to the battle of that great day of God Almighty.* To prepare and gather the people of the world to that battle, so abundantly predicted in the prophetic parts of the Bible; to the event, which may be called, the battle of *that* great day so well known.

And he gathered them together into a place called, in the Hebrew tongue, Armageddon. This text probably will be fulfilled both literally and mystically. There is to be a literal expedition under Gog, against the Church of Christ; consisting of the Jews and people of Israel in Palestine.* And Armageddon, or the mountain of Megiddo, may be the place literally where Gog and his bands will be destroyed.† Armageddon imports, the mountain of Megiddo, (or Megiddon, which is the same) or *the mountain, that declares.* Megiddo was a city of Manassah, 44 miles north of Jerusalem. It was there, that Jabin's army was routed by the few men under Barak and Deborah; Judges i, 27; and v, 19. It appears to have been a seat of the warring Canaanites. Ahaziah fled thither from Jehu; and there died of his wounds just before received; 2 Kings ix, 27. In this place Josiah was slain by Pharaoh Necho; 2 Chron. xxxii, 22; and all Judah mourned for him. This place was hence noted as a place of *slaughter*, and of *mourning;* Zech. xii, 11. Mr. Edwards remarks, that the words *waters of Megiddo,* and *valley of Megiddo,* imply a *mountain,* or *rise* of Megiddo. Probably this mountain or rise is small. Indeed, as mount *Carmel* was in the vicinity of Megiddo, this mountain *may* be alluded to, and in the prophecy, called the *mountain of Megiddon.* I conceive it to be of no great consequence, whether the word, importing *mountain,* and prefixed to Megiddon, relates *wholly,* or in part, to a mountain in that part of the country, as Carmel, or any other mountain or hill; or whether it is *wholly mystical.* Though I *do* conceive the text will have a kind of literal fulfilment, as it relates to Gog and his bands, who are to be destroyed in Palestine;—and a mystical fulfilment *only,* as it relates to the body of the Antichristian nations, to be destroyed at that period.

---

* See Ezek. xxxvii, xxxviii, and xxxix.
† See sec. ii, chap. iii, of the preceding dissertation.

Perhaps there is the same reason, and *only* the same, for this place to be called *mount Megiddon*, as for Perazim, in 'Isa. xxviii, 21, to be called *mount Perazim.* Predicting primarily the destruction of, the Jews, and ultimately the battle of that great day of God, the prophet says; "For the Lord shall rise up as in *mount Perazim.*"—We know not of any *mountain* in Perazim, where the Lord broke forth, before David, like a destroying flood, upon the Philistines; 2 Sam. v, 20. Yet in predicting the battle of that great day of God, it is said, in allusion to that ancient event, "The Lord shall rise up as in *mount Perazim.*" So the wicked of the world are to be gathered to *mount Megiddon.* In Joel iii, 9—12, they are gathered to the *valley* of Jehoshaphat. That valley likewise implies a mountain. Hence the men of war are there challenged, "let them draw near; let them *come up!*" Gog and his bands will be collected in Palestine. The numerous nations predicted to be in that vast coalition, will need the subtilest management, to excite and give direction to the event. But the object of this subtile agency will no doubt have a mystical fulfilment. Countless multitudes throughout the evangelized nations, will be prepared and marshalled, as in battle array against the Church, and the King of Zion; and will be cut off in fatal judgments, under the seventh vial. A general spirit of licentiousness, Infidelity, and of false religion, will be found cooperating over the world; producing the most fatal effects to the temporal, and especially to the eternal interests of men; leading the multitudes of the people to treasure up wrath against the day of wrath; and thus to be found in the mystic Armageddon, when the day of that battle shall arrive.

In the midst of the account concerning the three unclean spirits like frogs, we find a pause; and our Lord in heaven gives the solemn admonition to the world; *Behold I come as a thief. Blessed is he, that watcheth, and keepeth his garments, lest he walk naked, and they see his shame.* Most urgent warning! When such wickedness prevails, the chariot-wheels of justice are near! God will take his enemies on surprise. They believe not in his coming. And the event will be to them like the coming of a thief; yea, like lightning from heaven. And all, whose souls are not adorned with grace, will be exposed to sink with Infidels, under the shame of their wickedness, and the terrors of that day. Let this kind warning sink deep into the ears and hearts of Christians! Says inspiration to them, *Ye are not in darkness, that that day should overtake you as. a thief.* Our blessed Lord has repeatedly predicted, that his coming shall be as that of a thief; unlooked for; unexpected by the wicked world; like the flood upon the old world; and like the destruction of Sodom. Luke xvii, 26—30. The perils of those times are predicted, and the most wakeful vigilance enjoined. *Blessed is he that watcheth, and keepeth his garments. Blessed is that servant, whom his Lord, when he cometh, shall find so doing.*

THE SEVENTH VIAL.

And the seventh Angel poured out his vial into the air; and there came a great voice out of the temple of heaven from the throne saying, It is done. And there were voices, and thunders, and lightnings; and there was a great earthquake, such as was not since men were upon the earth, so mighty an earthquake, and so great. And the great city was divided into three parts, and the cities of the nations fell; and great Babylon came in remembrance before God, to give unto her the cup of the wine of the fierceness of his wrath. And every island fled away, and the mountains were not found. And there fell upon men a great hail out of heaven, every stone about the weight of a talent; and men blasphemed God because of the plague of the hail; for the plague thereof was exceeding great. (Rev. xvi, 17, to the end.)

WE have here a large assemblage of figures, and of the most terrific kind. This is the most tremendous of all the vials. It appears more terrible, than all the pre-

ceding vials united. About as much is said, to prepare the way for it, and to describe it, as with respect
to all the other vials. No such preparations appeared
for any, or all the other vials, as for this. And no such
warnings were given. This is called, *the battle of that
great day of God Almighty;* as being an event *well
known* through the prophets. In the original the THAT
is singularly emphatical. The article is twice used;
and the pronoun ekeinees, that, inserted beside: Indicating, that it is a day well known. The events of
this vial are future. The particulars are unknown to
man. But from the numerous predictions of it, many
probable things may be gathered. A great ʰvoice
from the temple of heaven proclaims, *It is done.* The
mystery of iniquity is finished.. The enemies have
had their day; and now God will vindicate his cause.
The subsequent *voices and thunders and lightnings* are
striking expressions of the terrors of that scene. A
great earthquake follows, *such as was not since men
were upon the earth, so mighty an earthquake, and so
great:* An emblem of a fatal shock of judgments, such
as man has never witnessed! As our Lord predicted of
the same event; *For then shall be great tribulation,
such as was not since the beginning of the world to this
time; no, nor ever shall be.* (Matt. xxiv, 21.). And
as Daniel predicts of the same event; *And there shall
be a time of trouble, such as never was since there was
a nation, even to that same time.* (Dan. xii, 1.) *The
great city is divided into three parts.* By the great
city here is meant probably the Empire of Antichrist.
His subjects revolt, and become each other's executioners. *The cities of the nations fall.* The Divine
vengeance, which breaks at Palestine, and destroys
Gog and all his bands, rolls and thunders through the
nations; demolishes their capitals; and lays their cities
in ruins. The Antichristian Babylon, including what
remains of the Papacy, comes into remembrance with
God. The cup of the wine of the fierceness of his
wrath is given. Every island flees away. The mountains of great kingdoms are no more found. They
are plunged in the sea of revolution and ruin. Psalm

xlvi, 2, 3. And even all these figures are inadequate to the events. Another is therefore added; that of terrible *hail* falling on man, every stone being of about an hundred and fourteen pounds weight; indicative of judgments as (much more fatal, than those usually known, as hailstones of this enormous size would be more terrible, than common hail. The other vials were local: This is general; *poured out into the air;* or upon the kingdom of the devil on earth, who is *the prince of the power of the air.* The vast armies of Atheists, Pagans, and the remains of the Papal and Mohammedan powers, collected in the Holy land, receive the first discharge of the artillery of Heaven, which sinks them in perdition. And the judgments will thence proceed, and will sweep off the *violent* enemies of the Church in every land. Probably violent, exterminating wars, civil dissentions, pestilences, and the raging elements let loose upon man, with other fatal judgments, will constitute the terrors of that day. The hand of God will be seen by all, in scenes of vengeance. Men will know, that those who fall, are *the slain of the Lord; whose carcasses, we are assured, shall be, at that day, from one end of the earth, even unto the other end of the earth* (Jer. xxv, 33.) *This is the day that shall burn as an oven; and all the proud, yea and all that do wickedly, shall be as stubble; and that day that cometh shall burn them up, saith the Lord of hosts, that it shall leave them neither root nor branch.* (Mal. iv, 1.) This is the day, *when God will gather the nations, and assemble the kingdoms, and pour upon them his indignation, even all his fierce anger; and all the earth shall be devoured with the fire of his jealousy.* (Zeph. iii, 8.) *And he shall sweep the sinners thereof out of it.* (Isa. xiii, 9.) *They shall be consumed as the fat of lambs; into smoke shall they consume away. And the meek shall inherit the earth, and delight themselves in abundance of peace.* The Scriptures, which predict this destruction of the enemies of the Church, are numerous, both in the Old and New Testaments; and they are *terrible!*

60

As to the *period* of this vial; it will not be poured out, till after the subversion of the Turkish empire, and the consequent return of Israel and the Jews; and the collection of the armies of Gog and Magog against them. (Ezek. xxxvii, xxxviii, xxxix.) These things must occupy some time. As to the precise time of the seventh vial, I do not feel great confidence. The old expositors, who have placed the introduction of the Millennium about A. D. 2,000, *may* prove correct. See section I, chapter II. But I believe it is hasten-ing on apace.

According to the preceding scheme of the vials, and in confirmation of it, it is observable, as before no-ted, that the three last vials fall successively upon the three great wicked powers, the *Papal*, the *Mohamme-dan*, and the *Antichristian;* giving to each a deadly blow; and the last vial deciding the controversy; sweeping from the earth all, who are found in array against the Church. The first four of the vials were poured upon the Papal see, and its supporters; and were minor, and preparatory events. The three last are capital events. The fifth gives a death blow to the Papal Beast, by the rise of Antichrist. The sixth sub-verts the Ottoman Empire. And the seventh plunges Antichrist, with the scattered remains of the two pre-ceding powers, into perdition; and decides the contro-versy between the Church and all her inveterate ene-mies through evangelized nations. The analogy be-tween the vials and the trumpets, has been noted under the fifth vial. The first four of the *trumpets* related to minor events, which fell upon the Christian Roman empire. The three last related to capital events, and hence were called *wo trumpets*. And each of these three related to a *different* power. The first to the rava-ges of the Saracens; the second to that of the Turks; the third to the destruction of Antichrist. The same thing is true of the vials, as they have been explained. The first four were minor judgments upon the Papal see, preparing the way for its destruction. And the three last are capital events, each relating to a *different* power.

I am constrained to think the venerable *Mede*, and those authors, to be correct, who have supposed the seventh trumpet, or third woe, *does not* comprise all the vials. It appears as though this trumpet and the seventh vial must *meet*, and receive their accomplishment in the same event.

Surely those writers, who carry the origin of the period of the vials back to the early days of the Papal see, are far from viewing all the vials included in the seventh trumpet. For they place a number of them even before the sixth trumpet. Pool's continuators, upon the seventh trumpet, (Rev. xi, 15,) observe; "Here ariseth a great question, whether the seven vials, of which we shall find the sixteenth chapter treating, do belong all to the seventh trumpet? or whether some of them belong to the sixth trumpet? Great divines are on *both sides of this question.* Mr. Pool, in his Latin synopsis, has collected together their reasons." The reasons offered in favor of all the vials being included in the last wo-trumpet, are, in my opinion, inconclusive. While the objections against this scheme are irresistible. And if the seventh trumpet does not contain all the vials, it can contain none but the seventh and last. For no objection can be offered against its containing only the *last* vial, which does not equally militate against its containing any number *more* than the last, but short of the *whole*. The third woe then, must probably comprise either the *whole* of the vials; or only the *last* vial. And the latter I apprehend will prove to be the fact.

It is striking to observe the *sameness* of the descriptions of the two events, the last wo-trumpet, and the seventh vial: And that this trumpet and vial appear to stand precisely in the same relation to the introduction of the Millennium. Let us compare together the two prophetic descriptions.

Seventh Trumpet.

Rev. x, 7; and xi, 15—19. "But in the days of the voice of the seventh angel, when he shall begin

Seventh Vial.

Rev. xvi, 17—21.

to sound, the mystery of God shall be finished."

"And the seventh angel sounded; and there were great voices in heaven, saying, The kingdoms of this world are become the kingdoms of our Lord and of his Christ; and he shall reign forever and ever."

"And the temple of God was opened in heaven; and there was seen in his temple the ark of the testimony; and there were lightnings, and voices, and thunderings, and an earthquake, and great hail."

"And the seventh angel poured out his vial into the air; and there came a great voice out of the temple of heaven saying, It is done."

"And there were voices, and thunders, and lightnings; and there was a great earthquake, such as was not since men were upon the earth, so mighty an earthquake, and so great. And there fell upon men a great hail out of heaven, every stone about the weight of a talent; and men blasphemed God because of the plague of the hail, for

ceeding great."

"And the four and twenty elders, who sat before God on their seats, fell upon their faces, and wor-

O Lord
who art,
to come,
taken to
and
na-

tions were angry, and thy wrath is come, and the time of the dead that they should be judged, (avenged) and that thou should-

"And the great city was divided into three parts; and the cities of the nations fell; and great Babylon came into remembrance before God, to give unto her the cup of the wine of the fierceness of his wrath; and every island fled away, and the mountains were not found."

est give reward unto thy
servants the prophets, and
to the saints, and to them
who fear thy name, small
and great; and shouldest
destroy them who destroy
the earth."

Who can believe, that these two portions of prophecy do not relate to precisely the same period and
event? Both introduce the Millennium. Both describe
the battle of that great day of God, in the same figures. And there is *no appearance*, that the description
of the seventh trumpet contains any thing more than
what is contained in the seventh vial. If it were designed to contain *all* the vials, or if the whole period
of the vials were then *future;* how could the voices in
heaven proclaim, *the kingdoms of this world are become
the kingdoms of our Lord, and of his Christ?* This does
not appear to be one of those prophecies which speak
of things far future, as though they were present.
To suppose it, is to destroy the very *occasion* of the
joys of the heavenly hosts there noted. Their joys
were, that the *time* for the introduction of the Millennium *had actually arrived.* They well knew *before,*
that this joyful event was *future,* and *certain,* and
would arrive in due time. This they knew every time
they turned their thoughts upon it. And were their
peculiar joys (expressed at the sounding of the seventh trumpet) occasioned only by a new turning of
their attention to that subject, which was still far future? A thing which they had done millions of times
before! How could this afford them any new source of
joy? But let themselves decide the question. Do they
not decide, that the occasion of their peculiar joy is
the *actual introduction* of the blessed millennial glory?
The kingdoms of this world are become *the kingdoms of
our Lord and of his Christ.* The same thing, which
is expressed upon the effusion of the seventh vial; "*It
is done.*"

In Rev. x, it appears to be *decided*, that the seventh
trumpet does not contain the whole period of the vials;

but is the same with the seventh vial. The seven thunders had uttered their voices; or the *wars and rumors of wars*, attendant on the rise of Antichrist, had been heard. The Angel now, (verses 5, 6,) as though to correct the mistake of those, who will now imagine, that the third woe has already commenced; and to check the impatience of the saints for the coming of Christ; as well as to assure them, that it should be in due time; lifts up his hand to heaven, and swears, with unusual formality and solemnity, that, Χρονος ουκ εσται ετι; *the time shall not be yet:* Or, the time shall not be prolonged. And he adds; *But in the days of the seventh Angel, when he shall begin to sound, the mystery of God shall be finished; as he hath declared to his servants the prophets.* In this passage several things are decided:

1. At the time of the seven thunders uttering their voices, the seventh trumpet, or third woe, is *still future.* In the preceding chapter the effects of the first and second wo-trumpets are described. In this xth chapter, instead of going on to a description of the *third* wo-trumpet, as would seem to be natural, and as he does in the course of the following chapter, a notable intervening event is introduced, by the crying of a mighty Angel with a loud voice; and by seven *thunders* uttering their voices.

Thunder is a striking emblem of war.* And seven shocks of thunder, breaking at once, must be a striking emblem of an unprecedented scene of wars. The import of this figure was sealed up, till it should be fulfilled. Then it was no doubt to be understood. These seven thunders, we may apprehend, have been heard in the wars of our day, attending the rise of the Antichristian Beast; and the formation of his horns. Our blessed Lord, when predicting his coming,† foretold that there should be *wars and rumors of wars,* which are but *the beginning of sorrows;* but the end he says "is not by and by;" or is not yet: As the Angel in this chapter swears, that *the time is not yet,* or immediate-

---

* See Isa. xxix, 6.　　† Mat. xxiv; Mark xiii; Luke xxi.

ly. These two passages, no doubt, relate to the same period and thing. And when the great events of the seven thunders, which must be viewed as opening a new era of affairs, *commence,* instead of introducing the events of the third woe, (as some would, from the greatness and terrors of the scenes, naturally expect,) the Angel announces, that the seventh trumpet is still future; that it shall not be quite yet; or shall not be long deferred. The great events of the seven thunders then, are *not* the seventh trumpet.*

2. In verse 7, we learn, that at the *beginning* of the seventh trumpet, when the Angel shall *begin* to sound, the mystery of God shall be *finished,* precisely the same idea with that in chap. xvi, 17; where upon the pouring out of the seventh vial into the air, the great voice from the temple of Heaven announces; *It is done.* But surely if the mystery of the prosperity and triumphs of the enemies of God, is *finished, in the days of the voice of the seventh angel, when he shall begin to sound;* his *beginning* to sound must be at a *later date,* than the introduction of the period of the vials! It must be the same with the *seventh vial;* which does indeed *finish* the mystery of iniquity. If the *beginning* of the seventh Angel to sound, or the commencement of the third woe, be but the *introduction* of the period of the vials, how could the Angel of the covenant announce, that when the seventh Angel shall *begin* to sound, the mystery of God shall be *finished?* The assertion would be utterly untrue; as would the assertion in chap. xi, 15, upon the sounding of the seventh trumpet before noted, *The kingdoms of this world are become the kingdoms of our Lord, and of his Christ.* Do not these Scriptures, viewed in this connexion, demonstrate that the seventh trumpet and the seventh vial relate to the same event?

3. The seventh trumpet, we here learn, relates to the great event, which God of old revealed to the prophets. *But in the days of the seventh angel, when he shall begin to sound, the mystery of God shall be*

---

* See remarks upon this, in the treatise upon the fifth vial.

finished, as he hath declared to his servants the· pro-
phets. What great events of these last days did, God
of old abundantly reveal to his servants the prophets
in Israel? The event of the *seventh vial,* the destruction of the final and mystical Babylon, to prepare the
way for God's Israel to build their millennial Jerusalem, was abundantly revealed of old to God's servants
the prophets. The battle of *that* great day was very
much by them predicted; as may be seen in the second
and following sections in chapter iii of this dissertation.
And lest any should say that *that* event, so much predicted in the ancient prophets, comprises *all the vials,* as they
have conceived that the seventh *trumpet* comprises
them; we find the dreadful event *restricted,* in Rev.
xvi, 14, to the *seventh* vial: *To gather them to . the*
battle . of that great day of God Almighty. What great
day? *That great day* so well known, as abundantly revealed in the prophetic parts of the Word of God.
This clause, (applied to the *seventh* vial) forcibly implies, that this vial is *that very event,* so abundantly
predicted in the prophets, that God would *gather the*
nations, and assemble the kingdoms, and pour out
upon them his indignation, even all his fierce anger;
and the whole earth should be devoured with the fire
of his jealousy. And that he would destroy the sinners
thereof out of it. The minor events of the preceding
vials probably were not much known in the prophets of
the Old Testament. But the decisive event of the
seventh vial was *well* known in the writings of the ancient prophets. And the predictions of this event
can by no means admit, that the judgments of *all* the
vials are included in that tremendous scene, called the
day of the Lord. For it is ever represented, not as
a long series of judgments, occupying some centuries;
but as of short duration;—a decisive event;—a day
that burns as an oven;—a gathering of the nations to
the valley of Jehoshaphat, where God will *soon decide*
the controversy with his enemies. ";He will finish the
work, and cut it short in righteousness, because a short
work will the Lord make upon the earth." These remarks are not to insinuate, that the interesting event

of that day of the Lord will be accomplished literally in *one day;* nor in *one battle.* It may be a work of *months,* if not *years.* But it is to be *short,* and of the most decisive kind;—too short and decisive, to be viewed as comprising all the vials. It can comprise only the *seventh;* which is accordingly called, "the battle of *that* great day of God Almighty; as being an event well known in the prophets. Yet the passage, Rev. x; 6, under consideration, decides that the seventh trumpet (the third woe) is the very same with that *day of the Lord,* in the prophets; which in fact fulfils the seventh vial. "But in the days of the seventh angel, when he shall begin to sound, the mystery of God shall be finished, *as he hath declared to his servants the prophets."* Here we learn, that the seventh trumpet does not comprise *all* the vials; but only the *seventh.* For the seventh *trumpet* is the very event noted in the prophets. Yet the seventh *vial* is "the battle of *that* great day of God Almighty," so well known in the prophets. Thus the seventh *trumpet* and seventh *vial* are fulfilled in the *same event.* The first concludes the septenary, or number seven, found in the first general division of the prophetic part of the Revelation; and the last concludes the septenary found in the last general division; as will appear in the next chapter, and on the first chart there exhibited. The idea, that the seventh trumpet and seventh vial are the same, is of some importance. It goes to decide that the notable judgment of the third woe is future of the sixth vial.

It is ascertained, in section i, chapter ii, of this book, that the reign of sin, under the gospel, or the time preceding the Millennium, was probably to be about 2000 years. In the course of this period, beside a variety of other judgments, there were to be three notable ones, called woes, as well as trumpets. The first of these took place about the close of the first third of the above 2000 years, as all expositors agree. The second woe took place about the close of the second third of the 2000 years, as is likewise agreed. The Turks were clearly committing their ravages, in the former part of the fourteenth century. What then does analogy suggest, relative to the time of the third woe? It suggests that it may rationally be expected not long before the close of the 2000 years. This woe then, must be at too late a period to be viewed as including all the vials. And if it do not include them all, it probably includes only the seventh vial; or is the same in the first great division of the book of Revelation, with "the battle of that great day of God Almighty, in the second division. For an account of this general division, see chapter v; *A concise view of the Revelation.*

The numerous predictions in the Old and New Testaments, of the awful and universal destruction of the contending enemies of Christ, to prepare the way for his millennial Kingdom on earth, *evince,* that the event will be of sufficient magnitude to fulfil the seventh trumpet, the third woe, the battle of that great day of God Almighty, and the seventh vial: Or, that these different representations *may* all relate to this *same event.* . Its extent and terrors will be such, that it is not to be esteemed strange, that in addition to its being called the seventh trumpet, if should be represented as the third woe, the battle of that great day of God Almighty, and the seventh *vial.* We do not imagine the third woe to be a different event from the seventh trumpet; nor the battle of that great day of God Almighty to be an event different from the seventh vial; although they are different representations. Why then should it be deemed improper to conclude, that the seventh trumpet and the seventh vial relate to the same event?

The supposition, that the seventh trumpet includes all the vials, involves the subject in inexplicable difficulties. We must then say, according to the foregoing scheme of the vials, that the third woe commenced, or the seventh trumpet was blown, at the time of the reformation, early in the sixteenth century. Consequently, that the slaying and the resurrection of the witnesses, and the earthquake, (see Rev. xi, 7—15,) preceded that period. How then could the witnesses be said to have prophesied in sackcloth, 1260 years, Rev. xi, 3. Or be said to have been given, for this period, into the hands of Popery? Dan. vii, 25. Or the witnesses, when they were slain, be said either to have *finished*, or even to be *about* to finish their testimony of 1260 years. And how could the Angel announce, (Rev. x, 5. 6,) *But in the days of the seventh angel, when he shall begin to sound, the mystery of God shall be finished, as he hath declared to his servants the prophets?* Or how could the great voices in heaven, chap: xi, 15, announce, at some period *before* the reformation, or *at* that time, *The kingdoms of this world are become the kingdoms of our Lord and of his Christ?* For the kingdoms have not *yet* become thus. And the commencement of the reformation was nearly three hundred years ago.

Or shall it be said the third woe commenced at the time of the revolution in France? and that the vials then began to be poured out? But can we exclude from the vials that regular series of fatal judgments upon the Papal see, which commenced at the time of the reformation, and which have been noted as fulfilling the four first vials? Have they not a most evident claim to be reckoned among the vials? Can it appear judicious to exclude them; and then to suppose (with a late author) that at least four of the vials were accomplished on France and her dependencies, in about *twenty years?* This appears too much to diminish the object of the vials. And has it not been shown, in section ii, chapter iii, in remarking upon the slaying of the witnesses, that no event took place antecedent to the French revolution, which can be viewed as answering to that representation?

It does appear indeed, from every consideration, that the seventh trumpet is still *future.* For the way is not yet prepared for the kingdoms of this world to become the kingdoms of our Lord, and of his Christ. But is it probable, that after all the fatal judgments inflicted on Papal Rome, the whole period of the vials is still future? This cannot be admitted. It follows then, that the seventh trumpet does *not* comprise all the period of the vials. It probably comprises only the *seventh* vial.

According to the foregoing scheme of the vials, we are yet under the second woe. According to Bp. Newton, the second woe continues, till the Turkish empire is broken. And this, I think, is evident. The sixth trumpet established that empire. And it is natural to view it as closing in the subversion of the same empire under the sixth vial. The voice *then* proclaims, "The second woe is past; and behold the third woe cometh quickly." Rev. xi, 14.

Four of the vials have been poured out. The effusion of the fifth has been introduced in our day; and is now, with unprecedented terrors, fulfilling the judgments of Heaven on Papal nations. The sixth vial may not be far distant. And the *seventh* (the terrific and decisive scenes of the third woe, and the battle of that great day of God Almighty) will be fulfilled at the close of the 1260 years, and will decide the controversy between Jesus Christ and his enemies.

This scheme concerning the vials accounts for all the late commotions in Europe; and ascertains that a new and most important era has commenced; although the third woe is still future. The tremendous scenes, which have recently taken place, are the judgments of the *fifth vial;* the subversion of the *seat* (throne) of the Papal Beast, by the rise of the Atheistical Antichrist, who denieth the Father and the Son. These are the *wars and rumors of wars,* foretold by our blessed Lord, as the harbingers of his coming, and as the beginning of sorrows. These probably are the seven thunders uttering their voices, at a period subsequent to the second woe, and not long antecedent to the third; whose import was to be sealed up, till they should be fulfilled; whose events would then be naturally mistaken for the coming of Christ in the *third woe;* but upon which the Angel *swears,* that *the time is not yet, the end shall not be by and by.* Events most interesting to the Church must intervene between this and the destruction of her enemies, to introduce her millennial glory. The *bitter* contents of the little book in the Angel's hand must be experienced. *And I took the little book out of the angel's hand, and ate it up; and* *it was in my mouth sweet as honey; and as soon as I had eaten it, my belly was bitter. And he said unto me, Thou must prophecy again before many peoples, and nations, and tongues, and kings.* The events here hinted, if they be *future*, (as must be apprehended, from the connexion of the events of the passage,) *future days must unfold!* The people of God need to be prepared for every event.* Never perhaps were the Christian armor, and holy vigilance and faithfulness, more necessary, than at the present period. Our Lord, when predicting this period, gives in charge; *Watch ye therefore; for ye know not when the Master of the house cometh, at even, or at midnight, or at the cockcrowing, or in the morning; lest coming suddenly, he find you sleeping. And what I say unto you, I say unto all,* WATCH.

---

* This representation is consistent with all that has been said of the Beast from the bottomless pit's *soon* going into perdition; and his damnation *slumbering not.* His reign will be short, compared with the events of prophecy; though in the view of the then present generation, it will not be so *immediate*, as they are inclined to hope.

A concise view of the Revelation of St. John.

THE following exposition of this mystical book is submitted. The brevity, which in one short chapter must be consulted, forbids the adducing of many arguments relative to the subjects exhibited, or of many objections against different schemes. I might state what authors have said on each point; but it would be unwieldy. Many of the expositions given, are such as accord with the most approved expositors. *Some are new.* Let these be examined by the word of God; and may the reader devoutly search, compare and judge for himself.

I shall give but a concise view of the contents of each chapter. The plan, chronology, and outlines of the book, in its several parts, will be my chief object. If these be correctly settled, more minute particulars will not be of difficult decision.

The revelation contains three subjects, of very unequal length. Christ denominates them, (chap. i, 19,) "The things which thou hast *seen;* and the things which *are;* and the things which *shall be hereafter.*" The first were contained in the first chapter, exhibited in the former part of the first scene, which was opened to St. John. This may be viewed as a *prologue*, or introduction to the whole.

The second subject, or the things which *then were,* are found in the second and third chapters, in continuation of the first scene. They were delivered from the mouth of Jesus Christ in his enditing of seven epistles, one to each of the seven churches then in Asia Minor. These were not designed as a prophetic part of the Word of God. But like the other admonitory parts of the sacred Scriptures, they equally apply to all people of characters similar to those here described, in every age.

The third subject, the things which were to be in times then future, follows. This was the great and signal object of the vision. By far the greater part of the vision is occupied in exhibiting these then future scenes.

The whole exhibition in the Apocalypse is in the form of a drama, in a succession of various scenes. The first scene, contained in the three first chapters, has been concisely noted. A preparation then follows, in the fourth and fifth chapters, to exhibit the events of futurity. The scenery appears to be laid in heaven, which is presented in the second scene, and fourth chapter, through a large opening, which seemed to be made high in the aerial region, or through that vault of the visible heaven, which bounds our sight. In this scene, the Actors, and some of the apparatus for the ensuing scenes, are presented. God the Father is represented as on his throne of glory, surrounded with a rainbow, an emblem of his covenant faithfulness; and attended with other insignia of the divine Majesty. Christ, under the emblem of a lamb, that had been slain, and under the name of "the Lion of the tribe of Judah," is presented. The gospel Church is exhibited under the emblem of four and twenty Elders. And the ministers of the gospel are represented by four living creatures; (as all agree that the word zoa, from zoo to live, ought to have been rendered.) By the different forms of these living creatures, different ministerial talents and gifts are symbolized.* The angels also as

---

* Pool's continuators, Guise, Scott, and others, have given their decided opinion, that these living creatures symbolize the ministers of the gospel. The evidence in favor of this appears conclusive. In Rev. v, 8—11, when the Lamb takes the book, the living creatures and elders adoringly fall before him, and sing a new song, saying, "Thou art worthy to take the book, and to open the seals thereof; for thou wast slain, and hast redeemed *us* to God by thy blood, out of every kindred and tongue and people and nation; and hast made *us* unto our God kings and priests; and we shall reign on the earth." Here it is decided that the four living creatures belong to the *human race.* They cannot be Angels. For the Angels are presented in the next verse, in their own names and forms, as distinct

Messengers of Providence, and ministering Spirits to the Church, are in this scene presented. The decrees of God, then about to be unfolded, are presented. under the emblem of a *book*, of ancient form, in the right hand of God the Father. This book was a *roll*, consisting of seven pieces of parchment, each written on one side, and rolled up, the writing inward; and each sealed down, on the last edge, and the back side. The seven pieces were thus rolled, and sealed; one over the other. The breaking of the outside seal, unrolling the parchment, and presenting its contents, was to commence the revealing of events then future. In the sixth chapter this solemn process begins. This is the first prophetic chapter. With this therefore, I shall begin my further explanations.

To prepare the way for this, let it be observed, that the prophetic part of this mystical book is found in two great general divisions. The first begins with the sixth chapter, and closes with the eleventh. It begins with events of the first century, and proceeds on, till at the close of the eleventh chapter, it reaches and describes the scene of judgments, which just precedes the Millennium, under the description of the seventh trumpet, and the third woe. This terrible event, and the introduction of the Millennium, are concisely announced, at the close of the first general division—the close of the eleventh chapter.

from the living creatures. In chap. iv, 9, 10, these living creatures are the smaller number, who stand between God and, the Elders, and lead in his worship. "And when these beasts give glory and honor and thanks to him that sat on the throne, who liveth forever and ever, the four and twenty elders fall down before him that sat on the throne, and worship him that liveth forever and ever, and cast their crowns before the throne.

Here are Christ's ministers leading in the worship performed in the Church. In chap. vi, 1--7, these living creatures are the monitors of God's people, who when the first seals are opened, call on their people to *"come and see."* Here is one important branch of the, duties of the ministers of Christ, to exhibit the opening events of Providence, and call on their people to behold them.

The second general division of the prophetic part of the Revelation, commences with the xiith chapter, and continues to the end of the book. It begins where the first division began, or with a reversion back to the first century; and proceeds to exhibit events from that time, to the end of the world. It closes with a descrip-tion of heaven, and a solemn epilogue, or finishing ad-dress, from Christ, relative to his coming to judge the world. And it is remarkable that the scenes, in the sec-ond general division, proceed in *pairs;* or, two scenes are appropriated to each period of events, as will be shown. Two scenes begin with the apostolic age;—two with the commencement of the reformation, in the sixteenth century; two with the rise of the Antichris-tian Beast of the last days; two with the introduction of the Millennium; and two with a description of the subsequent heavenly state. Each of these two general divisions has an internal arrangement, a process, and subdivisions, peculiar to itself. Each, while moving through the same periods, gives a different view, of syn-chronical events. Each therefore has its peculiar excel-lency, while it has its peculiar mode of instruction. The subdivisions, in each of the two general divisions, will be exhibited, as we pass along through the chapters, where the way will be prepared for them to be under-stood. Seven periods in the one general division, sev-en periods in the other, and seven periods presented by the two general divisions conjointly, will be noted.

I shall make use of two *charts*, of simple construc-tions, to exhibit and to render familiar the plan and contents of this book. The first exhibits the two *gen-eral divisions* above noted; and the periods or chronolo-gy of the contents of each prophetic chapter in this book. Here the peculiar arrangement of each general division will be *presented to the eye;* together with the septenary, or number seven, in the one, and in the other, and that resulting from both. The second chart ex-hibits the *seals, trumpets,* and vials; with a sketch of the events fulfilling each seal, trumpet and vial; and the analogy presented, between the descriptions of the six first trumpets, and their corresponding vials. This second chart gives a relative view of the seals, trumpets, and vials, and their fulfilments; and is a concise memorandum of the principal events of the' Apocalypse. See Chart first. (The charts for convenience sake are placed at the close of the volume.)

The following numbers, in answer to references on chart first, explains the prophetic chapters of the Revelation.

First General Division.

1. The sixth chapter, or first prophetic scene, commences the opening of the *seals*, in the first century; and contains six of the seals. The sixth seal closes in the revolution in the Roman empire under Constantine, about the year 320.

First Seal. "And I saw when the Lamb opened one of the seals; and I heard as it were the noise of thunder, one of the four beasts saying, Come and see. And I saw and beheld a white horse; and he that sat on him had a bow; and a crown was given unto him; and he went forth conquering and to conquer."

This hieroglyphic is differently explained by different great authors. One class of them suppose it to have related to the war between the Romans and the Jews, about 40 years after Christ, in which Jerusalem was destroyed, and the few of the Jews, who escaped the slaughter, were dispersed in the Roman empire. It appears indeed very natural, and consentaneous with the events of the following seals, to view this figure as fulfilled by that war, fatal to the Jews, under Vespasian. The Jews had crucified Christ. And here Christ came, and destroyed their temple, city and nation. Another class of authors suppose this figure to have been fulfilled in the blessed propagation of the gospel in heathen lands, under the ministry of the apostles, and of their early successors. Christ thus rode forth in the triumphs of his cause, in allusion to ancient victorious generals and conquerors, who rode on white horses, as emblems of victory. This figure under the first seal, (if these authors be correct) seems to be expressed in allusion to such scriptures as the following: Psalm xlv, 3—6, "Gird thy sword upon thy thigh, O most mighty: with thy glory and thy majesty. And in thy majesty ride prosperously, because of truth, and meekness, and righteousness; and thy right hand shall teach thee terrible things. Thine arrows are sharp in the heart of the King's enemies, whereby the people fall under thee." The Captain of our salvation early began to fulfil this prediction of him, (according to this explanation of it) in the salvation of his chosen in heathen lands, as we find in the Acts of the Apostles.

Jesus Christ did indeed ride forth in glorious prosperity, at that very period, in *both* the foregoing senses. Whether both therefore may not unite in the fulfilment of the figure, the reader will judge. The two great ideas, of destruction to the inveterate enemies of God, and the enlargement and salvation of his friends, do abundantly in the sacred oracles, and in divine Providence, go hand in hand, to accomplish the same general event,—the fulfilment of God's word in the salvation of Zion. In the last days, just preceding the Millennium, Christ is again presented upon his white horse of victory, for the salvation of his Church in the destruction of her enemies. See Rev. xix, 11—21.

Second Seal. "And when he had opened the second seal, I heard the second beast say, Come and see. And there went out another horse that was red; and power was given unto him that sat thereon to take peace from the earth, and that they should kill one another, and there was given unto him a great sword." This seal is thought to have been fulfilled in, and after the reign of Trajan and Adrian, in the bloody scenes occasioned by the insurrections of the Jews, in Egypt, Cyprus, and other parts of the Roman empire. Six hundred thousand, and some authors say, more than a million of Jews were cut off in those insurrections. And probably not a less number of Romans and Greeks were destroyed. The Jews and Romans had crucified Jesus Christ, and persecuted his followers. And now they were made to be each other's executioners. "The Lord is known by the judgments that he executeth."

Third Seal. "And when he had opened the third seal, I heard the third beast say, Come and see. And I beheld, and lo a black horse; and he that sat on him had a pair of balances in his hand. And I heard a voice in the midst of the four beasts say, A measure of wheat for a penny, and three measures of barley for a penny; and see that thou hurt not the oil and the wine." The figures here presented are symbols of *scarcity* and *famine*. And this judgment did indeed take place, at the very time to which these symbols allude, under the reign of the Antonines. Dreadful famines were occasioned by inundations, wars, mismanagement of public stores, devouring insects, fires, earthquakes, and other signal judgments, upon Rome, and her various provinces.

Fourth Seal. "And when he had opened the fourth seal, I heard the voice of the fourth beast say, Come and see. And I looked, and behold a pale horse: and his name that sat on him was death, and hell followed with him. And power was given unto them over the fourth part of the earth, to kill with sword and with hunger, and with death, and with the beasts of the earth." The events denoted by these symbols were fulfilled in the reign of Caracalla; and in days that followed, to the reign of Aurelius in the third century. In those times we find thirty competitors at once claiming the imperial crown. Emperors were set up, and deposed in thick succession. *Twenty,* some authors say *thirty,* different emperors were acknowledged in sixty years; most of whom came to violent deaths. Wars within and without raged. Also famines and most terrible pestilence raged for fifteen years together. Wild beasts (one of God's signal judgments; see Ezek. xv, 21,) invaded. Authors state, that five hundred wolves entered a city at one time: And that lions and tigers made signal war upon the inhabitants of various parts of the empire.

Fifth Seal. "And, when he had opened the fifth seal, I saw under the altar the souls of them that were slain for the word of God, and for the testimony which they held. And they cried with a loud voice, saying,

How long, O Lord, holy and true, dost thou not judge and avenge our blood on them that dwell on the earth?. And white robes were given unto every one of them; and it was said unto them, that they should rest yet for a little season, until their fellow servants also and their brethren, that should be killed as they were, should be fulfilled. This prophetic passage may have some special allusion to that persecution, for ten years, which was to take place under Dioclesian.* But the passage must be viewed as comprising things upon a wider scale. We hear in it the voice of the blood of martyrs generally crying to God from the ground for vengeance; as did that of Abel, Gen. iv, 10. The judgments of the preceding seals seem to be overlooked by these martyrs, as though those judgments were nothing, compared with those, for which their blood calls. It is remarkable that this seal does not exhibit an execution of judgments. It is a call only for judgments far more signal, than any previously executed. It is hence to be viewed as a *notice preparatory* to the more terrible judgments of the following or sixth seal; and indeed to all the judgments then future, till the introduction of the Millennium. It may be viewed as a divine denunciation of the tremendous judgments which shall issue in that effectual *"inquisition for blood,"* which God will institute, when he shall "come out of his place to punish the inhabitants of the earth for their iniquity; when the earth shall also disclose her blood, and shall no longer cover her slain:" Isa. xxvi, 21. The effectual judgments of the last days, introductory to the Millennium, are abundantly represented as an avenging of the blood

---

* This was the tenth and most terrible of the persecutions, under the Pagan empire. The first was by Nero, a little after the middle of the first century. The second was by Domitian, just at the close of the first century. The third was by Adrian, soon after. The fourth was by Antoninus Verus, after the middle of the second century. The fifth was by Antoninus who succeeded, near the close of the second century. The fifth by Maximin, the sixth by Desus, the seventh by Gallus, the eighth by Volusian, the ninth by Valerian, and tenth by Dioclesian, the most terrible of all.

of martyrs, and of all the blood wickedly shed upon the earth. Rev. xviii, 24; "And in *her* (mystical Babylon) was found the blood of prophets, and of saints, and of all that were slain upon the earth." As Christ denounced to the Jews, that the blood of prophets and saints, and of all wickedly slain upon the earth, should be required of that generation; so the blood of all the martyrs, shed in Antichristian Rome, will be in a most important sense required of the generation, that shall fall in the battle of the great day, according to the passage just quoted from Rev. xviii, 24. The fifth seal may be viewed as the first warning in the prophetic parts of this book, of that tremendous event; while, in its chronological order its immediate reference was to judgments then impending. Like the fifth trumpet then, which is the first wo-trumpet, the fifth seal begins the opening of things upon a wider scale, than any preceding seals.

Sixth Seal. "And I beheld when he had opened the sixth seal, and lo, there was a great earthquake; and the sun became black as sackcloth of hair, and the moon became as blood; and the stars of heaven fell unto the earth, even as a fig-tree casteth her untimely figs; when she is shaken of a mighty wind. And the heavens departed as a scroll, when it is rolled together; and every mountain and island were moved out of their places. And the kings of the earth, and the great men, and the rich men, and the chief captains, and the mighty men, and every bond man, and every free man hid themselves in the dens, and in the rocks of the mountains; and said to the mountains and rocks, Fall on us, and hide us from the face of him that sitteth on the throne, and from the wrath of the Lamb. For the great day of his wrath is come; and who shall be able to stand?"

This signal passage, it is agreed by all the best expositors, predicted the revolution in Rome, from Paganism to Christianity, which took place under the emperor Constantine, early in the fourth century of the Christian era. See a sketch of this revolution in the note, page 71 of this book. The ancient pagan Ro-

man Beast in this revolution, received a wound in his
sixth, his imperial head, and died. From that period,
for a course of centuries, the secular Roman Beast had
no actual existence. The Papal Beast arose, and with
his image of the Pagan Beast had his season of dominion.
This revolution was a far more notable event, than the
judgments of the preceding seals; as appears from the prophetic description of it; and from the history of the event.
The figures in this passage are bold, striking, complicated, and decisive. And events will be more fully adequate to them, when the same imperial head of the
Roman Beast, after being healed of its deadly wound,
and having again attacked the cause of Christ, and filled the world with terror, shall be utterly destroyed
in the battle of that great day of God Almighty.

The three last seals, like the three last trumpets,
relate to *capital events.* The fifth and sixth just described, clearly relate to more signal judgments, than
those of the preceding seals. And the seventh (which
is opened in the beginning of the eighth chapter) is
indeed the most capital of all; for it contains all the
trumpets.

2. The seventh chapter presents four Angels, at the
four corners of the earth, holding the four winds, that
they should not blow, till the servants of God were
sealed in their foreheads. One hundred and forty four
thousand are sealed from the twelve tribes of Israel.
An innumerable multitude then appear, of all nations, and kindred, and people, and tongues, standing
before the throne. And a description follows of the
heavenly state.

The holding of the four winds, is an emblem of the
deferring of further desolating judgments on the Roman empire, for a season, after the revolution before
noted. The dreadful judgments of the northern invasions were impending. But they were suspended for
a course of years. And this interval of peace the Holy
Spirit improved, to call in vast multitudes, (a certain
number put for an uncertain) of God's chosen. Their
being sealed in their foreheads, is an emblem of their
being renewed and sanctified. They are represented

as being literally of Israel. The Gentiles acceded to
the Jewish church or the visible kingdom of God.
They are hence called the children of Abraham. And
the portion of them then converted are here figuratively called by the name of the twelve patriarchs. The
Gentile church is God's *spiritual Israel.* Their number in the Roman empire, at that time was vast, represented by the square of the twelve patriarchs, or of
the apostles, in thousands. Yet the scene was increased. Far greater multitudes, which none could number, were then presented to the view of the evangelist,
as though they were already in heaven, collected from
all parts of the earth, and had begun, in the vast assembly above, their eternal work of praise. Their state of
glory is described. They had come out of great tribulation on earth. Their palm branches held in their
hands, are symbols of their eternal victory. And their
enjoyment of God and the Lamb is perfect, exquisite,
and everlasting.

The scene in this chapter was most animating to
the people of God, and probably designed to fortify
their souls against the terrors of the tremendous scenes,
that were to follow, under the trumpets.

3. The eighth chapter contains four of the trumpets
of judgment inflicted on the Roman empire.

Seventh Seal. "And when he had opened the seventh seal, there was silence in heaven about the space
of half an hour." This silence may be viewed as indicative of the solemn awe and suspense, occasioned by
an expectation of the terrible series of judgments then
opening upon the western branch of the empire, in the
invasions from the barbarians of the north; and the
bloody revolution to take place there between the last
of the third century, and the beginning of the seventh.
Some suppose this silence to have been expressed in
allusion to the silent worship performed in the ancient
Jewish temple, while the high priests, on the day of
expiation, was offering incense on the golden altar.
What follows seems to favor this idea. For Christ,
the Angel of the covenant, the great High Priest, is
represented as perfuming the prayers of the saints,

with his mediatorial incense offered on the golden altar before the throne; in allusion to the ancient offering of incense by the Jewish high priest, while the people worshipped in *silence*. Christ then casts from heaven to earth a censer full of fire from the altar, on which the prayers of the saints are perfumed; and voices, thunderings, lightnings, and an earthquake follow. These denote the judgments of God, upon the enemies of the church, inflicted through the intercession of Christ for his people, and in answer to their prayers for the protection of his cause. This seal, like the fifth, is a mere notice and preparation of tremendous succeeding judgments. It may be said to comprise, or relate to, all the judgments of the trumpets.

Seven Angels are presented, with seven trumpets, ancient emblems of war; and symbols of seven distinct scenes of divine judgment. And they prepare themselves to sound.

First Trumpet. "The first angel sounded: and their followed hail and fire mingled with blood; and they were cast upon the earth: and the third part of trees was burnt up, and all green grass was burnt up." This assemblage of figures predicted a vast destruction of the people; and the ruin of their tranquillity, and comforts. It was fulfilled by the terrible northern barbarous invasions upon the western wing of the Roman Empire, in the last part of the fourth century. The provinces of the empire were first attacked by those savage invaders, like a storm of hail and fire. Aleric with his Goths, and Attila (stiling himself the scourge of God, and the terror of men) with his hoards of Huns, made horrible devastations.

Second Trumpet. "And the second angel sounded; and as it were a great mountain burning with fire was cast into the sea; and the third part of the sea became blood. And the third part of the creatures which were in the sea and had life, died; and the third part of the ships were destroyed." This was fulfilled about the middle of the fifth century, when Genseric, king of the Vandals, with a great army from Africa, landed at the mouth of the Tiber, and took and plundered Rome, that had been so long the mistress of the world.

63

Third Trumpet. "And the third angel sounded; and there followed a great star from heaven, burning as it were a lamp, and it fell upon the third part of the rivers, and upon the fountains of water. And the name of the star is called Wormwood; and the third part of the waters became wormwood; and many men died of the waters, because they were made bitter." It may with some propriety be thought, that this trumpet was fulfilled by the bitter persecutions occasioned by the Arian heresy. These persecutions did indeed greatly imbitter the scenes of life, in the various nations of the Roman empire, which were symbolized by rivers and fountains of water. A star falling from heaven is a most fit symbol of an apostate teacher, a teacher of heresy. Such a star, in chapter ix, 1, symbolized Mohammed, or Sergius his aid, under the fifth trumpet, as will be noted. And in the third trumpet it may most aptly symbolize Arius. Both he and his followers might well be called wormwood. For, with all their sanctimonious phiz, and cry of persecution, they were *extremely bitter.* And they imbittered the blessings of life.

Arius denied the Trinity of Persons in the Godhead. He held that Christ was a mere creature, formed and dependent, but very exalted; a kind of middle link between God and creatures, though himself a real creature. Arius said, "We are persecuted, because we say *Christ had a beginning.*" And he seemed to think it sufficient to confute his antagonists, I say that they held, that Christ was not, in his divine Person, posterior, nor inferior to the Father.

His doctrines were very pleasing to the enemies of evangelical truth; and they spread with amazing celerity. Emperors and kings embraced his scheme, and became its furious advocates. The kings of the Goths and Vandals embraced Arianism, and treated the Church of Christ, in their opposition to it, with great severity. This was indeed a judgment; and has been supposed by some to have fulfilled one of the trumpets. And if so, it must have been the third. It is true Arius himself lived, and introduced his heresy, some time before the period of this third trumpet. But his heresy revived and became *more peculiarly distressing and bitter*, at the very time when we must look for the fulfilment of this trumpet. The second trumpet was fulfilled about the middle of the fifth century. The fourth trumpet was fulfilled in the latter part of the sixth century. The third trumpet then, must have occupied the space between these periods. And at this very time Moshiem informs, (vol. i, p. 467.) "Toward the commencement of this (the sixth) century, the Arians were triumphant in several parts of Asia, Africa, and Europe.—Their opinions were openly professed, and their cause maintained by the Vandals in Africa, the Goths in Italy, the Spaniards, the Burgandians, the Suevi, and the greatest part of the Gauls." The historian proceeds to speak of the Nicenians (Trinitarians,) as being rigorously treated by these adversaries, "particularly in Africa and Italy, where they felt, in a very severe manner, the weight of the Arian power, and the *bitterness* of their resentment." The ravages and triumphs of these furious heretics, however, were short, as Mosheim proceeds to inform. The storm was over, "when the Vandals were driven out of Africa (A. D. 534) and the Goths out of Italy, by the arm of Justinian." These events seem to accord with the description of the third trumpet.

Some however have been of opinion that this trumpet was fulfilled in merely *political events*. And the following have been selected as according with it. Odoacer, toward the close of the fifth century, collected an army in Germany, entered Italy by the Trentine, subdued the country, took Rome, deposed their last Emperor Momylus, and assumed the title of the king of Italy. But his kingdom was short. Theodoric with his Goths from Illyricum subdued Odoacer, and set up *his own* kingdom in Italy. These wars, revolutions, and barbarous governments, were indeed bitter judgments. Broils, confusion and distress, fill the histories of those times. The reader will judge for himself which of the above events, or whether both of them unitedly, fulfilled this trumpet.

Fourth Trumpet. "And the fourth angel sounded, and the third part of the sun was smitten, and the third part of the moon, and the third part of the stars; so that the third part of them was darkened, and the day shone not for a third part of it, and the night likewise." This is thought to have been fulfilled in the following events. After the above noted Gothic kingdom had for some time continued in Italy, Justinian, emperor in the east, by his general Belisarius took Rome. The next year Vitiges, king of the Goths, besieged it with 150,000 men, and reduced the Romans to the greatest extremity for more than a year. Twenty years after, Totilas, a succeeding Gothic king, took the city of Rome. Belisarius the next year took it again. Two years after, Totilas again recovered it. And five times in twenty years Rome was besieged and taken. And it was reduced to a miserable condition, being stripped of all its authority. For Narses, another general of Justinian, having subverted the Gothic kingdom in Italy, was constituted duke of Italy; and all the provinces, and Rome itself, (which till now had retained some small degree of its power) were subjected to him. The exarchate of Ravenna was soon after established. Ravenna became the seat of the new government. And upon this Rome lost all its authority and dignity, and was put upon a level with the other cities in Italy. That distinguishing political *luminary* was thus *darkened;* and darkness settled upon the advocates of the old government; or their political system was lost.

Thus the four minor trumpets were fulfilled. The three last were to be more capital events; and are called wo-trumpets; or the *first, second and third woes.* An Angel gives notice of this in the close of the eighth chapter. "And I beheld, and heard an angel flying through the midst of heaven, saying with a loud voice, *Woe, woe, woe,* to the inhabiters of the earth, by reason of the other voices of the trumpet of the three angels, which are yet to sound."

4. The ninth chapter gives a description of the two first woes, or the fifth and sixth trumpets.

Fifth Trumpet; or first Woe. A star falls from heaven, and unlocks the bottomless pit; whence a smoke pours forth, which darkens the sun and the air. From this smoke locusts of a dreadful description proceed, which have power as scorpions. They torment the men, who have not the seal of God upon their foreheads. All agree that this trumpet was fulfilled by the rise and progress of the Mohammedan delusion. The falling star was a symbol of Mohammed, as a false teacher: Or rather perhaps, of Sergius, an apostate monk, who aided him. His scheme did in fact open the bottomless pit. The smoke darkening the sun and the air, symbolized his wretched imposture. And the terrible locusts from this smoke denoted his vast armies of Saracens, or Arabian soldiers, by whom he propagated his delusion with fire and sword. This judgment rose with Popery in the seventh century, and continued many centuries. It soon overran a great part of the eastern world. Those frightful armies, in about 120 years, subdued and brought under the power of their delusion, Arabia, Palestine, Syria, both the Armenias, chief of Asia Minor, Persia, India, Egypt, Numidia, Barbary; and they made horrid ravages in Portugal, Spain, parts of Italy, Sicily, Candia, Cyprus; and they entered France with an army of 400,000 men. But they were there defeated by Charles Martel; and were driven from the west of Europe, with the loss, some say, of seven eighths of their army.

Sixth Trumpet, or second Woe. The sixth Angel looses four angels that are bound in the river Euphrates, and that are prepared for an hour, and a day, and a month, and a year, to slay a third part of men. An army, of two hundred millions is presented, who were horsemen, with breastplates of fire, and jacinth, and brimstone. Their horses have heads of lions; and from their mouths issue fire, smoke and brimstone, which kill a third part of men.

This trumpet was fulfilled in the rise and progress of the Turkish empire. Four sultanies of the Seljukian Turks, not far from the river Euphrates, were long restrained within their own bounds, by the Papal crusades, and the attacks of the Tartars. But in the beginning of the fourteenth century, these restraints having been taken off, those petty dynasties formed into an empire, and began to threaten Europe. Their armies became vast. They were composed chiefly of cavalry, or horsemen. They introduced the use of *fire-arms:*. And thus firing over the heads of their horses, they perfectly answered to the symbol, of fire and smoke and brimstone issuing from their horses' mouth, and killing men. They took Constantinople in the fifteenth century; and it has been the seat of their empire to the present day. In this siege the Turks used cannon of an enormous size; and thus further fulfilled the symbol of smoke, fire and brimstone issuing from their horses' mouths.

5. In the tenth chapter, a mighty Angel comes down from heaven, clothed with a cloud, with a rainbow upon his head, his face as the sun, and his feet as pillars of fire. He cries with a loud voice—upon which seven thunders utter their voices; the true import of which was to be sealed up *for that time.* Standing upon the sea and earth, the Angel decides with an oath, that the *time shall not be yet;* or shall not be *long deferred;* but in the days of the seventh trumpet, the scenes of wickedness shall be finished, as the prophets have foretold. The Angel has an open book in his hand, which John is directed to take and eat. The book is sweet in his mouth, but bitter in digestion: Which is explained, by his prophesying again before many peoples, and nations, and tongues, and kings.

In this chapter, it is believed, we have a clouded view of the terrible Empire of the last days. The ravages of the Turks had just been predicted, under the second woe. And now, before the account proceeds to note the third woe, the instrument of judgment, probably for the subversion of the Turks, as well as for the work of divine vengeance on Papal nations, is next adumbrated. A striking hint must be given of this *mighty Power,* and the terrible events of the last days, before the close of the first general division of the prophetic parts of this book. This chapter, in mystical hints, gives the same events, with those found in the second general division, in chapter xvii, and xviii;— the Beast from the bottomless pit; and the fall of Papal Babylon.

The period for the events of this chapter is clearly between the second and third woes, and not long before the third; and the events (it is strikingly hinted) are naturally mistaken for those of the third woe. This is implied in the oath of the Angel. The descent of a mighty Angel from heaven, crying with a loud voice, as when a lion roareth, is a striking symbol of the introduction of a scene of most interesting events. The descriptions of this angel decide that he is Christ. The rainbow upon his head, indicates that what he is going now to do, is in covenant faithfulness to his cause. Or some very important parts of the Bible are now to be fulfilled. A little book in his hand seems to indicate, that a new era is commencing in the history of man. The book's being *open*, may suggest, that the events of providence will now strikingly unfold the sense of the prophecies relative to the last days... The seven thunders uttering their voices, are a striking emblem of the commencement of a most terrible scene of wars. Their sense being sealed up, shows that the subject would not be understood, till it was unfolded by the events. The oath of the Angel seems to indicate that the terrible events of that day would naturally be mistaken for those of the seventh trumpet, or third woe. But the latter, he decides, is then *still future*. And in the mean time, the bitter contents of the little book must be experienced. For a more full explanation of this chapter, see fifth and seventh vials, in this second edition. And for the bitter contents of the little book, see section i, chapter iii, upon the trials of the church.

That this tenth chapter of Revelation is thus to be construed, as hinting in the first general division the events which in the second general division are given in more circumstantial detail, appears highly probable. The abominations of Popery are thus hinted in the first division, in chapter xi, 1—; as will be shown.

And in the second division the subject is resumed, and more fully illustrated, in chap. xiii, 11—to the end; and in chap. xvii, and xviii. The fatal judgments introductory to the Millennium, are announced in the close of the first division; chap. xi, 15—to the end. And in the second division this subject is resumed, and more largely and repeatedly described;—as in the close of the xivth chapter; the Angel on a white cloud, with his sharp sickle: In chap. xvi, the last vial: And in chap. xix, the battle with Christ. So in the case of this xth chapter. We have a prediction of the same events, which are afterward more definitely exhibited.

6. The eleventh chapter contains events from the seventh century, till the third woe, and the Millennium. A reed like a rod is given, by which to measure the temple of God, and the altar, and the worshippers. But the court without the temple must be left out; it is given to the Gentiles to be trodden under foot forty and two months. The two witnesses are described;— their mourning state; and their power over their enemies to inflict divine judgments. At the end of the term of their testimony, they are slain, by the Beast from the bottomless pit. After three days and an half, they rise, and ascend to heaven. A tenth part of the city falls in an earthquake. The third woe commences; and the kingdoms of this world become the kingdoms of Christ.

. The beginning of this chapter presents the unmeasurable corruptions of Popery. Their system does not accord with the rules of God's word: See Heb. viii, 5, where God's tabernacle must be made in all things according to the pattern given. The Romish church is symbolized by the outer court of the temple, where Gentiles worshipped. Their Romish religion is no better than Gentilism. It is a trampling of the true Church under feet. That apostacy should continue 1260 years. True followers of Christ, in this period, shall not be wanting. They are called God's two witnesses. These are especially Christ's true ministers; but include all his true followers. For 1260 years they are to be more or less depressed; yet shall exist, and their numbers be competent. At their prayers, God inflicts judgments on their enemies.' This is their *smiting* the earth with *plagues.* Just at the close of their depressed state, they are attacked by a new power represented as from hell. For three years and an half he prevails against them; and his nations and followers rejoice in their depression, because their wicked consciences have been tormented with evangelical truth; and they now imagine that they have obtained a complete triumph over it. But soon the cause of Christ is again revived, and rises superior to all the power of its enemies. New calamities are thundered upon the latter. And the way is soon found prepared for the third woe. If these events be future, and I apprehend they are, time will best explain them.

Seventh Trumpet, or third Woe. "And the seventh angel sounded; and there were great voices in heaven, saying, The kingdoms of this world are become the kingdoms of our Lord and of his Christ; and he shall reign forever and ever. And the four and twenty elders, who sat before God on their seats, fell upon their faces and worshipped God, saying, We give thee thanks, O Lord God Almighty, who art, and wast, and art to come, because thou hast taken to thee thy great power, and hast reigned. And the nations were angry, and thy wrath is come, and the time of the dead that they should be judged, and that thou shouldest give reward unto thy servants the prophets, and to the saints, and them that fear thy name, small and great; and shouldest destroy them, who destroy the earth. And the temple of God was opened in heaven, and there was seen in his temple the ark of the testimony; and there were lightnings, and voices, and thunderings, and an earthquake, and great hail." The commencement of the Millennium is here first exhibited to denote how soon, after the opening of the period of this trumpet, the way is prepared for the Church to arise. The figures, to denote the terrible scenes of judgment under the third woe, are multiplied and striking; and are such, as are used in the descrip-

64

tion of the same event, in the second general division, under the seventh vial; chap. xvi, 17—to the end. God had been before inflicting great judgments on wicked nations. But now his exterminating vengeance blazes at once against Antichrist, and all the nations of his confederacy, and the persecutors of the Church on earth. An effectual inquisition is made for the blood of the martyrs, and all the seas of human blood wantonly shed. Restraints are taken off from the fiery passions of the ungodly world; and they devour one another. Those, who have violently destroyed the peace of the earth, are now destroyed by God's vindictive power. Here the first general division of the prophetic part of this book, closes.

Second General Division.

The twelfth chapter begins with a reversion back, about 2000 years to the apostolic age, in order to traverse the period over again with new and different views of things most interesting to the people of God. In this division, two scenes are appropriated to each notable period exhibited in it. Things noted, or implied, in the first division, are here exhibited in more striking colors; and a more full view is given of various events.

In this twelfth chapter the Christian Church is symbolized by a woman in the aerial heaven, clothed with the sun, having the moon under her feet, and on her head a crown of twelve stars. The Church is abundantly known under the emblem of a woman, the spouse of Christ. She is adorned with righteousness, and clothed with his graces. She has indeed all sublunary things beneath her feet, being dead to the world, and her heart and conversation in heaven. And the gospel ministers, ordained by Christ in the twelve apostles, are gems in her crown. Her desires and exertions to propagate the gospel, and to bring converts to Christ, are symbolized by her being with child, and pained to be delivered. "My little children, for whom I travail in birth—till Christ be formed in you;" was the language of Paul. The devil opposing this bles-

sed work, is represented by a great red dragon standing before the woman to devour her offspring, having
seven heads, and ten horns, and seven crowns upon his
heads; and his tail drawing a third part of the stars, and
casting them to the ground. The devil has seven
heads and ten horns, as the secular Roman Beast, the
most noted agent of his mischievous operations, is
known under such a description. The devil has been
permitted to manage the crowns of the Roman empire,
for the promotion of his own cause; and has excited
those contentions, which have often hurled down rulers, kings and emperors, (symbolized by stars,) from
their stations; like stars falling to the earth. The man
child is born. The children of Zion have been brought
forth. And the succession of the Church has been rendered secure. This blessed truth, is, here denoted by
the man-child of the Church being caught up to the
throne of God. He is to rule all nations with a rod of
iron. Or Christ rules all nations with his rod of iron,
in behalf of the Church, and in answer to her prayers;
and hence he represents the Church as performing these
works of judgment. (See chap. ii, 26, 27; and xi, 5,
6; Ps. cxlix, 4—9; Isa. xli, 15.) The depressed
state of the Church, for 1260 years, under Papal corruption, and Antichristian tyranny, is denoted by the
woman fleeing into a wilderness, for that length of
time. The struggles between the apostate Romish
church and the true Church of Christ, during the dark
ages, is symbolized by a war in heaven between Michael, or Christ, and his angels, on the one hand; and
the dragon, and his angels on the other. The baffling
of Satan, in the reformation under Luther, is denoted
by the dragon's being overcome, and cast out of heaven.
The subsequent rage of the prince of darkness, man-
ifested in the Voltaire scheme of atheism, and the terrible events, which have followed in Christendom, is announced by a voice from heaven, saying, "Woe to the
inhabiters of the earth and of the sea; for the devil is
come down unto you having great wrath, because he
knoweth that he has but a short time. The Church
is represented, as again fleeing into the wilderness, to

remain the residue of her 1260 years, after these new
attacks of Satan in his agents of atheism. Floods of
lies, errors, heresies, armies, and violent measures, the
dragon excites through the civilized world, like floods
of water cast from his mouth, with a view to destroy
the Church. But the earth helps the woman, opens
her mouth, and swallows up these floods; or providential events blast and confound his diabolical designs.
In vexation and rage, the devil goes to make war
upon the remnant of the woman's seed. The fulfilment of this latter clause being future, time must unfold its import. Probably some branch of the Church,
distant from the ancient seat of the devil's operations,
will be violently attacked, either in Asia, or America.

8. The thirteenth chapter is synchronical with the
twelfth, just noted. It may be viewed as commencing in the apostolic age. And, with the preceding
chapter, it reaches *to*, but does not *describe*, the battle
of the great day. The preceding scene exhibits the
devil in his rage and operations against the Church.
This scene gives a description of those *Powers*, by
which the devil performs most of his mischievous operations. The one presents the great agent of mischief, and his object; the other his instruments of annoyance.

John in vision stands by the sea. He beholds a Beast
rising out of it, having seven heads and ten horns, and
upon his horns ten crowns, and upon his heads the
name of blasphemy. Here is the same Beast described
in Dan. vii, 3, 7, and symbolizing the secular Roman empire, in its hostility to the Church. The description in
Daniel relates perhaps more especially to the former
part of this empire; and the description in this chapter
to the latter, or the last days. This Beast appears with
a head that had been wounded to death; but is now
healed: And the world is wondering after him. The
devil gives him his power and seat and great authority.
He speaks great things and blasphemies. He makes
war upon the saints; and continues to the end of the
forty and two months; or the 1260 years. For an explanation of this symbol Beast, see section vi, chapter i,

of this dissertation. This pagan Beast was wounded to death under Constantine; and has his wound healed in modern France. While he lay dead, the Papal Beast arose, and had a long reign. This is the second Beast noted in this chapter, with two horns like a lamb, but that spake like a dragon. This is the same with the blasphemous horn of the secular Beast, in Dan. vii, 8. This Papal Beast makes an image to the pagan Beast; or establishes a system of idolatry, under the Christian name, essentially of the same nature with the preceding Pagan idolatry. For a fuller explanation of this Beast also, see section vi, chapter i. And for an exposition of the number of this Beast, and of his name, see section i, chapter ii. These two Beasts have been the great instruments of the devil in his opposition to the cause of Christ; and will continue to be thus, till both the Beast and the false prophet shall go into perdition, in the battle of the great day.

9. The fourteenth chapter leaves the fifteen first centuries, whose events had been predicted in the first division, and in the two preceding scenes in the second division, and leaps down to the beginning of the sixteenth century. This century opened with vast and portentous events, both to the false and to the true Church. The events of that period decide that it was to be the commencement of a new and important era in the fulfilment of the events of this mystical book; as is shown in the treatise on the first vial, in this dissertation.

In this chapter, Christ, the Lamb, appears on the mount Zion; and with him 144,000, having his Father's name written upon their foreheads. Here is represented Christ's glorious appearance in the reformation under Luther, after a long night of darkness under Papal delusion and tyranny. As in chap. vii, 1,—we are presented with a *sealing* time, after the revolution in Rome, and 144,000 are sealed; so here is another blessed sealing time. The purity of the Protestant doctrines and worship from Papal pollution, is next denoted, under the emblem of *chastity.* The pious Protestants were they, who were not defiled with women; "for they are

virgins." In process of time a missionary Angel commences his flight through the midst of heaven, having
the Gospel to preach to all nations, in the same hour
with the signal judgments of God on Papal nations.
This symbol has been fulfilled in the *late* and *present*
missionary spirit and exertions in the Christian world.
Another Angel proclaims that Papal Babylon is fallen.
And a third denounces to the world the fatal and eternal judgments, which will be executed on all who shall
worship the Beast, or have affinity with the abominations of the day. These faithful warnings, given by
the ministers and people of Christ, subject the Church
to *dangers* and *trials;* as is indicated by the following
hints; that *here is the faith and patience of the saints;*
and that "blessed are the dead who die in the Lord."
The Angel next appears on the white cloud, with his
sharp sickle. The harvest of the earth is reaped, and
its vintage gathered: Or the judgments introductory to
the Millennium are executed. Here is the same event
with the *seventh trumpet*, with which the first division
of the prophetic part of this book closes. For a more
full exposition of this chapter, see the note upon it, in
section vii, chapter i.

10. The fifteenth and sixteenth chapters belong to
one scene; and exhibit events, which synchronize with
those just noted. The fifteenth contains an *introduction* to the judgments of the seven vials; and the sixteenth presents the *execution* of those judgments. The
introduction presents seven Angels with their vials or
cups of wrath. Then by a prolepsis, or anticipation,
"the song of Moses and the song of the Lamb" is sung
by the Church, as introductory to the Millennium; indicating, that, at the close of the vials, is fulfilled the
antitype of the tremendous event at the Red Sea, celebrated by Moses and the tribes of the Lord; Exod. xv.

One of the four living creatures presents the seven
vials or cups of wrath, to the seven Angels, or ministers of Providence. An infinite honor God sees fit to
confer on his *ministers* and *people*, in representing that
his fatal judgments upon the enemies of the Church

are in a sense inflicted by *them;* being in their behalf, and in answer to their prayers. (See chap. ii, 26, 27; xi, 5, 6; xii, 5; Ps. cxlix, 4—9; Isa. xli, 15.)

In chapter sixteenth the seven vials are poured out.

Vial First. "And the first went and poured out his vial upon the *earth;* and there fell a noisome and grievous sore upon the men, who had the mark of the Beast, and upon them who worshipped his image." The earth here means the *Roman earth,* the field of Papal delusion,—the same that was meant by the *earth* in the judgment of the first trumpet. The first vial commenced the downfall of the Papal see. But the reformation early in the sixteenth century was clearly the commencement of this downfall. And it perfectly answered to the imagery of this vial. It occasioned a sore indeed, which has exhausted the life of the Papal Beast. It showed, in the language of the prophet, relative to that system, that "from the crown of the head to the sole of the foot there was no soundness; but wounds, bruises and putrifying *sores.*" See treatise on the first vial.

Vial Second. "And the second angel poured out his vial upon the *sea;* and it became as the blood of a dead man; and every living soul died in the sea." By the *sea* here, is meant the *seat* of the power marked out for judgment; the same on which the second trumpet was executed. The latter turned one third of the sea to blood. And the vial turned the whole of it to blood. This vial was fulfilled by the tremendous wars in Italy between Charles V, and Francis I, in the sixteenth century. This long series of furious wars, in the seat of the Papal delusion, afforded ample employment for the Pope, Charles, and other enemies of the reformation; so that the blessed word of God was not by them subverted. For nearly half a century Italy (and more than once Rome itself) was deluged in blood. See treatise on the second vial.

Vial Third. "And the third angel poured out his vial upon the *rivers and fountains of waters,* and they became blood. And I heard the angel of the waters say, Thou art righteous, O Lord, who art, and wast, and shalt be, because thou hast judged thus. For they have shed the blood of, saints and prophets; and thou hast given them blood to drink, for they are worthy." The third trumpet was executed on the rivers and fountains of water, and made them bitter. This vial turns them to blood This vial was fulfilled in the wars that raged in Europe in and after the latter part of the sixteenth century;—wars with the house of Austria;—wars relative to the Pregmatic Sanction;—and other furious wars and contests. After the wars in Italy were closed, other wars were kindled and raged in Europe. Says the historian, relative to the middle of the sixteenth century, "From this period Italy ceased to be the great theatre on which the monarchs of Spain, France, and Germany, contended for power and for fame. Their contentions and hostilities, though as frequent and violent as ever, were excited by new objects, and stained other regions of Europe with blood, and rendered them miserable in turn, by the devastation of war." (Dr. Robinson.) See treatise on the third vial.

Vial Fourth. "And the fourth angel poured out his vial upon the *sun;* and power was given unto him to scorch men with fire: And men were scorched with great heat, and blasphemed the name of God, who had power over these plagues; and they repented not to give him glory." The fourth trumpet darkened a third part of the *sun.* The fourth vial gives it power to scorch men with heat. This was probably fulfilled in the operations of the civil government in Christendom, against the interests of the Papal see. Many of them, instead of being obsequious to the Pope, to carry his laws and dogmas into execution, as before, wholly revolted from him, and established and defended the Protestant religion. And the other governments generally, that did not become Protestant, curtailed and withstood many of the usurpations of the Papal see; till that system became as it were *scorched,* and *withered.* The order of the Jesuits, those most efficacious defenders of the interests of the hierarchy, was finally subverted by the great governments of Europe. And the votaries of the Beast were so far from repenting, that they blasphemed God, by introducing the new and most abominable system of Illuminism. This soon prepared the way for the fifth vial, the first of the three capital vials; and has opened the flood gates of terror and devastation to the world. See treatise on the fourth vial.

Vial Fifth. "And the fifth Angel poured out his vial upon the *seat of the Beast;* and his kingdom was full of darkness; and they gnawed their tongues for pain, and blasphemed the God of heaven because of their pains, and their sores, and repented not of their deeds." The fifth trumpet opened the bottomless pit, darkened the world with a smoke from thence, and spread terror and devastation, far and wide, by its furious locusts. The fifth vial fills the Papal kingdom with darkness, by the rise of the Beast from the bottomless pit; and by the terrors of his armies, and violent measures. This vial has been fulfilled by the rise and measures of the French Empire. The Papal throne has indeed been subverted; his kingdom filled with darkness. Till the rise of the French Empire, the Papal Beast had a *throne*, and a *kingdom.* Since that he has had *none*. See treatise on the fifth vial.

Vial Sixth. "And the sixth angel poured out his vial upon the *great river Euphrates;* and the water thereof was dried up, that the way of the kings of the east might be prepared." The sixth trumpet gave rise to the Turkish empire, by *freeing*, and *uniting* the four Turkish sultanies, near the river Euphrates. And the sixth vial *overturns* this empire, to prepare the way for the restoration of God's ancient people; and perhaps for the conversion of the great eastern nations to Christ. See treatise on the sixth vial.

Vial Seventh. "And the seventh angel poured out his vial into the air; and there came a great voice out of the temple of heaven, from the throne, saying, It is done. And there were voices, and thunders, and lightnings; and there was a great earthquake, such as was not since men were upon the earth, so mighty an earthquake and so great. And the great city was divided into three parts, and the cities of the nations fell; and

65

great Babylon came in remembrance before God, to give unto her the cup of the wine of the fierceness of his wrath. And every island fled away; and the mountains were not found. And there fell upon men a great hail out of heaven, every stone about the weight of a talent; and men blasphemed God because of the plague of the hail; for the plague thereof was exceeding great." This is the *same*, in this second general division, with the seventh trumpet, or third woe, in the close of the *first*. In this event, the different series of the trumpets, the woes, the vials, and the great periods of the Revelation, (antecedent to the Millennium,) *meet*. Here each of those series finds its ultimate number; and all strike in unison. And the way is thence prepared for the millennial Kingdom of Christ. See treatise on the seventh vial.*

* It has been shown in the treatise on the *fifth* and *seventh* vials, that the judgment of the seventh vial, and that of the seventh trumpet, is *one* and the *same*. The seventh *trumpet* is a prediction of an event, in the *first* general division of the book; and the seventh *vial*, a prediction of the same event, in the *second* division. The judgment of the seventh trumpet is only "as God hath declared to his servants the prophets:" chap. x. 7. And the judgment of the seventh vial is "the battle of *THAT* great day of God Almighty;" alluding to the same predictions in the prophets. Both occupy the same period; and are predicted under the same figures.

The old opinion, that as the seventh seal comprises all the trumpets; so the seventh trumpet, or third woe, must comprise all the vials,—appears incapable of support; as is ascertained under the vials. The trumpets and the vials belong to different *divisions*, in the prophetic part of the Apocalypse. Each of these divisions has its arrangement peculiar to himself. The seventh trumpet closes the first division, and introduces the Millennium; precisely as the seventh vial closes the second division, and introduces the Millennium. The representation of the vials has no dependence on the seventh trumpet. The vials belong to a different system of arrangement. The old view of the subject, that the seventh trumpet contains all the vials, is attended with unanswerable objections and difficulties. There may seem, in the old opinion, a kind of mathematical *nicety*. But this is of no avail, when it is found incapable of being made to accord with the sacred Oracles. We must judge, not after the outward appearance, but judge righteous judgment, comparing scripture with scripture.

11th. The seventeenth chapter relates to a still later period; or to the commencement of the fifth vial, toward the close of the 18th century. It presents a new and blasphemous Roman Beast, just risen from the bottomless pit. His heads and horns identify him with the Roman Beast. Yet he is not (as was the old Roman Beast,) from the *"sea;"* but from the *infernal region.* His origin is not of *ancient,* but of *late* date. He *was,* and *is not,* and yet *is.* He *in a sense* formerly existed. He for a long time had no actual existence. Yet he mystically existed. "The Beast that thou sawest *was,* and is not, and shall ascend out of the bottomless pit, and go into perdition." He is mystically the Beast, that *was,* in his ancient Pagan form; but died of his wound in his Imperial head, in the revolution under Constantine. And in the last days ascends from the bottomless pit, just before he shall go into perdition, in the battle of that great day. He is mystically the old Imperial sixth head, healed of his deadly wound; and now symbolized by a *new Beast.* He is the *eighth* head of the Pagan Roman Beast, in numerical order. The ancient *Imperial* head was the *sixth.* The atheistical republican head was the seventh. And the new Imperial head the eighth. Yet the Roman Beast has really but seven heads of specific difference. This head in the last days therefore, is *"of the seven:"* or *one* of them. He is specifically the sixth, healed of his deadly wound. In *one* view he is a *new Beast,* directly from the infernal world. In *another* sense, he is the eighth head of the old Pagan Beast. And in a *third* sense, he is the sixth, the old Imperial head that was slain by Constantine, recovered to life. He has his ten horns, or vassal kingdoms. He is the executioner of the Papal harlot. He has her dressed out for execution, with her crimes written upon her forehead, after the manner of ancient Roman criminals, presented for execution. Her guilty characteristics are prominent upon her. She is mounted upon the Beast; and moving on to execution. The horns are goading her, as she passes. And they are to burn her with fire.

What can this Beast be, but the enormous Power, which has risen in France? And what *vial* can it fulfil, but the *fifth*, poured upon the throne of the Papal Beast, and filling his kingdom with darkness? For the evidence of this, see the treatise on vial fifth in the second edition of the dissertation. And for the explanation of this chapter, see section 6th, chapter i, *on the Roman, Papal, and Antichristian* Beasts. The *period* of this scene, is from the revolution in France, A. D. 1789;—till the battle of the great day of God.

12th. The eighteenth chapter belongs to the same period with the scene just noted. It it a more full illustration of the descent of the angel of the covenant, in chapter tenth, before noted in the first general division. To enlarge upon the same event, in this second general division, the Angel is again represented as descending from heaven, and announcing, *that Papal Babylon has indeed fallen; and has become the hold of every foul spirit, and the cage of every unclean and hateful bird.* The preceding scene presents the terrible instrument of the execution of Papal Babylon; and presents her on the way to execution. In this scene a description of the terrible event, as fulfilled is given. See explanation of this chapter, section 7th, chapter i, of the dissertation.

13th. The nineteenth chapter goes to a still later period;—the battle of the great day, and the introduction of the Millennium. The latter (as though to relieve the mind of the reader) is given first, under the emblem of the marriage of the Lamb. The battle, which precedes this blessed marriage of the Lamb, is thus described, in the last half of the chapter. An explanation is given of it in sec. 3d, chap. i, of this second edition; and in other parts of the dissertation. In describing the same events, in the close of the first general division, chap. xi, 15—19, the same method is adopted, of first noting the Millennium; and then the battle that precedes it.

14th. The twentieth chapter proceeds to describe the Millennium, under the view of the confinement of the devil to the bottomless pit, that he shall deceive the nations no more for a thousand years; and all the people of God, for this term, *reigning* *on the earth.* The dead, both martyrs, and all who escape the second death, are mystically represented as rising, and reigning. This is fulfilled, in the coming forward of bold, and zealous *successors;* as the resurrection of Elijah was fulfilled in John the Baptist. Christians are raised up in the spirit, zeal, and power of the martyrs, and deceased followers of Christ. The cause, in which the hearts of the martyrs and saints of past ages, were bound up, and in which they lived and died, revives and fills the world. The saints in heaven will see this event; and feel additional joy and glory. This is their mystical resurrection in this twentieth chapter, and their additional rewards noted in the corresponding passage in the first division, or in chap. xi, 18; "And that thou shouldest give reward unto thy servants, the prophets; and to the saints, and them that fear thy name, small and great." This twentieth chapter advances to events not noted in the preceding chapter; nor in the first general division. It predicts a second mystical resurrection, a resurrection of the wicked, in an apostacy toward the close of the thousand years. Gog and Magog (names under which Antichrist goes into perdition, in the battle preceding the Millennium) are raised again.* The last and a terrible scene of persecution follows Christ then comes to judgment. The dead are literally raised. All men are arraigned before him, judged, and awarded to bliss or woe.

15th. In the two last chapters, the scene unfolds the heavenly state, under the emblem of a vast city, the New Jerusalem. And the book closes with most solemn warnings to the world.

16th. In favor of the two general divisions of the prophetic part of the book, does any thing more need be said? The view of the contents of the chapters on the chart, evinces that the subject is thrown into these two grand divisions. The first division begins with the first century; and moves regularly on, through nearly two millenaries; and closes in the seventh trumpet or third woe, introductory to the Millennium.

* See 11. page 300 of this book.

This first general division has various subdivisions; as the seven seals; the seven trumpets; and the three woes. It moves forward through these, and closes in the battle of the great day, and the Millennium. These internal arrangements are such, as are, for the most part, peculiar to this first division; and show, that it is a part by itself. The first division admits of no reversion back to the period where it begins. It moves directly forward, (only with two collateral scenes) to its close in the Millennium.

*The second division then commences, on a new scale of internal arrangement. It reverts to the period where the first division commences; and traverses the same ground, with subdivisions wholly new, excepting where the first division begins, and closes. It gives events, which were either hinted, or implied in the first division, in more circumstantial description. Its uniform dualities of scenes, relating to the same periods, and the gradual advance of these scenes toward the end of the world, and into the future eternity, show it to be *a new division*, with arrangements peculiar to itself. This second division has five periods, with two synchronical scenes appropriated to each; as is seen upon the chart. And, with the first division, it has its *septenary*, or *series of seven*, the *seven vials*. These are on a new scale, and different from any septenary of the first division. I shall then rest on the evidence that these two divisions of the prophetic part of the Revelation, are founded in reality. And much aid is hence furnished in explaining this enigmatical book.

17th. The following things appear evident, relative to *periods*, in these two general divisions. The first division has its septenary of trumpets, which closes in the decisive judgments introductory to the Millennium. The second division has its septenary of vials, which closes in the same judgment. The first division has its septenary of seals; the last of which contains the seven trumpets. And beside these septenaries, both divisions unitedly contain a septenary of *notable periods*, which closes with the close of the septenary of the trumpets, and that of the vials. These notable periods resulting from both the divisions appear to be furnished from plain facts; as will be seen by casting an eye upon the first chart. The *first* period, commences with the *seals*, in the first century. The *second*, with the *trumpets*, in the fourth century. The *third* with the *first woe*, in the seventh century. The *fourth*, with the *second woe*, in the fourteenth century. The *fifth*, with the *period of the vials*, in the sixteenth century. The *sixth*, with the rise of the Antichristian Beast from the bottomless pit, in the eighteenth century. And the seventh with the battle of that great day of God Almighty. It has been our lot to behold the commencement of the sixth period, and fifth vial, in the rise of the Antichristian Beast from the bottomless pit, filling the Papal kingdom with darknes.

13. The following remarks are subjoined, relative to events, which occupied the long space of time between the fifth and sixth trumpets, or the first and second woes; as six of the vials occupy the space between the sixth and seventh trumpets, or the second and third woes.

The reign of sin, under the Christian era, and before the Millennium, was to occupy about two thousand years. Among the various divisions and judgments of this long period, there were to be three signal ones called *woes*; as has been shewn, section i, chapter ii. The first was introduced about the close of the first third of the above long period; or about the year 666. The second woe was introduced about the close of the second third of the above two thousand years; or in the year 1332. What then does analogy suggest relative to the time of the third woe? It suggests that it might naturally be expected to take place not long before the close of the two thousand years. According to this analogy, it must be still *future*, and is to be at too late a period to comprise all the vials. It has been shown in section i, chapter ii, that the battle of the great day may probably take place at the end of the 1260 years added to A. D. 666; or A. D. 1925; 75 years (the sum made by Daniel's two additional numbers) before the year 2000. Six of the vials must precede it, or occupy the space between the sixth and the seventh trumpets. This appears rational and probable, both from the length of time between the sixth and seventh trumpets; and also from analogy, that a similar succession of events did in fact occupy a similar space of time, between the fifth and sixth trumpets. Let them here be noted.

1. The complete establishment, and the progress, of the Papal delusion. This fatal apostasy, this curse to the world, was indeed synchronical with that judgment called the first woe, but distinct from it. After the period of the first woe opened, this horrid event appeared; the Papal Beast arose. This event was as great, as was the full development of the abominations of Popery, after the second woe, in the reformation, or first vial.

2. The wars of Charlemagne, tending to establish the Papal supremacy. "The life of that great prince (says Dr. Mosheim) was principally employed in the most zealous efforts to propagate and establish the religion of Christ among the Huns, Saxons and Frieslanders, and other unenlightened nations; but his piety was mixed with violence; his spiritual conquests were generally made by the force of arms; and this impure mixture tarnishes the lustre of his noble exploits." The fact was, he propagated the *Papal religion*, with *force* and *arms*. He was crowned, by the Pope, *king of the Romans*, with a view to give a permanency to the Papal cause. And he did as much toward confirming and extending the Papal delusion, as did Charles V, after the second woe, and under the second vial, toward executing divine judgments on the nations symbolized by the sea that was turned to blood.

3. The wars of succeeding princes in European nations. Those of Otho the great, in the tenth century, subduing the Danes, and others. Those of the Norman dukes, especially of William the conqueror.

4. The great readiness of the civil governments in Europe, and particularly in the German empire, to propagate the Papal religion, and to support the dogmas, and impositions of Popery. Dr. Mosheim, speaking of the idolatrous European nations, says, "the Christian kings and emperors left no means unemployed, to draw those infidels within the pale of the church. For this purpose, they proposed to their chiefs, alliances of marriage, offered them certain districts, and auxiliary troops—upon condition, that they would abandon the superstition of their ancestors," and embrace the catholic religion. "These offers were attended with the desired success." Those chiefs were proselyted; and they obliged their subjects to follow their examples. (Mosheim Vol. ii, p. 192.) The Papal harlot thus "reigned over the kings of the earth." Those civil governments did as much toward supporting her cause, as did the Protestant governments, in after days, or between the second and third woes, toward destroying it. See fourth vial.

5. The bitter and bloody contentions between the Popes and the emperors, relative to the right of investitures; and the prevalency of the Papacy in these contentions. These contentions, which drenched many provinces in blood, did much toward establishing the vast preponderancy of the Papal influence. Relative to this point then in contest, let it be remarked; the European emperors and princes made grants to the Papal clergy of certain territories, forests and castles. But they enacted, that, as a condition of holding those donations, those clergymen should take the oath of allegiance to their respective sovereigns, and receive from them a certain token, which should entitle them to the tenure of those respective grants. From this the emperors and princes undertook, in process of time, to assume to themselves the right of *election* of bishops and abbots, in their dominions, in violation of the customs and laws of the church. They would dispose of a bishopric or abbey, (when it became vacant) to some of their favorites; or even to the *highest bidder*. They thus assumed the whole power of the *ring* and

crosier, (or seal and shepherd's staff) of those sacred offices. This usurpation the hierarchy violently opposed. Armies were raised. Much blood was shed. These contentions in the tenth and eleventh centuries, were *violent*. But the hierarchy in some instances, prevailed. The emperor Henry IV was obliged to cross the Alps, in Feb. 1077, to seek pardon of Gregory VII. He had to stand at the gate of his holiness, with bare head and feet, and only a coarse woollen cloth to cover him, three days. The Pope then admitted him into his presence; but granted only a small part of his petition, after all his humility.

6. The horrible and bloody crusades to the Holy land, to recover it from the infidels, or the Mohammedan powers. These may be considered as the finishing scenes, previous to the second woe; as the *close* of *these* took off the restraints from the four Turkish sultanies near the river Euphrates, and prepared the way for the second woe in the rise of the Ottoman empire.

These events between the first and second woes, which attended the rise and zenith of Popery, seem indeed to bear some analogy to the sixth first vials, between the second and third woes; which bring down the Papacy, and the Mohammedan delusion. The following analogy, at least seems manifest between them; viz. The above series of events intervened between the first and second woes; and were distinct from the appropriate event of each. And in like manner the six first vials intervene between the second and third woes; and are distinct from the appropriate event of each.

The above considerations furnish an argument in favor of the opinion that six of the vials precede the third woe; or that the third woe does not contain all the vials; but is the same with the seventh vial. In further confirmation of this opinion, 1. Read and compare Rev. xi, 15—19, with chap. xvi, 17—21. The same events, in the same figures, and in the same connexion with the Millennium, are described. Both *finish* the kingdom of darkness, and thus prepare the way for that of Christ. 2. In Rev. x, 7, it is the *beginning* of the seventh trumpet to sound, that *finishes* the mystery of God. That mystery is not *yet* finished. Hence the *beginning* of the seventh trumpet is still future? But can all seven of the vials be still future? Is not the Papal Beast already destroyed by some of the vials? The affirmative appears evident. Hence some of the vials do precede the third woe. And if *some* of them thus precede, then six of them may precede the third woe or seventh trumpet. 3. Compare Rev. x, 7, with xvi, 14; and we find the seventh trumpet and seventh vial *are the same.* In the former passage, the seventh trumpet is only "as God hath declared to his servants the prophets." And in the latter passage, the seventh vial is called "the battle of THAT great day of God Almighty;" alluding to these very predictions in the prophets. 4. The 1260 *years,* of the witnesses' prophecying in mourning, expire, and the witnesses are slain, and rise again, and ascend up to heaven, and a vast earthquake follows, before the commencement of the *third woe;* Rev. xi, 3, 7—14. But the 1260 years are not *yet* expired. The Church is yet in the wilderness. Hence the commencement of the third woe must now be future.

On the Millennial Kingdom of Jesus Christ.

Section I.

Introductory remarks, to ascertain the true sense of the Kingdom of grace.

It. is a sublime sentiment of revelation, that God governs the world. "The Lord reigns, let the earth rejoice," is an epitome of the language of inspiration, upon this subject. God made all things; and made them for himself And all creatures and things, in heaven and earth, he has subordinated to a wise and good purpose. And he governs all things to the accomplishment of this purpose. Revelation and the light of nature conspire to evince the *particular*, the *universal*, and the *absolute* government of God; his government relative to every creature, thing and event. God governs the natural world; or the laws of nature; the heavens and the earth; the vegetable system; the animal; all insects; all the tribes of animated nature in the sea; every thing on land, wherein is the breath of life. He numbers our hairs; and sustains our frowns.

Is the *moral world* then overlooked of God? Is it without the circuit of the divine government? No verily! The kings heart is in the hands of the Lord, we are assured. And *every* man's heart is in the hands of the Lord: And as the streams of water he turneth it whithersoever he will. "The preparation of the heart of man, and the answer of the tongue, is from the Lord." The *mode* of the divine government is such, as to accord with that free moral agency, and just accountability, attributed to us in the word of God, and of which we are conscious. But the government of God exercised over the moral world, is *entire* and *perfect*. "There are many devices in a man's heart; nevertheless the counsel of the Lord that shall stand." "My counsel shall stand; and I will do all my pleasure." "He doeth his will in the armies of heaven, and among the inhabitants of the earth; and none can stay his hand." "Man's goings are of the Lord." I know, O Lord, that the way of man is not in himself; it is not in man that walketh to direct his steps. "All things are of God." "A man's heart deviseth his way; but the Lord directeth his steps:" "According to the purpose of him, who worketh all things after the counsel of his own will." "For of him, and through him, and to him are all things; to whom be glory forever."

This sentiment is the glory of heaven; the joy of the saints; the salvation of Zion; and the terror of the world of darkness. The Kingdom or government of God is in the hands of *Christ,* in his glorified humanity. *His* Kingdom ruleth over all. This wicked world, and devils, are perfectly in *his hands.* "Rule thou in the *midst of thine enemies.*"

But this universal divine government is not the *Kingdom,* which is to be the subject of this chapter. This universal divine government is essential to the Kingdom of grace. It is that, which will *secure* the Kingdom of grace; and without which the millennial Kingdom never would be introduced.

But the Kingdoms are *two,* and *distinct.* When we are taught to pray, "Thy Kingdom come;" the sense is not this; that God would *govern the world.* For *this* is not an *object* of prayer; but of *everlasting praise;* being an immutable fact, from the beginning to the end of time. And this Kingdom of God, extending over the universe, lays a blessed foundation for *prayer,* that the kingdom, now to be ascertained, *may come.*

What then, is the *Kingdom of Christ,* for which we are daily to pray? We read much of the Kingdom of God, and of heaven. In some passages it means the *Gospel dispensation.* "Repent; for the Kingdom of heaven is at hand." Here it meant that *new* and *last* dispensation of the covenant of grace, then about to be introduced. It sometimes means the *privileges* of the visible Church of God on earth, either under the Old or New Testament. This was the sense, when Christ said to the Jews, "The Kingdom of God shall be taken from you, and given to a nation, bringing forth the fruit thereof." And, "Suffer the little children to come unto me, and forbid them not; for of such is the *Kingdom* of heaven." "The *Kingdom* of heaven is like unto a net cast into the sea."—The Kingdom here, means the gracious cause of God on earth, from the time of the promise of Christ to Adam, to the end of the world.

It sometimes means the Kingdom of *glory*. "There shall be weeping and gnashing of teeth, when ye shall see Abraham, Isaac, and Jacob, and all the prophets, in the *Kingdom* of God; and you yourselves thrust out." "Flesh and blood cannot inherit the *Kingdom* of God."

From these remarks it appears, that the different *comings* of the Kingdom of grace, are but different *degrees* of the advancement of the *same* gracious Kingdom, which has existed from the days of Adam. This Kingdom of grace is the *Church*, in distinction from the world. It is the government of Christ in the *hearts of a willing people*, by his word and Spirit; with all the privileges of his visible Church.

This is the Kingdom of Christ, which is not of this world. "My Kingdom is not of this world." While he governs the *whole* world, yet his Kingdom of grace is a *different system*, under different government.

And this Kingdom of grace was to pass through various grades or degrees, from its first establishment, soon after the fall of man, to its consummation in heaven. Some of these grades were to be very *signal*. And these most signal grades or advances are repeatedly called the *coming* of that Kingdom. It was only in this sense, that the commencement of the gospel dispensation was called the *coming* of the Kingdom of heaven. While it was the coming of the Kingdom of heaven; it was attended at the same time with the taking of the Kingdom of heaven from the Jews, and giving it to a nation bringing forth the fruit thereof: Which shows that *that* coming of the Kingdom of heaven was not the coming of any new Kingdom; but was only a greater advancement of the *same* Kingdom of grace, which had been from the beginning.

Our Lord informed his disciples, that there were some standing *there*, "who should not taste of death, till they see the Kingdom of God." This must have related to a still further advancement of the same Kingdom, future of the commencement of the gospel dispensation. For the latter was then just at hand; and nearly all then present probably lived to see it. But when he says, "I tell you of a truth, that there be some standing here, who shall not taste of death, till they see the Kingdom of God;" we may conclude he related to that still further *advancement* of the Kingdom of God, which followed upon the destruction of Jerusalem. For in a parallel passage it is, that some were standing there, who should not taste of death, till they see the Son of man coming in his Kingdom; which must have related to his coming in the destruction of the Jews.

Hence it appears certain, that those different *comings* of the Kingdoms related only to the different advances of one and the *same* Kingdom. Accordingly we read, Rev. xii, 10, upon the event of the reformation from Popery, of voices in heaven, saying, "Now is come salvation and strength, and the *Kingdom* of our God, and the power of his Christ." Here, in the 16th century, was a *new* *coming* of the Kingdom of our God, in the language of Inspiration.

Upon the same principle it is, that the *Millennium* is abundantly predicted as the *coming* of the *Kingdom* of Christ. Not because it will be a *new* Kingdom; but a new *advancement* (and to a far greater degree than *ever)* of the Kingdom of grace and salvation. The preceding advancements, were but *shadows* of it. That event is a *great object* in the prophecies; as will be noted in the next section. And it is represented as the *coming* of the Kingdom of God. "In the days of those kings, shall the God of heaven set up a Kingdom." Upon the giving of the body of Antichrist to the burning flame, we read, "And behold one like the Son of man came with the clouds of heaven—

and there was given him dominion and glory, and a Kingdom, that all people, nations and languages should serve him; Dan. vii, 13, 14.

Christ foretold various events, which shall just precede and introduce the Millennium: And then said; "When ye see these things come to pass, know ye, that the Kingdom of God is nigh at hand;" Luke xxi, 31.

And the state of glory, after the resurrection, (it has been noted) is called the Kingdom of heaven.

A question occurs: For which of these advancements of the Kingdoms of grace, are Christians daily to pray, "Thy Kingdom come?"

As it relates to us, it is the *Millennium.* For *this* is the *next* great advancement of the Kingdom of grace. It is not only the greatest of all the advancements this side of heaven; but an advancement evidently not far distant.

As Christians of all the gospel ages were to pray, "Thy Kingdom come;" it was to be as though they had said; Let thy Kingdom of grace be supported, and advanced. May the next signal grade of its advancement soon arrive. And may it safely progress through all the rising degrees of prosperity, by heaven designed, till it shall reach its millennial, yea and its heavenly glory. This suggests what ought to be *our* ideas and desires, relative to this Kingdom, in our daily devotions. They must relate to those advancements of the Kingdoms, which are *still future;* and particularly to that stage of advancement next before us.

And for this event Christians may pray in *faith.* For the *millennial* glory of the Church is made certain; and is abundantly held up, in most animating prophetic descriptions.

Section II.

Predictions of the coming of Christ's Millennial Kingdom.

To adduce all the predictions of this joyful event, would be to transcribe a large portion of the prophetic scriptures. For it was a darling theme with the proph-ets. I can here touch only upon a few of those pre-dictions, as a specimen of the great body of them.

It might reasonably be expected, that God would make his gospel eventually to become prevalent through the world; that it should finally produce its proper ef-fect, in governing the hearts and lives of mankind on earth. It would be unaccountable, if this should not be the case. Would the merciful God suffer the cause of Satan, and the mystery of iniquity, to triumph and prevail against his darling cause, to the end of the world? Impossible! It would be most unaccountable. No! God will make the world to know what his Gospel and religion can do, for the happiness of man, *temporal*, as well as *eternal:*—That the *leaves* of the tree of life are for the healing of the nations from their madness and ru-in; and its fruit for their salvation. That this display will in due time be made, we are abundantly ascertain-ed in the prophets.

God engaged to Abraham, that in his *Seed*, (mean-ing *Christ*) *all nations*, and *all families of the earth*, should be blessed; (Gen xii, 3; Gal. iii, 8.) The time should come, when all nations and families, living on earth, should be blessed in *Christ*: An event, which is still future; but which will be accomplished in due time.

In Psalm xxii, is a prediction of the sufferings of Christ; and of the glory, that should follow. And in verse 27, it is said; "All the ends of the earth shall re-member and turn unto the Lord; and all the kindreds of the nations shall worship him."

Psalm xxxvii is a striking prediction of the destruc-tion of the enemies of the Church in the battle of the great day. And the great and blessed event to follow is, that "the meek shall inherit the earth, and delight themselves in the abundance of peace." With this idea the Church is there comforted, under all her per-secutions and trials.

The xlvith Psalm is a prediction of the same events. The political earth is removed. The mountains or kingdoms are plunged in the sea of revolution and ru-in. The heathen rage; the kingdoms are moved;

God utters his voice; the earth melts. Now the members of the Church call on each other, to "come and behold the works of the Lord; what desolation he hath made in the earth. He maketh wars to cease to the ends of the earth; he breaketh the bow, and cutteth the spear in sunder, and burneth the chariots in the fire." Now the Church exult; "The Lord of hosts is with us; the God of Jacob is our refuge. There is a river, the streams whereof shall make glad the city of God—God is in the midst of her; she shall not be moved."

Psalm lxvii, is a prediction of this Kingdom of Christ. There God will cause his face to shine, when his ways shall be known upon earth, and his saving health among all nations. All the people shall praise him. The nations shall be glad, and sing for joy. For God will govern the nations upon earth. The earth shall yield her increase. Over and over it is repeated, "God will bless us." And it is asserted; "All the ends of the earth shall fear him."

In Psalm lxxii, we have this blessed event. Among the predictions of it we read, that Christ "shall come down like rain upon the mown grass, and as showers that water the earth. In his days shall the righteous flourish; and there shall be abundance of peace, so long as the moon endureth. He shall have dominion also from sea to sea, and from the river unto the ends of the earth. All kings shall fall down before him; all nations shall serve him. Men shall be blessed in him; all nations shall call him blessed. The whole earth shall be filled with his glory."

In Psalm cii, 13—, we have the same. "Thou wilt arise and have mercy upon Zion. For the time to favor her, yea the set time, is come. So the heathen shall fear the name of the Lord; and all the kings of the earth thy glory. When the Lord shall build up Zion, he will appear in his glory."

David in his last words, delivers a sublime prediction of this Kingdom. Various of the saints of old, as they were about to leave the world, were wrapped up in prophetic extasy. The writer of the Psalms

was thus, relative to that Kingdom, which he had often predicted. 2 Sam. xxiii, 1—4. "Now these
be the last words of David. ' David the son of Jesse,
said, and the man who was raised up on high, the anointed of the God of Jacob, and the sweet psalmist of
Israel, said; The Spirit of the Lord spake by me, and
his word was in my tongue: The God of Israel said,
the Rock of Israel spake to me:"—Here let it be noted, that this very *remarkable* introduction must have
been for *no small purpose*. He must have been going
to express something far more weighty, than merely a
common-place-truth, such as, that *civil rulers ought to
be good men*. The sentence that follows, in the original, conveys the following sense; "He, who is 'to rule
over men (or the Messiah) will be just, ruling in the
fear of God." The best translators and expositors give
it this sense; and make it a prophecy of Christ. "There
shall be a Ruler over men," (says one noted interpreter) a just or righteous One, ruling in the fear of God."
It is thought the prophetic eye was upon this passage,
when various of the most sublime predictions concerning the Kingdom of Christ were uttered; particularly
the following; Jer. xxiii, 26; "Behold the days come,
saith the Lord, that I will raise up unto David a righteous Branch, and a King shall reign and prosper, and
shall execute judgment and justice in the earth. In
his days Judah shall be saved, and Israel shall dwell
safely: And this is the name whereby he shall be cal-
ed, *The Lord our righteousness*." And chap. xxxiii,
15; "In those days and at that time will I cause the
Branch of righteousness to grow up unto David; and
he shall execute judgment and righteousness in the
earth."

David, after predicting the Kingdom of this righteous Ruler, as above, adds; "*And he shall be as
the light of the morning when the sun riseth, even
a morning without clouds; as the tender grass
springing out of the earth, by clear shining after
rain*." The introduction of this kingdom of Christ
will be like a pleasant morning in the spring, after a
dark, stormy and dismal night. The grass is green;

the sky and air pleasant; the sun beautiful and reviving; and all nature smiles.

David then, as is usual, hints the tremendous scenes which just precede that blessed morning: "But the sons of Belial shall be all of them as thorns thrust away, because they cannot be taken with hands. But the men, that would touch them, must be fenced with iron, and the staff of a spear; and they shall be utterly burnt with fire in the same place." (See Mal. iv, 1 —, for an explanation of this burning of the sons of Belial.)

In Isaiah, this Kingdom is abundantly predicted. A few of the many predictions of it I will recite.

In chap. ii, 2—we read, "And it shall come to pass, in the last days, that the mountain of the Lord's house shall be established in the top of the mountains, and shall be exalted above the hills; and all nations shall flow unto it." It there follows, that wars shall cease from the earth: and all the people shall walk in the light of the Lord.

The xith chapter is upon this sublime subject. The Rod from the stem of Jesse, (i. e. from David) the Branch from his roots, is presented as governing in righteousness and faithfulness. He comes for the cause of the poor. He reproves for the meek of the earth. He smites the earth with the rod of his mouth; and with the breath of his lips slays the wicked. Then peace and salvation fill the world; predicted under the emblem of the harmony of animals of most discordant natures. The cow and the bear; the wolf and the lamb; the leopard and the kid, *unite in peace.* The infant plays with the asp; and the child is safe upon the den of the cockatrice. As one expresses it;

"The playful child shall ramble in the ring;"
"And from the crested serpent steal his sting."

"They shall not hurt nor destroy in all my holy mountain; for the earth shall be full of the knowledge of the Lord, as the waters cover the sea."

A description of the blessed consequences occupies the whole of the following chapter. And it closes thus;

"Sing unto the Lord; for he hath done excellent things.
This is known in *all the earth.* Cry out and shout,
thou inhabitant of Zion; for great is the Holy One of
Israel in the midst of thee."

In chap. xxiv, the earth is reeling to and fro like a
drunkard, because of the wickedness of man; till it
falls, to rise no more. Then salvation covers the earth.
"From the uttermost parts of the earth we have heard
songs, even glory to the righteous. Then the moon
shall be confounded and the sun ashamed, when the
Lord of hosts shall reign in mount Zion, and in Jerusalem, and before his ancients gloriously."

In chap. xxv, the blessed theme is pursued. And
the Lord of hosts is making to all people a feast of fat
things; of wines on the lees well refined. And the face
of the covering cast over all people, and the veil that
was spread over all nations, God destroys; and tears
are wiped from all faces.

In chapter xxxv, this Kingdom is the only theme.
The wilderness and the solitary place is glad. The desert blossoms as the rose. The glory of Lebanon is
given to it; the excellency of Carmel and Sharon.
They see the glory of the Lord, the excellency of our
God. Weak hands and feeble knees are made strong.
Fearful hearts too are comforted. Blind eyes are
opened; deaf ears unstopped. The lame leap; the
dumb sing. For streams of salvation break out in the
desert. Habitations of dragons become grass with
reeds and rushes. God's high way is opened through
the wilderness of the world; where no *unclean* shall
pass: and where no lion or ravenous beast shall enter:
But where the redeemed shall walk; where the simple
shall not err; and where "the ransomed of the Lord
shall return and come to Zion, with songs and everlasting joy upon their heads; they shall obtain joy and
gladness; and sorrow and mourning shall flee away."

In chap. xl, this Kingdom is predicted. God's people are comforted. Their warfare is accomplished.
The heralds of salvation have been heard in the wilderness of pagan lands; "Prepare ye the way of the Lord.
Make straight in the desert a high way for our God

Every valley shall be exalted; and every mountain and hill shall be made low; and the crooked shall be made straight; and the rough places plain: And the glory of the Lord shall be revealed; and all flesh shall see it together: For the mouth of the Lord hath spoken it."

In a considerable part of the remaining chapters of this book, the battle of the great day; and the subsequent Kingdom of Christ, are predicted. Some whole chapters are taken up upon the subject. And various of the descriptions are most brilliant. I will adduce a few passages, as a specimen. "Therefore shall they know in that day, that I am he that doth speak; behold it is I. How beautiful upon the mountains are the feet of him that bringeth good tidings; that publisheth peace; that bringeth good tidings of good; that publisheth salvation; that saith unto Zion, Thy God reigneth. Thy watchmen shall lift up the voice; with the voice together shall they sing: For they shall see eye to eye, when God shall bring again Zion. Break forth into joy; sing together, ye waste places of Jerusalem. The Lord hath made bare his holy arm in the eyes of all nations; and all the ends of the earth shall see the salvation of our God." "A little one shall become a thousand; and a small one a strong nation. I the Lord will hasten it in its time. Thy people shall all be righteous." "The Lord shall cause righteousness and praise to spring forth before all nations." "Behold the Lord hath proclaimed unto the end of the world; Say ye to the daughter of Zion, Behold thy salvation cometh." "And it shall come to pass, that from one—Sabbath to another—shall all flesh come to worship before me, saith the Lord."

Those things have never yet been fulfilled. But their fulfilment is *certain.*

Jeremiah predicts this Kingdom of Christ. I shall note but *one* of many passages. Chap. iii, 17; "At that time they shall call Jerusalem (or the Church) the throne of God; and all the nations shall be gathered unto it, to the name of the Lord, to Jerusalem; neither shall they walk any more after the imagination of their evil heart."

In Ezekiel this Kingdom of Christ is predicted. The last nine chapters are wholly devoted to this subject: But the descriptions are highly mystical.

In the prophecy of Daniel, this Kingdom is a great subject. In chap. ii, after the description of the great image, symbolizing the four great monarchies, it is added, verse 34—, "Thou sawest till that a stone was cut out without hands, which smote the image upon the feet, that were of iron, and clay, and break them to pieces. Then was the iron, the clay, the brass, the silver, and the gold, broken to pieces together; and became like the chaff of the summer threshing floor; and the wind carried them away; and no place was found for them. And the stone, that smote the image, became a great mountain, and filled the world." Here is a prediction of the destruction of the enemies of the Church, in the battle of the great day; and of the subsequent Kingdom of Christ.

In chap. vii, when the Roman Beast is slain, and his body destroyed, and given to the burning flame; Christ takes the kingdom; and all people, nations and languages, serve him. "And there was given him dominion, and glory, and a Kingdom, that all people, nations and languages, should serve him: His dominion is an everlasting dominion, which shall not pass away; and his Kingdom that, which shall not be destroyed." "And the Kingdom and dominion, and the greatness of the Kingdom, under the whole heaven, shall be given to the people of the saints of the Most High, whose Kingdom is an everlasting Kingdom, and all dominions shall serve and obey him."

The prophet Joel, chap. iii, 16—18, after describing the harvest and vintage of divine wrath upon the wicked, in the valley of decision, says; "The Lord also shall roar out of Zion, and utter his voice from Jerusalem; and the heavens and the earth shall shake; but the Lord shall be the hope of his people, and the strength of the children of Israel. So shall they know that I am the Lord your God, dwelling in Zion, my holy mountain. Then shall Jerusalem, (or my Church,) be holy; and there shall no stranger pass through her any more."

In Micah v, 1—4, is a repetition of the prediction of Isaiah, relative to the exaltation of the mountain of the Lord's house over the tops of the mountains, in the last days; and all nations flowing unto it:—That all wars thenceforward shall cease; and the instruments of slaughter shall be transformed into those of husbandry; and people shall sit every one under his vine and under his figtree: Or, religion, and the arts of husbandry and peace, shall fill the world."

The prophet Nahum, after noting the utter end, that God will make of the wicked, as an overflowing flood, and as stubble fully dry, says; "Behold upon the mountains the feet of him, that bringeth good tidings; that publisheth peace. O Judah, keep thy solemn feasts, perform thy vows; for the wicked shall no more pass through thee; he is utterly cut off."

Zephaniah predicts the overthrow of the enemies of the Church on earth; and the glory that shall follow. "The Lord will be terrible unto them; for he will famish all the gods of the earth; and men shall worship him, every one from his place, even all the isles of the heathen." "Therefore wait ye upon me, saith the Lord, until the day that I rise up to the prey: For my determination is to gather the nations, that I may assemble the kingdoms, to pour upon them mine indignation, even all my fierce anger; for all the earth shall be devoured with the fire of my jealousy. For then will I turn to the people a pure language, that they may *all* call upon the name of the Lord, and serve him with one consent."

With Zechariah this is an important subject. "The battle bow shall be cut off; and he shall speak peace to the heathen; and his dominion shall be from sea to sea; and from the river unto the ends of the earth." And the Lord shall be king over all the earth. In that day shall there be *one Lord*, and his name *one*.

The Old Testament closes, Mal. iv, with a striking prophecy of the ruin of Antichrist; and of the Millennial Kingdom. "Behold the day cometh, that shall burn as an oven; and all the proud, yea, and all that do wickedly, shall be a stubble; and the day that cometh shall burn them up, saith the Lord of hosts, that it shall leave them neither root nor branch. But unto you that fear my name, shall the Sun of righteousness arise, with healing in his wings; and ye shall go forth and grow up, as calves of the stall. And ye shall tread down the wicked; for they shall be as ashes under the soles of your feet, in the day, that I shall do this, saith the Lord of hosts."

In the New Testament, the subject is resumed. Our Lord in a parable, (Matt. xiii, 33) taught, that the Kingdom of heaven shall leaven the *whole* world. In John xii, 32, Christ promises, that he "will draw all men unto him." Not all the race of Adam, from first to the last. Those who are lost in hell will never be drawn to Christ. But the sense is this:—The time shall come, when *all*, living on earth, shall be drawn to him. All the ends of the earth shall look unto him, and be saved; as is taught in the Old Testament. "All the ends of the earth shall remember and turn unto the Lord;" as the psalmist predicted.

Paul to the Romans teaches, that the Jews and the "fulness of the gentiles, shall come in." And to Timothy; that at that period, God "will have all men to be saved; and to come to the knowledge of the truth."

In the Revelation, this is a great subject. Subsequent to the seventh trumpet, great voices in heaven proclaim, "The kingdoms of this world are become the Kingdoms of our Lord and of his Christ; and he shall reign forever and ever." Upon the dawn of this event we read; chap. xix; "And after these things, I heard a great voice of much people in heaven, saying, Alleluia, salvation, and glory, and honor, and power unto the Lord our God: For true and righteous are his judgments; for he hath judged the great whore, who did corrupt the earth with her fornication; and hath avenged the blood of his servants at her hand. And again they said, Alleluia. And her smoke rose up for ever and ever. And the four and twenty elders, and the four beasts, fell down and worshipped God upon the throne, saying *Amen; Alleluia.* And a voice came out of the throne, saying; Praise our God, all ye his

68

servants, and ye that fear him, both small and great.
And I heard as it were the voice of a great multitude,
and as the voice of many waters, and as the voice of
mighty thunderings, saying; Alleluia; for the Lord
God omnipotent reigneth. Let us be glad and rejoice,
and give honor to him: For the marriage of the Lamb
is come, and his wife hath made herself ready. And
to her was granted, that she should be arrayed in fine
linen, clean and white; for the fine linen is the righteousness of saints. And he saith unto me, Write;
Blessed are they that are called unto the marriage supper of the Lamb. And he saith unto me; These are
the true sayings of God." This is a brilliant prophetic description of the Church, in the commencement of
the Millennium.

Another description of the same is given in the following chapter. An Angel descends from heaven;
binds the devil; and shuts him up in the bottomless
pit; that he should deceive the nations no more for a
thousand years. Symbolic thrones are presented. The
event is now introduced, long before predicted by the
representatives of the Church; "And we shall reign
on the earth."

The souls of the martyrs, and of all, who had escaped the fatal snares of the kingdom of darkness, are now
raised, in their successors; and they live and reign with
Christ, a thousand years: Or, for *that term*, the
Church have a state of uninterrupted prosperity on
earth. The glory of the Lord is revealed, and all flesh
see it together.

SECTION III.

The desirableness of this Kingdom of Christ.

THE millennial Kingdom of Christ is held up,
through the prophetic scriptures, as an event *most desirable;* and the view of it most animating. The predictions of it were to animate the Church, under all
her trials, through all the preceding ages. What the
Savior said of Abraham, has been true, *in this sense,* of
the *children* of Abraham; they have rejoiced to see

Christ's *day.* They have seen his Kingdom by faith, and were glad. When its approach is near, the followers of the Lamb with joy obey the direction, to look up, and lift up their heads; for their redemption draws nigh. Such is the blessedness of the event, that the redeemed of the Lord will hail its dawn with songs and everlasting joys; they shall obtain joy and gladness; and sorrow and mourning shall flee away.

The object of this section will be, to note, in some particulars, the desirableness of that blessed day; or show *why* it will be as life from the dead.

. 1. *God will then be glorified on earth.* Now he is infinitely dishonored. He is set at nought by the multitudes of the wicked. Emperors, potentates, and the first men of the nations, despise God and his anointed;— and say, as was long since predicted of them, "Let us break their bands asunder, and cast their cords from us." Atheism raises its hydra forms, and brazen front. And millions unnumbered have the most contemptuous views of their Maker. They virtually blaspheme and deny him to his face. This is unspeakably dreadful in the view of all holy beings. The saints are *vexed* with such filthy conversation of the wicked; and are *grieved* for the honor of their God.

But in the Kingdom of Christ, God will be honored by all. He will be known, feared, obeyed, adored, and glorified, as God the great, the glorious, and the terrible.

Jesus Christ will then be honored. Instead of being denied, set at nought, derided, and all his benevolence, and his dying love despised; he will be embraced and adored, as the *divine Redeemer,* the *only* Savior of the world. Men will feel their need of him. They will duly appreciate his glorious grace. And the countless millions will live, preeminently, the lives they live in the flesh, by the faith of the Son of God. Their hearts, tongues and lives will resound the sacred sentiment; "This is my Beloved, and this is my Friend." "Worthy is the Lamb, who was slain, to receive power, and riches, and wisdom, and strength, and honor, and glory, and blessing."

2. *That will be a day of salvation.* The preceding ages are ages of dismal destruction. Hundreds of millions were ripening for ruin! People, with bright powers and amiable accomplishments, were moving down to endless woe! Nations were going abreast, in the broad way. Worshipping devils; and preparing to have their endless lot with them. Dear earthly friends were seen treasuring up wrath against the day of wrath. And those, as dear as our lives, were becoming vessels of wrath fitted for destruction. Most distressing case!

But that Kingdom of Christ will change the scene. It will bring *salvation* to the world. The hearts of the fathers will be turned to their children; and the hearts of the children to their fathers: And a people will be made ready prepared for the Lord. Nations will learn righteousness; and will participate in the salvation of God. Families and friends will have holy joy in each other. "Thy people shall *all* be righteous." "I will pour out my Spirit upon thy seed, and my blessing upon thine offspring." "All shall know the Lord from the least unto the greatest." "All thy children shall be taught of God; and great shall be the peace of thy children."

3. *The influence of Satan among men will be utterly restrained.* In the preceding ages, he *deceives* the nations; and *destroys* the world. He has vast influence to lead sinners captive at his will. He works in the children of disobedience. He is the father of lies; and leads his children to believe and propagate them. He comes with great wrath; upon which Heaven announces; "Woe to the inhabiters of the earth and of the sea." Spirits of devils collect the vast armies of the confederacy of the last days, against Christ. The wicked one thus has power to disseminate his infernal spirit, to deceive and to ruin.

But at the commencement of this Kingdom, he is bound and confined to hell, that he should not go out to deceive the nations any more, for a thousand years. This will be a blessed event; and renders that Kingdom *very desirable.*

4. *Pure religion will then every where prevail.* This will be most delightful. If there is now joy in heaven over one sinner that repenteth; how great will be the joy among those, who have the spirit of heaven, when all the millions on earth shall be penitent? Good people in all ages rejoice to hear, and much more to see, a shower of grace, where perhaps one to forty in a place is converted. How much greater will be the joy, when *all* are brought in, and Christ will "come down like rain upon the mown grass, and as showers that water the earth?" Christianity may be every where triumphant. The Church will "look forth as the morning, fair as the moon, clear as the sun, and terrible as an army with banners." Men will call her, the beauty of perfection; the glory of the world.

Sabbaths will be sanctified; and the ordinances and means of grace most faithfully improved. Men will universally obey the injunction; "Thou shalt keep my sabbaths, and reverence my sanctuary, I am the Lord." The vile scenes of irreligion, relative to sabbaths, and the ordinances of grace, which are now glaring before the face of heaven and earth, will then *be no more.* "And it shall come to pass, that from one sabbath to another, and from one new moon to another (i. e. on all proper occasions) shall all flesh come to worship before me." The numerous millions of people will flock to the house of God, as clouds, and as doves to their windows. And divine ordinances will be improved and honored. The following triumphant language relative to that day, will then be fulfilled. "Look upon Zion, the city of our solemnities; thine eyes shall see Jerusalem, a quiet habitation, a tabernacle which shall not be taken down; not one of the stakes thereof shall ever be removed; neither shall any of the cords thereof be broken. But there the glorious Lord shall be unto us, a place of broad rivers and streams. For the Lord is our Judge, the Lord is our Lawgiver, the Lord is our King, he will save us." "Thy teachers shall no more be removed into corners; but thine eyes shall see thy teachers."

5. *It will be a season of civil peace.* This is abundantly ascertained, in the prophecies of that day. There

will be no more the confused noise of the warrior, and garments rolled in blood. The bow will be broken; the spear cut asunder; the chariot burned in the fire; and wars will cease to the ends of the earth. The weapons of death will be turned into the implements of husbandry, and of the arts of peace. Nation will no more arm against nation. Neither shall they learn war any more.

The prophecies of this tenor, relative to that period, are express and abundant. Men will behold the past scenes of war, murder and blood, with horror and detestation.

6. *That will be a season of great health, longevity, and outward prosperity.* The following are among the predictions relative to that day. "And the inhabitant shall not say, I am sick:" "For as the days of a *tree*, are the days of my people; and mine elect shall *long* enjoy the work of their hands."

And much is said of the earth (at that day) yielding her increase; and the people dwelling in quiet habitations:—That they shall not build, and another inhabit the building; nor plant vineyards, and another possess them. But men shall long enjoy the work of their own hands. The earth, it is promised, shall yield her increase. Flocks and herds shall eat clean provender, and winnowed grain; Isa. xxx, 24; an indication of great prosperity and plenty. Many predictions indicate, that the curse will, in a degree, be taken off from the earth; so that the world will be a kind of Paradise. See Ps. lxxii, 16; Isa. vii, 22, 25. No more property will be lost in wars. Seas of wealth will not be expended for objects of pride, luxury, or ambition. But their merchandise and their hire shall be holiness to the Lord, (we are assured,) to eat sufficiently, and for durable clothing. There will be property enough to supply the wants of all men; and benevolence enough to have it wisely applied to this object.

7. *Civil government will then be perfectly subordinate to the interests of Zion.* This is abundantly ascertained, by the inspired Oracles. "Kings shall be thy nursing fathers, and queens thy nursing moth-

'ers.'' The sentiment, that civil government has nothing to do with religion; and religion has nothing to do with civil government, will then be found *banished*, with its *infernal instigator*, from the world. The sentiments of the Bible, upon this point, will then be every where admitted; that civil *rulers* must be *just*, ruling in the fear of the Lord; being ministers of God for good to *his people.* "The Gentiles shall come to thy light, and *kings* to the brightness of thy rising." "Thou shalt suck the breast of *kings*—I will make thine *officers* peace, and thine *exactors* righteousness." It then follows of course, "*Violence* shall no more he heard in thy land; wasting nor destruction within thy borders: But thou shalt call thy walls salvation, and thy gates praise." The nations will no more be tortured with systems of *perverse, crooked, hidden, designing,* and *mischievous* policy, tending to *violence, war* and *ruin.* They will experience the blessedness contained in the divine assurance,—"When the righteous are in authority, the people rejoice: As in the preceding times, people will have learned the truth of the sentiment, *to their cost,* that "when the wicked bear rule, the people shall mourn:" And, "the wicked walk on every side, when the vilest men are exalted." The most pernicious effects of the evil contained in this sentiment, or of having impious and most perverse rulers, will have been dreadful, and fatal to the wicked world. And a new and blessed order of things, relative to this, will have commenced. The kings and rulers of the world will then bring their glory into the new Jerusalem. They will be citizens of Zion: And will exert all their influence for her prosperity; as is fully implied, in her officers being peace, and her exactors righteousness; and in kings being her nursing fathers, and queens her nursing mothers.

8. *It will be a time of great knowledge.* Health, prosperity, leisure, benevolence and grace, with the best external advantages, will render application to study intense, and delightful; and knowledge easy, acute, and extensive. The face of the covering over all people, the veil over the nations, (we are assured,) shall be

taken off. And it follows of course, that "the light of the moon shall be as the light of the sun; and the light of the sun seven fold, as the light of seven days:"—A striking symbolic prediction of the vast increase of light and knowledge at that day, relative to the things of God, and relative to every thing beneficial to man. The Church are assured, in a comparative view, that the sun shall no more be their light, nor the moon; "but the Lord shall be thine everlasting light, and thy God thy glory." "The sun (it is said) shall be confounded, and the moon ashamed." "There shall no more thence, be an infant of days; nor an old man that hath not filled his days: But the child shall die an hundred years old." There shall no more be *ignorant old people:* But even a *child* shall have made great progress in knowledge.

And useful inventions and arts, for the benefit of man, we may believe, will far exceed all present conception.

9. *That day will be a season of eminent holiness; of intense benevolence.* The perilous times, because men are lovers of their *ownselves*, covetous, boasters, proud, blasphemers, unholy, covenant breakers, false, lustful, fierce, despisers of the good, traitors, heady, highminded, lovers of pleasure, and haters of God, with perhaps a form godliness, but denying its power;—these perilous days will have passed away. These horrible scenes, preparatory to the great day; "transgressing, lying against the Lord,—conceiving and uttering from the heart words of falsehood, so that truth is fallen in the streets, and equity cannot enter;"—these dismal scenes will have been swept from the earth. And a blessed contrast will appear. Men will "love the truth and peace." People will be "children that will not *lie*." "Neither shall a deceitful tongue be found in their mouths." "They will speak the truth every man to his neighbor." They will not walk in slander; neither deceive nor supplant. The reign of *sin* will have passed away; and the reign of *holiness* will have commenced. Love to God, and benevolence to man, will become triumphant through the world. Upon the bells of the

horses, and upon the pots of Jerusalem, we are assured, shall be written, *"Holiness to the Lord."* All their common utensils shall be employed for holy and benevolent purposes. Blessed period! And most desirable!

10. *That will be a season of great religious and spiritual enjoyment.* People will feel the rich sentiment of such passages as the following; "There is a river, the streams whereof shall *make glad* the city of God." "For the kindgom of God is righteousness, and peace, and *joy* in the Holy Ghost." "With *joy* shall ye draw water out of the wells of salvation." "Ye shall go out with *joy*, and be led forth with *peace*." "I create Jerusalem a *rejoicing*, and her people a *joy*." "And in this mountain (the Church) shall the Lord of hosts make unto all people a feast of *fat things;* a feast of wines on the lees; of fat things full of marrow; of wines on the lees well refined." People will have holy joy in God, and in one another, and in all the order of the Kingdom of grace. The passages will then be eminently fulfilled, "Peace I leave with you." "Thou wilt keep him in perfect peace, whose mind is stayed on thee." "And the peace of God, which passeth understanding, shall keep your heart and mind through Jesus Christ." "Behold, how good and how pleasant it is for brethren to dwell together in unity." "I sat down under his shadow with great delight; and his fruit was sweet to my taste." Then people will know the *blessedness* of the Christian life, the life of faith; will find it good to draw near unto God; and that a day in God's court is indeed better than a thousand in the scenes of the world.

11. *The systems of cavilling, error, schism and heresy, which now infest and disfigure the Church, will then be no more.* Inspiration assures, that "the watchmen shall see eye to eye." And God will "turn to the people a *pure language*, that they shall *all* call upon the name of the Lord, and serve him with *one consent*." "In that day shall there be *one Lord*, and his name *one*." No false prophet shall any more "wear a *rough garment to deceive:*" i. e. There shall be no more false prophets in sheep's clothing. As *Satan* is bound in the bottomless

69

pit, his *ministers cease.* And the one plain system of salvation is thus embraced by all.

12. *That millennial Kingdom will be a time when the characters and conduct of men, in the times preceding that kingdom will be duly estimated; and the wicked will be held in their merited abhorrence.* This is desirable. For it is painful, when the public sentiment is turned against the people of God; and impious characters are in the highest repute. However this will be the case, in the age preceding the Millennium, it will not continue to be the case in that blessed season. It is added, upon the prediction, that "from one sabbath to another, and from one new moon to another, shall all flesh come to worship before me, saith the Lord;—*And they shall go forth and look upon the carcasses of the men, who have transgressed against me; for their worm shall not die; neither shall their fire be quenched; and they shall be an abhorring unto all flesh.* The sense is this:— In sermons, and pious communications, the abominable characters and conduct of the enemies of God; and especially the infidelity, falsehood, perfidy, and violence, of the governments and nations, which will have opened the scenes of the battle of the great day, or have been just before the Millennium, will be clearly ascertained before the Church; and will be held by all classes of men, in the utmost *abhorrence.* The perverseness of the wicked, which is now labored to be concealed under every subtile disguise, will then be greatly unfolded. And the enemies of the Gospel will have their names and conduct go down to posterity, like the people of *Sodom* and *Gomorrha,* covered with *eternal infamy.* Many of such characters now wish to immortalize their names. And they will *do* it; but in a way the reverse of what they now design. They will be held in *merited* and *everlasting contempt.* And this universal and correct estimation of characters and things, is an event *greatly to be desired.* The turning of things upside down, by the wicked, is to be "esteemed as the *potter's clay;*" a brittle cover of their wickedness. Their putting darkness for light, and light for darkness; making a covenant with death, and an agreement with hell, and un-

der falsehood hiding themselves; (as Inspiration expresses it,) *will not stand;* but will appear, in all its horrid
impiety and madness, to the world of the Godly, in the
millennial Kingdom.

*In a word. That will be a season of great blessed-
ness.* "Glorious things are spoken of thee, O city of
God." "Arise, shine; for thy light is come; and the
glory of the Lord is risen upon thee. His glory shall
be seen upon thee. Gentiles shall come to thy light,
and kings to the brightness of thy rising." "Thou shalt
be, an eternal excellency." "The marriage of the Lamb
is come." "For thy Maker is thy husband." "I will
lay thy stones with fair colors; and thy foundations
with sapphires. I will make thy windows of agate, and
thy gates of carbuncle, and all thy borders of pleasant
stones. All thy children shall be taught of God; and
great shall be the peace of thy children." "Then the
moon shall be confounded, and the sun ashamed, when
the Lord of hosts shall reign in mount Zion and in Jerusalem, and before his ancients gloriously."

, This is the Kingdom, predicted for the animation of
the Church; and toward which she is moving *annually,*
and *daily,* upon the swift wings of time. This is the
Kingdom, the tokens of whose approach are now very
manifest.

SECTION IV.

Remarks and deductions, relative to this Kingdom.

1. *The advancement of this Kingdom is an important
object of prayer.* This appears, both from the great
excellency and desirableness of the event; and also from
the consideration, that God *commands* his people to
pray for it; and that he will prepare the way for this
Kingdom, and introduce it, in answer to prayer. When
the restoration of the Jews is predicted, (an event, which
may be viewed the immediate harbinger of this Kingdom) God says, "Yet for this I will be inquired of by
the house of Israel to do it for them." "Then shall ye
call upon me, and ye shall go and pray unto me, and I
will harken unto you. And ye shall seek me, and find

me, when ye shall search for me with all your heart. And I will be found of you, saith the Lord; and I will turn again your captivity; and will gather you from all the nations." And all the Church are directed daily to pray for this Kingdom; "*Thy Kingdom come.*"

This great event is the work of *God.* And it is made certain. Every thing will be made to give way to it. Every thing will be overruled to advance it. The rage of hell and earth against it will issue in its establish. ment.

But the mighty and blessed work is to be done, in answer to *prayer.* This is most evident. It is there. fore given in charge; "Ye that make mention of the Lord, keep not silence, and give him no rest, till he establish, and till he make Jerusalem a praise in the earth." It is predicted: "I have set watchmen upon thy walls, O Jerusalem, who will never hold their peace, day nor night." And the ministers and people of Christ thus *engage;* "For Zion's sake I will not hold my peace; and for Jerusalem's sake I will not rest, until the righteousness thereof go forth as brightness; and the salvation thereof as a lamp that burneth." Christ teaches, that his coming will be to avenge his elect, who *cry unto him, day and night.* And says the psalm. ist; "When the Lord shall build up Zion, he will ap. pear in his glory; he will regard the prayer of the des. titute, and not despise their prayer." We learn the great and urgent duty then, of daily, fervent and per. severing prayer for the advancement of this Kingdom.

2. *It is matter of joy, and a token for good, that a peculiar spirit of prayer for this event, is so widely dif. fused in the Church.* That this is happily the case is a thing too evident to all Christian observers, to need any further confirmation. And it appears like a fulfil. ment of some of the predictions, which relate to the dawn of the millennial glory. "Thus saith the Lord, it shall yet come to pass, that there shall come people, and the inhabitants of many cities; and the inhabitants of one city shall go unto another, saying, Let us go speed. ily to pray before the Lord, and to seek the Lord of hosts: I will go also."—"And many people and strong

nations shall come to seek the Lord of hosts in Jerusalem, and to pray before the Lord."—"In that day shall
ye call, every man his neighbor, under the vine and
under the 'fig tree;" i. e. into retirement, for special
prayer. Then the following predictions will be fulfilled. "Who hath heard such a thing? Who hath seen
such a thing? Shall' the earth be made to bring forth
in one day? Or shall a nation be born at once?' For
as soon as Zion travailed, she brought forth her children. Shall I bring to the birth, and not cause to bring
forth? saith the Lord." "It shall come to pass, that before they call, I will answer; and while they are yet
speaking, I will hear: The wolf and the lamb shall feed
together:" i. e. The millennial Kingdom shall then
speedily be introduced. "The effectual fervent prayer
of a righteous man availeth much." And truly, the
effectual, fervent, united and persevering prayers of the
body of the righteous, will avail much, for the introduction of the Millennium. Blessed be God, that such
prayers are now abundantly made.

3. *We find in this subject a criterion, by which to discern the true spirit of prayer.* The true spirit of prayer,
is a "spirit of grace, and of supplication;" or of intercession for the Kingdom of Christ. If this be wanting, we have no evidence of the spirit of prayer. If
Zion be overlooked, or the Kingdom of grace have no
interest in our hearts, our forms of devotion will be ineffectual. Hence we may learn our moral *state*, and
prospects.

4. *How wide is the difference between the gracious
and the graceless heart.* The former longs and devoutly
prays for the advancement of the Kingdom of grace.
While the latter is so far from this, that it is *hostile* to
this Kingdom. There can be no *neuter* in this case.
"He that is not for me, is against me: (Christ asserts)
He who gathereth not with me, scattereth abroad."
The two Kingdoms are hostile to each other. "The
carnal mind is enmity against God." "And there was
war in heaven; Michael and his angels fought against
the dragon; and the dragon fought, and his angels." It
is in vain to imagine we do not belong to the latter host,

if our souls be not engaged for the Kingdom of grace. We in that case, belong to the class, who *hate* the subjects of Christ's Kingdom. "Marvel not, if the world *hate* you. Ye know that it hated me, before it hated you. If ye were of the world, the world would love his own. But because ye are not of the world, but I have chosen you out of the world, therefore the world hateth you."

5. *Co operations with the people of God, in behalf of this Kingdom of grace, are to us vastly important.* People are to watch, as well as pray, for this object. Faith without works is dead." Christians have now an opportunity to be "workers together with God," in the promotion of the Kingdom of grace. Discrete systems for joint exertions, are instituted, and brought within our reach. And none can plead inability to contribute at least to the amount of the two mites of the poor widow, whom our Lord so highly commended. Who would decline to improve such an opportunity, and at such a day as this? The lines are drawing between the two Kingdoms. And these beneficent exertions of the Kingdom of Christ, are fast helping forward the separation. "Then shall ye return and discern between the righteous, and the wicked; between him that serveth God; and him that serveth him not." "Curse ye Meroz, saith the Angel of the Lord; curse ye bitterly the inhabitants thereof; because they came not to the help of the Lord, to the help of the Lord against the mighty." These words have a mystical import of vast weight, at this day.

6. *Various other tokens of the approach of this Kingdom, appear to be visible.* A variety of tokens, in the heavens and in the earth, are stated, in various parts of the sacred word, as evidential of the approach of this Kingdom. It would be long, and needless here to give them in detail. The best of judges believe them to be fulfilled, or fulfilling in a signal manner. This has excited a presentiment in the Church of Christ, that the day is drawing nigh. The signs in the heaven and in the earth have appeared; blood, and fire, and pillars of smoke.

These were *literally* fulfilled in the northern lights; and in other phenomena of modern date. And they are now *mystically* fulfilling in the terrible scenes among the nations to which the *northern lights* have *given way!* Wars most terrible, and rumors of wars; signs in the symbolic sun, moon and stars; famines, pestilences, and earthquakes in divers places; infidelity and licentiousness; perilous times; a spirit of falsehood, rage, and *crooked policy;* the unclean spirits like frogs, out of the mouth of the dragon, the Beast and the false prophet, gone through the nations, working miracles of revolution and ruin; together with a most violent disposition to break the bands of the Lord and of his anointed, and cast away the cords of their religion; kings, rulers and people, raging and imagining vain things against God, and his embassadors, and followers;—distress of nations, with perplexity; the symbolic sea and the waves roaring; men's hearts failing them for fear, and looking after those things, which are coming on the earth; while the powers of the symbolic heavens are shaken;—*these things are bursting upon a guilty world, with a flood of evidence, which nothing but atheism can deny!* The predictions of events, not long to precede the millennial Kingdom, are in a most evident and remarkable train of fulfilment.

7. *These tokens, while in various points of light they are full of terror and alarm, afford considerations of joy to the people of God.* Jesus Christ, when giving these very tokens, directs his people,—"And when these things begin to come to pass, then look up, and lift up your heads; for your redemption draweth nigh." The mystery of iniquity is then about to be finished. The wicked cause is then about to be swept from the earth. And the joyful Kingdom of grace is about to become triumphant. The following passages then become very important. "Fret not thyself because of evil doers; neither be thou envious against the workers of iniquity: For they shall soon be cut down as the grass; and wither as the green herb.—Rest in the Lord, and wait patiently for him: Fret not thyself, because of

the man who bringeth wicked devices to pass. For evil doers shall be cut off. But those who wait upon the Lord, they shall inherit the earth. For yet a little while, and the wicked shall not be, yea thou shalt diligently consider his place, and it shall not be: But the meek shall inherit the earth, and shall delight themselves in the abundance of peace. The wicked plotteth against the just, and gnasheth upon him with his teeth. The Lord shall laugh at him! for he seeth that his day is coming. The wicked have *drawn out the sword;* and have bent their bow, to cast down the poor and the needy, and to slay such as be of upright conversation. Their sword shall enter into their own heart, and their bows shall be broken.'' Truly *we* have no room to doubt, but this passage was inspired by Him, who searches all hearts. Nor need we doubt the correctness of those who deem this to be a prophecy of the very days, in which we live. And here are presented considerations to the Church, from the mouth of the Most High, full of support and consolation. God will soon rectify the whole scene. The cause of darkness shall ere long sink. And the meek shall inherit the earth, and delight themselves in abundance of peace.

The people of God then, in the midst of the gloom of these days, may well unite in the triumphant language of praise to their Redeemer, "Thou art *worthy* —For thou wast slain and hast redeemed us to God by thy blood, out of every kindred and tongue, and people, and nation, and hast made us unto our God, kings and priests, *and we shall reign on the earth.*" This was the triumph of the saints of old. They were *to reign on the earth*, by the triumphant reigning of their *Head*, and the universal prevalence of their *cause*, in the last thousand years. When the day is drawing nigh, and its dawn just ready to open upon us, what great occasion have present Christians to make that song of triumph their *own?* If *they* live not to *see* and *enjoy* the day, they may enjoy it by a holy fellowship with God and the Lamb. They may enjoy it, as near, by the holy anticipations of faith, which is the substance of things hoped for; and the evidence of things not seen. They may be the joyful instruments of preparing the way for the advancement of this Kingdom. And their souls will hence be prepared for the most perfect enjoyment of it in heaven. For if there is joy in heaven, over one sinner that repenteth; how much greater will be the addition of heavenly joy; when all on earth shall be penitent, and the earth be full of the knowledge and glory of the Lord, as the waters cover the seas?

The motives of joy and animation then, to the present people of God, from the view of the approach of the millennial Kingdom, are great and sublime.

CONCLUSION,

*In which some duties are suggested, which seem calcu-
lated to withstand the Infidelity of our times.*

I HAVE now finished my arguments and proofs in favor
of the points proposed in this dissertation.   Concerning the weight of the evidence, the reader will judge.
But proceeding on the ground, that the points proposed
are substantiated; what have the friends of Zion to do,
to withstand the Infidelity of this period?   They have
much to do; much with their own hearts; much with
their families; and much with their fellow men.   The
Divine precepts, now emphatically applicable, are
many, and most weighty.   One important direction
we find prefixed to the prophetic description of the rise
of Antichrist in Jude.   The Apostle exhorts, that we
contend earnestly for the faith once delivered to the saints.
The duty here enjoined implies, in addition to a faithful support of the *scheme* of Gospel grace, the diligent
use of all proper remedies against the insidious attacks
of all who aid the cause of Antichrist.   As these attacks
are concealed, oblique, and subtile; so the means of
withstanding them must be extensive; and must consist
much in guarding those principles, on the subversion
of which the enemies make their highest calculations.
These means ought to be wisely ascertained, and vigi-
lantly applied.

For this purpose, I shall now suggest some things,
which may be esteemed important.

1. *Repentance and reformation.*

If *these* be neglected, all other means will be of but
little avail.   For *God will wound the head of his enemies, and the hairy scalp of such an one as goeth on still
in his trespasses.*   This will hold true of *nations,* as well
as of individuals. However blamable may be the instru-

mental causes of our calamities, or public dangers; yet, they are a just punishment for our sins. Nothing but sin could betray us into the hands of the agents of Infidelity and disorganization. Our nation is deeply defiled with sin. We are guilty of ingratitude and impiety toward God; of undervaluing the Gospel of his Son; and of much contempt of his authority. Almost every species of vice and profanity is abounding. It is thought this nation has made unprecedented progress in wickedness; and this, notwithstanding our most signal Divine blessings, and our great obligations to God.

It has been but a short time since the first fathers of New England arrived in this western hemisphere, then a wilderness of savages and beasts. Their sole object in the perilous adventure was, the enjoyment of the liberty of conscience, and the mantaining and enjoyment of the Institutions of grace in their purity. Great things God did for them, in sustaining them under pressing calamities and dangers. And great things God has since done, in building us up into a great, independent and flourishing nation. Our obligations to God to be a *virtuous people*, are proportionably great. But alas! how have they been violated! When we compare the spirit and manners of our nation with those of our pious ancestors, the contrast is *dismal*. And it evinces that our degeneracy has been rapid and great.

God is angry with this nation. And justly may he exhibit his displeasure, by suffering the spirit of Antichrist to propagate his impositions in so guilty a land. But how dismal must be our prospects, should Antichristian influence find a permanent residence here! Our national judgments in that case would not linger; but we should be involved in the plagues of the infidel Power of the last days.

Permit me to enlarge a little upon this particular. To subvert this nation, this new world, this last and only republic on earth, and bring it under the grasp of the military Despot of the age, has certainly engaged the deepest intrigue and exertions of that enormous Power; and it is no doubt a prime object of the kingdom of

darkness. And considering the character and circumstances of our nation, nothing can prevent our falling before such an insidious host of dangers, but the omnipotent interposition of the God of our fathers.

But should that infernal influence, that dark and
crooked policy, that deep system of imposition, *here
prevail;* dreadful would be the consequences! We
should receive of Babylon's plagues, and sink with
her into perdition. *This* God decides, when he warns,
"Deliver thyself, O Zion, that dwellest with the daughters of Babylon." "Come out of her, my people, that
ye be not partakers of her sins, and that ye receive not
of her plagues." "If any man worship the Beast, and
his image, and receive his mark in his forehead, or in
his hand, the same shall drink of the wine of the wrath
of God, which is poured out without mixture." "Say
ye not, A confederacy, to all them, to whom this people shall say, A confederacy." "Woe to them that go
down to Egypt, or stay on Assyria." Such sacred
passages more than whisper our danger, and our duty.
An alliance with Antichrist is *ruin,* and inevitable
death! And the deepest intrigues of the Kingdom of
darkness are in the utmost exertion, to effect so fatal a
union. Every word spoken or step taken toward such
a union, is so much done toward our inevitable destruction. Would to God all people were sensible of this,
as they will be sensible of it, sooner or later! The
charms of delusion, at this period, are powerful, and of
unspeakable danger. God alone can save from falling
before them.

Every thing then, calls for repentance and reformation. The word of God, and the signs of the times,
enforce on us the following paternal language of heav-
en; "Amend your ways and your doings; and I will
"cause you to dwell in this place. Return unto me;
"and I will return unto you, saith the Lord of hosts. But
"if ye will walk contrary unto me, I will walk contra-
"ry unto you, and will punish you yet seven times for
"your sins. Return ye backsliding children, and I will
"heal your backslidings. If ye be willing and obedient,
"ye shall eat the good of the land. But if ye refuse

"and rebel, ye shall be devoured with the sword; for
"the mouth of the Lord hath spoken it." Should
such admonitions of Heaven be disregarded, we have
reason to tremble at such judgments as the following;
"And as they did not like to retain God in their knowl-
"edge, God gave them over to a reprobate mind, to do
"those things, which are not convenient. Because that
"when they knew God, they glorified him not as
"God, neither were they thankful; but became vain in
"their imagination, and their foolish hearts were darken-
"ed. Professing themselves to be wise they became
"fools." These, and the many similar warnings of Inspiration derive the greatest emphasis, (as they respect
us) from our national blessings, our Gospel privileges,
and our signal obligations to God. And nothing can
exempt us from their terrors, but *repentance* and *reformation.*

National sins are provoking to the God of nations.
This has ever been the case. And surely it cannot be
less so *now*, under the peculiar light and advantages of
this period. It was said of old, *Righteousness exalteth
a nation; but sin is a reproach to any people.* Civil
communities are punishable for their public sins, *only
in this world.* If sinful individuals continue to enjoy
prosperity in this world, it is not unaccountable. They
will be punished in the *next.* But if sinful communities escape Divine judgment here, one would be apt to
inquire, *Where is the God of judgment?* Is not *God to
be known by the judgments, which he executeth?* Terrible things were implied against an ungrateful and
wicked people of old, when we read; *Hear O heavens,
and give ear O earth; for the Lord hath spoken. I
have nourished and brought up children, and they
have rebelled against me. The ox knoweth his own-
er, and the ass his master's crib; but Israel doth not
know, my people doth not consider.*

Perseverance in sin, under signal calls of Providence,
is peculiarly provoking to God; and dangerous to an in-
corrigible people. *In that day did the Lord God call
to weeping and to mourning, and to baldness, and to
girding with sackcloth; and behold joy, and gladness,*

slaying oxen, and killing sheep, eating flesh, and drinking wine: let us eat and drink, for tomorrow we die. And it was revealed in mine ears, by the Lord of hosts, surely this iniquity shall not be purged from you till you die, saith the Lord of hosts. Were they ashamed, when they had committed abomination? Nay, they were not at all ashamed, neither could they blush. Therefore they shall fall among them that fall: at the time that I visit them, they shall be cast down, saith the Lord. A dreadful fulfilment these words will have, among Antichristian nations, at the battle of that great day, which is fast approaching.

No doubt our nation is highly favored with *praying people.* Their numbers have of late increased. And often has the Most High blessed whole nations, in answer to the prayers of individuals; or for his Church's sake. Ten righteous persons would have saved Sodom! But we read of a time's coming, with sinful nations, when the prayers of the pious among them, will cease to prevail. *Therefore pray not thou for this people—for I will not hear thee. Though Moses and Samuel stood before me, yet my mind could not be toward this people. Cast them out of my sight, and let them go forth.—Though these three men, Noah, Daniel, and Job were in it, they should deliver but their own souls, saith the Lord God.*

Every thing then calls on our great national community to repent and reform. "At what instant I shall "speak concerning a nation, and concerning a kingdom, "to pluck up, and to pull down, and to destroy it; if "that nation, against whom I have pronounced, turn "from their evil, I will repent of the evil, that I thought "to do unto them." Blessed encouragement! But read the alternative: "At what instant I shall speak concern-"ing a nation, and concerning a kingdom; to build and "to plant it; if it do evil in my sight, that it obey not "my voice; then I will repent of the good, wherewith "I said I would benefit them." These cannot be otherwise than words of alarm to our nation.

2. *Faithfulness in the government of our literary Institutions.*

These Institutions have a very powerful influence on the religious sentiments, and the morals of the community. Their members, and especially, their annual graduates, are capable of doing great good, or evil, in society; they can greatly withstand, or greatly promote the cause of Infidelity and licentiousness. How important is it then, that, while obtaining their education, they be duly impressed with a correct view of the dangers of this period, arising from the influence of Antichrist? And that they be diligently guarded, by pious instructions, against every impression of that philosophy, which is *falsely so called.* It is of high importance to the community, that they be led to imbibe the spirit, and correct sentiments, of the Christian religion. This is an object, which depends much on those, who have the government of our literary Institutions. And it is an object of great moment at this interesting period.

3. *Vigilance and faithfulness in the embassadors of Christ.*

Those, who are set for a defence of the Gospel, must in a special manner *contend earnestly for the faith once delivered to the saints.* Peculiar duties are attached to the office of the watchmen, to give notice when the enemy are approaching. If they sleep, or are unfaithful, ruin may ensue; and the watchmen must answer for it at the peril of their souls. The embassadors of Christ must watch the attacks of the enemy; and, at whatever risk, they must sound the alarm. *Blow ye the trumpet in Zion; sound an alarm in my holy mountain; let all the inhabitants of the land tremble for the day of the Lord; for it is nigh at hand.*

Ministers ought to use great plainness in preaching and supporting the distinguishing doctrines of the Gospel; and never to handle the word of God *deceitfully,* in order to render it palatable to the carnal heart. Infinite mischief has been done, and Infidelity greatly promoted, by such attempts to please men. The Aristotelian, Platonic, and other systems of ancient philosophy have been adopted in turn, or at different periods, to aid in unfolding the truths of revelation. But the consequences were fatal. Such attempts are nearly allied to Infidelity. They are a virtual rejection of the word of God.

In that form of Illuminism, called *The German Union,* the German divines, while they professed the warmest attachment to the Gospel, united to explain away its most offensive, or its peculiar doctrines. This was a signal for others to come forward, and deny the superiority of the Bible to natural religion; and thus to preclude the necessity of a revelation. And this again opened a door for a third class to deny all religion, and its Author. The first of these classes, Judas like! betrayed the Gospel into the hands of the other two, by stripping it of its blessed peculiarities. By numbers of such hands, under the mask of friendship, the sacred pillars of the Gospel were *there* undermined; and Infidelity obtained an easy triumph.

The faithful preaching of the distinguishing doctrines of grace must hold a prime rank among the means of withstanding the spirit of Antichrist, and of supporting the Christian Religion. This is a mean of God's appointment; and a mean, which God will bless. *Preach unto them the preaching, that I bid thee. Speak all the words that I command thee to speak unto them; diminish not a word.* This is an essential mean of salvation. A certain divine speaks of a twofold darkness;—*infidelity*, and a *corrupt theology.* The former, he says, has slain its thousands; the latter its ten thousands.

While the ministers of Christ at this day are wise as serpents, and harmless as doves; they will need to be *strong*, and *bold*, and very *courageous.* The wiles of Infidelity are so reduced to a system, and have taken such deep effect, that to expose them, is rendered unpopular with thousands, and dangerous to the undertaker. All the depths of Satan are interwoven with this scheme, to enable it to *defy* the friends of religion. Its pillars and bulwarks are numerous, and of long preparation. The last words of David, in his sublime prediction of the *Kingdom of the Righteous Ruler*, and of the scenes that shall precede it,* are here directly in point.

---

* 2 Samuel xxiii, 1, 6, 7.

"But the sons of Belial shall be all of them as thorns "thrust away, because they cannot be taken with hands; "but the man, that would touch them, must be fenced "with iron, and the staff of a spear; and they shall be "utterly burnt with fire in the same place." This is a prophetic description of the agents of the Infidelity of the last days. Ministers will be under great temptation to shrink from this important branch of their official duty; and to avoid the *task*, of *exposing the men of Belial.* But it is a duty, which the Great Head of the Church has assigned to his embassadors, to descry the approach of the enemy, and to give faithful warning. And they have no right to decline it, for any consideration. Neither flatteries, frowns, interests, nor dangers of death, can justify them in such neglect. Their Master endured the cross, and despised the shame. And they must follow him. *He, that would save his life shall lose it.*

The embassadors of Christ, of this generation, especially the younger part of them, may possibly see days of trial. Trials to the faithful will precede the Millennium. The feet of the ancient priests were dipped in the waters of Jordan, overflowing all its banks in the time of wheat harvest, before the waters divided to give a passage to the tribes of the Lord into the promised land.* It was the lot of these ministers of the Lord to lead the way, bearing the ark of the covenant before the people. That procession, divinely ordered, was about to take possession of the promised Canaan, and also to present us with a *type* of the *transition* of the Gospel Church from her wilderness state, to her millennial glory. They moved forward toward the foaming waters, which rolled furiously between them and the promised land, till the feet of the priests were plunged. Human wisdom saw no way of being transported over the flood. They confided in God. The command, given at the Red Sea, became again applicable; *Stand still, and see the salvation of the Lord!*

* Joshua iii, 10.

71

The floods were cut off. The waters were thrown asunder. Israel passed on dry land; and all was safe!

May the ministers of Christ, with a correct view of the present signs of the times, awake to duty and faithfulness; and cheerfully stand in their lot.

4. *Proper caution in the induction of men into the Gospel ministry.*

While a pious and learned ministry are to hold the first rank among the means of withstanding the Infidelity of the last days; unconverted and ignorant ministers are among the most fatal means of betraying the cause of Christ into the hands of Infidels. Hence the inspired caution, *Lay hands suddenly on no man.* This holy office is to be committed only to "faithful men, who "shall be able to teach others also. Holding fast the "faithful word, (says the apostle) as he hath been "taught, that he may be able, by sound doctrine, both "to exhort, and to convince the gainsayers." Surely none but men of grace, of abilities, and of good education, as well as of known and approved character, are adequate to this work. And none but such should be admitted to ordination, nor as candidates. False teachers, in such a land as this, are to be among the most fatal propagators of the Infidelity of the last days.

5. *A faithful support and improvement of the regular administration of the Gospel; avoiding erroneous and unknown teachers; and aiding the missionary cause.*

The enemies, aware that the administration of the Gospel is essential to the well being of Zion, and a prime bulwark of her defence, make this one of the first points of their attack. Their modes of attack are various. Where the way is prepared, the attack may be expected to be *direct* and *decisive;* as was the case in France, after the revolution. There the Protestant, as well as Catholic ministers were put to death in multitudes; or had to renounce their profession; or flee their country. In Holland also, after the French had gotten possession there, violence was used against the order of the Gospel. The people were forbidden to be called together, as had been usual, for Divine worship, by the ringing of bells. Ministers were forbidden to appear abroad in their distinctive dress. Yea, they were deprived of their salaries. Some of them were robbed of great sums of money; and were confined in prison. Cloots, a leading member in the French national Convention, used to say; "Kings and priests are worthless things: they are despots and corrupters."* If the Roman Catholic priests were corrupters, the French made no distinction between them, and the most unexceptionable Protestants. The whole order of the Gospel they utterly abjured.

Where the way is *not* thus prepared for an open attack; the operations of Infidelity against the administration of the Gospel, are more cautious, covert, and subtile; but calculated with vast design, to subvert the Christian religion, by first overturning its faithful ministry.

The native covetousness of the human heart is enlisted into this service. Many are induced to *withdraw*, or *withhold* the support of the Gospel ministry. Many under the name of teachers have artfully led the unwary to infer from the gratuity of some of Paul's missionary labors among the heathen, that, the ministry of the Gospel is *ever* to be free of all regular expense; and that all ministers, who stipulate for their regular support, in return for their being devoted to a people, are *hirelings* and *impostors.* This is a suggestion, than which nothing can be more opposed to the word of God; or injurious to man. It is a prime stratagem of hypocrisy, and of Infidelity. These words of Christ are perverted, and pressed into this service, *Freely ye have received; freely give.* In relation to the power of miraculous *healing*, which was superadded to the special commission of the apostles, our Lord gave them a charge; *Freely ye have received freely give.* (Matt. x, 8.) i. e. Make no merchandize of this special Divine delegation. Men would give almost any sum to be healed. Take nothing. But it is base wickedness to pervert these words of Christ into a prohibition to

* See Dr. Morse's Fast Sermon of 1799.

his ministers from asking their regular support. The words of Christ, which immediately follow, take this text out of the impostor's hands. "Provide neither gold, "nor silver, nor brass in your purses; nor scrip for "your journey; neither two coats; neither shoes; nor "yet staves: for the workman is worthy of his meat."

It is the express order of God, that those, who preach the Gospel, shall live of the Gospel; that people shall aid their support according to their several abilities; and that they shall do it to such a degree, as that their minister need not entangle himself with the affairs of this life, but may give himself wholly to the work of the ministry. When this support of the Gospel is covetously withholden, God charges the withholders with the sin of robbing him. (Mal. iii, 9.) And they may well expect judgments, delusion, and ruin, in return. The support of the Gospel then, and a faithful attention and obedience to its administration, are a most important remedy against the innovating, Antichristian principles of these last days.

And a firm rejection of all erroneous and irregular preachers, is an important mean of withstanding the Antichristian principles of this period. And this is solemnly enjoined in the word of God. Relative to the last days, Christ commands; "Take heed that no "man deceive you. For many shall come in my name, "and shall deceive many." Various predictions of the last days lead us to expect multitudes of false teachers. And that such will be most influential in propagating the Infidelity of that period. Peter, when about to predict the rise and agency of Antichrist, thus introduces the chapter; "But there were false prophets also "among the people, even as there shall be false teach- "ers among you, who privily shall bring in damnable "heresies; denying the Lord that bought them, and "bring upon themselves swift destruction. And many "shall follow their pernicious ways, by reason of whom "the way of truth shall be evil spoken of." Here we find *much* at least of that Infidelity is introduced by what the apostle calls, *false teachers.* This term may probably *here* be viewed as a word of considerable lat.

itude. It must comprise all, who are found in the active promotion of the Infidelity of this period; or of sentiments, that lead to it; whether they teach Atheism or Deism; or more special tenets under the notion of Christian doctrines; which yet are essentially erroneous: Whether they do it with an express design to propagate Infidelity; or, being given up to delusion and fanatacism, please themselves that they are doing God service: Whether they propagate their tenets under the guise of politics, or religion: Whether they act under pretence of a commission from Christ, or not; or whether their communications be made in private letters, secret assemblies, a sermon, a volume, a pamphlet, a tract, or a gazette. All, who *actively* undertake to *direct the public opinion*, so as to propagate Infidelity, or sentiments, which *in fact tend* to it, whether *they* perceive this tendency, or not, *are the false teachers in this passage of Peter.* They, from some motive, and in some form, undertake to *teach men;* and they teach them *falsehood;* which tends to unhinge their minds, and to prepare them for skepticism and licentiousness. These false teachers of various descriptions are predicted to be abundant in the last days; men of confidence and impertinence; as well as of base design: And many of them so subtile, that *if it were possible they would deceive even the very elect.*

Now the command of God is, that we should not be led by such persons, let them be of whatever profession; or let their zeal be what it may: "Take heed "that no man deceive you. Mark them, who cause di- "visions and offences, contrary to the doctrine, which ye "have learned; and avoid them. For they that are such, "serve not our Lord Jesus Christ, but their own belly; "and by good words and fair speeches deceive the "hearts of the simple."

Here it may, with great propriety, be added, that to unite in the missionary exertions of the present period, is an important duty, and a powerful antidote against the Antichristian influence of our times. A great missionary work, a remarkable propagation of the Gospel,

m

is to be effected. This is powerfully to aid the cause of Christ, under the darkness of Antichristian tyranny; and to prepare the way in due time to bring forward the introduction of the Millennium . And to this work men are called upon to put a helping hand. While the Most High will carry it forward, he will do it through the instrumentality of the friends of Zion, and of those, whom he will graciously incline to this purpose. God will show that the *silver* and the *gold* are *His.* He will incline the hearts of his chosen to bestow a portion of their attention and property upon the missionary object. This object has thus been promoted within eighteen years, to a degree unprecedented since the days of the apostles. The formation of the London Missionary Society, on the 21st of September, 1795, presented to the evangelized world a second *Pentecost.* Great numbers of Societies and associations have since been formed in different parts of what has been called the Christian world, to promote this most noble design, either in sending out missionaries; or in translating the Bible into the different languages of the heathen, and distributing this precious book among perishing millions. The particular and pleasing histories of these societies, the effectual doors opened, and the signal provisions and interpositions of Providence in the behalf of his servants, the people of God have perused with interest, pleasure, and wonder.

Ancient Divine predictions of this great event are express and striking. And they unite in fixing it about the present time. The Lamb appeared on the mount Zion, Rev. xiv, 1, at the reformation early in the sixteenth century. By and by, or after the Protestant cause had progressed through different nations for a convenient time, and the way was prepared, and the hour of God's judgment, in the subversion of the predominant Power of Papal Rome, had arrived, the *Angel* of the missionary cause, (verse 6,) begins his "flight "through the midst of heaven, having the everlasting "Gospel to preach to them, that dwell on the earth, to "every nation, and kindred, and tongue, and people; "saying, Fear God, and give glory to him; for the hour "of his judgment is come; and worship him, that made "heaven, and earth, and the sea, and the fountains of "water."

That this sublime emblem predicts a remarkable, general, and efficacious propagation of the Gospel through the nations, none I trust will dispute. And that it is to have its effect in *Pagan lands*, is evident from the last clause of the text; where the message is introduced, by unfolding the volume of *nature*. "Wor- "ship him, that made heaven, and earth, and the sea, "and the fountains of water." As if they should say, We have come to inform you *who* made the yonder visible heavens; this great earth; the sea; and the foun- tains of water; *what* he demands of you; and *how* you may worship and enjoy him. The prediction seems evidently to fix the event about the present time. The Protestant Religion *has* progressed through the nations. The hour of God's judgment has come. The accep- table year of the Lord is nearly connected with the day of vengeance of our God. Isa. lxi, 2. "For the day of vengeance is in my heart; and the year of my redeemed is come." Isa. lxiii, 4. The missionary An- gel has begun his flight. And the two great classes of events are collaterally progressing.

Parallel predictions of this blessed event corroborate the preceding exposition: And they show that this re- markable propagation of the Gospel is but a short season to precede the battle of that great day of God Almighty.

Now, shall we not *aid* this blessed work? Shall we not unite in it with the friends of Zion? Is it our inter- esting lot to have our season of probation at the im- portant period, when the blessed event of those ancient prophecies is beginning to be fulfilled? Gracious Parent of the world! Shall we not leap for humble joy and pious gratitude, that we are thus indulged the opportu- nity of being workers together *with thee* in so merciful and glorious an object, and at such a period as this? Who can withstand the motives of this blessed cause? Who will not lay his talents, all his powers of body and mind, his time, and his money, at the feet of Christ? This will be time, and money laid out to infinite ad-

vantage; diffusing salvation to perishing millions! This
will be making to ourselves friends of the mammon of
unrighteousness; that when we fail, they may be the
occasion of receiving us into everlasting habitations.
How suitable an employment, and how blessed a source
of consolation, when Antichrist is rising, and spreading
terror and devastation through the nations! While the
sea of revolution and tumult, and the waves thereof are
roaring, and men's hearts will be found failing them
for fear, and looking after those things, that are coming
upon the earth; yea while the Jordan of Antichristian
intrigue and violence may be found overflowing all its
banks, in the time of this harvest; *those*, who shall be
found thus following the Captain of salvation, may lift
up their heads, and sing; for their redemption draweth
nigh. But where shall we be safe, unless thus following the Lamb? *Where*, or *how* else can we, to such
advantage, withstand the attacks of the Infidelity and
licentiousness of this period? How else shall we escape
the displeasure of Him, who is *jealous* for his cause and
honor? "Curse ye Meroz, saith the angel of the Lord!
"Curse ye bitterly the inhabitants thereof; because they
"came not up to the help of the Lord, to the help of
"the Lord against the mighty." Say not you have no
property to spare for this object. Your property is *all
the Lord's.* You are but his stewards; and must give
an account to God for the improvement of every talent.
And shall we dare to withhold, when the great Master
calls for a little of his own property, which he has deposited in our hands? and this too from so noble an
object? "The earth is the Lord's, and the fulness
"thereof; the world and they that dwell therein." And
"God is able to make all grace abound toward us, that
"we having a sufficiency in all things, may abound to
"every good work. As it is written, He, that gathered
"much had nothing over; and he, that gathered little,
"had no lack." Withholding from God cannot be the
way to secure the divine benignity. When the enemy
are coming in like a flood, and the Spirit of the Lord is
lifting up a standard against them, shall we not flock to
that standard? Shall we not thus be found under the

banner of the King of Zion? Alas, the wicked will *not* *understand!* But the *wise will.* understand. And the latter will adopt this among the means of withstanding the torrents of Antichristian influence: They will aid the missionary exertions of the people of God.

6. *Due exertions to promote the sanctification of the Lord's day.*

Religion ever rises or. falls in exact proportion with the sanctification, or neglect of the Sabbath. The latter opens a wide door to Infidelity and licentiousness. These can no more exist with the due sanctification of this holy day, than darkness can co-exist with light. Hence men of an Infidel cast hate the Sabbath, and are, often found profaning it. One of the first deeds of French *liberty and equality* was, to abolish the Sabbath, by instituting their decade in its stead. And the same disposition is too prevalent among men on every side.

It is the duty of every civil government to restrain its subjects from the open violation of the Lord's day. The law of God and the general principle of civil legislation unite in demanding this. The law of God says: "Remember the Sabbath day to keep it holy;—the "seventh day is the sabbath of the Lord thy God; in it "thou shalt not do any work, thou, nor thy son, nor thy "daughter, nor thy man servant, nor thy maid servant, "nor thy cattle, nor thy stranger, that is within thy "gates." This latter clause clearly implies the duty of having civil laws to restrain from the open violation of the Sabbath. For strangers within our gates, when disposed to violate the Sabbath, will not be restrained by any thing short of civil laws. Yet the law of God *demands their restriction;* a law which is moral, perpetual, and binding on all men. The consequence is unavoidable. Every civil community ought to have laws to prevent all open violation of the Sabbath.

And the general principle of civil legislation establishes this duty. This principle can suffer nothing to be openly practised, which is evidently detrimental to the community. But what can be more detrimental to the community, than that flood of immorality and licentiousness, which are the *known* and *certain* consequen-

ces of a general profanation of the Sabbath? The proper improvement of this holy day has the most beneficial effects on the civil interests of men. The external observance of the fourth command then, is as proper a subject of legislation, as that of the third, the fifth,
the sixth, seventh, eighth, or any Divine command.
No precept in the decalogue is more founded in the nature of things, than the fourth.

And good laws enacted upon this subject ought to
be put in effectual execution. Shall the laws of God
and man be forced to retreat before the brazen front of
Infidelity and licentiousness? When this is the case,
officers of the civil peace are criminally deficient in
their duty. They ought, at whatever risk, to see good
laws relative to the Sabbath, as well as to other things,
put in effectual execution. This is an important means
of withstanding the impious designs of infidels, at this
interesting period.

And it is the command of Heaven, that we should
not forsake "the assembling of ourselves together, as
"the manner of some is; but that we should exhort one
"another; and so much the more, as we see the day
"approaching." It is no token for good, that public
worshipping assemblies are deserted by such multitudes. It is a circumstance, that calls for humility, and
exertion. Every one ought to exert all his influence,
in his own family, in his neighborhood, and among his
fellow men, to deter from this, and every breach of the
Sabbath; to bring people to the *courts of the Lord,* and
to induce them to *keep God's Sabbaths, and reverence
his sanctuary.*

7. *Proper caution in the admission of members into the
Church; and a faithful support of Christian discipline.*

While *the Spirit and the bride say,* Come, and the
arms of the Church are extended to receive every child
of God; the wicked are not to be received. "Unto the
"wicked God saith, What hast thou to do to declare
"my statutes, or that thou shouldst take my covenant
"into thy mouth? seeing thou hatest instruction, and
"casteth my words behind thee. And of the rest durst
"no man join himself unto them: But the people mag-

"nified them. And believers were the more added un-
"to the Lord. The Lord added to the church daily
"such as should be saved."

Unprincipled professors are in a situation effectually
to wound the cause of Christ, and to become dangerous tools of the enemy. A spy within the walls, un-
detected, is more dangerous than ten open enemies
without. Voltaire could boast, that his building a
church, and partaking of the eucharist, was a master
stroke of his policy in *crushing the wretch.* Better is a
small church of faithful members, than a large one of
the opposite character. The former will be terrible to
the wicked. While the latter may perhaps easily be
induced to open the gates to an insidious enemy. Hypocritical Jews were the most convenient and fatal tools
of the persecuting Antiochus, See Dan. xi, 30, 32.

A faithful support of the laws of Christ's house, is an
essential bulwark against the adversaries of religion.
A neglect of discipline betrays the cause of Christianity
into the hands of the enemy:—While a holy, strict,
judicious Church discipline renders a Church not only
*beautiful as Tirzah, and comely as Jerusalem; but terri-
ble as an army with banners.* Among the cavils of the
wicked, nothing is more common, than unfriendly remarks upon the failings of professors. The real failings of professors then, their stumbling blocks not
taken up, have a most pernicious effect toward bringing religion into contempt among the thoughtless and
vain, and to fix them in Infidelity. In opposition to
this, every Church ought to be a faithful court of Christ,
a city of his holiness; answering to the representation
given in holy Writ; *looking forth as the morning, fair
as the moon, and clear as the sun; the pillar and ground
of the truth.* This is of vast importance at the present
period. *Be blameless and harmless, the sons of God without rebuke, in the midst of a crooked and perverse nation,
among whom ye shine as lights in the world.*

Permit me here to add:—Every Church ought to be
a faithful *moral society* of Christ. They ought to unite
their efforts to dissuade from all vice, to discourage all
irreligion, all immorality. It seems hardly necessary

to say, that church members ought utterly to discountenance all vice by their *examples* and *lives.* When
this is not the case, such disorderly members ought
soon to be either recovered, or excluded from the
Church. But professors of the Christian religion ought
to be *active* and *diligent,* in prudent and faithful measures, to reclaim the immoral, to dissuade from every
species of vice and wickedness. This duty is enforced
by the commands of God, and the dictates of reason
and benevolence. God commands his people to *"walk
in wisdom toward them that are without."* Many things
are implied in this divine injunction; and particularly
the following; that professors maintain, in the consciences of those that are without, a clear conviction,
that they are followers of Christ; that they wish to do
them good; that they benevolently feel for their best
interest; and wish for their peace and salvation. And.
the above injunction implies, that the members of Christ
tenderly labor to recover those that are without, from
all wickedness, from that sin, which is a reproach to
any people. God gave it in express charge to his people of old, "Thou shalt in any wise rebuke thy *neighbor,* and not suffer sin upon him." Here a *neighbor,*
guilty of open sin, is to be by all means rebuked by
the people of God. What blessed effects might be expected to follow, if this duty were duly performed, with
a manifest tender concern for the temporal, and especially the eternal welfare of the transgressor? A band
of Christian brothers, acting under the influence of the
Spirit of Christ, and united under his authority, would
in this way be indeed "terrible (to the vicious) as an
army with banners." This is one instance of their
taking their proper stand; and is one instance of letting
their light shine before men. Why have so many of
the professed followers of Christ forgotten this part of
their duty? Was it enjoined upon the ancient Israelite, that if he saw his neighbor's ox or ass going astray,
he should give notice, or prevent the evil? And may
a professed Israelite indeed see his neighbor *himself*
going astray, and not attempt to reclaim him? This
is to conduct in a way unworthy of a follower of Him,

"who went about doing good," and who faithfully reproved the wicked. An inspired apostle said to the Thessalonians, "Now we exhort you, brethren, *warn them that are unruly.*" This must have meant not only the unruly *in the Church;* but also *those out of it.* The latter are especially intended. For something more is to be done to unruly members *in* the Church, than to *warn* them. Directions relative to them are differently expressed. But the *unruly without* are to be *warned,* by the followers of Christ;—warned of their *error,* their *folly* and *danger.* If your neighbor neglect the house of God, warn him, and entreat him to reform. If he violate the sabbath, by journeying, or attending to secular concerns, tell him his fault, and labor with him, to induce him to amend. If you find him contracting habits of idleness, intemperance, profanity, injustice, falsehood, or prevarication, or of any *vice,* or *error;* fail not to afford him tender, seasonable and solemn caution. Thus labor to recover him, Or you will find all his weight in the scale of Antichrist.

Would all the members of the Church of Christ kindly, piously and perseveringly perform these duties, the Church would be the most powerful moral society in the world. They would cultivate and improve every branch of morality, while they taught and propagated the true *principle* of morality, the love of God in Christ. Great things might thus be done in restraining their fellow creatures from vice. The effects on society would be most beneficial. And we have reason to be-. lieve such efforts would be blessed of God, as means of the *conversion* of many. The Church would then answer to her character, of being Christ's *witnesses;* unitedly, discreetly and firmly bearing their testimony for him, for the cause of religion and true morality. This would greatly tend to the moral health of communities; and the Church would indeed be "the *salt* of the earth;" and (in Christ) "the light of the world." If their light did but thus shine before men, others seeing their good works would be led to glorify their Father, who is in heaven.

Is there not much room and occasion for Churches generally to reform, relative to their performance of *these duties* toward them that are without? Is not their neglect of these duties one sad occasion of the prevalence of those floods of vice and immorality, which threaten to deluge the world? In one solemn description of the events, which lead on to the battle of that great day of God, (transgressing and lying against the Lord, departing away from our God, speaking oppression and revolt, conceiving and uttering from the heart words of falsehood, so that judgment is turned back, and justice standeth afar off, for truth is fallen in the streets, and equity cannot enter, yea truth faileth, and he that departeth from evil maketh himself a prey; Isa. lix, 13—16;) it is added; "And the Lord saw it, and it *displeased him, that there was no judgment; and he saw that there was no man, and wondered that there was no intercessor."* Does not this imply, that those who were set to *intercede for his cause on earth,* had become greatly deficient, as to the performance of this duty? The Church, in the way of this deficiency in duty, will perhaps bring upon herself the fiery trials, which she must experience in those days.

Ought not the professing people of God to reform in this thing? Would they not much better stand in their lot, adorn their Christian profession, and glorify God? Would not the Church appear more like the "*pillar and ground of the truth?"* Would they not present a much more formidable *phalanx* against the innovations of Antichrist?

And perhaps the people of God might with propriety induce people of *stability and good habits,* who have not united with the Church, to form into moral societies, or in some way, to lend their aid in the suppression of vice, and in counteracting the attacks of immorality and disorganization. Such an expedient might, no doubt, be of great benefit against the innovations of antichristian influence.

8. *Family Religion; and a pious, discreet family government.*

This is a remedy of the first importance against Antichristian influence. And the want of it is the mischievous occasion of much of the evils, which now threaten to inundate the civilized world. It is the order and the promise of God; *Train up a child in the way he should go, and when he is old he will not depart from it.* It was repeatedly given in charge by the God of Israel, relative to the doctrines, duties, and motives of their religion; "Thou shalt diligently teach them to thy chil-"dren, speaking of them when thou sittest in thine "house, and when thou walkest by the way; when thou "liest down, and when thou risest up." How *rational*, as well as *weighty* is the following inspired passage, relative to urging on children the things of God! "—Which we have heard and known, and our fathers "have told us:—We will not hide them from their chil-"dren, showing the generation to come the praises of the "Lord:—For he established a testimony in Jacob, and "appointed a law in Israel, which he commanded our "fathers, that they should make them known to their "children: That the generation to come might know "them, even the children that should be born; who "should arise and declare them to their children: That "they might set their hope in God, and not forget the "works of God; but keep his commandments." This is a law of God of prime importance at all times; and especially at this day of innovation and wickedness. When families neglect religion and a godly discipline, how soon do they become receptacles of vice and error; and society will groan under their baneful influence.

Voltaire and his disciples made their highest calculations on corrupting the rising generation, and directing the education of youth. Various of their first arrangements was to effect this object. Family prayer, the reading of the Bible, pious parental instructions and examples, the holy sanctification of the Sabbath, with salutary and effectual corrections and restraints, are most important to the proper education of a family. And these are means of the first importance towards withstanding the seductive arts of Infidelity. Happy, if all heads of families properly felt the weight of this sentiment. They *will* feel it, when they meet their children in the final judgment! They will feel it in eternity, where the infinitely weighty consequences of their faithfulness, or unfaithfulness will be clearly exhibited before the eyes of the universe.

9. *The employing of* PIOUS, *as well as able instructors of our children.*

School instructors have a great influence in forming the sentiments and morals of our youth. They have a great opportunity to sow the seeds of virtue, or of vice. On this principle, the Illuminees placed great dependence. Among the fatal arts of disseminating their sentiments, getting into their hands the management of reading schools held a high rank. In this way they gradually formed young minds to their views. And unsuspecting youth became an easy prey to their wiles.

The schoolmaster has an influence over the minds of his young charge, which ought never to be unguarded by their parents; nor misimproved by the teacher employed. His examples, and any remarks made by him, are weighty with the listening pupils, who are accustomed to reverence their instructor. Surely then he ought to be a person of correct *religious* sentiments and habits, as well as of good information. And those communities who have enacted strict laws relative to this object, have set an example worthy to be imitated by every part of the world. Would you hire a nurse, who would poison your children? Or is the poisoning of their souls of less importance than that of their bodies? The want of properly guarding this principle, and the exclusion of Bibles, of prayers, and of religious instruction from our schools, have opened a wide door to irreligion and Infidelity; the consequences of which *are alarming.* And a speedy and thorough reform in this particular, is a remedy of great importance against the present threatening evils.

And due caution relative to the *books* read by our youth, is a duty of no inconsiderable importance. It was a remark made by a shrewd observer of mankind, "Let me compose the ditties, and I care not who enacts the laws of a community." There is vast weight in this observation. The minds of youth may be imperceptibly perverted by ditties, songs, novels, tracts, and little books for children, (which appear beneath the notice of adults) as well as by subtile publications of more importance. The greatest dependence was placed, by the adepts of the Voltaire school, on this method of disseminating their poison through communities and kingdoms. And it is an avenue of corruption, which ought to be kept closed with caution.

10. *Wisdom and prudence in the choice of our civil rulers.*

The framers of the code of Illuminism combined in their object *"revolutions, and the doctrines of Atheism."* This is a point expressly ascertained by the developement of their scheme; and clearly exhibited in all their operations. And the subtilty of the old serpent is here displayed, to give the most deadly effect to this scheme of his operations against the cause of religion. Virtuous rulers are *a terror to evil doers*, and they constitute a bulwark to the cause of religion, which the propagators of Infidelity dread; while they naturally conjecture, that they have little or nothing to fear from rulers destitute of religious principles; but that they have much to hope from them. One great object of their scheme would therefore naturally be, to get rid of the restraints occasioned by virtuous rulers; and to bring forward men of the opposite character. In this way republics have been enslaved and ruined. And in many ways, revolutions and tumults aid the cause of Infidelity.

Our rulers proceed from ourselves And on their character our national weal, or woe depends. The sacred word will be fulfilled, which informs, that *When the righteous are in authority, the people rejoice; but when the wicked bear rule, the people mourn:* And that *The wicked walk on every side, when the vilest men are exalted.* In ancient sacred history we uniformly find, that good rulers were a blessing; and evil rulers were for judgment. The nation of Israel ever

73

found the truth of this remark. And it will not be
found less true under the blessings of Gospel light,
and of a free republican government. In the latter,
the moral character of the mass of the people will be
indicated by that of their rulers. If their rulers be
men of irreligion, and such be continued from time to
time in office, irreligion marks the character of the mass
of the people. In such a case, the Most High is insulted; and may be expected to manifest his displeasure in judgments. Notwithstanding the sentiment of
many in modern times, that an *infidel* will make as good
a civil ruler, as a *believer;* yet in sacred Writ, we find
it otherwise taught. It is a sentiment running through
the Bible, that *He that ruleth over men must be just,
ruling in the fear of God.* Hence men, notoriously of
the opposite character, ought never to be elected for
our rulers. And when they *are,* God is *contemned;*
and Infidelity is encouraged. The experience of men,
as well as the word of God, confutes the opinion, that
infidels, or openly irreligious men, may make the best
of rulers. The examples and influence of such men
will operate with *dreadful effect* against the cause of religion, and in favor of the cause of wickedness. Such
men are not to be confided in. They have no correct
principles of morality in their hearts. If men reject
the word of the Lord, we are divinely informed, that
there is *no wisdom in them;** unless it be a subtile
kind of wisdom to *do evil.* And the judgments of
Heaven in such a case may be expected. It is indeed
striking to read of wicked rulers, Jer. iv, 22; "They
are wise to do evil; but to do good they have no understanding." This is said of the abominable rulers of the last days.

The modern sentiment, that there is no connexion
between *religion* and *national concerns,* is among the
deceptive arts of the Infidelity of the last days. Had
the arch tempter believed this sentiment, he would not
have instigated his agents of Illuminism to have combined in their object, "revolutions, and the doctrines

* Jer viii, 9.

of Atheism." He well knows the connexion there is between religion and *good* civil government; and their kind influence on each other. The sentiment, that there is no connexion between them, however many well meaning people may be deceived into the belief of it, must have originated in *wicked design.* Listen to its import. What is it short of this? Religion has nothing to do with worldy concerns! And worldly concerns have nothing to do with religion! They are so disconnected, as to have no influence on each other. Consequently there is nothing of a moral nature in worldly affairs: And no religious discourse ought ever to contain any thing concerning them! Are such sentiments as these imbibed in a Gospel land? The ancient heathen, who believed there *were* gods, would have blushed at them! Would it do the above sentiments much injustice to read them in the following language; "God doth not see, neither doth the "Most High regard.—The Lord seeth us not; the Lord "hath forsaken the earth.—God hath forgotten; he hid-"eth his face.—The Lord shall not see; neither shall "the God of Jacob regard it.—Our tongue is our own; "who is Lord over us?—Thou wilt not require it.— "We are lords; we will come no more unto thee." In other words: We are not accountable for our conduct; and we will hear no more of any accountability.

We are sure this sentiment, of "no connexion be-"tween religion and the secular concerns of a nation," was not the sentiment of the god of ancient Israel. He ever taught that people, that religion and their national concerns *were most intimately connected.* Will it be said, *We have learned more wisdom, or are more correct?* The prediction of the Most High to the Church in the Millennium, that *Kings shall be thy nursing fathers, and queens thy nursing mothers,* indicates, that *He* is indeed "*of one mind*" upon this point; however *men have changed.* The above prediction more than hints the intimate connexion there shall be between religion and national concerns, when the unnatural distortions of Infidelity, and the days of licentiousness, shall cease; and things shall come to be as they ought. Rulers, whatever may be their *forms* of government, will be eminently pious, and *nursing fathers* to the Church; and all the concerns of nations will be made subordinate to her best interest. *The kings of the earth will bring their glory and honor into the new Jerusalem.*

In the choice of rulers, beware of flatterers. Remember the ambitious, deceptive flatteries of ancient Absalom.* Remember those of the great French assassin, Marat; whose profession of *republicanism*, and of concern for the people, in the midst of all his horrid murders of a countless throng of innocent men, women, and children, were in the most pathetic and soft strains of a *lover.* Men of the worst views may make the highest professions of concern for your welfare. Words are cheap. And such a profession is an old, and most convenient and fatal disguise. Judas betrayed the Son of God with a *kiss.* It must be done under cover of the purest friendship! The old serpent ruined the race of man, by seducing the woman in paradise with the kindest expressions of concern for the abridgement of their *rights,* and for their *liberty* and welfare. In histories, sacred and profane, we learn, that such professions have ever been the most convenient cover for the blackest designs. This cover is by no means excluded from the refined arts of modern innovation. On no one principle beside, is so much dependence made, as on this. And no other principle is so powerful and fatal, in "binding the world with invisible hands." Men are so fond of having *others regard them and feel for their interest,* that if one but *subtilly pretends* to do it, he may readily gain their confidence, and the management of their concerns. Remember, that real worth is *modest,* and must be sought for. Men of real virtue will not descend to flattery. While designing and ambitious men will force themselves, or be forced upon you under specious pretences. Such men are, in the Oracles of truth, set in direct contrast with men of *faithfulness. Most men will proclaim every one his own goodness; but a* faithful man *who can*

---

* 2 Sam. xv, 1—6.

find? Here the Holy Ghost teaches, that declaimers on their own goodness are the very *opposite* of *faithful* men. Why do not *this*, and similar Divine testimonies, put self eulogists to shame? Perhaps they never read them! Or do not view 'them' as of divine authority!

Let your solemn prayers, and your *influence*, ever be in favor of able men for civil rulers, who fear God, and hate covetousness.

11. *A vigilant eye upon the movements of the enemy; and a solemn attention to the signs of the times.*

Concealment is the policy and strength of the propagators of Infidelity and disorganization. Their scheme is subtilly calculated, while *binding the world*, to keep their hands *invisible*. One important mode of their defence is, to discourage, by rendering hazardous, every attempt to detect them. This principle, together with the native inattention of man to whatever does not address itself to his senses; and our usual lothness to believe that we are in danger from designing men, has rendered it unpopular with thousands, *to this day*, to speak of the existence of the modern system of disorganizers and infidels; even after all that profusion of evidence which has exposed this horrid system to the world. *But this is idle.* Such men *have* existed, and *do* exist. And the effects of their operations are *visible as the sun;* and are putting to hazard every thing most dear to man.

Shall such evil be disregarded? Shall hordes of latent enemies prey upon the vitals of a nation, and be unheeded? Such heedlessness has already rendered nations an easy prey to the devourer! Shall our great and fair Republic be added to the list? May gracious Heaven forbid! Let the evidence relative to this *wicked system* be weighed, and have its proper effect. Let it put us upon our guard. Let the fates of other nations induce us to apply with assiduity the proper means of escape. Concerning impostors, the Oracles of heaven inform us, *By their fruits ye shall know them.* Their profession will be *fair;* but *mischief* is in their hearts. Their words will be smoother than oil; yet are they drawn swords. Sheep's clothing is stolen to conceal ravening wolves. It is the part of the friends of Zion, to observe their fruits with a jealous eye.

And it is their duty likewise to observe with solemn awe the impending judgments of the present day; and not to overlook the hand and design of God in the signal events of this period. Such pious attention will discern powerful motives to diligence in withstanding the wicked agency of Antichrist; and in being prepared for every event. The Church, at the dawn of the Millennium, *adores* God in the following language, "Yea, in the way of thy judgments, O Lord, have we "waited for thee:"* In the way of *believing* in them; *seeing* them coming; and being *prepared* for them. The wicked are represented as being blind to the hand and judgments of God. "Lord, when thy hand is lifted "up, they will not see. Thy judgments are far above, "out of his sight." But so it ought not to be with us. Says our blessed Lord, "Ye can discern the face of the "sky; but can ye not discern the signs of the times? The "wise shall understand." To them it is said; "Ye are not "in darkness, that that day should overtake you as a "thief. When ye see all these things, then know that "it (the day of Christ) is nigh, even at the doors." The predictions relative to the last days clearly suggest that good people *will* discern and improve the signs of those times; will see Christ coming; and will look up with solemn joy, and attention, knowing that their redemption draweth nigh. And this believing, solemn attention is essential to a preparation for the trials of that day; to an escape from the snares of Infidelity; and to a maintaining of the character of the witnesses of Jesus Christ. This leads to note in the last place,

12. *Watchfulness and special prayer.*

By *watchfulness* here, I mean particularly, guarding the heart against the wiles of that system, which has been noted as in operation;—against the various impositions which are practised;—against those prejudic-

* Isa. xxvi. 8.

es, designed to be excited by public or private suggestions.

Here is probably the strongest hold of the agents of
Infidelity, the minions of Antichrist. "Armies of principle, (say they) can prevail, where armies of soldiers
cannot be introduced." Their highest expectations
have rested on what they have hoped to be able to effect among the mass of mankind, by a secret, disguised
dissemination of their principles; and by suggestions,
accusations, and innuendos, against characters and systems marked out for ruin. It is a known art of modern innovators, to *hint*, or *assert* things, however untrue, which make for their cause; and to persevere in the
assertions till they come to be believed. Read the letters and maxims of Voltaire, and of his associates, and
you will find this principle a prominent feature of
their scheme. This leads us to recollect some of the
characteristics of the agents of Antichrist, given in sacred Writ; "False accusers, fierce, despisers of them that
"are good; murmurers, complainers; speaking evil of
"dignities, and of things which they understand not;
"haters of them that are good; followers of Cain, of Ba-
"laam, and of Korah." With such conduct as is here
predicted, what evils have been done! Every republic
in Europe has been subverted and destroyed. Our own
republic is in this way violently attacked; though the
assailants are in disguise. Neighbors and brethren,
equally attached to the good of their country, have
been divided, and even inflamed against each other.
This evil has been long and systematically practised in
these States. And the consequences have become
alarming! The best characters, *civil* and *religious*, have
been vilified. The most inflammatory things have been
circulated, tending to fill the mind with disgust, if not
with rage, against the best of characters, by no means
excepting the ministers of Christ; and calculated to
subvert all order, *sacred* and *civil.* Has this been without design? Charity cannot believe that it has. Have
we not need then to *watch,* and guard our hearts against
the evil? How many have imbibed it, to their great
detriment, and that of the community? Whence orig-

inated the modern practice of traducing the best characters? Whom did we hear first publicly vilified?
and by whom? Washington groaned under this abuse!

A vigilant eye upon rulers, is not inconsistent with
duty to God, and the community. And the detection
of corrupt principles, in leading men, and leading
measures, is essential to the security of the civil rights
of a nation. But these things are different from a
torrent of groundless clamor and abuse poured forth
against men of the most established characters: Which
conduct *began the torrent of mischief in our nation.* Such
were the men marked out for ruin, by the leaders of
Illuminism. Surely if it is a duty to reverence civil
authority, and to be *subject, not only for wrath, but
also for conscience' sake;* it must be provoking to God,
and ruinous to a community to clamor against, and
weaken the hands of *good* civil rulers. This is repeatedly noted in prophecy, as among the fatal evils of the
last days: *Despising government—speaking evil of dignities.* A deep and dark system of this evil has been
framed, and set in motion; and has hurled the best of
men from office. Shall we be caught by it? Shall we
imbibe the poison, which has been, with so much
art and base design, prepared? Shall we *accede
with enthusiasm to grievances sketched out for us?* Shall
we not rather discover the mischief, and escape the
snare? Let our hearts be guarded against those prejudices, on the exciting of which our enemies have made
their highest calculations. Shall we permit ourselves
to be bound and immolated by "invisible hands?
Shall *strangers devour us and we know it not,* till it is
too late? Shall old neighbors and friends, who went
hand in hand through our revolutionary struggles, and
who never have felt or *had* but one interest, be alienated
from, and inflamed against each other, by foreign intrigue? This hateful game has been played upon us,
till we have appeared approaching the brink of ruin.
May the God of our fathers kindly interpose, and save
us from every species of delusion and imposition! Let
us pause, and consider. Let us awake to our dangers; and with wisdom and calmness use the best

methods of evading them. Let us distinguish between flattering professions, and real character; between our friends, and our enemies. Let us disdain, and repel every insinuation which is calculated to alienate us from our Christian teachers; or to excite our disgust against men and measures, the best adapted to our prosperity. That we may escape the snares deeply planted for our ruin, the heart must be kept with all diligence against every malignant passion. The angry spirit of the times must not be imbibed. We behold national, and even domestic bliss exposed to destruction. We read of the nations drinking of Babylon's cup, and of their being mad!* *There shall be five in one house divided, three against two, and two against three.* Parents and children are to be divided by the fatal arts of Antichristian imposition. *And the nations were angry, and thy wrath is come.* How weighty is the Divine admonition, which relates to the same period: "Seek ye "the Lord, all ye meek of the earth; seek righteousness; "seek meekness; it may be ye may be hid in the day of "the Lord's anger." This leads to the other particular under this head; which is,

Special Prayer. Never perhaps was special prayer more needful, than at the present day. The directions of our Savior are now emphatically applicable; "Watch "and pray, that ye enter not into temptation. Watch "ye, and pray always; that ye may be accounted wor-"thy to escape all those things which shall come to pass, "and to stand before the Son of man. Special dangers demand special prayers. *Call upon me in the day of trouble; I will deliver thee; and thou shalt glorify me.* Prayer is the girding on of the Christian armor. *Praying always, with all prayer and supplication.* This is a potent mean, which reaches the enemy, in a defenceless point. It disarms them, before they perceive that they are attacked; and defeats them in ways against which they have made no calculations.

God *taketh the wise in their own craftiness.* He disappointeth the devices of the crafty, so that their hands

* Jer. li, 7.

74

cannot perform their enterprises. This the Most High performs for his people, in answer to prayer. With prayer Jacob disarmed Esau; so that although Esau set out to meet Jacob with four hundred men, probably intent on revenge, he met him in peace, and did him no injury. Jacob *as a prince wrestled with God, and prevailed.* Prayer dispersed vast armies of old, combined against the people of God; *that* in the days of Gideon; *that* in the reign of Jehosaphat, and others. Prayer enabled men, who were marked out for ruin, to "quench the violence of fire; to escape the edge of the "sword; out of weakness to be made strong; to wax "valiant in fight; and to turn to flight THE ARMIES OF "THE ALIENS."

Prayer, no doubt, is an essential part of the means, by which the witnesses, in Rev. xi, 5,— are said to "devour "their enemies; and to smite the earth with all the plagues "as oft as they will. With *this weapon* the Church has always defeated her enemies. It is through the efficacy of prayer, that the burning bush has never been consumed; and the sheep among wolves never finally devoured. Prayer rescued Daniel from his intriguing accusers; and shut the mouths of the lions. It protected the three children of God under the violent rage of the king of Babylon; yea, in the burning fiery furnace. It delivered the Jews in Persia from the bloody decree of Haman; and hung that haughty courtier upon his own gallows. Prayer *cut Rahab, and wounded the dragon.* It parted the waters of the Red Sea for the rescue of God's oppressed people. Armed with this weapon, the Church will answer to the prophetic description; "Let the high praises of God be in their "mouths; and a two edged sword in their hands, to "execute vengeance upon the heathen, and punishment "upon the people; to bind their kings with chains, and "their nobles with fetters of iron; to execute upon them "the judgment written; this honor have all the saints."*

Prayer is the essential mean by which the Church will escape the ruin planned for her by her most potent

* Psalm cxliv, 6—9.

enemies of the last days. With this weapon, she will thresh the nations of her enemies to powder. "Behold "I will make thee a new threshing instrument having "teeth; thou shalt thresh the mountains, and beat them "small, and shalt make the hills as chaff. Thou shalt "fan them, and the wind shall carry them away, and "the whirlwind shall scatter them; and thou shalt re- "joice in the Lord, and shalt glory in the Holy One "of Israel.* This prediction, no doubt, relates to the same event with that in Dan. ii, 34, 35, where the stone cut out without hands, smites the feet of the image, and grinds *them,* and the remaining *materials* of the *whole image,* to powder, which like chaff is blown away. This is the dashing of the nations to pieces, as a potter's vessel. But the Church is represented as gaining this very victory over her enemies. Rev. ii, 26, 27. The truth is, Christ performs this work of signal judgment, to the glory of God, and the salvation of Zion, in answer to her prayers for the security and advancement of his cause. Thus we read, "And shall not God avenge "his own elect, who cry unto him day and night, "though he bear long with them? I tell you he will "avenge them speedily. Nevertheless, when the Son "of man cometh, shall he find faith on the earth?" Here the *coming* of Christ, in those decisive scenes of judgment, is to *avenge his elect;* and is in answer to their *long* and *persevering cries."*

Here then is the powerful weapon, which shall secure to Christians the victory. If *the effectual, fervent prayer of a righteous man availeth much;* surely the effectual, fervent and *special* prayers of all the righteous, under the oppressions of the last days, will avail more. "For the oppression of the poor, for the sighing of the "needy, now will I arise, saith the Lord; I will set him "in safety."

The following Divine directions and promises are accordingly given; "Ye, that make mention of the "Lord, keep not silence; and give him no rest, till he "establish, and till he make Jerusalem a praise in the

---

* Isa. xli, 15, 16.

"earth. Pray without ceasing. Be careful for noth-
"ing; but in every thing with prayer and supplication,
"with thanksgiving, let your request be made known
"unto God. Casting all your cares upon him; for he
"careth for you. It shall come to pass, that whosoev-
"er shall call on the name of the Lord, shall be saved:
"For in mount Zion, and in Jerusalem, shall be deliv-
"erance, as the Lord hath said, and in the remnant,
"whom the Lord shall call."

Therefore, "Blow ye the trumpet in Zion; sanctify
"a fast; call a solemn assembly; gather the people;
"sanctify the congregation; assemble the elders; gather
"the children, and those that suck the breast. Let the
"bridegroom go forth out of his chamber, and the
"bride out of her closet. Let the priests and ministers of
"the Lord weep between the porch and the altar; and
"let them say, Spare thy people, O Lord; and give
"not thine heritage to reproach, that the heathen should
"rule over them. Wherefore should they say among
"the heathen, Where is their God? Then will the
"Lord be jealous for his land, and pity his people."
Here is the duty of the people of God, and their only
path of safety, under the reign of Antichrist.

THE END.

"earth. Pray without ceasing. Be careful for noth-
"ing; but in every thing with prayer and supplication,
"with thanksgiving, let your request be made known
"unto God. Casting all your cares upon him; for he
"careth for you. It shall come to pass, that whosoev-
"er shall call on the name of the Lord, shall be saved:
"For in mount Zion, and in Jerusalem, shall be deliv-
"erance, as the Lord hath said, and in the remnant,
"whom the Lord shall call."

Therefore, "Blow ye the trumpet in Zion; sanctify
"a fast; call a solemn assembly; gather the people;
"sanctify the congregation; assemble the elders; gather
"the children, and those that suck the breast. Let the
"bridegroom go forth out of his chamber, and the
"bride out of her closet. Let the priests and ministers of
"the Lord weep between the porch and the altar; and
"let them say, Spare thy people, O Lord; and give
"not thine heritage to reproach, that the heathen should
"rule over them. Wherefore should they say among
"the heathen, Where is their God? Then will the
"Lord be jealous for his land, and pity his people."
Here is the duty of the people of God, and their only
path of safety, under the reign of Antichrist.

THE END.

Lightning Source UK Ltd.
Milton Keynes UK
UKHW011958050219
336746UK00011B/1570/P